MANAGING CHANGE

MANAGING CHANGE

A STRATEGIC APPROACH TO ORGANISATIONAL DYNAMICS

FIFTH EDITION

BERNARD BURNES

FT Prentice Hall

FINANCIAL TIMES

An imprint of **Pearson Education**

Harlow, England • London • New York • Boston • San Francisco • Toronto
Sydney • Tokyo • Singapore • Hong Kong • Seoul • Taipei • New Delhi
Cape Town • Madrid • Mexico City • Amsterdam • Munich • Paris • Milan

To Sue, Duncan, Stuart and Hobbes

Pearson Education Limited

Edinburgh Gate
Harlow
Essex CM20 2JE
England

and Associated Companies throughout the world

Visit us on the World Wide Web at:
www.pearsoned.co.uk

First published under the Pitman imprint 1992
Second edition published under the Pitman imprint 1996
Third edition published 2000
Fourth edition published 2004
Fifth edition published 2009

© Bernard Burnes 1992, 1996
© Pearson Education Limited 2000, 2004, 2009

ISBN 978-0-273-71174-2

British Library Cataloguing-in-Publication Data
A catalogue record for this book is available from the British Library

Library of Congress Cataloging-in-Publication Data
Burnes, Bernard, 1953–
   Managing change : a strategic approach to organisational dynamics /
Bernard Burnes. – 5th ed.
        p.   cm.
   Includes bibliographical references and index.
   ISBN 978–0–273–71174–2 (pbk. : alk. paper)   1. Organizational
change–Management.   I. Title
   HD58.8.B882 2009
   658.4′06–dc222

                                                                2009015909

10 9 8 7 6 5 4 3
14 13 12 11

Typeset in 10/12.5pt Sabon by 35
Printed by Ashford Colour Press Ltd. Gosport

Contents

Supporting resources

Visit **www.pearsoned.co.uk/burnes** to find valuable online resources

For instructors
- Complete, downloadable Instructor's Manual
- PowerPoint slides that can be downloaded and used for presentations

For more information please contact your local Pearson Education sales representative or visit **www.pearsoned.co.uk/burnes**

Acknowledgements

The fifth edition of this book, like the previous four, would not have been possible without the generous encouragement and assistance of a large number of people, especially my colleagues and students at the University of Manchester. I would like to express my thanks to all of them, and particularly to Adrian Nelson and Paul Whittle. In addition, Pearson Education, notably Matthew Walker, deserve many thanks for their encouragement and patience. However, and mostly, I am irredeemably indebted to my wife, Sue. Her painstaking reading and editing of draft after draft of this book have improved it beyond recognition. It is not too much to say that she deserves as much credit as I do for what is good about this book.

Nevertheless, despite all the help and assistance I have received, any faults or shortcomings in the final product are mine and mine alone.

Publisher's Acknowledgements

We are grateful to the following for permission to reproduce copyright material:

Figures

Figure 5.1 from *Organization Development and Change*, International Edition 9th Ed, South-Western (Cummings and Worley 2009) Cengage Learning Inc, From Cummings/ Worley. Organization Development and Change. International Edition, 9E. Copyright 2009 South-Western, a part of Cengage Learning, Inc. Reproduced by permission. www.cengage.com/permissions; Figure 6.3 adapted from Patterns in strategy formation, *Management Science*, 24(9), p. 13 (Mintzberg, H 1978), The Institute for Operations Research and the Management Sciences (INFORMS), Adapted with permission from Mintzberg, H (1978) Patterns in strategy formation, Management Science, 24(9), p. 13. Copyright 1978, The Institute for Operations Research and the Management Sciences (INFORMS), 7240 Parkway Drive, Suite 300, Hanover, Maryland 21076, USA.; Figure 7.1 from *Competitive Advantage*, Free Press: New York, USA (Porter, M 1985) Simon & Schuster, Adapted with the permission of The Free Press, a Division of Simon & Schuster Inc, from COMPETITIVE ADVANTAGE: Creating and sustaining superior performance by Michael E. Porter. Copyright (c) 1985, 1998 by Michael E. Porter. All rights reserved.; Figure 7.2 from *Competitive Strategy*, Free Press: New York, USA (Porter, M 1980) Simon & Schuster, Adapted with the permission of The Free Press, a Division of Simon & Schuster Inc, from COMPETITIVE STRATEGY: Techniques for analyzing industries and competitors by Michael E. Porter. Copyright (c) 1980, 1998 by The Free Press. All rights reserved.; Figure 7.4 adapted from *The Strategy Concept and Process: A Pragmatic Approach*, 2nd ed, Prentice Hall: New Jersey, USA (Hax, Arnoldo C and Majluf, Nicolas S 1996) p. 302 (Figure 17.15), Pearson Education Inc, Upper Saddle River, NJ, Adapted by permission of Pearson Education Inc., Upper Saddle River, NJ.; Figure 8.4 from *Managing Change in Organizations* 4th ed, FT/Prentice Hall: Harlow. (Carnall, CA 2003) p. 244, Pearson Education; Figure 9.1 from *Beyond the Boundaries: Leading and Re-Creating the Successful Enterprise* 2nd ed, McGraw-Hill: Sydney, Australia (Stace, D and Dunphy, D 2001) p. 107, Copyright 2001 Stace D and Dunphy D; Figure 11.3 adapted from Patterns in strategy formation, *Management Science*, 24(9), p. 13 (Mintzberg, H 1978), INFORMS, Adapted with permission Mintzberg, H (1978) Patterns in strategy formation, Management Science, 24(9), p. 13. Copyright 1978, The Institute for Operations Research and the Management Sciences (INFORMS), 7240 Parkway Drive, Suite 300, hanover, Maryland 21076, USA.; Figure 11.4 adapted from *Organisational Behaviour and Analysis* 2nd ed, FT/Prentice Hall: Harlow. (Rollinson, D 2002) p. 254, Pearson Education

Tables

Table 9.1 from *Managing Change in Organizations* 4th ed, FT/Prentice Hall: Harlow. (Carnall, CA 2003) p. 133, Pearson Education; Table 12.1 adapted from *The Art and*

Science of Leadership 5th ed, Prentice Hall: Upper Saddle River, NJ, USA. (Nahavandi, Afsaneh 2009) p. 10, Pearson Education Inc, Upper Saddle River, NJ, Adapted by permission of Pearson Education Inc., Upper Saddle River, NJ.; Table 12.2 adapted from *A Force for Change: How Leadership Differs from Management*, Free Press: New York, USA. (Kotter, J 1990) Simon & Schuster, Adapted with the permission of The Free Press, a Division of Simon & Schuster Inc, from A FORCE FOR CHANGE: How leadership differs from management by John P. Kotter. Copyright (c) 1990 by John P. Kotter, Inc. All rights reserved.

Text

Exhibit 5.7 from Understanding organisational culture and the implications for corporate marketing. *European Journal of Marketing*, p. 357 (Wilson, A M 2001), Emerald Group Publishing Limited, (c) Emerald Publishing Ltd, All rights reserved.; Exhibit 6.5 from *What is Strategy and Does it Matter?* Routledge: London (Whittington, R 1993); Exhibit 8.3 from It's just a phase we're going through: a review and synthesis of OD phase analysis. *Group and Organization Studies*, 10, December, pp. 383–412. (Bullock, RJ and Batten, D 1985), Sage publications, Copyright (c) 1985 by Sage Publications. Reprinted by permission of Sage Publications.; Exhibit 8.4 from Wanted: OD More Alive Than Dead! *Journal of Applied Behavioral Science*, 40 (4), pp. 374–391 (Greiner, L E and Cummings, T G 2004), Sage Publications, Greiner, LE and Cummings, TG, Journal of Applied Behavioral Science, 40 (4), pp. 374–391, copyright (c) 2004 by Sage Publications. Reprinted by permission of Sage Publications.; Exhibit 12.4 from BROKER'S CLIENTS DETAIL WEB OF DASHED DREAMS, *Boston Globe*, 20 January 2008, p. 1 (Blanton, K), PARS International, NY

The Financial Times

Case Study 3.1 from Tesco targets Aldi and Lidl with discount brand range *The Financial Times*, 17 Sept 2008, p. 22 (Rigby, E.); Case Study 4.1 from How we let down the diligent folk at the Halifax, *The Financial Times*, 24 September 2008, p. 13 (Kay, J.); Case Study 5.1 from The progressive power of thinking anew, *The Financial Times*, 22 November 2008, p. 14 (Witzel, M.); Case Study 6.1 from The master strategist: Michael Porter, *The Financial Times*, 15 August 2003, p/11 (Witzel, M.); Case Study 6.2 from The great iconoclast: Henry Mintzberg, *The Financial Times*, 5 August 2003, p. 11 (Witzel, M.); Case Study 7.1 from Row between Virgin and Sky is reignited, *The Financial Times*, 19 May 2007, p. 14 (Edgecliffe-Johnson, A.); Case Study 7.2 from Stewardship of a sprawling empire, *The Financial Times*, 18 November 2005, p. 13 (Bickerton, I. and Marsh, P.); Case Study 7.3 from Shoppers in clamour for Apple's 3G iPhone, *The Financial Times*, 12 July 2008, p. 10 (Minto, R.); Case Study 7.3 adapted from When some of the parts don't add up; Conglomerates that thrive are ruthless in their scrutiny of when to shed beloved but worn-out assets, *The Financial Times*, 7 August 2008, p. 10 (Baer, J. and Guerrera, F.); Case Study 7.4 from Divide and Conquer: Best Buy's Strategy *The Financial Times*, 31 October 2005, p. 10; Case Study 7.5 from Thin times for lean car production *The Financial Times*, 9 May 2008, p. 16 (Reed, J. and Soble, J.); Case Study 8.1 from Culture is key to CPA professional development, *The Financial Times*,

12 November 2007, p. 2 (Newing, R.); Case Study 10.1 adapted from Public sector innovation will take you by surprise, *The Financial Times*, 6 November 2007, p. 14 (Stern, S.); Case Study 11.1 adapted from BA struggles to escape T5 twilight zone, *The Financial Times*, 5 April 2008, p. 5 (Done, K. and Willman, J.); Case Study 11.2 from Microsoft's direct connection to the customer, *The Financial Times*, 31 December 2001, p. 7 (Harvey, F.); Case Study 12.1 from Manage with mother, *The Financial Times*, 2 March 1998, p. 14 (Kellaway, L.)

In some instances we have been unable to trace the owners of copyright material, and we would appreciate any information that would enable us to do so.

Introduction

> There is nothing so practical as a good theory. (Kurt Lewin)[i]
>
> All models are wrong, some models are useful. (George Box)[ii]

A recent McKinsey & Company (2008: 1) global survey which examined organisational transformation concluded that 'Organizations need to change constantly'. This is yet further evidence, if needed, that for society at large, and organisations in particular, the magnitude, speed, impact, and especially the unpredictability of change, are greater than ever before. Certainly, since the first edition of this book was published in 1992, new products, processes and services have appeared at an ever-increasing rate. In 1992, the VCR still ruled supreme, the DVD recorder was merely an interesting concept and the iPod was not even a twinkle in Steve Jobs's eye. Also, since 1992, local markets have become global markets, protected or semi-protected markets and industries have been opened up to fierce competition, and public bureaucracies and monopolies have either been transferred to the private sector or have themselves adopted much more market-orientated practices (Burnes, 2009).

When Hammer and Champy (1993: 23) declared that 'change has become both pervasive and persistent. It *is* normality', many people thought that this was something of an exaggeration. Most people would now see this as a statement of the blindingly obvious.

Certainly, the period since the publication of the first edition of this book has seen organisations having to cope with massive swings in their fortunes. The period began with a global recession and was followed in the mid-1990s by a takeover and merger boom of unprecedented proportions (Burton *et al*, 1996; *Economist*, 1998). Warner (1997: 3) commented that:

> *To find a similar period of economic change and merger frenzy, you might need to go back all the way to the 1890s . . . Out of it were born such companies as Standard Oil and American Tobacco, the very prototypes of the vertically integrated modern corporation.*

The period leading up to the new millennium saw the dotcom boom. This was rapidly followed by the dotcom collapse in which companies previously valued in billions of dollars suddenly became worthless – *see* the Marconi case study in Chapter 6 (Bryce, 2002; Cassidy, 2002; Cellan-Jones, 2003; Kaplan, 2002; Sirower, 2003). This period also saw the bankruptcy of Enron and the exposure of fraud on a massive scale by its leaders, yet another reminder of the fragility and unpredictability of organisational life. It was the spectacular collapse of companies such as Enron, which had grown rapidly and collapsed just as rapidly, that led the American investment guru, Warren Buffet, to make his now famous remark that 'It's only when the tide goes out that you see who has been swimming with their trunks off.'

[i] Lewin (1943/4: 169).
[ii] Quoted in Norrie (1993).

Nevertheless, after the first two years of the new millennium, the world economy began to recover and household names, such as Sainsbury and Marks and Spencer, began to signal that they were back to their competitive best. Then came the 2007 credit crunch, which began with the sub-prime scandal in the USA and quickly spread across the world (Clark, 2008; Doran, 2008; Hutton, 2008a). Not only has this led to the worst economic crisis since the Great Depression of the 1930s, but it also appears to have rolled back decades of economic orthodoxy. In particular, the mantra that free market competition was good and that publicly provided services were bad appears to have been overthrown with some force. Not only are the arch-exponents of the free market, the banks, queuing up for government handouts on a truly massive scale, but many of them have also been voluntarily nationalised – a fate which only a little while ago many of them saw as representing the worst excesses of state interference in the running of the free market (Hutton, 2008b).

Therefore, even in the relatively short period since the publication of the first edition of this book, organisations have had to cope with very different types of challenges. These range from globalisation, rapid growth, mergers and acquisitions, and the emergence of new technologies and new competitors, to falling markets, depressed economies, de-mergers and consolidations, and the collapse of some customers, suppliers, competitors and even the financial institutions who lend them money. It is the experience of organisations struggling to cope with events such as these, year in and year out, which underlies the quotation from McKinsey at the beginning of this Introduction: 'Organizations need to change constantly'. However, McKinsey & Company (2008) also found, in a recent survey of executives from around the world, that only a third of organisations managed change successfully.

This brings us to the purpose of this book – *Managing Change*. Though organisational change would not be considered particularly important if products and markets were stable and organisational change was rare, it would be considered even less of an issue if it were easily managed and success could be guaranteed. Alas, it is not just McKinsey who have found substantial evidence that managing change successfully is extremely difficult. Over the years, there have been a continuous stream of examples of change projects that have gone wrong, some disastrously so (*see* Brindle, 1998a; Burnes and Weekes, 1989; Bywater, 1997; Chatterjee, 2007; Chua and Lam, 2005; Cummings and Worley, 1997; Howarth, 1988; Kanter *et al*, 1992; Kelly, 1982a, 1982b; Kotter, 1996; Ojiako and Maguire, 2008; Stace and Dunphy, 1994; Stickland, 1998). Indeed, two of the most respected commentators in the field of organisational change, Beer and Nohria (2000), claim that nearly two-thirds of all change efforts fail, whilst one of the world's leading management consultancies, Bain & Co, claims the general failure rate is around 70 per cent (Senturia *et al*, 2008).

Though these seem staggeringly high rates of failure, studies of particular types of change initiatives appear to come to similar conclusions. For example:

Culture Change: A study of major European, Asian and North American companies by Bain & Co found that the failure rate for culture change initiatives was a shocking 90 per cent (Rogers *et al*, 2006).

Computerisation: The micro-electronics revolution of the 1980s, which saw the rapid expansion of computers and computer-based processes into most areas of organisational life, was the subject of a great many studies. These found that the failure rate of new technology change projects was anywhere between 40 per cent and 70 per cent (AT Kearney, 1989; Bessant and Haywood, 1985; McKracken, 1986; New, 1989; Smith and Tranfield, 1987; Voss, 1985). Nor do the problems in this area appear to be teething troubles limited to the 1980s (Goulielmos, 2003). In 1998, for example, the UK government had to admit that its £170 million programme to replace the computer system that holds the National Insurance records of everyone in the country was in such a mess that the system had collapsed, throwing its social security system into turmoil (Brindle, 1998a, 1999). Similarly, in 2007, one of the main reasons given for BA's Terminal 5 fiasco was the failure of its computerised baggage handling system (Done and Willman, 2008).

Total Quality Management (TQM): The move by Western organisations to adopt TQM began in the USA in the mid-1970s (Dale and Cooper, 1992). In the USA, one of the founders of the TQM movement, Philip Crosby (1979), claimed that over 90 per cent of TQM initiatives failed. Studies of TQM in European countries found a failure rate of 70 per cent or more (AT Kearney, 1992; Cao *et al*, 2000; Cruise O'Brien and Voss, 1992; Dale, 1999; Economist Intelligence Unit, 1992; Nwabueze, 2001; Patwardhan and Patwardhan, 2008; Whyte and Witcher, 1992; Witcher, 1993; Zairi *et al*, 1994).

Business Process Re-Engineering: This was hailed as 'the biggest business innovation of the 1990s' (Mill, 1994: 26). However, successful BPR initiatives seem rare (Cao *et al*, 2001; Tarokh *et al*, 2008). Bryant (1998) cites a reported failure rate for BPR initiatives of 80 per cent, Breslin and McGann (1998) put the failure rate at 60 per cent, whilst Bywater (1997) puts the figure at 70 per cent. Even the founding father of BPR – Michael Hammer – acknowledges that in up to 70 per cent of cases it leaves organisations worse off rather than better off (Hammer and Champy, 1993).

The striking factor about these four types of change is that there is a plethora of information, advice and assistance that organisations can and do call upon in planning and executing change, and yet, they still fail. This is perhaps why managers consistently identify the difficulty of managing change as one of the key obstacles to the increased competitiveness of their organisations (Hanson, 1993; Industrial Society, 1997; Worrall and Cooper, 1997; Dunphy *et al*, 2003; IBM, 2008; Senturia *et al*, 2008).

To many, this must seem paradoxical. On the one hand, there is now more advice on how to manage change than ever before. On the other hand, the failure rate of change initiatives is astronomical. The two quotations from Lewin and Box at the beginning of this Introduction hold the key to this paradox. What almost everyone would like is a clear and practical change theory that explains what changes organisations need to make and how they should make them. Unfortunately, what is available is a wide range of confusing and contradictory theories, approaches and recipes. Many of these are well-thought-out and grounded in both theory and practice; others, unfortunately, seem disconnected from either theory or reality. Also, though change theory requires an interdisciplinary perspective, each of the major approaches tends to view organisations from the disciplinary angle of their originators – whether it be psychology, sociology, economics, engineering or whatever – which can result in an incomplete and unbalanced picture. So, regardless of what their proponents may claim, we do not possess at present an approach to change that is theoretically holistic, universally applicable, and which can be practically applied. Nevertheless, we do know that, to paraphrase the George Box quotation, whilst all change theories are partial, some theories are useful. This means that for those wishing to understand or implement change, the prime task is not to seek out an all-embracing theory but to understand the strengths and weaknesses of each approach and the situations in which each can best be applied.

There can be few who now doubt the importance to an organisation of the ability to identify where it needs to be in the future, and how to accomplish the changes necessary to get there – although there is a great deal of dispute about how difficult or possible this is. Some might assume that managers do not need to understand organisation theory, strategy theory, change theory or any other theory in order to manage and change their organisations, but this would be to underestimate the extent to which managers and others in organisations are influenced, assisted or potentially misled by theory. Increasingly, managers are exhorted to adopt the teachings of the latest management guru. However, as Part 1 will demonstrate, and as Mintzberg and Quinn (1991: xii) observed:

> One can, however, suffer not just from an absence of theories, but also from being dominated by them without realizing it. To paraphrase the words of John Maynard Keynes, most 'practical men' are the slaves of some defunct theorist. Whether we realize it or not, our behavior is guided by the systems of ideas that we have internalized over the years. Much can be learned by bringing these out into the open, examining them more carefully, and comparing them with alternative ways to view the world – including ones based on systematic study, that is, research.

These 'systems of ideas', or organisation theories as they are more commonly called, are crucial to change management in two respects. First, they provide models of how organisations should be structured and managed. Second, they provide guidelines for judging and prescribing the behaviour and effectiveness of individuals and groups in an organisation.

To understand why and how to change organisations, it is first necessary to understand their structures, management and behaviour. As Mintzberg and Quinn indicate, it is clear that in many organisations there is no clear understanding of these theories. It follows that choices with regard to the appropriateness of particular structures and practices, the way they are chosen and implemented, are founded on limited knowledge and perhaps false assumptions. Change cannot hope to be fully successful under these circumstances. On the contrary, a full understanding of these theories is necessary if informed choices are to be made when instigating and implementing change. For this reason, these will be examined critically in relation to each other, and also in comparison with how organisations actually operate, as opposed to how theorists suppose them to. The aim is not to provide a 'hands-on' practical guide to organisational change – though readers should find this book useful in that respect as well. Rather the aim is to provide an understanding of the theories and approaches to change that are on offer, to indicate their usefulness and drawbacks, and to enable the reader to choose for her- or himself which 'models are useful' and when.

The central purpose of this book, then, is to aid this search for understanding both by describing and discussing the key approaches to organisational change, and by setting these within the broader framework of the development, operation and behaviour of organisations and those who populate them. The intention is to allow those who study and carry out organisational change to make their own judgements about the benefits, applicability and usefulness of the approaches on offer. Therefore, the key themes underpinning the book are as follows:

- There is a need to understand the wider theoretical and historical context within which organisations operate and the pressures and options they face for change.
- Organisational change cannot be separated from organisational strategy, and vice versa.
- Organisations are not rational entities *per se*, though those who manage them strive to present their deliberations and decisions as being based on logic and rationality.
- There is a strong tendency to present the various approaches to change as being limited in number and mutually exclusive. However, in practice, the range of approaches is wide, and they can be and often are used either sequentially or in combination.
- The appropriateness of each of the available approaches is dependent upon the type of change being considered and the constraints under which the organisation operates, although these constraints and objectives can themselves be changed to make them more amenable to an organisation's preferred approach to change or style of management.
- Organisations and managers can and do exercise a wide degree of choice in what they change, when they change and how they change.

The book is organised into three parts.

Part 1: The rise and fall of the rational organisation provides a comprehensive review of organisation theory and behaviour. Chapter 1 deals with the development of organisations from the Industrial Revolution through to the early years of the twentieth century, when the first fully fledged organisation theory, the Classical approach, appeared. This is followed in Chapter 2 with reviews of the next two organisation theories to appear: the Human Relations approach and Contingency Theory. Chapter 3 examines and compares the three main and most influential contemporary approaches to structuring and managing organisations: the Culture–Excellence and organisational learning approaches, primarily developed in the West, and the Japanese approach. Chapter 4 sets the review of organisational theories in a wider context by reviewing the postmodern, realist and complexity perspectives on organisations. Chapter 5 examines the importance and implications of culture, power and politics. Chapter 5, and Part 1, conclude that, by accident and design, organisation theories attempt to remove choice from organisations by specifying what they need to do in order to be successful. However, the review of culture, power and politics, together with evidence from the earlier chapters, shows that managers do have a wider scope for shaping decisions than much of the organisation literature suggests. This theme of managerial choice is continued in Part 2.

Part 2: Strategy development and change management: past, present and future comprises five chapters, examining the literature on strategic management and change management. Chapters 6 and 7 examine the dominant approaches to strategy, and the main tools and techniques available to organisations for its development and implementation. In particular, these two chapters draw attention to the differences between the Prescriptive and Analytical schools of strategy, and they highlight the importance of the relationship between organisational strategy and organisational change. Chapters 8 and 9 review the two dominant approaches to organisational change: the Planned approach and the Emergent approach. These chapters show that both approaches have their strengths and weaknesses, and that neither separately nor in combination do these approaches cover all change situations. Chapter 10 goes beyond the Planned and Emergent approaches to develop a *Framework for Change* that relates the various change situations organisations face to the range of approaches to managing change on offer. Chapter 10 concludes Part 2 by arguing that, though organisations face significant constraints on their freedom of choice, these constraints can be influenced and changed in order to allow organisations to choose the particular approach to strategy and change that best suits them.

Part 3: Managing choice comprises the concluding two chapters of the book. Chapter 11 combines the insights and perspectives from Parts 1 and 2 to create a Choice Management–Change Management model of organisational change. This model, which comprises three interlinked processes – choice, trajectory and change – provides an understanding of how managers and organisations can and do exercise choice and manage change. Given the importance attached to the role of managers in developing strategy and managing change, Chapter 12 reviews what managers do and how they do it. In particular, the role of leadership and management development is examined and related to approaches to change management. The chapter and the book conclude that if, as argued, managers have considerable choice over what to change and how to change it, then this lays a considerable responsibility on their shoulders. How organisations change and develop has enormous consequences, not just for their employees and owners but for society at large. In order to minimise social fragmentation and exclusion, and the destruction of the natural environment, managers need to act in the broader interests of all their stakeholders – employees, shareholders, themselves and the wider community.

The fifth edition

Since the publication of the fourth edition of this book, I have received many helpful comments and suggestions for improving and developing this book both from my own students and colleagues at the University of Manchester and from readers and users elsewhere. I am very grateful for these and have tried to utilise them in preparing this fifth edition. The main changes from the fourth edition are as follows:

- The case studies now appear at the end of each chapter. In the previous edition, the case studies were in three separate chapters plus a summary chapter.
- Consequently, the number of chapters has been reduced from 16 to 12.
- The number of case studies has been expanded from 10 to 12, and 5 of these are new to this edition. In addition, expanded versions of most of the case studies can be found on the book's website.
- The focus of each of the case studies has been linked to the topic of the chapter in which it appears. However, as in previous editions, the cases can still be used as stand-alone studies of change.
- Each of the chapters has been updated to reflect developments in the field since the fourth edition. The opportunity has also been taken to clarify and re-organise material to make it more accessible to readers, e.g. the section on culture in Chapter 5.
- The number of illustrations in each chapter has been expanded.

Part 1 The rise and fall of the rational organisation

CHAPTER 1

From trial and error to the science of management

The rise of organisation theory

Learning objectives

After studying this chapter, you should be able to:

- understand the development of work organisation from the Industrial Revolution until the beginning of the twentieth century;
- appreciate the reasons for the antagonistic relations between labour and employers in the nineteenth century;
- discuss the different roles played by technology and people in the development of the factory system;
- describe the main features of the Classical approach;
- understand why the Classical approach developed as it did in the USA, France and Germany;
- discuss the differences and similarities between the work of Taylor, Fayol and Weber;
- list the main advantages and disadvantages of the Classical approach to structuring organisations and designing jobs;
- describe the key features of the Classical approach to organisational change.

Ideas and perspectives 1.1
The case of Scientific Management

Frederick Taylor on Scientific Management

The principal object of management should be to secure the maximum prosperity for the employer, coupled with the maximum prosperity for each employé.

The words 'maximum prosperity' are used, in their broad sense, to mean not only large dividends for the company or owner, but the development of every branch of the business to its highest state of excellence, so that the prosperity may be permanent.

In the same way maximum prosperity for each employé means not only higher wages than are usually received by men of his class, but, of more importance still, it also means the development of each man to his state of maximum efficiency, so that he may be able to do, generally speaking, the highest grade of work for which his natural abilities fit him, and it further means giving him, when possible, this class of work to do.

It would seem to be so self-evident that maximum prosperity for the employer, coupled with maximum prosperity for the employé, ought to be the two leading objects of management, that even to state this fact should be unnecessary. And yet there is no question that, throughout the industrial world, a large part of the organization of employers, as well as employés, is for war rather than for peace, and that perhaps the majority on either side do not believe that it is possible so to arrange their mutual relations that their interests become identical.

The majority of these men believe that the fundamental interests of employés and employers are necessarily antagonistic. Scientific management, on the contrary, has for its very foundation the firm conviction that the true interests of the two are one and the same; that prosperity for the employer cannot exist through a long term of years unless it is accompanied by prosperity for the employé, and vice versa; and that it is possible to give the workman what he most wants – high wages – and the employer what he wants – a low labor cost – for his manufactures.

Source: Frederick Winslow Taylor, *The Principles of Scientific Management*, 1911, p. 1.

Introduction

In Britain and the rest of the industrial world today, it is almost impossible to imagine life without the plethora of organisations that comprise and make possible our everyday life. Yet organisations in their modern form – indeed, in almost any form – were virtually unknown before the beginning of the Industrial Revolution in the late eighteenth century. In the intervening period, as Morgan (1986) remarked, we have developed into an 'organizational society'. However, not only have organisations, in their many shapes, sizes and manifestations, come to reach into every facet of our lives, but they have also acquired an equally diverse range of theories, nostrums and semi-sacrosanct beliefs about how they should be structured, managed and changed.

This chapter sets out to explore and discuss the origins of organisations, from the Industrial Revolution to the early years of the twentieth century, when the first detailed and comprehensive organisation theory emerged. As Ideas and perspectives 1.1 shows, two of the overarching and complementary characteristics of this period were the conflict between workers and managers, and the search for a systematic, scientific, and above all efficient approach to running and changing organisations. The key themes of this chapter are as follows:

- Although industrialisation was primarily concerned with the move from a subsistence economy to a money-market economy, the main enabling mechanism for this was the creation of the factory system.
- The pattern and purpose of industrialisation varied from country to country. Whilst in Britain and the USA it was very much driven by individuals seeking profit maximisation, in mainland Europe a different approach can be seen. In Germany in particular, but also in France, industrialisation was largely state-sponsored, and aimed more to further the economic and military objectives of the state than to increase the profit-making capacity of individuals.
- The development of organisation theory was synonymous with the need by managers to legitimate and enhance their authority to initiate change.

The chapter begins by showing how the rapid expansion of national and international commercial activity created the conditions for the British Industrial Revolution, from which emerged the factory system, the precursor of all modern organisations. It is argued that the driving force behind this development was the merchant class. It will also be stressed that two key features of the early factory system were its *ad hoc*, trial-and-error nature, and the antagonistic relationship between owners and employees, or – to use the terminology of the times – masters and servants.

The chapter then goes on to show that British industrial practices, methods and technologies were 'exported' to other European countries and the USA, with similar results in terms of employer–employee relations. As the nineteenth century progressed, and organisations grew in number and size, trial and error increasingly gave way to more considered and consistent approaches to work organisation. This development was especially pronounced in the USA and continental Europe, as industrial leadership moved away from Britain and towards these areas.

What emerged, separately, were three different but complementary attempts by Frederick Taylor in the USA, Henri Fayol in France and Max Weber in Germany to replace the *ad hoc*, rule-of-thumb approach to organisations with a universally applicable blueprint or theory for how they should be managed. These three approaches, each focusing on different organisational aspects, coalesced into what later became known as the Classical school of organisation theory. This approach to organisations is characterised by:

- The horizontal and hierarchical division of labour.
- The minimisation of human skills and discretion.
- The attempt to construe organisations as rational–scientific entities.

It is argued that one of the key objectives of the Classical school, especially the Scientific Management component, was to legitimise the managerial right to plan and implement change by showing that it was the only group able to analyse the work situation scientifically and rationally, and to devise the most appropriate and efficient methods of operation.

The chapter concludes by arguing that the Classical approach, whilst being a significant advance on what went before, was badly flawed. In particular, its view of human nature and motivation was not only inaccurate, but also counterproductive in that it alienated workers from and made them resentful of the organisations that employed them. However, the precepts of the Classical school were not solely aimed at constraining workers' ability to make and block change; in addition, by laying down hard and fast rules of what was and was not best practice, they constrained management's freedom of action, thus alienating many managers as well as workers.

With hindsight, the attempt by Taylor, Fayol and Weber each in their own way to formulate a system of reciprocal obligations between managers and workers appears to be less a decisive break with the past and more an attempt to recast feudalism in a more scientific–rational framework. Certainly, in the late nineteenth century, French, German and American managers of European descent did share a recent and common feudal heritage which might make them well-disposed towards a system that replaced management–worker conflict with a code of joint obligation. Indeed, in Germany, the rise of bureaucracy that Weber described was itself a direct product of the Prussian feudal tradition. However, though many managers undoubtedly did long for and believe in an – albeit mythical – age when workers readily did as they were told, this ignored the fact that most American immigrants left Europe to escape just such a system, whilst French workers took pride in the belief that their Revolution had ended feudal despotism. Only in Germany was it possible to say that the feudal tradition remained strong, though not unopposed.

The rise of commerce and the birth of the factory

The pivotal event that shaped the world into the form we now see around us was the British Industrial Revolution, which began in the late eighteenth century. Before it, most societies were based on small-scale, self-sufficient agricultural production, with the vast majority of the population, some 80–90 per cent, living in the countryside. By the end of the nineteenth century, after the Industrial Revolution had run its course, the reverse became the case, in the leading industrialised countries at least, with most people living in urban centres and depending on industrial and commercial activities for their livelihood (Landes, 1969).

Britain was the pioneer industrial country; it was the model that other European nations and the USA sought to emulate in their attempts to transform traditional agrarian economies into urban societies based on science and technology (Kemp, 1979). The key development of the Industrial Revolution towards this process of societal transformation was the creation of the factory system. It was this that gave the impetus to and created the model for all that was to follow. As Weber (1928: 302) pointed out, the factory's distinguishing characteristic was:

. . . in general . . . not the implements of work applied but the concentration of owner-ship of workplace, means of work, source of power and raw materials in one and the same hand, that of the entrepreneur.

Or, to put it another way, it was the way the entrepreneur 'organised' the elements of production that distinguished it from what went before.

This tells us what changed, but it does not explain why or how in a few score years organisations came to dominate our lives. To answer this, it is necessary to appreciate the great surge of economic activity – especially the international trade in textile products – that arose in the seventeenth and eighteenth centuries. This trade gave an enormous impetus to textile production in Britain, which in turn had a knock-on effect in all other spheres of economic activity (Mathias, 1969).

Before and during the early part of the British Industrial Revolution, textile produc-tion was carried out as an agricultural by-occupation based on family units. However, as demand increased in the eighteenth century, some 'men and women [became] spe-cialist spinners or weavers, thinking first of wool, treating work on the land as, at most, a by-occupation' (Ashton, 1948: 23). Allied to this, a new mechanism sprang up to link producer and consumer: the 'putting-out' system, whereby a large merchant would 'put out' work to a number of independent domestic producers.

The advantage to the merchant was threefold:

- It was cheap – there were few overheads.
- It was flexible – production could be easily expanded or contracted.
- It avoided the difficulties involved in directly employing a workforce.

However, as demand continued to increase in the late eighteenth century, this system became more complex and more costly, and eventually it became too cumbersome (Pollard, 1965). The chain of intermediaries linking producer to consumer became increasingly difficult for the large merchant to control. There were many problems with the putting-out mechanism: dishonesty (on both sides) was rife; deliveries were late; and quality was often poor. Laws attempting to control producers could do nothing to rectify the fundamental weaknesses in the system. The incompatibility between the large and com-plex organisation of distribution and the multitude of tiny domestic workshop units, unsupervised and unsupervisable, was bound to set up tensions and drive merchants to seek new ways of production – ways whereby they could establish their own managerial control over the production process (Pollard, 1965).

There was also an incompatibility between different cultures. For the merchant, the expansion of markets was a chance to maximise profits in order to live in the grand style. For the rural domestic producer, involved in long hours of back-breaking work, it created the conditions for increased leisure. As Marglin (1976: 35) commented:

. . . wages rose and workers insisted on taking out a portion of their gains in the form of greater leisure. However sensible this may have been from their own point of view, it is no way for an enterprising capitalist to get ahead.

Therefore, it was the merchant who began the move towards the factory system – not because the merchant had an innate desire to run factories or exercise direct control over labour, but in order to take full advantage of expanding market opportunities to reap ever greater rewards.

Nevertheless, there was no headlong rush to create a new economic order overnight. The earliest factories, if that is not too grand a word for them, were small, unpowered weaving or spinning sheds that used existing technology and methods. A few very large factories – such as Wedgwood's Etruria Works in Stoke-on-Trent – were established, but these were the rare exceptions. Indeed, in 1780, the investment in fixed equipment and stock in the textile industry, which was the leading edge of the Industrial Revolution, was only £10 per worker, and the average factory employed no more than 10 or 12 people. By 1830, when the textile industry had grown to employ 100,000 people and the average factory size was 137, the investment in fixed equipment and stock had only increased to £15 per worker, and 50 per cent of the workforce were still home-based (Hobsbawm, 1968; Pollard, 1965; Tillett, 1970). Given this situation, it is hardly surprising that capital investment was quickly recovered and that it was running expenses, mainly wages and raw materials, which formed the bulk of manufacturing costs. It is this, and the original motive for moving to the factory system in the first place (to have greater control over labour), which explains the prevailing attitude of employers towards labour in the nineteenth century.

The relationship between employers and employees

British employers based their attitude towards employees on two basic propositions:

1. Labour is unreliable, lazy and will only work when tightly controlled and closely supervised.
2. The main controllable business cost is labour; therefore the key to increased profits is to make it cheaper, and/or increase its productivity, by getting employees to work harder, or for longer hours, for the same, or less, money.

In this respect, as contemporary writers such as Charles Babbage (1835) and Andrew Ure (1835) observed, workers' skill was seen as at best an inconvenience and at worst a threat, because it could be scarce, costly and allow workers a strong bargaining position.

As might be expected, employers' hostility was reciprocated by labour. Workers exhibited a strong dislike for, and reluctance to become part of, the factory system. As Pollard (1965) noted, this was for three main reasons:

1. It involved a wholesale change of culture and environment and the destruction of small, tightly knit communities in which they lived. Hard though the life of cottage industry was, it had given workers a measure of independence and some control over what they did, when they did it and how.
2. The discipline of the factory was harsh and unremitting with men, women and even small children all expected to work long hours, often seven days a week, in appalling conditions.
3. Given the lack of alternative organisational forms on which to establish factory life, employers often modelled them on workhouses or prisons. Indeed, to square the circle, some workhouses and prisons turned themselves into factories and their inmates into little more than slaves. Thus factories acquired the same stigma as was attached to prisons and workhouses.

Therefore, the antagonism that existed between owners and workers was based on a genuine clash of interests – one which has echoed through the industrial world ever since.

If this picture of the factory system in the nineteenth century seems bleak to us, it is nevertheless accurate, as is shown in the work of its proponents such as Charles Babbage and Andrew Ure, social reformers such as Seebohm Rowntree, political activists such as Frederick Engels and contemporary novelists such as Charles Dickens. Nor was this aspect of industrialisation restricted to Britain. Studies of other European countries and the USA have shown similar tensions, sometimes even more violent, between the old and the new methods of working, and between employers and employees (Bruland, 1989; Chapman and Chassagne, 1981; Mantoux, 1964; Pelling, 1960).

In defence of the factory owners, who must take responsibility for what emerged, it should be said that their own experience was limited and there were no textbooks to guide them. That they should 'copy' what models existed reflected both the common view of labour amongst the owning classes, and a lack of alternative organisational forms on which to base the emergent factory system. As other nations industrialised, notably Germany, France and the United States, they too adopted similar organisational forms and espoused similar attitudes towards labour. Partly this was because they were seeking to emulate Britain's success by copying her approach. It was also because these societies, like Great Britain, were riven by hierarchical and horizontal divisions that were inevitably reproduced in the workplace.

Industrialisation and the organisation of work

The system of organising work that came to characterise industrial life in Britain and most of continental Europe, and even the USA, by the end of the nineteenth century was based on the hierarchical and horizontal division of labour. Though this represented a significant break with the past in terms of how work had previously been organised, it was not out of step with the social stratification of European society nor with feudal traditions of obedience. The articulation and propagation of the principle of the division of labour owed much to the work of Adam Smith. In his book *The Wealth of Nations*, published in 1776, Smith used the now famous example of pin-making to illustrate what he saw as the advantages of the division of labour. He pointed out that a pin could be made entirely by one person doing everything, or by a number of people each specialising in one aspect of its production. For three reasons, he believed the latter was more efficient:

1. A worker who constantly performs one simple task will quickly acquire greater dexterity than one who performs a variety of tasks.
2. It avoids the loss of time necessitated by one person moving from one task to another.
3. The concentration of attention on one special task leads to the invention of machines that aid the productivity of labour and allow one person to do the work previously performed by many.

Smith's ideas were given flesh and form in Britain by pioneering factory owners such as Josiah Wedgwood, and Matthew Boulton and James Watt. At his Etruria pottery works, Wedgwood developed a production system that split the work process down into separate departments, each with its own specialist supervisor. Work was organised almost on a flow-line basis with the skill involved in each operation reduced to a minimum in order, in Wedgwood's own words, 'to make machines of men as cannot err' (quoted in Tillett, 1970: 37). Matthew Boulton and James Watt developed a similar approach at their Soho Works in Birmingham in the 1770s. They also kept detailed production records, a practice virtually unknown at the time (Roll, 1930). Wedgwood, Boulton, Watt and a few others were the architects of the factory system. By their organisation of work on and off the shopfloor, they created models that later managers would copy and adapt to their own needs and circumstances.

This approach to the organisation and control of work spread outwards from Britain. As Bruland (1989: 165) observed:

> There was a fairly direct international diffusion of these changes from Britain, the originating economy: British workers, in most parts of Europe, played a significant role in spreading the new work systems, in training local workers, and in the adaptation of the work force to the new rhythms of work.

As the nineteenth century progressed, this approach to work organisation became more developed and systematised. Charles Babbage (1835) developed a method of applying the division of labour principle to the detailed analysis of any job. He emphasised the need for and advantage of dividing tasks between and within mental and manual labour. He envisaged three 'classes' employed in the work process:

- The entrepreneur and his technical specialists who would design machines and plan the form of work organisation.
- Operative engineers and managers who would be responsible for executing such plans and designs, based on only partial knowledge of the processes involved.
- The mass of employees, needing only a low level of skill, who would undertake the actual work.

Thus, in Babbage's (1835: vii) view:

> . . . the master manufacturer, by dividing the work to be executed into different processes, each requiring different degrees of skill or force, can purchase exactly the precise quality of both which is necessary for each process . . .

Though coming from separate traditions, Smith's work was also in tune with the Prussian bureaucratic school, and undoubtedly the efficient organisation of German industry in the late nineteenth century owes much to a combination of the two approaches.

The pioneers of these developments in work organisation, whether in Britain, Germany or other European countries, tended to be strict disciplinarians who used their personal authority to impose the new working arrangements on a usually reluctant workforce (Chapman and Chassagne, 1981). Therefore, change tended to be managed by imposition and force rather than negotiation and agreement. Nor is it surprising that it should be so. In the main these were countries which had been, in the recent past, feudal economies dominated by warrior elites. In Germany, this was still the case. Even where, as in France, there had been a decisive break with the past, this seems merely to have reinforced rather than removed patterns of social rigidity and authoritarianism.

In such situations, resistance to or questioning of change was unlikely to be met by understanding or tolerance. Predictably, there was strong resistance, both active and passive, to the introduction of new working patterns and methods (Kriedte et al, 1981). Though this resistance could and did take the form of physical violence against factories and equipment, a more frequent manifestation was high labour turnover. One of the largest Manchester cotton spinning firms, McConnell and Kennedy, had an average turnover in the early nineteenth century of 100 per cent per year, a high but not uncommon rate (Fitton and Wadsworth, 1958; Pollard, 1965). A similar situation existed in other European countries. As Lee (1978: 460) noted, in Germany employers:

> . . . were generally satisfied if they achieved partial success in creating a stable core of skilled workers . . . Turnover was the most persistent labour problem confronting employers.

This situation clearly gave those workers whose skills were most in demand a significant bargaining position, which allowed them to raise their wages and determine the pace of work. However, it also acted as a spur to employers to seek methods of reducing their reliance on skilled labour (Bruland, 1989). One of the main ways that entrepreneurs responded was through technological developments aimed at replacing or reducing employers' reliance on skilled labour.

A contemporary observer of the nineteenth-century industrial scene, Andrew Ure (1836: viii–ix), drew special attention to the role that technology could play in this process:

> By developing machines . . . which require only unskilled instead of skilled labour, the cost of labour can be reduced [and] the bargaining position of the worker reduced.

It becomes clear why workers not only opposed the advent of the factory system but also, even when it became established, continued to oppose strongly changes in work practices and the introduction of new equipment. Even in the present day, where change tends to be preceded by consultation and its beneficial effects are stressed, there is still a tendency for those concerned to feel apprehensive of, if not downright resistant towards, change (Smith *et al*, 1982). Therefore, in a harsher and more authoritarian age, where organisational and technological change was seen as a weapon in the battle for control of the workplace, it is not surprising that change management should be achieved by imposition and coercion, and occasion the response that it did.

Nevertheless, despite the increasing opposition of 'organised' labour, the work practices associated with the factory system gradually permeated every aspect of industrial and commercial life, albeit only on a piecemeal basis. Even by the end of the nineteenth century, there was no unified or accepted approach that managers could apply to organisations in their entirety, though in Germany the application of the Prussian bureaucratic model allied to the approach to industrial organisation of Adam Smith was proving influential. Yet the developing factory system could not shake off the legacy of its origins or ignore the continuing battle between labour and management over control, rewards and skill. As the following shows, this was as much the case in continental Europe and the USA as it was in Britain.

Europe

The history of Europe since 1800, at least in economic terms, is essentially the history of industrialisation, of structural change through which industrial sectors grew and non-agricultural sectors came for the first time to dominate economic life. In general, for most of the nineteenth century, continental Europe lagged behind Britain in terms of industrial development. However, just as Britain was something of a patchwork quilt in terms of the pace of development of individual industries and regions, so too was the rest of Europe (Davis, 1989). As Pollard (1981) explained, European industrialisation developed from a few core regions. In Britain, southern Lancashire, the West Riding of Yorkshire and that part of the West Midlands called the Black Country were the engines of growth. In northern Europe, the area between the Scheldt, the Meuse and the Rhine rivers had a special role to play, whilst to the east, Silesia, Bohemia and Moravia became leading centres of industrial progress. In the south, it was northern Italy and Catalonia that led the way.

Nevertheless, though mainland Europe did have its pockets of progress, industrialisation did not spread from these at the same rate nor in the same manner as it had in Britain. The most outstanding feature of British industrialisation was its self-generating or autonomous nature. Nowhere else could these conditions be exactly reproduced. To use an analogy, once the wheel has been invented, others cannot reinvent it. What they can do is adopt it and adapt it to their needs and circumstances.

Therefore, Britain became a model to be consciously followed. In the same way that Japan became a focus for study, discussion and emulation by Westerners in the 1980s, so Britain was similarly regarded in the early nineteenth century. Regular visits were made by foreign governments and private entrepreneurs to discover and copy British methods and technologies. In some instances, British investors, entrepreneurs and inventors were encouraged by the governments of France, Germany and other European states to help develop their economies – all with the aim of reproducing and overtaking Britain's industrial lead.

For some, especially Germany and France, the process of industrialisation was less a matter of material progress by organisations and individuals pursuing profit maximisation, and more concerned with the maintenance of their position in the world. Just as they sought to challenge Britain's military might, so they sought to emulate her industrial power. They could not and would not let Britain dominate the world without a struggle. Therefore, though the advent of industrial capitalism was in all countries characterised by the rise of a class of industrialists who aggressively sought to maximise their own wealth, the context in which this occurred varied from country to country.

In Britain and the USA, the context favoured individual entrepreneurs pursuing their own self-interest. In Germany, and to a lesser extent France, industrialisation was sponsored by the state and for the state. The prime motive was to build the economic and military might of the state rather than the wealth of the individual. Where these were compatible, the state was happy to maintain a watching brief. However, where free enterprise and competition were seen as counter-productive to the objectives of the state, it intervened to reduce competition either through the creation of cartels and monopolies, or by state ownership or funding, as was the case with much of the European railway system. In Denmark, on the other hand, the operation of the market was constrained not by the state but by the creation of cooperatives, which allowed small-scale farming and business, and the way of life they represented, to survive where in other countries such enterprises were overwhelmed by larger competitors.

Therefore, though other countries used Britain as a model and benchmark, the actual process of industrialisation in each depended upon the unique political, social and economic circumstances that prevailed there. In some cases these gave primacy to profit maximisation, in others the interests of the state held sway, whilst in further cases sectional interests successfully challenged the power of the market. Consequently, influential though the British example was, once the necessary technique, capital and enterprise were introduced abroad and any element of conscious emulation had worn off, the industrialisation assumed a different character (Kemp, 1979). The continental countries did not and could not simply duplicate British experience.

There were, however, some fundamental similarities. All European societies, to a lesser or greater extent, were structured on a hierarchical basis, with those in positions of power strongly influenced in their view of the rest of society by feudal traditions of subservience and obedience. This was as much the case in post-revolutionary France as in Britain, and even more so in Prussia and Russia. It follows that the organisational forms and labour relations that characterised the emerging factory system in Britain found fertile ground elsewhere in Europe (Cipolla, 1973).

Despite this, other countries did not copy Britain unthinkingly or on a wholesale basis. As latecomers, they could, especially with the encouragement of the state, leapfrog some of the stages of industrialisation, which was one of their principal advantages, but they could not close the gap between themselves and Britain overnight. Ashworth (1987) commented that even as late as 1850, apart from Belgium, Europe had little mechanised industry to speak of; however, 50 years later, Germany had overtaken Britain as the leading industrial nation, and other nations were also poised to do so. The reasons for this are many and complex, involving social and political as well as economic factors (Mathias and Davis, 1989). A brief look at industrial development in Germany, France and Scandinavia illustrates this.

Germany

Within the space of a generation in the middle years of the nineteenth century, Germany was transformed from a collection of economically backward states forming a political patchwork in central Europe into a unified empire, driven forward by a rapidly expanding, technologically-centred industrial base (Kemp, 1979). Germany's progress was so rapid that, though it industrialised much later, by the end of the nineteenth century it had overtaken Britain as the world's premier industrial nation. This transformation, accompanied as it was by the deliberate resort to military force as an instrument of national policy, and an atmosphere of fierce nationalism, represented an event of major historical significance (Borchardt, 1973).

The two key factors that were primarily responsible for the nature and pace of German industrial development were the geographical and political conditions of the country, and the fact that German industrialisation was state-promoted rather than market-driven.

To look first at geography and politics: not until the late nineteenth century did Germany possess an integrated territory with an economic and administrative centre. Up to the nineteenth century, Germany was a collection of feudal fiefdoms that often warred with each other, rather than a unified nation. In 1789, 'Germany' comprised some 314 independent territories each with their own rulers, internal markets, customs barriers, currencies and trading monopolies. This internal fragmentation, as much as anything else, was probably the key obstacle to industrial progress. This did not change until the Congress of Vienna in 1815, which reduced the number of German states to 39. Each individual state then began to remove internal customs barriers and develop better communications systems, which opened the way for greater economic cooperation with other states.

However, unlike other countries, economic progress was neither driven nor accompanied by a democratisation of society. German society in the nineteenth century remained dominated by a feudal hierarchy. This was characterised by Prussian 'Junkerdom' with its military traditions and ambitions, and its autocratic behaviour. Unlike their counterparts in other countries, the German nobility were not diminished by industrial progress; rather they managed to seize the reins of commercial power to bolster their position. This was due, in many instances, to their retention of regional monopolies over trade, industry and the supply of labour.

This leads on to the second key feature of German industrialisation – the fact that it was state-promoted rather than free-market-driven. The drive for industrialisation, especially in Prussia, which came to dominate the rest of Germany, was not primarily motivated by economic reasons. Rather, industrialisation was seen as the process of building a strong and powerful state in which the old nobility continued to dominate. Therefore, for Germany, the fact that industrialisation was accompanied by the development of a strong military machine and the continued dominance of the Prussian Junkers was not an unfortunate coincidence, but its major objective.

Industrial progress in Britain exerted a strong influence on Germany. This was partly because it provided a model to emulate, but mainly because Germany saw industrial power and military power as two sides of the same coin. Unless Germany could catch up with and overtake Britain's industrial lead, Germany felt that it would be relegated to the status of a second-class state.

The transformation of Germany into an industrial superpower owed much to the role played by Prussia. From the early nineteenth century onwards, Prussia used its economic and military position as the most powerful German state to subdue the other German states and exclude possible rivals, especially Austria. The prime weapon in the Prussian arsenal was the creation of an all-German customs union (the *Zollverein*). Because of its size, Prussia could determine the rules for the *Zollverein* and, whenever and wherever it was extended, could ensure it was to Prussian advantage.

The customs union, because it opened up trade, also gave a boost to the development of better transportation and communication links, especially railway building (though the latter really took off once the Prussian military came to appreciate its strategic significance for the rapid transit of troops and materials). It seems very clear that, more than the emergence of any one industry, it was the creation of a single market and the boost to consumption that this brought about which was the key factor in Germany's economic progress in the nineteenth century (Kemp, 1979).

By 1834, practically all of Germany was included within the customs union and, though it did not come about until 1871, this provided the essential precondition for political unification. The fact that both political and economic unification were driven by and dominated by Prussia gave German industrialisation its unique character. The new German state that was established in 1871, for all its acceptance of universal suffrage and a national parliament, remained an autocracy ruled by the Hohenzollern dynasty, which still rested on the support of the traditional landed nobility of eastern Germany. It incorporated the bureaucratic and militarist traditions of the old Prussia and remained profoundly conservative.

Indeed, it was the adoption of the Prussian bureaucratic model by both state and industry, combined with close links between the two, which gave German industry its unique character. Unlike Britain, where the majority of firms remained relatively small and business operated in an *ad hoc* fashion, with each company pursuing its own interests, in Germany large, bureaucratically structured organisations became the norm. In addition, the state did not hesitate to intervene directly, for example when it nationalised the railways, if it believed the private sector could not or would not serve the national interest.

Given that the state saw German industry as almost an extension of government, it is not surprising that it sought to bolster managerial authority and restrict workers' rights. This also very much reflected the Prussian autocratic tradition of expecting and enforcing obedience from those lower down the social order. Therefore, in most – though not all – enterprises, employers took the view that they had a right to treat their workers however they pleased. A German employer regarded himself as a patriarch, as the master in his own house in pre-industrial terms, with total responsibility for the whole social organism of his enterprise and generally well beyond this. This type of self-esteem made German employers particularly unyielding in any situation of conflict.

One consequence of this was that the industrial and political climate became increasingly radical after the political and economic unification of Germany in 1871, though to no great effect. This period also saw the rapid development of the German economy. In 1870, the leading British enterprises were much bigger than their largest German competitors; by 1900, this position had been reversed. In many cases this was the result of governmental and banking encouragement to move to vertical integration. Also, cartels and monopolies, frowned upon elsewhere, received official endorsement in Germany, which allowed more orderly growth and longer-term investment decisions than might otherwise have been the case.

By the end of the nineteenth century the German economy had outstripped its British counterpart, but had not succeeded in avoiding either the same debilitating conflict between employers and employees, or the rise of political groups and parties which challenged the nature and purpose of capitalism. However, the influence of the Prussian autocratic tradition, the development of a strong bureaucratic approach within both private- and public-sector organisations, and the close relationship between industry and state, meant that industrial and political resistance was met by a unified and implacable alliance between employers and government. Though prepared to use welfare provisions, sickness benefit, old age pensions, etc., to reduce social tensions, the state was not prepared to cede one iota of industrial or political authority.

France

As in Germany, the process of industrialisation in France was driven by the desire to emulate Britain, rather than by any form of 'spontaneous combustion'. However, despite having the advantage of much earlier state encouragement than in Germany, France's industrial revolution was late in starting and did not reach maturity until towards the end of the nineteenth century (Dunham, 1955; Fohlen, 1973). The slow and late development of industry in France appears to have been caused by two key factors: political change and agrarian stagnation, both of which were inextricably linked with the French Revolution of 1789.

In the eighteenth century, little separated France and Britain in industrial terms. With much encouragement from the monarchy, French industry adopted British machines and equipment. British entrepreneurs and inventors were even persuaded to establish factories in France. During the last years before the French Revolution, the king paid great attention to the economy. A twin-track approach to industrial development was instituted. On the one hand, much state aid and encouragement were poured into industry; whilst on the other hand, there was the suppression of every obstacle to individual entrepreneurship, whether they be the privileges of the craft guilds or the ancient rights of the aristocracy.

Though these initiatives gave a significant boost to industrialisation, progress was halted, and even reversed, by the French Revolution in 1789 (Marczewski, 1963). To an extent this is surprising, given that those who dominated the Revolutionary Assemblies were men of property and substance, though drawn from the law and professions rather than the business world. They believed in upholding property rights, abolishing hereditary privilege and vested interests, and providing a favourable climate for entrepreneurship. They also introduced laws that placed employees in an inferior legal position to their employers and which prohibited them from combining for the purpose of bargaining. Nevertheless, the benefits of these to entrepreneurs were outweighed by other consequences of the Revolution. Foremost amongst these was the loss of most of France's colonial empire, together with its isolation, by the British naval blockade, from key markets such as the United States. The result was not only that France lost crucial imports and exports, but also that it was cut off from the prime source of technical and organisational innovation, Britain.

It was not until the final defeat of Napoleon in 1815 that France was once again able to concentrate on developing its economy rather than fighting wars. As before, the state took a lead in encouraging economic development, notably through the development of roads, canals and, later, railways. It also sought to stimulate the domestic economy by introducing import controls. However, this seems only to have allowed industry to keep outdated methods and equipment and maintain higher prices longer than might have been the case if it had not operated in a protected market. Only after 1850, with the upsurge in economic activity across Europe and the coming to power of Napoleon III, does the French economy really seem to have taken off.

The other main factor which held back industrialisation was the backward state of agriculture. The peasantry were already developing as an important group even before the French Revolution. However, the price they exacted for supporting the Revolution, the ownership of the majority of agricultural land, made them a powerful but reactionary force to which all sections of the property-owning classes had to pay attention. The consequences of this for industrialisation were twofold. First, the agricultural sector, unlike its counterparts in Britain and Germany, remained self-sufficient and inefficient for most of the nineteenth century. As such, it was incapable of generating either wealth for investing in industry or demand for manufactured goods produced by industry. Second, by depressing the rate of population growth, it prevented the mass population exodus from the countryside to the towns and thus starved industry of a ready supply of cheap labour. This situation was further exacerbated by the continuing opportunities for home work which, by supplementing agricultural incomes, extended the viability of rural life longer than might otherwise be the case.

Nevertheless, the continued existence of a large rural population, even up to the dawn of the twentieth century, was not just a product of land ownership and the presence of home work. It also owed a great deal to the presence of import barriers which allowed peasants to maintain, in comparison with their British counterparts, inefficient production methods, and reduced the need either to borrow money for new equipment or to sell plots that were too small to be viable.

Import barriers also produced a strong bond of self-interest between peasants and factory owners, both of whom saw free trade as a threat to their way of life. As one observer commented, 'Competition was always possible in France, it simply did not happen to be a preferred form of conduct' (Sheahan, 1969: 25).

For industrialists, the result was similar. The absence of foreign competition, allied to low levels of domestic demand, allowed the typical business to remain family-owned, and also relatively small. Finance for industrial expansion was raised from family members rather than financial institutions, which in turn restricted the size of the banking sector. Indeed, such was the shortage of domestically generated capital and risk-orientated entrepreneurs that the building of railways, so vital to the development of the French economy, could not have taken place without foreign capital and state support (Kemp, 1979).

Therefore, unlike in Britain, industrialisation in France was never driven by, or resulted in, individual enterprise or profit maximisation. For the state, the objective was a strong France. For the peasant and small entrepreneur, the objective was to make a reasonable living in the context of the rural and urban cultures they supported and valued.

Scandinavia

Having looked at how the three largest and most advanced European countries – Britain, Germany and France – industrialised, we shall now move on to examine how three of the smaller states – Sweden, Denmark and Norway – responded to the challenge of industrialisation. In 1800, the total population of these three countries was just over 4 million people: Sweden, 2.35 million; Denmark, 0.93 million; and Norway, 0.88 million. By 1910, it was still less than 11 million: Sweden, 5.5 million; Denmark, 2.8 million; and Norway, 2.4 million. The historical links between these countries were very close, and up to the First World War they operated a monetary union. Although, owing to their seafaring traditions, each had occupied a position of importance on the international stage, by the mid-nineteenth century the standing of all three countries had declined. In fact, Norway and Sweden had become two of the poorest countries in Europe, which was a prime reason for the large-scale emigration from these countries to the USA in the nineteenth century (Milward and Saul, 1973).

Despite growing pockets of industrial production, in the nineteenth century their domestic economies were weak, and all three countries depended heavily on exporting the products of their agricultural, mining and forestry industries to their more industrialised neighbours, especially Britain. That they were able to adapt their export efforts to the changing demands of the international economy bears witness to the entrepreneurial skills of these countries.

However, political, economic and social developments in these three countries in the nineteenth century, particularly in Denmark, laid the foundations for the creation of the

'Nordic model' of industrial relations, which emerged in the 1930s. This arose from the so-called 'historic compromise' between capital and labour, which extended cooperation between employers and social democratic governments over national economic policy into the industrial relations field. At a national level, it was agreed that the efforts of social democratic governments to bring about economic growth would not challenge the capitalist nature of production. Trade unions accepted this approach in exchange for basic trade union rights. This paved the way for an end to lock-outs and other such tactics by employers, and the creation of government-backed approaches to industrial democracy and further extensions of workers' rights (Dolvik and Stokland, 1992; Ferner and Hyman, 1992; Kjellberg, 1992).

These developments happened at different times and at a different pace in each country. Denmark led the way in the late nineteenth century, and Norway and Sweden followed a decade later, though the 'Nordic model' did not really establish itself fully until the 1930s and 1940s. However, the close ties between these three countries meant that political and industrial developments in one affected the other two. Hence the phrase 'Nordic model' was coined to describe similarities between the tripartite approaches adopted by government, employers and trade unions in each country, and the fact that these were distinct from practices elsewhere in Europe (or the rest of the world for that matter). However, for the moment, we are more concerned with the process of industrialisation in the nineteenth century and how this paved the way for these later developments.

For **Sweden**, the nineteenth century brought a rapidly rising population, which was matched by an increasingly productive agricultural sector that not only fully met domestic needs, but also developed a strong export market in grain, especially to Britain. The productivity of agriculture reflected the growing flexibility and commercialisation of this sector, facilitated by a series of gradual and peaceful rural reforms.

The iron trade also occupied an important position in the Swedish economy for much of the nineteenth century. This was due in no small part to its ability to adopt technological innovations, mainly from Britain, and the ability of Swedish ironmasters to seek out new international markets. By the end of the century, this had led to fewer but larger units of production, and the industry began to reflect the structures and methods of the leading European producers.

Despite the growth of agriculture and iron production, the most spectacular element in the growth of the Swedish economy was the boom in timber exports (Jorberg, 1973). Up to the 1830s, Swedish exports were only a fraction of those of Norway. However, the increasing urbanisation of Britain, and growing demand for timber from France and Germany, transformed the pattern of demand and supply. By the 1860s, softwood accounted for 40 per cent of all Sweden's exports, a situation that lasted well into the 1880s.

With over 20 million hectares of productive forest, Sweden possessed the largest such area in Europe, after Russia. The growth in markets was matched by the introduction of new methods and techniques, especially the use of steam engines and fine-bladed saws at the mills. The transfer of land ownership from the state to the private sector, in the early nineteenth century, also aided the development of the timber industry by allowing entrepreneurs to obtain timber rights often at ridiculously low prices, sometimes for no more than a sack of flour. Such a situation attracted many ruthless entrepreneurs whose regard for reforestation and conservation was negligible.

This combination of high demand, cheap wood and ruthless entrepreneurs created the conditions for a very sharp boom in timber exports, at least in the short term. Although after 1875 the state reversed its policy and began to reacquire forests, the timber companies also began to buy farmland, with its attendant forest rights. Gradually, the industry came to be dominated by a few large companies, some of which were foreign-owned. However, this concentration of ownership did make it easier for the state to oblige producers to take a more responsible approach to conservation and reforestation.

Given the dominance of the forestry industry, which relied almost exclusively on waterways for transportation, it is not perhaps surprising that railways came late to Sweden – not until the 1850s. It is also not surprising, given this situation, that it was government push rather than demand pull which gave the impetus to the Swedish railway system. Remarkably, by 1914, Sweden had 25 km of railway per 1,000 inhabitants, twice that of any other European country. It also had a thriving industry producing rolling stock and engines for both the domestic and export markets (Jorberg, 1973).

Nevertheless, in 1870, industry and handicrafts only employed 15 per cent of the population. There were no industrial centres to rival those of Britain, Germany and France. Even the iron districts were small separate communities. However, after 1870, there was a rapid expansion of the Swedish industrial base, so much so that in the 40 years up to 1914, the Swedish economy grew faster than any other in Europe. Even so, to put this picture into perspective, it should be noted that all the workers involved in Swedish engineering exports in 1912 totalled no more than those to be found in one large German railway works.

For a small country, dependent on its natural resources, Sweden's progress was significant. There were a number of reasons for this. First, changes in the eighteenth century had removed barriers to social mobility and created the conditions for the emergence of entrepreneurs. Second, these entrepreneurs showed an unrivalled ability to exploit Sweden's natural resources and take advantage of developing export markets. An additional factor was the high quality of the Swedish educational system. This provided an educated workforce able to adapt to changing industries, technologies and products. Therefore, though it would be wrong to underestimate the great asset of Sweden's natural resources, neither should one forget the contribution made by human capital. The combination of a less hierarchical society than elsewhere in Europe and a well-educated and skilled workforce clearly paved the way for the advent of the social democratic approach to society which became the hallmark of Sweden in the twentieth century.

On the other hand, it would be misleading to forget that, as elsewhere in Europe, industrialisation was a harsh process. Entrepreneurs could be very rapacious, and much of the technology and many of the methods they employed were imported from the more advanced nations, especially Britain. Consequently, though the Swedish government tended to be more keen to intervene than was the case in Britain, industrialisation was accompanied by the same sort of clashes between capital and labour, and the growing incompatibility between an agricultural economy based on self-sufficiency and a capitalist economy based on money.

By the end of the nineteenth century, Sweden had developed a small industrial base, by comparison with Britain, Germany and France, but one that was flexible and competitive. However, the organisation of labour and the technology deployed tended to be imported from the bigger industrial nations. It imported the poor labour relations that existed elsewhere as well.

Though Sweden's industrial base was modest by international standards, it was in advance of that of Denmark or Norway (Jorberg, 1973). For **Denmark**, as for Sweden, it was changes to agricultural production that gave a large boost to the economy in the nineteenth century.

Traditionally, Denmark had relied on the export of two commodities, grain and cattle (though, in the eighteenth and the first half of the nineteenth century, its economy also benefited considerably from its colonial possessions in Asia and the West Indies, particularly in terms of sugar production and the slave trade). Trade in the former grew rapidly in the nineteenth century. However, much of the grain was produced on marginal land, which was no longer economically viable after the collapse of world grain prices in the 1870s. After the early 1880s, imports outstripped exports.

On the other hand, the keeping of livestock and dairy produce showed a remarkable growth throughout the century. By the end of the nineteenth century, Denmark had a thriving export trade in butter and beef. By 1913, Denmark exported 80 per cent of its butter production, mainly to Britain where it had 40 per cent of the market; in that year, only Holland and Argentina exported more live cattle than Denmark. The latter part of the nineteenth century and the early twentieth century also saw a twelvefold rise in the production and export of pork (Milward and Saul, 1973).

One hindrance to the export of pork was the incompatibility between the large scale of the export market and the numerous small producers. However, this was over-come in the 1880s with the establishment of the first cooperative bacon factory. By 1914, 53 per cent of pig breeders were supplying to cooperatives. The idea of cooperatives to buy, process and sell produce had grown up in the dairy industry, and was later taken up by egg producers as well as pig breeders. Similar organisations were also used to purchase bulk feedstuffs and fertilisers. The impetus behind the development of cooperatives was the smaller farmers' fear of being exploited by their larger colleagues, who could afford to purchase the latest technology exclusively for their own use (Jorberg, 1973).

Therefore, unlike most other European countries, Denmark found a method of making small-scale farming production compatible with large-scale international demand. Nor were these cooperatives purely economic and technical organisations. Though this was their primary purpose, they also had a social and political role, and were anti-landowner. The growth of cooperatives along with their attendant 'folk high schools' was crucial, not only in educating farmers, but also in uniting them as an effective political force. Indeed, the party of small farmers, in alliance with the social democrats, headed governments from 1909 to 1910 and from 1913 to 1920. Not only does this show the political influence and socialist leanings of the cooperative movement, but it explains the emergence of the 'Nordic model' in Denmark some 20 years earlier than in the other two Scandinavian countries. The development of cooperatives was also one of the main reasons why there was no reduction in the numbers employed in Danish agriculture in the nineteenth century.

Though in some ways Denmark had a relatively thriving economy, its industrial base was, even relative to its size, on a more modest scale than in Britain, France or Germany. As an example, by 1911, the Danish cotton industry employed only 3,282 people, no more than one big mill in Britain. In total, there were only 108,000 workers employed in factories at this time.

In contrast, there was a tremendous growth in the service sector, not just in transport and communications, but also in financial and trading services. These latter tended to be concentrated in Copenhagen, where by 1910 half the country's population lived. By 1911, service activities accounted for 36 per cent of the occupied population, as opposed to 32 per cent in Norway and 19 per cent in Sweden.

One of the remarkable features of Danish industrialisation in the nineteenth century was the degree to which it preserved rather than destroyed the peasant and craft traditions. In agriculture, this was mainly due to the rise of cooperatives for processing and selling produce. In industry, the need to cater mainly for a small and discerning home market, allied to a well-educated workforce, kept alive the craft tradition, and – for most of the nineteenth century – the guild system. Even in 1914, 84 per cent of Danish workers were still in establishments employing five or fewer people. By contrast, in Sweden in 1912, only 24 per cent of workers were in establishments employing 10 or fewer people.

Therefore, if Denmark was less industrially advanced than some bigger European countries, it could however claim to have avoided the clash of cultures and the rise of industrial conflict that characterised the industrial revolution elsewhere in Europe.

Just as the process of industrialisation differed considerably between Sweden and Denmark, so was also the case with **Norway**. Like the other two countries, it was dependent on exports, but in Norway these were service-based rather than product-based. Shipping was its chief earner. In 1880, shipping accounted for 45 per cent of all exports.

Its links with Sweden and Denmark tended to be political rather than economic. Up to 1814, it was part of the Kingdom of Denmark, and in that year the King of Sweden also became the King of Norway. However, Denmark sided with France during the Napoleonic Wars and as a consequence of Napoleon's defeat lost the sovereignty of Norway to Sweden. Norway was given its own parliament and constitution, though its political and economic ties with Sweden were considerable until it achieved full independence in 1905.

Of the three Scandinavian countries, Norway was slowest to industrialise and, unlike the other two, this was neither preceded nor accompanied by the modernisation of agriculture. Nor was the stimulus to industrialisation generated internally. Rather, when industry really began to flourish, just before the First World War, it was brought about by an influx of foreign capital wishing to take advantage of Norway's potential for cheap hydroelectricity.

However, up to this point, Norway had made few steps towards becoming an industrial economy. In agriculture, Norway was held back by a combination of poor soils, difficult climate and extremely inefficient internal communications. Indeed, a marked feature of the Norwegian economy was the very poor contact and bad communications between various regions within the country, no doubt a consequence of the mountainous terrain, which meant that it was often easier to import goods from abroad rather than to move them from one part of Norway to another (Jorberg, 1973). This led to a dual economy: the increasingly prosperous urban areas which grew rich on the export of goods and services, and a subsistence agricultural economy in the countryside.

Accordingly, the towns prospered and the countryside stagnated with small peasant farmers tending to be the agricultural norm into the twentieth century. At the end of the nineteenth century, such was the low level of productivity of Norwegian agriculture that butter exports, worth 3.3 million kr, were dwarfed by imports of grain and animal feedstuffs worth 83 million kr. Norway had no other food exports of importance, except for fish (Milward and Saul, 1973).

On the other hand, Norway was mercifully free of the social rigidity of many other European countries where the nobility stood at the top of the social pyramid. Instead, uniquely, merchants and gentlemen-farmers formed the top layers of society, serfdom was rare, and there was a lack of the social injustice that seemed inevitably to accompany industrialisation in the more advanced countries. This may account for the willingness of employers and trade unions, particularly in the metal industries, to favour cooperation over conflict from the early 1900s (Dolvik and Stokland, 1992; Kjellberg, 1992).

The staple industries of the Norwegian economy in the nineteenth century were fishing, timber and shipping, along with a shipbuilding industry that was a product of all three. In the early years of the century, it also exported iron, but this trade was virtually killed by British and Swedish competition after Danish trade protection was abolished in 1814. The main employers were shipping, where some 33,000 were employed in the merchant marine in 1860, and fishing; both of these had only weak links to the rest of the economy. There was also a small, fragmented, engineering industry, which in 1850 only comprised 12 factories employing a total of 200 workers. From the 1840s there was a rapid growth in the textile sector. Even so, in 1860 this still only accounted for 3,000 workers out of a total of just under 20,000 industrial workers. The biggest industrial sector was forestry, employing almost one in three workers (Jorberg, 1973).

Therefore, because of its small population size, the lack of demand from the country-side, and the reliance of the towns on exports for their prosperity, Norway's industrial expansion was linked very closely to the export trades. When exports boomed, domestic demand increased; when exports fell, so did domestic demand. In addition, because its industrial sector was small, Norway found it difficult to generate capital domestically. As an example, in 1870, half of the mining industry was foreign-owned. However, with the development of closer economic links with Sweden in 1873, the market for Norwegian industry was expanded considerably.

Developing quite separately from the rest of the economy, the real growth industry of the nineteenth century was shipping. Shipping emerged during the eighteenth century as a subsidiary of the timber trade, but in the nineteenth century it developed entirely independently of Norway's own transport needs. Instead, it catered to the needs of other countries, especially Britain and Denmark and their colonies. It owed its existence to the country's shipbuilding tradition, the availability of local timber and the ready supply of cheap labour. From 1850, the industry grew rapidly, growing fivefold in the years up to 1880, by which time it was the third largest in the world, greater even than those of France and Germany. However, after 1900, the industry declined, owing to a fall in freight rates and to the advent of steam-powered vessels. The industry was very frag-mented, which meant that raising capital was difficult. Though this was not a problem with the small, wooden ships that had been the backbone of the industry, it became one with the need for larger, much more expensive, steam-powered vessels. Also, Norway lacked both the raw materials, iron and steel, and the skills to build steamships. Indeed, in the immediate pre-war years, only 20 per cent of the industry's requirements were met from home production. Even so, in 1914, the Norwegian shipping industry was the fourth largest in the world behind Britain, the USA and Germany, though there were signs that it was in decline.

The advent of hydroelectric power at the end of the nineteenth century did, however, make a significant difference to Norway's industrial development. Once the technology had been established, no country in Europe was better placed to exploit it than Norway, with its plentiful supply of waterfalls. However, to turn this into a reality required both capital and a use for the resultant cheap electricity. Both of these were to come from abroad. By 1914, hydroelectric power, financed by foreign capital, was used to produce synthetic fertiliser and aluminium. The attraction for foreign investors was cheap power. Almost all of the output was sold abroad, much of it without further processing. These developments had a significant impact in terms of increasing Norway's foreign earnings. The result was that some 14 per cent of the industrial labour force was directly employed by foreign firms by 1909, with considerable numbers being indirectly employed. These workers tended to be concentrated in the more capital-intensive industries and larger workplaces. This led to a law being passed which limited foreign ownership of Norwegian industry.

In many respects, with the stagnation of timber and shipping, the advent of modern chemical and metal industries was highly desirable. In another respect, though, they also showed the weakness of Norwegian industrialisation. Both these industries were heavily dependent on foreign capital; both were capital- as opposed to labour-intensive; and neither developed or needed a local supply or distribution network. Therefore, neither really impacted greatly, at least in the pre-war period, on the wider Norwegian economy. For this reason, in relation to its Scandinavian neighbours, Norway remained a relatively poor country, which certainly accounted for the large waves of emigration it experienced in the nineteenth and early twentieth centuries. In relation to political democracy and educational provision, though, particularly for women, it was in advance of most other European countries before 1914.

Considering these three Scandinavian countries as a whole, the picture of industrialisation by the early twentieth century was very mixed. Sweden was probably the most advanced, with Denmark not far behind but Norway trailing somewhat. However, because of population size, natural resources and history, none had developed an industrial base capable of competing with those of the leading European countries.

As elsewhere in Europe, all three tended to import methods and technologies from the more advanced countries, especially Britain. It would appear that the process of industrialisation, where it was reliant on foreign capital and methods, tended to reproduce the British experience of poor labour relations. However, particularly in Denmark, there were signs that different organisational forms allied to existing social structures and expectations, together with the growth of social democracy, held out the promise of avoiding the vicious employer–employee clashes experienced elsewhere.

Nevertheless, in Europe as a whole, for the most part, those who created and controlled the large business organisations that were becoming the norm still had to rely on their own experience and judgement, but with growing frustration over their inability to control and organise these bodies fully and effectively. There was also a realisation amongst some that, whilst change was inevitable, they lacked an effective and, as far as their employees were concerned, acceptable way of managing it. Therefore, by the end of the nineteenth century, there was a growing awareness of the need to develop an approach to organising work that was more systematic and less harsh and arbitrary than what had gone before. Although this was already, to an extent, taking place in Germany with the rise of bureaucracy, the USA was the country where the most conscious and consistent search was being pursued for a comprehensive theory of how to structure and run organisations.

The USA

In the USA, for a number of reasons, the need for a workable, overall approach to organisational design and control, which legitimised the authority of managers to initiate change, was perhaps more acute than anywhere else. The USA had industrialised far more rapidly and on a larger scale than any other nation. Only in the 1860s, after the Civil War, did the USA begin to industrialise in earnest, but by 1914 it had become the premier industrial nation, with the highest per capita income in the world. In the period 1860 to 1914, employment in manufacturing rose from 1.3 million to 6.6 million, and the population as a whole rose from 31 million to 91 million (Habakkuk and Postan, 1965). The USA at this time was still very much influenced by Europe, and initially at least adopted similar approaches and methods in organising and running industry. However, the size of the typical American organisation quickly grew much larger than those in Europe. Whilst the average British and French business was still the small, family-owned firm, in the USA it was the monopoly, which dominated an entire industry, or the conglomerate, which had substantial holdings in several industries. As an example, in 1900 Dale Carnegie sold his steel company for the enormous sum of $419 million to a group of financiers. They merged it with other steel concerns to create a monopoly steel producer employing 200,000 workers and valued at $1.3 billion. This was at a time when the British steel industry, which had led the world, comprised 100 blast furnaces owned by 95 separate companies.

As might be imagined, the numbers of Americans employed in factories and offices grew rapidly – almost tripling between 1880 and 1910 (Levine, 1967; Zinn, 1980). The rocketing increase in demand for labour could not be met by the existing population alone and was fuelled by successive waves of immigration. Whilst solving one problem – the shortage of labour – this created others. The culture shock of industrial work, a foreign language, and problems of housing and social integration created enormous pressures in American society. Alongside this was the arbitrary and ruthless discipline of the factory system, where workers were treated as so much industrial cannon fodder. It was a time of rapid social, technological and organisational change: a time where entrepreneurs did not so much expect to manage change as to impose it, and those who could not or would not accept this situation were treated harshly. Consequently, most industries found themselves sitting on a pressure cooker which could, and frequently did, explode in unexpected and violent ways. If management–labour relations were poor in most European countries, they were far worse in the USA (Pelling, 1960).

The American approach to industrial development owed little to government aid or encouragement, and much to individual entrepreneurship. For this reason American entrepreneurs had much more in common with the free market approach to industrial expansion of their British counterparts than to the state-sponsored traditions of Germany or France. Therefore, the German approach to industrial organisation, bureaucracy, which might seem appropriate given the size of American companies, was not attractive. In any case, it tended to operate best in situations where growth and demand were stable or predictable, which in Germany the government tried to facilitate. However, American growth patterns were volatile and unpredictable.

Consequently, there was great pressure to find organisational arrangements that would allow employers to control and organise their employees in a manner that reduced conflict, was cost-effective, and was applicable to the American environment and philosophy. It was also becoming recognised that it was not sufficient just to develop a more systematic approach to the organisation of work; there was also a need to develop an approach to managing change that would persuade workers to accept rather than reject or resist the introduction of new methods, techniques and technologies. Therefore, with the spirit of endeavour, determination and confidence that seemed so much a part of the American character at this time, managers and engineers set out to remedy this situation. Though similar developments were taking place in Europe, they lacked the intensity, commitment and scale of events in the USA. This is no doubt why one of the earliest and most enduring approaches to organisation theory emerged in the USA, and why the USA has continued to dominate the development of organisation theory.

Organisation theory: the Classical approach

As can be seen, at the end of the nineteenth century there was a clear need to replace the rule-of-thumb approach to organisational design and management with a more con-sistent and organisation-wide approach. This was not because of an academic interest in the functioning of organisations, though this was present, but in order to improve their performance, enhance their competitiveness and – an increasing concern at the time – to sustain and legitimate managerial authority. This was certainly the case in the USA, where explosive growth and a workforce suffering from culture shock had created dangerous social pressures that questioned the legitimacy of managerial power, and even the capitalist system itself. This was also true in Europe: although Europe industrialised earlier, it was not only having to come to grips with the increase in size and complexity of business life, but it was also facing considerable, and unexpected, competitive pressure from the United States.

Nevertheless, these difficulties could not quench the innate optimism of the age. It was a time, much more than now, when people dealt in certainties and universal truths. There was a feeling of confidence that any goal, whether it be taming nature or discern-ing the best way to run a business, could be achieved by the twin powers of scientific study and practical experience. All over the industrialised world, groups of managers and technical specialists were forming their own learned societies to exchange experiences, to discuss common problems, and to seek out in a scientific and rational fashion the solution to all organisational ills: to discover 'the one best way'.

Out of these endeavours emerged what was later termed the Classical approach to organisational design and management. As the name suggests, it was an approach that drew heavily on what had gone before, taking from writers such as Adam Smith and practitioners such as Josiah Wedgwood and leavening their ideas with contemporary experience, views and experiments. This approach, reflecting the age in which it emerged, portrays organisations as machines, and those in them as mere parts which respond to the correct stimulus and whose actions are based on scientific principles. The emphasis was on developing universal principles of organisation which would ensure the efficiency, stability and predictability of internal functions. Once these principles were established and in operation, organisations were seen as closed and changeless entities unaffected by the outside world. Though this approach first originated in the early part of the twentieth century, it influences on managerial practices and assumptions today, but its credibility amongst academics has long since waned (Kelly, 1982a, 1982b; Rose, 1988; Scott, 1987).

The Classical approach, or the Scientific–Rational approach as it is sometimes called, whilst not being homogeneous, is characterised by three common propositions:

- **Organisations are rational entities** – they are collectivities of individuals focused on the achievement of relatively specific goals through their organisation into highly formalised, differentiated and efficient structures.
- **The design of organisations is a science** – through experience, observation and experiment, it has been established that there is one best universal organisational form for all bodies. This is based on the hierarchical and horizontal division of labour and functions, whereby organisations are conceived of as machines which, once set in motion, inexorably and efficiently will pursue and achieve their pre-selected goals.
- **People are economic beings** – they are solely motivated by money. This instrumental orientation means that they will try to achieve the maximum reward for the minimum work, and will use whatever bargaining power their skills or knowledge allow to this end. Therefore, jobs must be designed and structured in such a way as to minimise an individual's skill and discretion, and to maximise management control.

The key figures in the development of the Classical approach were Frederick Taylor (1856–1915) and two of his main promoters, the pioneers of motion study, Frank and Lillian Gilbreth (1868–1924 and 1878–1972 respectively) in the USA, Henri Fayol (1841–1925) in France and Max Weber (1864–1920) in Germany. All were writing in the first two decades of the twentieth century, though Weber's work was not generally available in English until the 1940s. Below is an outline of their work.

Frederick Taylor's Scientific Management

Frederick Winslow Taylor was born into a prosperous Quaker–Puritan family in Germantown, Pennsylvania in 1856. Although he passed the entrance exam for Harvard Law School, instead of becoming a lawyer as his family wished, in 1874 he took a manual job in an engineering company and became a skilled pattern maker and machinist. In 1878, he joined the Midvale Steel Company as a labourer, but eventually rose to become its Chief Engineer. Having had enough of working for other people, in 1893 he set up his own consultancy (Sheldrake, 1996). Taylor was an accomplished and talented engineer, and became a leading authority on metal cutting and a successful inventor; however, it is for his contribution to work organisation that he is most famous (or infamous).

Taylor was a highly controversial figure during his lifetime and still remains so more than 90 years after his death. This was partly because his theory of management was a direct challenge to both workers and managers. However, a large part of the hostility he generated during his lifetime was due to his own character. Rose (1988: 23) stated that 'Taylor was a notorious neurotic – many would not hesitate to write crank; and there is even a case for upgrading the diagnosis to maniac.' He was certainly a zealot when it came to promoting his own ideas, and would brook no challenge to them, whether from workers or management. Not surprisingly, though he attracted devoted followers, he also engendered fierce dislike.

Through his experience as a shopfloor worker, manager and consultant, Taylor made a major contribution to the development of managerial theory and practice in the twentieth century (Locke, 1982; Rose, 1988). Yet his original attempts to improve productivity (or, as he put it, to stamp out 'soldiering') were less than successful. Not only was his use of sacking, blacklisting and victimisation counter-productive, but also the bitterness that this provoked haunted him for the rest of his life. It was his failure to achieve change by, as Rose (1988: 37) termed it, 'managerial thuggery' that led him to seek an alternative method of change management that the workers, and management, would accept because they could see that it was rational and fair. Thereafter, his prime preoccupation became the pursuit and promotion of a scientific approach to management.

Drawing on his work at the Midvale Steel Company and the Bethlehem Steel Company, Taylor constructed a general ideology of efficiency. It was only in 1911, when a group of his supporters met to discuss how better to promote his work, that the term 'Scientific Management' was first used to describe his approach to work organisation (Sheldrake, 1996). Though initially sceptical, Taylor embraced the term and there can be little doubt that the publication, in the same year, of his *Principles of Scientific Management* laid the foundation stone for the development of organisation and management theory. Taylor's primary focus was on the design and analysis of individual tasks; this process inevitably led to changes in the overall structure of organisations. Such was the impact of his work that it created a blueprint for, and legitimated, the activities of managers and their support staff. In so doing, he helped to create the plethora of functions and departments which characterise many modern organisations.

Before Taylor, the average manager tended to operate in an idiosyncratic and arbitrary manner with little or no specialist support. Taylor saw this as being at the root of much industrial unrest and workers' mistrust of management. Though criticised for his anti-labour postures, Taylor was also highly critical of management behaviour, which may account for this group's initial lack of enthusiasm for his ideas (Scott, 1987). After Taylor, managers were left with a 'scientific' blueprint for analysing work and applying his 'one best way' principle to each job in order to gain 'a fair day's work for a fair day's pay'.

These last two phrases sum up Taylor's basic beliefs:

- It is possible and desirable to establish, through methodical study and the application of scientific principles, the one best way of carrying out any job. Once established, the way must be implemented totally and made to operate consistently.
- Human beings are predisposed to seek the maximum reward for the minimum effort, which Taylor referred to as 'soldiering'. To overcome this, managers must lay down in detail what each worker should do, step by step; ensure through close supervision that the instructions are adhered to; and, to give positive motivation, link pay to performance.

Taylor incorporated those beliefs into his precepts for Scientific Management, comprising three core elements:

- The systematic collection of knowledge about the work process by managers.
- The removal or reduction of workers' discretion and control over what they do.
- The laying down of standard procedures and times for carrying out each job.

The starting point is the gathering of knowledge:

The managers assume . . . the burden of gathering together all the traditional knowledge which in the past has been possessed by the workman and then of classifying, tabulating and reducing this knowledge to rules, laws and formulae . . .

(Taylor, 1911a: 15)

This lays the groundwork for the second stage: increased management control. As long as workers possess a monopoly of knowledge about the work process, increased control is impossible. But once the knowledge is also possessed by managers, it becomes possible not only to establish what workers actually do with their time, but also by 'reducing this knowledge to rules, laws and formulae', to decrease the knowledge that workers need to carry out a given task. It also, importantly, paves the way for the division of labour.

The last stage is that 'All possible brain work should be removed from the shop and centred in the planning . . . department' (Taylor, 1911b: 98–9). The divorce of conception from execution removes control from the worker, who no longer has discretion as to how tasks are carried out.

Perhaps the most prominent single element in modern scientific management is the task idea. The work of every workman is fully planned out by management . . . and each man receives in most cases complete written instructions, describing in detail the task which he is to accomplish, as well as the means to be used in doing the work. . . . This task specifies not only what is to be done but how it is to be done and the exact time allowed for doing it.   (Taylor, 1911a: 39)

Allied to this last element was Taylor's approach to worker selection and motivation. Taylor carried out many experiments to identify and reward workers. He believed that organisations should only employ 'first class men' and they would only get the best results if they were paid by results. As he commented on his time as a consultant at the Bethlehem Steel Company (Taylor, 1911a: 18–21):

The Bethlehem Steel Company had five blast furnaces, the product of which had been handled by a pig-iron gang for many years. This gang consisted, at this time, of about 75 men. . . . Our first step was the scientific selection of the . . . proper workman to begin with. We therefore carefully watched and studied these 75 men for three or four days . . . A careful study was then made of each of these men. We looked up their history as far back as practicable and thorough inquiries were made as to the character, habits, and ambitions of each of them. Finally, we selected [Schmidt] . . . as the most likely man to start with. . . . Schmidt started to work, and all day long, and at regular intervals, was told by the man who stood over him with a watch, 'Now pick up a pig and walk. Now sit down and rest. Now walk – now rest,' etc. He worked when he *was told to work, and rested when he was told to rest . . . And throughout this time he averaged a little more than $1.85 per day, whereas before he had never received over $1.15 per day . . . One man after another was picked out and trained to handle pig iron . . . receiving 60 per cent more wages than other workmen around them.*

The 'task idea' allied to Taylor's approach to selecting and rewarding workers completes the process of gaining control over workers by managers. The workers become 'human machines', told what to do, when to do it and how long to take. But, more than this, it allows new types of work organisation to be developed, and new work processes and equipment introduced; thus workers move from having a monopoly of knowledge and control over their work to a position where the knowledge they have of the work process is minimal, and their control vastly reduced. The result is not only a reduction in the skills required and the wages paid, but also the creation of jobs that are so narrow and tightly specified that the period needed to train someone to do them is greatly reduced. This removes the last bargaining counter of labour: scarcity of skill.

According to Taylor, this transforms not only workers' jobs but also managers' jobs:

The man at the head of the business under scientific management is governed by rules and laws . . . just as the workman is, and the standards which have been developed are equitable. (Taylor, 1911b: 189)

Taylor stated that the 'scientific' basis and equal applicability of his methods meant they were neutral between labour and management; therefore they legitimated managerial action to analyse and change work methods, because managers are merely applying science to determine the best method of work. As Ideas and perspectives 1.1 shows, he claimed that his approach benefited both the worker and the company. The worker was enabled and encouraged to work to his maximum performance and be rewarded with a high rate of pay, whilst the company benefited from a high rate of output:

It is absolutely necessary, then, when workmen are daily given a task which calls for a high rate of speed on their part, that they should also be insured the necessary high rate of pay whenever they are successful. This involves not only fixing for each man his daily task, but also paying him a large bonus, or premium, each time that he succeeds in doing his task in the given time. . . . The remarkable and almost uniformly good results from the correct *application of the task and the bonus must be seen to be appreciated.* (Taylor, 1911a: 63)

Though seen as something of an anti-trade-unionist, which he probably was, as the above implies, he was also strongly critical of management. He believed that many of the problems organisations faced in implementing change were due to the arbitrary and inconsistent approach of managers. In fact, though trade unions were very suspicious of Scientific Management in general and Taylor in particular, managers seemed even more antagonistic. Indeed, after his death, Taylor's acolytes spent much time in the 1920s wooing the American unions with a considerable degree of success; they never achieved the same success with management (Rose, 1988). The main reason for this was that, though managers were anxious to find an approach that would curtail labour resistance to change and improve productivity, they were not prepared to subject themselves to a similar degree of discipline.

As Taylor's biographer, Copley (1923: 146) stated in relation to managerial resistance to Scientific Management at the Bethlehem Steel Company:

> Let us consider what Taylor was contending for. It was essentially this: that the government of the Bethlehem Steel Company cease to be capricious, arbitrary and despotic; that every man in the establishment, high and low, submit himself to law [i.e. that managers should obey the principles of Scientific Management].

Taylor believed passionately in the need to reform managerial authority: to base it on competence rather than the power to hire and fire. However, it is one thing to ask one's subordinates to change their ways and accept new rules and methods; it is another thing entirely for management to acknowledge that they too need to change, and change radically. No wonder that Taylor met managerial as well as worker resistance.

Nevertheless, even though managers resisted the full implementation of Taylorism, the new and rapidly expanding breed of industrial engineers, charged with developing and implementing new methods, techniques and technologies, found in Taylor and his contemporaries' work a blueprint for transforming the workplace and increasing their control and status. One consequence of this, brought about by the use of job cards and other forms of work recording and analysis systems, was a massive increase in the amount of paperwork that needed to be processed. Managers complained about the growth of 'industrial bureaucracy', but the benefits it brought by enabling average times and costs, etc., to be calculated easily outweighed the increase in clerical costs.

Nowhere was this demonstrated more dramatically than at Henry Ford's Highland Park plant – the home of the world's first mass-produced motor car, the Model T Ford. From 1909/10, when 18,664 Model Ts were sold, sales and production doubled year-on-year. However, every increase in production required a commensurate increase in the plant's workforce. In 1911/12, the plant produced 78,440 Model Ts with 6,867 employees. The next year production doubled and the number of employees doubled. Not surprisingly, Ford was desperate for ways of increasing employee productivity. The solution he adopted was to redesign the assembly operation around Scientific Management principles, and then couple this with the introduction of the moving assembly line. This allowed Ford once again to double production, but this time the workforce actually decreased (Lacey, 1986). So the 1910s saw the birth of the twin, and very much related, neologisms that both dominated and revolutionised industrial life for much of the twentieth century – Taylorism and Fordism.

Throughout the 1920s, the adoption of Scientific Management grew in America, though rarely in the full form laid down by Taylor. It was also introduced on a very limited basis into Europe, but met with much scepticism from managers and hostility from workers (Rose, 1988). Only in Russia did there seem any great enthusiasm for it. Indeed, Lenin saw Scientific Management combined with common ownership as the prime basis for Russian industrialisation: 'We must organize in Russia the study and teaching of the Taylor system and systematically try it out and adapt it to our own ends' (Lenin, 1918: 25). Taylor's work also attracted some interest in Japan. However, it was not until after the Second World War, through the auspices of the Marshall Plan for rebuilding Europe's war-torn economies, that Scientific Management was promoted and adopted on any significant scale outside America. Ironically, the contribution of

American trade unions, through their role in the Marshall Plan, was crucial in promoting Scientific Management in European enterprises (Carew, 1987).

Taylor claimed that his system was innovative and unique, which indeed it was in terms of the way he synthesised and systematised a host of previously disparate practices and presented them as scientific and neutral (Aitken, 1960; Rose, 1988). Yet in reality it can be seen that Taylor drew on many of the management practices and negative attitudes towards labour that were prevalent during the nineteenth century. He was also heavily indebted to many contemporaries and associates who helped develop the work study techniques necessary to implement Scientific Management, especially Henry Gantt and Carl Barth, who worked closely with him (Kempner, 1970; Sheldrake, 1996). Perhaps his greatest debt was to Frank and Lillian Gilbreth. As well as being the pioneers of motion study, they were the driving force in establishing the Society for the Promotion of Scientific Management, which was later renamed the Taylor Society, and did much to promote Taylor's work both before and after his death in 1915 (Rose, 1988; Sheldrake, 1996).

The Gilbreths and motion study

Much of modern work study (a central element of the Classical approach) owes its origins to the methods and techniques of motion study developed in the first quarter of the twentieth century by Frank and Lillian Gilbreth (*see* Gilbreth and Gilbreth, 1914). Their work on motion study was initiated by Frank Gilbreth, who was a contemporary of Taylor's. In many respects their careers were similar. Taylor, turning his back on Harvard Law School, began his career on the shopfloor and later rose to eminence as a manager and management consultant. Frank Gilbreth, after passing the entrance exam for but declining to enter the Massachusetts Institute of Technology, rose from being a bricklayer to running his own construction and consultancy companies. He was also, along with his wife, a leading campaigner for Scientific Management.

Although the development and promotion of motion study was begun by her husband, there is no doubt that Lillian Moller Gilbreth was an equal partner. Despite contemporary prejudices against women and education, she obtained Bachelor's and Master's degrees in English. She was only denied a doctorate in psychology by the University of California because family commitments prevented her, after her thesis had been approved, from spending the post-thesis year on campus that the regulations required (Sheldrake, 1996; Thickett, 1970).

In justifying their work, Frank Gilbreth stated in his 1909 book on bricklaying that motion study:

> . . . *will cut down production costs and increase the efficiency and wages of the workman . . . To be pre-eminently successful: (a) a mechanic must know his trade; (b) he must be quick motioned; and (c) he must use the fewest possible motions to accomplish the desired results.* (Quoted in Sheldrake, 1996: 28)

The Gilbreths developed a number of procedures for breaking work down into its constituent components. Flow process charts were used which split human motion into five basic elements: operations, transportation, inspection, storage and delay. Arising out of this, they developed a method of minutely analysing tasks which broke handwork into 17 basic elements. Examples of these are as follows:

Grasp Begins when hand or body member touches an object. Consists of gaining control of an object.

Release Begins when hand or body member begins to relax control of object. Consists of letting go of an object.

Plan Begins when hand or body members are idle or making random movements while worker decides on course of action. Consists of determining a course of action. Ends when course of action is determined.

The purpose of this microanalysis was not only to establish what was done, but also to discover if a better method of performing the task in question could be developed. In this respect, they did much original work in establishing the distinction between necessary and unnecessary movements. The latter were to be eliminated immediately and the former further analysed in more detail to see if they could be improved, combined or replaced by special equipment.

If this sounds remarkably similar to Adam Smith's observations on pin-making, mentioned earlier, this is no accident. The Classical approach is descended from Smith through the nineteenth-century pioneers of work organisation. Though remarkable in the level of minute detail to which they reduced the motions individuals make when undertaking manual tasks, the Gilbreths were only, as they saw it, taking Smith's maxims to their logical conclusion. If in the process they give the impression of dealing more with machines than people, that too is no accident. Like others who propounded the Classical approach, they viewed organisations and workers very much as machines. The work study methods developed by the Gilbreths and their successors are still widely used today, not just in manufacturing industries, but in all areas of life from hospitals to computer programming (Grant, 1983).

The Gilbreths were also concerned that, having established the best way to carry out a task, this should not be undermined by selecting the wrong person to carry it out or by creating the wrong environment. Therefore, they set about analysing employee selection and establishing environmental criteria with the same determination they had applied to analysing work performance. However, in neither case could they achieve the same microanalysis that characterised their work study technique; what finally emerged were effectively opinions based on their own 'experience', rather than being the product of experiment and observation.

The Gilbreths, like Taylor, were devoted to one objective – to discover the best method of doing any job. The difference was that whereas Taylor was concerned with reducing the time taken to perform a task, the Gilbreths were more concerned with reducing the motions taken to accomplish the task. Though this differing emphasis did lead to some friction with Taylor (Nadworthy, 1957), they were, none the less, among his main promoters and saw their efforts as complementary to, and aimed at enhancing, Scientific Management. The fact that work study is now often labelled 'time and motion' study perhaps shows this. Like Taylor, they saw themselves as creating a neutral system that benefited both labour and management. They felt that any increase in boredom or monotony brought about by their methods would be compensated for by workers' opportunities to earn more money.

While the Gilbreths and Taylor devoted their efforts to improving the productivity of individual workers, there were others who took a wider but complementary perspective.

Henri Fayol and the principles of organisation

Born in 1841 and educated at the *lycée* in Lyon and the National School of Mines in St Etienne, Fayol was promoting his ideas in France at the same time as Taylor was propounding his views on Scientific Management in the USA. He began his working life as a mining engineer in 1860 and, in 1888, was appointed Managing Director of an ailing mining company, which he quickly turned into a much-admired and financially strong enterprise. He retired as Managing Director in 1918, though he stayed on the Board until his death in 1925. In his 'retirement' he founded the Centre d'Etudes Administratives, whose role was to propagate Fayol's ideas through management education. He chaired weekly meetings of prominent industrialists, writers, government officials, philosophers and members of the military. This direct contact with opinion-formers and decision-makers is undoubtedly one of the main reasons why the Centre had such a profound influence on the practice and theory of management in both the public and private sectors in France.

Fayol's approach to managing organisations is described in his book *General and Industrial Management* which was published in France in 1916 but did not appear in English until 1949 (Lamond, 2004). Fayol did not draw his views on managing organisations solely from his own experience as a manager. His education at one of the *grandes écoles*, and his subsequent career as an executive of a large mining company, placed him among the elite of senior administrators in business, government and the armed forces. Therefore, though he spent his working life in the coal mining industry, his practical knowledge of business was informed by and fits within the intellectual and administrative traditions of French society.

His working life, in the late nineteenth and early twentieth centuries, coincided with a period of rapid industrialisation in France. It was a time when industrial unrest was rife, with frequent strikes by railway workers, miners and civil servants. As was the case in the USA, in this period of rapid growth and change, there was an unwritten consensus that French business and government needed a theory of management, no matter how basic (Cuthbert, 1970). Unlike Taylor and the Gilbreths, however, Fayol's focus was on efficiency at the organisational level rather than the task level: top-down rather than bottom-up (Fayol, 1949). Though this clearly reflects Fayol's own practical experience, it also shows the combined influence of the French intellectual tradition, with its preference for addressing philosophies rather than practicalities, and the administrative tradition, which sought to identify and lay down general rules and restrictions applicable to all situations.

Given his background, it is not surprising that Fayol was more concerned with general rather than departmental or supervisory management, and with overall organisational control as opposed to the details of tasks. This does not, however, place him in opposition to Taylor. Rather the combination of Taylor's work at the task level and Fayol's at the organisational level make their views complementary rather than contradictory. In addition, both emphasised strongly the need for professionally educated managers who would 'follow the rule' rather than acting in an arbitrary or *ad hoc* fashion.

As the following shows, Fayol (like all the Classical school) was concerned with developing a universal approach to management that was applicable to any organisation:

There is no one doctrine of administration for business and another for affairs of state; administrative doctrine is universal. Principles and general rules which hold good for business hold good for the state too, and the reverse applies.

(Quoted in Cuthbert, 1970: 111)

Therefore, in business, public administration, or indeed any form of organisation, the same universal principles apply (*see* Ideas and perspectives 1.2). According to Fayol (1949), it is the prime responsibility of management to enact these principles. Consequently, in order to achieve this, he prescribed the main duties of management as follows:

- **Forecasting and planning** – examining the future, deciding what needs to be done and developing a plan of action.
- **Organising** – bringing together the resources, human and material, and developing the structure to carry out the activities of the organisation.
- **Commanding** – ensuring that all employees perform their jobs well and in the best interests of the organisation.
- **Coordinating** – verifying that the activities of the organisation work harmoniously together to achieve its goals.
- **Controlling** – guaranteeing that all actions are correctly carried out in accordance with established rules and expressed commands.

Fayol was a gifted and highly successful businessman who attributed his success to the application of his principles rather than personal ability. Certainly, he was one of the pioneers of management theory, and many of his principles are still taught and practised today. However, part of the success of his work lay in the fact that he was writing for a receptive audience, and at a time when management practice and ideas were becoming international currency. Just as Taylor's system arose at the time when a need for a management theory had grown amongst the business community in the USA, so Fayol's was aimed at a similar demand in France, where the business community was developing rapidly but in an unplanned way.

Unlike Taylor, though, he attempted neither to denigrate trade unions openly nor to castigate managers. Nor did he share with Taylor a belief that the interests of managers and workers were necessarily the same or ultimately reconcilable. He did, however, believe that much industrial unrest could be eliminated by fairer, more consistent, and firmer management, particularly where this reduced the need for trade unions or their ability to organise. He also believed in the need to educate and train managers. His views were not seen as a direct attack on existing managers; rather, they were in harmony with the approach taken by managers in the larger private enterprises and those operating in government and the armed services. This is not surprising because, by and large, they and Fayol were educated in the *grandes écoles* and shared a common intellectual approach. In addition, Fayol did not generally try to impose his ideas directly on individual organisations. Instead, he preferred to influence managers indirectly through a process of education. In the light of the reaction in America to Taylor's attitude, many would consider this a wise move.

Ideas and perspectives 1.2
Henri Fayol's principles of organisation

1. **Division of work.** The object is to produce more and better work from the same effort, through the advantages of specialisation.
2. **Authority and responsibility.** Wherever authority is exercised, responsibility arises. The application of sanctions is needed to encourage useful actions and to discourage their opposite.
3. **Discipline.** This is essential for the efficient operation of the organisation. Discipline is in essence the outward mark of respect for agreements between the organisation and its members.
4. **Unity of command.** In any action, any employee should receive orders from one superior only; dual command is a perpetual source of conflicts.
5. **Unity of direction.** In order to coordinate and focus effort, there should be one leader and one plan for any group of activities with the same objective.
6. **Subordination of individual or group interests.** The interest of the organisation should take precedence over individual or group interests.
7. **Remuneration of personnel.** Methods of payment should be fair, encourage keenness by rewarding well-directed effort, but not lead to over-payment.
8. **Centralisation.** The degree of centralisation is a question of proportion and will vary in particular organisations.
9. **Scalar chain.** This is the chain of superiors from the ultimate authority to the lowest ranks. Respect for line authority must be reconciled with activities that require urgent action, and with the need to provide for some measure of initiative at all levels of authority.
10. **Order.** This includes material order and social order. The object of material order is avoidance of loss. There should be an appointed place for each thing, and each thing should be in its appointed place. Social order requires good organisation and good selection.
11. **Equity.** There needs to be fairness in dealing with employees throughout all levels of the scalar chain.
12. **Stability of tenure of personnel.** Generally, prosperous organisations have a stable managerial team.
13. **Initiative.** This represents a source of strength for the organisation and should be encouraged and developed.
14. **Esprit de corps.** This should be fostered, as harmony and unity among members of the organisation are a great strength in the organisation.

Source: Mullins (1989: 202–3)

Though there were attempts in France to promote '*Fayolisme*' in opposition to Taylorism, Fayol rejected this, preferring to see them as complementary (Sheldrake, 1996). As Urwick (1949: 9–10) commented in the Introduction to the English version of Fayol's book on *General and Industrial Management*:

The work of Taylor and Fayol was, of course, essentially complementary. They both realized that the problem of personnel and its management at all levels is the key to industrial success. Both applied scientific method to this problem. That Taylor worked primarily at the operative level, from the bottom of the industrial hierarchy upwards, while Fayol concentrated on the managing director and worked downwards, was merely a reflection of their very different careers.

The USA and France were not the only countries where developments in management practice and thought were being studied and documented. In Germany, at this time, Max Weber was charting the growth and merits of bureaucracy.

Max Weber on bureaucracy

Weber was born in 1864 into a well-to-do Prussian family. He pursued an academic career, obtaining a doctorate in 1889. In 1894, he was appointed Professor of Political Economy at the University of Freiburg, and in 1896 he accepted the Chair in Economics at Heidelberg. Unfortunately, in 1897, he suffered a mental breakdown, which plagued him for many years. He resigned from his university post and spent much of his time travelling in Europe and the USA. He also moved the focus of his academic studies from economics to sociology.

Weber was an ardent German nationalist, and, at the age of 50, he volunteered for military service in the First World War. Until his honourable discharge in 1915, he was responsible for establishing and running nine military hospitals. Despite this, he was a fierce and open critic of the Kaiser, whom he accused of being a dilettante hiding behind the divine right of kings. He believed that Germany's problems at home and abroad could only be solved if the monarchy were replaced with a constitutional democracy. After the war, he became a member of the Commission that drew up the Constitution for the Weimar Republic, and once again took up university teaching, this time in Munich. Unfortunately, when he died in 1920, most of his work was unpublished and his papers were in a state of chaos. It was not until the 1930s that his work began to be organised and published, and it was the 1940s before his work on bureaucracy was published in English (Sheldrake, 1996; Weber, 1948).

There is a considerable affinity between Weber's work on bureaucracy and Fayol's work on the principles of management. Both were concerned with the overall structuring of organisations, and the principles which guide senior managers in this task. Though a contemporary of Fayol and Taylor, it is unlikely that they were aware of his work on bureaucracy, though he may have been aware of their work.

However, unlike Taylor and Fayol, Weber was never a practising manager. His observations on administrative structures and organisational effectiveness arose from his study of the development of Western civilisation. From this, Weber concluded that the rise of civilisation was a story of power and domination. He noted (Weber, 1948) that each social epoch was characterised by a different form of political rule, and that for a ruling elite to sustain its power and dominance, it was essential for them both to gain legitimacy and to develop an administrative apparatus to enforce and support their authority.

Weber (1947: 328) identified what he called 'three pure types of legitimate authority':

1. **Rational–legal** – resting on a belief in the 'legality' of patterns of normative rule, and the right of those elevated to authority under such rules to issue commands.
2. **Traditional** – resting on an established belief in the sanctity of immemorial traditions and the legitimacy of those exercising authority under them.
3. **Charismatic** – resting on devotion to the specific and exceptional sanctity, heroism or exemplary character of an individual person, and of the normative patterns or order revealed or ordained by them.

For Weber, legitimacy is central to almost all systems of authority. He argued that there are five concepts on which rational–legal authority is based. According to Albrow (1970: 43), these are as follows:

1. That a legal code can be established which can claim obedience from members of the organisation.
2. That the law is a system of abstract rules which are applied in particular cases, and that administration looks after the interests of the organisation within the limits of the law.
3. That the man exercising authority also obeys this impersonal law.
4. That only *qua* [in the capacity of] member does the member obey the law.
5. That obedience is due not to the person who holds authority but to the impersonal order that has granted him his position.

Weber argued that, in the context of the rational–legal authority structures which prevailed in Western societies in the early twentieth century, the bureaucratic approach to organisation was the most appropriate and efficient. Under bureaucracy, laws, rules, procedures and predefined routines are dominant and not subject to the vagaries and preferences of individuals. They give form to a clearly defined system of administration – whether it be public administration, such as a government department dealing with pensions and social security payments, or private administration, such as an insurance company – where the execution of routine, pre-programmed procedures is all-important. Weber considered this approach to be both appropriate, because it was the ideal tool for a centralised administration where the legitimacy of those in power was underpinned by the rule of law, and efficient, because the bureaucratic approach mechanises the process of administration in the same way that machines automate the production process in factories.

Weber frequently asserted that the development of bureaucracy eliminates human fallibility:

> *Its [bureaucracy's] specific nature, which is welcomed by capitalism, develops the more perfectly the more bureaucracy is 'dehumanised', the more completely it succeeds in eliminating from official business, love, hatred, and all purely personal, irrational and emotional elements which escape calculation.* (Weber, 1948: 215–16)

Bureaucracy is characterised by the division of labour, a clear hierarchical authority structure, formal and unbiased selection procedures, employment decisions based on merit, career tracks for employees, detailed rules and regulations, impersonal relationships,

Ideas and perspectives 1.3
Rational–legal authority versus traditional authority

Characteristics of rational–legal authority	Characteristics of traditional authority
Areas of jurisdiction are clearly specified: the regular activities required of personnel are allocated in a fixed way as official duties.	The allocation of labour is not defined, but depends on assignments made by the leader, which can be changed at any time.
The organisation of offices follows the principle of hierarchy: each lower office is controlled and supervised by a higher one. However, the scope of authority of superiors over subordinates is circumscribed, and lower offices enjoy a right of appeal.	Authority relations are diffuse, being based on personal loyalty, and are not ordered into clear hierarchies.
An intentionally established system of abstract rules governs official decisions and actions. These rules are relatively stable and exhaustive, and can be learned. Decisions are recorded in permanent files.	General rules of administration either do not exist or are vaguely stated, ill-defined, and subject to change at the whim of the leader. No attempt is made to keep permanent records of transactions.
The 'means of production or administration' (e.g. tools and equipment or rights and privileges) belong to the office, not the office-holder, and may not be appropriated. Personal property is clearly separated from official property, and working space from living quarters.	There is no separation of a ruler's personal household business from the larger 'public' business under their direction.
Officials are personally free, selected on the basis of technical qualifications, appointed to office (not elected), and recompensed by salary.	Officials are often selected from among those who are personally dependent on the leader, e.g. slaves, serfs and relatives. Selection is governed by arbitrary criteria, and remuneration often takes the form of benefices – rights granted to individuals that, for instance, allow them access to the ruler's stores, or give them grants of land from which they can appropriate the fees or taxes. Benefices, like fiefs in feudalistic systems, may become hereditary and sometimes are bought and sold.
Employment by the organisation constitutes a career for officials. An official is a full-time employee and looks forward to a lifelong career in the agency. After a trial period, he or she gains tenure of position and is protected against arbitrary dismissal.	Officials serve at the pleasure of the leader, and so lack clear expectations about the future and security of tenure.

and a distinct separation of members' organisational and personal lives. It must, however, be borne in mind that Weber's bureaucratic model (or 'ideal' organisation), though inspired by developments in Germany at the time, was a hypothetical rather than a factual description of how most organisations were structured. It was his view of the characteristics that organisations should exhibit in modern societies based on rationality and law. How Weber saw these organisational characteristics supporting and reproducing rational–legal authority is best seen by contrasting them with the traditional administrative forms based on patronage (*see* Ideas and perspectives 1.3) (Weber, 1947 and 1948).

For Weber, therefore, bureaucracy provided a rational–legal form of organisation which distinguished itself from, and eradicated the faults and unfairness of, previous administrative forms by its mechanical adherence to set rules, procedures and patterns of authority. It removed the system of patronage and eliminated human variability, replacing it by the rule of law. In Weber's view, the principles of bureaucracy, especially the legitimation of authority and the subordination of all in the organisation to the same rules and procedures, were universally applicable to all organisations, big or small, public or private, industrial or commercial.

It can be seen that Weber's belief in the standardisation of, and obedience by all to, rules and procedures is the counterpart of the standardisation of production techniques advocated by Taylor and akin to the principles of administrative management prescribed by Fayol. Also, just as the work of Taylor and Fayol can be understood as representing a combination of their backgrounds and the state of the societies in which they lived, so is this the case with Weber. The Prussian bureaucratic tradition dominated both the public, and to a large extent, the private sectors in Germany. It was seen by the ruling elite as the ideal method for ensuring that the objectives of the state and the objectives of individual enterprises were adhered to. It also fitted in with the Prussian militaristic tradition of unquestioning obedience to superiors, which was a prevalent view in both public and private organisations. It must be remembered, of course, that the state and private enterprises in Germany were not primarily obsessed with profitability or individual aggrandisement. The key objective was to build Germany as the premier military and industrial power in Europe. Competition at the level of the individual or the individual enterprise was a concept that carried much less force in Germany, and even France, than in the USA or Britain. German industry and government were more concerned with ensuring that all sections of the country pulled in the same direction. Where competition threatened this, it was eliminated by the state, either by direct intervention, such as nationalisation of the railways, or by indirect intervention, through the formation of cartels and monopolies. In carrying out this grand plan for German development, bureaucracy was found to be the ideal tool.

In Germany, the advent of the First World War highlighted the incompatibility between industrial bureaucracies based on the rule of law, and a government run on autocratic lines for militaristic ends. Weber argued that the rule of law applied not only to the operation of organisations but also, and more importantly, to the running of society. If society was not based on the rule of law, if democratically elected governments did not hold power, then the authority of those who ruled must be called into question. This was the basis of Weber's attacks on the Kaiser and the military during the First World War. He believed that, in the modern age, rational–legal authority, based on democratically elected governments and laws governing property rights, was the best and most effective way for society and organisations to be governed. For Weber, the rise of bureaucracy and the rise of liberal democracy went hand in hand.

As can be seen, bureaucracy did not need a Taylor or a Fayol to develop or promote it; it already existed, was accepted by management, and was prospering, in Germany and other advanced countries, especially in the public sector. What Weber did was to give it intellectual respectability by arguing that it was particularly suited to the needs of (what he saw as) the rational, secular and increasingly democratic societies that were becoming the norm in the Western world.

The appeal of bureaucracy, to governments and large organisations at least, can be seen in the way that bureaucracy is an ever-present and pervasive feature of modern life. However, it would be misleading to give the impression that its development in Germany, or elsewhere, was uncontentious. In Germany, in the early years of the twentieth century, it tended to be the purpose and consequences of bureaucracy rather than its principles that were attacked. At an overall political level, the growth of radical parties of the left reflected growing concerns over Germany's military aims and the state's concomitant close links with business, and in particular its perceived preference for aiding capital rather than labour. At the level of the individual enterprise, the growth of militant trade unions, often linked to the parties of the left, reflected the growing frustration of workers who resented the autocratic approach of management and its resistance to collective bargaining.

Conclusions

It is not an inevitable fact of life that modern societies are characterised by organisations, of all shapes and sizes; this is the product of a particular combination of circumstances. The rise of capitalism in Britain and other European countries in the seventeenth and eighteenth centuries created new opportunities and new problems that could not be accommodated under the old order. The result was a move away from self-sufficient, autonomous, individual units to collective units of production controlled by an entrepreneur. It was entrepreneurs who, in pursuit of ever greater profits, created the factory system in Britain which became the basis of modern organisational life. The central features of the factory system were autocratic control, division of labour, and antagonistic relations between management and labour.

Though starting at different times and moving at their own pace, most European countries, followed by the USA, adopted and adapted the British approach to industrial organisation. However, as the nineteenth century progressed, the nature of industrialisation began to vary from country to country, reflecting the unique circumstances and needs of the host society. In Germany, the objectives of the state determined that large-scale public and private bureaucracies became the norm. In France, the state also played a role in shaping industrialisation, but in this case it was to perpetuate small-scale, inefficient business and agricultural operations. In both countries, individual pursuit of profit maximisation was less important than in either Britain or the USA. In Scandinavia, especially Denmark, the emergence of a more collective and less ruthless approach to industrialisation could be discerned.

Nevertheless, in the transition from a subsistence economy to a money economy, one clear image stands out above all else: the antagonism between employers and employees. The factory did not emerge because it was a more efficient means of production *per se*; it emerged because it offered entrepreneurs a more effective means of controlling labour. This meant that the factory was also a battleground, with employers seeking to impose new conditions and technologies, and workers – when they could – attempting to resist change.

As the nineteenth century progressed, managers became increasingly aware of the short-comings of their *ad hoc* and inconsistent responses to new challenges and opportunities, and the counter-productive nature of resistance to change. The need for a more coherent approach to structuring and running organisations was required: one that legitimated managerial authority, especially to initiate change. This crystallised into the Classical approach.

Though writing in different countries and from different perspectives, the proponents of what later came to be known as the Classical approach all adopted a similar perspective towards what they saw as one of the main issues for modern societies: how to create organisations that efficiently and effectively pursue their objectives. Taylor, supported by the work of the Gilbreths and others, concentrated very much on the operational level, arguing for his 'scientific' method of analysing, designing and managing jobs. However, his insistence on the consistent and unbiased application of scientific principles, and the emphasis he placed on all members of an organisation obeying rules and procedures, were as much a challenge to managerial beliefs and behaviour as they were to the beliefs and behaviour of shopfloor workers. Fayol, in contrast, was concerned less with operational issues and more with the overall administration and control of organisations. Therefore, to an extent, his could be called a top-down approach, whilst Taylor was working from the bottom up. Weber sought to put organisations in a wider historical and societal context, bringing together both the detailed tasks to be carried out in organisations and the general principles governing them.

Though Taylor's approach required a radical change in managerial behaviour and a significant increase in organisational bureaucracy, the objective of his system was to improve manual workers' productivity by redesigning their jobs. Everything else was, as Taylor would have put it, the outcome of pursuing this objective to its logical conclusion. The need to provide managers with rules and systems for running the entire enterprise, and not just that part of it dealing with manual labour, was a means of achieving his objective rather than a prime aim. This is where the work of Fayol and Weber has proved so crucial: together with Taylor's work, it comprises a system for running an entire business in a coherent, standardised and consistent fashion.

Therefore, taken together, their views are, broadly, complementary, and reflect an approach to organisations and people based upon a number of basic assumptions (*see* Ideas and perspectives 1.4).

Seen in the context of the early twentieth century, when there appeared to be a sub-stantial questioning of – and challenge to – managerial authority by workers, the Classical approach had many merits: not least in its attempt to replace arbitrary and capricious management with rules and procedures that apply equally to everyone in the organisation.

Similarly, it is important to see this work in terms of what went before. Weber explicitly drew on history to support his views; the historical debts of Taylor and Fayol,

Ideas and perspectives 1.4
The Classical approach – basic assumptions

- There is a 'one best way' for all organisations to be structured and operate.
- This approach is founded on the rule of law and legitimate managerial authority.
- Organisations are rational entities: collectivities consistently and effectively pursuing rational goals.
- People are motivated to work solely by financial reward.
- Human fallibility and emotions, at all levels in the organisation, should be eliminated because they threaten the consistent application of the rule of law and the efficient pursuit of goals.
- For this reason, the most appropriate form of job design is achieved through the use of the hierarchical and horizontal division of labour to create narrowly focused jobs encased in tight, standardised procedures and rules, which remove discretion, dictate what job-holders do and how they do it, and allow their work to be closely monitored and controlled by their direct superiors.

though not openly acknowledged in their work, are clearly there. From Smith, through Wedgwood, Boulton and Watt, Babbage and Ure can be traced key elements of the Classical approach: the division of labour, the distrust of human variability, the need for written rules, procedures and records, and the need for rational and consistent management and objectives. Parallel to these are key themes that run through other aspects of nineteenth-century life: the search for the rational, scientific, universal principles that govern the natural world, the belief in the Protestant work ethic, the emergence of Social Darwinism, the greater democratisation of societies, and the gradual reduction of laws favouring one class or group over another.

All these strands coalesced – not always neatly – in the Classical approach, creating (in retrospect) the first real and consistent attempt at a theory, a set of guidelines, for constructing, managing and changing organisations. However, given that it grew out of and was designed to meet particular circumstances, so its appropriateness began to be questioned and criticised as these circumstances changed.

Taylor and his adherents have been criticised both for their lack of scientific rigour and for their one-dimensional view of human motivation (Burnes, 1989; Kelly, 1982a, 1982b). Indeed, as Rose (1988) argued, Taylor portrayed human beings as 'greedy robots': indifferent to fatigue, boredom, loneliness and pain, driven solely by monetary incentive. For Taylor, material incentives are the only effective incentives to work. For this reason, he opposed everything else in the workplace that, in his opinion, undermined managers' attempts to introduce individual incentive systems, whether it be friendships, group loyalty, trade unions, or whatever. Taylor has also been attacked for over-emphasising the merits of the division of labour. The critics' argument is that the creation of jobs which have little intrinsic satisfaction leads to poor morale, low motivation and alienation. Indeed, such are the forces aligned against Scientific Management that it is difficult to find a facet of it that has not been attacked (Littler, 1978; Locke, 1982).

Fayol has been attacked on three fronts: first, that his principles are mere truisms; second, that they are based on questionable premises; and third, that the principles occur in pairs or clusters of contradictory statements (Massie, 1965; Mintzberg, 1973, 1975; Simon, 1947). In addition, Fayol, like Taylor, can be construed as being against trade unions. Certainly, he believed in the pre-eminence of management and its right to make changes how and when it wanted, so long as these were based on his general principles. He also believed, unlike Taylor, that management and labour were fundamentally in conflict. Therefore, his recommendations were partly aimed at eliminating the conditions in which trade unions can flourish, in the interests of his overall aim of establishing the legitimacy of managers to manage.

Weber's arguments for bureaucracy have also received criticism. For instance, Udy (1959) questioned Weber's assertion that bureaucracies are necessarily rational, whilst Parsons (1947) suggested that Weber puts forward contradictory arguments for the basis of authority within bureaucracies. Robbins (1987) pointed out that bureaucracy is most frequently attacked for encouraging goal displacement:

- Rules become ends in themselves rather than means to the ends they were designed to achieve.
- Specialisation and differentiation create sub-units with different goals which then become primary to the sub-unit members. Not only does this lead to conflict between sub-units, but the accomplishment of sub-unit goals becomes more important than achieving the organisation's overall goals.
- Rules and regulations become interpreted as setting minimum standards of performance rather than identifying unacceptable behaviour. Staff can become apathetic and merely perform the bare minimum of work.
- The unthinking and rigid application of standardised rules and procedures can lead to their being applied in inappropriate situations, with dysfunctional consequences.

Robbins (1987) also pointed out that bureaucracy can alienate both employees and customers or clients. For the former, being treated as mere cogs in a machine leads to a sense of powerlessness and irrelevance. For the latter, being presented with a rigid and faceless organisation, which appears to serve its own ends rather than those of its customers or clients, can be frustrating and, when the provision of welfare services is involved, even heartbreaking. Mullins (1993) also pointed out that bureaucracy is often associated with secrecy and attempts to prevent legitimate public access to vital information on the performance of government and large organisations. Weber's work on bureaucracy has also received criticism because of his lack of attention to informal and social processes, in particular the way that individuals and groups can and do struggle to promote their own interests and goals above those of others in the organisation (Crozier, 1964).

It should also be noted that, though broadly complementary, the approaches of Taylor, Fayol and Weber were developed separately and with different objectives in mind. There are, consequently, tensions and inconsistencies between them. Fayol stresses the importance of *esprit de corps* and individual initiative. Taylor and Weber would find the former irrelevant and the latter dangerous. Likewise, the unchanging rigidity of bureaucracy, as portrayed by Weber, leaves little scope for the continuous search for improvement in methods and productivity advocated by Taylor and Fayol. Taylor's advocacy of functional supervision, which in effect meant a worker being responsible to different supervisors for different aspects of his or her job (some four or five supervisors in total), would have been viewed as a threat to discipline and good order by both Weber and Fayol, who were fierce advocates of unity of command – each worker should receive orders from one superior only.

One of the main criticisms of the Classical approach as a whole is that its view of people is negative. Bennis (1959: 263) called the Classical perspective one of 'organisations without people' because it is founded on the belief that people can be reduced to the level of cogs in a machine. It can also be argued that, in any case, it is impossible to remove the element of human variability from the running of organisations and that attempts to do so are counter-productive. Rather than making people work more efficiently in pursuit of organisational goals, it alienates them from their work and makes them resentful of it (Mayo, 1933). This is a point developed by Argyris (1964), who argued that the Classical approach restricts the psychological growth of individuals and causes feelings of failure, frustration and conflict. Instead, he believes that the organisational environment should provide a significant degree of individual responsibility and self-control; commitment to the goals of the organisation; productiveness and work; and an opportunity for individuals to apply their full abilities. These developed as central issues for the proponents of the Human Relations approach, which emerged in the 1930s as a reaction to the 'de-humanised' Classical approach. This, together with Contingency Theory – the third approach to organisations to emerge in the twentieth century – will be discussed in the next chapter.

Test your learning

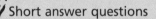

Short answer questions

1. What was Adam Smith's main contribution to the development of work organisation?
2. What was the putting-out system?
3. What was the main impetus for the move to the factory system?
4. What are the key tenets of Scientific Management?
5. According to Fayol, what are the prime functions of a manager?
6. What was Weber's main justification for advocating bureaucracy?
7. What are the main arguments for the Classical approach?
8. What are the main arguments against the Classical approach?
9. What are the implications for organisational change of the Classical approach?

Essay questions

1. To what extent can the move to the factory system be seen as a clash of cultures as opposed to a clash of economic systems?
2. Evaluate the case for seeing the work of Taylor, Fayol and Weber as forming a coherent school of thought.
3. Discuss the following statement: The Classical approach was appropriate to the time in which it was developed but it is no longer suitable to the needs of contemporary organisations.

Suggested further reading

1. Wilson, JF (1995) *British Business History, 1720–1994*. Manchester University Press: Manchester.

   Despite its title, this book neither confines itself to British history nor examines business in a narrow sense. Amongst other things, John Wilson's book provides an excellent review of the development of management in Britain, Germany, Japan and the USA from the early days of the Industrial Revolution.

2. Pollard, S (1965) *The Genesis of Modern Management*. Pelican: Harmondsworth.

   Though published over 40 years ago, Sydney Pollard's book still provides one of the best descriptions of the development of management, and the reaction of labour, in the eighteenth and nineteenth centuries.

3. Rose, M (1988) *Industrial Behaviour*. Penguin: Harmondsworth.

   Michael Rose's book provides a well-researched and thorough account of the rise and development of Scientific Management.

4. Sheldrake, J (1996) *Management Theory: From Taylorism to Japanization*. International Thompson Business Press: London.

   John Sheldrake gives an excellent summary of the lives and contributions of Taylor, Fayol and Weber.

5. Taylor, FW (1911) *The Principles of Scientific Management*. Dover (1998 edition): New York, NY, USA.

   This is perhaps the most cited, if least read, of all management books. However, as it numbers only 76 pages and is couched in quite accessible language, it is well worth reading.

CASE STUDY 1

Nissan's approach to supplier development

BACKGROUND

Nissan's Sunderland assembly plant is the most productive in Europe and produces almost one in every four cars built in the UK. However, when it opted for a UK base in 1984, the company faced a major challenge in bringing its European suppliers up to the same standard as those in Japan. Nissan recognised that European – especially UK – component suppliers fell far short of Japanese standards of quality, reliability and cost. Measuring suppliers' capabilities on a scale of 0 to 100, Nissan rated Japanese suppliers at 100, suppliers in mainland Europe were rated at 80 and UK suppliers were rated at 65–70. Nissan were required by the European Union to produce cars which contained, by value, 80 per cent local content. Therefore, it needed to improve the capabilities of its European suppliers, if it was to maintain the quality and cost standards achieved by its plants in Japan.

▶

To this end, Nissan decided in 1987 to form a Supplier Development Team (SDT) based at its Sunderland plant. The aim of the SDT was and is to help suppliers to develop their business to the stage where they can meet Nissan's present and future performance requirements. A similar function had been in operation for 15 years in Japan, and this was considered to be a suitable model for its UK operation.

Initially, two engineers were sent to Japan for a nine-week training course. This training included extensive practice in undertaking improvement activities within Nissan's Japanese suppliers. On their return, based on the techniques learnt in Japan, the engineers developed a 'ten-day improvement activity' for use with UK suppliers. Their aim was to establish an approach which, whilst achieving immediate productivity and quality improvements, would convince UK suppliers to adopt the Japanese approach to manufacturing. Consequently, though Nissan was concerned that the outcome of any improvement activity should be positive, its ultimate objective was for suppliers to recognise the value and benefits of adopting the Japanese approach, and to continue with it once the SDT had left.

The SDT approach was officially launched in the UK in November 1988, and involved a group of 12 medium-sized suppliers. Since these small beginnings, the size of the SDT has grown, and it has become an established and important part of Nissan's operations. It has worked with the majority of Nissan's suppliers, and has established a reputation amongst them for its expertise and commitment. Though it originally concentrated on shopfloor improvement projects, which still form the core of its work, it has also provided a broader range of assistance, such as cost reduction initiatives, joint product development, supervisory training and strategic planning programmes. In essence, it offers a consultancy service to Nissan's suppliers which is, normally, free of charge.

THE SDT IN ACTION

The SDT approach is to work co-operatively with suppliers to help them identify areas for improvement, and then to assist them to develop and monitor improvement plans. In particular, the SDT will train supplier personnel in quality and production improvement methods, and support supplier initiatives to improve production and reduce defects. The idea of free consultancy by an organisation such as Nissan sounds attractive, but suppliers can also perceive such an offer as either domineering or patronising. Nissan's relations with its suppliers were and are very positive; however, given the history of antagonism between customers and suppliers in the UK car industry, it tends to tread warily and prepare the ground carefully before offering assistance.

Initial Approach: Before undertaking the first improvement activity with a supplier, the SDT makes a presentation to the senior managers of the company concerned. This is because it regards senior management commitment and understanding as an essential precondition for success. Unless this commitment is gained, the SDT cannot and does not proceed further. Though the SDT approach is now well established among and valued by suppliers, in the early days of the SDT, some suppliers were sceptical and resistant to such an approach. Nevertheless, most suppliers respond favourably to the initial presentation.

The SDT's standard presentation begins by describing what continuous improvement (*Kaizen*) is and the benefits it brings. The SDT then outlines a typical improvement activity, including the various tools and techniques used. The Team stress that most improvement activities can be carried out at little or no cost, provided that the employees working in the area concerned are involved in planning and making the necessary changes.

If, after the presentation, senior managers are willing to proceed, the SDT briefs other staff and undertakes a factory assessment.

The Factory Assessment: The length of time devoted to a factory assessment varies, but typically it takes a day. Assessments are not compulsory, but most suppliers welcome an independent review of their operations, especially by a world-class company such as Nissan. The factory assessment does not form part of Nissan's formal supplier assessment procedure and, therefore, is less threatening than might otherwise be the case.

Factories are assessed under ten headings:

- Company Policy.
- Quality Performance and Procedures.
- Delivery Control Methods and Performance.
- Productivity.
- Equipment Maintenance Procedures.
- Stock Control.
- Production Process Development.
- Housekeeping (how tidy and orderly the factory is).
- Health and Safety.
- Employee Morale.

Each heading is scored out of five and the scores recorded on a factory assessment summary sheet. The assessment is then discussed with and explained to the supplier's management. From the assessment, the supplier and the SDT can begin to identify areas of concern and possible targets for improvement. The SDT then proceeds to suggest how it might be of assistance and, if this offer is accepted, agrees an improvement project with the supplier.

Improvement Activities: Though the ten-day improvement activity offered by the SDT is based on the tools, techniques and experience of Nissan in Japan, it has been tailored to meet the specific needs of its European suppliers (who are mainly based in the UK). Improvement activities usually include some or all of the following:

- Reducing assembly time and improving methods.
- Reducing overhead costs – including reducing inventory and improving equipment availability.
- Reducing work-in-process.
- Preventing defects.
- Improving productivity by reducing throughput times and introducing just-in-time scheduling.

As mentioned, most improvement activities are usually achieved at little or no cost to the supplier; however, the supplier does need to commit time and personnel to the activity. The improvement process revolves around a multi-functional team composed of the supplier's own staff, who are assisted by the SDT. The supplier's team includes operators and supervisors from the production area concerned as well as maintenance, process engineering, quality and sometimes administrative staff. The team is led by someone from the supplier. The SDT stress that the most important members of the team are the shopfloor employees working on the process which is to be improved. Not only does this prevent change simply being imposed on those who will be directly affected by it, with all the scope for resentment and mistrust that this can cause, but it also ensures that the valuable knowledge of the shopfloor employees is utilised. Perhaps more importantly, it provides them with the skills and motivation to continue to improve the process even after the SDT have ceased to be involved. An independent study (Lloyd *et al*, 1994) found that this approach led to greater commitment to the activity, and improved morale in the areas concerned. It also found that improvement activities helped to break down functional barriers, and assisted the development of greater co-operation and team spirit.

Once the process or activity which is to be improved has been agreed, targets for the improvement are then established (e.g. reductions in lead time, improvements in quality). The supplier prepares the ground for the activity by briefing staff and making any necessary resources available, such as a dedicated meeting room. If the improvement activity is likely to cause a disruption to production, a stock of components may be built up before the activity commences to compensate for this.

Day One of the ten-day improvement activity is devoted to providing training for the supplier's team. If it is the first time the supplier has been involved in such an activity, the SDT will take the lead in this. However, if the supplier has previous experience of SDT improvement activities, then a member of its staff is expected to take the lead. The SDT sees its prime purpose as ensuring that: everyone understands the concept of *kaizen*; the procedures for the ten-day activity are clear; and the team becomes familiar with the tools and techniques necessary for its task. In this latter respect, the most frequently-used tools and techniques are flow charts, work flow diagrams, pareto charts, cause and effect (fish bone) diagrams, brainstorming and critical path analysis. Where necessary, these are reinforced and supplemented as the ten-day improvement activity develops.

On **Day Two** of the improvement activity, the team splits into smaller groups to analyse and discuss the process to be improved. The groups use a combination of hard data, such as scrap rates, equipment down time and stock levels, and more subjective opinions, such as comments about layout, ease of use and the provision of information, to identify causes of waste and

possible counter-measures. The SDT encourages the use of stop watches and even video cameras to assist the supplier's team to analyse the process in question, though these can sometimes be viewed with suspicion by operators.

Once the individual groups have completed their deliberations, they reconvene as a team. The team usually makes a flow diagram of the entire process in order that everyone can appreciate what is involved and agree the changes which will bring the best benefits. The data that has been collected by the groups is analysed by the entire team. To make this easier, it is ordered and analysed under a number of standard headings:

1. **Quality:** Are quality problems due to material, process, design or training deficiencies?
2. **Technology:** Is the equipment appropriate, well-maintained, and used correctly?
3. **Ease of Operation:** Can work be made easier through ergonomic improvements such as by eliminating the need to bend, or through modifications to the equipment?
4. **Layout:** Does the layout of the process result in time delays or excessive work-in-process?

For each of the above categories, the team proceeds to identify *Concerns*, *Causes* and *Counter-measures*. Most suppliers' teams find this a demanding approach. In the space of two days, not only do they have to learn new tools and techniques, but they also have to deploy these in a rigorous and constructive fashion. Nevertheless, by the end of the second day, teams have normally identified what the problems are, what is causing them and the measures necessary to correct them. Sometimes, the outcome is a recognition that existing equipment is inadequate for its task, but it is more usually the case that the team comes up with a list of low cost/no cost changes which they can implement themselves. In some cases, other members of the supplier's staff may be called in to discuss the feasibility of some of the ideas generated. However, in the main, the suppliers' teams are usually capable of making their own judgements.

Days Three to Eight of the improvement activity are spent implementing the agreed improvements. Though the SDT does come back on day six to observe progress and can be contacted for assistance at anytime, the responsibility for this phase of the programme lies firmly with the supplier's personnel. The changes they make may be small and simple, or may involve the re-arrangement of complete areas of a factory. Where feasible, the team makes the changes in conjunction with personnel in the area concerned. The changed process is then tested, re-analysed and, if necessary, fine-tuned. To minimise disruption, any major changes in layout tend to take place during the weekend which falls in the middle of the improvement activity.

For **Days Nine and Ten** of the improvement activity, the SDT returns to help the team review what they have learnt and achieved, and to ensure that all changes are fully documented. They also discuss outstanding issues and concerns, and potential future improvement projects. The final task is to prepare and deliver a presentation to the company's senior managers describing the changes achieved and the benefits gained. Not only does this give staff the opportunity to show senior managers what they have achieved (and receive well-earned praise), but it also helps those unused to public speaking to develop their skills in this area.

SUMMARY

The SDT has come to be considered as a valuable resource by Nissan's suppliers, and there is always a queue for its services. From the suppliers' perspective, this is understandable. Improvement activities usually meet or exceed their targets. Productivity increases of between 20 and 40 per cent are quite common, as are similar improvements in quality and reductions in work-in-process. From Nissan's point of view,

it is not the individual improvement projects per se which are important, but the ability of suppliers to carry on making improvements once the SDT presence is removed. For many, this is the case, and individual improvement projects act as a catalyst to the development of continuous improvement both on and off the shopfloor. Nevertheless, this does not always occur, and some suppliers do appear to find difficulty sustaining and spreading the SDT philosophy which may affect their longer term position as a Nissan supplier. After all, Nissan is not a charity. It helps its suppliers to improve their competitiveness in order to improve its own competitiveness. Therefore, it would be misleading to believe that Nissan was in anyway 'soft' on suppliers. It promotes co-operative working with suppliers (and encourages suppliers to work co-operatively with their own staff) because it believes it makes sound business sense. Nissan is prepared to enter into long-term partnerships with its suppliers but the suppliers must reciprocate by continuously improving their performance – not an easy task. As Sir Ian Gibson, Nissan's former Managing Director, stated: 'Co-operative supply relationships are not an easy option, as many imagine, but considerably harder to implement than traditional buyer-seller relationships' (quoted in Burnes and Whittle, 1995: 10).

Questions

1. Compare Nissan's approach to performance improvement with that advocated by proponents of the Classical approach.

2. What are the benefits of Nissan's bottom-up approach to shopfloor performance improvement compared with the benefits of the Classical approach.

3. If Frederick Taylor's perception of human beings is as 'greedy robots', what is Nissan's? What are the implications of this for how staff should be managed?

(CHAPTER 2)

Developments in organisation theory

From certainty to contingency

Learning objectives

After studying this chapter, you should be able to:

- understand the reasons for the emergence of the Human Relations approach;
- identify the key features and key proponents of the Human Relations approach;
- list the advantages and disadvantages of the Human Relations approach;
- describe the differences between the Human Relations approach and the Classical approach to organisational design;
- discuss the reasons for the emergence and popularity of Contingency Theory;
- identify the key features and key proponents of Contingency Theory;
- state the advantages and disadvantages of Contingency Theory;
- appreciate how Contingency Theory seeks to incorporate both the Classical and Human Relations approaches;
- recognise the implications for organisational change of the Human Relations approach and Contingency Theory.

Ideas and perspectives 2.1
Organisations as cooperative systems

Functions of organisations

An organization is a system of cooperative human activities the functions of which are (1) the creation, (2) the transformation, and (3) the exchange of utilities. It is able to accomplish these functions by creating a cooperative system, of which the organization is both a nucleus and subsidiary system, which has also as components physical systems, personal systems (individuals and collections of individuals), and social systems (other organizations). Accordingly, from the viewpoint of creation, transformation, and exchange of utilities, the cooperative system embraces four different kinds of economies which may be distinguished as (a) a material economy; (b) a social economy; (c) the individual economies; and (d) the organization economy. . . . The individual economy . . . consists on one side of the power of the individual . . . to do work (physical acts, attention, thought); and on the other side the utilities ascribed by him to (1) material satisfactions, (2) other satisfactions which we shall here call social satisfactions.

The economy of the individual is constantly changing, because of (1) physiological needs, (2) exchanges made with others, (3) the creation of his own utilities, and (4) other changes in his state of mind, that is, his values or appraisal of utilities, physical and social.

Source: Chester Barnard, *The Functions of the Executive*, 1938, pp. 240–2.

Introduction

The emergence of the Classical approach to managing and changing organisations was one of the most significant events in the history of organisation theory and practice. From the 1920s until the 1960s, in the public sector, and in large private-sector concerns, bureaucracy was unquestionably seen as the 'one best way'. The other key element of the Classical approach, Scientific Management, had a more mixed reception. In the USA, the death of the irascible Taylor did much to overcome the early opposition to Scientific Management, especially among trade union leaders. It was enthusiastically taken up by capitalists in Japan and communists in Russia, though it met with stiff resistance in other European countries. In the 1930s, Scientific Management and a streamlined version, the Bedeaux system, were rejected by both unions and management in a large number of European countries, though after the Second World War, Scientific Management was heavily promoted as part of the Marshall Plan for the rebuilding of Europe (Carew, 1987; Rose, 1988).

Despite its growing dominance, from the 1930s, the Classical approach began to encounter both intellectual and practical opposition. This is shown clearly in Ideas and perspectives 2.1, which makes three assertions about the nature of organisations and individuals which strike at the very heart of the Classical approach:

1. Organisations are not machines but cooperative systems. To operate effectively and efficiently, they require the active cooperation of workers and not just their passive obedience.
2. People are motivated by a range of rewards, including social esteem, not just monetary ones.
3. Motivating factors change over time; what motivates a person one day may be in-effectual the next.

What makes many of these arguments, including Ideas and perspectives 2.1, more damaging to the Classical approach is that they came from practising managers rather than 'unworldly' academics.

Therefore, although the Classical school could claim much success, especially in the USA, there was also a rising tide of evidence against it. This could have led to the development and strengthening of the Classical approach, and clearly this did happen to an extent (*see* the work of Ralph Davis, 1928, on rational planning). However, as this chapter will show, what emerged were two new approaches to managing and chang-ing organisations: the Human Relations approach, which originated in the 1930s and in which Chester Barnard was a key figure, and the Contingency approach, which was developed in the 1960s.

The first half of this chapter describes the Human Relations approach. This approach was a reaction against the mechanistic view of organisations and the pessimistic view of human nature put forward in the Classical approach. It attempted to reintroduce the human element into organisational life, and claim for itself the title of the 'one best way'. In particular, it contended that people have emotional as well as economic needs, that organisations are cooperative systems that comprise informal structures and norms as well as formal ones, and that workers have to be involved in change if it is to be successful. This left managers with something of a dilemma as to which 'one best way' to adopt – the Classical or the Human Relations approach.

As the second half of this chapter will show, it was in response to this dilemma that Contingency Theory developed in the 1960s. Contingency Theory began by question-ing and rejecting the idea that there is a 'one best way' for *all* organisations. Instead, it argued for a 'one best way' for *each* organisation. It did not, therefore, reject the Classical approach and the Human Relations approach; instead it maintained that the structures and practices of an organisation are dependent (i.e. contingent) on the circum-stances it faces. Similarly, the approach to organisational change is also dependent on circumstance. In some situations change can be achieved successfully by Tayloristic imposition whilst in other cases the greater involvement advocated by the Human Relations school will be required. The main circumstances or contingencies which need to be taken into account are environmental uncertainty and dependence, technology and organisation size. After discussing the merits and drawbacks of the Human Relations approach and Contingency Theory, the chapter concludes that neither appears to be the solution to all known organisational ills that their proponents claim. In particular, it is argued that both fail to reflect and explain the complexities of day-to-day organisa-tional life.

The Human Relations approach

Even while the Classical approach was still struggling to establish itself, the seeds of a new approach to organisational design and change were already being sown. The origins of what later became known as the Human Relations approach can be traced to studies on work fatigue carried out in Britain during the First World War and work in the USA, at the same time, on employee selection, which gave new insights into employee motivation (Burnes, 1989). This work was developed and extended in the 1920s by Mayo (1933) in the USA and Myers (1934) in Britain, providing new perspectives on organisational life. These studies gave substance to a growing suspicion that the Classical view of organisations as being peopled by human robots motivated by money was badly flawed. Indeed, in 1915, the United States Congress took a stand against the use of Taylor's techniques in their establishments – although Scientific Management was becoming more accepted in private industry and was beginning to cross national boundaries, not always successfully (Rose, 1988). Similarly, though the growth of bureaucracy was gathering pace, so too was people's antagonism towards faceless, machine-like organisations where employees and customers alike lost their individuality and became numbers.

In addition, as Davis and Canter (1955) argued, it is necessary to recognise that jobs and work organisation are social inventions put together to suit the specific needs and to reflect the culture, ideology and the governing concept or ethos of the time. Therefore, to understand the emergence of the Human Relations movement, it is necessary to be aware of the changes taking place in Western society prior to and just after the Second World War.

In the 1930s, in many countries, there was the emergence of a more collectivist ethos than had previously been the case. In the USA, this was brought about by the reaction to the Depression of the 1920s and 1930s. The election of FD Roosevelt and the advent of his 'New Deal' introduced a new element of collective provision and concern into a previously highly individualistic nation. It also heralded the advent of 'Big Government' in the USA. In Europe, this collectivist ethos led to greater social concern; collective provision was led by the Scandinavian countries, and reflected the election of social democratic governments and a general mood of cooperation rather than conflict in industry in these countries. Similar developments became the cornerstone of the rebuilding of Western Germany after the end of the Second World War. The legacy of the collective effort needed to win the war was also evident in the UK with the construction of the Welfare State.

It was in the USA in the 1930s and 1940s that substantial evidence first emerged in print which challenged the Classical view of organisations and allowed the Human Relations approach to stand alongside, if not quite supersede, it. The basic assumptions of the Human Relations approach, as shown in Ideas and perspectives 2.2, were almost diametrically opposed to those of the Classical approach and its view of organisations as predictable, well-oiled machines in which people were relegated to the role of obedient cogs.

Therefore, in most respects, the Human Relations approach represents a distinct break from the ideas of the Classical school. However, in two important ways, similarities exist. The first is their shared belief in organisations as closed, changeless entities. Once

Ideas and perspectives 2.2
The Human Relations approach – basic assumptions

- **People are emotional rather than economic–rational beings.** Human needs are far more diverse and complex than the one-dimensional image that Taylor and his fellow travellers conceded. People's emotional and social needs can have more influence on their behaviour at work than financial incentives.
- **Organisations are cooperative, social systems rather than mechanical ones.** People seek to meet their emotional needs through the formation of informal but influential workplace social groups.
- **Organisations are composed of informal structures, rules and norms as well as formal practices and procedures.** These informal rules, patterns of behaviour and communication, norms and friendships are created by people to meet their own emotional needs. Because of this, they can have more influence on individual behaviour and performance, and ultimately on overall organisational performance, than the formal structure and control mechanisms laid down by management.

organisations have structured themselves in accordance with the correct precepts, then, regardless of external or even internal developments, no further changes are necessary or desirable. This leads on to the second similarity: proponents of both believed they had discovered the 'one best way' to run organisations; regardless of the type, nature or size of organisation, their precepts were the correct ones.

With that in mind, we can now begin to examine in detail the case for Human Relations. Despite the work of precursors, no one doubts that the Human Relations approach began in earnest with the famous Hawthorne Experiments.

Elton Mayo (1880–1949) and the Hawthorne Experiments

Elton Mayo was born in Adelaide, Australia in 1880. He had a somewhat chequered career. He failed three times to qualify as a medical doctor, and eventually became a lecturer in logic, psychology and ethics at the University of Queensland in 1911. There he developed a strong interest in the political problems of industrial society, and a life-long commitment to achieving social and industrial harmony. However, he was never very happy at Queensland and, in 1922, he emigrated to America. There, Mayo was fortunate in that his ideas on resolving industrial conflict attracted the attention of the Laura Spelman Rockefeller Memorial Foundation, which funded his entire career at the Harvard Business School. In effect, this meant that Mayo could pursue his own research without let or hindrance from university authorities. This was a major factor in the single-mindedness and success with which he undertook his work.

Elton Mayo is considered by many as the founder and leading light of the Human Relations movement. On his retirement as Professor of Industrial Research at Harvard Business School in 1947, Mayo was one of the most celebrated social scientists of the age. In praise of his achievements, the business magazine *Fortune* wrote of him:

Scientist and practical clinician, Mayo speaks with a rare authority that has commanded attention in factories as well as Universities. His erudition extends through psychology, sociology, physiology, medicine and economics, and his experience comes from a lifelong first-hand study of industry. (Quoted in Smith, 1998: 222)

Much of his fame rested on the 'Hawthorne Experiments' carried out at Western Electric's Hawthorne Works in Chicago in the 1920s and 1930s. However, within 10 years of his departure from Harvard, his reputation was in tatters: his expertise as a researcher was seriously questioned, his work was criticised for being too 'managerialist' and, perhaps most importantly, his contribution to the Hawthorne Experiments was considered as no more than a public relations exercise for Western Electric (Rose, 1988; Sheldrake, 1996; Smith, 1998).

The Hawthorne Experiments, as Gillespie (1991: 1) commented:

. . . are still among the most frequently cited and most controversial experiments in the social sciences . . . They are acclaimed as a landmark study in both sociology and psychology . . . Surveys in the key developments in organization and management theory consistently note the seminal contribution of the experiments to their field.

Yet, for most of the 80 years since the Hawthorne Experiments were initiated, it has been difficult to identify Mayo's exact role (Smith, 1987). That the name of Elton Mayo is inextricably linked with the Hawthorne Experiments is undeniable. That Mayo publicised and was given credit for masterminding them is also undeniable. Until recently, though, key questions have remained unanswered: did Mayo design and implement the experiments himself? What was the role of his colleagues at Harvard? How frequently did he visit the Hawthorne Works? Now, with the availability of family records and other archival material, Smith (1998) claims to have answered Mayo's detractors and to have re-established him both as the key figure in the Hawthorne Experiments and as the dominant figure in the Human Relations movement. Nevertheless, given the vehemence of Mayo's critics (Rose, 1988), one suspects that the debate over the 'Mayo mystique' is not yet over.

Despite the difficulty in separating out the myth from the man, we should not let that undermine the significance of the Hawthorne work or what we know of Mayo and his colleagues' contribution, even if we cannot clearly identify who did what. The Hawthorne programme was originally devised by Western Electric's own industrial engineers in 1924. Western Electric was the manufacturing division of the American Telephone and Telegraph Company. The Hawthorne Works, which at the time employed some 30,000 people, was considered a prime example of the application of the mass production techniques and work organisation methods advocated by Frederick Taylor and Henry Ford. However, this was tempered by the company's personnel and welfare policies which provided pension, sickness and disability benefits, a share purchase plan, medical treatment, extensive recreational facilities and a system of worker representation. This example of 'welfare capitalism' had the twin aims of reducing worker dissatisfaction and resisting trade union influence (Sheldrake, 1996).

The first phase of the Hawthorne Experiments, which lasted on and off until 1927, was the Hawthorne Illumination Tests (HIT), which were designed to examine the effects of various levels of lighting on workers' productivity. The engineers established control and experimental groups: the latter were subject to different levels of illumination as they carried out their work whilst the lighting of the control group was left unchanged. At the outset this looked like a standard Scientific Management experiment in the mould of Taylor and the Gilbreths. What the engineers were expecting was a set of unambiguous results that would allow them to establish the 'one best' level of illumination. This did not happen and, instead, data began to emerge that challenged the very basis of Scientific Management.

The engineers had expected the performance of the experimental group to vary with increases and decreases in illumination and for an optimum level to be established, but as the illumination was varied, so output continued to increase. Indeed, output only decreased in the experimental group when the lighting became so dim that it was difficult to see. More puzzling still, output in the control group, where no changes were made, also increased.

In 1927 the company began the second phase of the Hawthorne Experiments. Building on the HIT work, the company wanted to establish the effects on productivity of increased rest periods, a shorter working day, a reduced working week, free refreshments, changes to payment systems, better and friendlier communication, and a relaxation in the customary discipline usually imposed by first-line supervisors. The first group to be involved were six women in the Relay Assembly Test Room (RATR). As Gillespie (1991: 59) noted:

> [Their] privileged status and a modicum of control over work days brought about a strong identification with the test room among the workers . . . With the introduction of refreshments during the morning rest period, the women's status soared higher still.

By 1929, productivity in the RATR group had increased by some 30 per cent. In the interim, the company also initiated a further series of experiments in which, from 1928 onwards, Elton Mayo and his colleagues were closely involved. In the years that followed, successive groups of workers were subjected to changes in hours, payment systems, rest periods, etc. The subsequent changes in output, and the reasons put forward for these, undermined many of the assumptions regarding organisations and human behaviour previously perceived as sacrosanct (Mayo, 1933; Roethlisberger and Dickson, 1938).

The experiments were monitored continuously; from this work, Mayo and his colleagues concluded that it was not the changes in working conditions that affected output, but the fact that those workers involved had been singled out for special attention. This acted to increase their morale and make them want to perform better. It was the very fact that they were being studied which produced the increased performance; this later became known as the 'Hawthorne Effect'. This accounted for the improved performance by the original HIT control group, even with no changes to the lighting in their area: they also felt 'special' because they were being studied. These findings led Mayo and his group to move the focus of their work away from the reaction of individual workers to changes in their working conditions. Instead, they began to investigate the role and behaviour of the 'informal' groups that workers themselves established, and the norms and attitudes of these groups.

As a result of this work, Mayo and his colleagues put forward two major propositions that came to form the core of the Human Relations approach. The first related to the importance of informal groups within the formal structure of organisations. The Western Electric studies demonstrated the need to see the work process as a collective, cooperative activity as opposed to an individual, isolated one. The studies showed in particular the important effect that the informal, primary work group has on performance. These groups tend to develop their own norms, values and attitudes that enable them to exert strong social, peer group pressure on individuals within the group to conform to group norms, whether this be in relation to the pace of work or attitudes towards other groups and supervisors. Taylor, years before, had also noted the pressure that groups of workers could exert over their members to make them conform; however, he believed that this was abnormal behaviour which could be remedied by tight managerial control. What the Western Electric studies demonstrated was that far from being abnormal, such behaviour was perfectly normal.

The second proposition put forward by Mayo and his colleagues was that humans have a deep need for recognition, security and belonging. Rather than being purely economic beings, it was argued that the Hawthorne Experiments demonstrated that workers' performance and attitudes could be influenced more by their need for recognition and security, and also by the feeling of belonging engendered by informal groups. This latter point in particular reflected, in Mayo's view, a deep-seated desire by humans as social beings for intimacy, consistency and predictability. Where these social certainties were lacking, workers would deliberately seek to manufacture them by creating their own informal work groups. Therefore, rather than seeking to eradicate or undermine the workings of these informal groups, as Taylor had advocated, the Western Electric studies showed that management needed to gain the collaboration and cooperation of such groups if they were to get the best performance from workers.

It is generally agreed (Mullins, 1989; Rose, 1988) that the Western Electric studies had a dramatic effect on management and organisation theory. The studies ushered in an era where the Economic Man of the Classical approach was supplanted by Social Man. It was no longer possible for managers to ignore the effects of organisational structures and job design on work groups, employee attitudes and management–worker relations. The crucial issue became one of social relationships – Human Relations – in the workplace. In future, the focus of good management practice would shift to the importance of leadership and communication in order to win over employees. As the 1930s and 1940s progressed, other work began to emerge which both substantiated and broadened those findings.

Chester Barnard (1886–1961) and cooperative systems

Chester Barnard was born in Malden, Massachusetts in 1886. On leaving school, he became a piano tuner, but later attended Harvard University where he studied economics. On leaving university, he went to work for the American Telephone and Telegraph Company, in whose subsidiary, Western Electric, the Hawthorne studies were carried out. He was initially employed as a statistician, but quickly rose to hold a number of senior executive positions including, by the age of 41, becoming President of the New Jersey Bell Telephone Company. He also established his credentials as a prolific writer and lecturer with strong links to a number of universities, including Harvard. On retiring in 1948, he became President of the Rockefeller Foundation.

Barnard is best known for his book *The Functions of the Executive* (1938), which has a comparable place in the Human Relations literature to that of Fayol's work in the literature of the Classical school. In this work, Barnard put forward the idea of organisations as cooperative systems. In so doing, this gave him a double claim to fame: not only did he draw attention to the cooperative nature of organisational life, but he was also one of the first to treat organisations as systems rather than machines. He was in frequent touch with Mayo and his colleagues at Harvard, and closely followed their work at Western Electric. Therefore, although *The Functions of the Executive* was a personal and idiosyncratic work, reflecting Barnard's own distinct views and opinions, it was far from being bereft of academic substance. Indeed, his book was the first systematic attempt in English (Weber's work on bureaucracy was still not translated into English at this time) to outline a theory of organisations as a whole. In this respect, Barnard can claim both to have made a substantial contribution to the Human Relations approach and to have laid the groundwork for subsequent writers such as Selznick and Simon (Robbins, 1987; Scott, 1987).

Barnard had close links with Harvard Business School and, along with Elton Mayo, Talcott Parsons (who first translated Weber's work into English) and Joseph Schumpeter, was a member of the Harvard Pareto Circle. This group was established to discuss and promote the work of the Italian sociologist Vilfredo Pareto, whose writing placed great emphasis on social systems and social equilibrium (Sheldrake, 1996).

The influence of Pareto's social systems view can be seen in Barnard's depiction of organisations as cooperative systems. An organisation is a cooperative system, he argued, because without the willingness of its members to make contributions to and to pursue its goals, it cannot operate effectively. Like others who espoused the Human Relations approach, he believed cooperation could not be achieved solely by monetary incentives. Instead, he advocated a mixture of monetary and non-monetary inducements. Similarly, cooperation by itself would not be effective unless an organisation also possessed a common purpose: clear and realistic goals and objectives that the organisation's members could understand, relate to and pursue. Establishing this common purpose, in Barnard's opinion, had to be the responsibility of those at the top of the organisation, but achieving it required the cooperation of those at the bottom, and all levels in between. This leads to another of Barnard's assertions: the flow of authority is not from the top down but from the bottom up. He defined authority not as a property of management but as a response by subordinates to superiors. If subordinates did not respond willingly and appropriately, then no authority existed. In this example, as in many others, he both reflected the influence of and supported the findings of the Western Electric studies, which drew attention to the ability of workers through social groupings to facilitate or frustrate the will of management.

In order to avoid a negative response from workers, Barnard advocated systematic and purposeful communication. He saw communication, through both formal and informal structures, as being the key function of the executive. Indeed, he portrayed the organisation as a purposeful, coordinated system of communications linking all participants in a manner that not only encouraged the pursuit of the organisation's common purpose, but also legitimated the premises on which it was based. However, he argued that this does not happen automatically or accidentally; it is the product of effective leadership. This is why Barnard stressed the key role of the executive in leading the organisation by facilitating communication and motivating subordinates to high levels of performance; such developments could only come from the top. He also saw the executive as having a role in shaping and reinforcing the organisation's value systems or, as modern writers would put it, its culture.

Given the emphasis placed by Barnard on the setting and pursuit of clear objectives, and in his approach in general, there is a degree of overlap with the work of the Classical school. However, what significantly distinguishes him from them is his insistence on the non-rational, informal, interpersonal, and indeed moral basis of organisational life. His view of effective leadership also distinguishes him from the Classical school. Rather than seeing leadership as dependent on position, Barnard argued that successful leadership arose from the interplay between the individual leader, the followers and the context.

Above all, Barnard rejected the idea of material incentives being the only incentives to make people work purposefully. Indeed, he saw them as being 'weak incentives' that needed to be supported by other psychological and sociological motivators if organisations were to be successful in achieving their common purpose. In thus challenging the effectiveness of material incentives, he was to receive substantial support a few years later from a more academic source.

Abraham Maslow's (1908–1970) hierarchy of needs

Abraham Maslow was born in Brooklyn, New York in 1908. He trained as a psychologist at the University of Wisconsin and, apart from a brief period working in the family business, spent his working life in academia. Maslow was one of the first to differentiate between and classify different types of human need. For Taylor and his adherents, there was only one form of need: material or monetary need. Mayo *et al* and Barnard took a different view; they drew a distinction between material and non-material needs, but made no distinction within these two categories. Maslow (1943) identified five distinct forms of human need which he placed in a hierarchical order.

As Figure 2.1 shows, the five levels in Maslow's hierarchy of needs, in ascending order, are:

- **Physiological needs** – hunger, thirst, sleep, etc.; only when these basic needs have been satisfied do other needs begin to emerge.
- **Safety needs** – the desire for security and protection against danger.
- **Social needs** – the need to belong, to gain love and affection; to be in the company of others, especially friends.
- **Esteem needs** – these reflect a person's desire to be respected – esteemed – for their achievements.
- **Self-actualisation needs** – self-actualisation is the need to achieve one's full potential. According to Maslow, this will vary from person to person and, indeed, may differ over time, as a person reaches a level of potential previously considered unattainable and so goes on to strive for new heights. For these reasons, self-actualisation is a continuously evolving process throughout a person's lifetime.

Maslow argued that, beginning at the lowest level, a person had to satisfy substantially the needs at one level before they could move up the hierarchy and concentrate on 'higher-order' needs. Maslow (1943: 383) recognised that there were weaknesses in

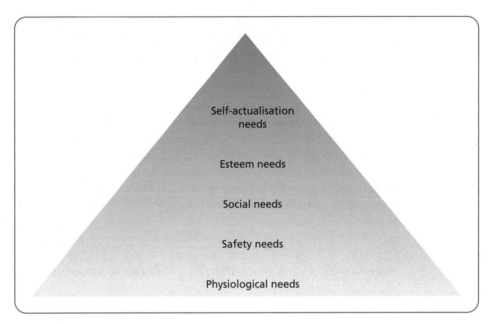

Figure 2.1 Maslow's hierarchy of needs

his theory of needs: 'Since, in our society, basically-satisfied people are the exception, we do not know much about self-actualisation, either experimentally or clinically.' He accepted that the strength of the hierarchy might differ with individual circumstances – some people's aspirations may be so deadened by their experiences that they would be satisfied by having enough to eat. He also saw that cultural differences between societies could have an impact on the extent and order of needs. Nevertheless, he did believe that his theory was generally applicable and that where people's higher aspirations were thwarted or unmet, the result was likely to be frustration and de-motivation.

Though not designed specifically for organisational analysis, but rather in the context of life in general, it can be seen why Maslow's work was so readily accepted by proponents of the Human Relations approach. For them, it explained why in some situations Tayloristic incentives were effective, whilst in other situations, such as the Hawthorne Experiments, other factors proved more important.

Applying Maslow's hierarchy of needs to human behaviour in organisations, it can be seen that people will first of all be motivated by the desire to satisfy physiological needs through monetary rewards. Once those have been substantially satisfied, however, workers will seek to satisfy – be motivated by – their safety needs, such as job security and welfare benefits. In a similar fashion, once safety needs are substantially met, these will fade into the background and social needs will come to the fore; people will want to be accepted as part of a group, to share common intents and aspirations with the group, to experience the bonds of friendship and loyalty. Clearly, these social needs played an important role in the Hawthorne Experiments, as did esteem needs. After social and esteem needs are substantially met, finally self-actualisation needs come to the fore. However, as mentioned above, the need for self-actualisation never wanes but tends to act as a continuing spur to further achievements.

Clearly, Maslow's work cannot be transferred fully into the organisational setting, given that the constraints on freedom of action imposed by most jobs do not allow individuals to approach, let alone attain, self-actualisation (Rose, 1988). Even very basic physiological needs are beyond the reach of many millions of people in the world. Nevertheless, in pointing to the negative effects of thwarting an individual's aspirations, and in distinguishing between types of intrinsic (non-material) and extrinsic (material) motivators, and arguing that, at any one time, it is the unmet needs which act as positive motivators, Maslow has had an enormous impact on job design and research (*see* Child, 1984; Smith *et al*, 1982). The influence of Maslow's theory of needs can be seen in the work of other exponents of Human Relations, especially Douglas McGregor.

Douglas McGregor (1906–1964) and Theory X–Theory Y

Douglas McGregor was born in 1906. He received his doctorate in psychology from Harvard, and spent much of his working life at the Massachusetts Institute of Technology where, from 1954 until his death in 1964, he was the first Sloan Fellows Professor. McGregor is one of the most widely cited Human Relations writers. He developed his views from his personal experience and observations as an academic, consultant and university administrator rather than from empirical research.

In his book *The Human Side of Enterprise* (1960), McGregor argued that decisions taken by top managers on the best way to manage people were based on their assumptions about human nature. McGregor maintained that there are basically two commonly held views of human nature: a negative view – Theory X; and a positive view – Theory Y (*see* Ideas and perspectives 2.3). He believed that managers' behaviour towards their subordinates was based upon one or other of these views, both of which consist of a certain grouping of assumptions about human behaviour.

McGregor saw Theory X, which he believed dominated the literature and practice of management, as a very negative view of human nature, whereas he saw Theory Y as a much more positive view of human nature. Theory X and Theory Y are not statements about what people are actually like, but rather the general assumptions that managers, and the rest of us, hold about what people are like. The fact that such views may not have a base in reality is irrelevant if managers act as though they are true. Managers who adhere to Theory X will use a combination of stick and carrot methods to control their subordinates, and will construct organisations that restrict the individual's ability to exercise skill, discretion and control over their work. Those managers who adhere to Theory Y will adopt a more open and flexible style of management. They will create jobs that encourage workers to contribute towards organisational goals and allow them to exercise skill and responsibility, and where the emphasis will be on non-material incentives.

Obviously, Theory X is akin to the Classical view of human nature and organisational design, whereas Theory Y falls more in the Human Relations tradition. Though McGregor favoured Theory Y, he recognised that it could not be fully validated. Instead, he saw Theory Y as a challenge to the orthodoxy of Theory X and, as he put it (McGregor, 1960: 53), as an 'invitation to innovate'. He argued that there was nothing inevitable about which approach to adopt. The choice lies with managers; those who adhere to Theory X will create a situation where workers are only able and willing to pursue material needs

Ideas and perspectives 2.3
Barnard's Theory X and Theory Y

Theory X assumptions	Theory Y assumptions
The average person dislikes work and will avoid it wherever possible.	Most people can view work as being as natural as rest or play.
Employees must be coerced, controlled or threatened with punishment if they are to perform as required.	Workers are capable of exercising self-direction and self-control.
Most people try to avoid responsibility and will seek formal direction whenever possible.	The average person will accept and even seek responsibility if they are committed to the objectives being pursued.
Workers place security above other factors relating to employment and will display little ambition.	Ingenuity, imagination, creativity and the ability to make good decisions are widely dispersed throughout the population and are not peculiar to managers.

(as Maslow observed). Such workers will be neither prepared nor in a position to contribute to the wider aims and objectives of the organisation that employs them. Managers who follow Theory Y precepts are likely to receive an entirely different response from their employees; workers will identify more clearly with the general interests of the organisation, and be more able and more willing to contribute to their achievement.

Though stressing the element of choice, McGregor, along with other Human Relations adherents, believed that changes in the nature of modern societies meant that organisations were moving, and should move, more in the direction of Theory Y.

Warren Bennis (1925–) and the death of bureaucracy

By the 1950s and 1960s, the Human Relations approach and the values it espoused were in the ascendancy. One clear sign of this was the widely held view in the 1960s that bureaucracy was dying and being replaced by more flexible, people-centred organisations that allowed and encouraged personal growth and development. One of the main exponents of this view is Warren Bennis.

Warren Bennis trained as an industrial psychologist and held a number of senior academic appointments, including Professor of Management at the University of Southern California. He is now best known for his work on leadership, and has acted as an adviser to four US presidents. In terms of the Human Relations movement, Bennis (1966) is credited with coining the phrase and making the case for 'the death of bureaucracy'. Bennis argued

Ideas and perspectives 2.4
The case against bureaucracy

- **Rapid and unexpected change** – bureaucracy's strength lies in its ability to manage efficiently the routine and predictable; however, its pre-programmed rules and inflexibility make it unsuitable for the rapidly changing modern world.
- **Growth in size** – as organisations become larger, then bureaucratic structures become more complex and unwieldy, and less efficient.
- **Increasing diversity** – rapid growth, quick change and an increase in specialisation create the need for people with diverse and highly specialised skills; these specialists cannot easily or effectively be fitted within the standardised, pyramid structure of bureaucratic organisations.
- **Change in managerial behaviour** – the increasing adoption of the Human Relations approach by managers challenges the simplistic view of human nature put forward by the Classical school, which underpins bureaucracy. If coercion and threats administered in a depersonalised, mechanistic fashion are counter-productive as a way of controlling people in organisations, then the case for bureaucracy is severely diminished.

that every age develops an organisational form appropriate to its time. Bureaucracy was, in his view, appropriate for the first two-thirds of the twentieth century but not beyond that. He believed that bureaucracy emerged because its order, precision and impersonal nature was the correct antidote for the personal subjugation, cruelty, nepotism and capriciousness that passed for management during the Industrial Revolution.

Bureaucracy, he stated, emerged as a creative and wholesome response to the needs and values of the Victorian Age. Up to this point, there is little to distinguish Bennis from Weber; however, he then went on to argue that the Victorian Age, and its needs, were dead and that new conditions were emerging to which bureaucracy was no longer suited (*see* Ideas and perspectives 2.4).

For Bennis and others such as Daniel Bell (1973), Alvin Toffler (1970) and EF Schumacher (1973), bureaucracy was rightly dying and being replaced by more diverse, flexible structures which could cope with the needs of the modern world.

Job Design: operationalising Human Relations

Though intellectually strong, the Human Relations school remained operationally weak up to the 1950s and 1960s because, unlike the Scientific Management element of the Classical school, it lacked a clear set of operational definitions and guidelines that allowed organisations to understand and implement it. The advent of the Job Design movement in both the USA and Europe rectified this to an extent, at least as far as the design of jobs was concerned.

In the last 50 years, Job Design, or work humanisation as it has also been called, has become a powerful technique for rolling back the worst excesses of the Classical school, especially in the area of manual work, where Scientific Management and its clones have had such an impact. It was in America in the 1950s that Davis and Canter (1955), influenced by the work of the Human Relations school, questioned the Tayloristic basis of job design and work organisation. They suggested that it would be possible to design jobs that satisfied not only human needs but also organisational ones as well. They argued that increased job satisfaction and increased organisational performance went hand in hand. Since then many other writers, especially in Europe, have contributed to the development of Job Design theory (Davis *et al*, 1955; Guest, 1957; Hackman and Oldham, 1980; Likert, 1961; Trist *et al*, 1963; Warr, 1987).

Job Design is a direct attack on the precepts of the Classical approach. Whereas Taylorist tradition seeks to fit people to rigidly defined and controlled jobs, Job Design theorists argue that jobs can and should be fitted to human needs. The basic tenets of Job Design are relatively straightforward and follow on from the work of the proponents of the Human Relations approach, especially Maslow. It is argued that the Classical approach to jobs, with its emphasis on fragmenting jobs and reducing workers' autonomy and discretion, is counter-productive to both individual fulfilment and organisational performance. This is because boring, monotonous and meaningless jobs lead to poor mental health and feelings of dissatisfaction. In turn, this can result in lack of motivation, absenteeism, labour turnover and even industrial unrest (Arnold *et al*, 1998).

The solution to these problems follows from the analysis. If Tayloristic trends in job design are counter-productive, then they should be reversed and 'variety, task completeness and, above all, autonomy' should be built into jobs (Wall *et al*, 1984: 15). Such a move would promote workers' mental health and job satisfaction, bringing in turn increased motivation and performance. Just as Taylor believed his approach would benefit both workers and management, so too do the proponents of Job Design; the difference is that the benefit to the worker is personal fulfilment rather than increased wages, though in both systems the benefit to management is increased productivity (Friedman, 1961; Hackman and Lawler, 1971; Herzberg *et al*, 1959; Kelly, 1982a, 1982b).

In practice, as Ideas and perspectives 2.5 shows, there are three main variants of Job Design.

Job Design emerged and attracted so much attention in the 1950s and 1960s for three main reasons:

1. The first flows from the work of Maslow (1943). As workers have become better educated and more affluent, their higher-order needs such as self-actualisation have come to the fore. This means that in order to obtain the best performance from workers, jobs have to be designed to meet their psychological as well as their financial needs (Kelly, 1982b).
2. As markets have become more global, more competitive and more volatile, organisations need to be more responsive to the needs of their customers. This requires workers to be more flexible, possess a greater range of skills, and be able to work as part of a team rather than on an individual basis (Aglietta, 1979; Streeck, 1987).
3. Low unemployment in the 1950s, 1960s and 1970s led to high rates of labour turnover and absenteeism and endemic industrial unrest in industries and organisations with poor job design (Pruijt, 1997). This was certainly a major reason for Volvo's adoption of Job Design in the 1970s (Blackler and Brown, 1978).

Ideas and perspectives 2.5
The three main variants of Job Design

- **Job enlargement**, which concentrates on increasing work variety by combining previously fragmented tasks together, or by rotating people between different types of work (Guest, 1957).
- **Job enrichment**, which concentrates on increasing workers' control over what they do by rearranging work so that some of the responsibilities previously borne by supervisors and support staff are given to individuals or, more often, semi-autonomous work groups (Herzberg, 1968).
- **Socio-technical Systems theory**, which is a variant on Job Design involving a shift of focus from the individual job to the organisation as a whole. Socio-technical Systems theory sees organisations as being composed of interdependent social and technical systems. The theory argues that there is little point in reorganising the social system in isolation from the technology being used, and that the level of performance achieved is dependent on the degree of fit between the two. This view sees technology as acting as a limitation on the scope for redesigning individual jobs (Davis, 1979; Dunphy and Griffiths, 1998; Trist *et al*, 1963). It follows, therefore, that Job Design must go hand-in-hand with technological change if it is to be successful.

Since the 1950s, the USA and most European countries have initiated some form of officially sponsored 'Work Humanisation' programme. Not surprisingly, Norway and Sweden, with their traditions of industrial cooperation and democracy, and what was West Germany, with its post-war commitment to industrial consensus and worker rights, led the way in terms of financial and legal backing. Norway initiated the process with its Industrial Democracy Project (1962–1975). Sweden has probably been the most consistent, however, establishing the Work Environment Fund in 1972, with a budget of SEK 500 million per year, and creating the New Factories Programme at the same time. In 1976 it enacted the Co-determination Act, which ensures that trade unions have a right to be consulted on all major changes in working conditions. In 1977, the Swedish government created the Centre For Working Life (later the Institute For Work Life Research) to initiate and promote work humanisation. In the 1980s, it initiated the Swedish Development Programme (1982–1987), the Leadership, Organisation and Co-determination Programme (1985–1990), and the People, Data, Working Life Programme (1987–1992). Germany has seen a similarly consistent approach with the Humanisation of Working Life Programme (1974–1989) and the Work and Technology Programme (1989–). Germany also provided subsidies (around DM 100 million per year) to encourage the adoption of Job Design practices (Pruijt, 1997).

Some of the Job Design initiatives in these countries were inspired by Norwegian researchers such as Einar Thorsrud, who propagated the concept of semi-autonomous work groups. Others derived from the work on the socio-technical systems approach carried out by the Tavistock Institute in London (Auer and Riegler, 1990). In the UK, however, despite the presence of the Tavistock Institute and the establishment of the Work Research Unit in 1974, official backing has been noticeably lukewarm. Indeed, even the modest expenditure devoted to the Work Research Unit was cut back considerably in the 1980s, and the Unit has now been disbanded. Successive UK governments now seem to share the American view that 'Quality of Working Life' programmes are the purview of individual organisations rather than something to be promoted by government.

To a great degree, the popularity of Job Design seems to have fluctuated with employment levels. In the full-employment era of the 1950s and 1960s, governments and employers in the West seemed relatively receptive to it. With the recessions of the 1970s and 1980s, however, interest fell away in most countries. The exceptions were Germany and particularly Sweden (*see* the Volvo case study at the end of the chapter), both countries where unemployment remained relatively low in the 1970s and 1980s. Despite this, there can be little doubt that Job Design precepts have permeated Western society on a significant scale, and provide the main operational alternative to the Classical approach; as Pruijt (1997) noted, however, Tayloristic work practices have proved far more persistent than the proponents of Job Design had expected.

The Human Relations approach: summary and criticisms

Though many tend to associate the Human Relations movement exclusively with the work of Mayo, the above shows that it is a much more diverse school of thought. Indeed, some have argued that to call it a school owes more to academic convenience than to reality (Rose, 1988). Nevertheless, there are continuing and overlapping themes in the work of the writers cited above which strongly bond them together. The first, and most obvious, is their almost total rejection of the Classical movement's mechanistic–rational approach towards people and organisation structures. As Dunphy and Griffiths (1998: 21) noted:

> *In particular, they attacked the notion of employees as interchangeable parts, stressing that individual employees had different motivations; that the specialisation of labour and deskilling had created widespread alienation and demotivation; and that excessive supervision had crushed employee initiative.*

The second and more fundamental feature is that whilst approaching the issues involved from different perspectives and emphasising separate aspects, the proponents of Human Relations create an organisational model that possesses both coherence and plausibility.

The Human Relations model stresses three core elements:

- leadership and communication;
- intrinsic job motivation (as well as extrinsic rewards);
- organisation structures and practices which facilitate flexibility and involvement.

These elements are underpinned by two central propositions:

- **Organisations are complex social systems**, with both formal and informal social structures, and are not mechanical contrivances. Therefore, they cannot effectively be controlled by close supervision, rigid rules and purely economic incentives.

- **Human beings have emotional as well as economic needs.** Organisation and job structures need to be designed in such a way as to enable workers to meet both their material and non-material needs. Only in this way will workers perform efficiently and effectively in the best interests of the organisation.

It is not difficult to see why the Human Relations approach proved popular. In a period when many people were becoming increasingly worried about the growth of impersonal bureaucracies, it provided an attractive alternative. It is an approach that stresses that human beings are not mere cogs in a machine but that they have emotional needs: humans want to 'belong', achieve recognition, and develop and fulfil their potential. As mentioned earlier, the Depression of the 1930s and the Second World War and its aftermath created, in the USA and Europe, a greater sense of collectivism and community than had hitherto been the case – another reason why the Human Relations doctrine found such a ready audience. Also, implicitly, it offers an approach to change management that has a surprisingly modern ring to it. The stress on organisations having clear objectives, effective communication systems and proactive leadership, coupled with the need to obtain the willing cooperation of employees, are central to many modern approaches to change management.

Despite its attractiveness and plausibility, a substantial and often vitriolic body of opinion came to be ranged against the Human Relations approach in the 1950s and 1960s (Rose, 1988). Economists rejected the argument that non-material incentives have a potentially stronger motivating influence than material incentives. The emphasis placed by the proponents of Human Relations on people's need for 'togetherness' and 'belonging' was seen by some as a denial of individualism. Others thought that it belittled workers and portrayed them as irrational beings who, given the chance, would cling to management as a baby clings to its mother. It was also attacked from both a management and a trade union viewpoint. Some of the former felt that its supposedly powerful manipulative techniques were either useless or inoperable, whilst representatives of the latter saw Human Relations as a vehicle for manipulating labour, and undermining – or attempting to eliminate – trade unions. Sociologists criticised it for attempting a sociological analysis of organisations without taking into account the larger society within which each organisation exists (Kerr and Fisher, 1957; Landsberger, 1958; Rose, 1988; Whyte, 1960).

Many of the criticisms were clearly directed at the work of Mayo and his colleagues, including inconsistencies between them. Landsberger (1958), for example, was one of the first to point out the difference between Mayo's (1933) interpretations of the Hawthorne Experiments and those of his colleagues, Roethlisberger and Dickson (1938), though Smith (1998) disputes this and many of the other criticisms of Mayo. However, by no means were all the criticisms levelled at Mayo and his colleagues. Maslow's work, a key theoretical cornerstone of the Human Relations approach, was found to lack empirical substance when researchers attempted to validate it, and certainly later theories of motivation seem to adopt a different approach (Arnold *et al*, 2005; Hall and Nougaim, 1968; Hitt *et al*, 2009; Lawler and Suttle, 1972; Sheldrake, 1996). Similarly, Bennis's views were attacked. The Aston Studies in the 1960s (Pugh *et al*, 1969a, 1969b) showed that bureaucracy was growing rather than declining. Also, Miewald (1970) argued that Bennis did not understand the nature of bureaucracy; in his view, far from being rigid, it could and did adapt to changing and dynamic environments. Kelly (1982b) also attacked the proposition that increased job satisfaction leads to increased performance.

There is one further criticism of the Human Relations approach, one that it shares with the Classical approach: it claims for itself the title of the 'one best way'. Yet, the question was posed, how can any approach claim that there is only one method of structuring and managing organisations, and that it holds good for all organisations and for all time? Indeed, the seed of this criticism can be found in Bennis's (1966) work, where he argued that organisations in the last third of the twentieth century would experience rapid and unexpected change, continue to increase in size – with the problems of complexity which this brings, and become more diverse and specialised. Clearly, whilst not explicitly advocating it, Bennis was making the case for an approach to organisations that recognised not only that they face different situations but also that these are not stable over time. Similarly, Trist *et al*'s (1963) argument regarding the need to fit social systems to technical ones can also be seen as making a case for a situationalist approach to job design. Indeed, the most telling argument against the 'one best way' approach is that presented by Davis and Canter (1955), mentioned earlier. If jobs and work organisation are social inventions designed to meet the needs of societies and organisations at particular points in time, then there can never be a one best way for all organisations and for all times. What is needed, instead, is an approach that links approaches to work design to the particular context to which they are best suited. In the 1960s and 1970s, such an approach emerged.

The Contingency Theory approach

Contingency Theory emerged in the 1960s out of a number of now classic studies of organisation structure and management (*see* Child, 1984; Mullins, 1989; Scott, 1987). Since the 1970s, it has proved – as a theory at least – to be more influential than either the Classical or Human Relations approach. In essence, Contingency Theory is a rejection of the 'one best way' approach previously sought by managers and propounded by academics. In its place is substituted the view that the structure and operation of an organisation is dependent ('contingent') on the situational variables it faces – the main ones being environment, technology and size (Burnes, 1989). It follows from this that no two organisations will face exactly the same contingencies; therefore, as their situations are different, so too should their structures and operations be different. Consequently the 'one best way' for *all* organisations is replaced by the 'one best way' for *each* organisation.

One of the earliest writers to lay the groundwork for Contingency Theorists was Herbert Simon. Writing in the 1940s (Simon, 1947), he criticised existing approaches as providing managers with nothing more than proverbs or lists of 'good practice' based on scant ideas, many of which contradicted each other. He argued that organisation theory needed to go beyond superficial and over-simplified precepts, and instead study the conditions under which competing principles could be applied.

Nevertheless, it was not until the 1960s that a considered approach emerged, which broke with the Classical and Human Relations movements' attempts to establish a universal approach suitable to all organisations. The former had concentrated on the formal structure and technical requirements of organisations, and had attempted to establish sets of general principles. The latter, the Human Relations movement, focused on the informal aspects of organisations and the psychological and social needs of their employees. As with the Classical approach, this produced lists of good practice and desired objectives, but it lacked precise guidance on how these should be applied.

Contingency theorists adopted a different perspective which created a clear distinction between them and proponents of the Classical approach and Human Relations school. Contingency theorists based their approach on systems theory, adopting the premise that organisations are open systems whose internal operation and effectiveness are dependent upon the particular situational variables they face at any one time, and that these vary from organisation to organisation. As Scott observed (1987: 23):

> *The previous definitions tend [implicitly] to view the organisation as a closed system, separate from its environment and comprising a set of stable and easily identified participants. However, organisations are not closed systems, sealed off from their environments but are open to and dependent on flows of personnel and resources from outside.*

Systems theory is not new: it has been used in the natural and physical sciences for years. However, its application to organisation only really emerged in the 1960s with the advent of Contingency Theory. As Robbins (1987) noted, there is wide agreement that the systems approach offers important insights into the working of an organisation. It views the organisation both as a whole, and as part of a larger environment. The idea is that any part of an organisation's activities affects all other parts. Organisations, rather than being closed (as previous theories implicitly assumed), are viewed as open systems operating within a wider environment and having multiple channels of interaction (Mullins, 1993). Therefore, organisations are not in complete control of their own fate; they can be, and often are, affected by the environment in which they operate, and this can and does vary from organisation to organisation.

This view is consistent with evidence that not all organisations – or even all successful ones – have the same structure, and that even within organisations, different structural forms can be observed (Mintzberg, 1979). Though many situational variables, such as the age of the organisation and its history, have been put forward as influential in determining structure, it is generally agreed that the three most important contingencies are environment, technology and size (*see* Ideas and perspectives 2.6).

The main figures in developing and establishing Contingency Theory were academics in Britain and the USA, among whom the pioneers were Burns and Stalker.

Tom Burns and George Macpherson Stalker: the importance of environment

The first major study to establish a relationship between organisations' environment and their structure was carried out by Burns and Stalker (1961) in Britain. They examined 20 firms in a variety of industries in order to assess how their structures responded to the environment in which they operated. Their findings were to have a major impact on organisation theory, and provide concrete evidence for rejecting a universal, 'one best way' approach to organisational structure and practice. They identified five different types of environment, based upon the level of uncertainty that was present, ranging from

Ideas and perspectives 2.6
The three main contingencies

- **Environmental uncertainty and dependence.** It is argued that the management of any organisation is undertaken in circumstances of uncertainty and dependence, both of which change over time. Uncertainty arises because of our inability ever to understand and control events fully, especially the actions of others, whether outside or inside an organisation. Because of this, forecasting is an inexact and hazardous enterprise. Similarly, the dependence of management upon the goodwill and support of others, whether they be internal or external groupings, makes an organisation vulnerable, and may in some circumstances even threaten its very existence. Levels of uncertainty and dependence will vary, but can never be totally eliminated, and must therefore be taken into account – treated as a contingency – when designing organisational structures and procedures (Burns and Stalker, 1961; Child, 1984; Lawrence and Lorsch, 1967; Pugh, 1984; Robbins, 1987; Thompson, 1967).

- **Technology.** The argument for technology being a key variable follows similar lines to that of environment. Organisations creating and providing different products and services use different technologies. Indeed, even those producing similar products may use differing techniques. Given that these technologies can vary from the large and expensive, such as a car assembly line, to the relatively small and cheap, such as a personal computer, the form of organisation necessary to ensure their efficient operation will also vary. If so, there is a need to treat technology as a contingent variable when structuring organisations. There are distinct variants of the case for technology, however, which reflect the different definitions of technology that theorists and researchers have employed. The two best-developed approaches are found in Woodward's (1965, 1970) studies of 'operations technology' and Perrow's (1967, 1970) analysis of 'materials technology'. The former refer to the equipping and sequencing of activities in an organisation's work flow, whilst the latter refer to the characteristics of the physical and informational materials used. Woodward's work tends to relate more to manufacturing organisations, whereas Perrow's is more generally applicable (Hickson *et al*, 1969; Thompson, 1967; Zwerman, 1970).

- **Size.** Some would argue that this is not just *a* key variable but *the* key variable. The case for size being a significant variable when designing organisations has a long antecedence within organisation theory, being first cited by Weber in the early part of the twentieth century when making the case for bureaucracy (Weber, 1947). The basic case is quite straightforward. It is argued that the structure and practices necessary for the efficient and effective operations of small organisations are not suitable for larger ones. For small organisations, centralised and personalised forms of control are claimed to be appropriate, but as organisations grow in size, more decentralised and impersonal structures and practices become more relevant (Blau, 1970; Mullins, 1989; Pugh *et al*, 1969a, 1969b; Scott, 1987).

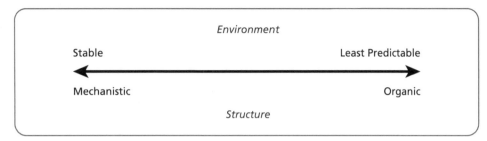

Figure 2.2 The environment–structure continuum

'stable' to 'least predictable'. They also identified two basic or ideal forms of structure: 'Mechanistic' and 'Organic'. Their data showed that Mechanistic structures were more effective in stable environments, whilst Organic ones were better suited to less stable, less predictable environments (*see* Figure 2.2).

Burns and Stalker neither reject nor accept what went before. Instead, they argued that both the Classical approach and the Human Relations approach can be appropriate, but that this depends on the nature of the environment in which the organisation is operating. As Ideas and perspectives 2.7 shows, Mechanistic structures are akin to the Classical approach, whilst Organic structures resemble the Human Relations approach. In this respect, they not only built on the past rather than rejecting it, but also restored

Ideas and perspectives 2.7
Burns and Stalker's ideal forms of structure

Characteristics of Mechanistic structures	Characteristics of Organic structures
• The specialisation of tasks. • Closely defined duties, responsibilities and technical methods. • A clear hierarchical structure with insistence on loyalty to the organisation and accountability to superiors. • Instructions and information flow (mainly) from the top to the bottom in a hierarchical manner. • Obedience to the organisations and its rules. • Importance and prestige determined by position in hierarchy.	• Job and task flexibility. • Adjustment and continual redefinition of tasks. • A network structure of control, authority and communication. • Lateral consultation based on information and advice rather than instructions and decisions. • Commitment to the work group and its tasks. • Importance and prestige determined by an individual's contribution to the tasks of their work group rather than their position in the hierarchy.

some responsibility to managers. Instead of being called on to adopt blindly the orthodoxy with regard to structure, managers would in future have to assess their organisation and its needs, and then adopt the structure and practices suitable to its situation (Child, 1984; Mullins, 1989; Scott, 1987).

Paul Lawrence and Jay Lorsch: the case for environment continued

Burns and Stalker's findings on the relationship between organisational environment and structure were examined and developed by a number of researchers in Europe and the USA. One of the most significant pieces of work was that carried out by Lawrence and Lorsch (1967) in the USA. Their work went beyond that of Burns and Stalker, in that they were interested not only in the relationship between environment and a company's overall structure, but also how individual departments within companies responded to, and organised themselves to cope with, aspects of the external environment that were of particular significance to them. They undertook a study of six firms in the plastics industry, followed by a further study of two firms in the container industry and two in the consumer foods industry. The structure of each of the firms was analysed in terms of its degree of 'differentiation' and 'integration':

- Differentiation refers to the degree to which managers and staff in their own functional departments see themselves as separate and have distinct practices, procedures and structures from others in the organisation.
- Integration refers to the level and form of collaboration that is necessary between departments in order to achieve their individual objectives within the environment in which the firm operates.

Therefore, differentiation is the degree to which departments are distinct from each other, whilst integration refers to the degree to which they have common structures, procedures, practices and objectives at the operational level. Generally, the greater the interdependence among departments, the more integration is needed to coordinate their efforts in the best interests of the organisation as a whole; this may not always be easy to achieve, however. In a rapidly changing environment, the conditions faced by individual departments may differ greatly, and a high degree of differentiation may be necessary. In such a situation, the need for integration is also likely to be great, but the diversity and volatility of the environment are likely to push individual departments in the opposite direction (Cummings and Huse, 1989).

In their study of the plastics industry, Lawrence and Lorsch (1967) found clear differentiation between key departments such as research, production and sales. Research departments were more concerned with long-term issues and were under pressure to produce new ideas and innovations. These departments, in Burns and Stalker's terminology, tended to adopt an Organic form of structure. Production departments on the other hand were, for obvious reasons, concerned with short-term performance targets relating to output, costs, quality and delivery. Such departments tended to operate in a fairly stable environment and had Mechanistic structures. Sales departments tended to fall in between research and production in terms of environment and structure. They operated in a moderately stable environment and were concerned more with getting production to meet deliveries than with long-term issues.

Whilst highlighting the degree of differentiation between key departments, the study also found that the degree of integration was critical to a firm's overall performance. Indeed, the two most successful firms in their sample were not only amongst the most highly differentiated, but also had the highest degree of integration. These findings were confirmed by their studies of the container and consumer foods industries, which showed that differentiation and integration in successful companies varies with the demands of the environment in which they operate. The more diverse and dynamic the environment, the more the successful organisation will be differentiated and highly integrated. In a more stable environment, the pressure for differentiation is less, but the need for integration remains. Therefore, Lawrence and Lorsch found that the most effective organisations had an appropriate fit between the design and coordination of departments and the amount of environmental uncertainty they faced. The most successful firms, however, were the ones that, whilst operating in an environment that required a high level of differentiation, also managed to achieve a high level of integration.

Clearly, in a situation where departments have dissimilar structures, practices and procedures, achieving integration is not easy or conflict-free. Indeed, in such situations, organisational politics can be rife. Lawrence and Lorsch found that the effective firms avoided such a situation by openly confronting conflict, and by working problems through in the context of the overall needs of the organisation. In addition, in firms that dealt successfully with conflict, the success of those responsible for achieving integration was based mainly on their knowledge and competence rather than their formal position. This was because their colleagues in the different departments respected and responded to their perceived understanding of the issues involved. It follows that to achieve high levels of integration and differentiation, an organisation cannot rely solely on the formal managerial hierarchy. This must be supplemented with liaison positions, task forces and teams, and other integrating mechanisms.

As with Burns and Stalker, Lawrence and Lorsch did not reject the Classical and Human Relations approaches *per se*, but instead saw them as alternative options, depending on the environment in which an organisation operates. In looking at the internal operations of organisations in this way, Lawrence and Lorsch raised the issue of dependence as well as uncertainty. This was a subject that James Thompson tackled in greater depth.

James Thompson: environmental uncertainty and dependence

Thompson's (1967) influential work took the environmental perspective forward in three important ways. The first was to argue that although organisations are not rational entities, they strive to be so because it is in the interests of those who design and manage the organisation that its work be carried out as effectively and efficiently as possible. In order to achieve this, organisations attempt to insulate their productive core from the uncertainty of the environment. However, it is not possible to seal off all, or perhaps even any, parts of an organisation, given that it must be open to and interact with its environment if it is to secure resources and sell its products. This leads on to Thompson's second major contribution: different levels of an organisation may exhibit, and need, different structures and operate on a more rational or less rational basis. Thompson's third contribution was to recognise that organisational effectiveness was contingent not

Ideas and perspectives 2.8
Thompson's classification of internal dependence

- **Pooled interdependence** – where each part of an organisation operates in a relatively autonomous manner, but by fulfilling their individual purposes they enable the organisation as a whole to function effectively.
- **Sequential interdependence** – where the outputs from one part of an organisation constitute the inputs for other parts of the system.
- **Reciprocal interdependence** – where overall effectiveness requires direct interaction between an organisation's separate parts.

only on the level of external environmental uncertainty, but also on the degree of internal dependence present. This echoes Lawrence and Lorsch's argument for integration and differentiation; however, Thompson made this point much more explicitly and related it to different structural forms. He formulated a three-type classification in relation to internal dependence (*see* Ideas and perspectives 2.8).

Thompson went on to argue that the type of interdependence could be related to the degree of complexity present: simple organisations rely on pooled interdependence; more complex organisations demonstrate both pooled and sequential interdependence; and in the most complex organisations, all three forms of interdependence may be present. Thompson envisaged that each form of interdependence would require distinct methods for coordinating activities. Pooled interdependence would be characterised by standardisation through the use of rules and procedures. Sequential interdependence would require the use of detailed plans and written agreements, whilst reciprocal interdependence would achieve coordination by means of personal contact and informal agreements between members of those parts of the organisation involved.

Therefore, in a nutshell, Thompson's main arguments are as follows:

- Different sections of an organisation will be characterised by varying levels of complexity, rationality and formalisation, depending on the extent to which managers can shield them from the level of uncertainty present in the environment.
- The higher both the overall level of uncertainty and that faced by each area of an organisation, the greater will be the dependence of one area on another.
- As this interdependence increases, coordination through standardised procedures and planning mechanisms will become less effective and the need for more personal contact and informal interaction will grow.
- The more that coordination is achieved through mutual reciprocity in this manner, the less rational will be the operation of the organisation.

Thompson's work is of seminal importance in the development of organisation theory, not only because of the case he made for linking external uncertainty to internal dependence, but also, as a number of writers have observed (*see* Robbins, 1987; Scott, 1987), because of the attention he drew to the fact that technology can influence organisation structures as well as environmental factors. Thompson's contribution in this respect lay in creating a classification scheme for technology, and arguing that technology determines the selection of the specific structural arrangements for reducing the effect of uncertainty on the various functions of an organisation. The issue of technology and structure had been raised earlier in a major study by Joan Woodward published in 1965.

Joan Woodward: the case for technology

In the 1960s, Joan Woodward carried out a major study of 100 UK manufacturing firms in south-east Essex, in order to establish the validity of the claims made by advocates of the Classical approach that the adoption of a bureaucratic–mechanistic structure was essential for organisational success (Woodward, 1965, 1970). After much work, Woodward concluded that no such correlation existed; what she found, however, was that the more successful companies adopted an organisational form that varied according to their main production technology. By technology, Woodward meant not only the machinery being used, but also the way it was organised, operated and integrated into a distinct production process. From her sample, she identified three distinct types of production technology, ranging from least to most complex (*see* Figure 2.3).

Woodward defined these three types of production technology as follows:

- **Small batch (or unit) production** – where customers' requirements were for one-off or small-volume specialist products.
- **Large batch (or mass) production** – where standardised products were made in large numbers to meet a forecast demand.
- **Process production** – where production was in a continuous flow, such as an oil refinery.

When the firms were grouped in this manner, a pattern emerged that showed that though they apparently differed considerably in terms of their organisational structure, many of the variations for the more successful firms could be explained by reference to the technology employed. Among firms engaged in small batch production, the most appropriate structure appeared to be one with relatively few hierarchical levels and wide middle management spans of control (i.e. an Organic-type structure). Woodward noted that technology became more complex as firms moved from small batch to large batch and finally process production. In turn, structures became taller and more narrowly based, with smaller middle management and larger chief executive spans of control (i.e.

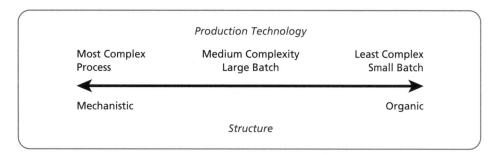

Figure 2.3 Woodward's technology–structure continuum

a Mechanistic-type structure). Within each category of technology, the best-performing companies were those closest to the median in the type of structure adopted. Therefore, Woodward's work clearly established a link between technology, structure and success which ran counter to the notion that there was a 'one best way' for all organisations.

Though qualified by later studies (*see* Child, 1984; Handy, 1986; Smith *et al*, 1982), Woodward's research remains a milestone in the development of Contingency Theory. In particular, she demonstrated the need to take into account technological variables in designing organisations, especially in relation to spans of control. Nevertheless, a major drawback of her work was the difficulty of applying it to non-manufacturing companies. This was remedied by the work of Charles Perrow.

Charles Perrow: the case for technology continued

In the USA, Charles Perrow (1967, 1970) extended Joan Woodward's work on technology and organisation structure by drawing attention to two major dimensions of technology:

- the extent to which the work being carried out is variable or predictable;
- the extent to which the technology can be analysed and categorised.

The first dimension, *variability*, refers to the incidence of exceptional or unpredictable occurrences, and the extent to which these problems are familiar and can be easily dealt with, or are unique and difficult to solve. For example, an oil refinery should experience few non-routine occurrences, whilst an advertising agency will encounter many unpredictable and exceptional occurrences. The second major dimension, *analysis and categorisation*, refers to the extent to which the individual task functions can be broken down and tightly specified, and also whether problems can be solved by recourse to recognised, routine procedures or if non-routine procedures have to be invoked. Bringing these two major dimensions of technology together, Perrow constructed a technology continuum ranging from routine to non-routine (*see* Figure 2.4). With the latter, there are a large number of exceptional occurrences requiring difficult and varied problem-solving techniques to overcome them. Routine technology, on the other hand, throws up few problems, which can be dealt with by recourse to standard, simple techniques.

Perrow argued that by classifying organisations according to their technology and predictability (routine to non-routine) of work tasks, it is then possible to identify

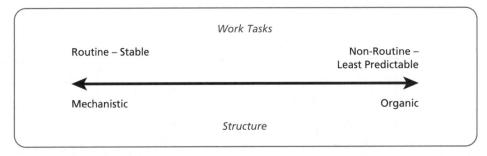

Figure 2.4 Perrow's technology–structure continuum

the most effective form of structure in any given situation or for any activity. Perrow's routine–non-routine continuum can be equated with Burns and Stalker's Mechanistic and Organic dimensions for organisation structures. In routine situations, where few problems arise and those that do are easily dealt with, a Mechanistic structure is more effective because of the stable and predictable nature of the situation. In a dynamic and unpredictable situation, however, a more flexible, Organic form of structure will be more effective in dealing with the non-routine and difficult problems that occur. By formulating his work in this manner (i.e. by combining technology and predictability) it became possible to apply it to non-manufacturing situations. Therefore, Perrow's work both reinforced and extended Woodward's case for recognising technology as a key situational variable to be taken into account when designing organisations. Nevertheless, whilst Perrow was developing his ideas, a further group of researchers were making the case for yet another 'key' contingency – size.

The Aston Group: the case for size

Though there are many proponents of the case for organisational size being a key contingency (*see* Child, 1984; Robbins, 1987), perhaps the earliest and most ardent were a group of British researchers based at the University of Aston in Birmingham (who became known as the Aston Group). In the 1960s, they carried out a series of studies to examine and identify the relationship between different forms of organisational structures and their determinants (*see* Pugh *et al*, 1969a, 1969b). The Aston Group began in the early 1960s by examining a sample of 87 companies, and, as the work developed, further samples were added to their eventually very impressive database. In analysing their results, the Aston Group found that size was the most powerful predictor of specialisation, use of procedures and reliance on paperwork. In effect, what they found was that the larger the organisation, the more likely it was to adopt (and need) a mechanistic (bureaucratic) structure. The reverse was also found: the smaller the organisation, the more likely it was to adopt (and need) an organic (flexible) structure (*see* Figure 2.5).

This was clearly a major finding. Not only did it support (at least in terms of larger organisations) Weber's earlier work on bureaucracy, but it also struck a blow against those, such as Bennis, who saw bureaucracy as dysfunctional and dying. The work of the Aston Group, along with that of others such as Blau and Schoenherr (1971), who also argued that size is the most important condition affecting the structure of organisations, gave bureaucracy if not a new lease of life then, at least, a new lease of respectability.

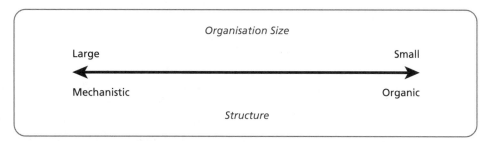

Figure 2.5 The size–structure continuum

Bureaucracy, according to the Aston results, was both efficient and effective, at least for larger organisations; and, given the tendency for the average size of private-sector companies and public bodies to increase throughout the twentieth century, its applicability would grow.

There are two explanations for the relationship between size and bureaucracy, both of which have similar implications for organisational efficiency and effectiveness:

1. That increased size offers greater opportunities for specialisation – the Adam Smith argument, in effect. This will manifest itself in terms of greater structural differentiation and a high degree of uniformity amongst sub-units. In the first instance, this will make managerial coordination more difficult, especially with the emergence of functional autonomy. To counter this, senior managers will move to impose a system of impersonal controls through the use of formal procedures, standardised reporting and control systems, the written recording of information, etc.
2. The difficulty of directing ever larger numbers of staff makes it highly inefficient to continue to use a personalised, centralised style of management. Instead a more decentralised system, using impersonal control mechanisms, has to be adopted. The introduction of such a system inevitably leads to the expansion of the administrative core (the bureaucracy) in organisations (Child, 1984).

As with all the Contingency theorists, those who argued for size as the key situational variable were not attempting to reinvent the 'one best way' approach for *all* organisations. Rather they were rejecting it in favour of an approach that saw organisational performance as dependent upon the appropriateness of the organisation's structure for its size. Therefore, like all the Contingency theorists, the Aston school adopted an approach which stressed that there is a 'one best way' for *each* organisation.

Contingency Theory: summary and criticisms

The Contingency approach can be considered much more a cohesive school of thought than either the Classical or Human Relations approach. It has three unifying themes:

- organisations are open systems;
- structure, and therefore performance, is dependent upon the particular circumstances, situational variables, faced by each organisation;
- there is no 'one best way' for *all* organisations but there is a 'one best way' for *each* organisation.

The attractions of Contingency Theory are obvious. First, it was in tune with the times in which it emerged – the 1960s and 1970s. This was a period of rapid economic and technological change, with a tendency towards much larger organisations, and a significant increase in domestic and international competition. In this situation, Contingency Theory offered a plausible explanation of not only why these events were causing problems for organisations, but also how to resolve them (Burnes, 1989). Second, on the surface at least, it was simpler to understand and apply than the Human Relations approach. As Figure 2.6 shows, if organisations adopt a structure which aligns with their environment, technology and size, the result will be good performance. However, if they do not, the result will be poor performance.

Environment Technology Size Structure	Stable Process Large	Dynamic Unit Small
Mechanistic	Good Performance	Poor Performance
Organic	Poor Performance	Good Performance

Figure 2.6 Matching structure to contingencies

Finally, like the Classical approach, Contingency Theory seeks to apply rationality to organisation design. In order to achieve good performance, organisations are told that they need to rationally analyse their situation and adopt the organisation structure which is most appropriate for the contingencies they face, i.e. as Figure 2.6 shows, they have to align their structure with their size, technology and environment.

In terms of implementing an appropriate organisation structure and of maintaining its appropriateness in the face of changing circumstances, the approach to change management offered by Contingency theorists was similar to that of the Classical school. In a rational fashion, managers should collect and analyse data on the situational variables the organisation faces and match these to the appropriate structural option. The theory then implies that for employees, faced with a plan for change based on such a 'scientific' approach, the only rational course of action is to accept the validity of the situation and cooperate with managers to achieve the required structural changes. However, it is at this point – the attempt to apply Contingency Theory rationally and mechanically – that problems and drawbacks emerge which give rise to a number of major criticisms of this approach, the main ones being as follows:

- Difficulty arises in relating structure to performance. A number of writers have pointed out that there is no agreed definition of 'good performance', and it therefore becomes difficult to show that linking structure to situational variables brings the benefits claimed (Hendry, 1979, 1980; Mansfield, 1984; Terry, 1976). Indeed, there are a wide range of factors other than structure which can influence performance, not least of which is luck. Davis and Star (1993) showed that seven of the twelve most profitable firms in the world are pharmaceutical companies, and that three of these are producers of anti-ulcer drugs. They conclude that the profitability of the pharmaceutical sector is attributable less to the nature of these organisations than to governments' over-generosity – clearly a case of an industry that is in the right place at the right time.

- Despite the length of time that Contingency Theory has been in circulation, there is still no agreed or unchallenged definition of the three key situational variables – environment, technology and size. The literature gives a wide and conflicting range of definitions of these, making it difficult not only to establish a link between them and structure, but also to apply the theory (Dastmalchian, 1984; Mullins, 1989; Pugh and Hickson, 1976; Robbins, 1987; Warner, 1984; Wood, 1979).

- Whilst, as argued above, a relationship has been established between size and structure, it has proved difficult to show that this relationship has an appreciable impact on performance. Some researchers have suggested that the link between size and structure relates to preferred systems of control, which may have more to do with the political and cultural nature of organisations than any attempt to improve performance (Allaire and Firsirotu, 1984; Child, 1984; Mansfield, 1984; Pugh and Hickson, 1976; Salaman, 1979).

- In examining the link between structure and contingencies, researchers use the organisation's formal organisational structure for comparison purposes. Yet, as the Hawthorne Experiments showed, the actual operation of an organisation may depend more on the informal structures created by workers than the formal ones laid down by management. This was a point made by Woodward (1965) in her study of technology and structure. She noted that organisation charts failed to show important relationships that, taken together, can have a significant impact on performance (Argyris, 1973; Burawoy, 1979; Selznick, 1948).

- Structure and associated practices and policies may be strongly influenced by external forces (Mullins, 1993). In the UK, privatised utilities are subject to regulation and face restrictions that have a significant influence on how they are structured and operate. Similarly, in the UK, financial service organisations are required to establish 'Chinese walls' between different parts of their business to avoid market-sensitive information being passed from one area to another.

- Rather than managers being the virtual prisoners of organisational contingencies when making decisions regarding structure, the reverse may be the case. Managers may have a significant degree of choice and influence over not only structure but also the situational variables. Whether this is called 'strategic choice' (Child, 1972), 'organisational choice' (Trist *et al*, 1963) or 'design space' (Bessant, 1983), the meaning is the same: those senior managers responsible for such decisions can exercise a high degree of freedom in selecting and influencing the technology to be used, the environment in which they operate and even the size of the organisation. Indeed, one of the architects of the technology–structure hypothesis, Charles Perrow, later claimed that technology is chosen and designed to maintain and reinforce existing structures and power relations within organisations rather than the reverse (Perrow, 1983). Other writers made the case for size and environment being manipulated in similar ways (Abell, 1975; Clegg, 1984; Hendry, 1979; Leifer and Huber, 1977; Lorsch, 1970).

- The postmodernists (*see* Chapter 5) also make a case for managerial choice. They argue that an organisation's environment is socially constructed and managers have the ability to 'construct' an environment which serves their needs (Hatch, 1997). As Grint (2005: 1467) comments:

  . . . decision-makers are much more active in the constitution of the context than conventional contingency theories allow, and that a persuasive rendition of the context . . . legitimizes a particular form of action that often relates to the decision-maker's preferred mode of engagement, rather than to what 'the situation' apparently demands.

- It is assumed that organisations pursue clear-cut, well-thought-out, stable and compatible objectives that can be fitted into a Contingency perspective. Researchers and practising managers argue that this is not the case, however – in fact, even two of the proponents of Contingency Theory, Lawrence and Lorsch (1967), highlighted the presence and danger of conflicting objectives. In reality, objectives are often unclear, and organisations may pursue a number of conflicting goals at the same time. Clearly, the objectives of an organisation will impact on its situation and its structure. If these objectives are arbitrary, conflicting or open to managerial whim, it becomes difficult to apply a Contingency approach (Abodaher, 1986; Edwardes, 1983; Hamel and Prahalad, 1989; Mintzberg, 1987; Sloan, 1986).

- The last criticism is that Contingency Theory is too mechanistic and deterministic, and ignores the complexity of organisational life. As argued by the Human Relations school, organisations are by no means the rational entities many would like to believe (a point also made by Thompson (1967) in his support of Contingency Theory). There is a need to see organisations as social systems, with all the cultural and political issues that this raises. In this view, structure is the product of power struggles between individuals and groups within the organisation, each arguing and fighting for their own perspective and position (Allaire and Firsirotu, 1984; Buchanan, 1984; Hickson and Butler, 1982; Morgan, 1986; Pfeffer, 1981; Robbins, 1987; Salaman, 1979).

Therefore, despite its attractiveness, Contingency Theory, like the Classical and Human Relations approaches, fails to provide a convincing explanation for the way in which organisations do and should operate.

Conclusions

For organisations, if not for academics, the key purpose of any organisation theory or approach is to help them analyse and rectify the weaknesses and problems of their current situation, and to assist them in bringing about the changes necessary to achieve their future objectives. Over the past 100 years, the design and management of organisations has moved from an *ad hoc* process based on – at best – guesswork, to one that is highly complex and informed by a host of practical and theoretical considerations. To the uninitiated, it might appear that this has made running organisations an easier and more certain process; yet a close examination of most organisations will reveal that this is far from being the case. Not only are organisations, in general, larger and more complex than in the past, but also the practical and theoretical reference points on which managers can draw are diverse and give conflicting and confusing signals.

Not surprisingly in such a situation, many managers look for simple, foolproof solutions: often ones that, as Douglas McGregor noted, appeal to their own basic orientation – whether that be Theory X or Theory Y. This is one of the reasons why the Classical approach, with its deep roots in the Industrial Revolution and its straightforward mechanical approach to organisations and their members, has proved so enduring – despite strong evidence of its lack of suitability in many situations. This search for simple, often quick-fix, solutions to the problems of organisational life has been manifested in many ways in the last three decades, not least the emergence of a series of 'panaceas' such as new technology, human resources management, Total Quality Management, culture change, etc. This is not to deny the benefits these can bring but, taken on their own, at best they encourage a fragmented approach, and at worst they create an atmosphere of resignation within organisations as one 'fad' is succeeded by yet another, and none is given the time necessary to prove itself (Collins, 2000). Clearly, in such situations, without an overall, long-term plan, the result of these various 'solutions' is to make the situation worse rather than better (Burnes, 1991; Burnes and Weekes, 1989).

Organisations clearly need to reject a short-term piecemeal approach, and instead see themselves in their totality and adopt a consistent and long-term approach. But which approach should they choose? We have seen in this and the previous chapter that well-thought-out and well-supported cases exist for a number of different approaches, but each has its drawbacks and critics. It may well be that each is capable of assisting organisations to analyse and understand the strengths and weaknesses of their present situation. Whether they can provide more effective organisational arrangements for the future is more debatable, however. Similarly, it is not obvious how organisations should actually achieve the process of transformation.

The Human Relations movement offers pertinent advice with regard to having clear objectives, good communication and leadership, but is less forthcoming on how change objectives should be set, and the concomitant changes planned and implemented. Contingency Theory, though, does give a procedure for setting objectives. It stresses the need to identify and analyse the situational variables an organisation faces in order to choose the most appropriate structure. However, it is also silent on the issues of planning and implementation, other than to imply that rational workers will accept rational propositions for change. In addition, even if organisations do manage to implement the recommendations of the Human Relations or Contingency advocates, it is not clear what degree of benefit they would derive from this, given the criticisms of these approaches.

In short, neither of the approaches discussed in this chapter appears to be the solution to all known organisational ills that their proponents seem to claim. They fail to reflect and explain the complexities of day-to-day organisational life that we all experience. In particular, the issue of organisational culture (Allaire and Firsirotu, 1984) barely gets a mention; yet, over the last three decades, its importance as both a promoter of and a barrier to organisational competitiveness has become apparent. Nor do they appear to take account of national differences and preferences, or for that matter pay regard to many of the wider societal factors that now impact on our lives, such as the need to show greater social responsibility, whether it be in the area of 'green' issues or equal opportunities. Yet, it is clear that enormous changes are taking place in the world, and that others will be necessary if some of the worst predictions for the future are to be avoided. In the face of these changes and challenges facing organisations, the Classical approach, the Human Relations school and Contingency Theory have all fallen out of favour. The next chapter describes the three newer perspectives on organisational life that have become increasingly influential in the last 30 years.

Test your learning

Short answer questions

1. What were the main findings of the Hawthorne Experiments?

2. Describe Maslow's hierarchy of needs.

3. Briefly discuss Theory X and Theory Y.

4. State Bennis's reasons for declaring the 'Death of Bureaucracy'.

5. Define the term 'contingency' as used by Burns and Stalker.

6. What are the respective attributes of Mechanistic and Organic structures?

7. How did Perrow define technology?

8. According to the Aston Group, size is the key contingency; state their case for this assertion.

9. What are the key arguments for and against the Human Relations approach?

10. What are the key arguments for and against Contingency Theory?

11. For each of the following, briefly state its implications for organisational change: (a) Human Relations and (b) Contingency Theory.

Essay questions

1. In what ways can the Human Relations approach be said to be superior to the Classical approach?

2. In what manner can Contingency Theory be said to incorporate both the Classical and Human Relations approaches?

Suggested further reading

1. Rose, M (1988) *Industrial Behaviour*. Penguin: Harmondsworth.

   Michael Rose gives an invaluable account of the development of the Human Relations movement and provides an interesting review of the work of Joan Woodward and the Aston Group.

2. Sheldrake, J (1996) *Management Theory: From Taylorism to Japanization*. International Thompson Business Press: London.

   John Sheldrake also provides an excellent review of the lives and work of the key figures in the Human Relations movement.

3. Hendry, C (1979) Contingency Theory in practice, I. *Personnel Review*, 8(4), 39–44.

   Hendry, C (1980) Contingency Theory in practice, II. *Personnel Review*, 9(1), 5–11.

   Wood, S (1979) A reappraisal of the contingency approach to organization. *Journal of Management Studies*, **16**, 334–54.

   Taken together, these three articles provide an excellent review of Contingency Theory.

CASE STUDY 2

Volvo's approach to job design

BACKGROUND

As shown in this chapter, Job Design has become the operational arm of the Human Relations movement. One of the prime example of Job Design in action is the Swedish motor company Volvo (now owned by Ford). Volvo has been seen as a leader in innovations in work organisation since the 1970s. Indeed, it is probably not an exaggeration to say that in the 1970s, when it began moving away from traditional methods of car assembly, Volvo was more famous for its commitment to work humanisation than for the actual vehicles it manufactured (Blackler and Brown, 1978).

Volvo's approach to reorganising vehicle production has evolved through a number of distinct phases: the abandonment of the assembly line in favour of group-based static assembly; the extension of group roles to include more collective responsibility and some decision-making autonomy; and the introduction of self-paced assembly work (Pontusson, 1990).

Volvo's move to end assembly-line production was not and is not a marginal activity – it has become embedded in the culture of the company. The decision to adopt Job Design at Volvo was and remains driven by management, regardless of later union and legislative encouragement, though to what extent they foresaw how extensively it would develop is not known. What is clear is that, in the 1960s, Volvo was as committed as any car company to the Classical approach to work organisation espoused by Taylor and embodied in the assembly-line approach to car production devised by Henry Ford. Yet, in the 1970s, it chose to break away from this industry-standard

approach and embark on (what has turned out to be) a long-term programme of increasingly radical work reorganisation.

Initially, Volvo's conversion to Job Design was inspired by commercial considerations relating to the costs of absenteeism and labour turnover, allied to pressure from public opinion in Sweden for it to embrace a less 'inhuman' form of work organisation. Although these appear to be the principal reasons for Volvo's management embarking on its commitment to Job Design, since then the process has developed its own momentum, to the extent that (as noted by Auer and Riegler, 1990: 14): 'group work is the basic concept for all changes in the organisation of production work at Volvo'. However, this did not come about overnight, without hesitation and backtracking, or in a fully planned and coordinated fashion; rather it has evolved or emerged through a number of distinct phases.

PHASES OF CHANGE

Volvo's adoption of Job Design principles began over 30 years ago. It has now reached a stage where group work has become the standard approach to work design, and assembly-line working is not considered appropriate for any new Volvo plant. When dealing with events spanning such a long period, it is often difficult to form an accurate picture of what has taken place and why; particularly when, as in this case, these events have been played out on different sites by different groups of managers and workers. Nevertheless, as Auer and Riegler (1990) and Pontusson (1990) pointed out, by examining major change programmes involving large investments in new or remodelled plants, it is possible to identify a number of distinct phases in the evolution of Volvo's approach to Job Design.

These phases are related to major investment projects which occurred in the 1970s, 1980s and 1990s, namely:

- **Phase 1: Kalmar** – This plant opened in 1974 and was the company's first, and most cited, attempt to move away from assembly-line work.
- **Phase 2: Torslanda** – This was Volvo's main car plant which, since the late 1970s, has seen a number of increasingly radical attempts to move away from the traditional assembly-line approach to car production. The original plan was to have car assembly being carried out by autonomous work groups who would be responsible for their own quality and pace of work. It was planned that work groups would also have responsibility for job rotation, managing material supplies and some maintenance tasks. However, these latter responsibilities were not achieved.
- **Phase 3: Uddevalla** – This new assembly plant opened in 1990, and exemplifies Volvo's decisive break with traditional motor industry jobs. As Karlsson (1996: 11) remarked:

  What was created was an extremely horizontal organisation, but also some vertical integration. This included responsibilities for quality and some integration with sales, because in the result-oriented team the idea was that the worker should be able to experience what he delivered to the customer. Hence the members of the assembly group could meet and talk directly to the customer.

- **Phase 4: Gent and Born** – The introduction of new cars in these existing plants in the late 1980s allowed Volvo the opportunity to introduce the team-based assembly methods developed in its other plants, thus showing Volvo's commitment to extending its Job Design philosophy across all areas of its operations. In addition, the assembly teams carry out their own maintenance as well as other support tasks. Indeed, so successful was this that Gent became the first plant outside Japan to gain the Total Productive Maintenance Award. In 1996, similar developments took place in Volvo's Dutch plant at Born.

This case study will examine the first of these four phases, Kalmar.

PHASE ONE – KALMAR

Those committed to challenging the 'inhuman' approach to work, epitomised by the Classical school in general and Henry Ford's moving assembly line in particular, came to look on Volvo's Kalmar car plant as a sort of promised land – a blueprint for the future of work. This was not only because Kalmar was seen as a model of human-centred work organisation, but also because it struck at the very heart of the industry which, through its use of the moving assembly line with its severe division of labour and short cycle times, had taken Taylorist work practices to their ultimate extremes. In addition, and just as importantly, it was heralded as a commercial success. Indeed, Kalmar was famous throughout the world for its 'revolutionary' approach to Job Design even before it opened (Blackler and Brown, 1978).

Perhaps the main reason for the perception that Kalmar was making a decisive break with the past was due to the way Volvo approached its design. The original management concept for Kalmar attempted to incorporate many of the progressive Job Design ideas circulating in the early 1970s. A project team composed of managers, engineers and architects was given responsibility for designing and building the plant. Each decision of this team had to be approved by a committee which included trade union representatives, health and safety experts, doctors and outside Job Design experts, including colleagues of Einar Thorsrud, the noted Norwegian work psychologist.

The 'revolutionary' image of Kalmar also owed much to the efficiency of Volvo's own publicity machine. This can be seen from statements about the ethos of the plant made by Pehr Gyllenhammar, Volvo's former Chief Executive, before it opened:

The objective of Kalmar will be to arrange auto production in such a way that each employee will be able to find meaning and satisfaction in his work.

This will be a factory which, without any sacrifice of efficiency or the company's financial objectives, will give employees opportunities to work in groups, to communicate freely among themselves, to switch from one job assignment to another, to vary the pace of their work, to identify with the product, to be conscious of a responsibility for quality, and to influence their own working environment.

When a product is made by people who find meaning in their work, it must inevitably be a product of high quality.

(Quoted in Aguren et al, 1984: 13)

Opened in 1974, Kalmar was Volvo's second largest final assembly plant. The differences between Kalmar and a traditional car plant are that, in the latter, the pace of work is determined by the moving assembly line, jobs are extremely fragmented and have cycle times of a few minutes or less, and workers are dedicated to one task only. At Kalmar there is no assembly line, workers operate in teams, with each team having its own dedicated area of the factory. Within the team, workers can move between tasks, and each task has a cycle time of between 20 and 30 minutes. In place of the assembly line, cars are mounted on automated carriers which move around the plant and serve both as a means of transport and as a work platform. This arrangement allowed Kalmar originally to operate two alternatives to the moving assembly line:

- **Straight-line assembly**. Work within each team area is split up into four or five work stations placed in a series along the production flow. Two team members work at each station, following the carrier through all the stations and carrying out all the necessary assembly operations.
- **Dock assembly**. This is where one carrier at a time is guided into the 'dock' assembly areas where all of the team's tasks are carried out on the stationary carrier by two or three people.

The main difference between the two approaches is that the first, straight-line assembly, still bears some relation to the moving assembly line in that the car carriers move automatically from station to station thus determining the pace of work. In the second approach, the dock system, the car is stationary all the time, giving workers more control over the pace of work. Nevertheless, both forms revolve around teamwork and offer variety and task completeness.

There can be very little doubt that, for its time, Kalmar represented a significant break with the past. However, there are those who question whether the original high hopes for the plant, in terms of the humanisation of work, have been met. Pontusson (1990) argued that the economic consequences of fluctuations in output levels led the plant management to retreat from its original ambitions and, in the latter part of the 1970s, to tighten managerial control over the work process. It was certainly the case that, compared to its conventional plants, there was no significant improvement in output. Also, as Berggren (1992: 123) noted, the ability of work teams to change the pace of work led to some 'mischief', and a team might change the pace of work of another team 'for fun'. For these reasons, according to Pontusson (1990), dock assembly was abandoned, and the potential for workers to influence the pace of work by taking automated carriers out of the main flow was ended.

Blackler and Brown (1978) argued that, with the abandonment of dock assembly, and despite longer cycle times, some fundamental elements of the assembly line (i.e. machine-paced work) have been maintained. Auer and Riegler (1990) made a similar point. They argued that, over time, changes such as new work evaluation methods, the removal of time buffers between stages and the general speeding up of the carriers (which are controlled by a central computer) have intensified the pace of work and have returned the production process much closer to the assembly-line concept than was originally intended.

Before it opened, Kalmar was being hailed as a revolution in Job Design. The reality is that Kalmar does not appear to have represented the dramatic break with the Fordist–Taylorist production process that many had hoped for (Auer and Riegler, 1990; Blackler and Brown, 1978; Pontusson, 1990). However, this does not mean that Kalmar was a failure. Given that Volvo, hitherto very much a traditional car company, was trying to invent a new concept in car assembly, it would have been surprising if they had managed to rewrite the rules of car production at the first attempt. It must be remembered that, although Kalmar was a social experiment, it was also expected to be an economic success. If the social dimension appeared to threaten financial performance, it was the former rather than the latter that would be sacrificed. The true measure of Kalmar's success lies not in the degree to which it achieved its 'revolutionary' goal, but in the extent to which it encouraged

Volvo's management to continue with and accelerate the move away from Fordist–Taylorist approaches to work. As Auer and Riegler (1990: 27) concluded, despite some disagreement among managers over the effectiveness of the organisation of the Kalmar plant, there were sufficient supporters for Volvo to proceed with the development of 'far more progressive' and 'radical' attempts to distance itself from the traditional assembly-line approach to car production. This is a point also made by Gyllenhammar:

> Volvo Kalmar is no final solution. It is the first step on the road. But much remains to be done in the field of work organisation. I could imagine much greater freedom and independence at work.
>
> (Quoted in Berggren, 1992: 127)

Nevertheless, in 1992, at the time of a major recession in the European car industry, Kalmar was closed.

SUMMARY

Volvo's commitment to Job Design did not end with Kalmar, rather it was the beginning of a process of work humanisation which, through successive phases, has humanised car production and given shopfloor workers an increasing level of control over the pace and content of their work. The progress of redesigning jobs at Volvo has been remarkable in comparison with the Tayloristic–Fordist nature of the company in the 1960s. The fact that it has continued and intensified over a period of 30 years, and that any organisational changes at Volvo are expected to revolve around group work, speaks volumes for the degree to which it has become embedded in the culture of the company. This is not to say that the result is perfect. It must be remembered that assembling cars and trucks will always be a physically demanding job. Also, Volvo is not an altruistic organisation; it exists

CASE STUDY 2 CONT.

to make a profit, and the way it organises work must reflect and facilitate this (regardless of pressures from trade unions, government legislation and public opinion). Nevertheless, as Pontusson (1990: 315) observed of Volvo, the 'stages of workplace reform involve a cumulative process of innovation, with a trajectory which adds up to a more or less definitive break with Fordism'. This conclusion, of course, makes the takeover of Volvo's car division by Ford in 1999 all the more ironic.

Questions

1. To what extent does the Volvo case support the arguments of the Human Relations school in terms of human motivation?

2. To what extent and why do you agree with the following statement: 'Job Design at Volvo has now become embedded in the culture of the company?'

3. Does the Volvo case support or undermine the arguments of the Contingency theorists in terms of aligning structures and practices with the situational variables the organisation faces?

CHAPTER 3

In search of new paradigms

Learning objectives

After studying this chapter, you should be able to:

- understand the reasons for the emergence of new organisational paradigms in the 1980s and 1990s;
- describe the principal features of the Culture–Excellence approach;
- list the core advantages and disadvantages of the Culture–Excellence approach;
- describe the central elements of the Japanese approach to management;
- understand the key advantages and disadvantages of the Japanese approach;
- discuss the main features of organisational learning;
- appreciate the chief advantages and disadvantages of organisational learning;
- compare the similarities and differences between Culture–Excellence, organisational learning and Japanese management;
- appreciate the implications for organisational change of these three paradigms.

Mini Case Study 3.1
The rise of consumer power

Tesco targets Aldi and Lidl with discount brand range

Tesco is moving to claw back lost ground from hard discounters such as Aldi and Lidl with the launch of a new 'discount brands at Tesco' range. Richard Brasher, commercial director of Britain's biggest retailer, said price was now more important to consumers than it had been for 20 years as he announced a range of 350 cheaper branded goods that will go into Tesco stores today.

'The centre of gravity in the marketplace has moved, even for people who have money, so they are demanding value at every part of the shopping trip', said Mr Brasher, as data showed Tesco had lost another chunk of market share in the 12 weeks to September 7.

▶

Mr Brasher conceded that the discounters had been enjoying a growth spurt during the past nine months – this was the third consecutive 12-week period that Tesco's market share had fallen, according to TNS – but said the new lines would be a worthy response to the threat.

'The relevance of that particular format [the hard discounters] is changing in the current climate. We respect them but they are quite limited and what consumers are saying to us is we want the things we get in these places but we want to get them from Tesco.' The new branded lines are not as cheap as Tesco's 'value' range but they undercut branded products. 'There is an opportunity between various levels to make sure there is a different proposition for consumers. There is an opportunity in the range to come up with something that is better quality and better presented but a little bit cheaper [than the main brands].'

The introduction of cheaper brands, which will be showcased in 'power aisles' from today, comes 15 years after Tesco introduced its red, white and blue 'value range' to stores in response to the arrival of continental hard discounters on British shores. 'This is the biggest thing since the launch of "value" 15 years ago and I think Tesco discount brands will be very important', said Mr Brasher. He said Tesco would extend the range if customers liked it. The supermarket chain is planning to use Clubcard data to identify and target shoppers it believes might be visiting rival stores with vouchers, while it is also launching a television and press campaign to woo back customers.

Asda, which has also been using its 'value credentials' to pick up market share from rivals, is also going on the offensive with plans to add a further 5,000 products in its stores.

Hard discounters see market share rise as shoppers vote with their feet. Consumers are applying a 'credit crunch' mindset to their shopping, with Tesco, Waitrose and J Sainsbury all losing market share while Asda rose to new heights over the past 12 weeks. Asda saw its share increase to 17.3 per cent in the 12 weeks to September 7, compared with 17 per cent last year.

Hard discounters Aldi and Lidl both increased their market share, with Aldi's up a fifth to 2.9 per cent and Lidl's up 11.1 per cent to 2.4 per cent. That left Tesco, Britain's biggest supermarket chain, suffering a 30 basis point fall in share to 31.5 per cent, while Sainsbury's dipped from 16 to 15.8 per cent. Dresdner, using TNS data, estimated that Marks and Spencer's underlying second-quarter food sales were down about 7 per cent, suggesting that life is getting tougher for the retailer's struggling food business.

Source: Elizabeth Rigby, *Financial Times*, 17 September, p. 22.

Introduction

Organisations have come a long way from the days when Henry Ford could famously declare: 'A customer can have a car of any color he wants, so long as it is black' (Witzel, 2003a: 113). Nowadays, the boot is on the other foot; it is a case of consumers dictating to organisations that they should meet their ever-changing tastes (Denegri-Knott *et al*, 2006). As Mini Case Study 3.1 shows, even organisations such as Tesco which appear to stand head and shoulders above their rivals have to react to customer pressure. When money is plentiful, customers tend to prefer quality over price; when money is in short supply, they target price over quality, and woe betide the organisation which tries to buck the trend. This is why successful organisations expend so much effort on identifying and meeting customer needs. Tesco has not reached its pre-eminent position as the UK's largest supermarket by ignoring what its customers want. It might prefer to compete on quality rather than price but, as Mini Case Study 3.1 demonstrates, if its customers want lower prices, Tesco will give them lower prices. Indeed, the essence of Tesco's success has been that its strategy, structure and culture are all geared to serving the needs of its customers. Henry Ford must be turning in his grave.

Tesco is not alone in seeing the customer as king. This is a lesson that successful organisations in all industries have learnt. Indeed, such has been the change in attitudes towards customers in the past three decades that many now speak of organisations as having gone through a paradigm shift. If this is so, what do we mean by a paradigm shift and what brought it about? Although he did not invent the word, it was the American philosopher of science Thomas Kuhn (1962) who, in his book *The Structure of Scientific Revolutions*, gave a new importance to the notion of 'paradigms'. He defined a paradigm as a universally recognised scientific achievement that over a period of time provides model problems and solutions to a community of practitioners. Kuhn was interested in how new ideas and frameworks for carrying out scientific work (i.e. paradigms) supplant old ones in the physical sciences. However, from the late 1960s onwards, a growing body of social scientists adopted the Kuhnian approach to their own disciplines with great enthusiasm. In the intervening period, new, varying, competing and controversial definitions of the term have been put forward (Burrell, 1997). As far as its applicability to organisations is concerned, a paradigm can be defined as a way of looking at and interpreting the world: a framework of basic assumptions, theories and models that are commonly and strongly accepted and shared within a particular field of activity at a particular point in time (Collins, 1998; Mink, 1992; Reed, 1992). However, as situations change and people's perceptions change, existing paradigms lose their relevance and new ones emerge. Handy (1986: 389) noted that:

> *When Copernicus suggested that the earth was not at the centre of the universe he was, though he knew it not, a paradigm revolutionary. But it was the minds of men that changed, not the motions of the planets, and the way in which they now viewed that same universe had a profound effect on their beliefs, values and behaviour.*

In the previous two chapters we have discussed the paradigms that, in the West at least, have emerged and become common currency in the field of management and organisation theory. Though these paradigms have their adherents as well as critics, increasingly managers have experienced real difficulties in achieving competitive success when applying them in today's turbulent, complex and diverse business world. In consequence, especially over the last three decades, both academics and practitioners have been searching for new recipes for organisational success.

It was in the USA that the search for new paradigms first became apparent. It was the rise of Japanese industrial and economic might that forced American businesses to question what they did and how they did it, as Morgan (1986: 111) observed:

During the 1960s the confidence and impact of American management and industry seemed supreme. Gradually, but with increasing force, through the 1970s the performance of Japanese automobile, electronic, and other manufacturing industries began to change all this. Japan began to take command of international markets . . .

The productivity gap between Japanese and American companies was starkly highlighted in a *Harvard Business Review* article by Johnson and Ouchi (1974). The authors claimed that Japanese workers, assembling the same product using the same technology, were some 15 per cent more productive than their American counterparts.

For an American audience this was a shocking statement, confirming the worst fears of a decline in the USA's competitive edge over the rest of the world. Since the Second World War American manufacturers had grown accustomed to out-producing and out-performing every foreign competitor. The era of the Cold War had led Americans to believe that the only danger to their general security sprang from communism and specifically the Soviet Union. The notion that their comprehensively vanquished enemies and strategic clients, the Japanese, might be poised to overhaul them technically and even economically was unpalatable, even unbelievable.

(Sheldrake, 1996: 185)

It was not only the USA that took fright; in the 1970s and 1980s, all over the Western world, businesses and governments too woke up to the Japanese challenge. Even West Germany, which prided itself on producing well-engineered and high-quality products such as BMW and Mercedes cars, found that the Japanese were producing cars such as the Lexus that were not only half the price, but also better-engineered and of far superior quality (Williams *et al*, 1991).

Nor was it just the Japanese challenge that frightened the West. The 1970s also saw the return of unemployment and inflation, both assumed to have been eliminated, and the occurrence of the two 'oil shocks', which highlighted most Western nations' precarious reliance on imported energy. Therefore, old certainties were being challenged and new orthodoxies began to arise. Rather like Copernicus, Japan made the West see the world, and its place in it, from a new perspective.

Organisations have become increasingly aware that in the last 20 years or so, the world has turned on its axis. The days of the mass production of standardised products appear to be over; the key words for the future are variety, flexibility and customisation. Perez (1983) and Freeman (1988) argued that a new techno-economic rationale was emerging (*see* Ideas and perspectives 3.1).

This new techno-economic rationale has been given a variety of names. In the 1970s, Daniel Bell (1973) heralded *The Coming of Post-Industrial Society*. In the 1980s, other writers spoke of the 'post-Fordist' or 'post-Taylorist' era (Whitaker, 1992). Increasingly, in the 1990s, the term 'postmodernism' was used to describe the changes taking place in the world in general and organisations in particular (Hassard, 1993). These terms, particularly the debate around postmodernism and its alternatives, will be discussed in Chapter 4. For now, however, what we need to recognise is that it is not necessarily that

Ideas and perspectives 3.1
The new techno-economic rationale

- A shift towards information-intensive rather than energy- or materials-intensive products.
- A change from dedicated mass production systems towards more flexible systems that can accommodate a wider range of products, smaller batches and more frequent design changes – 'economies of scale' are being replaced by 'economies of scope'.
- A move towards the greater integration of processes and systems within companies and between suppliers and customers, which permits a more rapid response to market and customer requirements.

Source: Perez (1983) and Freeman (1988)

the nature of organisations themselves has changed fundamentally, though significant changes in size, technology and complexity have certainly taken place. It is rather that, like those who listened to Copernicus, we are seeing their role in the established order from a different perspective and beginning to see new possibilities and new challenges.

It is the emergence of these new possibilities and challenges that has motivated Western organisations to undertake a fundamental reassessment of their objectives and operations, rather than a mere change in fashion or managerial whim – though this is obviously present as well (Collins, 2000; Huczynski, 1993; Kennedy, 1994). In effect, what we can see from the beginning of the 1980s is the emergence of a paradigm shift, or, to be more accurate, the search for new, more appropriate paradigms. It seemed as if the changes taking place in the business environment were so enormous and rapid that existing paradigms, whatever their past merits, were breaking down and new ones emerging.

In this chapter, we examine the three proto-paradigms that have come to dominate Western managerial thinking and writing since the 1980s: the Culture–Excellence approach, the Japanese Management approach and the Organisational Learning approach. As Mini Case Study 3.1 shows, there is a tendency to link them together or treat them as though they are largely the same. However, as this chapter will show, they are distinct approaches to running organisations with different origins and differing implications for management. Culture–Excellence arose as an attempt to counter Japanese competitiveness by drawing on and re-shaping the American and British traditions of individualism and free market liberalism. It emerged in the early 1980s, and its principal exponents (Tom Peters and Robert Waterman, 1982; Rosabeth Moss Kanter, 1989; and Charles Handy, 1989) have attempted both to predict and to promote the ways in which successful (excellent) companies will and should operate in the future.

The Japanese management paradigm is a very different animal. It has been developed in Japan over the last 50 years, and not only is it being extensively practised there, but, at least until recently, its success was not disputed. Because of the success of the Japanese economy and Japanese companies in the 1960s, 1970s and 1980s, the Japanese approach attracted much interest in the West – a classic case of 'if you can't beat them, join them'. This was especially the case in the UK, where Japanese inward investment (by household names such as Honda, Nissan and Toyota) generated a great deal of debate regarding the impact and merits of 'Japanisation' (Ackroyd *et al*, 1988; Dale and Cooper, 1992; Hannam, 1993; Turnbull, 1986; Whitehill, 1991). This was also the case in the USA, where Japan and Japanese methods were seen, in turn, as either a threat or a lifeline to American industrial pre-eminence (Kanter *et al*, 1992; Pascale and Athos, 1982; Peters, 1993; Schonberger, 1982).

The third approach, organisational learning, came to the fore in the early 1990s. Leading management thinkers, in particular Chris Argyris (1992), have been interested in organisational learning for over 40 years. However, it is only in the last 20 years that the concept has become popularised as an engine for organisational competitiveness through the work of Senge (1990) in the USA and Pedler, Boydell and Burgoyne (1989) in the UK. One of the key benefits claimed for organisational learning is that it is a universal approach which draws on and is consistent with both Western and Japanese organisational traditions (Hedlund and Nonaka, 1993; Probst and Buchel, 1997).

Though the Culture–Excellence and Japanese approaches have some similarities, for example the resemblance between the Japanese passion for quality and the Culture–Excellence school's fervent advocacy of the pursuit of excellence, the two also have significant differences, as will be shown. Whilst the Japanese approach has clearly influenced the Culture–Excellence thinkers, the influence of the latter in Japan has been small. The two may be competing approaches in the West, but certainly not in Japan. Nevertheless, both are dynamic and developing paradigms, with some common elements, and consequently a merging or a blending of the two, at least in some Western organisations, is quite possible. The organisational learning approach, though it draws on both Western and Japanese organisational traditions, is not an attempt to fuse or merge the Culture–Excellence and Japanese approaches. Instead, it represents yet another attempt to provide Western countries, particularly the USA, with an approach to managing organisations that will allow them in the twenty-first century to enjoy the sort of dominance they enjoyed for much of the twentieth century.

Nevertheless, it will be argued in the conclusion to this chapter that, although these three proto-paradigms offer new possibilities, they also raise familiar controversies, not least regarding the role and treatment of people. Therefore, as the following discussion of the three approaches will show, whilst attempting to become new paradigms, they still have to answer old questions.

The Culture–Excellence approach

The core of the Culture–Excellence approach can be summed up by a quote from a recent report by the management consultants Bain & Company:

> . . . *culture is at the heart of competitive advantage, particularly when it comes to sustaining high performance. Bain & Company research found that nearly 70 percent of business leaders agree: Culture provides the greatest source of competitive advantage. In fact, more than 80 percent believe an organization that lacks a high-performance culture is doomed to mediocrity.*
>
> (Rogers *et al*, 2006: 1)

Though predominantly a North American perspective, the Culture–Excellence approach has also found its adherents in Europe. Therefore, the examination of this approach will draw on the work of key writers from both sides of the Atlantic, namely Tom Peters and Robert Waterman, Rosabeth Moss Kanter and Charles Handy. These writers are all practising and internationally recognised management consultants; Handy and Kanter are distinguished academics as well. Consequently, though their work is attempting to predict and promote the way firms will or should operate in the future, it is firmly based on what they believe the best companies are doing now or planning to do in the future.

These three perspectives formed the spearhead of the movement that simultaneously charted and created the new organisational forms that have begun to appear over the last 30 years. Their work – though both complementary and distinct – is of profound influence in shaping our understanding of what the future holds in the field of management. This work will now be examined in detail, starting with the American perspectives of Peters and Waterman, and Kanter, and concluding with Handy's British perspective.

Tom Peters and Robert Waterman's search for excellence

Tom Peters has been, arguably, the most influential management consultant of the last 25 years. His books sell in millions, his seminars fill auditoriums, and his newspaper column is syndicated across the world (Collins, 2008). He is also said to be one of the highest-paid management consultants in the world, reputedly charging some US$25,000 per seminar back in 1987 (Huczynski, 1993). He catapulted to international fame when he co-authored, along with Robert Waterman, *In Search of Excellence: Lessons from America's Best-Run Companies* (Peters and Waterman, 1982). Not only is this the best-selling business book of all time, it has also been called the greatest business book of all time (Collins, 2008). It is difficult to overestimate the impact this book has had. At a time when Western economies were on the rocks and Japanese companies appeared to be sweeping all before them, *In Search of Excellence* seemed to offer a way, perhaps the only way, for Western companies to regain their competitiveness (Crainer, 1995).

The origins of the book lie in a major study of the determinants of organisational excellence, which Peters and Waterman carried out when working for the management consultants McKinsey and Company. They used the now-famous McKinsey 7 S Framework (*see* Ideas and perspectives 3.2), which they had developed jointly with Richard Pascale and Anthony Athos, to study 62 of America's most successful companies.

Peters and Waterman concluded that it was the four 'soft' Ss (staff, style, shared values and skills) that held the key to business success. In stressing the 'soft' Ss, they challenged the rational theories of management described in previous chapters. They argue that the rational approach is flawed because it leads to the following:

- **Wrong-headed analysis** – situation or information analysis that is considered too complex and unwieldy to be useful. This is analysis that strives to be precise about the inherently unknowable.
- **Paralysis through analysis** – the application of the rational model to such an extent that action stops and planning runs riot.
- **Irrational rationality** – where rational management techniques identify the 'right' answer irrespective of its applicability to the situation in question.

Ideas and perspectives 3.2
The 7 S Framework

Strategy: plan or course of action for the allocation of scarce resources in order to achieve specified goals.

Structure: the main features of the organisation chart and how the various parts of an organisation are linked.

Systems: the organisation's formalised procedures and processes.

Staff: the composition of the workforce, i.e. engineers, managers, etc.

Style: the behaviour of key managers and also the cultural style of the organisation.

Shared values: the guiding concepts and meanings that infuse the organisation's members.

Skills: the distinctive capabilities possessed by individuals, groups and the organisation as whole.

Source: Peters and Waterman (1982)

In the light of these criticisms, Peters and Waterman argue that the analytical tools that characterise the rational approach should only be used as an aid to, rather than a substitute for, human judgement. They believe that it is the freedom given to managers and employees to challenge the orthodox and to experiment with different solutions which distinguishes the excellent companies from the also-rans. In place of the rational approach, Peters and Waterman argue that there are eight key attributes that organisations need to demonstrate if they are to achieve excellence:

1. A bias for action.
2. Closeness to the customer.
3. Autonomy and entrepreneurship.
4. Productivity through people.
5. Hands-on, value-driven.
6. Stick to the knitting.
7. Simple form, lean staff.
8. Simultaneous loose–tight properties.

These are discussed in detail below.

1 A bias for action

One of the main identifiable attributes of excellent companies is their bias for action. Even though they may be analytical in approach, they also favour methods that encourage rapid and appropriate response. One of the methods devised for achieving quick action is what Peters and Waterman term 'chunking'. Chunking is an approach whereby a problem that arises in the organisation is first made manageable (i.e. broken into 'chunks') and then tackled by a small group of staff brought together specifically for that purpose. The main reason for the use of such groups, variously called project teams, task forces or quality circles, is to facilitate organisational fluidity and to encourage action. Key characteristics of these groups are as follows:

- They usually comprise no more than ten members.
- They are voluntarily constituted.
- The life of the group is usually between three and six months.
- The reporting level and seniority of the membership is appropriate to the importance of the problem to be dealt with.
- The documentation of the group's proceedings is scant and very informal.
- These groups take on a limited set of objectives, which are usually determined, monitored, evaluated and reviewed by themselves.

Chunking is merely one example of the bias for action that exists in excellent companies and reflects their willingness to innovate and experiment. These companies' philosophy for action is simple: 'Do it, fix it, try it.' Therefore, excellent companies are characterised by small, *ad hoc* teams applied to solving designated problems which have first been reduced to manageable proportions. Achieving smallness is the key, even though the subject or task may be large. Smallness induces manageability and a sense of understanding, and allows a feeling of ownership.

2 Close to the customer

Excellent companies really do get close to the customer, while others merely talk about it. The customer dictates product, quantity, quality and service. The best organisations are alleged to go to extreme lengths to achieve quality, service and reliability. There is no part of the business that is closed to customers. In fact, many of the excellent companies claim to get their best ideas for new products from listening intently and regularly to their customers. The excellent companies are more 'driven by their direct orientation to the customers rather than by technology or by a desire to be the low-cost producer. They seem to focus more on the revenue-generation side of their services' (Peters and Waterman, 1982: 197).

3 Autonomy and entrepreneurship

Perhaps the most important element of excellent companies is their 'ability to be big and yet to act small at the same time. A concomitant essential apparently is that they encourage the entrepreneurial spirit among their people, because they push autonomy markedly far down the line' (Peters and Waterman, 1982: 201). Product champions are allowed to come forward, grow and flourish. Such a champion is not a blue-sky dreamer, or an intellectual giant. The champion might even be an ideal thief. But above all, the champion is the pragmatist, the one who latches on to someone else's idea, and doggedly brings something concrete and tangible out of it.

In fostering such attitudes, the excellent companies have what they label 'championing systems' which comprise three key elements (*see* Ideas and perspectives 3.3). The essence of championing system is to foster, promote and sustain the budding entrepreneur. It is claimed that the three elements of the championing system are essential to its operation and credibility.

Ideas and perspectives 3.3
The three elements of the championing system

- **The product champion** – a zealot or fanatic who believes in a product.
- **A successful executing champion** – one who has been through the process of championing a product before.
- **The godfather** – typically, an ageing leader who provides the role model for champions.

Source: Peters and Waterman (1982)

Another key part of this system is that, in some companies, product champions tend to be allocated their own 'sub-optional divisions'. These are similar to small, independent businesses and comprise independent new venture teams, run by champions with the full and total support of senior management. The sub-optional division is independent in that it is responsible for its own accounting, personnel activities, quality assurance and support for its product in the field. To encourage entrepreneurship further, teams, groups and divisions are highly encouraged by the companies' reward structures to compete amongst themselves for new projects.

Autonomy and entrepreneurship are also encouraged by the type of no-holds-barred communications procedures adopted by excellent companies. These exhibit the following characteristics:

- **Communication is informal** – even though there are lots of meetings going on at any one time, most meetings are informal and comprise staff from different disciplines gathering to talk about and solve problems.
- **The communication system is given both physical and material support** – blackboards, flip-charts and small tables that foster informal small group discussions are everywhere. The aim is to encourage people to talk about the organisation: what needs changing; what is going on; and how to improve things around the place. There are also people, variously described as dreamers, heretics, gadflies, mavericks or geniuses, whose sole purpose is to spur the system to innovate. Their job is to institutionalise innovation by initiating and encouraging experimentation. They can also call on staff in other divisions of the organisation to assist them in this process, as well as having financial resources at their disposal.
- **Communication is intensive** – given the freedom, the encouragement and the support (financial, moral and physical) in the organisations, it is no wonder that the level of communication between and amongst workers is not only informal and spontaneous but also intense. This is borne out by the common occurrence of meetings without agendas and minutes. Also, when presentations are made in these meetings, questioning of the proposal is unabashed and discussion is free and open. Those present are expected to be fully involved in such meetings and there are no 'sacred cows' that cannot be questioned.

This intense communication system also acts as a remarkably tight control system, in that people are always checking on each other to see how each is faring. This arises out of a genuine desire to keep abreast of developments in the organisation rather than any untoward motive. One result of this is that teams are more prudent in their financial expenditure on projects. Another is that the sea of inquisitors act as 'idea generators', thereby ensuring that teams are not dependent entirely on their own devices to innovate and solve problems. This usually also ensures that all options are considered before a final decision is made. The concomitant result of this fostering of creativity is that senior management is more tolerant of failure, knowing full well that champions have to make many tries, and consequently suffer some failures, in the process of creating successful innovations.

4 Productivity through people

A cherished principle of the excellent companies is that they treat their workers with respect and dignity; they refer to them as partners. This is because people, rather than systems or machines, are seen as the primary source of quality and productivity gains. Therefore, there is 'tough-minded respect for the individual and the willingness to train him, to set reasonable and clear expectations for him, and to grant him practical autonomy to step out and contribute directly to his job' (Peters and Waterman, 1982: 239). There is a closeness and family feeling in such companies; indeed many of the 'partners' see the organisation as an extended family. The slogans of such companies tend to reflect this view of people: 'respect the individual', 'make people winners', 'let them stand out', 'treat people as adults'.

5 Hands-on, value-driven

Excellent companies are value-driven; they are clear about what they stand for and take the process of value-shaping seriously. There is an implicit belief that everyone in the organisation, from the top to the bottom, should be driven by the values of the organisation; hence the great effort, time and money spent to inspire people by and inculcate them with these values:

> . . . these values are almost always stated in qualitative, rather than quantitative, terms. When financial objectives are mentioned, they are almost always ambitious but never precise. Furthermore, financial and strategic objectives are never stated alone. They are always discussed in the context of the other things the company expects to do well. The idea that profit is a natural by-product of doing something well, and not an end in itself, is almost always universal.
>
> (Peters and Waterman, 1982: 284)

Implanting these values is a primary responsibility of the individual members of the management team. They set the tone by leading from the front. Coherence and homogeneity must, however, first be created among senior management by regular meetings (both formal and informal). The outcome of this is that management speaks with one voice. They are passionate in preaching the organisation's values. They unleash excitement, not in their offices, but mainly on the shopfloor where the workers are. Inculcating these values, however, is a laborious process and persistence is vital in achieving the desired goal.

6 Stick to the knitting

Acquisition or internal diversification for its own sake is not one of the character-istics of excellent companies. They must stick to the knitting – do what they know best. But when they do acquire, they do it in an experimental fashion, by first 'dipping a toe in the water'. If the water does not feel good, they get out fast. Acquisitions are always in fields related to their core activities and they never acquire any business that they do not know how to run. As a general rule, they 'move out mainly through intern-ally generated diversification, one manageable step at a time' (Peters and Waterman, 1982: 279).

7 Simple form, lean staff

A guiding principle in excellent companies is to keep things simple and small. Structurally, the most common form is the 'product division'. This form, which is rarely changed, provides the essential touchstone that everybody understands and from which the com-plexities of day-to-day life can be approached. Since the use of teams, groups and task forces for specific projects is a common stock-in-trade of these companies, most changes in structure are made at the edges, such as by allocating one or two people to an *ad hoc* team. By adopting this approach, the basic structure is left in place, while all other things revolve and change around it. This gives these organisations great flexibility but still enables them to keep their structures simple, divisionalised and autonomous.

Such simple structures only require a small, lean staff at the corporate and middle management levels. This results in there being fewer administrators and more doers: 'it is not uncommon to find a corporate staff of fewer than 100 people running a multi-billion-dollar enterprise' (Peters and Waterman, 1982: 15). Therefore, in excellent companies, flat structures, with few layers, and slimmed-down bureaucracies – which together allow flexibility and rapid communication – are the order of the day.

8 Simultaneous loose–tight properties

This is the 'firm and free' principle. On the one hand, it allows the excellent companies to control everything tightly, whilst on the other hand allowing and indeed encourag-ing individual innovation, autonomy and entrepreneurship. These properties are jointly achieved through the organisation's culture – its shared values and beliefs. By sharing the same values, self-control and self-respect result in each person becoming their own, and everyone else's, supervisor. The individual members of the organisation know they have the freedom, and are encouraged, to experiment and innovate. They also know that their actions will be scrutinised and judged, however, with the utmost attention paid to the impact they have on product quality, targets and, above all, the customer. The focus is on building and expanding the frontiers of the business. The ultimate goal is to be the best company, and in the final analysis, this is the benchmark against which the discipline and flexibility of the individual will be measured.

Therefore, Peters and Waterman maintain that the main attributes of excellent companies are flat, anti-hierarchical structures; innovation and entrepreneurship; small corporate and middle management staffs; reward systems based on contribution rather than position or length of service; brain power rather than muscle power; and strong, flexible cultures.

Peters and Waterman's vision of the organisation of the future, based on their study of leading American companies, has proved extremely influential, not only in the business world but in academia as well. This is not to say (as will be shown later) that they are without their critics; however, there is little doubt that they laid the groundwork, especially in highlighting the important role played by culture, for other leading thinkers whose work draws on and gels with theirs.

Their vision of the future has not stood still. Peters formed his own consultancy, The Tom Peters Group, and has used this as a vehicle for developing and implementing the Culture–Excellence approach. Though not fundamentally changing his view of the need for excellent organisations, in *Thriving on Chaos* (Peters, 1989) he argued that none existed in the USA. In *Liberation Management* (Peters, 1993), he placed more emphasis on the need to break organisations into smaller, more independent, more flexible units. Only by doing this, he argued, would managers be 'liberated', and thus able to achieve their – and their organisation's – full potential. In this book, Peters maintains that the age of the large corporations such as IBM and General Motors is over. He sees such companies as outmoded and uncompetitive dinosaurs, which are doomed to extinction unless they change rapidly and irreversibly. Peters argues that only rapid structural change can create the conditions for entrepreneurial cultures to emerge that both liberate managers and empower workers. Indeed, this book is nothing short of an out-and-out attack on the very existence of corporate America.

The Circle of Innovation: You Can't Shrink Your Way to Greatness (Peters, 1997a) is perhaps his most iconoclastic book. Even the format of the book is different from what has gone before. Indeed, its use of a multitude of different images, font types and font sizes and, in some cases, almost surreal page layouts, makes it more like a pop video than a traditional book. The message could not be clearer: just as this book is innovative in its format, so organisations must be innovative if they are to survive. His attack on present and past organisational practices, stability and any sense of permanence is keener and more vitriolic than ever. Professionalism, rules, balance, propriety, logic and consensus are all outmoded concepts, he argues. Peters (1997a: 76) quotes Dee Hock, founder of the Visa Network, who said: 'The problem is never how to get new, innovative thoughts into your mind, but how to get the old ones out.' For Peters, organisational forgetting is far more important than organisational learning. Future success, he argues, is not related to what an organisation has done in the past, nor what is bringing it success now, but how innovative it will be in identifying new products, services and markets. He makes a strong, almost messianic, plea for organisations to centre themselves on innovation. Peters argues that innovation demands obsession, tension, being provocative, and having no market peers looking over your shoulder. As firms achieve parity in terms of quality and costs, he believes that only a constant commitment to being different, to continuous innovation, will allow companies to differentiate themselves from their competitors. Just as quality was seen as everyone's job in the 1980s,

Ideas and perspectives 3.4
The Circle of Innovation

- Distance is dead.
- Destruction is cool.
- You can't live without an eraser.
- We are all Michelangelos.
- Welcome to the white-collar revolution.
- All values come from the professional services.
- The intermediary is doomed.
- The system is the solution.
- Create waves of lust.
- Tommy Hilfiger knows.
- Become a connoisseur of talent.
- It's a woman's world.
- Little things are the only things.
- Love all, serve all.
- We're here to live life out loud.

Source: Peters (1997a)

so Peters maintains that innovation must also become everyone's job now. In terms of structure, organisations must adopt a network or even a virtual structure, where small groups and even individuals have the freedom to self-manage themselves, to make connections and break connections as they see fit. Indeed, the subtitle of this book could well be 'Anarchy rules!'

Whereas in *In Search of Excellence*, he and Robert Waterman put forward their eight attributes of excellence, this book is structured around his 15 points on The Circle of Innovation (*see* Ideas and perspectives 3.4).

Trying to follow Peters's train of thought through his various books is like trying to catch mist – just when you think you have got it, it slips through your hands. Indeed, Peters (1997a: xv) takes pride in his inconsistency: ' "They" call me inconsistent. I consider that a badge of honor.' Originally he saw the pursuit of 'excellence' as the only way to save corporate America from annihilation by its Japanese competitors (and thus maintaining the USA as the premier industrial nation). Then, in *Liberation Management*, Peters (1993) argued that corporate America needed to be destroyed in order for America to survive. The message from *The Circle of Innovation* is that, with the business world in a permanent state of chaos, the only way for any organisation to survive is by constantly reinventing itself through a ceaseless process of innovation and change.

Nevertheless, though he offers some new tools and techniques, and the tone of his work has become more strident and zealot-like over the years, in essence he is still promoting the concepts first developed in *In Search of Excellence*. He argues (Peters, 2006) that the eight key attributes of excellence which formed the core of the book have proved their staying power and become the way that winning businesses organise themselves and motivate their people. He continues to maintain that the market is not simply the final arbiter of success, but the only arbiter. Meeting the ever-increasing appetite for instant gratification is the only way to survive. Innovation, i.e. autonomy and entrepreneurship, is now the prime attribute of excellence and the only guarantee of success. For Peters, large, bureaucratic organisations based on command and control systems are the enemy of excellence. Peters's (1997a: 493) view of how organisations should be run is, perhaps, best summed up by a quotation he cites from the racing driver Mario Andretti: 'If things seem under control, you're just not going fast enough.'

Yet for all Peters's continued stridency in presenting his recipe for corporate resurgence, his later books also seem to contain a greater sense of frustration. More than 25 years after *In Search of Excellence*, Peters's message has still not been acted upon by the vast majority of the business world and, as Collins (2008: 331) recently noted: 'Peters' relationship with the corporate world is strained, and, increasingly, unproductive.'

Rosabeth Moss Kanter's post-entrepreneurial model

Kanter is a professor at the Harvard Business School. Her early work concerned Utopian communities, such as the Shakers, but she then went on to study business organisations. O'Hara (2008: 1) recently commented that:

> At 65, Kanter boasts an impressive CV. She has 22 honorary doctorates, was editor of the Harvard Business Review in the early 1990s, was named one of the '50 most influential business thinkers in the world', and has spent decades studying corporate governance and advising governments and business.

Kanter first came to prominence with her (1977) book, *Men and Women of the Corporation*. This was an intensive examination of corporate America, which she saw as bureaucratic, unimaginative and uninspiring. In her next book, *The Change Masters* (Kanter, 1983), she offered her personal recipe for overcoming what she saw as the malaise and lack of competitiveness of the USA. The book painted corporate America as being in transition; it recognised that the corporatism of the past no longer worked, but was not sure where the future lay. Kanter (1983) argued that it lay in American and not Japanese ideas, and particularly in unleashing individual dynamism through empowerment and greater employee involvement.

Though her earlier books were clearly in tune with Peters and Waterman's work, it is Kanter's (1989) *When Giants Learn To Dance: Mastering the Challenges of Strategy, Management, and Careers in the 1990s* that most complements and develops their work by attempting to define what organisations need to be like in the future if they are to be successful. Kanter called for a revolution in business management to create what she termed post-entrepreneurial organisations. She used this term:

> . . . because it takes entrepreneurship a step further, applying entrepreneurial principles to the traditional corporation, creating a marriage between entrepreneurial creativity and corporate discipline, cooperation, and teamwork.   (Kanter, 1989: 9–10)

Kanter maintained that:

> If the new game of business is indeed like Alice-in-Wonderland croquet, then winning it requires faster action, more creative maneuvering, more flexibility, and closer

partnerships with employees and customers than was typical in the traditional corporate bureaucracy. It requires more agile, limber management that pursues opportunity without being bogged down by cumbersome structures or weighty procedures that impede action. Corporate giants, in short, must learn how to dance.

(Kanter, 1989: 20)

She argues that today's corporate elephants need to learn to dance as nimbly and speedily as mice if they are to survive in our increasingly competitive and rapidly changing world. Companies must constantly be alert and on their guard, and keep abreast of their competitors' intentions. By evaluating the response of modern organisations to the demands placed upon them, Kanter produced her post-entrepreneurial model of how the organisation of the future should operate. She sees post-entrepreneurial organisations as pursuing three main strategies:

1. Restructuring to find synergies.
2. Opening boundaries to form strategic alliances.
3. Creating new ventures from within: encouraging innovation and entrepreneurship.

These are detailed below.

1 Restructuring to find synergies

Synergy occurs where the whole adds up to more than the sum of its constituent parts. In an age where resources are scarce, one of the priorities of organisations is to make every part of the business add value to the whole. The essence of this approach is to identify and concentrate on the core business areas and to remove all obstacles and impediments to their efficient and effective operation. Therefore, all non-core activities are eliminated, and authority is devolved to the appropriate levels of the business: those in the front line. In practice this means selling off a company's non-core activities and ensuring that what remains, especially at the corporate and middle-management levels, is lean and efficient. Nevertheless, it is not sufficient merely to have a strategy of reducing the size of the organisational bureaucracy. Companies must also ensure that the essential tasks that these people previously carried out are still undertaken. This can be accomplished in a number of ways, such as the use of computers to carry out monitoring and information-gathering; devolving greater responsibility and power down to individual business units; and contracting out services and tasks previously carried out in-house.

The result is to create flatter, more responsive and less complex organisations that have a greater degree of focus than in the past. Kanter argues that such radical changes need to be well planned, however, and executed with care and in a way that ensures that employee motivation is increased, not eliminated.

2 Opening boundaries to form strategic alliances

With the slimming-down of the organisation and the contracting-out of some of its functions, there arises the need to pool resources with other organisations; to band together to exploit opportunities and to share ideas and information. These alliances take three forms: service alliances, opportunistic alliances and stakeholder alliances. The first, a service alliance, is where two or more organisations form a cross-company consortium to undertake a special project with a limited lifespan. Such alliances are usually considered when the resources of the various partners are insufficient to allow them to undertake the project by themselves. For this reason, and not surprisingly, many such alliances involve research and development (R&D) projects. The collaboration between Ford and General Motors on research into the development of new materials for making cars is an example of this. This approach allows organisations to mobilise resources, often on a large scale, whilst limiting their exposure and protecting their independence. It is the limited purpose of the consortium that makes it possible even for competitors to join together for their mutual benefit.

The second form, an opportunistic alliance, comprises a joint venture whose aim is to take advantage of a particular opportunity that has arisen: 'the two principal advantages behind this kind of alliance are competence-enhancing ones: technology transfer or market access or both' (Kanter, 1989: 126). An example of such an alliance was the link-up between the Rover Group and Honda Motors; the former gained access to Japanese know-how, whilst the latter gained greater access to the European market. However, as Kanter (1989: 126) pointed out, such alliances are not always equally beneficial: 'once one of the partners has gained experience with the competence of the other, the alliance is vulnerable to dissolution – the opportunity can now be pursued without the partner'.

The third form, a stakeholder alliance, unlike the previous two, is seen as a continuing, almost permanent partnership between an organisation and its key stakeholders, generally considered to be its employees, customers and suppliers. There is a growing awareness among employees, trade unions and management of the need to see each other as partners in the same enterprise rather than rivals. A similar case is made for treating customers and suppliers as partners too. The main reason for the organisation to exist is to serve its customers; therefore, there is a need to keep close to them, not only to be aware of their present concerns and future needs, but also to gain ideas regarding potential joint product development. In the same way, the organisation relies on its suppliers, who will in any case want to get closer to them as their customers. Stakeholder alliances have gained a growing band of adherents in Britain in recent years, especially, though not exclusively, amongst Japanese companies such as Nissan Motors (Partnership Sourcing Ltd, 1991a; Wickens, 1987). As Kanter points out, major innovations in technology and organisational systems require longer-term investments. Companies can only enter into such investments if they are secure in the knowledge that their key stakeholders are themselves committed to the same aims and approach.

The result of these alliances is that structures and positions within organisations will change, sometimes quite dramatically. This is especially the case amongst senior and line managers, but even previously protected groups – such as R&D specialists – will also see their roles and responsibilities change. They will have to work more closely not only with colleagues internally, but also with external groupings.

3 Creating new ventures from within – encouraging innovation and entrepreneurship

Traditional organisations face a difficult balancing act between gaining the full benefits from existing mainstream business, and, at the same time, creating new activities that will become the mainstream business of the future. Kanter argues that there is a feeling in many traditional companies that opportunities are being missed owing to their inability to give staff the flexibility to pursue new ideas and develop new products. The job of creating new products or ventures used to be the sole domain of the strategic planners or the R&D departments. However, in the post-entrepreneurial organisation, this will no longer be the case: innovation will move from these specialised domains to the centre stage. As the case studies in this book show, some organisations are deliberately forming new, independent units or entirely restructuring themselves to nurture innovation and entrepreneurship. New cultures are being created which encourage and aid innovation, and old barriers and restrictions are being eradicated. As a result of such changes, the innovative potential of employees is being tapped, and a proliferation of new ideas, products and ways of working are emerging.

The consequences of the post-entrepreneurial model

There is no doubt that the post-entrepreneurial model carries profound implications for both organisations and their employees. However, Kanter, unlike Peters and Waterman, does not see these new developments as being an unalloyed blessing, especially in the case of employees. In particular, she draws attention to three areas where the changes will have a major impact on employees: reward systems; career paths and job security; and lifestyle.

Reward systems

Employers and employees will increasingly come to look for new and more appropriate ways of rewarding and being rewarded. Indeed, with the advent of performance-related pay, in both the private and public sectors, there is already a gradual change from determining pay on the basis of a person's position and seniority to basing it on their contribution to the organisation. These changes are being driven by four main concerns: cost, equity, productivity and entrepreneurial pressure (*see* Ideas and perspectives 3.5).

Ideas and perspectives 3.5
Drivers for changes to reward systems

Cost – the concern is that the present system is too expensive for companies that must conserve resources to be competitive.

Equity – organisations are concerned to ensure that employees are fairly rewarded for their efforts.

Productivity – organisations want to adopt reward systems that motivate high performance from employees.

Entrepreneurial pressure – companies are aware that the present system does not always adequately reward entrepreneurs for their efforts.

Source: Kanter (1989)

These concerns are being approached through the application of three different, though not necessarily mutually exclusive, payment methods:

- The first is profit-sharing, whereby the pay of the employee is pegged to the company's performance. This means that salaries are not fixed but instead are related, by the use of a predetermined formula, to the profit of the organisation over a given period of time, usually the previous financial year.
- The second method is the use of individual performance bonuses, which are paid on top of basic salary and are related to a predetermined performance target. This method has the advantage of enabling individuals to establish a direct correlation between their personal effort and the bonus payment they receive. Though this method is not new, the sums involved are – sometimes as much as twice basic salary.
- The last is the venture returns method, which represents perhaps the most radical break with the past. This is a scheme whereby entrepreneurs and inventors within an organisation are given the opportunity to earn returns based on the performance, in the marketplace, of the particular products or services for which they are responsible. Through this mechanism, the entrepreneur or inventor remains within the corporate fold but is paid on a similar basis to the owner of a small, independent business. The advantage is that they get the personal satisfaction and reward of running their 'own' business, whilst the larger organisation benefits from having highly motivated and innovative people in charge of part of its operations.

The picture created by new reward systems is not, of course, totally rosy. Where there are winners, there may also be losers; not everyone will have the opportunity or drive to be an entrepreneur, or will be in a position that lends itself to some form of bonus system. Also, many people who currently benefit from reward systems based on seniority and position may find they lose out. Older workers, established in organisations and well down their chosen career path, could be particularly adversely affected by such changes. In addition, such payment systems may be divisive and create conflict. Kanter stresses the need for teamwork, yet a situation where some members of the team are receiving high bonuses is bound to create tensions which undermine cooperation and collaboration. It may be that profit-sharing schemes, which encompass everyone in the organisation, overcome this threat to teamworking, but if everyone receives the same share of the profits irrespective of their individual contribution, the motivating effect is likely to be diminished. The result of these various approaches to pay could be minimal in terms of motivation, or could even be demotivating and indeed drive out the most experienced people in the organisation.

Careers and job security

As organisations have become slimmer and more tasks are contracted out, organisation structures are becoming flatter as entire layers of hierarchy are dispensed with. The resultant effect threatens the demise of traditional forms of career path. Kanter argues that the idea of staying with one organisation and climbing the corporate career ladder is being replaced by hopping from job to job, not necessarily in the same organisation. Therefore, instead of people relying on organisations to give shape to their career, in future the onus will be on individuals to map out and pursue their own chosen route.

This change is also affecting skill development in organisations. It will no longer be sufficient just to be skilled in a particular job or specialism, because these will certainly change over time or even entirely disappear. Increasingly, individuals are finding that the concept of job security is being replaced by 'employability security' – the ability to adapt and enhance one's skills so as to be able to perform well in different types of jobs and organisations. Careers, therefore, are being shaped by professional and entrepreneurial principles: the ability to develop and market one's own skills and ideas, rather than by the sequence of jobs provided by one company. People will join organisations or accept particular jobs not, as in the past, because of job security or career progression, but in order to develop their skills, add to their knowledge and enhance their future employability.

Kanter argues that:

> . . . what people are increasingly working to acquire is the capital of their own individual reputation instead of the organisational capital that comes from learning one system well and meeting its idiosyncratic requirements. For many managers, it might be more important, for example, to acquire or demonstrate a talent that a future employer or financial investor might value than to get to know the right people several layers above in the corporation where they currently work.
>
> (Kanter, 1989: 324)

Having painted this picture, it must also be acknowledged that there are contradictions and dilemmas that need to be resolved. What is being created are organisations and cultures that facilitate innovation and entrepreneurship, and change and flexibility. These will be organisations where employability and loyalty are transient concepts and what matters, almost exclusively, is the individual's present performance rather than their past or potential future contribution. The two main dilemmas from the organisational perspective are, therefore, how to reconcile the above with their stated objective of treating employees as long-term partners, and how to motivate employees to work in the organisation's interest rather than their own interest. This is an especially pointed dilemma in the case of the champions and entrepreneurs on whom it is argued the future of organisations depends. This is because it is this group of highly marketable individuals who are most likely to see their careers in terms of many different jobs and organisations.

Workers' lifestyle

There are now many organisations where people have been given greater freedom to innovate and experiment, where there are strong financial rewards for increased performance levels and where people are given greater control over their area of the business. There is little doubt that in such situations people are expected, and indeed wish, to work longer hours and centre what social life they have around their work. Indeed, there is now much evidence that in most developed countries people are working longer hours than they did a decade ago (Kodz *et al*, 2003). To encourage this, many companies now provide key employees with 'concierge' services that do their shopping, find them plumbers, sort out their new car and even find them a new house and arrange the move. The purpose of this is, of course, to allow staff to focus more effectively on their job.

Nevertheless, where there are benefits to the organisation, there may also be disbenefits to the individual:

> *The workplace as a centre for social life and the workmate as a candidate for marriage mate is, on one level, a convenience for overloaded people who have absorbing work that leaves little time to pursue a personal life outside. It is also an inevitable consequence of the new workforce demographics. But on another level, the idea is profoundly disturbing. What about the large number of people whose personal lives are not contained within the corridors of the corporation? What about the people with family commitments outside the workplace?* (Kanter, 1989: 285)

We already know the adverse cost that such work patterns can have on people's physical and mental health and on their family life. Indeed, there is now a growing tendency among senior managers of both sexes to give up work or move to less well-paid but less demanding jobs (downshifting) in order to spend more time with their families (Carvel, 2002; Etzioni, 2004; Frith, 2003). One particularly high-profile example of this in the UK was the decision in 2008 by the then Minister of Transport, Ruth Kelly, to resign as an MP in order to spend more time with her children as they grow up. However, as a survey by Hamilton (2003: vii) revealed, downshifting is not just for the rich and powerful:

> *The results show that 25 per cent of British adults aged 30–59 have downshifted over the last ten years. This is remarkably high and much higher than previous estimates. The proportion rises to 30 per cent if those stopping work to look after a baby or set up their own businesses are included.*

The downshifting phenomenon may be the reason why Kanter believes unmarried or divorced executives are thought to be preferred to their married counterparts by some companies because it is assumed they can focus more on their job and that they are less likely to downshift given their lack of home life. Indeed, one of the UK's most high-profile businessmen, Sir Alan Sugar, recently said that he was reluctant to hire women because they might take time off to have children (Ashley, 2008). However, the consequence of this approach for organisations that have a long-hours, high-pressure culture is that they may find themselves fishing for talent in a smaller and smaller pool. On the other hand, those who seek to promote a work–life balance for their staff may find it much easier to recruit and retain the best people. The consequence, therefore, of crossing the line between motivation and exploitation may prove detrimental for both staff and the organisations which employ them.

Kanter shares Peters and Waterman's view that traditional, bureaucratic organisations stifle creativity and innovation (*see* Ideas and perspectives 3.6) and enthusiastically agrees with their call for radical organisational change. Furthermore, on the issues of innovation and entrepreneurship, culture and flexibility, and structure and jobs, they share much common ground. To an extent we might expect this, given that they are all writing from an American perspective, and basing their views on the experience and plans of leading American companies. Where she differs from them is that Kanter is aware that such developments have a downside as well as an upside. In particular, she draws attention to the contradiction that lies at the heart of the post-entrepreneurial model: are people – their skills, motivation and loyalty – central to the success of the organisation

Ideas and perspectives 3.6
Rules for stifling innovation

1. Regard any new idea from below with suspicion – because it's new, and because it's from below.
2. Insist that people who need your approval to act first go through several other layers of management to get their signatures.
3. Ask departments or individuals to challenge and criticize each other's proposals. (That saves you the job of deciding; you just pick the survivor.)
4. Express your criticisms freely, and withhold your praise. (That keeps people on their toes.) Let them know they can be fired at any time.
5. Treat identification of problems as signs of failure, to discourage people from letting you know when something in their area isn't working.
6. Control everything carefully. Make sure people count anything that can be counted, frequently.
7. Make decisions to reorganize or change policies in secret, and spring them on people unexpectedly. (That also keeps people on their toes.)
8. Make sure that requests for information are fully justified, and make sure that it is not given out to managers freely. (You don't want data to fall into the wrong hands.)
9. Assign to lower-level managers, in the name of delegation and participation, responsibility for figuring out how to cut back, lay off, move people around, or otherwise implement threatening decisions you have made. And get them to do it quickly.
10. And above all, never forget that you, the higher-ups, already know everything important about this business.

Source: Kanter (1983: 100–1)

of the future, or are they just another commodity to be obtained and dispensed with as circumstances and their performance require?

In *The Challenge of Organizational Change*, Kanter and her co-authors (Kanter *et al*, 1992) turn their attention to the issue of managing change, and propose 'ten commandments for executing change' (*see* Ideas and perspectives 3.7).

Looking at approaches to change, Kanter *et al* (1992) distinguished between 'Bold Strokes' and 'Long Marches' (*see* Ideas and perspectives 3.8). The former relate to major strategic decisions or economic initiatives. These, they argue, can have a clear and rapid impact on an organisation, but they rarely lead to any long-term change in habits or culture. The Long March approach, on the other hand, favours relatively small-scale and operationally focused initiatives that are slow to implement and whose full benefits are achieved in the long term rather than the short term. The Long March approach can impact on culture over time. Bold Strokes are initiatives taken by a few senior managers, sometimes only one; they do not rely on the support of the rest of the organisation for their success. The Long March approach, however, does. Without the involvement and commitment of the majority of the workforce, such initiatives cannot succeed.

Ideas and perspectives 3.7
Ten commandements for executing change

1. Analyze the organization and its need for change.
2. Create a shared vision and a common direction.
3. Separate from the past.
4. Create a sense of urgency.
5. Support a strong leader role.
6. Line up political sponsorship.
7. Craft an implementation plan.
8. Develop enabling structures.
9. Communicate, involve people, and be honest.
10. Reinforce and institutionalize change.

Source: Kanter *et al* (1992: 383)

Ideas and perspectives 3.8
Bold Strokes and Long Marches

	Bold Strokes	Long Marches
Objective	Major strategic or economic change	Behavioral/cultural change
Timescale	Rapid, short-term change	Slow, long-term change
Involvement	Senior managers	The whole organization

Source: Kanter *et al* (1992)

Kanter *et al* argue that Bold Strokes and Long Marches can be complementary, rather than alternatives. For example, a major restructuring can lead to short-term economic benefits, but if the organisation is to prosper in the long term it may need to transform its culture through a Long March. However, in practice, companies appear to favour one or the other.

Kanter's, unlike Peters's, works go far beyond the confines of the individual business enterprise to look at the workings of society as a whole. She co-authored a book, *Creating the Future*, with Michael Dukakis, the former Governor of Massachusetts (Dukakis and Kanter, 1988) and worked on his failed campaign for the US Presidency. The influence of Dukakis and successive Democrat administrations in Massachusetts can be seen in Kanter's *World Class: Thriving Locally in the Global Economy* (Kanter, 1997). Here she argues that if local communities and regions are to achieve economic security, they must see themselves as competing bodies in a mercilessly competitive global economy. Kanter paints a picture of the global economy as one where free enterprise reigns supreme and where goods, and many services, can be supplied from anywhere in the world. She points out that in the 1980s and 1990s, both blue- and white-collar American jobs were exported to whichever part of the world offered the lowest labour costs. Though supporting this example of the working of the free enterprise system as being ultimately to everyone's benefit, Kanter argues that if local communities and regions are to survive and prosper in such a fierce climate, they must learn how to defend themselves. In particular, she argues for an interventionist local state which forms alliances with local private enterprises and manipulates the local economy. By creating a business-friendly taxation system and by the selective use of public expenditure for education and infrastructure projects, it can aim to attract and retain employers, especially large corporations.

In *Innovation: Breakthrough Thinking at 3M, DuPont, GE, Pfizer, and Rubbermaid* (Kanter *et al*, 1997), Kanter returned to the internal world of the organisation and the tried and tested ground of the Culture–Excellence approach. The core arguments of the book are neatly summed up on the dust jacket, which states that inside you will discover:

- Why it is impossible to approach innovation from a business school mentality.
- Why investigations of any cost or size will fail if tied too tightly to current market-place needs.
- Why managers must learn to operate more intuitively.
- Why cross-functional teams are more productive than any other organisational configuration.
- How fostering a competitive internal environment results in a healthy, creative tension and hungry, entrepreneurial employees.

These points are fleshed out by drawing upon the practices of the companies in the book's title and the editors' own, anecdotal, experiences. In a book whose Foreword is written by Tom Peters, it is not perhaps surprising that many of the arguments mirror those of Peters's own book on innovation (Peters, 1997a). Indeed, the key thrust of the book is succinctly summed up in a phrase from Tom Peters's (1997b) Foreword: 'Tomorrow's victories will go to the masters of innovation! Period!' It speaks volumes for the credibility which the Culture–Excellence approach has achieved in the business world that, after nearly two decades, its two leading American proponents are still in agreement about what it takes to achieve success.

Over the last decade, Kanter has continued to develop these views (*see* Kanter, 2006). However, she has also given increased attention to issues of social and corporate responsibility, especially the relationship between what she refers to as 'principled' business practices, robust democracy and a healthy civil society (O'Hara, 2008). In her recent *Harvard Business Review* article (Kanter, 2008), she examines the practices of leading global companies, such as IBM, Proctor and Gamble and Cisco, to show how they are meeting business and societal challenges such as maintaining economic growth whilst achieving environmental sustainability. As Ideas and perspectives 3.9 shows, she argues that these organisations are achieving this by resolving long-standing contradictions, such as between innovation and standardisation, and business value and societal value. As always with Kanter, the key to resolving these contradictions is the marriage of culture and excellence.

Ideas and perspectives 3.9
Having it both ways

When do you know a paradigm is shifting? When long-standing contradictions begin to resolve. In the giants my research team and I studied, I was struck by the number of areas in which they achieved a balance between seemingly opposing goals.

- *They both globalize and localize, deriving benefits from the intersections.*
- *They both standardize and innovate, endeavoring to prevent consistency from becoming stifling conformity.*
- *They foster a common universal culture but also respect for individual differences, seeking inclusion and diversity.*
- *They maintain control by letting go of it, trusting people educated in the shared values to do the right thing.*
- *They have a strong identity but also a strong reliance on partners, whom they collaborate with but do not control.*
- *They produce both business value and societal value.*
- *They bring together the 'soft' areas (people, culture, and community responsibility) and the 'hard' areas (technology and product innovation).*
- *They do not abandon values in a crisis; in fact, as leaders put them to the test, crises serve to strengthen commitment to values.*

Source: Kanter (2008: 48)

In the next (and last) section on Culture–Excellence, we will examine the emergence of new organisational forms from the perspective of a British theorist: Charles Handy.

Charles Handy's emerging future organisations

Charles Handy is one of Britain's leading management thinkers. Indeed, in a 1997 European league table of global management gurus, he was placed third; all the others in the top ten were American (Rogers, 1997). Handy was educated at Oxford University and the Sloan School of Management at the Massachusetts Institute of Technology. He has been an oil executive, an economist and a professor at the London Business School. He has also acted as a consultant to a wide range of organisations in business, government, the voluntary sector, education and health.

Handy's first book, *Understanding Organizations*, which was published in 1976, has become a standard text on management courses and is now in its fourth edition (Handy, 1993). However, the book that brought him to public prominence and where he first began to articulate his views about the future direction of organisations was *The Future of Work* (Handy, 1984). As with Kanter and Peters, his work was inspired by the rise of Japan and the apparent decline of the West. In particular, he was concerned with the high level of unemployment in the UK at that time. Handy argued that if organisations were to survive and meaningful jobs were to be created for all those who wished to work, then both organisations and individuals would have to change the way they perceived jobs and careers. It was in his book *The Age of Unreason* (1989) that Handy fully articulated his views on the requirements for organisational success. He argued that profound changes were taking place in organisational life:

> *The world of work is changing because the organisations of work are changing their ways. At the same time, however, the organisations are having to adapt to a changing world of work. It's a chicken and egg situation. One thing, at least, is clear: organisations in both private and public sectors face a tougher world – one in which they are judged more harshly than before on their effectiveness and in which there are fewer protective hedges behind which to shelter.*   (Handy, 1989: 70)

He asserted that British companies were fast moving away from the labour-intensive organisations of yesteryear. In future, new knowledge-based structures, run by a few smart people at their core who will control a host of equally smart computerised machines, will be the order of the day. Already, he noted, leading British organisations were increasingly becoming entities that received their added value from the knowledge and the creativity they put in, rather than from the application of muscle power. He contended that fewer, better-motivated people, helped by clever machines, could create much more added value than large groups of unthinking, demotivated ones ever could.

Like Peters and Kanter, Handy believes that the emerging future organisations will be smaller, more flexible and less hierarchical. Similarly, he also believes that the new organisations will need to treat people as assets to be developed and motivated, rather than just so much industrial cannon fodder. However, he does not assume that the future will be without diversity in relation to the organisational forms that emerge. Unlike Peters and Waterman, and to a lesser extent Kanter, he recognises that companies will continue to face differing circumstances and will need to respond in different manners. Therefore, instead of trying to re-establish a new 'one best way' for all organisations, with all the contradictions that arise from such attempts, Handy identifies three generic types of organisation that he argues will dominate in the future (*see* Ideas and perspectives 3.10).

Ideas and perspectives 3.10
Handy's generic organisations

Organisation type	Core principles
1. Shamrock	Three distinct groups of staff – Core, Contractual Fringe and a Flexible Labour Force.
2. Federal	A collection or network of individual organisations allied together to achieve a common purpose.
3. Triple I	Information, Intelligence and Ideas = Added Value

Source: Handy (1989)

---

1 The Shamrock organisation

This form of organisation, like the plant of the same name with three interlocking leaves, is composed of three distinct groups of workers who are treated differently and have different expectations: a small group of specialist 'core' workers; a contractual fringe; and a flexible labour force.

The *core workers* are the first leaf, and the main distinguishing feature of the Shamrock form of organisation. These are a group of specialists, professional workers who form the brain, the hub or what we might call the 'nerve centre' of the organisation. These are people who are seen as being essential to the organisation. It is these few intelligent and articulate personnel in whose hands and heads reside the secrets of the organisation. They are both specialists and generalists, in that they run the organisation and control the smart machines and computers that have replaced, to a large extent, much of the labour force. This 'all puts pressure on the core, a pressure which could be summed up by the new equation of half the people, paid twice as much, working three times as effectively' (Handy, 1989: 118–19).

For their well-rewarded jobs, they are expected to be extremely loyal to the organisation, and to live and breathe their work. It is their responsibility to drive the organisation forward to ever greater success; to be flexible enough to meet the constantly changing challenge of competitors and the equally changing and sophisticated needs of customers. Core workers operate as colleagues and partners in the organisation, as opposed to superiors and subordinates. In a very real sense, it is their company, and as such they expect to be recognised and rewarded for their roles and achievements, rather than the position they occupy on the organisation's ladder. It follows that they are managed differently – by consent: asked and not told what to do.

The *contractual fringe* is the second leaf of the Shamrock. A central feature of Shamrock organisations is their smallness in relation to their productive capacity. This is achieved by two methods: first, as mentioned above, by the use of machines to replace people; and secondly, by the contracting-out to individuals and other organisations of services and tasks previously done in-house. This leads to the creation of a contractual fringe, who may or may not work exclusively for the company in question. They are contracted to carry out certain tasks, for which they are paid a fee based on results, rather than a wage based on time taken. The arguments put forward in favour of such arrangements are numerous, but tend to boil down to three main ones:

- **It is cheaper** – companies only pay for what they get.
- **It makes management easier** – why keep the people on the payroll with all the attendant human management problems if it is not necessary?
- **Workload balancing** – when business is slack, it is the contractor who bears the impact of the reduced workload.

The *flexible labour force* is the third and fastest-growing leaf of the Shamrock and comprises a pool of part-time workers available for use by organisations. These are people with relevant skills who are not in need of, or who cannot obtain, full-time employment, but who are prepared to work on a part-time basis.

Increasingly, among this group of flexible workers are women who left their skilled jobs to raise families, but who are willing to return to work on a part-time basis, while still maintaining their child-rearing commitments. Included in this also is the growing army of young or retired executives, who prefer to hop from one job to another, doing bits and pieces of work on a part-time basis. These workers are sometimes referred to as temps (temporaries) or casuals. The growth of this group can be measured by the proliferation of employment agencies, catering solely for these groups, which have been established in the United Kingdom since the early 1980s. However, the flexible work-force never

> . . . *have the commitment or ambition of the core. Decent pay and decent conditions are what they want, . . . They have jobs not careers and cannot be expected to rejoice in the organisation's triumphs any more than they can expect to share in the proceeds, nor will they put themselves out for the love of it; more work, in their culture, deserves and demands more money.* (Handy, 1989: 80–1)

The picture, therefore, of the Shamrock organisation is one where structure and employment practices allow it to be big in terms of output, whilst being small in terms of the number of direct employees. For the latter reason, it is lean with few hierarchical layers and even less bureaucracy. It achieves this by the application of smart machines and a combination of part-time staff and subcontractors, whose work can be turned on and off as circumstances dictate. However, in a departure from past practice, the people involved may be highly skilled and competent. This also has the advantage of requiring much less office and factory accommodation than more traditionally organised companies. Other than the core staff, the rest are all scattered in different organisations or their own homes, often linked through sophisticated communication systems.

Such organisations, with their flexibility and skills, are well-suited to the provision of high-performance products and services to demanding and rapidly changing markets. The beauty of it all, as Handy argues, is that they do not have to employ all of the people all of the time or even in the same place to get the work done. According to Handy, small is not only beautiful but also increasingly preferable.

2 The Federal organisation

This is the second type of generic organisation that Handy sees as becoming dominant in the future. He defines this type of organisation as a collection or network of individual organisations allied together under a common flag with some shaped identity. Federations arise for two reasons. The first is that, as Shamrock organisations grow bigger, the core workers begin to find the volume of information available to them to make decisions increasingly difficult to handle. Secondly, they constitute a response to the constantly changing and competitive environment of the business world. Modern organisations need not only to achieve the flexibility that comes from smallness, but also to be able to command the resources and power of big corporations.

As Handy (1989: 110) puts it:

> It [Federalism] allows individuals to work in organisation villages with the advantages of big city facilities. Organisational cities no longer work unless they are broken down into villages. In their big city mode they cannot cope with the variety needed in their products, their processes, and their people. On the other hand, the villages on their own

have not the resources nor the imagination to grow. Some villages, of course, will be content to survive, happy in their niche, but global markets need global products and large confederations to make them or do them.

Federalism, therefore, implies the granting of autonomy to Shamrocks. Autonomy requires that Shamrocks are headed by their own separate chief executives, supported by a team of core workers, who take full responsibility for running the company. In such situations the Shamrocks become separate, but related, entities, under the umbrella of the Federal Centre. With the devolving of power to the Shamrocks, which still remain in the Federal portfolio, the Federal Centre is left to pursue the business of providing a common platform for the integration of the activities of the Shamrocks. The Federal Centre has the role of generating and collating ideas from the different Shamrocks and making them into concrete, achievable strategic objectives. Therefore, the Federal Centre is concerned mainly with the future; with looking forward, generating ideas, and creating scenarios and options of what the future will look like. All this is done with the ultimate aim of moving the organisation forward and keeping it ahead not only of its rivals, but also of its time.

Another feature of the Federal organisation is what Handy refers to as the 'inverted do'nut'.

> *The do'nut is an American doughnut. It is round with a hole in the middle rather than the jam in its British equivalent . . . This, however, is an inverted American do'nut, in that it has the hole in the middle filled in and the space on the outside; . . . The point of the analogy begins to emerge if you think of your job, or any job. There will be a part of the job which will be clearly defined, and which, if you do not do, you will be seen to have failed. That is the heart, the core, the centre of the do'nut . . . [but] . . . In any job of any significance the person holding the job is expected not only to do all that is required but in some way to improve on that . . . to move into the empty space of the do'nut and begin to fill it up.* (Handy, 1989: 102)

Through this approach, the Federal organisation seeks to maximise the innovative and creative potential of staff members. It does this by specifying the core job, the target and the quality standard expected of a given product or service. Outside of this specified domain, within the do'nut's empty space, however, staff members are given enough room and latitude to challenge and question existing ideas, to experiment and to come up with new methods of doing things, and new products or services. The aim is to encourage enquiry and experimentation that lead to higher standards. It follows from this that the essence of leadership under a Federal system is to provide a shared vision for the organisation; one which allows room for those whose lives will be affected by it – either directly or indirectly – to modify it, ponder over it, expand it, accept it and then make it a reality. Leadership in such situations is about providing opportunities for staff to grow and test their potential to the limit.

3 The Triple I organisation

This is the third of Handy's new organisational forms, although in fact it comprises a set of principles rather than a structural model. From the above, it is clear that both

Shamrock and Federal organisation types introduce new dimensions into the world of work. Traditional perspectives are being transformed, and the established criteria for judging organisational effectiveness are being re-evaluated. Issues such as the definition of a productive contribution to work, reward systems, managerial skills and many more are being examined in the light of new management ideas. Indeed, according to Handy, we appear to be on the verge of a revolution in management thought and practice.

An examination of the attributes of the core workers in both Shamrock and Federal organisations gives an indication of what will constitute the new formula for success and effectiveness in tomorrow's companies. The core workers, as seen by Handy, use their *Intelligence* to analyse the available *Information* to generate *Ideas* for new products and services. Thus we find that Handy's first two organisational forms contain the seeds to produce his third form, the Triple I – organisations based on Intelligence, Information and Ideas. Since the three Is constitute the prime intellectual capital of the new organisations, clearly the Triple I principle applies most importantly to the core group of workers who are in a position to possess these attributes.

In future, it is argued, the equation for organisational success will be:

Triple I = AV

Intelligence, Information and Ideas = Added Value

A Triple I organisation will be 'obsessed with the pursuit of truth, or, in business language, of quality' (Handy, 1989: 113). This will not depend solely on human ability but will be a combination of smart people and smart machines. Therefore, organisations of the future will increasingly have to:

- Invest in smart machines to remain competitive and effective.
- Recruit skilled and smart people to control the machines.
- Ensure that this group of skilled people is rewarded equitably.

For the Triple I organisation to emerge and remain successful, it must keep the skills, knowledge and abilities of its staff up to date. This means that it must become a learning organisation; one that provides a conducive environment for the development of its intellectual capital. Time and effort must be consciously and officially devoted to learning and study, at all levels of the organisation. The core, especially, must spend more time than their equivalents in more traditional companies on thinking and study: meeting with other external professionals and experts, going on study tours and listening more to 'partners' within the organisation, all with the objective of improving the organisation's human capital. The new organisations will be dynamic, interactive societies where information is open to all, freely given and freely received. In the Triple I organisation, everyone will be expected to think and learn as well as to do. Nevertheless, it is the core worker from whom most will be demanded. Such people will be increasingly:

> . . . expected to have not only the expertise appropriate to his or her particular role, but will also be required to know and understand business, to have the technical skills of analysis and the human skills and the conceptual skills and to keep them up to date.
> (Handy, 1989: 124)

This is one of the key features that make the Triple I organisation unique; it is a hotbed of intellectual discourse, where the prevailing culture is one of consent rather than instruction. Staff are unsupervised in the traditional sense, and instead are trusted to do what is right and given room to experiment with new ideas and concepts. Finally, the flexibility of such organisations, and the unpredictability of the environments in which they operate, mean that careers will become more variegated and less permanent.

As can be seen, therefore, Handy's view of the future shape of organisations does not appear dissimilar to that of Kanter, and Peters and Waterman. However, he does depart from their views in at least two crucial respects. Firstly, he explicitly acknowledges that not all organisations will adopt the same form or move at the same pace. His three generic forms indicate that organisations will have to exercise choice and judgement in order to match their particular circumstances to the most suitable form. Also, it is clear that he views this as an evolutionary as well as a revolutionary process: companies cannot immediately become a Triple I type of organisation; they have to develop into one over time. Secondly, he explicitly states what is only hinted at by the other writers, namely that in the new organisations where everyone is to be treated as an equal 'partner', some will be more equal than others, i.e. the core workers will be treated and rewarded in a more preferential manner than the contractual fringe or the flexible labour force.

Handy does not give specific guidance as to how existing organisations can adapt themselves to take on these new forms, although he does indicate that a lack of empowerment and self-belief amongst individuals in organisations presents a major obstacle to change. However, in an earlier work (Handy, 1986), he does state very clearly that fundamental change is a long-term process and that people tend to react emotionally rather than rationally to change.

After the publication of *The Age of Unreason*, Handy appeared to grow increasingly concerned with the unanticipated consequences of his prescriptions for the world of work. This is made clear in the first paragraph of his 1994 book, *The Empty Raincoat*:

> *Four years ago, my earlier book,* The Age of Unreason, *was published. In that book I presented a view of the way work was being reshaped and the effects which the reshaping might have on all our lives. It was, on the whole, an optimistic view. Since then, the world of work has changed very much along the lines which were described in the book. This should be comforting to an author, but I have not found it so. Too many people and institutions have been unsettled by the changes. Capitalism has not proved as flexible as it was supposed to be. Governments have not been all-wise or far-seeing. Life is a struggle for many and a puzzle for most.*
>
> *What is happening in our mature societies is much more fundamental, confusing and distressing than I had expected.* (Handy, 1994: 1)

In *The Empty Raincoat*, Handy returns to and restates many of the themes of his earlier work, but with two differences. Firstly, he explicitly acknowledges that the types of careers that these new organisational forms will create will have a severely adverse effect on the home life of employees, especially senior managers. They will be called on to be company men and women above all else, including their families.

Secondly, there is an almost evangelical feel to the book. This is especially noticeable in the later section of the book, where Handy argues that the modern world has taken meaning out of people's lives and that, whilst the pursuit of profit may motivate senior managers:

Not many in the lower realms of the organisation can get excited by the thought of enriching shareholders. 'Excellence' and 'quality' are the right sort of words, but they have been tarnished by repetition in too many organisations.

(Handy, 1994: 265)

This more pessimistic view of the future is still there in his 1997 book, *The Hungry Spirit* (Handy, 1997: 3):

Many of us are, I believe, confused by the world we have created for ourselves in the West . . . the new fashion for turning everything into a business, even our own lives, doesn't seem to be the answer. A hospital, and my life, is more than just a business. What good can it possibly do to pile up riches which you cannot conceivably use, and what is the point of the efficiency needed to create those riches if one third of the world's workers are now unemployed or under-employed as the ILO calculates? And where will it end, this passion for growth? . . . I am angered by the waste of so many people's lives, dragged down by poverty in the midst of riches. I am concerned by the absence of a more transcendent view of life and the purposes of life, and by the prevalence of the economic myth which colours all we do. Money is the means for life and not the point of it.

In the book, Handy argues that, in the West, people's spiritual needs have been sacrificed to the pursuit of their material needs; and he examines the options, and where the responsibility lies, for putting balance back into people's lives. In particular he is concerned with the distribution of wealth, the role that education can play in giving everyone a good start in life, and how we can look after ourselves whilst having a care for others as well. He even touches on, perhaps, the biggest question of all: 'What, ultimately, is the real purpose of life?' (Handy, 1997: 5). In addressing these issues he ranges widely, looking at markets, organisations and the role of business, government and religion. He believes the answer lies in the pursuit of 'Proper Selfishness'. This is a redefinition of individualism; he sees individuals as moving away from the pursuit of narrow self-interest, and instead realising that it is in their best interests to pursue a fairer society for all. Though he identifies a role for government and business in creating Proper Selfishness, he believes it is individuals themselves who bear the main responsibility for its achievement. In particular, he draws attention to the role of individual entrepreneurs in changing the world:

Entrepreneurs, whether social or commercial, often discover aspects of themselves in the pursuit of something beyond themselves. Such people are not content to let the status quo be the way forward. They itch to make a difference . . . Almost accidentally, corporations have become the nursery for frustrated entrepreneurs. They should turn this to a positive account and do it more deliberately, in the hope that they can retain some of the best for themselves, including women, while seeding the community with the others. The workplace has always been the real school for life. Perhaps it just needs to change its curriculum a little to tune in with the new age of personal initiative.

(Handy, 1997: 262)

In recent years, Handy has seen himself less as a management guru and more as a social philosopher (Handy, 2007a, 2007b). He is concerned that blind greed still drives many people and that the pursuit of riches has created a mercenary society which lacks a moral or spiritual compass. Handy calls for a new sense of purpose for individuals, organisations and society. He wants to see a strong ethical approach to business and society, and a re-creation of the concept that people exist to help and serve each other as well as themselves. These are sentiments that many of us would probably share but, unfortunately, he fails to show how the unleashing of individual entrepreneurship and the creation of the new organisational forms he advocates will aid this search for meaning. Instead, he asks us to put our faith in the goodness of people and to be optimistic about the future. A recurrent theme in Handy's work, however, has been the many paradoxes thrown up by contemporary society, especially the presence of dire poverty amidst extreme wealth, and the potential of technology for creating meaningful work compared with the increasing tendency for the quality of life to decline. Therefore, it seems strange that the one paradox that Handy appears to ignore is that the forms of organisations that he advocates may well be creating the poor jobs and poverty he deprecates.

Culture–Excellence: summary and criticisms

In its third biennial Global CEO Study, IBM (2008: 54) stated that 'The Enterprise of the Future constantly searches for new ways to compete.' In particular, IBM notes that such an enterprise:

- Thinks like an outsider.
- Draws breakthrough ideas from other industries.
- Empowers entrepreneurs.
- Experiments creatively in the market, not just the lab.
- Manages today's business while experimenting with tomorrow's model.

Such phrases could have been written by Tom Peters or any of the proponents of Culture–Excellence. The IBM Study shows that Culture–Excellence has had a major impact on the thinking and practice of businesses globally, and not just in the UK and the USA. This is not surprising. *In Search of Excellence* has sold over six million copies, making it the best-selling management book of all time. Largely as a result of its success, its authors, especially Tom Peters, have become successful and influential consultants and, in Peters's case, arguably the leading business guru of his day (Collins, 2008). Rosabeth Moss Kanter and Charles Handy have likewise achieved the pre-eminence in business circles that they had previously only occupied in academia. A look in the business section of any bookshop will show that there are also many more authors who have jumped on the bandwagon. Indeed, barely a day seems to go by without the publication of yet another blockbuster proclaiming that it has discovered the recipe for success. Some of these achieve a degree of prominence in business circles, though many seem to disappear without trace. Nevertheless, the fact that publishers keep publishing them, and that in different ways and shapes they repeat and project the Culture–Excellence message, emphasises the thirst by managers for the message.

As the IBM (2008) Study shows, it is not just a case that managers buy them to leave them on the shelf. Over the last 25 years, on both sides of the Atlantic, managers have been attempting to reshape their companies along the Culture–Excellence lines. In 1997, a survey by the Industrial Society showed that in the UK alone some 94 per cent of respondent organisations either had recently been through or were going through a culture change programme (Industrial Society, 1997).

The reason for its emergence, and for its continuing popularity, was that in a world where old certainties had disappeared, where new and more dangerous competitors seemed to appear every day, it rejected the communal and corporatist approach of the Japanese, and offered instead a recipe for success that was in tune with the free market liberalism, with its stress on individualism, that has dominated much of the West for the last three decades. Nor was it merely a rehash of what had gone before. The Culture–Excellence approach to organisations is significantly different from previous approaches; although we might note that the new forms, especially Handy's Shamrock type, bear an interesting resemblance to the first budding of organisational life during the Industrial Revolution. The entrepreneurial style of management, the stress on a privileged core of skilled workers, and the contracting-out of whole areas of organisational activities are all hallmarks of the early industrial organisations. However, the big differences between then and now relate to the level of sophistication and complexity of the new organisations that are emerging, the degree of integration of both internal functions and external relationships, the grade of intelligence and skill required of all staff, whether they be core or periphery – and, of course, the conditions of employment. For Watson (1986: 66), who coined the term 'Culture–Excellence school' to describe proponents of this approach, there is one further and crucial difference:

> [In these new organisations] what brings the activities of the organisational members to focus upon those purposes which lead to effective performance is the existence of a strong and clearly articulated culture.　　　　　　　　　　　　　　　(Watson, 1986: 66)

It is this which makes it clear that the Culture–Excellence approach that has been developing since the early 1980s is remarkably different from most of the theory and practice that has grown up in the last 100 years.

Peters, Kanter and Handy argue that organisations are entering a new age, where familiar themes are taking on different meanings and are being expressed in a new language. Contrasting the old with the new, they argue that what is important in the new is not muscle power, but brain power: the ability to make intelligent use of information to create ideas that add value and sustain competitiveness. The new organisation is flatter in structure, though it might be more accurate to say that structure is decreasing in importance and that its role as a directing and controlling mechanism is being taken over by cultures that stress the need for, and facilitate, flexibility and adaptation (though in passing we should note that Peters (1993) also sees the dismembering of hierarchical structures as an important step in creating these new cultures). The Culture–Excellence approach wishes to sound the death knell of hierarchical organisations and the concept of promotion through the ranks. Careers and skills are taking on new meanings, as are established ideas of reward.

In future, it is argued, careers are likely to depend on the individual and his or her ability to remain employable. In turn, the skills needed for 'employability' will tend to be generic and broad-based rather than organisation- or function/specialism-specific. Likewise, career paths and promotion will no longer be shaped by the particular employing organisation and its structures and criteria, but will be driven more by individuals creating their own opportunities by taking on new roles and responsibilities, either in one organisation or, more likely, by moving from company to company. As for pay, it seems that this will take the form not so much of a wage related to the particular post occupied, but more that of a fee paid for actual performance.

On human relations, the message being transmitted is that the new forms of organisations will treat their employees in a more responsible and humane fashion than has been the norm. Employees will be seen and treated as 'partners', capable of making a substantial contribution to the growth of the organisation. This approach, it is argued, will manifest itself in a tough-minded respect for the individual, who will receive training, be set reasonable and clear objectives, and be given the autonomy to make his or her own contribution to the work of the organisation. The new organisations will seek to develop open, flexible and pragmatic cultures, which help to maintain a learning environment that promotes creativity and entrepreneurship amongst all employees.

Another feature of the new organisational forms, it is claimed, will be their ability to grant autonomy and encourage flexibility and initiative whilst at the same time keeping tight control of their operations. Like so much else, this is to be achieved through culture rather than structure, and values rather than rules. Everything is to be monitored closely, not by the watching eye of superiors, but by the creation of a homogeneous environment in which all take an equal responsibility for, and legitimate interest in, the work of their colleagues.

Clearly, the new organisation forms that are being promoted offer much that is admirable and worth supporting. Equally clearly, their adherents and promoters raise more questions than they answer. To an extent this is inevitable when dealing with something that is emerging rather than an existing and concrete reality. However, as this concept has been around for nearly two decades, this is no longer the case. Therefore, it would be remiss to ignore or gloss over the questions and dilemmas that seem apparent. Many writers have drawn attention to the shortcomings of the Culture–Excellence approach. Carroll (1983) and Lawler (1985) were both scathing about the methodological shortcomings of the research on which Peters and Waterman's (1982) book was based. Indeed, Peters himself appears to have admitted that he and Waterman 'faked' some of the data in order to obtain their results (Kellaway, 2001). This would seem to give additional support to Wilson's (1992) claim that the book lacks any apparent empirical or theoretical foundations. Though Wilson's criticisms may seem somewhat exaggerated, it is certainly arguable that the Culture–Excellence approach does have serious weaknesses, especially in three areas that are crucial to the operation of organisations:

1. **People**. There are serious concerns and contradictions regarding the role and behaviour of people in the new organisations. On the one hand, they are proclaimed as the chief asset of the new organisations. On the other hand, there are clearly different grades of employee, from core to periphery, and these different grades will be treated and rewarded in a markedly dissimilar manner; furthermore, none of the different grades can expect any real job security. The new organisations will only value employees as long as they and their areas perform to the highest of standards. Not only does this pit individual against individual, but also one part of the organisation against another. Whilst healthy competition may enhance organisational competitiveness, from what we know of motivation theory (Arnold *et al*, 1998) it is not clear that the Culture–Excellence approach is that healthy. The Culture–Excellence approach

also encourages teamwork, yet the pursuit of individual advancement and reward often leads to conflict rather than cooperation (Schein, 1988).

2. **Politics**. Though Western companies traditionally either deny the existence of internal struggles or argue that such behaviour is perverse, it is clear that the struggle for resources, power and survival is as great within organisations as it is between them (Buchanan and Badham, 1999; Pfeffer, 1981; Robbins, 1986). As stated above, the recommendations of the Culture–Excellence school would seem to exacerbate political behaviour by and between individuals and groups, yet in the main they ignore this drawback to their approach, even though it is potentially damaging to both organisational and individual performance.

3. **Culture**. The proponents of Culture–Excellence are advocating a 'one best way' (one best culture) approach for all organisations, irrespective of their size, environment and other circumstances. Also, as Wilson (1992) pointed out, Culture–Excellence assumes a simple causal relationship between culture and performance. Nevertheless, for the proponents of the Culture–Excellence school, culture is the great cure-all – the creation of a culture of excellence is seen as answering all questions and solving all problems. This assumes that the creation of new cultures will itself be unproblematic. However, as Chapter 5 will show, culture and politics appear to be the Achilles heel of approaches to managing organisations.

It would also be remiss of us if we ignored the differences between the main proponents of Culture–Excellence. Peters is a free market liberal in the classic American mould. He believes that individual and organisational competition untrammelled by government is what makes societies strong. Kanter agrees with most of this, but believes that local communities, working with big business, have a positive role to play in attracting and keeping well-paid jobs for their communities. She has also become more increasingly concerned with issues of social justice and environmental sustainability but believes that these are best tackled by enlightened big business. Handy is also committed to the free market, but has become increasingly concerned with the outcome of his prescriptions. He appears to be turning his back on pure individualism, arguing instead for a less rapacious, more caring capitalism, driven by what he terms 'Proper Selfishness' and more concerned with the collective good than individual wealth creation. Though Peters and Kanter may continue to hold to the Culture–Excellence line, it is difficult to see that the direction which Handy is now taking is consistent with it.

There is one final concern that is wider than the Culture–Excellence approach *per se* or its impact on organisations, but which is reflected in the differences between Peters, Kanter and Handy. The move towards creating segmented workforces of the type described by Handy (1989), and the emphasis on the temporary nature of employment championed by Peters and Waterman (1982) and Kanter (1989), are part of a continuing trend in the West, driven by neo-liberal economic and social policies, towards worsening job security and conditions of service, in order to create a vast pool of under-employed, especially part-time, labour that can be turned on or off as the situation dictates.

This trend can be seen in figures from the 1990s. In the UK in 1993, for example, some 9.7 million workers (38 per cent of all UK workers) were part-time, temporary, self-employed, on a government training scheme, or unpaid family workers – an increase of 1.25 million since 1986. Similarly, the proportion of men in employment who were part of the flexible workforce rose from 18 per cent in 1981 to 27.5 per cent in 1993 (Watson, 1994). This trend to temporary employment has continued apace. It is now a global business which, in 2005, was worth some US$240m and is dominated by a group of 10 multinational corporations (EWERC, 2007).

This rise in temporary, part-time employment tallies with Hutton's (1995) argument that the UK is now more socially divided than at any time since the Industrial Revolution. In particular, he maintains that the UK is a 30/30/40 society – the marginalised, the newly insecure and the advantaged – and that this not only raises the spectre of increased social tensions, but is a positive disadvantage to wealth creation. Hutton's attack on the adverse effects of neo-liberal market policies is supported by others, notably Saul (1997), who pointed out that the income gap between the highest- and lowest-paid workers in the UK was greater in 1997 than at any time since 1880, when records began. Figures published by the UK government (Brindle, 1998b) show that between 1979 and 1998 the richest 10 per cent of the population saw their incomes grow by 70 per cent in real terms whilst the bottom 10 per cent of the population suffered a cut in real income of 9 per cent. In the same period, poverty in the UK almost tripled. As White (1999) noted, this increase in poverty has had an especially adverse impact on children. In 1979, 1 in 10 children lived in poverty. In 1996/7, the figure was 1 in 3. Even in the last decade, despite the New Labour government, which came to power in 1997, spending billions of pounds attempting to reduce child and adult poverty, the battle seems to be being lost. Child and pensioner poverty is growing, the richest 20 per cent of society is now taking a larger share of national income than in 1997 and the poorer households have seen their share fall (Elliott, 2008). For example, in 2007, the CEOs of the UK's biggest companies saw their salaries rise by over 30 per cent (Green, 2008). Perhaps not surprisingly, the gap between rich and poor is now wider than at any time in the last 40 years (Dorling *et al*, 2007).

This bleak picture is not restricted to the UK. As Dunphy and Griffiths (1998) point out, in 1980, the Chief Executive Officers of the 300 largest US companies had incomes 29 times that of the average manufacturing worker; ten years later, their incomes were 93 times greater. By 2000, the average CEO salary was 531 times greater (AFL-CIO, 2003). Nor does the pace of executive pay increases appear to have slowed down. In 2006, the CEOs of America's largest companies saw their salaries rise by an average of 38 per cent (DeCarlo, 2008). As a consequence, the gap between rich and poor in the USA is now bigger than at any time since 1928 (Johnston, 2007). The founder of Microsoft, Bill Gates, has a personal fortune that is greater than the combined wealth of the 106 million poorest Americans (Elliott and Brittain, 1998). Globally, the poorest 40 per cent of the world's population receives 5 per cent of global income and the richest 20 per cent get three-quarters of global income (United Nations Development Programme, 2007). Indeed, the estimated wealth of the 11 richest individuals is more than the combined GDP of the 49 least developed countries (*Trade*, 2003).

Much of the economic and labour market liberalisation we have seen since the 1980s was justified by 'trickle-down' economics – the view that as the rich got richer, then some of this wealth would trickle down to the rest of society and, therefore, society as a whole would become wealthier. This clearly does not appear to be the case. Not surprisingly, if one looks at the poorest nations in the world, the situation is much worse, with malnutrition, poverty and disease on the increase (Gittings, 1998). In the 1990s, the number of people in sub-Saharan Africa living on less than $1 a day increased from 47 to 49 per cent, and in eastern and central Europe it increased from 7 to 20 per cent (Elliott, 2003). Nor does the situation appear to be abating. Despite the economic promise of globalisation, and despite high-profile campaigns such as *Make Poverty History*, and despite the promises of the world's richest nations, child and adult poverty are growing across the world. Half the world – nearly three billion people – live on less than two US dollars a day and some one billion live on less than one US dollar a day (United Nations Development Programme, 2007). For example, in Egypt some 2.7m children are working in appalling conditions for up to 10 hours a day for as little as 20p (McDougall, 2008). Couple such low incomes with rising food costs, and 2008 may be remembered as the year when the world's poor began to run out of food (Cooper, 2008; Tibbs and Bailey, 2008).

In the USA, Robert Reich, who was Secretary of Labor in the first Clinton administration, and other leading figures have warned of the dangers of a social chasm opening up between an ever-increasing rich elite, holed up in guarded compounds, and a jobless, impoverished majority (Elliott, 1997; Reich, 1997). As a sign of this, there are now more private security guards in the USA than there are publicly employed police (Dunphy and Griffiths, 1998). Contrast this with the case of Japan, discussed next, where, traditionally, at government and organisation level, full employment has taken precedence over profit and underpinned its voracious appetite for economic expansion (Holden and Burgess, 1994). Given this, Guest's (1992) assessment of *In Search of Excellence*, 'Right enough to be dangerously wrong', may well find favour with many people.

Despite these concerns and criticisms, Culture–Excellence has become the most influential approach to running organisations in the USA and Europe, as is apparent from the many articles on its merits and case studies of its use that appear regularly in management journals. However, since the 1950s, the Japanese have been developing an alternative approach to structuring and managing organisations that is not only markedly different from the Culture–Excellence one but also has a proven track record of success.

The Japanese approach to management

The last 60 years have seen the rebirth of Japan. Reduced almost to ashes at the end of the Second World War, by the 1980s Japan had built an industrial empire second to none (Francks, 1992). Even now, despite its economic ills of the last two decades, it is still, astoundingly, the second largest economy in the world (*Economist*, 2008). As Morgan (1986: 111) stated:

> *With virtually no natural resources, no energy, and over 110 million people crowded in four small mountainous islands, Japan succeeded in achieving the highest growth rate, lowest level of unemployment and, at least in some of the larger and more successful organizations, one of the best-paid and healthiest working populations in the world.*

Though writers suggested many reasons for Japan's success, ranging from culture to economic institutions, time and again, its approach to managing organisations was cited as the key factor (Hunter, 1989; Laage-Hellman, 1997; Sako and Sato, 1997; Schonberger, 1982; Smith and Misumi, 1989; Whitehill, 1991).

Before proceeding to examine what is meant by the Japanese approach to management, it is useful briefly to trace Japan's development as an industrial nation. Up to the middle of the nineteenth century, Japan was an intensely nationalistic society which practised a deliberate policy of isolating itself from the outside world. Therefore, for most of its inhabitants, Japan was the world. It was a feudal country that laid strong emphasis on obligation and deference, and where obedience to authority in general, and to the Emperor in particular, was unquestioned (Sheridan, 1993).

For all its deliberate isolation, Japan was a sophisticated and well-educated country with a high degree of literacy. Education was based on a set of Confucian principles which stressed unquestioning obedience to the family; total loyalty to one's superiors; and reverence for education and self-development. The abiding influence of these can still be seen in Japanese society today, and underpins the strength of Japanese organisations (Smith and Misumi, 1989). However, from the mid-nineteenth century, Japan began to experience internal tensions. The feudal aristocracy experienced escalating financial difficulties whilst the merchant class, considered social inferiors, began to prosper. At the same time, it became clear that the growing military might of other countries posed a potential threat to Japan. In response to these developments, Japan adopted a twin-track policy of economic and military growth, not dissimilar to that being developed in Germany at this time (Hunter, 1989).

Missions were dispatched abroad to study and bring technologies and practices back to Japan. On one such visit in 1911, Yukinori Hoshino, a director of the Kojima Bank, became acquainted with the work of Frederick Taylor and obtained permission to translate his work into Japanese. Following this, Taylor's Scientific Management principles, and allied approaches to work study and production management, were rapidly and enthusiastically adopted by the Japanese (McMillan, 1985). Indeed, such was the impact of Taylor's work that, according to Wren (1994: 205), it 'led to a management revolution, replacing the entrepreneur-dominated age'. By the 1920s, Japan had moved from being an agrarian economy to one dominated by industry. As in many Western countries, industrialisation was accompanied by considerable industrial conflict, sometimes violent (Urabe, 1986). However, unlike in most Western countries, this was not accompanied by a growing democratisation of society. Instead, democratic tendencies were quashed by a growing coalition between industry and the military that promoted intense nationalism and led, almost inexorably, to Japan's involvement in the Second World War. After Japan's defeat, its shattered society was occupied by the USA, which stripped the Emperor of his traditional powers and established a Western-style democracy (Sheridan, 1993; Whitehill, 1991).

Given the state of the Japanese economy after the Second World War, the success of its reconstruction is nothing short of miraculous. The Korean War in the 1950s proved a stroke of good fortune for Japan, in that the USA used Japan as an important staging post for troops and supplies. This injected billions of American dollars into Japan's economy. However, perhaps much more important was America's contribution to management education in Japan. In the immediate post-war years, Japanese companies acquired a reputation for bitter industrial disputes, shoddy workmanship and poor quality. The main responsibility for tackling these problems lay with American engineers working for the Civilian Communications Section of the Occupation Administration (Sheldrake, 1996). Four men in particular have been credited with turning this situation around and creating the basis of Japan's fearsome reputation for the productivity of its workforce and quality of its products: Charles Protzman, Homer Sarasohn, Joseph Juran and W Edward Deming. Interestingly, the last three of these had all worked at Western Electric's Hawthorne Works and were, therefore, familiar, though not necessarily always in agreement, with the Human Relations approach. All of them were far removed from the narrow concept of the engineer. They took a wide view of how enterprises should be run and in particular of the need for managers to show leadership and gain the commitment of their workforces. Their approach, which covered business policy and organisation as well as production methods and techniques, was enthusiastically received, adopted and disseminated by the senior managers who attended their courses and lectures. As Horsley and Buckley (1990: 51) noted, Deming, especially, met with enormous success:

> WE Deming became a legend in Japan. He gave hundreds of lectures . . . to eager managers on the vital importance of statistical quality control . . . Among his pupils were many who were to become captains of Japanese industry in the 1960s and 1970s, heading firms like Nissan, Sharp and the Nippon Electric Company (NEC). The annual Deming Prize for good management was highly coveted in the 1950s, and is still being awarded today.

Nevertheless, despite the economic and technical assistance of the USA, there is little doubt that the main credit for the country's success can be attributed to the hard work, commitment and intelligence of Japanese managers and workers. Under the umbrella of a supportive economic and political framework, Japanese enterprises overcame their severe industrial relations and quality problems of the 1950s and created the distinctive and hugely successful Japanese approach to developing and managing their businesses that allowed them to take the world by storm in the 1970s and 1980s (Fruin, 1992; Pascale and Athos, 1982; Sako and Sato, 1997; Sheldrake, 1996; Smith and Misumi, 1989).

What is the Japanese approach to management?

As one might expect, it is difficult to find an all-embracing definition of the Japanese approach to management that satisfies all commentators or can be found in all Japanese companies. In particular, there are distinct differences between larger and smaller enterprises in Japan, and in the treatment of full-time and part-time, and male and female employees in all enterprises (Cole, 1979; Laage-Hellman, 1997; Sako and Sato, 1997). Indeed, such are these differences that some argue there is either no such thing as a distinctive Japanese approach to management or that, if it does exist, no one has been able to capture it accurately (Dale, 1986; Keys and Miller, 1984; Sullivan, 1983). Nevertheless, the vast majority of observers do seem to agree that it exists and can, broadly, be defined (Abegglen and Stalk, 1984; Ackroyd *et al*, 1988; Hatvany and Pucik, 1981; Holden and Burgess, 1994; Pascale and Athos, 1982; Smith and Misumi, 1989).

Perhaps the most influential work, and still the best-selling book, on Japanese management was William Ouchi's (1981) *Theory Z: How American Business Can Meet the Japanese Challenge*. Drawing on the theoretical insights of Douglas McGregor and Chris Argyris, Ouchi argued that Japanese success stemmed from:

- The involvement and commitment of the entire workforce.
- A set of internally consistent norms, practices and behaviours based on trust and strong personal ties between the individual and the organisation, particularly their immediate work group.
- Practices such as lifetime employment, slow evaluation and promotion and collective decision-making.
- The belief that workers want to build cooperative and close working relationships.

Many other writers have also tried to capture the essence of Japanese management. McKenna (1988) believes that the key elements are:

- Lifetime employment,
- The seniority principle with regard to pay and promotion,
- Enterprise unionism (which will be explained later).

Pang and Oliver (1988) agree with McKenna but also draw attention to:

- Training and education.
- Company-based welfare schemes.
- Quality circles.
- Manufacturing methods such as Just-in-Time production.

Keys and Miller (1984) argue that the hallmarks of Japanese management are:

- Long-term planning.
- Lifetime employment.
- Collective responsibility.

Laage-Hellman (1997) emphasises the presence of:

- A consensus-seeking decision-making process.
- Incremental planning through the development of a long-term vision.
- The use of short-term action plans.
- Passive owners who do not usually interfere with managers.
- Strategies that give priority to long-term growth and survival.
- The effective use of external resources through partnerships with suppliers and customers.

Other commentators have also come up with similar lists. One of the most quoted of these is by Pascale and Athos (1982) who used the McKinsey 7 S Framework (*see* Ideas and perspectives 3.2), which they had developed jointly with Tom Peters and Robert Waterman, to analyse Japanese management. Like Peters and Waterman's Culture–Excellence approach, Pascale and Athos stressed the four 'soft' Ss (staff, style, shared values and skills). This was not to dismiss the 'hard' Ss (strategy, structure and systems), but to emphasise that the real difference between Japanese companies and their Western counterparts was that the latter tended to concentrate on the 'hard' Ss and ignore the 'soft' Ss. Pascale and Athos argued that, in contrast, Japanese companies had developed the ability to combine and blend the 'soft' and 'hard' Ss to their competitive benefit. Their work differed from other studies of Japanese management at the time by examining the management style of Japanese companies operating in the USA. In a similar vein, Peter Wickens, who was Personnel Director of Nissan Motor Manufacturing (UK) Ltd for over 10 years, also commented on the transfer of Japanese management to the West. In his 1987 book, *The Road to Nissan*, written when he was still at Nissan, he argued that the Japanese approach can be characterised by three factors:

- Teamwork.
- Quality-consciousness.
- Flexibility.

Interestingly, after he left Nissan, Wickens (1995) commented that Ouchi and others tended to miss, or underplay, one very important element of Japanese companies:

- A very strong control culture, especially in relation to shopfloor workers.

As Figure 3.1 shows, the factors identified by the above writers can be separated into two categories: those relating to personnel issues and those relating to business practices.

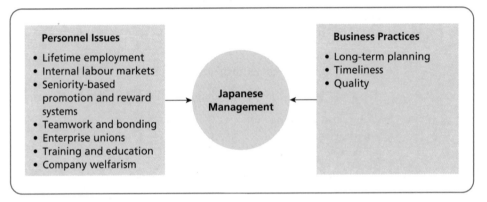

Figure 3.1 The key elements of Japanese Management

Personnel issues

The dedication, commitment and ability of Japanese workers is seen as a major factor in the success of Japanese companies. Though much credit for this has been given to the culture of Japanese society, especially its Confucian tradition of obedience and loyalty, similar levels of motivation have been reproduced in Japanese companies operating in the West (Wickens, 1987), which would imply that other factors are also at work. Chief among these is the crucial role played by the personnel policies prevalent in many Japanese enterprises, especially the larger ones. The core of the Japanese approach to personnel comprises a combination of practices and policies designed to align their behaviour with, and bind employees to, the organisation, and promote their long-term development and commitment. The principal practices and policies concerned are listed below.

1. **Lifetime employment.** Many employees are recruited straight from school or university, and expect, and are expected, to spend the rest of their working lives with the same organisation. This 'guarantee', based as it is on an age-old sense of mutual obligation and belonging, creates an intense sense of loyalty to and dependence on the organisation. Indeed, Holden and Burgess (1994) observed that whilst a Japanese

worker might survive the loss of his family, the collapse of his employing organisation would be unbearable. Therefore, lifetime employment is a central feature of the Japanese approach and supports so much else, including a willingness to change and the maintenance of a stable organisational culture. However, the fact that organisations prefer to recruit school or university leavers also makes it difficult for individuals to move between companies once they have accepted an appointment. It follows that if someone is fired, their chances of securing other employment are negligible.

2. **Internal labour markets.** Most positions are filled from inside the company. This is a corollary to lifetime employment which demonstrates to the employee that satisfactory performance will bring promotion, and it eliminates the potential for tension which can be brought about by the recruitment of outsiders.

3. **Seniority-based promotion and reward systems.** Employees are ranked and rewarded primarily, but not exclusively, on their length of service, and independent of the precise nature of the job they perform.

4. **Teamwork and bonding.** Although Japanese employees are made to feel part of the organisation and see it as some sort of extended family, they are first and foremost a member of a particular work group or team. The group is not just a collection of individuals; it is constructed and developed in such a way that it comprises a single entity which takes collective responsibility for its performance. Japanese companies use a variety of techniques, both at work and in a social setting, for bonding team members to each other and to the organisation.

5. **Enterprise (single-company) unions.** Unlike in the West, Japanese companies tend to allow only one union to represent the interests of the workforce. In addition, Japanese unions tend to be single-company or enterprise unions. Indeed, from a Western point of view, they are not so much trade unions as company associations. This is illustrated by the practice of senior managers, at some stage in their careers, being expected to serve as union officials.

6. **Training and education.** Extensive and continuous training and education form an integral part of Japanese personnel policies. This emphasis on the continuous development of employees, to enable them to carry out their work better and to prepare them for promotion, represents a significant investment by Japanese companies in their human capital. Much of the training is done on the job and is always geared to the twin aims of improving organisational performance and individual development. Though encouraged by the company, employees are expected to take responsibility for their own self-development.

7. **Company welfarism.** Many Japanese companies provide a wide range of welfare benefits for their employees. These can cover medical treatment, education for children and even housing. Some of the larger companies are almost mini-welfare states in themselves.

Many other practices and policies could be added to the list, but these appear to be at the core. They are designed to instil the following in employees:

- Loyalty and gratitude to the company and a commitment to its objectives.
- A sense of security.
- A strong commitment to hard work and performance improvement;
- An atmosphere of cooperation and not conflict.
- A belief in self-development and improvement.

These are the cornerstones of Japanese company life; their presence is the reason why Japanese national culture is often cited as being at the heart of Japan's ability to compete in a world market. These operate within organisation structures which, to Western eyes at least, appear complex, highly formalised and very hierarchical (Whitehill, 1991). However, these personnel issues cannot be seen in isolation from the working practices that Japanese companies use or the objectives they pursue. It is the combination of the two that makes Japanese companies so effective (Wood, 1991). Without overall direction and the appropriate work systems, even the best skilled and motivated workers are ineffective. This is why Japanese business practices and work systems should receive as much attention as personnel issues.

Business practices

The Japanese ability to satisfy customers, and thereby capture markets, by developing and producing products to a higher specification and at a lower cost than their competitors, is staggering considering the state of their industry in the 1940s and 1950s. Indeed, even as recently as the 1960s, 'Made in Japan' was synonymous with poor quality. What has changed, or rather what has come to fruition, has been the methods they apply to all aspects of business, but especially to manufacturing (Hannam, 1993). The fact that some of these methods have, quite naturally, Japanese names (such as *Hoshin Kanri* – policy deployment; *Genba Kanri* – workshop management; *Kaizen* – continuous improvement; *Kanban* – a paperless form of scheduling) tends, for the Western audience, to cloak and mystify the core principles and systems being used, and also to disguise the extent to which these have been adopted from the West. Leaving aside the jargon and terminology, Japanese business practices and work systems can be characterised by three interrelated elements: long-term planning, timeliness and quality.

1. **Long-term planning.** This will be discussed further in Chapters 6 and 7, but for now, in brief, let us say that the timescale on which Japanese enterprises operate is far longer than that of many of their Western competitors, and their focus on building a strong market position similarly contrasts with the short-term profit maximisation objectives prevalent in the USA and UK in particular (Hamel and Prahalad, 1989). Needless to say, this is an enormous advantage when considering investment decisions, whether this be for products, processes or people (Smith and Misumi, 1989).

2. **Timeliness.** The Japanese are seen as having a crucial competitive edge in their ability to develop products and bring them to market faster than their competitors. Part of the explanation for this relates to teamwork. Whilst many Western companies are still designing and developing products on a sequential basis (whereby one part of the design is completed before another is begun), the Japanese work in teams to undertake these tasks simultaneously. This form of teamwork extends to working jointly with customers and suppliers as well (Laage-Hellman, 1997). Not only does this cut the overall time required, but it also leads to fewer errors and misunderstandings because all the relevant parties are involved (Womack *et al*, 1990). Another major contribution to the timeliness of the Japanese is a series of practices designed to cut manufacturing lead times. The main one is Just-in-Time

production. Under Just-in-Time, parts are supplied and used only as and when required. This method reduces stock and work-in-progress and thus reduces cost. However, to achieve this (as proponents of lean/agile manufacturing have stressed) requires everything to be 'right first time', otherwise such a system would quickly grind to a halt for lack of usable parts (Kidd and Karwowski, 1994; Lamming, 1993). Therefore, it is necessary to drive waste and inefficiency out of the system, and the key mechanism for achieving this is the Japanese commitment to quality (Dale and Cooper, 1992).

3. **Quality.** The Japanese commitment to quality is now legendary. Their approach owes much to the inspiration of three Americans: MacArthur, Deming and Juran (Wilkinson, 1991). General MacArthur, who (on behalf of the USA) virtually ruled Japan in the early post-war years, encouraged Japanese industry to improve production quality as part of the rebuilding of their shattered industrial base. Deming (1982) showed the Japanese that statistical process control (SPC), and other such techniques, are powerful methods of controlling quality. Juran (1988) showed the Japanese that quality was determined by all departments in an organisation, and thus set them on the road to developing Total Quality Management. Though imported, the Japanese developed the original concepts considerably. In particular, they introduced the concept of continuous improvement – *Kaizen*. Despite the widespread acceptance of the need for improved quality in the West, the Japanese appear to be the only nation so far capable of diffusing successfully the ideas and practices throughout their industry (Dale and Cooper, 1992; Hannam, 1993; Schonberger, 1982; Womack *et al*, 1990).

In any investigation of the Japanese approach to long-term planning, timeliness and quality, it is necessary to recognise the role played by employees in decision-making. Most discussions of Japanese management emphasise the occurrence of upward influence, particularly through the *ringi* system (*see* Ideas and perspectives 3.11).

Ideas and perspectives 3.11
The *ringi* system

This is a procedure whereby proposals for new policies, procedures or expenditure are circulated throughout the firm for comment. The proposal is circulated in written form, and is then sent to all who might be affected if it were to be implemented, in ascending order of seniority. The proposal is modified in line with comments, and only when all agree is it implemented. This joint approach to decision-making is also operated through production councils and quality circles, and covers the planning and scheduling of production, work allocation, changes to production methods, problem-solving, etc. (Inagami, 1988). This system of involving large numbers of people in decision-making is the reason why the Japanese are notorious for the slowness with which they make decisions, and famous for their ability to get it right first time (Hannam, 1993; Smith and Misumi, 1989).

As well as aiding decision-making, the *ringi* system has another equally important benefit:

> *The ringi is as much a process for exploring and reaffirming values as it is for setting a direction . . . In the American view objectives should be hard and fast and clearly stated for all to see. In the Japanese view they emerge from a more fundamental process of exploring and understanding the values through which a firm is or should be operating. A knowledge of these values, the limits that are to guide actions, defines a set of possible actions. An action chosen from this set may not be the very best, but it will satisfy parameters deemed crucial for success.*
>
> (Morgan, 1986: 93)

One factor only mentioned briefly so far is the importance – or not – of culture to the Japanese approach to management. Certainly, early studies laid great stress on the relationship between Japanese culture and business success (Abegglen, 1958). The argument emerged that it was the nature of Japanese society and its impact on individuals and companies that gave Japan its competitive edge. For this reason, it was argued, the West would never be able to replicate Japanese practices and competitiveness successfully. Indeed, one reason why Pascale and Athos (1982) chose to study Japanese companies operating in America was that Pascale doubted whether American companies could learn much from the Japanese in Japan because their cultures were so different (Crainer, 1995). Obviously, as Hofstede (1980, 1990) showed, national cultures do impinge on organisational practices. However, whether or not this means that such practices cannot successfully be adopted in other societies is another question. A number of studies have undermined the argument for considering the Japanese approach to management to be dependent on Japanese culture. It has been shown that many of the distinctive practices of Japanese companies are relatively new and not embedded in Japanese history, that the role of culture is less influential than other factors, and that the Japanese approach can be successfully replicated outside Japan (Ackroyd *et al*, 1988; Buckley and Mirza, 1985; Cole, 1979; Marsh and Mannari, 1976; Pascale and Athos, 1982; Smith and Misumi, 1989; Urabe, 1986; Wickens, 1987).

The future of the Japanese approach

In discussing the distinctive Japanese approach to management, we must not forget the strong reciprocal links between government and business, especially the importance of Japanese industrial policy in stimulating and guiding the country's economic progress. This is seen most clearly in the close links between business and the Ministry of International Trade and Industry (MITI). As part of its remit to establish Japan as a leading industrial nation, MITI played a crucial role in establishing national programmes in key industries to encourage joint action, to develop the country's science and technological base, amongst companies and public research institutions. The ultimate goal of these programmes has been to create a strong, competitive and world-class industrial base for Japan. These collaborative programmes have not been at the expense of competition between companies; rather they have helped to improve the competitiveness of all the companies both in relation to each other and, importantly, in relation to international rivals (Laage-Hellman, 1997).

Nevertheless, despite the competitiveness of Japanese firms and the active support of the Japanese government, the economic bubble burst in 1991. After successfully coping with the second oil crisis of 1979 and the effects of a rapidly appreciating currency in the mid-1980s, Japan enjoyed sustained economic growth until the early 1990s. However, since then the economy has been in protracted recession, though it has shown occasional signs of recovery (McCormick, 2007; Statistics Bureau, 2003). Nevertheless, successive banking and political scandals have undermined the stability of the political and financial system on which Japan's industrial might was built (Barrie, 1999; Shirai, 1997). This has led to a flurry of political and business reforms, and attempts to introduce Western-style deregulation in order to foster competition and cut costs.

Many explanations have been put forward for the decline of the Japanese economy. One of the most persuasive is that whilst Japan developed a world-class manufacturing base, this was undermined by a failure to develop the rest of its economy to similar standards (Pilling, 2003). In particular, the service sector, especially retailing, is only half as productive as its US counterparts. Similarly, the Japanese public sector is seen as being far less efficient than its Western equivalents. The banking sector also did the Japanese economy no favours by making vast loans to property companies to purchase over-priced land and buildings, which became worth only a fraction of what they paid for them when the asset bubble burst in the 1990s. This helps to explain why, despite all its economic problems, even in the worst years of the 1990s, Japan's economy, and its leading industrial companies, generally continued to outperform those of its competitors in the West (Pilling, 2003; Shirai, 1997). Therefore, its economic problems over the last decade do not appear to invalidate the Japanese approach to management as developed in, and applied to, the manufacturing sector. However, low growth, domestic recession, increasing international competition, technological developments that have led to changes in industrial and job structures, and an ageing population have all created pressures to change the Japanese approach to management (Harukiyo and Hook, 1998; Sako and Sato, 1997; Thomas, 2003).

In the larger Japanese companies, these pressures have led to structural changes designed to flatten the hierarchy and create greater flexibility (Koji, 1998). In the motor industry, in particular, there has also been a weakening of the previously strong supply chain links, with second- and third-tier suppliers being exposed to greater levels of competition (Masayoshi, 1998). Looking at the Japanese approach to production systems, here too there have been changes; but these do not seem to have radically changed the main characteristic of the Japanese approach, which has been one of blending mass production with flexibility (Masayuki, 1998).

Perhaps the area where the pressures for change have been the greatest is in personnel practices, especially those relating to lifetime employment, seniority-based promotion and rewards systems, and the treatment of female workers (Sako and Sato, 1997). As far as lifetime employment is concerned, there is some evidence that the economic, industrial and technological changes of the 1980s and 1990s have had an effect on this (Barrie, 1999). For white-collar workers, especially the older and higher-paid ones, there is evidence that continuous employment within one enterprise is giving way to continuous employment within a group of enterprises (Inagami, 1995; Sako, 1997). In the past, if a worker's job was eliminated, they would be given another one in the same workplace. Increasingly, the tendency is now to transfer redundant workers to another job within the same group or affiliated group of companies but not necessarily the same workplace. In some cases, this can be hundreds of miles away, and can also involve a reduction in pay (Watts, 1998). However, for blue-collar male workers, where the distinctions between East and West were always the most marked, job security seems to have improved, if anything. This is because of the falling birth rate, which has also led to an increase in the retirement age from 55 to 60 or even 65 (Seike, 1997). Research has also shown that whilst the use of part-time (mainly women) and contract labour may be increasing, job security in this area is also increasing (Wakisata, 1997). Therefore, overall, it appears that stability of employment may actually be increasing. In terms of lifetime employment for male workers, though there have been some changes to the system, it appears that most Japanese corporations have maintained this (McCormick, 2007). Certainly, most Japanese managers, as well as workers, do seem to believe it is desirable and feasible to maintain it, especially as it is seen as essential to manager–worker cooperation (Ohmi, 1997; Sako, 1997; Sugeno and Suwa, 1997). As the Finance Director of a large Japanese corporation commented:

> *To secure our employees living life in good shape is one of the corporation's duties ... We cannot believe in cutting employees to sustain profitability. It is a kind of failed management philosophy.* (Quoted in Barrie, 1999: 13)

In the area of the seniority principle, there does seem to be a greater willingness to make changes. There is growing pressure from both employers and unions to consider other criteria, such as ability, as well as seniority when determining pay and promotion (Sugeno and Suwa, 1997). In a 1995 survey, two-thirds of responding managers saw the introduction of ability-based reward and promotion systems as a priority in order to create greater flexibility, although very few managers seemed prepared to abandon the seniority principle totally (Kawakita, 1997; Sako, 1997). A recent study has confirmed that the seniority principle still applies quite widely in Japan but that meritocracy is on the increase (Fukushige and Spicer, 2007). However, it must be remembered that though seniority plays an important part in promotion and reward, ability has always been taken into account as well. Therefore, what seems to be taking place is fine-tuning of the traditional Japanese reward system rather than its dismantling.

Significant changes do, however, seem to be taking place with regard to female workers (Fukushige and Spicer, 2007). As in the West, there has been a significant increase in the proportion of women in the workforce in Japan in the last 40 years. In 1960, there were 18.1 million working women (40.8 per cent of the adult female population); by 1992, this had grown to 26.2 million (75.4 per cent of the adult female population) (Wakisata, 1997). This growth was accompanied by legal changes to promote equal opportunities and practical assistance with child care arrangements. Like men, women have also benefited from greater security of employment. The average length of service of women workers increased from 4.5 years in 1970 to 7.4 years in 1992; the respective figures for men are 8.8 and 12.5 years. In addition, there seems to be a gradual reduction in the very significant gap between male and female rates of pay: in 1970, women earned on average some 50 per cent of male wage levels; by 1992, this had increased to around 60 per cent. However, for female university graduates in their 20s, the figure was over 90 per cent (Wakisata, 1997). As can be seen, a combination of legal, economic and demographic drivers does seem to have led to a significant rise in gender equality in Japanese workplaces (Fukushige and Spicer, 2007).

Therefore, there have been and remain significant pressures on the Japanese economy, which have led to changes in how companies are structured and run, especially their human resource practices, and in their relations with customers and suppliers (McCormick, 2007; Thomas, 2003). However, these do not seem designed to undermine or alter significantly the core of the Japanese approach to management (Harukiyo and Hook, 1998). The strong ties that bind workers and Japanese enterprises together and which lie at the heart of the Japanese approach to management have not weakened (Sako and Sato, 1997). As Shirai (1997: xv) commented, 'it appears from all the indicators that the foundations of stable labour–management relations in Japan remain unshaken and intact'. Therefore, though there has been much talk of Japan becoming more like the USA in terms of its business practices and personnel policies, recent research suggests that there are still distinct differences between the two countries and that a distinct Japanese model still exists (McCormick, 2007). Indeed, overall, there seems little evidence for the case that globalisation is bringing about the convergence of national cultures and business practices (Leung *et al*, 2005). This does not mean that the Japanese approach to management is not changing – it is; but it is still recognisably a Japanese approach to management and not a Western one (Fukushige and Spicer, 2007).

The Japanese approach: summary and criticisms

It can be seen, therefore, that there are distinctive practices and policies which have a coherence and can be described as 'the Japanese approach to management'. However, it is not simply the merits of the individual practices that have given the Japanese their competitive edge. Rather it is that they are devised and adopted in such a way that they are integrated and mutually supportive of each other; in particular, Japanese companies have a unique way of combining hard and soft practices (Laage-Hellman, 1997; Ouchi, 1981; Pascale and Athos, 1982; Sako and Sato, 1997). This is not to say that this approach is universal in Japan or that all elements are present in those companies that do practise it. However, there is sufficient evidence available to justify stating that it is the dominant approach in Japan at the moment, and has been since at least the 1960s (McCormick, 2007; Smith, 2008).

This does not imply that it will not change. Indeed, given that most of these practices have been evolving over the last 50 years, it would be surprising if they did not continue to evolve (McCormick, 2007; Smith, 2008; Smith and Misumi, 1989; Thomas, 2003; Whitehill, 1991). Already, as described above, there is strong evidence to show that changes are taking place. Even in large companies, such as Toyota and Honda, policies of lifetime employment and the reluctance to recruit staff mid-career are being modified, owing to the need to recruit skills that are in short supply, and because of economic and social pressures. These include especially the pressures for equal opportunities for men and women, the implications of an ageing population, and the need to recruit foreigners (Dawkins, 1993, 1994; Thomas, 1993; Wakisata, 1997).

Nevertheless, although the dynamic and innovative nature of Japanese organisations and their passionate devotion to competitiveness are likely to lead to changes in the way organisations are run, it is unlikely that these changes will undermine the core construct of mutual obligation between organisation and employee that lies at the heart of the Japanese system (McCormick, 2007; Ohmi, 1997; Sako, 1997; Sugeno and Suwa, 1997).

It also seems more than likely that the changes which are taking place and will take place in the future will enhance, rather than detract from, Japan's economic strength.

The Japanese approach has delivered impressive economic results, but there are those who would question the social cost involved. Japanese workers are expected, some would say coerced, to work much longer hours than their Western counterparts, and in addition are expected to participate in many work-related social events (Clark, 1979; Smith, 2008). There is also considerable evidence to show that Japanese workers are less satisfied with their lot than their Western counterparts, especially in relation to working hours and pay (Kamata, 1982; Lincoln and Kalleberg, 1985; Luthans *et al*, 1985; Naoi and Schooler, 1985; Odaka, 1975).

In many respects this is not surprising. From a Western standpoint at least, Japanese companies appear to operate very oppressive and authoritarian regimes that, through the combination of personnel practices and work systems discussed above, together with peer group pressure, leave workers little option but to conform and perform to very high standards (Kamata, 1982; Smith, 2008; Smith and Misumi, 1989). This accounts, in part at least, for the common observation that the Japanese are a nation of workaholics. However, there are other serious criticisms of the Japanese approach:

- Most companies operate a two-tier labour market, whereby a significant minority of the workforce have good conditions and lifetime employment, at the expense of less well-paid and less secure jobs for the majority, especially women. However, there is now some evidence that this is changing, especially for women (Wakisata, 1997).
- Even those with lifetime employment are little more than slaves to the corporation because they cannot move to other jobs (Morgan, 1986; Smith, 2008).
- The merits of teamwork are only gained thanks to the unremitting peer group pressure on individuals continually to improve their performance (Kamata, 1982).
- The lack of independent trade unions leaves workers defenceless in the face of managerial pressure to work ever harder (Kazunori, 1998; Yutaka, 1998). Indeed, chronic overwork has now reached such levels in Japan that cases of death by overwork are common, and the Japanese have now coined an expression for this phenomenon: *karoshi* (Smith, 2008).

Whatever the merits or demerits of the Japanese approach, there is little doubt that it has had an enormous impact on organisational performance; consequently, many attempts have been made to introduce 'Japanisation' into Western companies (Ackroyd *et al*, 1988; Hannam, 1993; McCormick, 2007; Pang and Oliver, 1988; Pascale and Athos, 1982; Schonberger, 1982; Thomas, 2003; Turnbull, 1986). Despite some reservations about how well the system might travel, Japanese companies have shown that they can transfer their approach to the West. Nissan's Sunderland car assembly plant in the UK was judged by the Economist Intelligence Unit to be the most productive in Europe for the second year running in 1998, whilst in the same year its Smyrna, Tennessee plant was cited as the most productive in North America by the Harbour Report.

On the other hand, transferring the Japanese approach to indigenous Western companies appears to have been more problematic. Even the UK car components industry, which, owing to the presence of Nissan, Honda and Toyota, has received more support and encouragement than probably any industry outside Japan, seems to have failed to adopt the Japanese approach successfully (Hines, 1994; Lamming, 1994). This may be a major reason why many companies in the West, whilst not rejecting the lessons of Japanese management *per se*, are now turning to other approaches to increase their competitiveness, especially organisational learning.

Organisational learning

Though Culture–Excellence and the Japanese approach continue to exert a powerful influence over Western companies, in the 1990s a third approach to organisational success came forward to challenge them: organisational learning. Despite its new-found popularity in the 1990s, organisational learning was not a new concept. The highly respected American academic Chris Argyris has been writing about organisational learning for over 40 years (Argyris, 1992). However, there can be no doubt that interest in the concept of organisational learning, or the learning organisation as it is sometimes called, grew considerably in the 1990s. As Crossan and Guatto (1996) noted, there were as many academic papers published on the topic in 1993 as in the whole of the 1980s. Many of these articles are dotted with emotive statements such as 'the rate at which individuals and organizations learn may become the only sustainable competitive advantage' (Stata, 1989: 4). Though statements like this have the power to attract the attention of business leaders, there are really two factors which appear to have moved organisational learning from being a subject for serious academic study to a hot boardroom topic: the pace of change, and the rise of corporate Japan.

There is considerable support for the view that the pace of change is accelerating as never before, and that organisations have to chart their way through an increasingly complex environment. Organisations are having to cope with the pressures of globalisation, climate change, changes in technology, the rise of e-commerce, situations where customers and suppliers can be both competitors and allies, and a change in emphasis from quantity to quality and from products to services. To cope with this growing complexity, organisations are recognising the need to acquire and utilise increasing amounts of knowledge if they are to make the changes necessary to remain competitive (Chawla and Renesch, 1995). As Pautzke (1989) stated:

> *Careful cultivation of the capacity to learn in the broadest sense, i.e. the capacity both to acquire knowledge and to develop practical abilities, seems to offer a realistic way of tackling the pressing problems of our time.*

> (Quoted in Probst and Buchel, 1997: 5)

The second, and perhaps main, factor that generated such interest in organisational learning is the rise of corporate Japan. In attempting to explain and/or combat Japanese penetration of Western markets, many commentators argued that one of the main strengths of Japanese companies is the speed with which they gather information on markets and competitors, and disseminate and act upon this information internally (Nonaka, 1988; Pascale and Athos, 1982). However, Japanese companies' ability to learn, adapt and develop also extended to their commitment to continuous improvement, in processes as well as products, both internally and jointly with customers and suppliers (Laage-Hellman, 1997; Sako and Sato, 1997). The result, as described earlier in this chapter, is their fearsome reputation for producing the right product, in the right time and at the right price.

Underpinning this is an ability to translate a commitment to individual learning into organisational learning (Hedlund and Nonaka, 1993; Nonaka, 1988; Ouchi, 1981; Whitehill, 1991). This idea, that the promotion of collective learning is crucial to organisational success, has not only led to the upsurge in interest in organisational learning, but it also provides a bridge between Western and Eastern approaches to managing organisations. For these reasons, Probst and Buchel (1997: 1) argue that 'Organizational learning offers an alternative paradigm by which systems can change, thus permitting us to redefine the economy and society.'

What is organisational learning?

The term 'organisational learning' is often used interchangeably with the term 'learning organisation'. The difference, according to Tsang (1997: 74–5), is that:

> Organizational learning is a concept used to describe certain types of activity that take place in an organization while the learning organization refers to a particular type of organization in and of itself. Nevertheless, there is a simple relationship between the two – a learning organization is one which is good at organizational learning.

In effect, the difference appears to be between 'becoming' and 'being'. Organisational learning describes attempts by organisations to become learning organisations by promoting learning in a conscious, systematic and synergistic fashion that involves everyone in the organisation. A learning organisation is the highest state of organisational learning, in which an organisation has achieved the ability to transform itself continuously through the development and involvement of all its members (Argyris and Schön, 1978; Burgoyne et al, 1994; Chawla and Renesch, 1995; West, 1994).

A further, and perhaps more significant, distinction between the two terms relates to those who use them. Argyris (1999: 1) asserts:

> We divide the literature that pays attention to organizational learning into two main categories: the practice-oriented, prescriptive literature of 'the learning organization,' promulgated mainly by consultants and practitioners, and the predominately skeptical scholarly literature of 'organizational learning', produced by academics.

In fact the term 'learning organisation' is used much less now than in the 1980s and 1990s. This appears to be because very few organisations, if any, appear to have achieved learning organisation status (Easterby-Smith, 1997; Probst and Buchel, 1997; Tsang, 1997). For this reason, organisational learning now appears to be the term of choice for both the sceptical and prescriptive camps.

Having said that, one of the problems in coming to grips with organisational learning is that its advocates appear to offer a multitude of definitions or models of what it is. Ideas and perspectives 3.12 gives a sample of the definitions that have been advanced, but it is probably not an over-exaggeration to say that there are nearly as many definitions of organisational learning as there are writers on the topic (Tsang, 1997).

Easterby-Smith (1997) attempts to explain this confusion of definitions by identifying the different disciplinary backgrounds of those writing on organisational learning. He argues that most writers come from one of six disciplines: psychology, management science, sociology, organisation theory, production management and cultural anthropology. Wang

Ideas and perspectives 3.12
Organisational learning

Organizational learning is the process by which the organization's knowledge and value base changes, leading to improved problem-solving ability and capacity for action.
(Probst and Buchel, 1997: 15)

A learning organization is an organization skilled at creating, acquiring and transferring knowledge, and at modifying behavior to reflect new knowledge and insights.
(Garvin, 1993: 80)

Organizational learning means the process of improving actions through better knowledge and understanding.
(Fiol and Lyles, 1985: 803)

An entity learns if, through its processing of information, the range of its potential behaviors is changed.
(Huber, 1991: 89)

Organizational learning occurs through shared insight, knowledge and mental models and builds on past knowledge and experience, that is, on memory.
(Stata, 1989: 64)

and Ahmed (2003) note that it is not just the different disciplinary backgrounds of the proponents of organisational learning that leads to confusion. They identify five different focuses on the concept, and argue that researchers tend to centre their attention on only one of these. The five focuses are: 'focus on the collectivity of individual learning; focus on the process or system; focus on culture or metaphor; focus on knowledge management; and focus on continuous improvement' (Wang and Ahmed, 2003: 9).

Like Argyris (1999), Easterby-Smith (1997) also draws attention to the difference between the long-established contributors to the field, the academic sceptics, who have been attempting to analyse, describe and understand learning processes within organisations, without necessarily wishing to change them (e.g. Argyris, 1992; Bateson, 1972), and the relatively newer entrants, the practitioners and consultants, who are attempting to prescribe what an organisation should do to maximise learning (e.g. Pedler *et al*, 1989; Senge, 1990). This is a point also made by Tsang (1997), who notes that, up to the 1980s, it was the analytical writers who dominated the field, but in the 1990s, with the upsurge in interest in organisational learning, it was the prescriptive writers who came to the fore. Though the variety of disciplinary backgrounds and perspectives of those writing about organisational learning helps to explain the plethora of definitions, it does not help to resolve them. For this reason, as Probst and Buchel (1997) state, there is as yet no comprehensive theory of organisational learning. Nevertheless, there is one area where there is growing clarity and agreement: 'In today's environments . . . learning is directed increasingly at transformational change' (Cummings and Worley, 2001: 520). It is the potential of organisational learning to enable organisations to reinvent themselves in order to compete in the changing and increasingly uncertain and competitive environment that is making it such an attractive proposition for many managers.

Although many writers have contributed to the concept of the organisational learning, those who have done most to popularise the concept in the UK are Pedler, Boydell and Burgoyne (1989). Perhaps the most influential writer of the 1990s was Peter Senge in the US, whose book *The Fifth Discipline* (1990) caught the imagination of corporate America. Its success motivated a whole host of consultants and academics to follow suit and produce books and articles extolling the virtues of the learning organisation, and the steps necessary to become one (Tsang, 1997). Part of the success of his book lies in the fact that it combines the individualism of the Culture–Excellence approach with the knowledge-generating ability of the Japanese approach. Senge argues that there are five interrelated disciplines that organisations need to foster amongst individuals and groups in order to promote learning and success (*see* Ideas and perspectives 3.13).

Ideas and perspectives 3.13
Senge's five disciplines

1. **Personal mastery** – individual growth and learning.
2. **Mental models** – deeply ingrained assumptions that affect the way individuals think about people, situations and organisations.
3. **Shared visions** – the development of a common view of the organisation's future.
4. **Team learning** – the shift from individual learning to collective learning.
5. **Systems thinking** – the 'Fifth Discipline' that links the others together and which, he argues, is missing in most organisations:

The art of systems thinking lies in being able to recognize increasingly (dynamically) complex and subtle structures . . . amid the wealth of details, pressures and cross-currents that attend all real management settings. In fact, the essence of mastering systems thinking as a management discipline lies in seeing patterns where others see only events and forces to react to.

Source: Senge (1990: 73)

In contrast to Senge, who stresses the attributes an organisation needs to possess in order to learn, others stress the learning styles of individuals and organisations. Perhaps the most influential in this area are Argyris and Schön (1978) who, building on the work of Bateson (1972), proposed a three-level evolutionary model of learning (*see* Ideas and perspectives 3.14).

Burgoyne (1995) suggests that the importance of learning at Level III, Argyris and Schön's (1978) triple-loop learning, lies as much in its ability to allow an organisation to create and transform its environments as it does in allowing it to transform itself. He also considers that this is reflected in the ability of the organisation to stabilise the context in which it operates and/or its relationship with it. It is at this level that the concept of the learning organisation can fully emerge.

Cummings and Worley (2001) argue that there are a number of learning interventions designed to help an organisation's members move from adaptive, Level I, learning

Ideas and perspectives 3.14
Three levels of learning

- **Level I – single-loop learning.** This is adaptive learning, which involves detecting and rectifying errors or exceptions within the scope of the organisation's existing practices, policies and norms of behaviour in order to ensure its objectives are met. Typical examples of this would be the monitoring of quality standards or adherence to sales targets in order to detect and correct variance. However, this would not feed back into the questioning of, or amendment to, the organisation's original objectives.
- **Level II – double-loop learning.** This goes beyond correcting variance in standards and targets and, instead, involves challenging the appropriateness of the organisation's basic norms, values, policies and operating procedures that create these standards and targets in the first place. This is reconstructive learning, which involves reconstructing basic aspects of an organisation's operations. Typically, this might involve questioning whether some functions should be outsourced rather than continuing to be performed in-house or whether the organisation should adopt a flatter, more open structure to remain aligned with its environment. Out of such changes, new practices, policies and norms of behaviour are generated.
- **Level III – triple-loop learning.** This involves questioning the rationale for the organisation and, in the light of this, radically transforming it. A typical example of this might be a traditional manufacturing organisation attempting to reinvent itself as a service company with all the implications for culture, structure and practices that such a move would require.

Source: Argyris and Schön (1978)

to transformative, Level III, learning. These comprise three phases, but Cummings and Worley (2001: 522–4) warn that:

Although the phases are described linearly below, in practice they form a recurrent cycle of overlapping learning activities.

1. Discover theories in use and their consequences. *This first step involves uncovering members' mental models or theories in use and the consequences that follow from behaving and organizing according to them. . . .*
2. Invent and produce more effective theories in use. *Based on what is discovered in the first phase of this change process, members invent and produce theories in use that lead to more effective actions and that are more closely aligned with [Level II and Level III] learning. . . .*
3. Continually monitor and improve the learning process. *This final phase involves . . . learning how to learn. Here learning is directed at the learning process itself and at how well [Level II and Level III] learning characteristics are reflected in it. This includes assessing OL strategies and the organizational structures and processes that contribute to them.*

Ideas and perspectives 3.15
Promoters of organisational learning

- **Structure** – this needs to be flat and teamwork-based in order to promote networking both internally and externally.
- **Information systems** – these need to be geared toward the rapid acquisition, processing and sharing of information.
- **Human resource practices** – these need to include appraisal and reward systems which promote the acquisition and sharing of new skills and knowledge.
- **Organisational culture** – this needs to be based on values and norms which promote openness, creativity and experimentation in order to support successful learning.
- **Leadership** – managers throughout the organisation must lead, promote and be involved in organisational learning.

Source: Cummings and Worley (2001)

Cummings and Worley (Ideas and perspectives 3.15) also identify five organisational characteristics that promote organisational learning.

Therefore, as can be seen from Ideas and perspectives 3.15, Cummings and Worley identify both the phases that organisations need to go through to move from adaptive to transformational learning, and the characteristics which promote organisational learning. Probst and Buchel (1997: 16), on the other hand, take a very different view, claiming that 'Organizational learning is unique to an institution.' That is to say that each organisation can and should find its own way to become a learning organisation. They argue that there are at least four different generic approaches (*see* Ideas and perspectives 3.16).

Ideas and perspectives 3.16
Approaches to organisational learning

- **Learning by developing a strategy** – shaping the organisation's future through a participative and practical learning exercise.
- **Learning by developing a structure** – developing structural forms, such as matrix and network structures, that promote learning.
- **Learning by developing a culture** – the creation of shared values, norms and attitudes that promote collective success over individual attainment.
- **Learning by developing human resources** – developing staff through participative and group-orientated learning.

Source: Probst and Buchel (1997)

Despite the diversity and contradictions evident among those promoting the concept of organisational learning, one thing is clear: they all see the main purpose of learning as facilitating organisational change. As with the Culture–Excellence and the Japanese approaches, its popularity owes much to its posited beneficial link to organisation performance. However, unlike them, it is the only organisation theory whose main purpose is to enable organisations to cope with and promote change. As Probst and Buchel (1997: xi) comment:

> . . . *learning is attracting increasing attention both in academic circles and business practice. One of the main reasons for this is the increasing pressure of change on companies . . . The rate of change accelerates steadily, and companies must find their bearings in an increasingly complex environment. The ability to learn is thus of paramount importance. Companies which do not successfully implement organizational changes, and which fail to cultivate their potential to develop, may soon find themselves amongst the losers.*

As can be seen, there are considerable arguments in favour of the learning approach; yet there are also arguments against it.

Organisational learning: summary and criticisms

Though there has been considerable interest in the concept of organisational learning, this does not seem to have created the clarity one might have wished for. As Antonacopoulou and Chiva (2007) comment:

> *The OL debate appears to have reached a point of stalemate where little progress seems to be noticeable in terms of some of the prominent questions that still remain unresolved. Although there seems to be some agreement that emotion, power and politics are part of the OL process and support learning in the presence of diversity there is still lack of agreement about how OL takes place and the mechanisms or processes involved, what factors facilitate its development, or what aspects to look for when we investigate OL.*

Consequently, as Huczynski and Buchanan (2001) assert, for every positive statement about organisational learning, one can also find a negative one (*see* Ideas and perspectives 3.17).

It is, therefore, difficult to summarise a concept that has been defined in so many different ways, from so many different perspectives and about which there is so much dispute. However, there are perhaps five aspects of organisational learning that most writers would agree upon:

- An organisation's survival depends on its ability to learn at the same pace as or faster than changes in its environment.
- Learning must become a collective and not just an individual process.
- There must be a fundamental shift towards systems (or triple-loop) thinking by an organisation's members.
- By adopting organisational learning, an organisation not only acquires the ability to adapt quickly and appropriately to changing circumstances, but it can also transform itself if necessary.

Ideas and perspectives 3.17
Organisational learning

Positives	Negatives
A rich, multi-dimensional concept affecting many aspects of organisational behaviour	A complex and difficult set of practices, difficult to implement systematically
An innovative approach to learning, to knowledge management and to investing in intellectual capital	An attempt to use dated concepts from change management and learning theory, repackaged as a management consulting project
A new set of challenging concepts focusing attention on the acquisition and development of individual and corporate knowledge	A new vocabulary for encouraging employee compliance with management directives in the guise of 'self-development'
An innovative approach to organisation, management and employee development	An innovative approach for strengthening management control
Innovative use of technology to manage organisational knowledge through databases and the Internet or intranets	A technology-dependent approach that ignores how people actually develop and use knowledge in organisation

Source: Huczynski and Buchanan (2001: 135)

- As well as the ability to transform itself, an organisation can adapt to, influence and even transform its environment.

Presented in this way, it is easy to appreciate the attractiveness of organisational learning. Nevertheless, Huczynski and Buchanan are not the only ones to draw attention to the more problematic aspects of organisational learning, in fact there are six major criticisms which have been levelled against it; these are as follows:

1. As is apparent from the above review, there is no agreed definition of organisational learning (Burnes *et al*, 2003; Easterby-Smith, 1997; Probst and Buchel, 1997; Tsang, 1997; Wang and Ahmed, 2003). Even Tom Peters (1993: 385), who might be expected to be attracted to the concept, stated that: 'Most talk about "learning organisations" is maddeningly abstract or vague – and perpetually falls short on the specifics.'

2. Despite the volume of publications on the subject, there is a scarcity of rigorous empirical research in the area. As Tsang (1997) pointed out, one of the main reasons for this is that many of those writing on organisational learning are practitioners and consultants seeking to prescribe and sell rather than describe or analyse. He argues that, as well

as promoting the concept, they are also trying to promote themselves and the organisations they work for. A similar point was also made by Easterby-Smith (1997: 1107):

> *Much of the existing research into learning organizations is based on case studies of organizations that are said to be successful, and these sometimes seem to rely more on public relations than on any rigorous and grounded studies.*

If this is the situation, then much of the research on organisational learning, and the recommendations and conclusions that flow from it, have to be treated with a degree of scepticism.

3. As Thompson (1995) pointed out, 'The term organizational learning is actually a misnomer. In fact an organization itself doesn't learn – people learn.' It follows that, in most organisations, the achievement of a high level of organisational learning will necessitate a fundamental shift in how individuals learn. This is not just a case of collecting and sharing information in new ways but, crucially, of thinking in new ways (Argyris and Schön, 1978). This requires individuals to undergo difficult and sometimes painful changes involving unlearning old ways of thinking and the redrawing of their cognitive maps – the way they perceive and make sense of the world around them. Many writers have commented on the serious obstacles to achieving such changes (Argyris, 1990; Hedberg, 1981; Probst and Buchel, 1997; Wang and Ahmed, 2003). However, above and beyond these difficulties lies a further issue. In engineering such changes in an individual's thought processes, it is not just their perception of the organisation that is being changed, but their perception of the world outside work and how they relate to it and to others around them. What are being tampered with are deep-rooted personality traits and constructs that are fundamental to an individual's psychological make-up. In such cases, one has to question not only the extent to which such attempts can ever be successful, but also whether it is even ethically justifiable to try.

4. Probst and Buchel (1997) maintain that organisational learning requires the generation of diversity of opinion and, at the same time, the creation of consensus. They argue that these contradictory tasks can be reconciled and achieved through the development of a collective view of reality. Their view assumes that it is in everyone's interest to participate in organisational learning and the ensuing changes. Although some writers, especially Argyris (1990) and Easterby-Smith *et al* (2000) recognise that there are major barriers to organisational learning, the assumption is that these can be overcome. However, as Chapter 1 demonstrated, much of our organisational experience since the Industrial Revolution has shown that managers view knowledge and control as almost synonymous. To this end, managers have systematically attempted to reduce workers' knowledge and increase their own (Rose, 1988). As will be discussed further in Chapter 5, organisations are riven by political battles, and the possession and selective use of knowledge is a potent weapon in such situations (Pfeffer, 1981). Beyond that, however, many traditional managers are unlikely to welcome the creation of organisations which encourage openness, and allow subordinates to seek out their own knowledge and question the expertise and authority of their superiors. As Garratt (1999: 205) put it:

> *A few, often senior, people can see the concept as highly challenging and unnerving. They are concerned that existing organisational power balances may be upset by too much 'transparency' . . .*

Given what we know about resistance to change, given what we know about power and politics in organisations, it is surprising, as Blackler and McDonald (2000) and Coopey and Burgoyne (2000) note, that so little attention has been paid to these issues by those investigating and promoting organisational learning.

5. Though Japanese companies are often held up as exemplars of organisational learning, most theory and practical advice in this area has been developed in the West, especially the US. The proponents of organisational learning argue that the recipes they have developed are applicable to all organisations and cultures; nevertheless, many writers have drawn attention to the problem of transferring theories and practices developed in one culture to another (Deresky, 2000; Fagenson-Eland *et al*, 2004; Hedlund and Nonaka, 1993; Hofstede, 1993; Rosenzweig, 1994; Thomas, 2003; Trompenaars, 1993). For example, openness and the encouragement of public debate and criticism are seen as an essential part of organisational learning (Chawla and Renesch, 1995). Although US managers might not find this too difficult to accept, it is doubtful whether, for example, Japanese or Chinese managers, with their tradition of preserving face, would find it so easy (Deresky, 2000). Face involves both maintaining one's own dignity and decorum and, at the same time, not undermining or attacking the dignity and decorum of others. Therefore, Japanese and Chinese managers, and managers from other non-Western countries, might find it very difficult openly to challenge and criticise the behaviour and ideas of others or for others to do this to them (Ho, 1976; Jones *et al*, 2000; Tsang, 1997). Similarly, as was noted in the previous chapter, proponents of Contingency Theory argued against universal approaches to organisational effectiveness and in favour of a context-based approach (Burns and Stalker, 1961; Woodward, 1965; Child, 1984). In particular, they maintain that theories and practices developed with one sort of organisation or situation in mind may be much less effective in a different set of circumstances (Burnes, 1991).

6. Burnes *et al* (2003) point out that the case for the general adoption of organisational learning is based on the assumption that all organisations operate in a fast-moving and unpredictable environment. In such a situation, the ability to learn and adapt must be possessed by all members of the organisation and not just a few at the top. Burnes *et al* argue that this may be the case for companies in the IT sector, but other sectors may experience a much lower level of environmental disturbance. Also, they maintain, even in fast-moving sectors such as IT, there are companies, such as Microsoft, whose dominant position allows them a degree of predictability and stability (Coupland, 1995; Wallace and Erickson, 1992). In addition, Burnes *et al* pose the question: if an organisation can develop the ability to transform its environment, what is to stop it creating an environment where organisational learning is unnecessary? After all, given the many obstacles and barriers to developing and maintaining organisational learning, this would appear an attractive proposition.

Given the intense debate over the nature and utility of organisational learning, we can perhaps agree with Probst and Buchel (1997: xi) who warn that:

We should be wary of dismissing it [organisational learning] as the latest fad, since the topic of learning is attracting increasing attention both in academic circles and in business practice.

However, we can perhaps also agree with Mintzberg *et al*'s (1998b: 228) double-edged compliment that:

> . . . *[organisational learning] is all the rage right now, and mostly for good reasons. But it is no panacea for anything. People have to learn, but they also have to get on with doing the regular work efficiently. (Horses wear blinders for good reasons.) There can be a time to learn and a time to exploit previous learning . . . So learning is wonderful, but there can be too much of a wonderful thing!*

Conclusions

This chapter has examined the three main approaches to managing and structuring organisations that have dominated Western thinking and practice over the last three decades. The proponents of all three approaches claim that theirs is a new paradigm that contrasts sharply and favourably with the organisational theories discussed in Chapters 1 and 2. This does not mean there are not some similarities with what has gone before. For example, the Japanese use the industrial engineering concepts developed by Taylor and his contemporaries to study and design jobs. However, the context in which they are deployed (the lack of payment by results, the use of teamwork and worker involvement, and above all else, guaranteed jobs) is markedly different. In a similar way, the Culture–Excellence approach can be seen to bear some similarities with the Human Relations movement, especially in its emphasis on leadership and communication. However, the emphasis on culture, individual achievement and all-round excellence make it a distinct approach. The same can be said of organisational learning, which builds on, but develops in a wider context, past practices for encouraging individual and group learning.

There are also points of contact between the three approaches themselves. Organisational learning consciously draws on the methods used by the Japanese to gather and use information speedily. In addition, it stresses, as with Culture–Excellence, the importance of individuals in promoting innovation. However, it also clashes with the other two approaches. Advocates of organisational learning stress that it can enable companies to shape and create their environment, whilst supporters of Culture–Excellence stress that organisations have no choice but to adapt to their environment. It is at odds with the Japanese approach in terms of change. The Japanese favour directed continuous incremental change, whereas the organisational learning approach encourages continuous but often undirected adaptation and also transformational change.

There are also points of contact between the Japanese approach and the Culture–Excellence approach (the emphasis on excellence, the importance of culture); but, again, there are marked differences. Lifetime employment and loyalty to the organisation contrast strongly with the stress on the transient nature of jobs proposed by the proponents of Culture–Excellence. As an example, contrast the threat to thousands of jobs posed by the merger of the Halifax and Leeds Building Societies in the UK (in order to form the UK's fourth largest bank) with the case of the merger of the Mitsubishi Bank and the Bank of Tokyo in Japan (to form the world's largest bank), where it was stated that maintaining all jobs was a matter of honour (Hughes, 1995; Rafferty, 1995). Likewise, payment by seniority and payment by performance are significant points of departure (though there is an increasing, but still small-scale, use of performance pay in Japan). It is noticeable as well that neither the Culture–Excellence nor the organisational learning approach really concerns itself with the sort of hard, manufacturing and quality practices so common in Japan.

Finally, the Culture–Excellence school seems obsessed with downsizing and arguing for smallness. The Japanese, on the other hand, are committed to growth. As Ferguson (1988: 57) remarked, in the 1970s and 1980s the USA was not outperformed by small, nimble organisations, but by 'high industrial complexes embedded in stable, strategically-co-ordinated alliances often supported by protectionist governments'.

On balance, though there are similarities, these three approaches conflict with, rather than complement, each other. The Japanese approach, with its combination of tried-and-tested hard and soft techniques, provides a coherent and comprehensive approach to organisations which stresses both innovation and stability. The Culture–Excellence approach tends to emphasise soft techniques, innovation, dynamism and unpredictability, and, particularly, draws attention to the role of culture. Organisational learning, as an attempt to provide a coherent paradigm for organisational competitiveness, is the newest and least concrete of the three. At one level it has affinities with the other two approaches, but its emphasis on learning as the principal source of competitiveness also distinguishes it from them. This does not mean that if Western organisations become more adept at adopting Total Quality Management and other such techniques, and if Japanese companies broaden their use of external labour markets and adopt more flexible structures, the three may not coalesce, especially given the common emphasis on learning. At the moment, however, they remain competitors rather than collaborators.

Needless to say, none of the three approaches is without its drawbacks or criticisms. In particular, there are five concerns that should be highlighted, relating to 'one best way', people, politics, culture and change management.

One best way

The first three chapters of this book have been concerned with approaches to managing and structuring organisations. The one clear message that has emerged so far is to beware of any theory or proposition which claims that it is the 'one best way' for all situations and all organisations. Yet all three of the approaches we have discussed in this chapter appear to advocate just that.

People

The Culture–Excellence and Japanese approaches also leave much to be desired with regard to people. Both approaches rely on a workforce split into a privileged core and a relatively unprivileged periphery. Under both approaches there is a strong emphasis on commitment to the organisation taking precedence over all else, even family life. Therefore, long hours and short holidays are the norm under both systems. The Japanese approach appears to offer more job security, at least for the privileged core. However, the price of this is that competition for jobs in the better organisations begins, quite literally, at birth. To get a job with the best companies, applicants have to have been to the best universities; to enter those, they have to have been at the best schools; and to enter the best schools, they have to have been at the best nurseries (Bratton, 1992; Fruin, 1992). The lack of clarity of the organisational learning concept makes it difficult to be certain what the implications of it are for people. However, it does project an intensity of work and commitment that aligns it with the Culture–Excellence approach. Also, its emphasis on restructuring individuals' cognitive processes in order to overcome their resistance to learning is, potentially at least, very worrying. Therefore, taking all three approaches together, one cannot escape the conclusion that the social cost of achieving excellence, in either West or East, is high.

Politics

The issue of organisational power and politics has received extensive attention over the last 30 years (Buchanan and Badham, 1999; Dawson, 2003; Huczynski and Buchanan, 2001; Kotter, 1982; Minett, 1992; Pfeffer, 1992; Willcocks, 1994; Yammarino and Dansereau, 2002) and will be explored in Chapter 5. Given that organisations are social entities and not machines, power struggles and political infighting are inevitable. They may not always be prominent, but tend to come to the fore in situations where resources are scarce or organisations are in transition (Morgan, 1986). It is perhaps here that Peters and Waterman, with their notion of total openness and trust to the extent of employees effectively allowing others to monitor their work, could most easily be accused of being out of touch with reality. There is a tendency in the West to treat politics and conflict as illegitimate; but, as Pascale (1993) and Thompkins (1990) argued, conflict is part and parcel of the creative process, and political skills may be a key competence for managers if they are to be successful leaders and persuaders. To ignore the presence of conflict or underestimate its tenacity is usually a recipe for disaster (Kanter *et al*, 1992; McLennan, 1989; Pfeffer, 1992; Robbins, 1986).

However, in the Japanese, Organisational Learning and Culture–Excellence approaches, little is said on the subject of organisational politics and conflict. As far as the Culture–Excellence and organisational learning perspectives are concerned, there appears to be an assumption that employees working in smaller business units, having greater autonomy and more satisfying jobs, will work with each other, pursuing a common purpose. As Chapter 5 will show, this is perhaps an unrealistic expectation. It may well be that in Japanese organisations, with their consensual and open approach to decision-making, strong commitment to organisational goals, high peer group pressure and, for some at least, lifetime employment, conflict is either minimised or channelled into creative directions; though Ishizuna (1990), Kamata (1982) and Sakai (1992) have shown that this is not always the case. However, in the West, with companies reshaping their businesses, where job security is being eroded, where an individual's current performance outweighs all other considerations, and where only the fittest and fleetest of foot can expect to survive, it is foolish to deny or underestimate the importance of power and politics or to believe that culture can act as a cure-all.

Culture

This brings us to the next concern to which these three approaches give rise. Proponents of all three approaches treat culture in a rather simplistic fashion. For the Culture–Excellence school, all problems are resolved through the creation of strong, flexible, pragmatic cultures which promote the values of trust, cooperation and teamwork. A similar point can also be made with regard to the creation of a learning culture. In neither approach is there any real discussion or acknowledgement of the difficulties in defining or changing culture, despite much evidence to the contrary (Allaire and Firsirotu, 1984; Schein, 1985; Wilson, 1992). Nor do those who seek to promote the Japanese approach treat the subject of culture any more thoroughly. Either it is portrayed as an immutable feature of Japanese companies which prevents the West from adopting the Japanese approach or, more frequently these days, the Japanese approach is seen as somehow independent of culture (Sheldrake, 1996; Smith and Misumi, 1989). Very few writers acknowledge that Japanese companies, like their Western counterparts, can find themselves with apparently inappropriate cultures that they wish to change (Ishizuna, 1990). Therefore, all three approaches clearly leave themselves open to the accusation that they gloss over the difficulty of changing culture. The role of organisational culture will be examined in Chapter 5.

Change management

There is one last issue that should be touched on: the management of change. Organisation theories are also theories of change. Most organisation theories claim to show organisations how to identify where they are and where they should be. They also, either explicitly or implicitly, address the issue of change management.

For the Classical school, change management is relatively easy: it tells organisations what they should be and, because managers and workers are rational beings, they should accept any concomitant changes because it's the logical thing to do! A similar approach is adopted by the Contingency theorists. The Human Relations movement, on the other hand, sees change as more problematic. Organisations are social systems, change is not a rational process, emotions come into play as well. Therefore, persuasion and leadership play a key role in changing organisations.

The Culture–Excellence approach has little to say about how change should be achieved, despite acknowledging the radical transformation it is advocating. Peters (1993) advocated a 'Big Bang' approach to change: 'change radically and do it quickly' seems to be his advice. Handy (1986), on the other hand, seemed to adopt a more gradualist approach to change – big changes over long periods. Kanter *et al* (1992) advocated a combination of both; they argue that major changes, especially in behaviour, can only be achieved over time. However, they also believe that dramatic gestures are also necessary to improve performance in the short term. Therefore, their approach to change is a combination of 'Bold Strokes and Long Marches'. Taken as a whole, the message from the Culture–Excellence school is somewhat mixed and the process and details are lacking, notwithstanding Kanter *et al*'s (1992) book on change.

Though organisational learning is explicitly directed at enabling organisations to change, its proponents are vague and inconsistent in specifying how one leads to the other, and particularly how the ultimate goal, of becoming a learning organisation, can be achieved (Probst and Buchel, 1997). Nor is it clear how the plethora of change initiatives generated by learning will lead to effective, coordinated and complementary overall change (Easterby-Smith, 1997; Tsang, 1997).

The Japanese approach, however, is more specific. Proponents of the Japanese approach advocate creating a vision of the future and moving towards it in incremental steps (*Kaizen*) at all levels of the organisation. The Japanese are extremely able at this process, which has given them a reputation as a nation that makes ambitious long-term plans which are slowly, relentlessly and successfully achieved. However, it is debatable whether this approach could work in many Western countries. In the USA and UK in particular, competitive pressures appear to require radical change over a short timescale, and at the same time there appears to be a built-in aversion to long-term thinking, especially amongst the financial institutions that play a pivotal role in the life of most firms.

Therefore, though the Organisational Learning, Japanese and Culture–Excellence approaches have their strong points, they also have their drawbacks, at least as far as Western companies are concerned. For this reason, none has achieved the same intellectual dominance enjoyed by past paradigms, though the Culture–Excellence approach has come to exert a powerful influence on managerial attitudes and behaviour over the past two decades. However, this lack of a dominant paradigm is not necessarily a cause for despair. Developing paradigms by their very nature will contain dilemmas and contradictions that can only be resolved with experience and the passage of time. This is not a case for ignoring them; rather the reverse. The future is not, hopefully, immutable. Managers are not powerless: they do have some freedom of choice and action, and the possibility does exist to influence the future shape of work by promoting the good and avoiding the bad.

Parts 2 and 3 of this book will further consider managerial choice and the degree to which organisations are free to shape their own future. Before moving on to this, however, the final two chapters in Part 1 will round off the review of organisation theory by examining, in Chapter 4, the case for and alternatives to the postmodern perspective on organisations and, in Chapter 5, the role of culture, power and politics in constraining and enabling organisational choice.

Test your learning

Short answer questions

1. What is a paradigm?

2. Why did *In Search of Excellence* become an instant best-seller when it was first published?

3. List the main tenets of the Culture–Excellence approach.

4. What is a Shamrock organisation?

5. What are the main personnel and business issues that make up Japanese Management?

6. What are seen as the main benefits of the Japanese approach?

7. Define organisational learning.

8. State the key arguments in favour of organisational learning.

9. For each of the following, briefly state its implications for organisational change: (a) Culture–Excellence, (b) the Japanese approach and (c) organisational learning.

Essay questions

1. What are the main similarities and differences between the Culture–Excellence approach and Japanese Management?

2. What are the core tenets of organisational learning and what difficulties might an organisation encounter in introducing it?

Suggested further reading

1. Peters, TJ and Waterman, RH (1982) *In Search of Excellence: Lessons from America's Best-Run Companies*. Harper & Row: London.

   In order to capture the essence of Culture–Excellence, there is no better book to read than the one that began it all.

2. Wilson, DC (1992) *A Strategy of Change*. Routledge: London.

   David Wilson's book provides a pithy and critical analysis of the shortcomings of the Culture–Excellence approach.

3. Sheldrake, J (1996) *Management Theory: From Taylorism to Japanization*. International Thompson Business Press: London.

   John Sheldrake provides a brief but good review of the work of Charles Handy and also of the rise of Japanese Management.

4. A more comprehensive review of Japanese management can be found in Sako, M and Sato, H (eds) (1997) *Japanese Labour and Management in Transition*. Routledge: London.

5. Probst, G and Buchel, B (1997) *Organizational Learning*. Prentice Hall: London.

   For a brief, comprehensive and comprehensible look at organisational learning, this book is excellent.

CASE STUDY 3

The transformation of XYZ Construction

PHASE 1 – CULTURE CHANGE

Background: XYZ Construction employs 500 staff and is part of a European-based multinational enterprise. Its main business is the provision of specialist services to major construction projects. As is typical for the construction industry, XYZ operates in a highly competitive and at times hostile and aggressive environment. Disputes between contractors and subcontractors can become bitter and frequently end in litigation, though there have been a number of attempts over the last decade to create better relationships. Just as relationships between organisations tended to be hostile, so relationships within organisations were also less than friendly. Up to 1996, XYZ had been run by an autocratic Managing Director who was feared by his colleagues and who treated the company as his own personal fiefdom. His style of management was not liked and many felt that it was counterproductive but, as one manager commented, 'You didn't challenge him, you didn't put your head above the parapet, or he'd make life hell for you.' When he retired, the parent company took the view that XYZ was underperforming and that much of this was due to poor management and a lack of cooperation within the company. His replacement was appointed with the remit to improve the performance of the company and develop its managerial competency. This he did to great effect. Over a four-year period, he transformed the operation, culture and structure of the organisation.

Focusing on people and performance: The new Managing Director was appointed in 1996. He had trained as an engineer at XYZ but had then left and worked for a number of other companies in the construction industry. Construction is a close-knit industry, however, and he still knew XYZ and its staff quite well. He came with a reputation as an enlightened manager who could deliver performance improvements. The construction industry was notorious for the antagonistic relations between the main contractors and subcontractors such as XYZ, who specialise in one aspect of the construction process. The Managing Director recognised, however, that the industry was attempting to change, and conflict was being replaced by 'partnership' initiatives – contractors and subcontractors working in a more cooperative and team-based manner (Burnes and Coram, 1999). The Managing Director also recognised that external partnerships needed internal partnerships and teamworking if they were to be successful. In turn this would require a new style of participative management in XYZ. Therefore, the Managing Director set out not just to upgrade XYZ's management but to undertake a root-and-branch overhaul of the company's operations and culture.

As a signal of his way of working, as a first step in creating better relationships amongst managers, he broadened out the Senior Management Team to include key staff who were not directors. In what had been a very hierarchical and status-conscious company, this was a significant change. The Managing Director knew that the staff in the company,

particularly at a senior level, were experienced and competent people. He believed it was in the company's interest to retain staff rather than replace them. However, he also believed that they would need to change their attitudes and behaviours and upgrade their managerial skills if the company was to achieve the changes he believed were necessary. His strategy for transforming the company rested on carrying out two crucial activities in parallel: to introduce new practices and techniques into the company in order to provide a better service to customers (and thus improve the company's overall performance), and to change attitudes and behaviours within the company, especially those of managers. He did not see these as being separate activities or pro-grammes: he saw them as being linked. New practices, such as customer care and customer partnering, were not mere technical exercises. They required behavioural changes and new managerial skills. Therefore, the Managing Director wanted to create a change programme whereby any change designed to improve the organisation's performance, whether it be new skills, new techniques or whatever, also had to promote and reinforce behavioural and culture change. The converse was also the case: any effort designed to change culture or behaviour also had to have the objective of improving the organisation's performance.

Between 1996 and 2000, the company undertook a series of organisational, management and staff development initiatives designed collectively to transform the organisation's performance and culture. The main initiatives are as follows:

Date	Event
June 1996	New Managing Director appointed
August 1996	*Kaizen* Phase 1
October 1996	Customer Care Programme launched

CASE STUDY 3 CONT.

Date	Event
March 1997	Investors in People launched
April 1997	*Kaizen* Phase 2
September 1997	Customer Care Programme extended to construction sites
January 1998	Construction Supervisors' new role launched
June 1998	New Senior Management Team formed
November 1998	*Kaizen* Phase 3
March 1999	Site-based trainers appointed
June 1999	XYZ culture redefined
July 1999	Leadership and behaviours review

The Managing Director's first initiative was to introduce a small-scale *Kaizen* programme. *Kaizen* is a Japanese technique for achieving small-scale improvements through teamwork (Witzel, 2002). The Managing Director saw his *Kaizen* initiative as delivering four benefits: it would show the organisation that improvements could be achieved on a quick low-cost/no-cost basis; it would promote teamworking; it would give managers confidence to delegate to and empower their staff; and it would allow both staff and managers to acquire new skills. In a traditional company such as XYZ, it was not easy to introduce new ideas and new ways of working, especially where managers might perceive them as a threat. But the Managing Director made it clear he was committed to this initiative and that it had to work. Over the next few years the *Kaizen* approach was rolled out throughout the organisation.

The next initiative, in October 1996, was a customer care programme. This was designed to engender a positive view of customers by promoting joint teamworking. In an industry where antagonism between customers and suppliers (contractor and subcontractors) was the order of the day, where settling disputes through the courts was almost a standard practice, it was never going to be easy to promote customer care. The Managing Director knew, however, that the future of the company depended on working with customers to understand what they wanted and to give it to them. Once again, this initiative was a combination of organisational change and management development; but, much more than the *Kaizen* initiative, it was also central to changing the culture of the organisation. It began with a few key customers and a few key managers, but such was its perceived success that a year later it was extended to the actual construction sites.

Other initiatives were introduced over the next few years, including Investors in People, and a redesigning of the Construction Supervisors' role to ensure that the post-holders possessed the skills, competencies and behaviours necessary to work closely with customers and staff under the new regime. Once again this was designed to achieve a combination of aims, including changes to working practices, the upgrading of managerial competency on the construction sites, and the promotion and development of a more team-based culture in the organisation.

By the end of 1999, the Managing Director felt the company had made sufficient changes to its behaviour and practices to believe its culture was very much different from when he took over in 1996. However, he felt that the new culture needed to be formalised and consolidated. Therefore, he initiated a company-wide review of each manager's leadership abilities and behaviours in order to ensure they were compatible with and promoted the new culture. However, he was aware that the basic structure of the company was unchanged and that he would need to address this issue in the near future (*see* Case Study 8 at the end of Chapter 8).

Questions

1. Evaluate and comment upon the extent to which XYZ can be said to have adopted the Culture–Excellence approach to running its business.

2. The transformation of XYZ appears to have taken place with very little resistance or opposition from staff and managers. Discuss why this should be so.

3. To what extent and why do you agree with the following statement: the new Managing Director has not changed the culture of XYZ but has merely introduced a new management style.

CHAPTER 4

Critical perspectives on organisation theory

Postmodernism, realism and complexity

Learning objectives

After studying this chapter, you should be able to:

- discuss the contribution of postmodernism to organisational theory;
- list the strengths and shortcomings of postmodernism with regard to the design and management of organisations;
- understand the main tenets of the realist perspective;
- discuss the strengths and weaknesses of the realist perspective for organisations;
- describe the influence of complexity theories on our understanding of organisations;
- state the main advantages and disadvantages of the complexity approach to organisations;
- appreciate the limitations of rational approaches to organisations;
- comprehend how postmodernism, realism and complexity widen the scope for organisational choice.

Mini Case Study 4.1
Realism replaces grand visions

How we let down the diligent folk at the Halifax

I once gave away more money than Andrew Carnegie or Bill Gates. Ten years ago, as a director of the Halifax Building Society I authorised the distribution of almost £20bn to its 8m members on flotation of the business. Last week, the story reached a sad denouement and much of the windfall slipped away. The organisation, now part of HBOS, agreed to a rescue bid from Lloyds TSB.

The business I joined gathered deposits from small savers, mostly through its branches. It lent the proceeds to house buyers. Founded as a self-help organisation by provident Yorkshire folk 150 years ago, the Halifax became the world's largest mortgage lender. Its quality of service and competitive interest rates trounced conventional banks in the UK retail savings market. The simple business model was very robust. In the early 1990s, a combination of high interest rates, recession and falling house prices posed much more serious problems for UK homeowners than anything seen, or likely, in the current credit crunch. But the Halifax remained profitable and mortgages readily available.

Accepting deposits and underwriting and administering mortgages requires that millions of records should be maintained and updated every day with almost no errors. This activity does not require flair or imagination but does require conscientious individuals with integrity and loyalty. The Halifax was a precision machine that made the most of the talents of ordinary people. I came to understand the fundamental incompatibility of the cultures of retail and investment banking and why the marriage of the two so often leads to tears.

The road to nemesis began, not at conversion, but earlier – on the day it was decided that treasury should be a profit centre in its own right rather than an ancillary activity. Legal restrictions on UK mortgage lenders were relaxed in 1986. Halifax's main rival, Abbey, converted to a public company and leveraged its deposit base to build a large balance sheet. Most bankers were incredulous that the Halifax had been so slow to take advantage of this opportunity.

For an economist who taught that profit could be sustained only as a result of competitive advantage, this diversification raised a simple question. Some businessmen on the board, accustomed to a world in which profit is earned only by meeting customer needs, saw the same difficulty. Trading in short-term money market instruments is essentially a zero-sum game – one party's gain is another's loss. So what was the source of the trading profits that not just our company, but every company in this business, claimed to make? The experienced bankers would shake their heads at this naivety. If they deigned to answer the question at all, it was to say that our traders were uniquely perceptive and prescient, although it was difficult to remain convinced of that once you had met them. Large banks derived an informational advantage from the volume of business they transacted for their main customers. But it was hard to understand why those customers tolerated it, or how newcomers could muscle in.

Most apparently successful trading strategies involve what I now call Taleb processes, after Nassim Taleb's book The Black Swan. A series of small profits is punctuated by occasional large losses. Then cognitive dissonance combines with short memories. The profits are attributed to successful trading, the losses are the result of unforeseeable events.

There, in a nutshell, is the story of the credit crunch. And there is the story of how a business that had grown for 150 years forfeited its independence. When the dust settles, many banks and hedge funds will have lost more money on their trading activities in the past year or so than they had made in their entire history. Those conscientious people who process deposits and issue mortgages are still there, though many have had the worst weekend of their lives. The business they do continues to make money. Customers mostly remain loyal. The pursuit of shareholder value damaged both shareholder value and the business. We let them all down.

Source: John Kay, *Financial Times*, 24 September 2008, p. 13.

Introduction

It is now commonly believed that our world is changing significantly and that we are entering a new era (Berkeley Thomas, 2003; Cooper and Jackson, 1997; Deresky, 2000; Giddens, 2002; Handy, 1997; Hardaker and Graham, 2002; Hatch and Cunliffe, 2006; IBM, 2008; Kanter, 2006; Peters, 2006). Whether we refer to this development as 'the Information Age', 'the Age of the Internet', 'the Age of Innovation', 'the Age of Unreason', 'Post Industrial Society', 'the Postmodern Age' or 'Globalisation', the message is the same: what worked in the past will not work in the future, and organisations, like society at large, will have to change in unprecedented and unanticipated ways if they are to survive. However, despite all this talk of a brave new world, in the wake of the oil crisis and credit crunch, more and more companies are searching for some form of twenty-first century financial realism and rejecting the grand visions of easy money which dominated the last 20 years or so. As Kay's description of the demise of the Halifax Building Society, Mini Case Study 4.1, illustrates, the leaders of many financial institutions appeared to have lost touch with reality in their belief that huge profits could be made by creating and packaging debt into esoteric and little-understood financial instruments such as derivatives that few understood and which ultimately proved worthless. As with the DotCom collapse in 2000, reality eventually caught up with the financial institutions, many of which, like the Halifax, went out of business or were taken over at a fraction of their previous market value. As a recent Financial Times (2007: 15) headline put it: *Dreams are no basis for a sound corporate strategy*. Of course, there are many in the financial sector who will argue that their grand visions were realistic and that the post-credit crunch reality will prove too pedestrian and lacking in ambition. In a sense, this sums up the problem many organisations now face, in a world of competing realities, whose reality should they believe? This chapter will examine three critical perspectives on organisation theory with a view to understanding how they view 'reality' and the implications of their differing views for organisations.

The previous three chapters have described the development of organisations and organisation theory from the Industrial Revolution through to the present day, in order to show the various approaches to and options for designing and running organisations so as to meet the challenges they face. What has emerged is a somewhat confusing picture of theories which claim, each in their own way, to be the answer to all organisational ills, yet which are all open to potentially damning criticisms. All the theories we have examined claim to give practical and coherent advice to managers on how to structure and run their organisations. Yet, as Ideas and perspectives 4.1 shows, it is in their limited applicability to the range and complexity of situations found in everyday organisational life that these theories are most open to criticism.

This, and the following chapter, which is devoted to an examination of culture, power and politics, will address the issues raised in Ideas and perspectives 4.1, especially the final three points. This chapter examines three important and critical perspectives on organisations: postmodernism, realism, and complexity (*see* Ideas and perspectives 4.2, 4.3 and 4.4).

Ideas and perspectives 4.1
Criticisms of organisation theories

- The tendency to assume a unitary frame of reference, in which the interests of workers and managers, blue-collar and white-collar staff, and people of different genders, ethnicity and religions either coincide or can be easily reconciled, is a clear shortcoming in all these theories.
- The belief of the Classical school and the Human Relations movement that contextual factors – the external environment, size, technology, etc. – are either irrelevant or easily accommodated is another obvious flaw.
- The assumption by both the Contingency theorists and the proponents of Culture–Excellence that managers are powerless to change the situational variables they face, and have no choice but to accept the prevailing recipe for success, is not borne out in reality.
- There is a growing scepticism regarding the ability of rational, objective science to provide an explanation for the many and fundamental changes taking place in organisations and the wider society.
- One of the most serious drawbacks is that only the Culture–Excellence school, and to a lesser extent the organisational learning and Japanese approaches, give any importance to the role of organisational culture – and even then it is treated in a simplistic fashion.
- None of the theories gives serious consideration to the role of power and politics in influencing decision-making in organisations. Not only does this go against a great deal of research that has been produced over the last 20 years, but it also runs counter to most people's own experience of organisational life.
- Lastly, these theories explicitly or implicitly reject the notion of choice. Their basic argument is that organisations need to follow 'their' recipe for success or they will fail. Yet, if we look at the population of organisations, we can see a vast variety of approaches to their design and management. Some, for periods of time at least, may seem more successful than others, but most organisations appear capable of surviving whether they adopt the current recipe in full, in part or totally reject it.

Ideas and perspectives 4.2
Postmodernism

This is a loosely defined philosophical movement which, though originally based in the arts, has become increasingly influential in the social sciences over the last 25 years. It is a way of looking at the world that rejects rationality and objectivity. Instead, it concentrates on the ways in which human beings attempt to shape reality and invent their world. Therefore, for postmodernists, reality is socially constructed and for this reason, there is not one reality but multiple realities.

Ideas and perspectives 4.3
Realism

Like postmodernism, realism is a philosophical doctrine that was first applied to the arts but has in the last decade been taken up by organisation theorists. Also like postmodernists, realists believe that reality is socially constructed. But, unlike the postmodernists, realists reject the notion of multiple realities. The essence of realism is that there is only one reality and it exists even if we have not yet discovered it. They see both the natural and social worlds as consisting of complex structures which exist even if we are not aware of them or how they influence our behaviour. For realists, events and patterns of events are generated or caused by mechanisms and powers that exist independently of the events they generate. Therefore, realists do not deny the ability of human beings to shape their world, but they see this ability as being limited by an ensemble of real and concrete structures, practices and conventions in society.

Ideas and perspectives 4.4
Complexity

Contrary to postmodernism and realism, complexity arose from the natural sciences before being taken up by social scientists. Complexity theories are concerned with how order is created in dynamic non-linear systems. In particular, those applying this approach to organisations maintain that successful organisations need to operate at the 'edge of chaos' and can only maintain this position by the presence of appropriate order-generating rules.

The chapter concludes by arguing that, whilst these three approaches differ significantly, what they have in common is that they open up the prospect that organisations have choices in what they do and how they do it. Rather than being the prisoners of organisation theories or contingencies, managers (potentially) have considerable, though by no means unconstrained, freedom of choice over the structure, policies and practices of their organisations, and even over the environment in which they operate. This then leads on, in Chapter 5, to an examination of the role of culture, power and politics in the identification, shaping and pursuit of choices.

The postmodern perspective

From modernism to postmodernism?

As was described in Chapter 3, a sea change has taken place over the last 30 years in terms of how we view organisations. The Culture–Excellence model, the Japanese approach and organisational learning all have links with the past but they also represent a break with what has gone before. Running alongside these developments and to a large extent giving them a theoretical respectability, albeit mainly an unacknowledged one, is the view that we have moved from the modern to the postmodern world (Boje, 2006).

For Alvesson and Deetz (1996: 191–2), it was the changing nature of work and competition in the 1980s that forced organisation theorists to question existing and entrenched assumptions about the world:

> *The increased size of organizations, rapid implementation of communication/ information technologies, globalisation, changing nature of work, reduction of the working class, less salient class conflicts, professionalization of the workforce, stagnant economies, widespread ecological problems and turbulent markets are all part of the contemporary context demanding a research response.*

Initially, in the 1980s, much of the debate about the changing nature of the modern world revolved around the posited move from 'Fordist' to 'post-Fordist' or 'neo-Fordist' forms of work organisation. This debate, over the move from mass production to flexible specialisation, initially centred on the work of Piore and Sabel (1984). Their argument was that the age of Taylorism and Fordism, the age of mass production, was dead. Mass production was concerned with the production of standardised goods for stable mass markets using a form of work organisation that was characterised by the intense division of labour, the separation of conception from execution and the substitution of unskilled for skilled labour (Tomaney, 1990). It was argued, however, that the market conditions that allowed Fordism to thrive have passed. The emergence of segmented and highly volatile markets, brought about by changes in consumer tastes and technological innovation, require organisations to be highly flexible in order to succeed in these post-Fordist conditions (Laudon and Starbuck, 1997).

According to Piore and Sabel (1984), only decentralised, worker-run firms have the flexibility, skills and commitment to cope with sudden shifts in consumer demands, volatile input prices and rapid changes in technology. They drew on the operation of loose alliances of small firms in Italy to substantiate their case. Though an attractive proposition to some, there does not appear to have been any great movement to create the decentralised worker cooperatives envisaged by Piore and Sabel, as Williams *et al* (1987) showed. Instead, other writers began to argue in favour of the emergence of neo-Taylorist or neo-Fordist organisational forms (Smith, 1994; Whitaker, 1992). Rather than the age of industrial bureaucracy coming to an end, it was argued that it was going through a two-pronged programme of change. On the one hand, computerised automation was linking together machines and processes and thus eliminating labour. On the other hand, where this was not possible, managers were shifting production to low-wage regions of the world (Froebel *et al*, 1980).

As Smith (1994) argued, the problem with this perspective is that though it fits, for example, General Motors, it does not fit Toyota, which has proved by far the more successful car company in the world. Sayer (1989) complained that the post-Fordist literature was confused, riddled with speculation and is selective in its use of evidence. Piore and Sabel (1984) in particular have come in for much criticism, especially in relation to what some see as their over-optimistic view of the developing nature of work. As Amin and Robins (1990: 202) commented: 'what we are seeing in the present period are organisational developments that are in significant ways an extension of Fordist structures. What is at work is not corporate fragmentation, but, in fact, more effective corporate integration.' Therefore, though their supporters can point to examples of flexible specialisation and post- and neo-Fordism, the explanations they gave for these and the implications they drew from them have attracted much criticism (Whitaker, 1992). Indeed, given the breadth and magnitude of the new organisational developments and forms discussed in Chapter 3, terms such as flexible specialisation, post-Fordism and neo-Fordism seem to have only a limited ability to explain the many changes taking place in organisational life. Nevertheless, what this debate did was to create a receptivity amongst a wider audience for the work of the postmodernists, who provided a more substantial and complex explanation for the changes taking place in the world around us.

Depending on whom one reads, postmodernism is either a relatively new concept or it has been around at least since the 1930s, if not longer (Appignanesi and Garratt, 1995; Featherstone, 1988a). Certainly, the term became fashionable among young writers, artists and critics in New York in the 1960s. In the 1970s and 1980s, the term became more widely used in architecture, music and the visual and performing arts (Hassard, 1993). However, its adoption by organisation theorists stems from the work of the poststructuralist movement in French philosophy, which emerged in the 1960s. The interest in meaning and interpretation by symbolic-interpretive organisation theorists, drawing on linguistic, semiotic and literary theory, also served to increase interest in postmodernism (Hatch, 1997). In the 1970s and 1980s, it became most closely associated with the work of Jean Baudrillard (1983), Jacques Derrida (1978), Michel Foucault (1977) and Jean-François Lyotard (1984).

Researchers in organisation and management studies came relatively late to postmodernism. It was only in the late 1980s, with, for example, the work of Smircich and Calás (1987) and Cooper and Burrell (1988), that postmodernism started to impact on organisation theory. The interest in postmodernism by many social scientists and organisation theorists stemmed from their growing belief that existing, modernist, theories, such as the Contingency approach, could no longer account for the changes taking place in the world of work and society in general. In particular, there was an increasing scepticism concerning the ability of rational, objective science to provide absolute and unitary knowledge of the world. In its place, postmodernists argue for a relativist position that emphasises multiple realities, fragmentation and subjectivity (Linstead, 1993).

Postmodernism, as the term implies, is something that carries on from, succeeds or takes its frame of reference from modernism. Therefore, it is necessary to understand how the proponents of postmodernism define modernism in order to appreciate their arguments. Modernism is a term used to describe the values, rationale and institutions that have dominated Western societies since the Age of Enlightenment in the eighteenth century. This was the period in which European thought, led by France and Great Britain, is seen as making a decisive break with the superstition, ignorance and tradition of the Middle Ages. In its place emerged a strong belief in progress, economic and scientific rationality, a search for the fundamental rules and laws that govern both the natural world and human nature, and a commitment to a secular, rationalist and progressive individualism (Gergen, 1992; Hassard, 1993). As Hobsbawm (1979: 34) noted, 'Liberty, equality and (it followed) the fraternity of all men were its slogans.' Linstead (1993: 99) commented that the Enlightenment:

. . . produced a commitment to the unfolding of progress through history, the incremental growth of knowledge through science and the resulting inevitable subordination of nature to culture and the control of man.

Also, as Gergen (1992: 211) stated, modernist 'presumptions remain vital throughout contemporary culture, and have left an indelible mark on theories of organization from early in the [twentieth] century to the present'. Modernists, therefore, assume that the world, both social and natural, and its structuring principles, are accessible through the correct (scientific) methods of observation and analysis. In relation to organisational life, the term modernism is used to describe the form of organisation that has dominated both the public and private sectors over the past 100 years (Biberman and Whitty, 1997). In the previous chapters, we have termed this the Classical or bureaucratic model, though others use terms such as Taylorist, Fordist or the machine-era paradigm (Fox, 1994; Smith, 1994; Tomaney, 1990). It is an organisational form which, its proponents argue, is based on rationality, logic and the pursuit of scientific rules and principles. Such organisations are characterised by mechanistic and hierarchical structures based on the extreme division of labour, and control systems that suppress people's emotions and minimise their scope for independent action.

Ideas and perspectives 4.5
Some features of postmodernism

Fragmentation: the breaking up of established structures into fragments.
De-differentiation: the blurring or dissolution of established boundaries.
Hyper-reality: confusion and mixing of the real with artificial/virtual realities.
Chronology: interest in the past and its imitation alongside/instead of the future.
Pastiche: the playful mixing of styles of decoration, dress, expression, etc.
Anti-foundationalism: rejection of all basics, absolutes, fundamentals, universals, etc.
Pluralism: all of the above happening simultaneously!

Source: Berkeley Thomas (2003: 214)

As can be seen from Ideas and perspectives 4.5, postmodernism offers a very different view of the world from that of the modernists. Postmodernism opposes or denies the validity of the Enlightenment's emphasis on reason, logic and rationality as the foundation of scientific method and the basis for the establishment of truth. Postmodernism challenges the claim of science to establish authoritative or absolute knowledge. Instead, it argues that scientific knowledge is a social construction by the scientific community, and that new scientific paradigms are brought about by changes in the community of scientists rather than scientific discoveries *per se* (Hassard, 1990).

Therefore, for postmodernists, knowledge is relative, not absolute. Postmodernism is, as Watson (1997: 383) states:

A way of looking at the world which rejects attempts to build systematic explanations of history and human activity and which, instead, concentrates on the ways in which human beings 'invent' their worlds, especially through language and cultural innovations.

One of the crucial distinctions between modernists and postmodernists is how they view the nature of language:

For the modernist, language was simply a tool for the logical representation of the real . . . Within the postmodernist view, language . . . gains its meaning and significance through its placement within social interchange. Words fail to make sense (they remain nonsense) until there is at least one other person to give assent to their meaningfulness. (Gergen, 1992: 213–14)

Therefore, if language is a social construct, one cannot take the statements, rules and practices of particular groups and organisations at face value. Instead, taking their cue from Derrida (1978), postmodernists often begin their analysis of a situation or event by 'deconstructing' the language used. Deconstruction is an approach that seeks to reveal and overturn the assumptions underlying an argument, proposition or theory. Overturning assumptions opens up space for previously unconsidered alternatives. In the postmodernist approach, alternatives are left open to multiple interpretations, and the acceptance of multiple, fragmented realities is seen to displace the idea of one unitary transcendent reality (Hatch, 1997). Like many others, postmodernists recognise that the various stakeholders in an organisation each have different perceptions of what the organisation should do and whose views and interests should be paramount. Where they differ, however, is that they do not believe that there is a correct view or that one view has a right to be paramount. Instead, postmodern management and organisation theory, beginning with a process of deconstruction, 'seeks to reconstruct organizations by restoring a sense of harmony and balance in our species, our institutions, and our theories' (Gephart *et al*, 1996: 364).

This leads on to another prevailing theme within postmodernism: self-reflexivity – a critical suspicion of one's own suppositions. If reality and language are social constructs, then, so the postmodernist argument goes, to avoid the modernist error of believing they have discovered a fundamental truth or reality, postmodernists must constantly question and be suspicious of their own assumptions, statements and actions (Lawson, 1985).

Moving on to the links between postmodernism and organisation theory, the concept of self-reflexivity has similarities to Argyris and Schön's (1978) notion of double- and triple-loop learning, which promotes the questioning and challenging of existing organisational assumptions (*see* Chapter 3). Other aspects of Argyris's work also show postmodernist leanings, particularly his questioning of the inner contradictions of research methods (Argyris, 1980). We can also see postmodernist tendencies in Morgan's (1986) *Images of Organizations*, in which he treats existing organisation theories as metaphors.

Moving into the heartland of organisation theory, Linstead (1993) argues that under postmodernism, hierarchies of merit, legitimacy and authority give way to networks, partnerships and organisational structures of a shifting, fluid and social nature. These are driven by external forces, such as markets or competition, and are *ad hoc*, short-term, fragmentary and localised. According to Daft (1998), necessity will force postmodern organisations to develop more flexible and decentralised organisation structures with fuzzy boundaries both internally and externally. In such organisations, he believes, leaders will become facilitators who will communicate through informal, oral and symbolic channels, control will be exercised through self-regulation, planning and decision-making will be inclusive and egalitarian principles will hold sway. In a similar vein, Boje (2006: 27) argues that:

> . . . *postmodern theory holds out the possibility for a liberatory, non-predatory version of capitalism, if you will, a liberatory-grand narrative. This postmodern grand narrative professes democratic governance, transparency in monitoring corporate ethics, and a revision to the surplus value equation of maximizing exploitation that favors worker rights, community sovereignty over corporations, and eco-sustainability.*

Consequently, as Clegg (1990) maintains, there are clear distinctions between modernist and postmodernist organisational forms (*see* Table 4.1).

Table 4.1 Comparison of modernist and postmodernist organisational forms

	Modernist organisations	Postmodernist organisations
Structure	Rigid bureaucracies	Flexible networks
Consumption	Mass markets	Niche markets
Technology	Technological determinism	Technological choice
Jobs	Differentiated, demarcated and deskilled	Highly de-differentiated, de-demarcated and multi-skilled
Employment relations	Centralised and standardised	Complex and fragmentary

Clegg acknowledges that postmodern forms of organisation are somewhat ill-defined. Nevertheless, he argues that they are associated with developments such as flexible specialisation and post-Fordism, and that examples of postmodern organisations can be found in Japan, Sweden, East Asia and Italy. However, he does point out that whilst they can be associated with progressive developments, such as the extension of industrial democracy in Sweden, they can also be linked to more repressive and elitist developments, such as the segmented labour force policies adopted by Handy's Shamrock organisation (*see* Chapter 3). In the Shamrock organisation, there are three classes of employees – *core workers*, the *contractual fringe* and the *flexible labour force*. Each of these three segments of the organisation's workforce has very different conditions of employment and is treated and valued very differently. Therefore, for Clegg, and an increasing number of organisation theorists, postmodernism has arrived, it is having a major impact on the nature and functioning of organisations, and it will continue to do so (Addis and Podesta, 2005).

There are two areas of organisational life to which the postmodernists have paid particular attention: culture and power. The postmodern approach to organisational culture rejects both the integrationist perspective, which sees culture as being shared by all members of an organisation, and the differentiation perspective, which sees organisational unity as being broken by coherent and stable subcultures. Instead, it takes a fragmentation perspective, believing that organisational cultures are inconsistent, ambiguous, multi-plicitous and in a constant state of flux (Martin, 1992; Meyerson and Martin, 1987). Hatch (1997: 231) observes of the postmodern perspective on culture that:

> *In this view, alliances or coalitions can never stabilize into subcultures and certainly not into unified cultures because discourse and its focal issues are always changing – hence the image of fragmentation.*

Therefore, for postmodernists, organisational culture is important, and indeed is clearly linked to their interest in symbols and language. However, postmodernists are sceptical of attempts to manipulate and change culture, as Hatch (1997: 235) points out:

> *When you attempt to change organizational culture, while it is true that something will change, generally the changes are unpredictable and sometimes undesirable (e.g., increases in employee cynicism towards cultural change programs) . . .*

Where power is concerned, postmodernists take a very different view from most other writers on organisations. They are less concerned with the power that individuals or groups possess, acquire or deploy. Rather they believe that power resides in the combination of linguistic distinctions, ways of reasoning and material practices which make up the body of taken-for-granted knowledge that exists in society and organisations (Alvesson and Deetz, 1996). Perhaps the most influential postmodernist writer on power has been the French philosopher, Michel Foucault (1983). Foucault argues for a strong link between knowledge and power. He believes that knowledge, when it becomes socially legitimised and institutionalised, exerts control over what we think and do. However, there is a power struggle between different bodies of knowledge each fighting for legitimacy and supremacy. For Foucault, though these bodies of knowledge are seeking to represent reality, at the same time they socially create it. He argues that power moulds everyone, both those who use it and those who are used by it. He maintains that power and know-ledge depend on each other, so that an extension of a group's power is dependent upon and accompanied by an extension of its knowledge, and *vice versa* (Appignanesi and Garratt, 1995). Gergen (1992: 221) takes a similar perspective, arguing that:

> *. . . power is inherently a matter of social interdependence, and it is achieved through the social coordination of actions around specified definitions.*

The postmodernist perspective on power has important implications for how a particular view of reality comes to the fore and is maintained in an organisation. Rather than being the product of an objective and rational process, it is the product of power and politics in an organisation. In some organisations, there does not appear to be a settled and generally agreed view of reality; rather what we see are competing inter-pretations put forward by competing groups and individuals. In other organisations, however, a definite view does appear to be held and does appear to be maintained. This is achieved when a coalition of groups and forces is able to wield power and use political processes to achieve a dominant position over others in the organisation. When this occurs, it is their view of reality which takes shape and comes to be accepted. Therefore, not only is power deployed to legitimate their view of the world, but, in turn, its legitimacy bolsters their power.

The implications for organisations

What we can see from this review of postmodernism is the influence that both modernism and postmodernism have had on organisational theory and practice in the twentieth century. Clearly, the Classical approach, and especially Weber's contribution, with its emphasis on rationality and scientific knowledge, is very much within the tradition of modernism. Indeed, one can also say that much of the Human Relations literature, with its use of scientific methods to identify the 'one best way', and certainly the literature on Contingency Theory would appear to fall squarely into the modernist camp. On the other hand, the Culture–Excellence approach seems much more comfortable with the rhetoric of postmodernism. Not only does it share a similar view of the current state of the world, i.e. chaotic and unpredictable, but it also shares some of the language. For example, Charles Handy (1989) entitled one of his books *The Age of Unreason*, whilst Rosabeth Moss Kanter (1989) writes of 'post-entrepreneurial' organisations. Though Tom Peters does not necessarily use the language of the postmodernists, the essence of his message, and certainly the pastiche style of his books, sits comfortably with postmodernism (e.g. Peters, 1997a). The same can be said of organisational learning, with its emphasis on knowledge acquisition, rapid change and, most importantly, the ability of organisations to create their own realities (Hatch, 1997). The Japanese approach, with its inclusion of hard and soft elements, on the other hand, seems to contain happily elements of modernism and postmodernism. Indeed, it may be that one of the main criticisms of modernism and postmodernism is that both come from a Western, especially European, intellectual and cultural tradition and, consequently, may not lie easily with other, particularly Eastern and Islamic, intellectual and cultural traditions (Appignanesi and Garratt, 1995).

Nevertheless, at least in the West, postmodernism does appear to be having a powerful and pervasive impact on both theory and practice in organisations. However, perhaps the main reason why it is having such an impact is that there are many forms of postmodernism which have a multiplicity of meanings and have been utilised in a wide variety of ways (Alvesson and Deetz, 1996). In particular, postmodernism seems to have fragmented into something of a smorgasbord from which both left and right, capitalists and anti-capitalists, can choose those morsels which take their fancy. As one of the key writers in the field of postmodernism and organisations noted:

> *What is the postmodern approach to organizations? There is no one approach. Postmodern approaches fragmented into naive postmodern (calling late modern postindustrialism or complex/adaptive organizations postmodern); more radical approaches (Baudrillard and Lyotard's era-breaks with modernity and some of Foucault); more critical theory approaches (Jameson, Debord, and Best and Kellner, etc. combine critical theory with postmodern theory).Then there are approaches I would call post-postmodern: hybridity (Latour's thesis that we have never been modern, instead there is hybridity of discourses, mostly modern with some postmodern); dark side of postmodern (global reterritorialization, postmodern warfare, and Biotech Century).*
>
> (Boje, 2006: 22)

In summary, despite the somewhat impenetrable and contradictory nature of the literature, the core of postmodernism concerns the nature of reason and reality. For postmodernists, reason and logic have proved illusory and reality is a social construct. In organisational terms, an organisation, or rather those individuals and groups that dominate it, create their own reality – their own view or views of the world. Whether they see themselves as successful or not, whether they view the world as chaotic, whether they believe they can shape their own future, is to a large part determined not by any objective data or what is happening in their environment as such, but by their own ability to shape their own reality. The extent to which they can impose their view of reality on others both inside and outside will, to a large degree, determine whether they and the organisation are seen as successful or not.

Seen in this light, postmodernism has three important implications for the organisation theories and practices discussed in the previous three chapters:

1. **Culture**. As we saw in Chapter 3, the Culture–Excellence school has been highly influential in bringing the issue of organisational culture to the forefront of management thought and practice over the last two decades. In essence, what they argue is that, in order to achieve excellence, managers need to create a strong, unified and appropriate culture for their organisation. A core component of this approach is to manipulate and use language and symbols to create a new organisational reality. Though acknowledging the importance of culture, and sharing a concern with symbols and language, postmodernists, however, view the results of attempts to manipulate and change culture as generally unpredictable and sometimes undesirable. This is because the outcomes depend upon the multiplicity of meanings and interpretations that others in the organisation put on such attempts, which are inherently unmanageable (Hatch, 1997).

2. **Reality**. How does a particular view of reality come to the fore and how is it maintained in an organisation? The answer for postmodernists concerns the role of power and politics. In some organisations, there does not appear to be a settled and generally agreed view of reality; rather what we see are differing interpretations put forward by competing groups and individuals. In other organisations, however, a definite view does appear to be held and does appear to be maintained. This is achieved when a coalition of groups and forces is able to wield power and use political processes to achieve a dominant position over others in the organisation. When this occurs, it is their view of reality that takes shape and comes to be accepted.

3. **Choice**. As we saw in the three previous chapters, most organisational theorists and practitioners in the twentieth century tended to believe that there was a 'one best way' to run organisations. The postmodernist debate, however, has raised significant questions about whether these 'one best ways' represent some form of objective knowledge, or whether they are socially constructed realities which pertain to particular times, countries, industries and organisations. If organisational reality is socially constructed, then, in theory at least, it is open to organisations to construct whatever reality they wish. From this perspective, organisations have a wide degree of choice about what they do, how they do it and where they do it.

The influence of postmodernism, on organisational thinking and practice cannot be denied (Boje, 2006). Nevertheless, despite its attractions, there are some serious reservations about its validity and usefulness.

Postmodernism – some reservations

Perhaps the main reservation and drawback of postmodernism is the difficulty in defining the concept (Boje, 2006). In the social sciences, the term has acquired a wide and often conflicting set of definitions, including a social mood, a historical period filled with major social and organisational changes, and a set of philosophical approaches to organisational and other studies (Alvesson and Deetz, 1996; Featherstone, 1988b; Hassard and Parker, 1993). Hatch (1997: 43) believes postmodernism has been defined in so many different ways that:

> *It is impossible to choose a core theory, or a typical set of ideas, to exemplify post-modernism – the incredible variety of ideas labelled postmodern defies summarization, and the postmodern value for diversity contradicts the very idea of unifying these different understandings into a single, all-encompassing explanation.*

As Appignanesi and Garratt (1995: 4) observe:

> *The confusion is advertised by the 'post' prefix to 'modern'. Postmodernism identifies itself by something it isn't. It isn't modern anymore. But in what sense exactly is it post . . .*

- *as a result of modernism?*
- *the aftermath of modernism?*
- *the afterbirth of modernism?*
- *the development of modernism?*
- *the denial of modernism?*
- *the rejection of modernism?*

> *Postmodern has been used in a mix-and-match of all these meanings.*

The confusion and variety of postmodernism can be seen in Ideas and perspectives 4.6 which shows a list of terms which postmodernists use instead of *modern* and *postmodern*.

Ideas and perspectives 4.6
Terms used by postmodernists

modern	postmodern
modernity	postmodernity
modernité	postmodernité
modernisation	postmodernisation
modernism	postmodernism

Source: Featherstone (1988a: 197)

However, there is little consistency in how these terms are used or defined. Not only are postmodernity and postmodernism used to describe different phenomena, but there is also no agreement or even consistency as to what the individual terms mean either (Boje, 2006; Featherstone, 1988a). Indeed, Burrell (1988: 222) remarked of one of the key influences on the postmodernist debate, Michel Foucault, that:

> . . . it is important to note that Foucault's iconoclasm takes him into positions which are not readily defensible and his refusal to retain one position for longer than the period between his last book and the next is certainly problematic.

As well as the difficulty in defining postmodernism, there are also powerful voices that defend modernism and attack postmodernism as a form of intellectual nihilism or of neo-conservatism (Aronowitz, 1989; Callinicos, 1989). Hassard (1993: 119) states that:

> The most influential critic of postmodernism, however, is Jürgen Habermas . . . [He] argues that theories of postmodernism represent critiques of modernity which have their ideological roots in irrationalist and counter-Enlightenment perspectives . . . Habermas suggests that as many French writers [especially Derrida, Foucault and Lyotard] take their lead from the counter-Enlightenment statements of Nietzsche and Heidegger, this can be interpreted as a disturbing link with fascist thinking . . . Habermas wishes to defend robustly 'a principle of modernism', which he suggests is an unfinished project that holds great, unfulfilled emancipatory potential.

For Lyon (2000), the main critics of postmodernism fall into three camps (*see* Ideas and perspectives 4.7).

However, no matter how one groups the criticisms of postmodernism, it cannot be denied that a number of serious reservations have been expressed regarding the validity of the concept. These include its lack of consistency and clarity, that its proponents mis-read the current state of the world, that it may be correct but it is not important, and its posited alignment on the far right of the political spectrum. Its proponents accept that the postmodernist message is not always clear and consistent but, in the main, they would reject most of the other criticisms, especially that it is an ideology of the right. On the other hand, there can be little doubt that the postmodernist message has provided some justification and encouragement for the neo-liberal policies, such as privatisation and deregulation, adopted by most Western governments in the last

Ideas and perspectives 4.7
Critics of postmodernism

1. Those who claim there has never been a fully modernist era and claim there cannot, consequently, be a 'post' modernist one.
2. Those who maintain that the current developments in society are merely an extension of what has gone before rather than any significant break with the past.
3. Those who accept that the world is entering a new age, but believe globalisation (*see* Chapter 12) and not postmodernism is its defining characteristic.

Source: Lyon (2000)

30 years. Nevertheless, regardless of the merits or not of postmodernism, there are two other non-modernist perspectives on organisations which are also having a significant impact on organisation theory: realism and complexity.

The realist perspective

What is realism?

As the above showed, there appear to be two dominant philosophical perspectives on the social world: the modernist, or positivist, perspective which believes in objective reality, logic and reason, and the postmodernist perspective, which sees multiple and competing realities which are socially constructed. In the field of organisations, over the past 20 to 30 years, it is the postmodernist perspective which has come to the fore. However, Ackroyd and Fleetwood (2000a) argue that there is an alternative to both. They point out that there is much substantive research on organisations that is based on neither modernism (positivism) nor postmodernism. This work is based on a long-established seam of social science which strongly maintains that, in order to understand and explain events, it is necessary to take into account both social structures, such as organisations, routines, rules and power, and the meaning that individuals and groups apply to these. Underpinning this work are well-developed philosophical doctrines that are neither modernist nor postmodernist. One of the most important of these is realism, which offers support for a non-modernist and non-postmodernist approach to organisations and management (*see* Ideas and perspectives 4.8).

The essence of realism, as Easton (2000: 207) notes, 'is that there is a reality "out there" waiting to be discovered'.

Since the 1970s, realism has been applied to the social sciences by a number of writers (Bhaskar, 1979, 1986; Collier, 1994; Dobson, 2001; Harré, 1972; Outhwaite, 1987; Sayer, 2000). However, though few have explicitly applied it to management, it is said to underpin much work in the field of institutional and regulation theory, and there is now a growing interest in its application to the wider issues of management and organisations (Ackroyd and Fleetwood, 2000b). As with postmodernism, the term realism has influenced many areas such as the arts, literature, philosophy and the social sciences,

---

Ideas and perspectives 4.8
Realism

To be a realist is, minimally, to assert that many entities exist independently of us and our investigations of them. Clearly, then, most people are realists in this basic sense: we differ in what entities we are realists about. The realist social scientist, however, is likely to claim that social entities (such as markets, class relations, gender relations, social rules, social customs or discourse and so on) exist independently of our investigations of them.

Source: Ackroyd and Fleetwood (2000a: 6)

and the term tends to be used differently in each of these areas. However, the core belief of realists is that many entities exist independently of us and our investigation of them. Therefore, unlike postmodernists, realists assert that social entities, such as markets, class relations, gender relations, ethnic groupings, social rules, etc., exist, are real and can be discovered, though this does not mean that discovering them will be easy. As Easton (2000: 207) succinctly puts it, 'We see through a glass darkly but there is something there to see.'

Realism and organisations

In applying realism to organisations, there is an increasing tendency to prefix the term with the word *critical* (Fleetwood and Ackroyd, 2004). This follows on from Bhaskar's use of the term critical realism in his work on science and social science (Collier, 1994). Those using this form of words in relation to organisations appear to do so in order to signal that they approach the study of organisations from a critical rather than dogmatic or naive standpoint (Dobson, 2001). They are signalling that their attitude is one of self-reflection and that they are aware of the hidden presuppositions which abound in social systems. However, the use of the 'critical' prefix is not always consistent. For example, Ackroyd and Fleetwood (2000b) in their edited book on realism and organisations do not use the prefix whilst in their later edited book on the same topic (Fleetwood and Ackroyd, 2004) they do use the prefix. Whilst keeping this in mind, we will continue to use the term without its prefix.

Tsoukas (2000) states that realist philosophers see both the natural and social worlds as consisting of complex structures that exist independently of our knowledge of them. For realists, events and patterns of events are generated (are caused to be brought about) by causal mechanisms and causal powers that operate independently of the events they generate. Realists seek to identify the generative structures, i.e. the causal mechanisms that bring about events, and to identify their capabilities, i.e. their causal powers (Harré and Madden, 1975; Harré and Secord, 1972). However, though these causal mechanisms possess certain capabilities, causal powers, the actual outcome of their operation will be dependent, i.e. contingent, on circumstances. For example, the Japanese approach to management has the potential to engender teamworking and organisational commitment, but whether it will or not depends on a whole host of situational variables, such as the nature of the society in which the organisation operates and the expectations of the employees concerned (Delbridge, 2004). Organisations also contain competing and contradictory organising principles, such as class, gender and ethnicity, and they are composed of different groups with their own distinct priorities and agendas that can undermine the dominant causal mechanisms (Reed, 2000). Nevertheless, despite the potential of these competing forces and groups to create disorder, in many cases the interaction between them occurs in such a way that it produces organisational integration, a degree of continuity and stability, and sufficient change to maintain the organisation's viability (Ackroyd, 2000).

In terms of organisations and management, a central issue is the extent to which organisations and their practices are produced by human beings but still exist externally to them and shape their behaviour. Realists are very clear on this point. They argue that whilst the social world, including organisations, is a product of human action, it is not necessarily a product of human design but exists independently of human beings (Connelly, 2000; Easton, 2000). Realists also argue that social phenomena can exist without those involved having any knowledge of them. For example, markets only exist in and through human activity, yet there is no necessity that those people involved should be conscious of the part they play in sustaining them.

Therefore, realists acknowledge the socially constructed nature of the world but, unlike postmodernists, do not see the world as being merely a social construction (Ackroyd and Fleetwood, 2000b; Fleetwood and Ackroyd, 2004). This can be seen in terms of the structure and operation of organisations. Realists argue that a structure is a set of simultaneously enabling and constraining rules and resources which shape the inter-actions of those who work in or have to deal with the organisation. That is to say, a structure can be considered as a causal mechanism which has the potential and capability to act in certain ways, i.e. it has causal powers (Giddens, 1984; Manicas, 1980; Tsoukas, 2000). Consequently, as Tsoukas (1992) observes, just because a person may have friendly relations with a bank manager does not by itself mean that the person will be able to obtain a loan – the key issues are the lending rules of the bank and the creditworthiness of the borrower. Organisations may give groups and individuals certain powers but they also prescribe how and when these powers are to be deployed (Whittington, 1989). This does not imply that those concerned know how the rules are generated, the obvious and less obvious ways in which compliance is ensured, or their role in maintaining and developing these rules. Therefore, to continue the banking example, the bank manager knows the lending rules but not necessarily why they are as they are. Also, though he or she is aware of the penalties for non-compliance, they are less likely to be aware of the subtle pressures exerted by cultural norms to behave in certain ways. Yet the lending decision is not a mechanical process. The manager does have the ability to exert judge-ment and a degree of discretion in what they do. Likewise, the potential borrower can present their case in a more or a less convincing fashion. This is why the causal powers possessed by a causal mechanism are seen as capabilities and not determinants. Whilst causal powers limit what can be done, and whilst they have the potential to bring about (cause) certain actions to occur, whether they do occur or not is dependent on a range of other factors as well, not least human action or inaction. As a result, when studying management and organisations, realists stress the need to give due weight to both people and structure, and the complex interplay between them. They argue that human action is shaped by the simultaneous constraining and enabling nature of an organisation's structure, which tends to favour certain types of outcome, but that any actual outcome is contingent on the prevailing circumstances (Tsoukas, 1989; Whittington, 1994). In addi-tion, as Kumar (1995) notes, not only do these constraining and enabling forces lie outside the control of those concerned, but those concerned are often unaware of them.

Realists seek to understand and explain events by focusing on the mechanisms, struc-tures, powers and relations that bring them about. In seeking an explanation in this way, realists begin by postulating the existence of a possible mechanism and proceed by collect-ing evidence for or against its existence and evidence of possible alternative mechanisms (Outhwaite, 1987; Reed, 2000). In revealing the mechanisms which bring about events, realists also seek to engender debates about alternative ways of structuring the social world and alternative forms of relationships, be they concerned with class, gender or power.

The use of realism in the field of management and organisations is most closely associated with the work of Bhaskar. His argument (Bhaskar, 1989: 36) is that nothing happens out of nothing:

. . . people do not create society. For it always pre-exists them and is a necessary condition for their activity. Rather society must be regarded as an ensemble of structures, practices and conventions which individuals reproduce and/or transform, but which would not exist unless they did so. Society does not exist independently of human activity . . . But it is not the product of it . . .

Bhaskar (1986) makes a distinction between human action and social structure. He argues that common propositions which are applied to people assume such a distinction: 'He cashed a cheque' assumes a banking system, 'He pleaded guilty' assumes a legal system (Bhaskar, 1979; Connelly, 2000). The two are mutually influential and interdependent but can be analysed separately, and are fundamentally different in that social structures pre-exist and are sustained and changed through human action, but human action is constrained and enabled by social structures. Realists do not deny that there are multiple perspectives or competing claims about the nature of the social world. They also share with postmodernists a recognition of the role of culture, power and politics in shaping organisational choices. However, they reject the possibility that there are multiple realities. Therefore, unlike the postmodernists, they claim that truth exists and what exists can be found, though the finding may be very difficult (Easton, 2000). As Stacey (2003: 7) comments:

. . . realists do not see any inherent limitation on human ability to comprehend reality in its entirety. For them, it is only a matter of time before research progressively uncovers more and more of reality.

Realism – some reservations

Realism is a riposte to both modernism and postmodernism. It attacks the former for placing too much reliance on science, rationality and logic, whilst criticising the latter for rejecting reality in favour of multiple and competing realities. Though it would be unfair to characterise realism as being a halfway house between modernism and postmodernism, it does tend to open itself up to criticism from both camps (Klein, 2004). The modernists object to the social construction side of the realists' reality, whilst the postmodernists object to the realists' claim that there is only one reality and it can be discovered. However, the battle as to which perspective on the world will carry most weight with organisation theorists is not just between postmodernists and realists; over the last decade or so, a third perspective, complexity, has entered the fray, which, unlike modernism and postmodernism, owes its origins not to philosophy but to the natural sciences.

The complexity perspective

What is complexity?

Over the last decade or so, an increasing number of academics and practitioners have come to view organisations through the lens of complexity theories, and this is having a profound impact on views of how organisations should be structured and changed (Arndt and Bigelow, 2000; Bechtold, 1997; Black, 2000; Burnes, 2005; Fitzgerald, 2002a; Lewis, 1994; MacIntosh and MacLean, 2001; Morgan, 1997; Stacey, 2003; Tetenbaum,

1998; Wheatley, 1992b). Complexity serves as an umbrella term for a number of theories, ideas and research programmes that are derived from many different disciplines in the natural sciences (Rescher, 1996; Stacey, 2003; Styhre, 2002). To emphasise the diversity of viewpoints amongst complexity researchers, we will follow Black's (2000) lead and use the term complexity theories rather than theory.

Complexity theories are concerned with the emergence of order in dynamic non-linear systems operating at the edge of chaos, such as weather systems, which are constantly changing and where the laws of cause and effect appear not to apply (Beeson and Davis, 2000; Haigh, 2002; Wheatley, 1992b). Order in such systems manifests itself in a largely unpredictable fashion, in which patterns of behaviour emerge in irregular but similar forms through a process of self-organisation, which is governed by a small number of simple order-generating rules (Black, 2000; MacIntosh and MacLean, 2001; Tetenbaum, 1998). Many writers have argued that organisations are also complex systems that, to survive, need to operate at the edge of chaos and have to respond continuously to changes in their environments through just such a process of spontaneous self-organising change (Hayles, 2000; Lewis, 1994; Macbeth, 2002; MacIntosh and MacLean, 1999, 2001; Stacey, 2003; Stickland, 1998).

Complexity theories stem from attempts by meteorologists, biologists, chemists, physicists and other natural scientists to build mathematical models of systems in nature (Gleick, 1988; Lorenz, 1993; Styhre, 2002). In the process, a number of different but related theories have emerged, the key ones being chaos theory (Bechtold, 1997; Haigh, 2002; Lorenz, 1979, 1993), dissipative structures theory (Prigogine and Stengers, 1984; Prigogine, 1997), and the theory of complex adaptive systems (Goodwin, 1994; Stacey *et al*, 2002). The main difference between these three theories, according to Stacey (2003), is that chaos and dissipative structures theories seek to construct mathematical models of systems at the macro level (i.e. whole systems and populations), whilst complex adaptive systems theory attempts to model the same phenomena at the micro level by using an agent-based approach. Instead of formulating rules for the whole population, it seeks to formulate rules of interaction for the individual entities making up a system or population. However, all three see natural systems as both non-linear and self-organising. There are three central concepts that lie at the heart of complexity theories – the nature of chaos and order; the 'edge of chaos'; and order-generating rules.

Chaos and order

Chaos is often portrayed as pure randomness, but from the complexity viewpoint, it can be seen as a different form of order (Arndt and Bigelow, 2000; Fitzgerald, 2002b; Frederick, 1998). Fitzgerald (2002a) states that chaos and order are twin attributes of dynamic, non-linear (complex) systems, and, within chaos, a hidden order may be concealed beneath what looks completely random. For complexity theorists, chaos describes a complex, unpredictable and orderly disorder in which patterns of behaviour unfold in irregular but similar forms; snowflakes are all different but all have six sides (Tetenbaum, 1998). Stacey (2003) identifies three types of order–disorder:

- **Stable equilibrium** – such systems can become so stable that they ossify and die.
- **Explosive instability** – such systems can become too unstable and, as with cancer, get out of control and destroy themselves (Frederick, 1998).

- **Bounded instability** – these are complex systems which, torn between stability and instability, have the ability to transform themselves in order to survive.

Edge of chaos

Under conditions of 'bounded instability', systems are constantly poised on the brink between order and chaos. Elsewhere, Stacey (Stacey *et al*, 2002) refers to this as a 'far-from-equilibrium' state, whilst Hock (1999) uses the term 'chaordic'. However, the term most commonly used to describe this condition is 'the edge of chaos':

> . . . *complex systems have large numbers of independent yet interacting actors. Rather than ever reaching a stable equilibrium, the most adaptive of these complex systems (e.g., intertidal zones) keep changing continuously by remaining at the poetically termed 'edge of chaos' that exists between order and disorder. By staying in this intermediate zone, these systems never quite settle into a stable equilibrium but never quite fall apart. Rather, these systems, which stay constantly poised between order and disorder, exhibit the most prolific, complex and continuous change* . . .
>
> (Brown and Eisenhardt, 1997: 29)

It is argued that creativity and growth are at their optimal when a complex system operates at the edge of chaos (Frederick, 1998; Jenner, 1998; Kauffman, 1993; Lewis, 1994). It is the presence, or not, of appropriate order-generating rules, which permits self-organisation to take place, that allows some systems to remain at the edge of chaos, whilst others fall over the edge.

Order-generating rules

In complex systems, the emergence of order is seen as being based on the operation of simple order-generating rules which permit limited chaos whilst providing relative order (Frederick, 1998; Lewis, 1994; MacIntosh and MacLean, 2001; Reynolds, 1987; Stacey *et al*, 2002; Wheatley, 1992b). As Gell-Mann (1994: 100) puts it:

> *In an astonishing variety of contexts, apparently complex structures or behaviors emerge from systems characterized by very simple rules. These systems are said to be self-organized and their properties are said to be emergent. The grandest example is the universe itself, the full complexity of which emerges from simple rules plus chance.*

Therefore, the concept of order-generating rules explains how complex, non-linear, self-organising systems manage to maintain themselves at the edge of chaos even under changing environmental conditions. Complex systems have a further trick up their sleeve. Under certain conditions they can even generate new, more appropriate, order-generating rules when the old ones can no longer cope with the changes in the system's environment (Bechtold, 1997; MacIntosh and MacLean, 1999; Wheatley, 1992b).

The implications for organisations

A growing number of academics and practitioners maintain that organisations are complex, non-linear systems, the behaviour of whose members is characterised by spontaneous self-organising underpinned by a set of simple order-generating rules (Arndt and Bigelow, 2000; Bechtold, 1997; Black, 2000; Fitzgerald, 2002a; Lewis, 1994; MacIntosh and MacLean, 2001; Morgan, 1997; Stacey, 2003; Tetenbaum, 1998; Wheatley, 1992b).

Frederick (1998) argues that companies that relentlessly pursue a path of continuous innovation succeed because they operate at the edge of chaos, and, indeed, because they inject so much novelty and change into their normal operations, they constantly risk falling over the edge. Brown and Eisenhardt (1997) draw a similar conclusion from their research into innovation in the computer industry. They maintain that continuous innovation is necessary for survival and that this is brought about by a process that resembles self-organisation in nature.

Perhaps the most well-known example of a self-organising organisation is Visa. Visa has grown by 10,000 per cent since 1970, comprises 20,000 financial institutions, operates in 200 countries and has over half a billion customers (Hock, 1999). However, as Tetenbaum (1998: 26) notes:

> . . . you don't know where it's located, how it's operated, or who owns it. That's because Visa is decentralized, non-hierarchical, evolving, self-organizing and self-regulating. . . . it is a chaordic system conceived as an organization solely on the basis of purpose and principle. Its structure evolved from them.

If organisations are complex systems, management and change take on a new dimension. Beeson and Davis (2000) make the point that whilst it might be fruitful to see organisations as non-linear systems, to do so will require a fundamental shift in the role of management. Like many others (e.g. Boje, 2000; Stacey et al, 2002; Sullivan, 1999; Tetenbaum, 1998; Wheatley, 1992b), they point out that self-organising principles explicitly reject cause-and-effect, top-down, command-and-control styles of management. Brodbeck (2002) suggests that the belief by managers that order and control are essential to achieve their objectives needs to be redressed. Morgan (1997) maintains that complexity will require managers to rethink the nature of hierarchy and control, learn the art of managing and changing contexts, promote self-organising processes, and learn how to use small changes to create large effects. For Tetenbaum (1998), the move to self-organisation will require managers to destabilise their organisations and develop the skill of managing order and disorder at the same time. Managers will need to encourage experimentation and divergent views, even allow rule-breaking, and recognise that 'people need the freedom to own their own power, think innovatively, and operate in new patterns' (Bechtold, 1997: 198). For Jenner (1998: 402), the key to achieving this is a flexible, decentralised structure.

Brown and Eisenhardt (1997: 29) refer to such flexible structures as 'semistructures', which they maintain 'are sufficiently rigid so that change can be organized, but not so rigid that it cannot occur'. They claim that organisations can only survive in highly competitive environments by continuously innovating and improvising, which, they argue, relies on intensive, real-time communication within a structure of a few, very specific, rules. Beeson and Davis (2000) echo this point and argue that, in such situations, change becomes an everyday event undertaken by all in the organisation. Brown and Eisenhardt (1997: 28) also claim that in the firms they studied:

> The rate and scale of innovation . . . was such that the term 'incremental' seemed, in retrospect, stretched. Yet it was not radical innovation [but] . . . a third kind of

process that is neither incremental nor radical and that does not fit the punctuated equilibrium model . . .

Similarly, Brodbeck (2002) draws attention to studies that cast doubt on the effectiveness of large-scale change programmes (*see* Clarke, 1999; Harung *et al*, 1999). For Styhre (2002), the problem is that such programmes assume that it is possible to predict the outcomes of change and attempt to plan, control and manage it in a rational, top-down, linear fashion.

These writers are depicting organisations operating at the edge of chaos and, therefore, needing to respond continuously to changes in their environments through a process of spontaneous self-organising change in order to survive. However, as in the natural world, this process is driven by order-generating rules that themselves can be subject to transformation in certain situations (Lewis, 1994; MacIntosh and MacLean, 1999, 2001; Stacey, 2003). When this takes place in nature, it is an automatic process; in organisations, this is rarely likely to be the case. As Stacey (2003) argues, people are not unthinking molecules; they can and do exercise free will, they can and do pursue their own objectives, they can and do utilise power and political manoeuvring to gain their own ends, and they can and do interpret events in widely differing ways. Therefore, self-organisation may not occur even when appropriate order-generating rules are present, nor, if such rules cease to be appropriate, can it be assumed that they will automatically be transformed. Instead both will depend on the nature of the organisation (Griffin, 2002).

MacIntosh and MacLean (2001) provide evidence of the existence and importance of order-generating rules, based on a case study of a long-established manufacturing company that had been in decline for over 30 years. This decline appeared to be caused by a combination of inappropriate order-generating rules (such as 'don't innovate unless it leads to cost reduction') and a rigid structure that stifled innovation. Once this was recognised, the company evolved more appropriate order-generating rules (such as 'better, faster, cheaper') and implemented a new structure that gave greater freedom for self-organisation to its constituent parts.

In order for organisations to promote change through self-organisation, a number of writers have argued that organisations need to operate on democratic principles, i.e. their members will have to have the freedom to self-organise. For example, Bechtold (1997) argues that organisations seeking to adopt a complexity approach need a balanced distribution of power, strong customer focus, a strategy of continuous learning and an orientation towards community service. A further strand in this argument is provided by Kiel (1994), who argues that because small actions can have large and unpredictable consequences, individual human activity assumes great importance. Jenner (1998) claims that for self-organisation to work, authority must be delegated to those who have access to the broadest channels of information that relate to the issue concerned. Nevertheless, Stacey (2003: 278) sounds a note of caution:

This seems to assume that self-organisation is some new form of behaviour rather than a different way of understanding how people have always behaved. The question is whether such self-organising behaviour produces patterns that block or enable change.

In considering complexity theories and organisational change, one of the key questions is to ask: 'What's new?' (Frederick, 1998). If we look at what appears to be being said about management, structure, behaviour and change, much of it seems very familiar.

Ideas and perspectives 4.9
Applying complexity theories to organisations

Implication 1 There will be a need for much greater democracy and power equalisation in all aspects of organisational life, instead of just narrow employee participation in change (Bechtold, 1997; Jenner, 1998; Kiel, 1994).

Implication 2 Small-scale incremental change and large-scale radical-transformational change will need to be rejected in favour of 'a third kind' which lies between these two, and which is continuous and based on self-organisation at the team or group level (Brodbeck, 2002; Brown and Eisenhardt, 1997).

Implication 3 In achieving effective change, order-generating rules have the potential to overcome the limitations of rational, linear, top-down, strategy-driven approaches to change (MacIntosh and MacLean, 1999, 2001; Stacey, 2003; Styhre, 2002).

Writers from Peters and Waterman (1982) onwards have been arguing that managers need to abandon top-down, command-and-control styles, that organisational structures need to be flatter and more flexible, and that greater employee involvement is essential for success (Handy, 1989; Kanter, 1989, 1997; Kanter *et al*, 1997; Kotter, 1996; Peters, 1989, 1993, 1997a). However, as the implications listed in Ideas and perspectives 4.9 show, there are three areas where those seeking to apply complexity theories to organisations appear to depart from, or significantly extend, the received wisdom of the last 20 years.

The basis for *Implication 1* is that unless employees have the freedom to act as they see fit, self-organisation will be blocked and organisations will not be able to achieve continuous and beneficial innovation. The rationale for *Implication 2* is that neither small-scale incremental change nor radical-transformational change work: instead, innovative activity can only be successfully generated through the 'third kind' of change, such as new product and process development brought about by self-organising teams. *Implication 3* is based on the argument that because organisations are complex systems, which are radically unpredictable and where even small changes can have massive and unanticipated effects, top-down change cannot deliver the continuous innovation that organisations need in order to survive and prosper. Instead, it is argued that organisations can only achieve continuous innovation if they position themselves at the edge of chaos. This position can only be achieved and maintained through self-organisation, which in turn depends on the possession of appropriate order-generating rules. However, should these rules cease to be appropriate for the organisation's environment, the process of self-organisation allows new, more appropriate, rules to be generated. Therefore, in a chicken-and-egg fashion, order-generating rules create the conditions for self-organisation, and self-organisation creates the conditions that enable order-generating rules to be transformed (Bechtold, 1997; Hoogerwerf and Poorthuis, 2002; Tetenbaum, 1998).

Complexity – some reservations

Like postmodernism and realism, complexity has much to commend it. It offers an explanation of the apparent complexity and chaos of modern life and, potentially at least, a way of managing this complexity and chaos. Also, for managers, it is an approach based on 'hard' science and not 'airy-fairy' philosophy. Nevertheless, writers have raised three significant reservations about the application of complexity theories to organisations (Burnes, 2005):

1. The complexity approach requires a significant shift towards greater organisational democracy and power equalisation. This appears to go far beyond the more limited, and often failed, attempts to redistribute power through empowerment, flatter organisational structures and quality improvement programmes which have been called for over the last 20 years (Eccles, 1993; Foegen, 1999; Lawler *et al*, 1998; Lee, 1999; Pfeffer, 1996; Stohl and Cheney, 2001; Wetlaufer, 1999; Whyte and Witcher, 1992; Witcher, 1993; Zairi *et al*, 1994). Therefore, convincing organisations that they are complex systems is likely to prove far easier than for organisations to achieve the profound internal realignments necessary to implement this concept (Beeson and Davis, 2000; Stacey, 2003).

2. In applying complexity theories to organisations, it is important to bear in mind that, even in the natural sciences, there are variants of these and disputes about their definition and implications (Black, 2000; Stacey *et al*, 2002; Stacey, 2003). As Arndt and Bigelow (2000: 36) observe, they have 'caused consternation as well as delight'. Therefore, one needs to be extremely careful not to treat complexity theories as though they are established, unitary, unquestioned and uncontroversial (Houchin and MacLean, 2005; Stickland, 1998).

3. There appears to be a lack of clarity or explicitness regarding how writers are applying complexity theories to organisations (Arndt and Bigelow, 2000; Brodbeck, 2002; Burnes, 2005; Hayles, 2000; Morgan, 1997; Stacey *et al*, 2002; Stacey, 2003). For example, some see them as a metaphorical device which provides a means of gaining new insights into organisations, whilst others see them as a way of mathematically modelling how and why organisations operate as they do (Stickland, 1998). If the former, then it could be argued that the complexity perspective is just another of the multiple realities so beloved of the postmodernists. If the latter, then its proponents will have to show how mathematical modelling techniques can be applied to complex and dynamic human processes in organisations, though there is no indication that anyone has yet attempted to do so (Stacey, 2003).

As Burnes (2005) has noted, though complexity theories may be bringing about a fundamental re-evaluation of how we view the natural world, there is as yet insufficient evidence to support the claim that they also have the potential to bring about the same sort of fundamental re-evaluation of the nature, purpose and operation of organisations.

Conclusions

In Chapters 1–3, we reviewed the main theories and approaches to structuring and running organisations. These three chapters showed that, over the past 100 years, organisation theory had moved a long way from the mechanical certainties of the Classical school as exemplified by the work of Frederick Taylor. We no longer perceive organisations as simple machines, nor of people as cogs, or 'greedy robots', in those machines. We now recognise the convoluted nature of organisations and their environments, and the even more convoluted nature of human beings. Contemporary approaches to running organisations have attempted to move away from the mechanical certainties of Frederick Taylor and co. by developing theories that focus on, or incorporate, the human–social dimension of organisational life. Consequently, for the Culture–Excellence school, the key issue has been organisational culture; for the Japanese, the key issue has been to blend together the 'hard' and 'soft' elements of organisational life; whereas for the learning school, the main topic has been to understand how humans learn, and how this can be translated from individual learning to collective, organisational learning. Though there are some common elements between all three approaches, there are also major differences. Nevertheless, this has not stopped proponents of all three from seeking to promote their approach as the 'one best way'.

What this chapter has shown is the need to set and understand approaches to running and designing organisations into a wider theoretical frame. None of the three perspectives on organisations reviewed in this chapter was developed specifically with organisations in mind; indeed, their originators might have been somewhat surprised to see this development. Two of them, postmodernism and realism, are based on well-developed philosophical doctrines, and the other, complexity, comes from a great deal of research carried out in a wide variety of disciplines in the natural sciences. All three are inspired by the desire to understand the world around us in its widest context, whether this be art, history, science or why it always seems to rain in Manchester. All three have significant implications for structuring and managing organisations.

- Postmodernism, with its denial of an absolute reality and promotion of competing, and socially constructed, multiple realities, offers enormous scope for the emergence of alternative strategies and choices, but it also stresses the importance of culture, power and politics in how the strategies are selected and legitimised, and how choices are made.

- The realists reject the concept of multiple realities in favour of just one. They do not deny the socially constructed nature of their reality, though they claim that it is no less real for all that. Nor do they deny that this social construction offers organisations a great deal more scope for choice and manoeuvre than conventional approaches appear to acknowledge. The difference between these two perspectives is that while the postmodernists believe that anything is possible, the realists see organisations' room for manoeuvre and choice as limited by intricate structures in both the natural and social worlds which exist even if we are not aware of them.

- The complexity perspective sees organisations as complex, self-organising systems that, in order to maximise their innovative capacities, need to operate at the edge of chaos (bounded instability). In order to remain in this position, rather than falling off the edge, they need to develop and maintain appropriate order-generating rules. In order to develop and maintain appropriate order-generating rules, organisations are required to become far more democratic than they are now and allow 'people the freedom to own their own power, think innovatively, and operate in new patterns' (Bechtold, 1997: 198). In effect, choice moves from the few to the many. Though it does appear to be the case that organisations can survive for long periods of time without appropriate rules, complexity theorists maintain that this will reduce the organisation's innovative capacity and threaten its long-term survival.

As can be seen, all of these three critical perspectives have important but different implications for organisational life, and each has fundamental differences from the other two. Nevertheless, there is one very important implication which all three perspectives share; this is that organisations do have a wide range of options and choices open to them as to how they are structured and operate. This is the case even if one concedes that some postmodernist realities are more dominant than others, that 'real' social entities, such as markets, class relations, gender relations, social rules, etc., limit choice, or that eventually organisations need to adopt or develop appropriate order-generating rules. If choice is far wider than most organisation theories acknowledge, this poses questions as to how to identify options, and who will make the decisions as to which ones to choose? In Chapter 3, we drew attention to the importance of culture in shaping organisations and the actions of those in them. Chapter 3 also drew attention to the lack of interest paid to power and politics in running organisations and making decisions. In this chapter, especially in considering postmodernism, we have also drawn attention to the role of culture, power and politics in shaping decisions in organisations. In the next chapter, we will return to these issues and show how they impact on the choices made by those who run organisations.

Test your learning

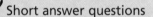

Short answer questions

1. What is flexible specialisation?

2. Give three definitions of postmodernism.

3. Using Clegg's (1990) distinction between modernist and postmodernist organisation forms, identify the significant differences between job design under a modernist regime and that under a postmodernist regime.

4. What is realism?

5. What do realists mean by the terms 'causal mechanism' and 'causal powers'?

6. What do complexity theorists mean by the 'edge of chaos'?

7. What are the implications of the complexity perspective for organisational democracy?

8. For each of the following, briefly state their implications for organisational change: (a) postmodernism, (b) realism and (c) complexity theories.

Essay questions

1. What are the implications for organisations of differences between postmodernists and realists in terms of how they view reality?

2. What are 'simple order-generating rules', and how might an organisation identify and modify these?

Suggested further reading

1. Hatch, MJ (1997) *Organization Theory: Modern, Symbolic and Postmodern Perspectives.* Oxford University Press: Oxford.

   Stacey, RD (2003) *Strategic Management and Organisational Dynamics: The Challenge of Complexity.* Financial Times Prentice Hall: Harlow.

   Taken together, these two books provide a good overview of the postmodernist slant on organisations.

2. Ackroyd, S and Fleetwood, S (eds) (2000) *Realist Perspectives on Management and Organisations.* Routledge: London.

   This edited collection of essays provide an excellent introduction to realism and how it can be applied to organisations.

3. Black, JA (2000) Fermenting change: exploring complexity and chaos. *Journal of Organizational Change Management* (Special Edition), **13**(6).

   Fitzgerald, LA (2002) Chaos: applications in organizational change. *Journal of Organizational Change Management* (Special Edition), **15**(4).

   These two special editions of the *Journal of Organizational Change Management* offer a thought-provoking and informative overview of complexity theories.

CASE STUDY 4

File sharing and the music industry[1]

BACKGROUND

Though the creation of music is as old as mankind itself, in its commodity form, as a saleable product, it is a relatively recent phenomenon. The market for music began with the sale of sheet music in the nineteenth century. In the twentieth century, with the emergence of and demand for recorded music in the form of vinyl records, cassettes, CDs, etc., the market expanded enormously to become a global industry. However, though the physical product itself may have changed, the distribution channels and the division of labour within the industry have remained relatively stable: artists create music, record labels promote and distribute it and the fans consume it. As this case study will show, however, the advent of the Internet and file-sharing technologies are causing a seismic shift in the way music is distributed, and is facilitating music piracy on a massive scale.

The credit or blame, depending on whether you are a music industry executive or a music fan, will go to Shawn Fanning. Fanning is the classic American computer geek who dropped

[1] This case study is based on work carried out with Gary Graham of the Manchester School of Management and Glenn Hardaker of Huddersfield University Business School. A fuller version of this case can be found in Graham *et al* (2002).

CASE STUDY 4 CONT.

out of college because he wanted to spend his time developing a computer program which would make it easier to find and swap music via the Internet. He called the program, and the company he launched, Napster after his school nickname. Napster quickly became one of the legends of the Internet. As Alderman (2001a: 4) commented:

The program launched in June 1999 and took off with unprecedented speed. For many, using Napster was an epiphany. One would fire it up, type in a song and instantly be connected with possibly thousands of other users who had what you wanted. Sure, you could get the studio version of Led Zeppelin's Whole Lotta Love. But if you were on at the right time, you could also get live versions of the song recorded in LA in 1977, San Francisco in 1975 or Tokyo in 1972. You might also get the new Radiohead or Eminem album weeks before their official release dates. Millions did. Using Napster was easier than going to a record store, and easier than ordering records online, and it allowed the discovery of music in ways that had not existed before. Record stores, for instance, didn't give you the opportunity to identify the cool people and investigate what else they were listening to. If there was another Napster user whose songs you liked, you could check what other music they had on their hard drive and send them instant messages. As a bonus, the whole Napster experience (excluding the computer and net costs) was free. The industry's response was incredulity and, initially, inaction.

The Napster software was very simple to use. You installed it, you placed your favourite music files in a folder on your hard disk and

then connected to the Internet. Immediately, you could share every other Napster user's music files and they could share yours. At its height in 2000, more than 80 million users per month were treating themselves to free music. Not surprisingly, the industry was not inactive for long. Whilst Napster might seem a good idea to its millions of users, to the big record labels it meant piracy on a scale that could eventually lead to their bankruptcy.

THE MUSIC INDUSTRY AND THE INTERNET

Record-making is economically as well as technically a complex process. Like books, films, television and other art forms, music is rarely just a product. Not only is it difficult to identify, develop and manage successful artists, the artistic value (and therefore the commercial value) of records depends upon their consumers' aesthetic preferences, which are neither stable nor predictable. Just because an artist has sold millions of records in the past does not mean they will in the future. The reverse is also the case. Before getting a record contract, even the biggest-selling artists, such as the Beatles, have usually been turned down by a number of record companies who failed to spot their sales potential.

For organisations involved in any form of distribution, the Internet offers the opportunity to replace 'bricks' with 'clicks' and thus improve their competitiveness (profitability) by removing stages in the distribution process. This issue is particularly acute for the music industry in that the on-line delivery of music is transforming the way music is distributed and could lead to the elimination of its physical manifestations such as CDs, record shops, etc.

Prior to the advent of the Internet, the supply chain for music comprised three main activities: the creation of music; the marketing of music; and the distribution of music. It is the big record labels that dominate the music industry rather than the artists who actually create the music. This is because it is the record labels that control access to, and in some cases actually own, the major distribution and marketing channels. According to Parikh (1999), it is the dominant position of the labels that prevents artists from independently distributing their own material, and it is this dominant position that explains why the labels collect approximately 85–90 per cent of the profit from music sales.

Parikh (1999) also argues that the current structure works against the interests of consumers. This is because the number of intermediaries and elements between the artist and the consumer make it relatively inefficient. Whilst each stage in the chain adds costs, it is not clear to what extent they provide any added value for the consumer. It is this potential to remove cost, without necessarily removing value to the final consumer, that makes the supply chain for music ripe for transformation by the Internet.

As Amazon.com has shown with books, and latterly with music, the Internet does offer the potential to remove some layers and elements in the distribution channel for music. As with books, the need physically to produce and distribute music, in the form of CDs and cassettes, has nevertheless limited the extent to which intermediaries can be eliminated and costs reduced. However, the advent of digital technology in the 1980s, which enabled music to be recorded and stored digitally in the form of CDs and minidiscs, also allows it to be transmitted digitally via the Internet. This development is taking layers out of the supply chain for music, and thus threatening the livelihood of those involved in manufacturing and distributing physical products such as CDs. But, as such, it does not threaten or challenge the dominance of the record labels, which still retain control over production and distribution.

By itself, so long as consumers download and pay for copyrighted musical content through legitimate online trading organisations, this would not be a problem for the record companies. Indeed, the Internet offers enormous scope for the music industry to bring music to a wider public, afford niche artists access to their audiences, and distribute old, new and unusual music at affordable prices.

What does threaten the dominance of the labels, however, is the advent of file-sharing technologies such as Fanning's Napster. These developments enable consumers to bypass the record labels by swapping music files directly between themselves without any money flowing to the record labels. Music piracy is not new; however, what really scares the music industry is the sheer scale and ease of the piracy allowed by the Internet. In theory, and increasingly in practice, it is possible to download (i.e. pirate) any piece of music without paying for the privilege of doing so.

SUMMARY

On the one hand, the Internet offers an enormous potential to reduce the complexity and the cost of music production and distribution by eliminating the need for CD manufacturers, music shops, transportation, etc. Certainly, the popularity of online music stores such as Apple's iTunes shows that this is increasingly the preferred way for customers to purchase music.

On the other hand, it is estimated that 19 out of 20 downloads are from illegal sites. Therefore, the Internet facilitates piracy on a scale previously unknown, which threatens to have a significant and adverse impact on the income of the record labels. Consequently, the music industry is faced with a major strategic dilemma. How does it maximise the use of the Internet to generate revenue whilst minimising the use of the Internet for piracy?

▶

CASE STUDY 4 CONT.

Questions

1. Imagine that you are a consultant with Postmodern Perspectives, a management consultancy which offers its clients a postmodern approach to strategy. You have been asked by a major record label to provide it with advice on how to maximise income and minimise piracy from the Internet. What advise would you offer, why and what would be specifically postmodern about it?

2. Imagine that you are a consultant with Realist Consultants, a management consultancy which offers its clients a realist approach to strategy. You have been asked by a major record label to provide it with advice on how to maximise income and minimise piracy from the Internet. What advise would you offer, why and what would be specifically realist about it?

3. Imagine that you are a consultant with Complexity Management, a management consultancy which offers its clients a complexity-based approach to strategy. You have been asked by a major record label to provide it with advice on how to maximise income and minimise piracy from the Internet. What advise would you offer, why and what would be specifically complexity based about it?

CHAPTER 5

Culture, power, politics and choice

Learning objectives

After studying this chapter, you should be able to:

- understand the main tenets of organisational culture;
- discuss the strengths and weaknesses of the cultural approach to organisations;
- describe the role of power and politics in organisations;
- state the main advantages and disadvantages of the power-politics perspective on organisations;
- understand the scope, methods and limitations for the exercise of choice in terms of organisational design and change.

Mini Case Study 5.1
Managerial choice

The progressive power of thinking anew

When we think of innovation, we usually think first of technology. We think of new products and services, technological processes, computer systems and software, and disruptive technologies that sometimes have the power to reshape the entire business landscape. Or we think of artefacts, such as Bluetooth and the BlackBerry, that change how we communicate.

But innovation concerns more than technology. As Michael Mol and Julian Birkinshaw point out in *Giant Steps in Management*, the most important innovations in business concern how we think about and do management, how we organise, solve problems, make strategy and lead people. The authors . . . believe these 'management innovations' are more important than usually credited. It is these, rather than new technologies, that have been the biggest influences in the way we do business today.

What is a 'management innovation'? The definition Mol and Birkinshaw offer is 'innovation in management principles and processes that ultimately change the actual process of what managers do, and how they get it done'. A management innovation changes the way we all work.

▶

Why is this important? Because, Mol and Birkinshaw argue, management innovation is directly connected to sustainable competitive advantage. . . . For Toyota and P&G, it did [lead to sustainable competitive advantage]. But there are other examples of management innovators surrendering their lead: Ford is a classic case in point. And while the divisional structure played a significant role in the rise of General Motors, it was not the only factor – good marketing, cost control and capable leadership were equally important.

This qualifies the thesis, but does not invalidate it. Management innovation can be a source of competitive advantage, if you know how to exploit it. In that respect, it is no different from any other innovation: the winner is not the one who invents the technology, but the one who gets it to market. In the same way, a management innovation is not in itself the key to lasting success.

Source: Morgan Witzel, *Financial Times*, 22 November 2007, p. 14.

Introduction

The first three chapters of this book described the main and most influential approaches to running organisations that have emerged in the last 100 years. Using the terminology of Mini Case Study 5.1, these are all major 'management innovations'. If they can be said to have one common feature, it is that each of them claims to have discovered the 'one best way' to run organisations. As such, the result of these innovations ought to be the reduction or elimination of managerial choice and discretion. If there is a sure-fire way of running organisations, the main job of senior managers is to see that it is implemented and that no one, especially themselves, deviates from it. If there is a sure-fire recipe for success, then we should see the elimination, or at the very least the downgrading, of senior managerial posts because almost anyone should be capable of implementing the recipe. However, given the dramatic increase in executive salaries on both sides of the Atlantic in the last 15 years, this is clearly not the case (AFL-CIO, 2003; DeCarlo, 2008; Finch and Treanor, 2003; Green, 2008). Similarly, if such sure-fire recipes exist, why is there such a wide disparity in organisational success and why do so few, if any, companies manage to achieve long-term prosperity? In the 80 years from 1917 to 1997, only 2 of America's largest 100 companies, GE and Kodak, outperformed the market (Foster and Kaplan, 2003).

As Witzel comments in Mini Case Study 5.1, 'Management innovation can be a source of competitive advantage, if you know how to exploit it.' In essence, 'management innovations', though important, are no replacement for 'management resourcefulness'. Consequently, the choices that managers make regarding which innovations to adopt and how to implement them are at least as important as the innovations themselves. For example, as Sheldrake (1996) notes, the Japanese approach to quality was developed by Americans but American companies have signally failed to gain the same level of competitive advantage from it that their Japanese rivals have.

The importance of managerial choice was noted in the conclusion to the previous chapter when discussing postmodernism, realism and complexity. It was argued that rather than being the prisoners of circumstances, rather than being hemmed in by successful recipes, rather than rational beings unquestioningly following rational recipes, managers may have a surprisingly wide degree of choice and discretions. Even if one rejects the 'boundless' view of choice advocated by the postmodernists in favour of the 'bounded' view of the realists and complexity theorists, managers are still far from the 'executive robots' implied by those who promote 'one best way' approaches to running organisations. However, if the recipes for success are not straitjackets, if managers are not rational beings, if they do have scope for choice, on what do they base their choices? In this chapter, we will examine the argument that the answer lies in the areas of culture, power and politics.

The chapter begins with a review of organisational culture. It is shown that many organisations lack a cohesive culture that bonds them together in a common purpose. However, contrary to the arguments of the Culture–Excellence school, even where strong cultures exist, they may not always be appropriate; they may also be undermined owing to the absence of clear or uncontested organisational goals. The review of culture concludes that:

- Although organisational culture may have important implications for organisational performance, there is little agreement about the nature of culture, whether it can be changed or the benefits to be gained from attempting to change it.
- Instead of culture being seen as an all-important and malleable determinant of performance, organisational life in many cases is dominated by political power battles which may be more influential than culture in shaping key decisions.

Consequently, the review of culture leads on to an examination of the nature and role of power and politics in organisations. This view maintains that organisations are essentially political entities. In reviewing the arguments for this view, the chapter shows that:

- The decisions, actions and major developments of organisations are influenced and determined by shifting coalitions of individuals attempting to protect or enhance their own interests.

The behaviour of managers in attempting to protect their own interests raises the issue of the degree to which they can exert choice over what they do and how they do it. The issue of choice is examined in the final section of this chapter. The examination draws not only on the review of culture, power and politics from this chapter but also on the conclusions of the previous chapter. In summing up the implications for managerial choice of the two chapters, it is argued that:

- Rather than being the prisoners of organisational theories or contingencies, managers (potentially) have considerable, though by no means unconstrained, freedom of choice over the structure, policies and practices of their organisations, and even over the environment in which they operate.
- In exercising choice, managers are influenced by organisational theories and constraints, but they are also influenced by their concern to ensure that the outcome of decisions favours, or at least does not damage, their personal interests.

The conclusion to this chapter – and indeed of Part 1 of the book – is that, whether illegitimate or useful, political behaviour is an ever-present part of organisational life, and that such behaviour is particularly prevalent when major change initiatives are being considered or implemented.

The cultural perspective

What is organisational culture?

As can be seen from the discussion in Chapter 3 of the Culture–Excellence school and, to a lesser extent, organisational learning and Japanese management, many writers point out that managers and employees do not perform their duties in a value-free vacuum. Their work and the way it is done are governed, directed and tempered by an organisation's culture – the particular set of values, beliefs, customs and systems that are unique to that organisation. Though Peters and Waterman's (1982) view that organisational culture is the prime determinant of organisational performance has been highly influential, and received much support (Flamholtz, 2001; Kotter and Heskett, 1992; Rogers *et al*, 2006), other writers stress different, but no less important, aspects of culture. Keuning (1998: 46), for example, argues that the two most important functions of culture are: 'To provide relatively fixed patterns for handling and solving problems . . . [and to] . . . reduce uncertainty for members of the organization when confronted with new situations.' Nevertheless, as Wilson (1992) noted, so influential has Peters and Waterman's view become that culture has come to be seen as the great 'cure-all' for the majority of organisational ills.

The fascination of business with organisational culture began in the 1980s with the work of writers such as Allen and Kraft (1982), Deal and Kennedy (1982), and above all Peters and Waterman (1982). Academics, however, had drawn attention to its importance much earlier; as Allaire and Firsirotu (1984) and Albrow (1997) have shown, there was already a substantial academic literature on organisational culture well before the work of Peters and Waterman (*see* Eldridge and Crombie, 1974; Turner, 1971). Blake and Mouton (1969), for example, were arguing that there was a link between culture and excellence in the late 1960s. For all this, organisational culture remains a highly contentious topic whose implications are far-reaching.

Turner (1986) traced the 'culture craze' of the 1980s to the decline of standards in manufacturing quality in the USA, and the challenge to its economic supremacy by Japan. He commented that the concept of culture holds out a new way of understanding organisations, and has been offered by many writers as an explanation for the spectacular success of Japanese companies in the 1970s and 1980s. Bowles (1989), amongst others, observed that there is an absence of a cohesive culture in advanced economies in the West, and that the potential for creating systems of beliefs and myths within organisations provides the opportunity for promoting both social and organisational cohesion. The case for culture was best summed up by Deal and Kennedy (1982), who argued that culture, rather than structure, strategy or politics, is the prime mover in organisations.

Silverman (1970) contended that organisations are societies in miniature and can therefore be expected to show evidence of their own cultural characteristics. However, culture does not spring up automatically and fully formed from the whims of management. Allaire and Firsirotu (1984) considered it to be the product of a number of different influences: the ambient society's values and characteristics, the organisation's history and past leadership, and factors such as industry and technology. Other writers have constructed similar lists but, as Brown (1995) commented, there does seem to be some dispute over which factors shape organisational culture and which are an integral part of it. Drennan (1992), for example, lists company expectations as a factor that shapes culture, but these might just as easily be seen as a reflection of an organisation's values which, as Cummings and Huse (1989) point out, are a key component of the organisation's culture. However, the difficulty in distinguishing between the factors that shape culture and those that comprise culture is a reflection, as Cummings and Huse (1989: 421) also point out, of the 'confusion about what the term culture really means when applied to organizations'. Brown (1995: 6–7) estimated that there are literally hundreds of definitions of culture: examples of these are shown in Ideas and perspectives 5.1.

Ideas and perspectives 5.1
Definitions of culture

The culture of the factory is its customary and traditional way of thinking and doing things, which is shared to a greater or lesser degree by all its members and which new members must learn, and at least partially accept, in order to be accepted into service in the firm.
(Jaques, 1952: 251)

Culture describes patterns of behavior that form a durable template by which ideas and images can be transferred from one generation to another, or from one group to another.
(Haggett, 1975: 238)

Culture . . . is a pattern of beliefs and expectations shared by the organization's members. These beliefs and expectations produce norms and powerfully shape the behavior of individuals and groups in the organization.
(Schwartz and Davis, 1981: 33)

A quality of perceived organizational specialness – that it possesses some unusual quality that distinguishes it from others in the field.
(Gold, 1982: 571– 2)

By culture I mean the shared beliefs top managers in a company have about how they should manage themselves and other employees, and how they should conduct business(es).
(Lorsch, 1986: 95)

Culture represents an interdependent set of values and ways of behaving that are common in a community and that tend to perpetuate themselves, sometimes over long periods of time.
(Kotter and Heskett, 1992: 141)

Culture is 'how things are done around here'.
(Drennan, 1992: 3)

Whilst there is a similarity between the definitions shown in Ideas and perspectives 5.1, there are also some distinct differences: is culture something an organisation is or something it possesses? Does it mainly apply to senior managers or does it embrace everyone in the organisation? Is it a weak or a powerful force? Perhaps the most widely accepted definition is that offered by Eldridge and Crombie (1974: 78), who stated that culture refers:

> . . . to the unique configuration of norms, values, beliefs, ways of behaving and so on, that characterise the manner in which groups and individuals combine to get things done.

Therefore, what we can say of culture is that it:

- Defines how those in the organisation should behave in a given set of circumstances.
- Affects all, from the most senior manager to the humblest clerk.
- Ensures that the actions of a member of an organisation are judged by themselves and others in relation to expected norms of behaviour.
- Legitimises certain forms of action and proscribes other forms.

This latter view is supported by Turner (1971), who observed that cultural systems contain elements of 'ought' which prescribe forms of behaviour or allow behaviour to be judged acceptable or not. Other writers have suggested a wide variety of different aspects of culture as being important in shaping behaviour. For example, Martin *et al* (1983) pointed to the role of organisational stories in shaping the actions and expectations of employees. They identified seven basic types of story prevalent in organisations which provide answers to seven fundamental questions of behaviour (*see* Ideas and perspectives 5.2).

Alongside stories, much attention has been paid to the role of ceremonies, rites and rituals in reinforcing behaviour. Trice and Beyer (1984) found that these include the following:

- **Rites of passage** – designed to facilitate and signal a change in status and role through events such as training and induction programmes.
- **Rites of questioning** – to allow the status quo to be challenged through the use of, for example, outside consultants.

Ideas and perspectives 5.2
Fundamental questions of behaviour in organisations

1. Can employees break the rules?
2. Is the big boss human?
3. Can the little person rise to the top?
4. Will I get fired?
5. Will the organisation help me if I have to move?
6. How will the boss react to mistakes?
7. How will the organisation deal with obstacles?

- **Rites of renewal** – to enable the status quo to be updated and renewed through participative initiatives including strategy development, vision building and job redesign programmes.

Another common theme in the literature is the role of 'heroes'. Peters and Waterman (1982) stressed the importance of corporate heroes in shaping the fortunes of their 'excellent' companies. Deal and Kennedy (1982) likewise saw the corporate hero as the great motivator, the person everyone looks up to, admires and relies on. Indeed, there is a tendency, not just in the USA, to attribute much of business success to the actions and personality of individuals, such as Pierre du Pont, Henry Heinz, Henry Ford, Alfred Sloan, Toyoda Kiichiro, Matsushita Konosuke, Edward Cadbury and Sir John Harvey-Jones. Current corporate heroes include Richard Branson at Virgin, Ratan Tata at Tata Group, Steve Jobs at Apple, Stuart Rose at Marks and Spencer and Rupert Murdoch at News Corp and, perhaps the biggest of them all, Warren Buffet at Berkshire Hathaway. Of course, heroes can also become villains, most notably Jeff Skilling at Enron. *Fortune* magazine named Enron as 'America's Most Innovative Company' for six years in a row until 2001, when it was revealed that its spectacular growth was an illusion created by fraud on a truly massive scale. Skilling quickly moved from being the CEO that everyone should copy to the villain whose behaviour should be avoided at all costs.

Leadership is just one aspect of culture. Brown (1995) compiled a long list of 38 key elements of culture that have been identified by writers in the field, which include organisational climate, metaphors, attitudes, history and basic assumptions. Identifying these separate elements of culture helps us to flesh out and better understand how organisational culture manifests itself and impacts on individual and group behaviour. However, Brown also shows that producing lists of elements or focusing on the role of particular elements tends to present a confusing and partial picture of culture. It becomes difficult to determine which are the more and which are the less important elements and, in terms of changing culture, which elements can be easily altered and which are more immutable.

To overcome this lack of clarity, there have been a number of attempts to identify and categorise the constituent elements of culture. Hofstede (1990) developed a four-layered hierarchical model of culture which ranged from *values* at the deepest level through *rituals*, *heroes* and, at the surface level, *symbols*. In a similar way, Schein (1985) suggested a three-level model, with *basic assumptions* being at the deepest level, *beliefs*, *values* and *attitudes* at the intermediate level, and *artefacts* at the surface level. Based on an analysis of the different definitions of culture, Cummings and Huse (1989) produced a composite model of culture, comprising four major elements existing at different levels of awareness (*see* Figure 5.1).

Cummings and Huse (1989: 421) define these four major layers of culture as follows:

1. *Basic assumptions.* At the deepest level of cultural awareness are unconscious, taken-for-granted assumptions about how organizational problems should be solved . . . They represent nonconfrontable and nondebatable assumptions about relating to the environment, as well as about the nature of human nature, human activity and human relationships. [. . .]
2. *Values.* The next higher level of awareness includes values about what *ought* to be in organizations. Values tell members what is important in the organization and what they need to pay attention to. [. . .]

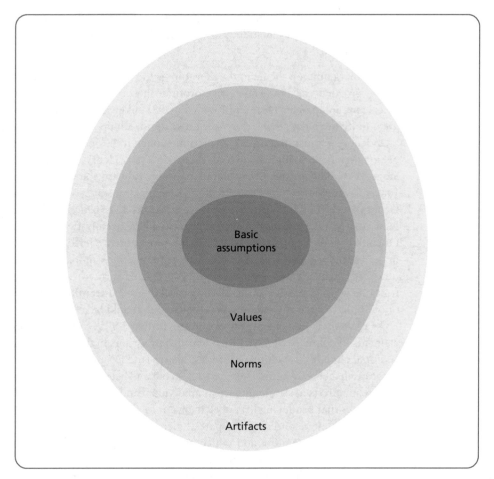

Figure 5.1 The major elements of culture

3. *Norms.* Just below the surface of cultural awareness are norms guiding how members should behave in particular situations. These represent unwritten rules of behavior. [. . .]

4. *Artifacts.* At the highest level of cultural awareness are the artifacts and creations that are visible manifestations of the other levels of cultural elements. These include observable behaviors of members, as well as the structures, systems, procedures, rules, and physical aspects of the organization.

While the various hierarchical models of culture elements are useful, we should always remember that, as Brown (1995: 8–9) observes, 'actual organisational cultures are not as neat and tidy as the models seem to imply'. Indeed, Fang (2005–6) questions the usefulness of what he calls the 'onion' view of culture, i.e. that culture comprises a number of layers which can be peeled back in order to reveal the true essence of an organisation. Instead, Fang (2005–6: 82) views culture as an 'ocean':

It is useful to conceive of culture as having a life of its own. Seen longitudinally or historically, every culture has a dynamic life full of energies, sentiments, dramas, and contradictions. In its entire life span, every culture encompasses an ocean of infinite potential value orientations. . . . At a given point, many cultural values have been endorsed, promoted, and legitimized, while other 'value cousins' are dampened, suppressed, and destroyed.

Where there are cultures, there are also usually subcultures, and where there is agreement about cultures there can also be disagreements and counter-cultures (de Chernatony and Cottam, 2008). In particular, there can also be significant differences between espoused culture and culture-in-practice (Yaniv and Farkas, 2005). All of this can adversely affect an organisation's performance.

This lack of neatness and tidiness has not prevented numerous attempts to define organisational culture, nor attempts to categorise the various types of culture. Deal and Kennedy (1982) identified four basic types of culture, as did Quinn and McGrath (1985) – but the two categorisations are very different (*see* Ideas and perspectives 5.3 and 5.4).

Ideas and perspectives 5.3
Deal and Kennedy's four types of culture

- The *Tough Guy, Macho culture*, characterised by individualism and risk-taking, e.g. a police force.
- The *Work-Hard/Play-Hard culture*, characterised by low risks and quick feedback on performance, e.g. McDonald's.
- The *Bet-Your-Company culture*, characterised by high risks and very long feedback time, e.g. aircraft companies.
- The *Process culture*, characterised by low risks and slow feedback, e.g. insurance companies.

Source: Deal and Kennedy (1982)

Ideas and perspectives 5.4
Quinn and McGrath's four types of culture

- The *Market*, characterised by rational decision-making and goal-orientated employees, e.g. GEC under Arnold Weinstock.
- The *Adhocracy*, characterised by risk-orientated and charismatic leaders and value-driven organisations, e.g. Apple and Microsoft in their early days.
- The *Clan*, characterised by participation, consensus and concern for others, e.g. voluntary organisations.
- The *Hierarchy*, characterised by hierarchical, rule-based authority that values stability and risk avoidance, e.g. government bureaucracies.

Source: Quinn and McGrath (1985)

These two examples show the difficulty researchers encounter when trying to describe and categorise something as nebulous as culture. This difficulty can also be seen with Handy's (1979) attempt to categorise culture. This is perhaps the best-known typology of culture and the one which has been around the longest. Handy developed it from Harrison's (1972) work on 'organization ideologies'. Handy (1986: 188) observed that 'There seem to be four main types of culture . . . *power*, *role*, *task* and *person*.' As shown in Ideas and perspectives 5.5, he relates each of these to a particular form of organisational structure.

Handy (1986) believes that *role* cultures (with their accompanying mechanistic structures) and *task* cultures (with their accompanying organic structures) tend to predominate in Western organisations. Relating these two types of culture to Burns and Stalker's (1961) structural continuum, with *mechanistic* structures at one end and *organic* at the other, we can see that Handy is in effect seeking to construct a parallel and related cultural continuum, with *role* cultures at the *mechanistic* end and *task* cultures at the *organic* end (*see* Figure 5.2).

Ideas and perspectives 5.5
Handy's four types of culture

A *power culture*, Handy states, is frequently found in small entrepreneurial organisations such as some property, trading and finance companies. Such a culture is associated with a web structure with one or more powerful figures at the centre, wielding control.

A *role culture* is appropriate to bureaucracies, and organisations with mechanistic, rigid structures and narrow jobs. Such cultures stress the importance of procedures and rules, hierarchical position and authority, security and predictability. In essence, role cultures create situations in which those in the organisation stick rigidly to their job description (role), and any unforeseen events are referred to the next layer up in the hierarchy.

A *task culture*, on the other hand, is job- or project-orientated; the onus is on getting the job in hand (the task) done, rather than prescribing how it should be done. Such types of culture are appropriate to organically structured organisations where flexibility and teamworking are encouraged. *Task* cultures create situations in which speed of reaction, integration and creativity are more important than adherence to particular rules or procedures, and where position and authority are less important than the individual contribution to the task in hand.

A *person culture* is, he argues, rare. The individual and his or her wishes are the central focus of this form of culture. It is associated with a minimalistic structure, the purpose of which is to assist those individuals who choose to work together. Therefore, a person culture can be characterised as a cluster or galaxy of individual stars.

Source: Handy (1986)

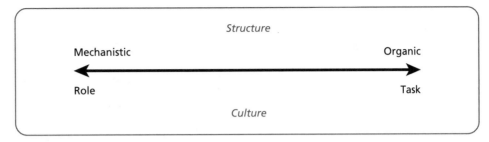

Figure 5.2 A structure–culture continuum

This categorisation certainly accommodates the five Western approaches to organisation theory discussed in the previous chapters. However, it is difficult to accommodate Japanese organisations within this framework, as their cultures contain elements of each extreme. As was described in Chapter 3, Japanese companies have very tightly structured jobs, especially at the lower levels; they are very hierarchical and deferential, whilst at the same time achieving high levels of motivation, initiative and creativity in problem-solving. They tend to be heavily group- or team-orientated, with such teams having a great deal of autonomy.

This difficulty of where to place Japan highlights one of the main criticisms of the various attempts to categorise culture, which is that they appear to give insufficient weight to the influence of national cultures on the types of organisational culture that predominate in particular countries. Increasingly over the last decade, and to an extent before, strong reservations have been expressed about the ethnocentric nature of organisational theory; the main reservation concerns the generalisability and applicability of management theories developed in the West, predominately the USA, to the very different cultures and societies of Asia, the Middle East and Africa (Deresky, 2000; Fagenson-Eland *et al*, 2004; Fang, 2005–6; Ho, 1976; Rosenzweig, 1994; Sullivan and Nonaka, 1986; Thomas, 2003; Trompenaars, 1993). Lowe *et al* (2007: 246), looking at the various approaches to culture, believes that the problem is that:

> . . . *they all unconsciously adhere to the structuralist inheritance of western philosophy and the rationalist consequences of Enlightenment thinking. They are all, therefore, western culture-bound accounts of culture, and . . . ignore possible alternative models of culture from other perspectives. They describe culture using a western rationalist world-view . . .*

Such criticisms have not and should not stop Western researchers from attempting to study the differences between national cultures. In this respect, one of the most comprehensive and influential studies was carried out by Hofstede (1980, 1990, 2001). He suggested that national cultures can be clustered along the lines of their similarities across a range of cultural variables, as follows:

- the prevailing sense of individualism or collectivity in each country;
- the power distance accepted in each country (the degree of centralisation, autocratic leadership and number of levels in the hierarchy);
- the degree to which uncertainty is tolerated or avoided.

Ideas and perspectives 5.6
Hofstede's national clusters

1. Scandinavia (primarily Denmark, Sweden and Norway): these cultures are based upon values of collectivity, consensus and decentralisation.
2. West Germany (prior to unification), Switzerland and Austria: these are grouped together largely as valuing efficiency – the well-oiled machine – and seeking to reduce uncertainty.
3. Great Britain, Canada, the USA, New Zealand, Australia and the Netherlands: these lie somewhere between 1 and 2 but cluster on the value they place on strong individuals and achievers in society.
4. Japan, France, Belgium, Spain and Italy: these are clustered on bureaucratic tendencies – the pyramid structure – favouring a large power distance.

Based on these cultural variables, Hofstede (1980 and 1990) classified industrialised countries into four broad clusters (shown in Ideas and perspectives 5.6). However, his findings have to be treated with some caution as his sample was drawn from just one multinational company, IBM.

Hofstede's work has come in for its fair share of criticism in the way it portrays different national cultures (*see* Fang, 2005–6; Lowe *et al*, 2007; McSweeney, 2002). Wilson (1992: 90) nevertheless observed that 'The similarity of the factors in [Hofstede's] national culture study to Handy's (1986) four organizational forms is striking.' Yet whilst one can see that Scandinavia can be classed as exhibiting *task* culture characteristics, and the group containing West Germany can be seen as exhibiting *role* culture characteristics, the other two groupings (Great Britain *et al* and Japan *et al*) are more difficult to place. Rather than placing Great Britain and the USA in one category, according to where they are positioned on Hofstede's dimensions, it might be more accurate to follow Handy's own lead and say that both *task* and *role* cultures are prevalent. This still leaves us with where to place Japan *et al*. From the point of view of Hofstede's dimensions, Japan appears to exhibit characteristics of Handy's *role* culture but, as pointed out above, this is only part of the story of Japanese organisational life.

The impact of different national cultures on the management of organisations will be returned to in Chapter 12 when discussing globalisation. However, for now, it is important to recognise that Handy's categorisation of types of culture is very useful, in that it takes us beyond vague generalisations and gives us a picture of differing cultures. It must still be recognised that Handy's classification is merely one amongst many. A number of researchers have attempted to rationalise the plethora of types of culture by attempting to group the various classifications. Wilson (2001) attempted to make sense of the literature on culture by identifying the perspective of those writing about it. As Ideas and perspectives 5.7 shows, he identifies three main perspectives on culture: integration, differentiation and fragmentation. Taking a very different tack, the Organizational Culture Inventory (OCI) (Jones *et al*, 2006) attempts to group types of culture by how they impact on the behaviour of individuals and groups in an organisation (*see* Ideas and perspectives 5.8).

Ideas and perspectives 5.7
Wilson's culture perspectives

The integration perspective: This portrays a strong or desirable culture as one where there is organisation wide consensus and consistency (e.g. Schein, 1985; Deal and Kennedy, 1982; Peters and Waterman, 1982). Espoused values are consistent with formal practices, which are consistent with informal beliefs, norms and attitudes. Cultural members share the same values, promoting a shared sense of loyalty and commitment. Where inconsistencies, conflict or subcultural differentiation occur, this is portrayed as being a weak or negative culture.

The differentiation perspective: This emphasises that rather than consensus being organisation-wide, it only occurs within the boundaries of a subculture. At the organisational level, differentiated subcultures may co-exist in harmony, conflict or indifference to each other (e.g. Van Maanen, 1991). These sub-cultures related to different jobs, different levels of organisational status, gender and class. Claims of harmony from management masked a range of inconsistencies and group antagonisms. What is unique about a given organisation's culture, then, is the particular mix of subcultural differences within an organisation's boundaries.

The fragmentation perspective: This approach views ambiguity as the norm, with consensus and dissension co-existing in a constantly fluctuating pattern influenced by events and specific areas of decision making (e.g. Frost *et al*, 1991). Consensus fails to coalesce on an organisation-wide or subcultural basis, except in transient, issue-specific ways. Rather than the clear unity of the integration perspective, or the clear conflicts of the differentiation viewpoint, fragmentation focuses on that which is unclear.

Source: Wilson (2001: 357)

Ideas and perspectives 5.8
Organizational Culture Inventory classifications

Constructive cultures. Cultures in which members are encouraged to interact with others and approach tasks in ways that will help them to meet their higher-order satisfaction needs (includes Achievement, Self-Actualization, Humanistic-Encouraging and Affiliative cultures).

Passive/Defensive cultures. Cultures in which members believe that they must interact with people in defensive ways that will not threaten their own security (includes Approval, Conventional, Dependent and Avoidance cultures).

Aggressive/Defensive cultures. Cultures in which members are expected to approach tasks in forceful ways to protect their status and security (includes Oppositional, Power, Competitive and Perfectionist cultures).

Source: Jones *et al* (2006: 18)

What this review of culture types and classifications highlights is both the difficulty of defining cultures clearly, and also the profound implications of the cultural approach to organisations. These implications fall under four main headings.

- Firstly, Deal and Kennedy (1982) argue that behaviour, instead of reacting directly to intrinsic and extrinsic motivators, is shaped by shared values, beliefs and assumptions about the way an organisation should operate, how rewards should be distributed, the conduct of meetings, and even how people should dress.
- Secondly, if organisations do have their own identities, personalities or cultures, are there particular types of cultural attributes that are peculiar to top-performing organisations? As discussed in Chapter 3, the Culture–Excellence school replies to this question with a resounding *yes*!
- Thirdly, Sathe (1983) argues that culture guides the actions of an organisation's members without the need for detailed instructions or long meetings to discuss how to approach particular issues or problems; it also reduces the level of ambiguity and misunderstanding between functions and departments. In effect, it provides a common context and a common purpose for those in the organisation. However, this is only the case when an organisation possesses a strong culture, and where the members of the organisation have internalised it to the extent that they no longer question the legitimacy or appropriateness of the organisation's values and beliefs.
- Fourthly, one of the most important implications is that it is possible to change or manage a culture (Barratt, 1990; O'Reilly, 1989).

This last implication is particularly contentious, with many writers supporting the view that organisations can deliberately change their culture but with others arguing strongly against it.

Changing organisational culture?

That cultures do change is not in question. No organisation's culture is static: it tends to evolve in a slow and unplanned fashion as a result of the turnover of group members, changes in the organisation's environment and general changes in society (Fang, 2005–6; Kotter and Heskett, 1992). However, this is a far cry from saying that organisations can deliberately choose to change their culture, which is what many writers do claim. In order to examine this issue, three questions will be addressed:

1. Why should an organisation wish to change its culture?
2. Is culture, or significant elements of it, amenable to deliberate change?
3. Are there established approaches available for changing culture?

We will begin by examining the first of these questions.

1. **Why should an organisation wish to change its culture?** Given that culture is locked into the beliefs, values and norms of each individual in the organisation, and because these are difficult constructs to alter, natural (unplanned) culture change will be slow, unless perhaps there is some major shock to the organisation (Boddy, 2002; Brown, 1995; Burnes, 1991; Keuning, 1998; Schein, 1985). This in itself may not be problematic for organisations, provided that other factors change in an equally

slow fashion. However, the argument put forward by the proponents of Culture–Excellence is that a successful culture is one based on values and assumptions appropriate to the unpredictable and fast-moving environment in which they believe modern organisations operate. In addition, it has been argued that, to operate effectively and efficiently, an organisation's culture needs to match or be appropriate to its structure (Allaire and Firsirotu, 1984; Handy, 1986). Looking at Figure 5.2, we can see that organisations with *mechanistic* structures are said to operate effectively and efficiently if they have *role* cultures (Handy, 1986). If we refer back to the work of Burns and Stalker (1961) discussed in Chapter 2, we can merge Figure 2.2 with Figure 5.2 to show how different structures relate to different environments and, by extension, how different cultures relate to different environments (*see* Figure 5.3). As can be seen, *mechanistic* structures and *role* cultures are suitable for *stable* environments and *organic* structures and *task* cultures are suitable for *least-predictable* (highly dynamic) environments.

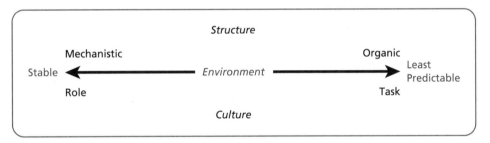

Figure 5.3 A structure–culture–environment continuum

Given that an organisation's environment can change rapidly, situations will arise where an organisation's culture and structure may be out of step with its environment, e.g. it may have a *mechanistic* structure and a *role* culture but find itself operating in a *least-predictable* environment. In response to this, an organisation can change its *mechanistic* structure deliberately and relatively quickly to an *organic* one which would be more suitable to its new environment. However, if it assumes that its culture will adjust to the new circumstances in a natural (unplanned) manner, it is likely to find that this is a slow and unpredictable process. Consequently, a company that moves quickly to replace a *mechanistic* structure with a more *organic* structure, to cope with increasing uncertainty in its environment, might find that the change does not improve its effectiveness and efficiency because it still has a *role* culture which is not only incompatible with its changed environment but which also clashes with its new *organic* structure (*see* Figure 5.4).

As Handy (1986: 188) commented, this mismatch between culture and other key organisation variables is not uncommon or unimportant:

Experience suggests that a strong culture makes a strong organisation, but does it matter what sort of culture is involved? Yes, it does. Not all cultures suit all purposes or people. Cultures are founded and built over the years by the dominant groups in an organisation. What suits them and the organisation at one stage is not necessarily appropriate for ever – strong though that culture may be.

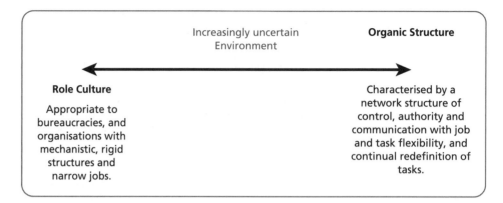

Figure 5.4 A structure–culture mismatch

Flynn (1993) described how, with the introduction of a more market-orientated philosophy, such situations arose across organisations in the public sector in the UK. Jack Welch faced the same situation at GE in the 1980s. He had delayered, downsized and got rid of underperforming units. In the process he had reduced the workforce by 70,000 employees and earned the nickname 'Neutron Jack'. However, as he stated to a group of GE employees, he came to recognise that:

> *A company can boost productivity by restructuring, removing bureaucracy, and downsizing, but it cannot sustain high productivity without cultural change.*
>
> Quoted in Ghoshal and Bartlett (2000: 201)

Many similar cases can be found elsewhere in the private sector (*see* Boddy, 2002; Brown, 1995; Cummings and Worley, 2001; Dobson, 1988; Industrial Society, 1997). In such situations, rather than facilitating the efficient operation of the organisation, its culture may obstruct it.

Therefore, the answer to the question *Why should an organisation wish to change its culture?* is 'because its existing culture is no longer fit for purpose and is having a detrimental effect on its competitive performance'. This now leads on to the second question.

2. **Is culture, or significant elements of it, amenable to deliberate change?** The literature on culture is extensive and confusing, with many writers arguing the case for culture being something that can be deliberately and successfully changed, but with a substantial number of other writers taking either an openly hostile view or a much more cautious one. Ogbonna and Harris (2002) label these three groups of writers as the optimists, the pessimists and the realists. For the optimists, there are those, such as Barratt (1990: 23), who claim that 'values, beliefs and attitudes are learnt, can be managed and changed and are potentially manipulable by management'. O'Reilly (1989) takes a similar view, arguing that it is possible to change or manage a culture by choosing the attitudes and behaviours that are required, identifying the norms or expectations that promote or impede them, and then taking action to create the desired effect. Therefore, there is a body of opinion that sees culture as something that can be managed and changed. There are also many, many organisations in which, for a variety

of reasons, senior managers have decided that their existing culture is inappropriate or even detrimental to their competitive needs and, therefore, must be changed (Deal and Kennedy, 1982; Industrial Society, 1997; Peters and Waterman, 1982).

For the pessimists, Filby and Willmott (1988) questioned the notion that management has the capacity to control culture. They point out that this ignores the way in which an individual's values and beliefs are conditioned by experience outside the workplace – through exposure to the media, through social activities, as well as through previous occupational activities. Hatch (1997: 235) is also very dubious about attempts to change organisational culture:

Do not think of trying to manage culture. Other people's meanings and interpretations are highly unmanageable. Think instead of trying to culturally manage your organization, that is, manage your organization with cultural awareness of the multiplicity of meanings that will be made of you and your efforts.

A further concern expressed by a number of writers relates to the ethical issues raised by attempts to change culture (Van Maanen and Kunda, 1989; Willmott, 1995). This concern is succinctly articulated by Watson (1997: 278) who concludes that:

Employers and managers engaging in these ways with issues of employees' self-identities and the values through which they judge the rights and wrongs of their daily lives must be a matter of serious concern. To attempt to mould cultures – given that culture in its broad sense provides the roots of human morality, social identity and existential security – is indeed to enter 'deep and dangerous waters' . . .

The realists seem to take a position somewhere in between those who see culture as something that is amenable to managerial choice and those who see it as immutable. These writers appear to agree that culture as a whole cannot be changed, but argue that certain key elements, such as norms of behaviour, can be influenced by management (Schein, 1985). This viewpoint is summed up by Meek (1988: 469–70), who argues that:

Culture as a whole cannot be manipulated, turned on or off, although it needs to be recognised that some [organisations] are in a better position than others to intentionally influence aspects of it.

As the labels they ascribe to the three groups might imply, Ogbonna and Harris (2002) tend to believe that the realists have the best of the argument; culture as a whole cannot be changed but it is possible intentionally and successfully to change key aspects of culture. In essence, what the realists appear to be arguing is that those wishing to change culture should concentrate on changing the behaviour of staff by manipulating the two upper layers of culture as depicted in Figure 5.1, i.e. artefacts and norms. Fang (2005–6) notes that, according to Leon Festinger's (1957) theory of cognitive dissonance (*see* Chapter 10), if one can change behaviour, this can then lead to a change in values, the third layer in the culture 'onion' depicted in Figure 5.1. Burnes and James (1995:17) sound a cautionary note with regard to cognitive dissonance and behaviour change:

It has been argued that, where individuals are required to change their behaviour in such a fashion that it clashes with their attitudes and gives rise to dissonance, an attitude change will only occur if the people concerned believe, rightly or wrongly, that they have a choice as to whether to adopt the new behaviour or not. If, on the other hand, they feel that they are being compelled against their will to change their behaviour, this can lead to high levels of dissonance and perhaps open defiance.

This view is also supported by many of the writers on power and politics (see the following section of this chapter) who see the use of remunerative and coercive power as counter-productive, because those on the receiving end of such power tend to view it negatively and resent it (Rollinson, 2002).

Therefore, the answer to the question *Is culture, or significant elements of it, amenable to deliberate change?* is yes. There is considerable evidence that the surface elements of culture, i.e. artefacts and norms, can be changed. There is also some evidence that changes to behaviour can lead to changes in values (the third layer in the culture 'onion') but only if those concerned feel that they have choice and are adopting the new behaviours of their own free will. If this is not the case, attempts to change culture may result in resistance rather than cooperation. The actual practice of culture change can be understood more easily by moving on to examine the third question.

3. **Are there established approaches available for changing culture?** Over the last 25 years, many organisations have attempted to change their culture in order to improve or regain their competitiveness. A survey of the UK's 1,000 largest public- and private-sector organisations, carried out in 1988 by Dobson (1988), revealed that more than 250 of them had been involved in culture change programmes in the preceding five years. A similar survey by the Industrial Society in 1997, covering over 4,000 organisations, found that over 90 per cent of respondents were either going through or had recently gone through a culture change programme (Industrial Society, 1997). Nor does there seem to be any slacking of the pace of culture change. A survey of 365 companies in Europe, Asia and North America by the management consultants Bain & Co found that 76% believed that their cultures could be changed and 65% believed that they needed to change their cultures (Rogers *et al*, 2006).

However, whilst many organisations perceive the need to change their culture, it often requires a major shock to the system before they actually embark on such a change. It was only following the Enron crash, with the subsequent severe criticisms of its auditors, that the Big Four accounting companies in the USA began to change their cultures to become more risk-averse (Michaels, 2004). Similarly, it was only with the onset of the 'credit crunch' in 2007, brought about by reckless sub-prime loans (Hutton, 2008a), that the rest of the institutions in the financial services sector also followed suit. Banks and other financial bodies make their money by lending money. In the boom times of the 1990s and 2000s, they very much adopted a lend, lend, lend culture. However, the credit crunch triggered a stampede from a risk-inclined to a risk-averse culture (Balakrishnan and Collinson, 2007; Elliott, 2007).

In examining how organisations change their cultures, the Industrial Society (1997) found that this was promoted through a variety of methods including strategic planning, training, organisation redesign to promote teamwork, and changes to appraisal systems. Based on his 1988 survey, Dobson identified a four-step approach to culture change involving shaping the beliefs, values and attitudes of employees (*see* Ideas and perspectives 5.9).

Ideas and perspectives 5.9
Dobson's guide to changing culture

Step 1   Change recruitment, selection and redundancy policies to alter the composition of the workforce so that promotion and employment prospects are dependent on those concerned possessing or displaying the beliefs and values the organisation wishes to promote.

Step 2   Reorganise the workforce to ensure that those employees and managers displaying the required traits occupy positions of influence.

Step 3   Effectively communicate the new values. This is done using a variety of methods such as one-to-one interviews, briefing groups, quality circles, house journals, etc. However, the example of senior managers exhibiting the new beliefs and values is seen as particularly important.

Step 4   Change systems, procedures and personnel policies, especially those concerned with rewards and appraisal.

Source: Adapted from Dobson (1988)

Drawing on the work of a wide range of researchers, Cummings and Worley (2001) offered their own six 'practical' steps for achieving cultural change (*see* Ideas and perspectives 5.10). Though wider in scope in that their approach sets change in a strategic context, the actual mechanics are very similar to those adopted by the organisations Dobson studied.

Many other writers advocating culture change adopt a similar approach. Some of these, including Peters and Waterman (1982) with their eight steps to excellence, take a very prescriptive line. Some appear to view changing culture as a relatively easy process. An example of this was an article in *Management Today* (Egan, 1994) which took just four pages to show how organisations could quickly, and with apparent ease, identify and change their cultures. No matter how its supporters interpret or apply it, this type of generic approach to culture change has been criticised as being too simplistic, and putting forward recommendations which are far too general to be of use to individual organisations (Brown, 1995; Gordon, 1985; Hassard and Sharifi, 1989; Nord, 1985; Uttal, 1983).

However, regardless of whether the approaches to culture change are more or less prescriptive, regardless of whether they are simplistic or sophisticated, they all appear to be attempting to manipulate or change the two upper elements of culture – artefacts and norms of behaviour – rather than attempting to change basic assumptions or even values (*see* Figure 5.1). This can be seen very clearly from Ideas and perspectives 5.9 and 5.10. If one examines the concrete actions that these approaches propose, they cover changes to:

- Organisational structures, systems and policies (artefacts), designed to change people's behaviour.
- The composition of the workforce designed to recruit or promote staff who exhibit the desired behaviours (norms) or to get rid of staff who don't.

Ideas and perspectives 5.10
Cummings and Worley's six steps to culture change

1. **Formulate a clear strategic vision.** Effective cultural change should start from a clear vision of the firm's new strategy and of the shared values and behaviour needed to make it work. This vision provides the purpose and direction for cultural change.

2. **Display top-management commitment.** Cultural change must be managed from the top of the organisation. Senior managers and administrators need to be strongly committed to the new values and the need to create constant pressure for change.

3. **Model culture change at the highest level.** Senior executives must communicate the new culture through their own actions. Their behaviours need to symbolise the kind of values and behaviours being sought.

4. **Modify the organisation to support organisational changes.** Cultural change must be accompanied by supporting modifications in organisational structure, human resource systems, information and control systems, and management style. These organisational features can help to orientate people's behaviours to the new culture.

5. **Select and socialise newcomers and terminate deviants.** One of the most effective methods for changing culture is to change organisational membership. People can be selected in terms of their fit with the new culture, and provided with an induction clearly indicating desired attitudes and behaviour. Existing staff who cannot adapt to the new ways may have their employment terminated, for example, through early retirement schemes. This is especially important in key leadership positions, where people's actions can significantly promote or hinder new values and behaviours.

6. **Develop ethical and legal sensitivity.** Most cultural change programmes attempt to promote values that emphasise employee integrity, control, equitable treatment and job security. However, if one of the key steps in pursuing culture change is to replace existing staff with new recruits, not only can this send out the wrong message to newcomers and the remaining staff but, depending how staff are selected for replacement, it could also contravene employment laws. Therefore, organisations need to be especially aware of these potential ethical and legal pitfalls.

Source: Adapted from Cummings and Worley (2001: 509–11)

There are two final and very important issues that need to be recognised when looking at approaches to culture change. The first is that it is a brutal process. There is a tendency to think that because culture is seen as encompassing the 'soft' side of the organisation, culture change is in some way about winning hearts and minds through the persuasive power of transformational leadership: people are not forced to change – they want to change (Burns, 1978). Ideas and perspectives 5.9 and 5.10 show that the reality is very different. The key actions involve restructuring the organisation and its workforce. As Dobson states, the first step is to:

Change recruitment, selection and redundancy policies to alter the composition of the workforce so that promotion and employment prospects are dependent on those concerned possessing or displaying the beliefs and values the organisation wishes to promote.

Cummings and Worley are even more explicit when they speak of the need to *terminate deviants*. Culture change is mainly focused on getting rid of those who oppose or cannot fit in with the new culture, putting supporters in key positions and ensuing that reward systems reward those who support the new culture. Careers are destroyed, people either sacked or sidelined, and power and rewards are redistributed to supporters of the new order. This is not participative change, but directive and coercive change: there is nothing soft and cuddly about it. Take for example these starkly illustrative words of Stuart Rose describing his actions in transforming Marks and Spencer's culture:

[Each of] The stores were run differently, as if by their own management teams, and the different divisions were five or six robber barons, all competing under the umbrella of one retailer. Anyone coming in from the outside was strangled at birth. But I had already worked at M&S and I knew which levers to pull. I got the company by the balls and squeezed very hard until one or two people took notice. I butchered the Board . . . (In conversation with Grant, 2006: 24)

The second issue relates to the extent that changes to artefacts and norms will lead to changes in values and thus to an overall change in an organisation's culture. As mentioned above when discussing question 2, according to the theory of cognitive dissonance, behaviour change can lead to a change in values, but only if free will is involved, i.e. only if those affected feel that they have a choice. In examining the various approaches to culture change, what is striking is the directive and coercive nature of the process. It may well be that newcomers to the organisation feel they have a choice in whether to join the organisation and sign up to the new behaviours. It may also be that those who see themselves as benefiting from the culture change may feel that they have chosen to adopt the new ways. However, for the majority of an organisation's members, they are likely to feel that they had no choice, which in turn may lead to a degree of resentment and even resistance. This may be why a large proportion of culture change efforts are seen to fail (Brown, 1995; Jones *et al*, 2006; Rogers *et al*, 2006).

Therefore, the answer to the question *Are there established approaches available for changing culture?* is yes, but . . . The 'but' is that these approaches tend to focus on changing behaviour and not culture *per se*. These approaches may though lead to changes in values but only if those involved feel they have a choice. However, the approaches to culture change tend also to be directive and coercive and, therefore, do not promote choice for many of those involved. The difficulty of accomplishing culture change has led many writers to express reservations about attempting to change culture.

Changing organisational culture: some reservations

Though there are many writers who believe that culture can be changed, some take a more cautious view of the results of such attempts. A major study of cultural transformation in 530 organisations by Gilmore *et al* (1997) found that organisations experienced both positive and negative outcomes, with senior managers reporting that quality and productivity improved and employees reporting that morale decreased and workload increased. Even more worrying for proponents of culture change were the results of the 2006 survey by Bain & Co, which found that fewer than 10% of organisations were successful in changing their cultures (Rogers *et al*, 2006). Such findings underlie Brown's (1998) warning that organisations must be sure that the problems they wish to address through cultural change are actually caused by the existing culture. He maintains that there is a tendency to assume that culture is the root cause of organisational problems, when in fact they might arise from inappropriate organisational structure. By pursuing culture change instead of the real cause of their problems, organisations doom themselves to failure. Brown also points out that senior managers may use the issue of culture to redirect blame for poor performance away from themselves and onto the rest of the organisation. In addition, he warns against taking an overly simplistic view of culture by believing that organisations have a single unitary culture, or by assuming that all employees can be made to share a single purpose or vision. This was also a point made by Hatch (1997) on behalf of the postmodernists. One of the most influential writers on the subject of culture, Schein (1985), takes a similarly cautious view. He warns that before any attempt is made to change an organisation's culture, it is first necessary to understand the nature of its existing culture and how this is sustained. According to Schein, this can be achieved by analysing the values that govern behaviour, and uncovering the underlying and often unconscious assumptions that determine how those in the organisation think, feel and react. Difficult though he acknowledges this to be, he argues that it can be achieved by:

- analysing the process of recruitment and induction for new employees;
- analysing responses to critical incidents in the organisation's history, as these are often translated into unwritten, but nevertheless very strong, rules of behaviour;
- analysing the beliefs, values and assumptions of those who are seen as the guardians and promoters of the organisation's culture;
- discussing the findings from the above with staff in the organisation, and paying especial attention to anomalies or puzzling features which have been observed.

Schein's approach, therefore, is to treat the development of culture as an adaptive and tangible learning process. His approach emphasises the way in which an organisation communicates its culture to new recruits. It illustrates how assumptions are translated into values and how values influence behaviour. Schein seeks to understand the mechanisms used to propagate culture, and how new values and behaviours are learned. Once these mechanisms are revealed, he argues, they can then form the basis of a strategy to change the organisation's culture.

Hassard and Sharifi (1989) propose a similar approach to that advocated by Schein. In particular, they stress two crucial aspects of culture change:

Before a major [cultural] change campaign is commenced, senior managers must understand the implications of the new system for their own behaviour: and senior management must be involved in all the main stages preceding change. In change programmes, special attention must be given to the company's 'opinion leaders'.

(Hassard and Sharifi, 1989: 11)

Schwartz and Davis (1981), on the other hand, adopt a different stance with regard to culture. They suggest that, when an organisation is considering any form of change, it should compare the strategic significance (the importance to the organisation's future) of the change with the cultural resistance that attempts to make the particular change will encounter. They term this the 'cultural risk' approach. They offer a step-by-step method for identifying the degree of cultural risk involved in any particular change project. From this, they argue, it is then possible for an organisation to decide with a degree of certainty whether to ignore the culture, manage round it, attempt to change the culture to fit the strategy, or change the strategy to fit the culture. Although Schwartz and Davis's method relies heavily on managerial judgement, they maintain that it constitutes a methodical approach to identifying, at an early stage, the potential impact of strategic change on an organisation's culture, and vice versa.

It should, of course, be pointed out that though Schein's approach and Schwartz and Davis's approach are different, this does not mean they are in conflict or are not compatible. Indeed, both could be considered as different aspects of the same task: deciding whether culture needs to be changed, and, if it does, in what way.

No one should dispute the difficulty of changing an organisation's culture. The work of Schein (1985), Schwartz and Davis (1981), Cummings and Huse (1989) and Dobson (1988) provides organisations with the guidelines and methods for evaluating the need for and undertaking cultural change. Schein's work shows how an organisation's existing culture, and the way it is reinforced, can be revealed. Schwartz and Davis's work shows how the need for cultural change can be evaluated and the necessary changes identified. Finally, the work of Cummings and Huse (1989) and Dobson (1988) shows how cultural change can be implemented.

Taking a different tack, Schein (1984, 1985) also argues that there is a negative side to creating (or attempting to create) a strong and cohesive organisational culture. He argues that shared values, particularly where they have been seen to be consistently successful in the past, make organisations resistant to certain types of change or strategic options, regardless of their merit.

Schein is also critical of the idea that culture change can be achieved by a top-down, management-led approach (Luthans, 1989). Instead, he appears to advocate a contingency or context-specific view of culture (Schein, 1989). Taking an organisational life-cycle approach, he argues that an organisation may need a strong culture in its formative years to hold it together whilst it grows. However, it may reach a stage where it is increasingly differentiated geographically, by function and by division. At this stage, managing culture becomes more a question of knitting together the warring factions and subcultures. In such a case, a strong culture may outlive its usefulness.

Salaman (1979) also pointed out that whilst there may be a strong or dominant culture in an organisation, there will also be subcultures, as in society at large. These may be peculiar to the organisation or may cut across organisations. Examples of the latter are groups such as doctors and lawyers who have their own professional cultures which extend beyond the organisations that employ them. Davis (1985) examined the culture of white- and blue-collar lower-level employees. He found that not only do these groups have their own distinctive cultures, but these can often be in conflict with the dominant (managerial) culture of their organisation. Therefore, subcultures exist in a complex and potentially conflicting relationship with the dominant culture. If that dominant culture is seen by some groups to have lost its appropriateness (and thus legitimacy), then potential conflicts can become actual conflicts. The reverse can also be the case; cultural values and methods of operation which one group adopts may be seen as being out of step with 'the way we've always done things'. This in turn can lead to an undermining of the authority of managers and specialists – endangering the efficient operation of the organisation (Morieux and Sutherland, 1988).

Uttal (1983) is another who expressed caution with regard to the difficulties and advisability of culture change. In particular, he observed that even where it is successful, the process can take anywhere from 6 to 15 years. Meyer and Zucker (1989) went further, arguing that whilst managing cultural change may result in short-term economic benefits, in the longer term it may result in stagnation and demise. Another difficulty in achieving culture change, according to Brown (1995: 153), is that:

> . . . most employees in an organisation have a high emotional stake in the current culture. People who have been steeped in the traditions and values of the organisation and whose philosophy of life may well be caught up in the organisation's cultural assumptions will experience considerable uncertainty, anxiety and pain in the process of change . . . Even if there are personal gains to be made from altering the habits of a lifetime these are likely to be seen as potential or theoretical only, as against the certainty of the losses.

Therefore, any attempt to change an organisation's culture is inevitably going to meet with some resistance. Sometimes this will be open and organised; often it will be covert and instinctive with people trying to hold on to old ways and protect the old order. Unlike many other forms of change, the main resistance may well come from middle and, especially, senior managers who see their status, power and personal beliefs challenged. This is a point made by Cummings and Worley (2001), who observed that culture change programmes often result in or require the removal of managers from key leadership positions.

A further reservation expressed by a number of writers relates to the ethical issues raised by attempts to change culture. Van Maanen and Kunda (1989) argued that behind the interest in culture is an attempt by managers to control what employees feel as well as what they say or do. Their argument is that culture is a mechanism for disciplining emotion – a method of guiding the way people are expected to feel. Seen in this light, attempts to change culture can be conceived of as Taylorism of the mind. Frederick Taylor sought to control behaviour by laying down and enforcing strict rules about how work should be carried out. Van Maanen and Kunda in effect argue that culture change programmes attempt to achieve the same end through a form of mind control. Willmott (1995) expresses similar concerns. He believes that the overriding aim of culture change is to win the 'hearts and minds' of employees by achieving control over the 'employee's soul'. Watson (1997: 278) concludes that:

> Employers and managers engaging in these ways with issues of employees' self-identities and the values through which they judge the rights and wrongs of their daily lives must be a matter of serious concern. To attempt to mould cultures – given that culture in its broad sense provides the roots of human morality, social identity and existential security – is indeed to enter 'deep and dangerous waters'.

Changing organisational culture: conflicts and choices

As in so much else to do with organisations, there is no agreement amongst those who study culture as to its nature, purpose or malleability. Certainly, few writers doubt its importance, but beyond that there is much disagreement. The result, to quote Brown (1995: 5), is that we are presented with 'an embarrassment of definitional riches'. The Culture–Excellence proponents argue that there is only one form of culture that matters in today's environment – strong and flexible – and that organisations should adopt it quickly or face the consequences. The proponents of the Japanese approach to management and the organisational learning camp adopt a similar, though less strident, view. Schein (1984, 1985, 1989) agreed that culture is important and that in certain cases a strong culture is desirable. However, in other situations, shared values and strong cultures may have a negative effect by stifling diversity and preventing alternative strategies arising. He also doubts that managers acting in isolation from the rest of an organisation have the ability by themselves to change the existing culture or impose a new one. Salaman (1979) also drew attention to the presence and role of subcultures, particularly their potential for creating conflict. Meek (1988) took the view that culture as a whole is not amenable to conscious managerial change but that elements of culture might be open to deliberate change. The postmodernists take a firmer line against deliberate culture change. Though they consider organisational culture to be important, they are sceptical of attempts to manipulate and change culture, believing that the outcomes of such attempts are unpredictable and can alienate rather than motivate employees – remember Hatch's (1997: 235) warning not even to 'think of trying to manage culture'.

As cited earlier, Ogbonna and Harris (2002) believe that the writers on culture can be divided into three groups: the optimists, the pessimists and the realists. They argue that the realists probably have the best of the argument, i.e. that culture as a whole cannot be changed but that certain elements, such as artefacts and norms, can be changed. However, the lack of consensus amongst writers has to be acknowledged. Bearing this in mind, there are three main conclusions we can draw from the above review of the culture literature:

- Firstly, in the absence of unambiguous guidelines on organisational culture, managers must make their own choices based on their own circumstances and perceived options as to whether or not to attempt to change all or part of their organisation's culture.
- Secondly, directive and coercive approaches to culture change may be successful in changing the behaviour and values of some existing members of an organisation, and they may allow the recruitment of staff more amenable to the new ways of working. However, such approaches may also alienate a considerable number of staff who feel they are being forced to change. In such cases, covert and overt resistance to change may arise with the organisation dividing into warring camps rather than a unified body.
- Lastly, in the absence of strong or appropriate cultures that bind their members together in a common purpose and legitimate and guide decision-making, managers may find it difficult either to agree amongst themselves or to gain agreement from others in the organisation. As Robbins (1987) argued, in such a situation, there is a tendency for conflict and power battles to take place.

Therefore, in understanding how organisations operate and the strengths and weaknesses of the theories we have been discussing in the previous chapters, it is necessary to examine the power–politics perspective on organisations.

The power–politics perspective

Political behaviour in organisations

The cultural perspective on organisational life reinforces the argument developed in previous chapters that organisations are not rational entities where everyone subscribes to, and helps to achieve, the organisation's overarching goals. The power–politics perspective puts forward a similar view, arguing that organisations often act irrationally, that their goals and objectives emerge through a process of negotiation and influence, and that they are composed of competing and shifting coalitions of groups and individuals (Brown, 1995; Buchanan and Badham, 1999; Mintzberg *et al*, 1998a; Robbins, 1986, 1987). This perspective began to emerge strongly in the late 1970s and early 1980s, and is especially associated with Jeffrey Pfeffer's (1981) book *Power in Organizations*. Before then, as Gandz and Murray (1980) discovered when they reviewed the literature on organisational politics, there was very little general interest in the topic, and very few publications on it.

Of the early work in the field, Lindblom's (1959) work on the 'science of muddling through' and Cyert and March's (1963) book, *A Behavioral Theory of the Firm*, can be said to have really laid the basis for the later explosion of interest in power and politics in organisations. Writing from the viewpoint of public-sector organisations, Lindblom argued that political constraints on policy make a rationalist approach to decision-making impossible. Cyert and March extensively developed Lindblom's work, showing that private-sector firms were no less political entities than public-sector organisations. The intention behind their work was to provide a better understanding of decision-making by supplementing existing theories, which tended to focus on market factors, with an examination of the internal operation of the firm. Cyert and March characterised firms as competing and shifting coalitions of multiple and conflicting interests, whose demands and objectives are constantly, but imperfectly, reconciled and where rationality is limited or bounded by uncertainty over what is wanted and how to achieve it. Under such circumstances, managers 'satisfice': rather than searching for the best solution, they select one that is satisfactory and sufficient (Simon, 1947).

Cyert and March's work on the political dimension of decision-making and the nature of organisational life now forms part of the received wisdom on organisational behaviour (Mallory, 1997). This is not to refute or marginalise the role of organisational culture. As Handy (1993) observes, the extent to which agreement exists about the tasks an organisation undertakes, how it undertakes them, and the extent to which members of the organisation are committed to achieving them, will be affected by the strength and the perceived legitimacy or suitability of the organisation's culture. Willcocks (1994: 31) takes the view that diverse interests are part of organisational culture. They include, he argues, 'for example, the goals, values and expectations of the organizational participants and have been described as cognitive maps or personal agendas'. The importance of the power–politics perspective is that it shows that, even where a strong culture may be present, the cohesiveness, willingness and stability of an organisation's members is unlikely to be uniform either across an organisation or over time. Rather the extent of cooperation and commitment they exhibit will vary with the degree to which they perceive the goals they are pursuing as broadly consistent with their own interests (Mullins, 1993; Rollinson, 2002). Therefore, as Pfeffer (1978: 11–12) commented:

> *It is difficult to think of situations in which goals are so congruent, or the facts so clear-cut that judgment and compromise are not involved. What is rational from one point of view is irrational from another. Organizations are political systems, coalitions of interests, and rationality is defined only with respect to unitary and consistent ordering of preferences.*

It might be comforting to believe that individuals and groups within organisations are supportive of each other, that they work in a harmonious and cooperative fashion. Such a non-political perspective portrays employees as always behaving in a manner consistent with the interests of the organisation. In contrast, as Robbins (1986: 283) remarked,

> *. . . a political view can explain much of, what may seem to be, irrational behavior in organizations. It can help to explain, for instance, why employees withhold information, restrict output, attempt to 'build empires' . . .*

Handy (1986) also observed the tendency for individuals and groups to pursue courses of action that promote their interests, regardless of the organisation's formal goals and objectives. He noted that where individuals perceive that the actual or proposed goals of the organisation or the tasks they are asked to perform are out of step with their own interests, they will seek where possible to bring the two into line. In some cases, individuals and groups may be persuaded to change their perceptions; in others, they may seek to change or influence the goals or tasks. It is this phenomenon of individuals and groups, throughout an organisation, pursuing differing interests, and battling with each other to shape decisions in their favour, that has led many commentators to characterise organisations as political systems (Buchanan and Badham, 1999; Dawson, 2003; Mintzberg *et al*, 1998a; Morgan, 1986; Pettigrew, 1985, 1987; Pfeffer, 1981, 1992). Bradshaw-Camball and Murray (1991: 380), in describing the conditions necessary for political behaviour to occur, demonstrate why so many commentators see it as an intrinsic part of organisational life:

> *. . . virtually all [writers] agree that for politics to occur, certain conditions must exist. There must be two or more parties (individuals, groups or large entities), some form of interdependence between the parties, and a perception on the part of at least one of the parties that divergent interests exist between them such that there is, or may potentially arise, conflict between the parties. Once these conditions exist, the subsequent actions of the parties involved will be deemed 'political'.*

This echoes Zaleznik's (1970) view that where there are scarce resources (which is the case in most organisations), the psychology of scarcity and comparison take over. In such situations, possession of resources becomes the focus for comparisons, the basis for self-esteem and, ultimately, the source of power. Such situations will see the emergence not only of dominant coalitions but also, Zaleznik argues, of unconscious collusion based on defensive reaction. Therefore, whilst some individuals will perceive their actions as 'political' or self-interested, others may act in the same manner, but believe they are pursuing the best interests of the organisation.

Drory and Romm (1988) argued that those in managerial positions are less likely than those in non-managerial positions to define (or recognise) their actions as political. This may be explained by the findings from a survey of 428 managers carried out by Gandz and Murray (1980). They found that managers are more involved in political behaviour, and therefore tend to see it as a typical part of organisational life. If this is the case, it could be argued that the more individuals and groups are involved in political behaviour, the more it becomes the norm, and they become blind to its political nature and see it merely as standard practice. Those less involved in such behaviour, on the other hand, recognise its political nature because it stands out from their normal practices. It is also the case that those lower down the organisation, whilst affected by resource allocation decisions, are less likely, on a regular basis, to be in a position to influence such decisions. For managers, however, arguing for additional resources or allocating existing resources is the currency of everyday life. This is reflected in Gandz and Murray's survey, where 89 per cent of respondents thought that successful executives had to be good politicians. Despite this, over 50 per cent of respondents also thought that organisations would be happier places if they were free of politics, and a similar number thought that political behaviour was detrimental to efficiency. As Kanter (1979) and Pfeffer (1992) note, this ambivalent attitude, i.e. believing that political behaviour is necessary but deploring its use, is rife in organisations.

As mentioned in Chapter 4, postmodernists take a very different view of power and politics to that of most other writers on organisations. They are not greatly concerned with the way individuals and groups acquire and hold on to power as such. Instead, they focus on the relationship between power and knowledge, and on the way that power is used to promote particular views of reality and to legitimate particular forms of knowledge in organisations.

Power and politics: towards a definition

It is relatively easy to provide simple definitions of power and politics:

Power – the possession of position and/or resources.
Politics – the deployment of influence and leverage.

However, it is more difficult to distinguish between the two, as was shown by Drory and Romm (1988). They argued that the two concepts are often used interchangeably and that the difference between the two has never been fully settled. Indeed, a brief examination of each shows the difficulty, and perhaps danger, in separating them. First, however, it is also necessary to understand the difference between power and authority.

Robbins (1987: 186) drew an important distinction between them:

Authority: '. . . the right to act, or command others to act, toward the attainment of organizational goals. Its unique characteristic, we said, was that this right had legitimacy based on the authority figure's position in the organization. Authority goes with the job.'

Power: 'When we use the term power we mean an individual's capacity to influence decisions. . . . the ability to influence based on an individual's legitimate position can affect decisions, but one does not require authority to have such influence.'

In support of his view, Robbins quotes the example of high-ranking executives' secretaries, who may have a great deal of power, by virtue of their ability to influence the flow of information and people to their bosses, but have very little actual authority. Pfeffer (1992) extends this view by pointing out that power can stem from three sources:

* Formal authority to act.
* Control over information.
* Control over resources.

However, he believes this last source of power is particularly important. We must, Pfeffer (1992: 83) argues, recognise the truth of the 'New Golden Rule: the person with the gold makes the rules.'

Moving from power to politics, Robbins (1987: 194) defines organisational politics as the:

. . . *efforts of organizational members to mobilize support for or against policies, rules, goals, or other decisions in which the outcome will have some effect on them. Politics, therefore, is essentially the exercise of power.*

Robbins's argument, then, is that:

* Power is the capacity to influence decisions.
* Politics is the actual process of exerting this influence.

This view, that politics is merely the enactment of power, is held by many writers. Gibson *et al* (1988: 44), for example, stated that organisational politics comprises:

. . . *those activities used at all levels to acquire, develop or use power and other resources to obtain individual choices when there is uncertainty or disagreement about choices.*

This view is also central to Pfeffer's (1981: 7) widely accepted definition, that organisational politics:

. . . *involves those activities taken within organizations to acquire, develop and use power and other resources to obtain one's preferred outcome in a situation where there is uncertainty or descensus about choices.*

Pfeffer, like many writers, refers to organisational politics as games. In his major work *Power in Organizations* (Pfeffer, 1981), he took the view that decisions in organisations are the result of games among players with different perceptions and interests. This was a theme developed by Mintzberg (1983) in his comprehensive review of power and politics in organisations. He lists 13 political games that are common in organisations, the key ones being:

* Games to resist authority.
* Games to counter resistance.
* Games to build power bases.
* Games to defeat rivals.
* Games to change the organisation.

Ideas and perspectives 5.11
Political ploys

- **Reason** – facts and information are used selectively to mount seemingly logical or rational arguments.
- **Friendliness** – the use of flattery, creation of goodwill, etc., prior to making a request.
- **Coalition** – joining forces with others so as to increase one's own influence.
- **Bargaining** – exchanging benefits and favours in order to achieve a particular outcome.
- **Assertiveness** – being forceful in making requests and demanding compliance.
- **Higher authority** – gaining the support of superiors for a particular course of action.
- **Sanctions** – using the promise of rewards or the threat of punishment to force compliance.

Source: From Kipnis *et al* (1980, 1984), Schilit and Locke (1982)

Like all games, political ones have particular tactics associated with them. Ideas and perspectives 5.11 lists the seven most common ploys used by managers when seeking to influence superiors, equals and subordinates.

Robbins (1986) observed that the most popular tactic or ploy is the selective use of reason, regardless of whether the influence was directed upwards or downwards. Although cloaked in reason, arguments and data are deployed in such a way that the outcome favoured by those using the tactic is presented in a more favourable light than the alternatives. Therefore, though reason may be deployed, it is not done so in an unbiased or neutral fashion; it is used as a screen to disguise the real objective of the exercise. In deciding which tactic to use, Kipnis *et al* (1984) identified four contingency variables that affect the manager's choice:

- The manager's relative power.
- The manager's objectives in seeking to influence others.
- The manager's expectations of the target person's/group's willingness to comply.
- The organisation's culture.

Having gained a clearer picture of power and politics, we can now move on to examine one of the central issues that arises from this: the distinction between the legitimate and illegitimate use of power and politics.

Power, politics and legitimacy

Thompkins (1990) firmly believes that the use of politics is a direct contravention of or challenge to the legitimate rules of an organisation. Many, however, see organisational politics as existing in a grey area between prescribed and illegal behaviour (Drory and Romm, 1988). Porter *et al* (1983) differentiate between three types of organisational behaviours: prescribed, discretionary and illegal. They believe that political behaviour falls within the discretionary rather than the illegal category. The most common view is that the use of politics in organisations can best be described as non-sanctioned or informal or discretionary behaviour, rather than behaviour that is clearly prohibited or illegal (Farrell and Petersen, 1983; Mayes and Allen, 1977). This definition of politics helps to distinguish between the formal and legitimate use of officially sanctioned power by authorised personnel, and power that is exercised either in an illegitimate manner by authorised personnel or used by non-authorised personnel for their own ends.

Most organisations and many writers see political behaviour as dysfunctional (Drory and Romm, 1988). Batten and Swab (1965), Pettigrew (1973) and Porter (1976) believed that political behaviour goes against and undermines formal organisational goals and interests. Thompkins (1990), though, argued that political manoeuvring in organisations is due to a failure by senior managers to set and implement coherent and consistent goals and policies in the first place. This results in uncertainties, which in turn lead to conflict between groups and individuals. In such a situation, Thompkins (1990: 24) argues:

> Management is then left without top level guidance to run company operations. They will, then, by their own nature of survival, over a period of time, make decisions that will perpetuate their own safety and security. This is the beginning of political power, where legitimate discipline begins to decline and illegitimate discipline begins to strangle the organisation. In short, the tail begins to wag the dog. 'Politics' in this form is created by the neglect of top executive management.

Pfeffer (1981) took a different view of organisational politics. Rather than political behaviour arising from a lack of clear-cut goals and policies, he suggests that the construction of organisational goals is itself a political process. Nevertheless, this does not always mean that political behaviour is detrimental to organisational effectiveness. Mintzberg (1983) maintains that, when used in moderation, political games can have a healthy effect by keeping the organisation on its toes. Mayes and Allen (1977) took a similar view. Pascale (1993) went further, putting forward the view that conflict and contention are necessary to save an organisation from complacency and decline. The argument that the use of politics and power are central to the effective running of organisations has been most strongly put by Pfeffer (1992: 337–8) in his book *Managing with Power*, in which he argued that:

> Computers don't get built, cities don't get rebuilt, and diseases don't get fought unless advocates for change learn how to develop and use power effectively. . . . In corporations, public agencies, universities, and government, the problem is how to get things done, how to move forward, how to solve the many problems facing organizations of all sizes and all types. Developing and exercising power requires both will and skill. It is the will which often seems to be missing.

For Pfeffer, will and skill are exercised through the pursuit of a focused and consistent personal agenda which is implemented through a seven-step programme (*see* Ideas and perspectives 5.12). However, Mintzberg (1983) sounds a note of warning. He argues that if too many people pursue their own personal agenda, or if the use of power and politics becomes too aggressive and pervasive, it can turn the whole organisation into a political cauldron and divert it from its main task.

Ideas and perspectives 5.12
The use of power and politics

1. Decide what your goals are, what you are trying to accomplish.
2. Diagnose patterns of dependence and interdependence; what individuals are influential and important in your achieving your goal?
3. What are their points of view likely to be? How will they feel about what you are trying to do?
4. What are their power bases? Which of them is more influential in the decision?
5. What are your bases of power and influence? What bases of influence can you develop to gain more control over the situation?
6. Which of the various strategies and tactics for exercising power seem most appropriate and are likely to be effective, given the situation you confront?
7. Based on the above, choose a course of action to get something done.

Source: From Pfeffer (1992: 29)

To an extent, the degree to which the balance between positive and negative benefits is tipped one way or the other in an organisation is dependent on the type of power deployed and how it is used. Etzioni (1975) identified three distinct types of power used in organisations:

- **Coercive power** – the threat of negative consequences (including physical sanctions or force) should compliance not be forthcoming.
- **Remunerative power** – the promise of material rewards as inducements to cooperate.
- **Normative power** – the allocation and manipulation of symbolic rewards, such as status symbols, as inducements to obey.

Robbins (1986) developed this further by identifying not only types of power but also the sources of power. To Etzioni's three types of power, he added a fourth:

- **Knowledge power** – the control of information.

> We can say that when an individual in a group or organization controls unique information, and when that information is needed to make a decision, the individual has knowledge-based power. (Robbins, 1986: 273)

Robbins suggests that these four types of power stem from four separate sources:

- A person's position in the organisation.
- Personal characteristics.
- Expertise.
- The opportunity to influence or control the flow of information.

All four types of power can be and are deployed in organisations. The degree to which they will be effective is likely to depend upon the source from which they spring. Coercive power is usually the prerogative of those in senior positions, whilst even quite junior members of an organisation may, in particular circumstances, control or possess information that enables them to exert knowledge power. The interesting point to note is that the use of knowledge power – the selective and biased use of information (often deployed under the guise of reason) – is shown to be effective in gaining willing compliance and cooperation from those at whom it is directed. According to Huczynski and Buchanan (2001), however, the favourite influencing strategies are:

- For influencing up (managers) – the use of reason.
- For influencing across (co-workers) – the use of friendliness.
- For influencing down (subordinates) – the use of reason.

This appears to fit in well with the view of many observers that the use of remunerative and coercive power, i.e. the opposite of reason and friendliness, is often counter-productive because those on the receiving end of such power tend to view it negatively and resent it (Bachman *et al*, 1968; Ivancevich, 1970; Robbins, 1986; Student, 1968).

This is perhaps why the most detrimental outcomes from the deployment of power arise when people feel they are being coerced into a particular course of action that goes against their beliefs or self-interest (Rollinson, 2002). Therefore, irrespective of the source or type of power, it is perhaps the willingness to use it in situations where there will be clear winners and losers, and where the covert activities of warring coalitions turn into open warfare, which leads to the more dysfunctional and damaging consequences. Such battles, where groups and individuals fight to influence key decisions and in so doing bolster their own position, especially where the stakes are high, can end with senior figures either leaving or being forced out of the organisation.

The case of Liverpool Football Club is a case in point. The club was bought jointly by the American entrepreneurs Tom Hicks and George Gillett in March 2007. However, since the takeover, the two men appear to have become bitter enemies and have fallen out repeatedly and publicly over the running and ownership of the club. Each has tried to buy out the other by involving a third party and both have resisted attempts to buy them out. The Chief Executive has been caught in the middle, with Hicks demanding his resignation for apparently siding with Gillett. This has had an unsettling effect on the team, especially as it seems that at least one of the co-owners has tried secretly to hire a replacement for the existing team manager (Hunter, 2008). All in all, it seems impossible to see how such a power battle can end without one, if not both, of the co-owners departing the club.

In the mainstream business world, there are many such examples. Take the case of BMW when it was considering selling Rover. The battle over the future of Rover's Longbridge plant in the UK led to both Bernd Pischetsrieder, BMW's Chairman, and his long-time boardroom rival, Wolfgang Reitzle, BMW's Marketing Director, being forced to resign (Gow, 1999a; Gow and Traynor, 1999). A similar situation occurred with Pehr Gyllenhammar, the man who ran Volvo for more than two decades. His 1993 attempt to merge Volvo with Renault, the French state-controlled car company, was opposed by a coalition of shareholders and managers, who felt that it was not so much a merger of equals as a takeover by Renault. Both shareholders and managers felt that in such a situation their interests would be damaged, and a very public power struggle ensued, with both sides claiming to act in Volvo's best interests (Done, 1994). Both these cases could be classed as battles between individuals fighting to maintain their own power. However, the reality was that in both cases major issues concerning the future viability of these organisations were at stake. The irony in Volvo's case was that six years after rejecting a merger with Renault because it was seen as disadvantageous to the company's interests, the company sold its car division to Ford Motors, whose work practices were seen as the antithesis of all that Volvo held dear.

The battle for control of the advertising agency Saatchi & Saatchi, which resulted in the founders leaving, also shows how a power struggle can leave an organisation damaged (Barrie, 1995; Donovan, 1995). Another very public example of a power clash was the on–off merger of SmithKline Beecham and Glaxo. In 1998, the two companies announced that they planned to merge and form the largest pharmaceutical company in the world, worth an estimated US$165 billion. However, the merger was quickly called off owing to a rumoured clash between SmithKline's Chief Executive, Jan Leschley, and Glaxo's Chairman, Sir Richard Sykes, over who would run the merged company (although given that it later emerged that Mr Leschley's pay, perks and shares package was worth over £90 million, one can understand why he would be reluctant to step down in favour of Sir Richard Sykes (Buckingham and Finch, 1999)). It was only when Leschley and Sykes both announced their retirements that the merger proceeded. In some cases, such clashes can become endemic and linger on even after the initial cause has long gone. Lonrho is a case in point. After the successful battle to oust Tiny Rowland from the company he founded and for so long dominated, Lonrho was split up and sold off. Yet the political battles for control still rumbled on even amongst its demerged parts (Laird, 1998).

Clearly, as the above examples show, the deployment of coercive power can be very damaging; however, other forms of power can also have adverse effects, though perhaps in a more insidious fashion. The use of remunerative power by senior managers in the UK and the USA is a good example. Over the last two decades, executive salaries in both countries have run far ahead of inflation, the pay of salaried staff and company profits (Business Notebook, 2003; DeCarlo, 2008; Dunphy and Griffiths, 1998; Green, 2008). This caused much controversy, especially in the privatised, but once public, utilities such as gas, electricity and water. In these organisations, executives, the so-called 'fat cats', appeared to use their power to give themselves extremely generous remuneration packages; whilst at the same time, they cut jobs and wages for many staff elsewhere in their organisations (Smithers, 1995). In general, though, this practice was condoned by both shareholders and governments because the UK economy and UK companies were doing well and those controlling them could argue that they were being rewarded for success. However, the criticisms of fat-cat salaries became more strident and widespread after the economy started to falter. Government, shareholders and trade unions began to sing with one critical voice that those leading companies were being rewarded for failure. Given that amongst the UK's top 100 companies, the pay of directors rose 84 per cent in the three years to 2003 but the stock market value of these companies fell by 50 per cent, one can understand the outcry (Finch and Treanor, 2003). This disgruntlement became even more strident when it was realised that some companies were giving big payoffs to executives who appeared to have failed in their jobs, such as Gerald Corbett, who walked away from Railtrack with a payoff of £3.7m (Treanor and Finch, 2003). The issue is not so much whether the way executives distribute rewards in their organisations is fair or not, but the corrosive effect such a blatant use of power has on employee morale, shareholder support and customer loyalty. One of the best (or worst) examples of this is the case of Bob Nardelli's reign at Home Depot (*see* Mini Case Study 5.2).

Mini Case Study 5.2
Nardelli's style helps to seal his fate

Four months ago, a defiant Bob Nardelli said he had no intention of resigning as chairman and chief executive of Home Depot. 'I love this company', he told the Financial Times. 'I've been in business 35 years and I've never been in a company with more growth potential. As long as I have my health and support from the board I will continue.' It now seems likely that, even as Mr Nardelli spoke those words, the support of the board was already wavering. Home Depot's directors accepted his resignation, by mutual agreement, at a board meeting on Tuesday following a traumatic year for the home improvement retailer.

Mr Nardelli's departure marks a second low point for the combative executive who arrived at Home Depot from General Electric six years ago after losing out in the race to succeed Jack Welch, his mentor, as chairman of GE. His fate may have been sealed as early as last May, when he infuriated many investors by refusing to answer questions at its annual meeting about his hefty compensation package and the company's sagging share price. Mr Nardelli was already a target for shareholder activists, having received more than $120m in compensation, excluding stock options, during his first five years as chief executive, while the share price slumped. But the anger was intensified by his belligerent attitude towards rebel shareholders and activist investors who were preparing a fresh campaign against him ahead of this year's annual meeting.

Adapted from A Ward (2007): Nardelli's style helps to seal his fate.
Financial Times, 4 January, p. 22.

These very public manifestations of power battles in organisations represent merely the tip of the iceberg. They illustrate the tendency for such battles to be fought under the banner of 'the best interests of the organisation'. Political infighting, the seeking of allies, the influencing of decisions, and the protection or promotion of one's own or one's group's interests are nearly always justified by recourse to the best interests of the organisation (just as the parties involved in any armed struggle always seem to justify it on the grounds that they have justice on their side). It is not that the participants necessarily believe their own propaganda, though often they do; it is that, without it, they would find it very difficult to justify, to themselves and their allies, the use of blatantly illegitimate tactics such as challenging, undermining or explicitly ignoring their organisation's official goals and policies.

Therefore, in opposing or promoting a particular decision or development, those indulging in even a low level of political behaviour rarely openly declare their own personal interest in the outcome. As Pfeffer (1981) maintained, a major characteristic accompanying political behaviour is the attempt to conceal its true motive. This can be seen from Buchanan and Badham's (1999: 27–9) list of power tactics shown in Ideas and perspectives 5.13. Concealing motives is essential because, as Allen *et al* (1979), Drory and Romm (1988) and Frost and Hayes (1979) observe, those involved believe that such tactics would be judged unacceptable or illegitimate by others in the organisation, and as such resisted. Accordingly, a false but acceptable motive is presented instead.

Ideas and perspectives 5.13
Power tactics

- **Image building** – action that enhances a person's standing, such as backing the 'right' causes.
- **Selective information** – withhold unfavourable information from superiors.
- **Scapegoating** – blame someone else.
- **Formal alliances** – form or join a coalition of the strong.
- **Networking** – make friends with those in power.
- **Compromise** – be prepared to give in on unimportant issues in order to win on the important ones.
- **Rule manipulation** – interpret rules selectively to favour friends and thwart opponents.
- **Other tactics** – if all else fails, use dirty tricks such as coercion, undermining the expertise of others, playing one group off against another, and get others to 'fire the bullet'.

Source: Buchanan and Badham (1999: 27–9)

The picture of power and politics that emerges from Ideas and perspectives 5.13 tends to be a negative one, portraying individuals and groups as using power and politics purely to pursue their own selfish interests. However, others take a more positive view. Morgan (1986) offered a model of interests, conflicts and power, accepting that diversity of interests can create conflict. In such circumstances, power and influence are, he suggests, the major means of resolving conflict. Buchanan and Boddy (1992) argue that the use of power and politics is a necessary component in the toolkit of those responsible for managing change in organisations. Seen in this light, political behaviour can have a positive effect on improving the working of organisations by enabling them to manage change more effectively. Pfeffer (1992), in a similar vein, maintains that the use of power is an important social process that is often required to get things done in interdependent systems. In fact, he maintains that a failure to deploy power and politics is harmful:

By pretending that power and influence don't exist, or at least shouldn't exist, we contribute to what I and others (such as John Gardner) see as the major problem facing many corporations today, particularly in the United States – the almost trained or produced incapacity of anyone except the highest-level managers to take action and get things accomplished. (Pfeffer, 1992: 10)

Perhaps Gardner (1990: 57) summed up the issues involved in the power–politics debate most succinctly when, in relation to those who possess and deploy power, he argued that:

The significant questions are: What means do they use to gain it? How do they exercise it? To what ends do they exercise it?

We can see from the above why writers have found it difficult to separate power from politics. Whilst it is possible to examine the potential for power without also examining how power is or might be exercised, for students of organisational life this is rather a sterile endeavour. For the purpose of understanding what makes organisations tick, how decisions are arrived at, why resources are allocated in a particular way and why certain changes are initiated and others not, we have to comprehend both the possession and exercise of power, whether it be by official or political means.

Though Robbins rightly draws a distinction between formal authority and the possession and deployment of power, we should not fall into the trap of assuming that there is not a close relationship between the two. An examination of the ability to exert influence (power) over key decisions and the possession of position (authority) shows that these tend to lie within dominant coalitions rather than being spread evenly across organisations (*see* Buchanan and Badham, 1999; Pfeffer, 1978, 1981, 1992; Robbins, 1987). The dominant coalition is the one that has the power to affect structure. The reason why this is so important is that the choice of structure will automatically favour some groups and disadvantage others. This is why, as shown earlier in this chapter, restructuring organisations is one of the first steps taken by those seeking to create a new culture – they need to destroy the power base of those who benefit from the old order and are likely to resist the new order. A person's or group's position in the structure will determine such factors as their influence on planning, their choice of technology, the criteria by which they will be evaluated, allocation of rewards, control of information, proximity to senior managers, and their ability to exercise influence on a whole range of decisions (Morgan, 1986; Perrow, 1983; Pfeffer, 1981, 1992; Robbins, 1987). Though the post-modernists would not disagree with this analysis *per se*, as mentioned earlier, their view of power in organisations is a much broader one. For them, power is the mechanism by which groups in organisations create and reinforce their view of reality. In turn, post-modernists maintain, it is this shaping and construction of reality that, in the main, allows dominant groups in organisations to impose their will on others rather than the use of sanctions and other control mechanisms (Reed and Hughes, 1992).

Managing and changing organisations: bringing back choice

In the previous chapter we examined the postmodernist, realist and complexity perspectives on organisations. The postmodernists argue that reason and logic have had their day, and that organisations are social organisms in which individuals and groups construct their own views of reality based on their own perceptions of the world and their place in it. Realists, whilst accepting the social construction hypothesis, argue that reality does exist and that it imposes limits, though sometimes very broad ones, on what individuals and organisations can do. The proponents of complexity, for their part, see organisations as complex, self-organising systems where, in order to maintain appropriate order-generating rules, choice and decision-making must move from the few to the many. What Chapter 4 showed, with its review of these three perspectives, was that organisations have a great deal more choice and freedom in what they can do and how they can do it than the organisation theories discussed in Chapters 1–3 allowed.

In this chapter we have sought to develop this argument further by looking at how choices are made in organisations and on what basis. The chapter began by examining the literature on organisational culture, which revealed that, despite its popularity as a promoter of organisational excellence, culture is difficult to define, change and manipulate. Strong cultures may have a positive effect on organisations, in that they can bond disparate groups together in a common purpose; and weak cultures may have a negative impact, in that individuals and groups can pursue separate and conflicting objectives. In some situations, however, especially where there is major environmental disruption, the reverse may also be true, with strong cultures being a straitjacket on innovation and weak ones allowing new ideas and new leaders to come to the fore. In such situations, where the organisation's dominant coalition is split, or is so ossified it cannot entertain change, power and politics come to the fore.

As the examination of the literature on power and politics showed, in cases where a clash of interests and a clash of perspectives is present, where the status quo is being challenged, major decisions about the future direction, structure and operation of an organisation are likely to be dominated by issues of power and politics (Buchanan and Badham, 1999).

Murray (1989: 285), reporting on a major study of the introduction and use of information technology, commented that:

> . . . the use of new technology is subject to processes of organizational decision-making and implementation characterized by often conflicting managerial objectives, rationalities and strategies developed through the mobilization of organizational power.

Therefore, as far as Buchanan and Badham (1999), Dawson (1994), Morgan (1986), Pfeffer (1992), Robbins (1987) and many others are concerned, the process of organisational change is inherently a political one.

Though the postmodern, realist, complexity, cultural and power–politics perspectives on organisational life are very different, there are also strong overlaps. In particular, the management of meaning and the creation of legitimacy through the construction and manipulation of symbols is an area of common ground. This can be seen in Pettigrew's (1985) study of organisational change in ICI. He maintains that the process of change is shaped by the interests and commitments of individuals and groups, the forces of bureaucratic momentum, significant changes in the environment, and the manipulation of the structural context around decisions. In particular, Pettigrew (1987: 659) argues:

> The acts and processes associated with politics as the management of meaning represent conceptually the overlap between a concern with the political and cultural analyses of organizations. A central concept linking political and cultural analyses essential to the understanding of continuity and change is legitimacy. The management of meaning refers to a process of symbol construction and value use designed to create legitimacy for one's ideas, actions and demands, and to delegitimate the demands of one's opponents . . . [Therefore] structures, cultures and strategies are not just being treated here as neutral, functional constructs connectable to some system need such as efficiency or adaptability; those constructs are viewed as capable of serving to protect the interests of the dominant groups. . . . The content of strategic change is thus ultimately a product of a legitimation process shaped by political/cultural considerations, though often expressed in rational/analytical terms.

This view that the choice and use of structure, and other key decisions, is the outcome of a political process rather than the application of rational analysis and decision-making has significant implications for organisation theory. Whilst it does not necessarily invalidate the appropriateness or otherwise of particular approaches, it does mean that managerial aspirations and interests are seen as more important than might otherwise be the case. It also means that, rather than being the prisoners of organisation theory (as some might suppose or hope), managers do have significant scope for the exercise of choice with regard to structure and other organisational characteristics.

In his review of the influence of power and politics in organisations, Robbins (1987) noted that no more than 50 to 60 per cent of variability in structure can be explained by strategy, size, technology and environment. He then went on to argue that a substantial portion of the residual variance can be explained by those in positions of power choosing a structure that will, as far as possible, maintain and enhance their control. He pointed out that proponents of other determinants of structure, such as size, technology, etc., assume that organisations are rational entities: 'However, for rationality to prevail an organization must have either a single goal or agreement over the multiple goals. Neither case exists in most organizations' (Robbins, 1987: 200). Consequently, he argued that structural decisions are not rational. Such decisions arise from a power struggle between special-interest groups or coalitions, each arguing for a structural arrangement that best suits them. Robbins (1987: 200) believes that whilst strategy, size, technology and environment define the minimum level of effectiveness and set the parameters within which self-serving decision choices will be made, 'both technology and environment are chosen. Thus, those in power will select technologies and environments that will facilitate their maintenance of control.' As both the realists and complexity advocates argue, however, the extent to which those in power can please themselves has limits. Markets do exist, economies can fall as well as rise and, as the dotcom collapse in 2000 and the credit crunch in 2007 showed, new technologies do not always deliver on their promise and market bubbles can and do burst. The power–politics perspective, therefore, does not totally undermine the case against the rational view of management but it might explain the dismal long-term performance of America's largest companies mentioned earlier in this chapter (Foster and Kaplan, 2003). After all, if executives are busy pursuing their own (usually) short-term interests, they can hardly be pursuing the long-term interests of their organisations.

There is also other strong and significant evidence that challenges the view of management as rational and neutral implementers of decisions determined by objective data. In particular, the detailed case studies of organisational decision-making and change at ICI and Cadbury Ltd carried out, respectively, by Pettigrew (1985, 1987) and Child and Smith (1987) lend a great deal of weight to the view that management in general, and the management of change in particular, is inherently a political process. Murray (1989) made the telling point that, given the insecurity of many managers' positions, particularly during periods of major upheaval and change, it is not surprising that managers and other groups attempt to influence decisions in order to protect, enhance or shore up their position in the organisation.

Nevertheless, one needs to be wary of ascribing the purpose of all organisational decisions and actions to self-interest. Politics plays a part but, to view Robbins's (1987) finding from another perspective, so too do strategy, size, technology and environment.

As the realists would argue, these can act as a constraint on the freedom of action of groups and individuals, as can the need to be seen to act in the organisation's best interests, in line with agreed goals and in a rational manner. Therefore, though the political perspective has become very influential in the last 30 years, it does not explain all actions and all decisions in organisations. We need to see power and politics as an important influence on organisations but not the only influence. Indeed, we need to remember the original objective of Cyert and March's (1963) work on organisational politics. They sought to show that external factors were not the only factors that affected decision-making in organisations. This is not, of course, the same as saying that external factors do not matter. As Child and Smith (1987) show with their firm-in-sector perspective (*see* Chapter 6), the external environment does matter. In a whole host of concrete and symbolic ways, it constrains and impinges on organisational decision-making and behaviour. It may well be, as Robbins (1987) commented, that strategy, size, technology and environment only define the minimum level of effectiveness and set the parameters within which decisions are taken, but this is still a very important constraint on managers. It is also an important rejoinder to those management theorists who have become, according to Hendry (1996: 621), 'overfocused on the political aspects of the change [decision-making] process'.

In summary, therefore, power and politics are amongst the most important factors influencing decision-making in organisations. Indeed, by linking the arguments of Robbins, Pettigrew and Murray regarding managerial choice of structure to the discussion on culture, two very interesting points arise:

- Firstly, it was argued by Allaire and Firsirotu (1984), and others, that culture and structure need to be mutually supportive if an organisation is to operate efficiently and effectively. If, as the power–politics perspective argues, structure is in part at least the outcome of self-interested choice by the dominant coalition, the degree of congruence between the two may be due more to accident than design.
- Secondly, it was also argued earlier that organisational culture is the product of long-term social learning in which dominant coalitions play a key role. This clearly opens up scope for choices over both structure and culture. However, the development of culture and approaches to changing it are long-term processes. Dominant coalitions, on the other hand, change their composition and priorities over time, sometimes over quite short periods of time.

Therefore, although it can be argued that the possibility exists for managers to choose both the structure and culture that best suit their own self-interests, this is only likely to result in a balanced and effective structure–culture nexus if the dominant coalition holds sway and is consistent in its aims over long periods of time.

As many observers have noted, whilst these conditions may exist in some Western companies (e.g. News International under Rupert Murdoch, General Electric under Jack Welch, Virgin under Richard Branson), these are the exception. In any case, as the departure of Arnold Weinstock from GEC showed (*see* Marconi case study in Chapter 6), such situations often rely on dominant individuals to hold coalitions together; when they go, the dominant coalition falls apart and a new one emerges with a radically different vision for the organisation (Brummer and Cowe, 1998; Brummer, 1999). Sometimes the departure of such individuals can even bring an organisation perilously close to collapse, as was the case with GEC when Weinstock stepped down, Apple Computers when Steve Jobs was fired in 1985, and with Tiny Rowland's forced departure from Lonrho in 1995 (Laird, 1998; Morgan, 1986). Indeed, in some companies, so forceful and coercive is the personality of a dominant individual that their will cannot be questioned, and fundamental problems are only discovered once they depart, as was the case with Robert Maxwell and Mirror Group Newspapers (Bower, 1996).

The Japanese experience seems at first glance to follow a similar pattern of dominant coalitions relying on one key person for their legitimacy and direction. In their case, however, when such a person departs, the dominant coalition appears to maintain the unity of purpose (Fruin, 1992; Pascale and Athos, 1982; Whitehill, 1991). Yet even the Japanese are not immune from problems when changing leaders. For example, Nissan's appointment of a new chief executive in 1985 was followed by an attempt to change its culture in order to overcome what were seen as major mistakes by the previous incumbent (Ishizuna, 1990). This and other changes failed and, in the end, Nissan was, in effect, taken over by the state-owned French car-maker Renault.

To sum up, what we can see is that managers have a degree, arguably a wide degree, of choice or influence over major organisational variables such as structure, technology, environment and perhaps even culture. Despite the arguments of the postmodernists, however, their freedom of action is constrained by a whole host of factors such as market conditions, technological development, organisational goals, policies and performance, their own and other people's self-interests, and the need to portray their actions as being rational and in the best interests of their organisation. In addition, in a reciprocal way, some of the factors over which they have a degree of choice, such as structure and culture, can also limit managers' freedom of manoeuvre. These constraints will vary from organisation to organisation at any one time and, within and between organisations, over time but will never be fully absent. Strong though these constraints may be, however, choice will never be totally absent.

Conclusions

In reviewing the main approaches to and perspectives on organisation theory, Part 1 of this book has shown that, by succeeding stages, these have moved from the mechanical–rational outlook of the Classical school to the, arguably, culture-based perspectives of the Culture–Excellence, Japanese and Organisation Learning approaches, passing through the social perspective of the Human Relations school and the rational perspective of the Contingency theorists. They all argue for a 'one best way' approach (though the Contingency theorists believed in this for 'each' rather than 'all' organisations). Because of this approach they all, in effect, seek to remove choice from managers: do as we tell you, or else! Indeed, it was one of the main claims of the Classical school that it removed discretion not only from workers, but also from managers. As Frederick Taylor (1911b: 189) stated:

> *The man at the head of the business under scientific management is governed by rules and laws . . . just as the workman is, and the standards which have been developed are equitable.*

The role of managers, from these perspectives, is to apply rationally the dictates of the particular theory promoted. To do otherwise would be sub-optimal and irrational.

By building on the discussions of postmodernism, realism and complexity in Chapter 4, this chapter has sought to move managerial choice back to centre stage. By exploring organisational culture, it was shown that the degree to which culture influences behaviour is dependent upon the presence of clear and consistent organisational goals. If these are not present, which appears to be the case in many companies, conflict and disagreement emerge regardless of the nature of the culture. Similarly, if the environment changes to the extent that existing ways of working are no longer appropriate, once again, conflict and disagreement may emerge. In such situations, it is the political perspective on organisational life that offers the better opportunity for understanding how and why decisions are taken, particular courses of action are embarked upon, and why some changes to the management and structure of the organisation are pursued and others discarded.

The examination of organisational politics and power added further weight to the criticisms of the approaches to organisation theory considered in previous chapters, particularly concerning the scope for rational decision-making and choice. To an extent, the key issue was raised when discussing Contingency Theory, namely the question as to whether managers are the prisoners of the situational variables they face, or whether they can influence or change these. Certainly some critics of Contingency Theory argue that managers can, partly at least, influence or choose the contingencies they face. This casts doubts not only on the deterministic nature of Contingency Theory, but also on all organisational theories, because – either openly or implicitly – they are all founded on the notion that organisations face certain immutable conditions that they cannot influence and to which they must therefore adapt.

This does not necessarily mean that the various theories and their attendant structures and practices we have discussed so far in this book are invalid, unhelpful or inapplicable. It does, however, mean that it may be possible, within limits, for organisations, or rather those who control organisations, to decide upon the structure and behaviours they want to promote, and then shape the conditions and contingencies to suit these, rather than *vice versa*. Indeed, as far as the public sector in the UK is concerned, this appears to be exactly what governments have done. From 1979 to 1997, successive Conservative governments took the view that they wanted managers in the public sector to be cost-focused and entrepreneurial, and shaped the conditions in which the public sector operates (i.e. its environment) in order to promote those attributes (Ferlie *et al*, 1996; Flynn, 1993). Following its election in 1997, the 'New Labour' government similarly manipulated the public-sector environment to encourage a more market-orientated approach to service delivery (Salauroo and Burnes, 1998; Vidler and Clarke, 2005).

If – contrary to the dictates of most management theories – organisations are *not* the prisoners of situational variables, as most organisation theories maintain, if those who manage them do have a degree of leeway in what they do, one then has to ask what factors do influence the actions of decision-makers. The review of the power–politics literature showed organisations as shifting coalitions of groups and individuals seeking to promote policies and decisions that enhanced or maintained their position in the organisation. From the literature, a persuasive argument is mounted for seeing politics and power – usually promoted under the cloak of rationality, reasonableness and the organisation's best interests – as a central, though not exclusive, determinant of the way organisations operate.

In particular, though political behaviour appears to be an ever-present feature of organisational life, politics comes to the fore when major issues of structural change or resource allocation are concerned. Such decisions have crucial importance for achieving and maintaining power or position, or even – when the chips are down – for keeping one's job when all around are losing theirs.

Therefore, it is surprising that much of organisation theory, which after all is primarily concerned with major decisions concerning structure and resource allocation, seems to dismiss or gloss over power and politics. Nevertheless, what is clear from this chapter is that managers, despite the constraints they face, have a far wider scope for shaping decisions than most organisation theories acknowledge, and that the scope for choice and the deployment of political influence is likely to be most pronounced when change, particularly major change, is on the managerial agenda.

Having examined the merits and drawbacks of the main organisation theories, and in particular having raised the issue of the way in which major decisions are decided upon and implemented, we can now turn our attention in the following chapters to an in-depth examination of how organisations decide upon and carry out change.

Test your learning

Short answer questions

1. What are Cummings and Huse's four elements of culture?

2. Briefly describe Handy's four types of culture.

3. List three implications of Hofstede's work on national cultures for Western approaches to organisation theory.

4. What does the term 'satisfice' mean?

5. Give three benefits of Robbins's addition of *knowledge power* to Etzioni's three types of power.

6. Define organisational power.

7. Define organisational politics.

8. For each of the following, briefly state their implications for organisational change: (a) organisational culture and (b) power and politics.

Essay questions

1. Discuss the following statement: organisational culture is the prime determinant of organisational performance.

2. Explain the concept of dominant coalitions, and discuss how these can prevent organisations dividing into warring factions with individuals and groups pursuing their own personal agendas.

Suggested further reading

1. Brown, A (1998) *Organisational Culture* (2nd edition). Financial Times Pitman: London.

   Andrew Brown's book gives a useful introduction to the uses and abuses of organisational culture.

2. Pfeffer, J (1992) *Managing with Power: Politics and Influence in Organizations.* Harvard Business School Press: Boston, MA, USA.

   This is an entertaining and very useful guide to the power–politics perspective on organisations.

CASE STUDY 5

GK Printers Limited

BACKGROUND

GK Printers Limited is a small, family-run printing business. It was established just after the Second World War by the present Managing Director's father. The company was originally a jobbing printers; which is to say they would print anything. 'No job too large or too small' might well have been their motto, although in fact, the mainstay of their business was producing stationery, business cards and publicity brochures for local companies. Unlike many other small printers, it had updated its equipment and processes which enabled it to grow its business whilst similar companies struggled. Nevertheless, its customers, old and new, were becoming increasingly demanding with regard to price and delivery. In addition, there were signs that its competitors were beginning to win back some of the work they had lost to GK.

Eventually, it became clear that GK was beginning to lose a significant amount of business. This was partly due to increased competition, but mainly it was because its customers, in seeking to cut their own costs, were reducing the size and frequency of their orders (though when orders were placed, they were often required far faster than previously). This presented a double threat to GK. Firstly, the fall in overall volumes was having an adverse effect on turnover and profit. Secondly, the reduction in size of individual print runs was having an adverse effect on costs because, though the actual volume was smaller, the design, order processing and set-up costs remained constant. In effect, as volumes decreased, the cost of each printed item increased. In addition, there were worrying signs that some customers were using word-processing packages and colour printers to produce their own publicity material instead of going to a printer.

At a time when its customers were pressurising it to cut costs, GK was faced with the dilemma of whether to increase its prices to offset rising costs (and risk customers going elsewhere or developing their own facilities), or to maintain or reduce prices and see its profits plunge. The knee-jerk reaction of many in the company was, 'If customers want smaller runs, the price goes up.' However, the Managing Director and the other managers in GK came reluctantly to accept that, whilst the logic was impeccable, the result could be disastrous. After much seemingly futile discussion, it was the Marketing and Design Manager who eventually came up with a suggestion that, though laughed at initially, later turned out to be the key to GK's survival. He pointed out that to maintain its existing volume of business, and perhaps even increase it, GK needed to improve on its already good level of service. In particular, it needed to cut costs in order to cut prices and improve the efficiency of its internal operations to cut delivery times. The initial reaction to these suggestions was, perhaps predictably, very negative. After all, if volumes decrease, unit costs must increase because set-up costs are constant; also, an increase in the number of smaller print runs actually extends turnaround times for a similar reason – more set-ups are required. So the Marketing and Design Manager was attempting to turn the conventional wisdom regarding printing on its head. In addition, he was a relatively newcomer to the company and, in some people's eyes, he was believed to lack an in-depth knowledge of the printing industry. Finally, GK had already made significant strides in improving efficiency and cutting costs, and there was some doubt as to the scope for any real improvements in these areas.

A FALSE START

Despite the initial adverse comments, the Managing Director began to wonder if it might be possible to reduce set-up times and costs. If it could, he reasoned, the company would be able to attract more business, prevent customers seeking in-house solutions, and undermine their competitors. In the past, the Managing Director had brought in outside consultants to help improve the company. However, in this instance he asked the Marketing and Design Manager to put forward some suggestions for reducing costs and set-up times. This was for two reasons. Firstly, he wanted to

give him a chance to prove himself to the rest of the team. Secondly, the Managing Director wanted to demonstrate that they had the managerial talent to dispense with outside assistance.

The Marketing and Design Manager quickly responded and within a fortnight presented his proposals to the Managing Director and other senior staff. He began by identifying what he saw as the main problem the company faced:

1. Though there had been a slight decline in the number of individual orders, the actual reduction in the volume of business was much greater because customers were ordering shorter print runs.
2. The result of this was that, whilst office staff, marketing, design, administration, etc., were as busy as ever, the print shop was short of work, and it was not unusual to see printers sitting reading the paper with nothing else to do.
3. However, though the printers were underworked, this did not provide much scope for reducing delivery times, because most of GK's lead time was accounted for by non-printing activities – especially design, which could take anything up to two weeks.

Having laid out what he saw as the problem, the Marketing and Design Manager went on to offer a solution. He argued that the key to solving the company's problems lay in speeding up design time. He pointed out that there was always a backlog of design work ranging from one to two weeks. Given that everything, even repeat orders, went through design, total lead time could be anything from three to five weeks. Whilst this was considerably better than in the past, it was no longer acceptable as customers were cutting stock to a minimum. Many customers were asking to have their printing back within seven days, sometimes even sooner where promotional

CASE STUDY 5 CONT.

material was concerned. The solution, therefore, he argued, was to have more design staff. If one extra designer was employed the Marketing and Design Manager believed that design lead time could be reduced to two or three days.

The Managing Director and other managers, especially the Printing Manager, who had been arguing unsuccessfully for new equipment for some time, were taken aback by this proposal. The analysis, they believed, was correct but the solution, they felt, was an outrageous piece of opportunism. The case for more design staff had been raised and rejected in the recent past. The Marketing and Design Manager's colleagues felt that he was blatantly using the company's current problems to empire-build. Not surprisingly, he vigorously denied this. Nevertheless, the meeting ended acrimoniously and no decision was taken.

The Managing Director was particularly infuriated, as he had genuinely been expecting an acceptable solution to emerge from the meeting. Instead, the friendly working atmosphere he valued, and which he felt he did much to promote, had been shattered. Nor did he see an easy way to bring his managers back together to seek a cooperative solution. He was also annoyed because he realised that he had made a mistake in asking only one person to put forward their view. Not only would a team have avoided favouring one area rather than another; it would not even occur to anyone to make the accusation. Having made the mistake, however, he was not sure how to remedy it. If a team was set up to examine the options that did not include the Marketing and Design Manager, he would rightly see it as a snub and probably attack any solution that was put forward. If he was included, it was likely that

he would continue to push his proposal and the other managers would react badly. His inclination was to impose a solution and tell everyone to get on and implement it. Unfortunately, he did not have a solution to impose.

Questions

1. Imagine that you are an outside consultant brought in to advise the Managing Director:
   a. What are the key issues he needs to address and resolve?
   b. What are the main steps he needs to take to agree and implement a solution?
   c. What obstacles might he expect to encounter and how might he overcome these?

2. Imagine that you are the Managing Director. You have decided to take direct charge of resolving the situation without the aid of any outside assistance:
   a. What is your analysis of what has gone wrong so far and who is to blame?
   b. What are the main steps you need to take to agree and implement a solution successfully?
   c. What obstacles might you expect to encounter and how might you overcome these?

3. Imagine that you are the Marketing and Design Manager. The Managing Director has asked you to reflect on the response of your colleagues and produce a revised and acceptable plan for resolving the company's problems.
   a. What is your analysis of why the first proposal was so strongly rejected?
   b. What are the main steps you need to take to develop a proposal acceptable to your colleagues?
   c. What are the main obstacles to achieving an acceptable proposal?

Part 2: Strategy development and change management: past, present and future

CHAPTER 6

Approaches to strategy

Managerial choice and constraints

Learning objectives

After studying this chapter, you should be able to:

- discuss the origins, development and popularity of organisation strategy;
- describe the main features of the Prescriptive stream of strategy;
- list the strengths and weaknesses of the Prescriptive stream;
- discuss the key elements of the Analytical stream of strategy;
- state the major advantages and shortcomings of the Analytical stream;
- understand the key differences between the Prescriptive and the Analytical streams of strategy;
- describe the constraints faced by organisations and whether these can be manipulated or overcome;
- appreciate the relationship between strategy and change.

Mini Case Study 6.1
Michael Porter

The master strategist: Michael Porter

Michael Porter became famous in the 1990s as a consultant on competitiveness to business and governments. In the 1980s, however, he wrote several popular and respected books on business strategy, introducing basic tools of strategic thinking such as the 'five forces' model and the value chain.

It is for this work on strategy that he is likely to be remembered, and his ideas have had a wide impact. In 1999, *Fortune* called him the single most important strategist working today, and possibly of all time.

Prof. Porter was born in Ann Arbor, Michigan, in 1947. He studied at Princeton and Harvard and joined the faculty at Harvard in 1973. He has also become a highly respected consultant, working with companies such as DuPont and Shell, and the US, Canadian, New Zealand and Swedish governments.

▶

Prof. Porter views strategy from the standpoint of economics, and his ideas on how strategy should be implemented are based on an understanding of competition and other economic forces. Strategy is not devised in isolation; a company's options will always be limited by what is going on around it.

His famous 'five forces' model shows the constraining impact that competition and environment have on strategy.

The five forces identified by Prof. Porter are: the threat of new entrants and the appearance of new competitors; the degree of rivalry among existing competitors in the market; the bargaining power of buyers; the bargaining power of suppliers; and the threat of substitute products or services that could shrink the market.

The strength of each of these forces varies from industry to industry, but taken together they determine long-term profitability. They help to shape the prices companies can charge, the costs they must pay for resources and the level of investment that will be needed to compete.

From the external environment, he turns to the company itself. Companies make products and deliver them to consumers, but they can also add value to the basic product in a variety of ways and through different functions.

Value can be added directly, for example by giving a product new technology features, or indirectly, through measures that allow the company to become more efficient. Prof. Porter argues that every product follows a critical path through the company, from its inception to its delivery as a finished article. At every stage along this path there are opportunities to add value. This path he calls the 'value chain'.

The value chain is crucial, he says, because it demonstrates that the company is more than just the sum of its parts and activities: all activities are connected, and what is done at one stage affects work at other stages.

The company needs to examine its value chain and decide where it can add value most effectively to meet competitive pressures in the industry.

These concepts can be applied to entire sectors and national economies as well as individual companies, and Prof. Porter went on to develop his theories of national competitiveness in great detail.

Source: Morgen Witzel, *Financial Times*, 15 August 2003, p. 11.

Mini Case Study 6.2
Henry Mintzberg

The great iconoclast: Henry Mintzberg

Henry Mintzberg had been called 'the great management iconoclast' for his willingness to attack previously sacred concepts in business and management. But his commonsense approach to management problems has won him a broad following, particularly among students and working managers. He is best known for his work on business strategy, where he exposed the gap between academic concepts of strategy and reality.

Born in Montreal in 1939, Mintzberg studied engineering and worked for Canadian National Railways before obtaining a doctorate from the Massachusetts Institute of Technology in 1968. He joined the faculty of management at McGill University, Canada, where he has remained. Mintzberg was interested in defining what managers really do and how they carry out their tasks. He discovered a vast body of what he termed 'managerial folklore': research studies that considered managers rational beings who made decisions based on careful analysis of all available information.

Experience told Mintzberg that managerial work was not like that. Not only was it less structured and ordered than assumed but its true nature was also hard to define. His observations of managers in action confirmed this. He found that decisions were made quickly, often on the move, usually based more on intuition and experience than on considered analysis. Action was more important than reflection. Half the daily management tasks he observed took less than 10 minutes each and only 10 per cent took more than an hour.

The portrait of the manager and his task that emerges from Mintzberg's work is a sympathetic one. Managers are constantly 'firefighting', dealing with problems under pressure. Rather than the best possible solution, they seek the best solution that can be implemented given the resources available. And, says Mintzberg, because each organisation has its own culture and needs, managers' responses to problems will vary. There may be no one 'right' way to manage a business.

These affect strategy. Academic conceptions of strategy regarded it as the province of top management, who consider and make strategic decisions with detachment. Again, Mintzberg disagrees. In the real world, strategy-making is ad hoc and instinctive, not structured and planned. The concept of 'strategic planning' becomes an oxymoron.

Mintzberg sees this approach to strategy as a virtue. 'Emergent strategy', as he calls it, is strategy that evolves according to need, constantly adjusted and adapted. He also speaks of 'crafting strategy', a process by which managers develop strategy according to the needs of their organisation and environment. Here, strategy creation and implementation are interdependent. He compares the art of strategy making to pottery and managers to potters sitting at a wheel moulding the clay and letting the shape of the object evolve in their hands.

Successful management is about knowing the business – in all its aspects and not just in specialist areas – and an ability to manage through discontinuity.

Source: Morgen Witzel, *Financial Times*, 5 August 2003, p. 11.

Introduction

In Part 1 of this book, we discussed the options open to organisations in terms of their structures, cultures, behaviours and practices. By examining the development of organisational theory in the 200 years since the Industrial Revolution, we saw that, in the beginning, management was almost exclusively concerned with strict labour discipline and long working hours. The methods used to pursue these were *ad hoc*, erratic, short-term and usually harsh and unfair. As the period progressed, more structured and consistent approaches came to the fore. Up to the 1960s, it was the Classical and Human Relations approaches that dominated organisational thinking. With the advent of these two approaches, the emphasis moved more to the effectiveness and efficiency of the entire organisation, rather than focusing purely on discipline and hours of work.

Both these approaches tended to dwell on internal arrangements and to assume that organisation structures and practices were in some way insulated from the outside world. The development of Contingency Theory in the 1960s, with its underlying Open Systems perspective, changed all this. The nature of the environment (both internal and external) in which organisations operate emerged as a central factor in how they should structure themselves. This theme has been continued with the development of new paradigms in the last 30 years, and the importance of situational variables, especially environmental turbulence, which organisations face, is seen by many as an unchallenge-able fact (Kanter, 2006; Peters, 2006).

As argued in Part 1, the degree to which organisations are the prisoners of these situational variables (as opposed to being able to exercise influence and choice) is certainly open to debate. Similarly, as shown in Chapters 4 and 5, the credibility of the rational approach to decision-making has been considerably undermined in the last three decades. The increasing appreciation of the complexity of organisational life has been paralleled by a growing recognition that organisations cannot cope successfully with the modern world and all its changing aspects purely on an *ad hoc* and piecemeal basis. Whether decision-makers operate on the basis of rationality or are influenced by personal con-siderations or organisational cultures, the received wisdom is that for organisations to succeed there must be a consistency and coherence to the decisions taken – which is another way of saying that they must have a strategy (Johnson and Scholes, 2002). Unfortunately, it is easier to say that an organisation needs a strategy than it is to say what that strategy should be or how it should be derived. Perhaps the two most influ-ential writers on strategy over the past 25 years have been Michael Porter and Henry Mintzberg, yet, as Mini Case Studies 6.1 and 6.2 show, their portrayal and understand-ing of strategy is significantly different.

In this chapter, we shall examine the development and shortcomings of the main approaches to strategy that have been put forward in the last 60 years. It will be shown that, since the end of the Second World War, organisations have begun to take a strategic perspective on their activities. They have increasingly sought to take a long-term over-view in order to plan for and cope with the vagaries of the future. In many respects, the development of strategic management has tended to mirror the development of organisational theory. In the 1940s and 1950s, the strategy literature only considered one aspect of an organisation's activities – the external environment. It tended to seek rational, mathematical approaches to planning. With the passing of time, more intuitive and less rational approaches to strategic management have been developed which claim to incorporate the totality of organisational life.

The chapter concludes by arguing that, rather than managers being the prisoners of mathematical models and rational approaches to strategy development, they have con-siderable freedom of action and a wide range of options to choose from. They are still not totally free agents; their freedom of action is seen as being constrained or shaped by the unique set of organisational, environmental and societal factors faced by their particular organisation. Fortunately, these constraints are not immutable. As argued in Part 1, it is possible for managers to manipulate the situational variables they face with regard to structure. Similarly, managers can exert some influence over strategic constraints and, potentially at least, can select the approach to strategy that best suits their preferences.

Understanding strategy: origins, definitions and approaches

The origins of strategy

It is commonly believed that our concept of strategy has been passed down to us from the ancient Greeks. Bracker (1980: 219) argued that the word strategy comes from the Greek *stratego*, meaning 'to plan the destruction of one's enemies through the effective use of resources'. However, they developed the concept purely in relation to the successful pursuit of victory in war. The concept remained a military one until the nineteenth century, when it began to be applied to the business world, though most writers believe the actual process by which this took place is untraceable (Bracker, 1980; Chandler, 1962). Chandler (1962) put forward the view that the emergence of strategy in civilian organisational life resulted from an awareness of the opportunities and needs – created by changing population, income and technology – to employ existing or expanding resources more profitably.

Hoskin (1990) largely agrees with Chandler's view of the development of modern business strategy since the Industrial Revolution. However, he does take issue with both Chandler and Bracker on two crucial points. Firstly, he argues that the modern concept of organisational strategy bears little resemblance to military strategy, at least as it existed up to the First World War. Secondly, he challenges the view that the origins of business strategy are untraceable. When investigating the emergence of modern strategy he did find a link with the military world, though it was not quite the link that Bracker and Chandler proposed. Like Chandler, Hoskin argues that one of the most significant developments in business management in the nineteenth century occurred in the running of the US railways. Unlike Chandler, however, Hoskin gives the credit for initiating business strategy to one of the Pennsylvania Railroad's executives, Herman Haupt. He states that Haupt:

> . . . *changes the rules of business discourse: the image in which he reconstructs business, on the Pennsylvania Railroad, is that of the proactive, future-oriented organization, which is managed by the numbers . . . How does he do so? By importing the practices of writing, examination and grading . . . On the Pennsylvania Railroad we find for the first time the full interactive play of grammatocentrism [writing and recording] and calculability [mathematical analysis of the recorded data].*
>
> (Hoskin, 1990: 20)

This approach created the bedrock on which strategic management grew in the United States, especially after the Second World War. It also ensured that strategic management became a quantitatively orientated discipline, whose focus was on the use of numerical analysis to forecast market trends in order to plan for the future. Hoskin also points out that Haupt was a graduate of the US military academy at West Point, which pioneered the techniques of 'writing, examination and grading' in the military world. From there its graduates, particularly Haupt, took them out into the business world – hence the link between military and civilian management techniques.

Thus it is possible to see why strategic management developed in the way it did – as a quantitative, mathematical approach. We can also see that there are links between the military and business worlds, but that they are not as some have claimed. Management strategy has not developed from the approach to military campaigns of the ancient Greeks; instead it has adopted and made its own the techniques of record-keeping and analysis that were developed at West Point in order to measure the performance, and suitability for military life, of the US army's future officer class.

The contribution of the American armed forces to this quantitative approach to strategy did not end with West Point or in the nineteenth century. In 1945, with the end of the Second World War, America experienced an extraordinary trading boom. McKiernan (1992) commented that this forced many American companies to rethink their business planning systems. In order to justify and implement the capacity expansion necessary to cope with the boom, companies began to abandon short-term, one-year, budgeting cycles in favour of more long-range planning techniques. The development of this strategic approach to planning and investment was given a significant impetus when some of the people involved in the USAAF's wartime strategic planning activities returned to civilian life – most notable amongst them was Robert McNamara, who became Chairman of the Ford Motor Company, Secretary of State under John F Kennedy and President of the World Bank (Moore, 1992). Their main vehicle for influencing business was the Harvard Business School's approach to business policy teaching, which steadily moved the focus of management away from a preoccupation with internal organisational issues (as proposed by the Classical and Human Relations schools) towards an external orientation. This was best exemplified by the development of two important concepts: marketing, with its emphasis on analysing demand and tailoring products to meet it; and systems theory, with its emphasis not only on the interconnectedness of different parts of an organisation, but also the links between internal and external forces.

In the intervening years, first in the USA and later across the Western world, these techniques and approaches have become more widely disseminated and used (Bracker, 1980). Much credit for this must go to three key figures, Kenneth R Andrews, Alfred D Chandler and H Igor Ansoff, for their work in developing and fleshing out the concept of strategic management, and especially for demonstrating the importance of product–market mix. Nevertheless, in highlighting the importance of the outside world, and thus breaking managers' Classical school-inspired fixation with internal structures and practices, they can be criticised for not making the link between the two. So managers moved from believing that internal arrangements alone would bring success to believing that an external, market focus was the key.

The rise and fall of long-range planning

In order to cope with the new and rapidly changing technological, economic and organisational developments that followed the end of the Second World War, American organisations, which were at the forefront of these developments, began to adopt long-range planning techniques. This necessitated first defining the organisation's objectives, then establishing plans in order to achieve those objectives, and finally, allocating resources, through capital budgeting, in line with the plans. A key aim of this process was to reduce the gap that often occurred between the level of demand that a firm expected, and planned for, and the level of demand that actually occurred (Fox, 1975). Therefore, long-range planning was a mechanism for plotting trends and planning the actions required to achieve the identified growth targets, all of which were heavily biased towards financial targets and budgetary controls. However, this process proved incapable of accurately forecasting future demand, and the problem of the gap between the level of expected demand and actual demand remained.

Long-range planning failed for a variety of internal and external reasons (McKiernan, 1992). Internally, many planning systems involved little more than an extrapolation of past sales trends. Little attention was paid to wider external economic, technological or social changes, or even changes in the behaviour of competitor firms. Thompson (2008: 15) cites Queen Victoria's funeral as a classic example of this type of planning:

> *The route of her funeral procession was laid down as exactly the same route as for her uncle, the previous monarch. The dress rehearsal was by all accounts either hilarious or a farce, depending on your sense of humour. The planners had not taken into account the fact that London had changed considerably in the 60-odd years of Victoria's reign. Some streets were no longer accessible. Many were not even there any more!*

Externally, in the 1960s, the relatively comfortable conditions of high market growth gave way to lower levels of growth, which led to increased competition as companies tried to increase, or at least maintain, their market share to compensate for lower growth. One outcome of this was that strategic planners had to adapt to a world where growth was not steady; it could slow down, increase or be interrupted in an unpredictable and violent manner. Also, unforeseen opportunities and threats could and did emerge. Furthermore, it became evident that closing the gap between the plan and what actually occurred was not necessarily the most critical aspect of strategy formulation. Indeed, since the early 1970s, volatile markets, over-capacity and resource constraints have taken over as dominant management considerations.

Long-range planning techniques could not cope with such environmental turbulence which, to say the least, limits forecasting accuracy. In addition, the nature of American business had begun to change. Slower growth and increased competition led to a situation where large single-business firms, which in the past might have dominated a single industry, were being replaced by multinational conglomerates operating in a wide range of increasingly competitive industries and markets. Therefore, rather than managing a single, unified enterprise, corporate managers found themselves managing a diverse portfolio of businesses. Richard Branson's Virgin empire is a good example of this sort of development:

> *Virgin, a leading branded venture capital organisation, is one of the world's most recognised and respected brands. Conceived in 1970 by Sir Richard Branson, the Virgin Group has gone on to grow very successful businesses in sectors ranging from mobile telephony, to transportation, travel, financial services, leisure, music, holidays, publishing and retailing. Virgin has created more than 200 branded companies worldwide, employing approximately 50,000 people, in 29 countries. Revenues around the world in 2006 exceeded £10 billion (approx. US$20 billion).* (Virgin.com, 2008)

In response to the emergence of conglomerates and the failure of long-range planning, in the late 1960s, the concept of strategic management began to emerge. Unlike long-range planning, strategic management focuses on the environmental assumptions that underlie market trends and incorporates the possibility that changes in trends can and do take place, and is not based on the assumption that adequate growth can be assured (Elliot and Lawrence, 1985; Mintzberg and Quinn, 1991). Consequently, strategic management focuses more closely on winning market share from competitors, rather than assuming that organisations can rely solely on the expansion of markets for their own growth (Hax and Majluf, 1996). As Johnson and Scholes (2002: 15–16) comment:

> *Strategic management is concerned with complexity arising out of ambiguous and non-routine situations with organisation-wide rather than operations-specific implications. . . . Nor is strategic management concerned only with taking decisions about major issues facing the organisation. It is also concerned with ensuring that the strategy is put into effect. It can be thought of as having three elements within it . . .* under-standing the strategic position *of an organisation,* strategic choices *for the future and turning* strategy into action.

Strategic management sought to take a broader and more sophisticated view of an organisation's environment than long-range planning. Initially at least, it was closely associated with a number of portfolio planning techniques which also emerged in the late 1960s (Hax and Majluf, 1996; McKiernan, 1992). The most famous of these is the Boston Consulting Group's Growth Share Matrix (*see* Figure 7.2 in Chapter 7). As will be described in Chapter 7, this and other portfolio planning techniques was developed to assist managers in running large, diversified enterprises operating in complex environments. Much of this work was sponsored and used by big American corporations, such as General Electric, in order to identify the market position and potential of their strategic business units (SBUs) and to decide on whether to develop, sell or close them down. This 'positioning' approach to strategic management, the latest variant of which is Porter's (1980, 1985) 'competitive forces model' (*see* Figure 7.1 in Chapter 7), dominated the practice of strategic management from the 1960s onwards, and to a large extent still does (Galagan, 1997; Rigby and Gillies, 2000). It has also led many companies to adopt a harsh, and to an extent unthinking, approach to business success, epitomised by the words of Jack Welch when he was CEO of GE: 'We will run only businesses that are number one or two in their markets' (quoted in Kay, 1993: 339). Therefore, if businesses are not, or do not have the potential to become, leaders in their field, they are sold off or closed down (Koch, 1995).

As Kay (1993), and many others, point out, this approach to strategic management portrays strategy as a rational process whereby managers gather hard, quantitative data on their companies, and from this information come to rational decisions regarding their future. However, from the late 1970s onwards, the rational perspective on strategy has come under increasing attack, not least by the leading management thinker of his generation, Henry Mintzberg (1976, 1978, 1983, 1987, 1994, 1998, 2001, 2007). The main criticisms of the rational approach to strategy are threefold:

- that hard data are no more reliable, and in some cases less so, than qualitative data;
- that organisations and managers are not rational entities and do not apply a rational approach to decision-making; and

- that an organisation's strategy is as likely to emerge from unplanned actions and their unintended consequences over a period of time as it is from any deliberate process of planning and implementation (Child and Smith, 1987; Hatch, 1997; Mintzberg *et al*, 1998a; Pettigrew *et al*, 1992; Stacey, 2003; Whittington, 1993).

Defining strategy

As the above shows, like many other concepts in the field of management, there are many approaches to strategy but none are universally accepted (Stacey, 2003). Indeed, as Khalifa (2008: 894) recently commented:

> *The plethora of strategy concepts, theories, frameworks, and claims of superiority dazzles many who may not be able to see the forest from the trees. Managers and practitioners are overwhelmed by the flood of advice coming from different directions and each dismisses the other as out of date, short sighted, incomplete, inadequate, or even misleading.*

Even one of the pioneers of business strategy, Igor Ansoff (1987), warned that strategy is an elusive and somewhat abstract concept. This must be expected when dealing with an area that is constantly developing. Nor should this inhibit the search for a definition, or definitions, because in doing so we can see how the debate on strategy is developing and where the main areas of dispute lie.

Rather than leading to clarity, the eclipse of long-range planning merely heralded the arrival of a range of different and often confusing perspectives on strategy (Kay *et al*, 2003). As early as the 1960s, two schools of thought vied with each other: the Planning school and the Design school (Mintzberg *et al*, 1998a). The Planning school was based on formal procedures, formal training, formal analysis and a large dose of quantification. Its underlying assumption was that a strategy could be put together and work in the same way as a machine. It led to the creation of strategic planning departments in large organisations, reporting directly to the chief executive; that person's role – though notionally to be the architect of strategy – was to approve the planners' plan. The chief proponent of the Planning school was Igor Ansoff. Ansoff was a Russian–American engineer, mathematician, military strategist and operations researcher whose *Corporate Strategy* was published in 1965 to great acclaim (Koch, 1995). In this book he assumes that the purpose of a firm is profit maximisation, and he portrays strategic management as being primarily concerned with the external, rather than internal, concerns of the firm, especially the matching of products to markets (the product–market mix). As Figure 6.1 shows, Ansoff sought to show that organisations needed to tailor their strategies to the mix of markets they were operating in or wished to operate in, and the products they produced or intended to produce. So for example, as quadrant 1 shows, he argued that where an organisation was selling existing products into existing markets, it needed a market penetration strategy aimed at enabling them to take a greater share of the market. However, as quadrant 4 shows, where the company wished to sell new products into new markets; it would need a diversification strategy. Ansoff's book provided managers with a plethora of checklists and charts to enable them to derive objectives, assess synergy between different parts of an organisation, appraise its competence profile and decide how, where and in which way to expand. Nevertheless, as

	Existing Products	*New Products*
Existing Markets	Market Penetration Strategy	Product Development Strategy
New Markets	Market Development Strategy	Diversification Strategy

Figure 6.1 Product–market mix

Koch (1995) remarked, from today's viewpoint, the book, and indeed the precepts of the Planning school as a whole, have not aged well.

The Design school, though sharing some features with the Planning school, adopted a different, less formal and machine-like approach. It proposed a model of strategy that emphasises the need to achieve a fit between the internal capabilities of an organisation and the external possibilities it faces. The foundations of the Design school lay in the work of Alfred Chandler, one of the most eminent and influential American economic historians of his generation. His main contribution to the Design school is encapsulated in his 1962 book, *Strategy and Structure*, which was based on a major study of US corporations between 1850 and 1920. In the book, Chandler defined strategy as the determination of the basic long-term goals and objectives of an enterprise, and the adoption of courses of action and the allocation of resources necessary for carrying out these goals. The book also suggested three important precepts for running organisations which challenged the conventional wisdom of the time:

- Firstly, that an organisation's structure should flow from its strategy rather than being determined by some universal 'one best way'.
- Secondly, that the 'visible hand of management' was more important than Adam Smith's 'invisible hand of the market' in meeting customer need.
- Lastly, that large organisations need to decentralise and divisionalise in order to remain competitive.

Though Chandler's work proved very influential in shaping the strategy debate, the real impetus for the Design school came from the work of the General Management group at Harvard Business School, especially the work of Kenneth R Andrews (Mintzberg *et al*, 1998a). The model of strategy developed by Andrews and his colleagues places primary emphasis on the appraisal of an organisation's external and internal situations. To facilitate this, Andrews developed the now-famous SWOT technique (*see* Figure 6.2 and also Chapter 11).

The purpose of a SWOT analysis is to enable an organisation to assess its internal Strengths and Weaknesses in the light of the Opportunities and Threats posed by the

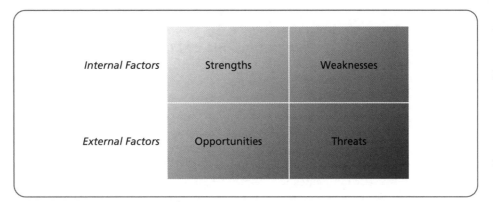

Figure 6.2 SWOT analysis

environment in which it operates (Andrews, 1980). Based on this assessment, organisations then generate and evaluate a number of strategies in order to choose the best one (Rumelt, 1997).

Like the Planning school, the Design school has attracted its fair share of criticism (*see* Mintzberg *et al*, 1998a). In particular, Chandler's view that structure should follow strategy has been heavily criticised. Tom Peters (1993: 148), for example, remarked that:

> *I understand Chandler's reasoning, but I think he got it exactly wrong. For it is the structure of the organization that determines, over time, the choices that it makes about the markets it attacks [i.e. its strategy]. Give me a vertically integrated, hierarchically steep organization and perhaps, even today, I can do a few things well. But one thing is certain: I can't shift course very rapidly! A McKinsey or EDS or CNN chooses to do what it does – i.e. continually reinvent itself, with apparent ease – because of its 'structural' shape much more than its chosen strategy.*

Regardless of the criticisms levelled at it, the Design school can be seen as an advance on the Planning school. Whereas Ansoff and the Planning school regard strategy as almost exclusively concerned with the relationships between the firm and its environment, Chandler, Andrews and the Design school take a broader view. Its approach takes account of internal as well as external factors. In particular, the Design school sees issues such as organisational structures, production processes and technology as being essentially strategic. The key point proponents of the Design school make is that the external and internal cannot be separated, as the Open Systems theorists would be the first to point out (*see* Scott, 1987 and Chapter 8). The external affects the internal, and vice versa. Therefore, strategic management must encompass the totality of the organisational domain and must not be restricted to one aspect, such as determining the product–market mix (Andrews, 1980).

This brings us a little nearer to a definition but still leaves us with a hazy concept. Henry Mintzberg argued that it is necessary to recognise explicitly that there are multiple definitions of strategy and that we need to use these to manoeuvre through this difficult field. According to Mintzberg *et al* (1998b), there are five main and interrelated definitions of strategy: *plan, ploy, pattern, position* and *perspective* (*see* Ideas and perspectives 6.1).

Ideas and perspectives 6.1
Mintzberg's five definitions of strategy

- **Strategy as a plan.** According to this view, strategy is some form of consciously intended course of action which is created ahead of events. This can be either a general strategy or a specific one. If specific, it may also constitute a ploy.

- **Strategy as a ploy.** This is where strategy is a manoeuvre to outwit an opponent. An example of this is when a firm threatens to lower its prices substantially to deter new entrants into its market. It is the threat to lower prices that is the consciously intended course of action, and not any actual plan to do so.

- **Strategy as a pattern.** This is where we observe, after the event, that an organisation has acted in a consistent manner over time; i.e. whether consciously or not, the organisation exhibits a consistent pattern of behaviour. We can say from this that an organisation has pursued a particular strategy. This may not be the strategy it intended to pursue, however, but it is the one that has emerged from the action of the organisation. Therefore, though the organisation's realised strategy could be the product of a conscious and deliberate plan, this is often not the case.

- **Strategy as a position.** From this perspective, strategy is about positioning the organisation in order to achieve or maintain a sustainable competitive advantage. Mintzberg *et al* argue that most organisations try to avoid head-on competition. What they seek to achieve is a position where their competitors cannot or will not challenge them. In this sense, strategy is also seen as a game: groups of players circling each other, each trying to gain the high ground.

- **Strategy as perspective.** This definition sees strategy as a somewhat abstract concept that exists primarily in people's minds. For members of an organisation, the actual details of its strategy, as such, are irrelevant. What is important is that everyone in the organisation shares a common view of its purpose and direction which, whether people are aware of it or not, informs and guides decision-making and actions. Consequently, without the need for detailed plans, the organisation, through a shared understanding, pursues a consistent strategy or purpose.

Source: Mintzberg *et al* (1998b)

In a manner that has a postmodernist feel to it, Mintzberg *et al* (1998b) do not argue that one definition should be preferred to the others. In some senses they can be considered as alternatives or complementary approaches to strategy. Also, they are useful in adding important elements to the discussion of strategy. They draw our attention to the distinction between conscious and unconscious strategy, and between emergent and planned strategy. They also highlight the role of the organisation's collective mind in developing and implementing strategy.

In a similar way to Mintzberg *et al*, Johnson (1987) also distinguishes between different views of the strategic management process. As Ideas and perspectives 6.2 shows, he argues that there are three basic views that reflect more general distinctions in the social

Ideas and perspectives 6.2
Johnson's three basic views of strategy

- **The rationalistic view** – which sees strategy as the outcome of a series of pre-planned actions designed to achieve the stated goals of an organisation in an optimal fashion.
- **The adaptive or incremental view** – which sees strategy evolving through an accumulation of relatively small changes over time.
- **The interpretative view** – which sees strategy as the product of individual and collective attempts to make sense of, i.e. interpret, past events.

Source: Johnson (1987)

sciences. One way of considering these various definitions or views of strategy, following on from Morgan (1986), is as metaphors. Morgan (1986) identified eight influential metaphors that are applied to organisations (*see* Ideas and perspectives 6.3).

Morgan (1986: 12–13) comments that:

. . . our theories and explanations of organizational life are based on metaphors that lead us to see and understand organizations in distinctive yet partial ways. . . . By using different metaphors to understand the complex and paradoxical character of organizational life, we are able to manage and design organizations in ways that we may not have thought possible before.

In a similar way to Morgan's use of metaphors, the postmodernist viewpoint, as discussed in Chapter 4, would see the varying definitions of strategy as competing realities which managers attempt to impose on their organisations. Realists would acknowledge that these are different perspectives that do influence organisational strategy, but would also argue that there is a 'real world out there' which has to be addressed if strategies

Ideas and perspectives 6.3
Morgan's organisational metaphors

- Organisations as machines
- Organisations as organisms
- Organisations as brains
- Organisations as cultures
- Organisations as political systems
- Organisations as psychic prisons
- Organisations as flux and transformations
- Organisations as instruments of domination

Source: Morgan (1986)

are to be successfully realised. Complexity theorists would take a similar view, acknowledging that different perspectives do exist and are influential, but claiming that the social world, like the natural world, is governed by order-generating rules which organisations ignore at their peril. Therefore, whilst most would see Mintzberg *et al*'s and Johnson's definitions of strategy as metaphors or alternative perspectives, some would also argue that they represent competing realities, whilst others would argue that there is only one reality (though this can and does change with circumstances and time).

Nevertheless, the explicit recognition that there are multiple definitions of strategy can help us to make sense of the confusion of terms which litter the literature and which different writers use in different ways. Many writers seem to treat corporate planning, long-range planning, strategic planning and formal planning as synonymous. However, not all would agree. Naylor (1979), for example, defined strategic planning as long-range planning with a time horizon of three to five years. Litschert and Nicholson (1974) took the opposite view: they stated that strategic and long-term planning are not synonymous, arguing that strategic planning is a process which involves making a sequence of inter-related decisions aimed at achieving a desirable future environment for an organisation. Andrews (1998: 51), similarly, defined strategy as a:

> . . . *pattern of decisions in a company that determines and reveals its objectives, purposes, or goals, produces the principal policies and plans for achieving those goals, and defines the range of business the company is to pursue, the kind of economic and human organisation it is, or intends to be, and the nature of the economic and non-economic contribution it intends to make to its shareholders, employees, customers and communities.*

What we can see from the above is that, knowingly or not, writers are using different definitions of strategy and thus interpreting particular terms or phrases in the light of their own implicit or explicit definition. Yet despite the use of these various terms, a certain consensus of opinion does emerge with regard to the basic features of strategic management and strategic decisions. Most of the writers would agree with Johnson and Scholes (1993), who described strategy as:

- concerning the full scope of an organisation's activities;
- the process of matching the organisation's activities to its environment;
- the process of matching its activities to its resource capability;
- having major resource implications;
- affecting operational decisions;
- being affected by the values and beliefs of those who have power in an organisation;
- affecting the long-term direction of an organisation.

Approaches to strategy: the Prescriptive versus the Analytical stream

In defining strategy, especially bearing in mind Mintzberg *et al*'s (1998b) and Johnson's (1987) various definitions, there are two further issues to be considered:

1. Is strategy a process or the outcome of a process?
2. Is strategy an economic–rational phenomenon or is it an organisational–social phenomenon?

Taking these two questions together, it can be seen that there are two parallel, competing and, to an extent, interacting streams of ideas. The first, the Prescriptive stream, sees strategy as a controlled, intentional, prescriptive process, based on a rational model of decision-making, which produces complete deliberate strategies (Ansoff, 1965; Argenti, 1974; Steiner, 1969). The second, the Analytical stream, which is more interested in understanding how organisations actually formulate strategy rather than prescribing how they should formulate it, argues that it is the outcome of the complex social and political processes involved in organisational decision-making (Hamel and Prahalad, 1989; Miles and Snow, 1978; Mintzberg, 1987; Pettigrew, 1980; Quinn, 1980a).

The Prescriptive stream grew out of the long-range planning initiatives of the 1940s and 1950s, and is aimed primarily at the practitioners of strategy. Through the work of the Planning and Design schools, this stream dominated the practice of strategy in the 1960s and 1970s. They not only saw strategy as an economic–rational process, but also considered its options and usefulness as primarily restricted to issues relating to market share and profit maximisation (Ansoff, 1965; Porter, 1980). However, with growing disillusionment amongst academics and practitioners over the ability of this approach to deliver competitiveness, a new variant of this approach came to the fore in the 1980s: the Positioning school. This school is most closely identified with Michael Porter (1980, 1985) whose *competitive forces framework* reinvigorated the Prescriptive approach and allowed it to maintain its dominance on the practice of strategy in the 1980s and 1990s (Teece *et al*, 1997). The main difference between the Positioning school and the earlier Planning and Design schools was that:

> *Both the planning and design schools put no limits on the strategies that were possible in any given situation. The positioning school, in contrast, argued that only a few key strategies – as positions in the economic market place – are desirable in any given industry: ones that can be defended against existing and future competitors. Ease of defense means that firms which occupy these positions enjoy higher profits . . . By thereby dispensing with one key premise of the design school – that strategies have to be unique, tailor-made for each organization – the positioning school was able to create and hone a set of analytical tools dedicated to matching the right strategy to the conditions at hand . . .* (Mintzberg *et al*, 1998a: 83)

The work of Porter and the Positioning school will be discussed in more detail in Chapter 7. However, for now, the key points to note are that the three schools that comprise the Prescriptive stream have dominated the practice of strategy within organisations since the 1960s. The reason for this is threefold:

- Firstly, the proponents set out deliberately to address the needs of industry and commerce by providing them with a blueprint for strategy formulation and implementation.
- Secondly, they interacted closely with a number of leading consultants, notably the Boston Consultancy Group, and business schools, notably Harvard, to promote their work and tailor it to the needs of organisations. By reinforcing and promoting each other, this triple alliance of researchers, consultants and educators created an iron orthodoxy that organisations, especially large ones, felt they ignored at their peril.

- Lastly, because all three groups in this triple alliance were in effect engaged in a business activity, selling strategy as a product, they were able to invest in promoting and developing their product in a way that others were not. As the following examination of the Analytical stream of strategy will show, though, this did not mean that other important perspectives on strategy were not developed or did not achieve acceptance by a wide audience. It did, however, mean that these alternative perspectives have never had the same impact on practice within organisations as those promoted by the Prescriptive stream.

The Analytical stream, which began to appear in the 1970s and represents a more sceptical and more academically orientated face of strategic management, views strategy not as a process, but as an outcome of a process. Its proponents' emphasis is not on the construction of detailed plans, which in any case they believe to be a misdirected approach, but on the organisational and social aspects of strategy formation. Their argument is that the capabilities of an organisation, in terms of its structure, systems, technology and management style, restrict the range of strategic options the organisation can pursue. Consequently, in a very real sense, it is the day-to-day stream of decisions regarding the development of its capabilities that determines an organisation's strategic direction, rather than the reverse (Mintzberg, 1994). This can be seen in Mintzberg's (1978) concept of emergent strategy. As Figure 6.3 shows, organisations may start out with an intended strategy – objectives they set out to achieve. However, due to unrealistic expectations or changing circumstances, many of these fall by the wayside. In responding on a day-to-day basis to changing events, existing capabilities influence the decisions which are taken and from these decisions emerge new strategies. These emergent strategies combine with surviving elements of the original intended strategy to form the realised strategy.

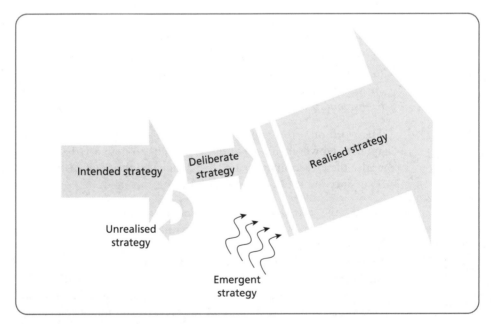

Figure 6.3 Emergent strategy
Source: Adapted from Mintzberg (1978: 13)

A good example of how events conspire to defeat intended strategies is the recent turmoil in the financial services sector. At the beginning of 2007, the intended strategies of most organisations in the sector revolved around sales growth and profit increase. By the end of 2007, with the advent of the credit crunch, the realised strategies focused on coping with falling growth and decreased profit – in some cases, the key strategy issue was survival (Doran, 2008). However, the decisions taken by financial service organisations in responding to the credit crunch were influenced by their existing capabilities, which allowed some to survive relatively unscathed whilst others went out of business or had to be rescued by competitors or governments.

One of the oft-cited examples of how capabilities shape strategies is that of Japanese management. Pascale and Athos (1982) and Hamel and Prahalad (1989) argued that Japanese business success is not based on detailed and well-thought-out strategies *per se*, but on strategic intent – the commitment of Japanese managers to create and pursue a vision of their desired future. The vision is then used to bind an organisation together and give it a common purpose to which all can contribute. A key part of this common purpose is the identification and development of the core competences and capabilities necessary for the achievement of the organisation's vision.

This theme has been taken up by other Western writers on strategy. Kay (1993) used the term 'distinctive capabilities' rather than 'core competences', but is clearly describing the same thing. He argued that a firm's distinctive capabilities fall under four headings: reputation, architecture (i.e. internal and external structures and linkages), innovation and strategic assets. Kay asserted that an organisation's competitiveness is dependent not upon any strategic plan as such, but upon the uniqueness and strength of its capabilities. It is these that allow an organisation to take advantage of opportunities and avoid threats, whether foreseeable or not. In a similar way, Stalk *et al* (1992) used the term 'core capability' in referring to an organisation's practices and business routines; and Grant (1991a) proposed a framework for analysing a firm's competitive advantage in terms of its resources and capabilities.

To an extent, the case made by Kay, Stalk *et al* and Grant is complementary to Mintzberg's (1987) concept of emergent strategy. Based on the many Western companies he had studied, Mintzberg argued that successful companies do not start out with detailed strategic plans. Instead, their strategies emerge over time from the pattern of decisions they take on key aspects of their activities. Mintzberg *et al* (1998a: 189–90) draw a distinction between planned or deliberate strategies and emergent ones:

Deliberate strategy focuses on control – making sure that managerial intentions are realized in action – while emergent strategy emphasizes learning – coming to understand through the taking of actions what those intentions should be in the first place. . . . The concept of emergent strategy . . . opens the door to strategic learning, because it acknowledges the organization's capacity to experiment. A single action can be taken, feedback can be received, and the process can continue until the organization converges on the pattern that becomes its strategy.

Clearly, there are similarities between the Japanese intent and/or competence approach to strategy, Mintzberg's view of strategy and Kay and co.'s distinctive capabilities. However, the Japanese consciously work out their shared vision and consciously pursue it. The emergent approach, at least in its pure form, lacks the concept of 'vision' and doubts the presence of conscious intent. Even so, Mintzberg (1994: 25) does recognise that in practice some organisations pursue:

> . . . *umbrella strategies: the broad outlines are deliberate while the details are allowed to emerge within them. Thus emergent strategies are not bad and deliberate ones good; effective strategies mix these characteristics in ways that reflect the conditions at hand, notably the ability to predict as well as the need to react to unexpected events.*

Kay (1993) takes a similar view. Whilst doubting the efficacy of corporate vision *per se*, he does stress that the development of capabilities is, or at least can be, a conscious and planned process.

As mentioned in Chapter 4, complexity theories have had an increasing influence on organisation theorists over the last decade. However, their influence on the strategy literature has been limited by the fact that complexity theorists do not appear to share a common view of complexity and organisational strategy. For Stacey (2003: 319–20):

> *Strategy comes to be understood as the evolving patterns of an organisation's identity. . . . Strategy as the identity of an organisation is continuously constructed and enacted in the interaction of organisational practice.*

For MacIntosh and MacLean (2001), strategy also has an emergent dimension to it but, for them, a key feature of strategy is to identify and maintain the appropriateness of the organisation's order-generating rules. It is the presence of appropriate order-generating rules that allows a consistent, and beneficial, pattern of action to emerge which forms the organisation's strategy. Bechtold (1997) and Brown and Eisenhardt (1997) stress that the purpose of order-generating rules is to keep an organisation operating at the edge of chaos. For them, the purpose of strategy is to create an organisation where self-organisation can take place. It is the ability to self-organise that they see as being crucial to maintaining and/or developing appropriate order-generating rules and thus bringing about beneficial change.

As with complexity theories, population ecology is borrowed from the physical sciences. It is a Darwinist-type approach that focuses on how organisations adapt and evolve in order to survive within the general population of organisations to which they belong (Carroll, 1988; Morgan, 1990). Watson (1997: 273) comments that:

> *One way of considering the relationship of organisations to other organisations in the environment is to regard them as involved in a process of natural selection: a fight for survival within the ecological system of which they are part. . . . They go through both planned and unplanned 'variations' in their form, and, largely through processes of competition, the environment 'selects' the form which best suits the organisation. Organisations then 'retain' the form which best suits their particular 'niche' or 'domain'. . .*

Population ecologists do not, therefore, challenge the importance of the fit or correspondence between an organisation and its environment, but they do question the extent to which achieving this is a conscious and planned process. In particular, as Pettigrew *et al* (1992: 25) maintain: 'Ecologists are unimpressed by the possibility that managers can turn their organizations round, and instead stress organizational inertia.' This argument echoes Hannan and Freeman's (1977: 957) assertion that:

. . . for wide classes of organizations there are very strong inertial pressures on structure arising from both internal arrangements (for example, internal politics) and from the environment (for example, public legitimation of organizational activity). To claim otherwise is to ignore the most obvious feature of organizational life.

Population ecologists argue that an organisation's survival, the extent to which it achieves a fit with its environment, depends on a combination of the organisation's own (planned and unplanned) actions, the activities of other organisations in its field and a strong element of luck (i.e. being in the right place, with the right combination of characteristics and at the right time).

The stress on luck or serendipity is also present in the work of writers such as Williamson (1991) and Weick (1979). Weick, in particular, views the world as an essentially ambiguous place in which it is unrealistic, and indeed impossible, to make detailed plans. This is clearly a strong challenge to those who emphasise the need for, and ability of, organisations to pursue environmental match or correspondence. However, Child's (1972) concept of equifinality takes this challenge even further. Equifinality, as Sorge (1997: 13) notes:

. . . quite simply means that different sorts of internal arrangements are perfectly compatible with identical contextual or environmental states. The principle goes against the idea of a quasi-ideal 'match' which is inherent in the principle of correspondence. Whereas correspondence [i.e. Contingency] theory suggests that rigid and bureaucratic structures are not a good match for volatile and shifting product markets, equifinality theorists claim that it may very well turn out to be a good match but only if the level and diversity of the workforce is large and organization culture produces motivated and flexible actors.

As Mintzberg *et al* (1998a) note in relation to equifinality, managers need to recognise that achieving a successful outcome is more important than imposing the method of achieving it.

Pettigrew (1985, 1987) and Child and Smith (1987), through their respective studies of ICI and Cadbury, also offered important insights and perspectives on approaches to strategic management and environmental fit. Pettigrew argues that there is a need for a change theory that sees organisations and how they operate in their entirety, one that recognises the importance and influence of the wider environment and appreciates the dynamic and political nature of strategy development and change. He is critical of theories which assume that organisations are rational entities pursuing agreed goals that reflect their best interests. Instead, he argues that organisations have to be understood in the context of the constraints and possibilities offered by the environment in which they operate and in relation to the self-interests of the individuals and groups that compose them.

Pettigrew, therefore, sees organisations primarily as political systems in which groups and individuals, under the guise of rationality, seek to mobilise support for, and legitimate the pursuit of, strategies and actions that promote or sustain their personal or sectional interests. Particular groups or individuals may achieve a position of dominance, but that dominance is always subject to prevailing intra-organisational and environmental conditions. Therefore, Pettigrew rejects the view that strategy is a rational process of deliberate calculation and analysis. Instead he believes that organisational strategy – though often cloaked in rational and analytical terms – is in reality the outcome of a combination of internal political struggles, between groups and individuals seeking to influence policy in their favour, and external environmental pressures and constraints (this argument was examined in more detail in Chapter 5).

Child and Smith's (1987) firm-in-sector perspective has some similarities with Pettigrew's work; however, they take a more realist perspective, arguing for a stronger determining link between the individual firm and the sector in which it operates, and a lesser role for organisational politics. As shown in Ideas and perspectives 6.4, they suggest three areas of firm–sector linkage that shape and constrain the strategies organisations pursue.

Child and Smith's (1987) view draws on economic theories of the firm and suggests that the sector, particularly when strongly competitive, determines the path, the trajectory, a firm must take for its future success. Though not denying a role for organisational politics, they claim that, unless the strategic decisions a firm takes are consistent with the conditions prevailing in its sector, success may be jeopardised. Therefore, though falling in the Analytical stream, Child and Smith appear to exhibit a greater faith in a rational and linear progression from market sector analysis to strategy formulation and implementation than Pettigrew and many other writers.

Ideas and perspectives 6.4
Child and Smith's firm-in-sector perspective

1. **The 'objective conditions' for success.** In essence, this is an argument for 'sector or environmental determinism'. Though each firm within a sector may pursue a different strategy, these will all tend to focus on or be determined by similar success factors such as customer satisfaction, quality, profitability, etc. Therefore, 'a firm's viability depends upon the extent to which its behaviour is appropriate to those environmental conditions'.

2. **The prevailing managerial consensus.** '[A]t least within well-established sectors, the senior managers of constituent firms hold very similar constructs of the sector's operational dynamics which effectively furnish the rules of the game for the sector.' It follows that 'the sector is the bearer of external exemplars against which a firm's current strategy and structure, and the ideology underlying these, can be compared . . .'.

3. **The collaborative networks operating in the sector.** Firms do not exist in isolation from the rest of the sector but are joined together in patterns of cooperation and affiliation with other firms in the sector. Consequently, 'a sector does not only consist of product competitors; it is also a *network* of potential and actual collaborators'. Such collaborations may be with customers, suppliers, outside experts or even competitors.

Source: Child and Smith (1987: 566–9)

The Analytical stream also has a number of other variants, most notably those that see the role and personality of leaders as being the key determinants of successful strategy (Bennis and Nanus, 1985). Leadership will be touched on later in this chapter, and covered more extensively in Chapter 12; nevertheless, merely mentioning it here serves to emphasise the somewhat disparate nature of the Analytical stream of strategy. Proponents of this stream are united by a number of factors such as their attempt to understand rather than prescribe strategy; their orientation, mainly, to an academic rather than a business audience; and their view of organisations as complex social entities operating within dangerous, dynamic and unpredictable environments. On the other hand, the proponents of the elements which make up the Analytical stream are divided by their emphasis on different aspects of strategy, such as politics, the industry sector, the general environment, organisational and national cultures, leadership, etc. They are also divided by their explicit or implicit adherence to postmodernist, realist or complexity perspectives. So, although it is true to say that proponents of the Japanese-inspired strategic intent and/or competence argument came to the fore in the 1990s, it is also true to say that they are challenged by the proponents of the other elements in this stream who still exert a powerful influence on the debate over strategy. It follows that their differences with each other are as important as their differences with proponents of the Prescriptive stream of strategy.

Understanding strategy: choices and constraints

Whilst the above identifies key themes in the debate over organisational strategy, it still presents a somewhat confusing picture. Clearly there is a distinction between those who adhere to the Prescriptive stream of strategy, which arose from the long-range planning approach of the 1940s and 1950s, and the Analytical stream as represented by, amongst others, the strategic intent and/or competences approach of the 1980s and 1990s. What is not clear, however, is the degree to which a common understanding and perspective exists amongst those collected under the Analytical umbrella. Certainly, a number of writers have tried to argue that a common perspective does exist. Brown and Jopling (1994) believed that the main distinction lies between the writers of the 1950s and 1960s who, they argue, saw strategy as basically concerned with fitting the organisation to its environment, and the writers of the 1980s and 1990s who, they argue, see strategy as focusing on internal issues, mainly to do with the development of core competences. They base their case on a Contingency perspective. The earlier approach, they argue, was suitable to organisations operating in relatively stable and predictable environments, who had a limited product range, and where competition was restricted. With the advent of greater competition and more unstable environments, this approach was no longer viable, and firms had to look internally at how they could organise themselves to cope with the new situation. To an extent, this is an attractive analysis. However, though it is true that the earlier writers on strategy – such as Ansoff and company – did concentrate on product–market mix issues, it is also true that they later came to appreciate the link between the outside and the inside (Moore, 1992). Also, whilst Mintzberg and others have concentrated on internal capabilities, the Japanese approach has been to see the internal and external as two sides of the same coin, which is why they emphasise the importance of the strategic outward-looking vision driving the development of internal capabilities.

All the same, such a simple distinction, based on one dimension of organisational life, cannot resolve the complex differences between and within the Prescriptive and Analytical streams. Mintzberg *et al* (1998a) noted that the strategy field is more eclectic and more populous, in terms of different approaches, than ever before. In such a situation, attempts to fit writers into two camps, whether they be early and late, external and internal, are bound to fail. The multiple-definition view of strategy argued by Mintzberg *et al* (1998b), and particularly their proposition that the various definitions of strategy are both competing and complementary, offers another perspective. Strategy can be considered as either a process or an outcome. It can also be considered as either a rational approach or a political and/or social phenomenon. The various approaches to strategy do not reflect some underlying truth; rather they are different approaches that organisations can choose (consciously or not) to adopt, depending on their circumstances, objectives and management.

If this is the case, it may be that instead of looking for a theory of or approach to strategy that unifies and encompasses all the others, we should turn the argument on its head and ask, as we did with organisational theory, whether there is a 'one best way' for strategy?

In approaching this question, it is valuable to return to Child's (1972) concept of equifinality. As stated earlier, Sorge (1997: 13) writes that equifinality 'quite simply means that different sorts of internal arrangements are perfectly compatible with identical contextual or environmental states'. To paraphrase this definition, and to stretch the concept a little further than Child might have intended, it could be argued that different approaches to strategy formulation may be perfectly compatible with positive outcomes. This may especially be the case if one takes account of the growing opinion, as expressed in this and the previous chapters, that though organisations are constrained by their circumstances, they do possess the ability to manipulate and influence these circumstances to their own benefit. If this is the case, then, as Mintzberg *et al* (1998a: 365) maintain, 'the question is not whether there exists strategic choice, but how much'. To approach this question, we need to attempt to classify the various approaches to strategy in order to establish the degree to which they incorporate or exclude choice.

Though the above review of approaches to strategy cannot claim to be all-embracing, it does cover the key protagonists in the area. Whilst it separates the main approaches into two streams, however, it does not provide a classification or taxonomy of the various approaches. Whittington (1993) attempted to make sense of the many definitions and categories of strategy by identifying four generic approaches to strategy: the Classical, Evolutionary, Processual and Systemic (*see* Ideas and perspectives 6.5).

Whittington's categorisation of generic approaches to strategy is extremely useful in making sense of the plethora of approaches on offer. As one would expect, it is not perfect; some writers, such as Mintzberg, could fall under more than one heading, whilst others, like Child and Smith, are difficult to locate. Nevertheless, the Classical approach, with its modernist leanings, would clearly incorporate the work of the Planning, Design and Positioning school and the early Western writers on strategy. The Evolutionary approach has links with both the work of the complexity theorists and population ecologists; Mintzberg's (1994) work on emergent strategy might also

Ideas and perspectives 6.5
Whittington's generic approaches to strategy

- **The Classical approach.** This is the oldest and most influential approach to strategy. It portrays strategy as a rational process, based on analysis and quantification, and aimed at achieving the maximum level of profit for an organisation. It argues that, through rigorous analysis and planning, senior managers can predict future market trends and shape the organisation to take advantage of these.

- **The Evolutionary approach.** As the name implies, this uses the analogy of biological evolution to describe strategy development. It believes that organisations are at the mercy of the unpredictable and hostile vagaries of the market. Those organisations that survive and prosper do so not because of their ability to plan and predict, which is impossible, but because they have been lucky enough to hit on a winning formula. From this perspective, successful strategies cannot be planned, but emerge from the decisions managers take to align and realign their organisations to the changing environmental conditions.

- **The Processual approach.** This perspective concentrates on the nature of organisational and market processes. It views organisations and their members as shifting coalitions of individuals and groups with different interests, imperfect knowledge and short attention spans. Markets are similarly capricious and imperfect but, because of this, do not require organisations to achieve a perfect fit with their environment in order to prosper and survive. Strategy under these conditions is portrayed as a pragmatic process of trial and error, aimed at achieving a compromise between the needs of the market and the objectives of the warring factions within the organisation.

- **The Systemic approach.** This approach sees strategy as linked to dominant features of the local social system within which it takes place. The core argument of this perspective is that strategy can be a deliberate process, and planning and predictability are possible, but only if the conditions within the host society are favourable. Therefore, to an extent, this is a contingency approach to strategy which can accommodate situations where firms do not seek to maximise profit or bow to market pressures. If the conditions within the host society are supportive, markets can be manipulated, financial considerations can become a secondary issue, and stability and predictability can be achieved. Also, under such conditions, the objectives managers seek to pursue may be related more to their social background, degree of patriotism or even professional pride, than to profit maximisation. Therefore, from the Systemic perspective, the strategy an organisation adopts and the interests managers pursue reflect the nature of the particular social system within which it operates.

Source: Whittington (1993)

fall under this heading. The Processual approach could also cover Mintzberg's work, certainly includes Pettigrew's (1985, 1987) work on organisational politics and sits reasonably comfortably with the postmodernists. The Systemic perspective, which has a realist tinge to it, clearly owes much to the Japanese approach to strategy as described by Hamel and Prahalad (1989).

Whittington (1993) also categorises these four approaches to strategy in terms of how they view outcomes and processes. He argues that the Classical and Evolutionary approaches see profit maximisation as the natural outcome of strategy. The Systemic and Processual approaches, on the other hand, believe other outcomes are both possible and acceptable, such as stability, environmental responsibility or maintenance of an organisation's dominant coalition. With regard to processes, the groupings change. Here the Classical and Systemic approaches both agree that strategy can be a deliberate process. The Evolutionists and Processualists, though, see strategy as emerging from processes governed by chance and confusion.

Whittington's four categories of strategy can be summarised as follows:

* Classicists see strategy as a rational process of long-term planning aimed at maximising profit.
* Evolutionists also believe that the purpose of strategy is profit maximisation, but regard the future as too volatile and unpredictable to allow effective planning. Instead, they advise organisations to focus on maximising chances of survival today.
* The Processualists are equally sceptical of long-range planning, and see strategy as an emergent process of learning and adaptation.
* The Systemic perspective argues that the nature and aims of strategy are dependent upon the particular social context in which the organisation operates.

To an extent, the four approaches to strategy have some similarity to the Western approaches to organisation theory discussed in Part 1. The Classical, Evolutionary and Processual approaches are clearly 'one best way' or 'only possible way' approaches, whereas the Systemic approach offers a Contingency perspective on strategy. They also share some common ground with organisation theory on the issue of rationality. The Classical and Systemic approaches argue that strategy is or can be rational and intentional in its development and objectives. The Processualists believe that it is rational in neither aspect; the Evolutionists take a similar view of process, but appear to adopt a rational perspective on outcomes, in that profit maximisation is seen as the only outcome that guarantees survival.

In their view of the scope for managerial choice and judgement, three of these four approaches to strategy do appear to be more permissive than organisation theory. Clearly, the Classical strategy theorists leave little scope for either: their instruction seems to be to follow the textbook in terms of outcomes and processes or else! However, both the Evolutionists and the Processualists emphasise the need for managers to be fleet of foot and percipient in making key decisions responding to opportunities or threats; although the Evolutionists (rather like Napoleon in his view of generals) appear to believe that, at the end of the day, a lucky manager may be more desirable than an able one. For advocates of the Systemic approach, choice and judgement are important, but tend to be constrained by the limits and objectives of the society in which they are located.

It would appear, therefore, that managerial choice, preference and judgement, for all but the Classicists, do have a role to play in determining not just an organisation's strategy, but also the particular approach to strategy it adopts. In our examination of the strategy literature, however, it is clear that choice is constrained and can only be exercised within limits (from some perspectives, very narrow limits indeed). As Figure 6.4 shows, these limits or constraints, which are suggested by or inferred from the literature, can be classified under four headings.

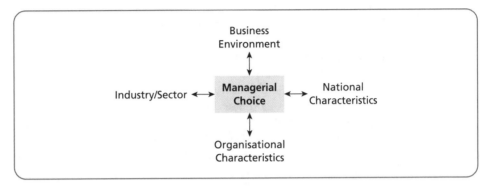

Figure 6.4 Constraints on managerial choice

National objectives, practices and cultures

The case for country-specific constraints very much follows the argument of the Systemic perspective on strategy. This view sees the operation of organisations as strongly influenced by the social system in which they operate. In some cases, such as in Japan and Germany, patriotism, national pride and a collectivist ethos have created a business environment that supports the pursuit of long-term national objectives. This is reflected in the behaviour of individual firms and financial institutions that favour stable growth over the medium to long term, rather than short-term profit maximisation. In Britain and the USA, on the other hand, the climate is far more supportive of individual endeavour and short-term profit maximisation rather than the national interest *per se*.

The difference between these two approaches is neatly summed up in the old saying that 'What's good for General Motors is good for America'. The Japanese would, of course, transpose this to read 'What is good for Japan is good for Toyota'. This view also draws support from Hofstede's (1980, 1990) work on national cultures discussed in Chapter 5. The implication, therefore, is that organisations ignore national norms at their peril: the pursuit of short-term profit maximisation in Japan and Germany is likely to be as difficult, and perhaps as counter-productive, as the pursuit of a long-term strategy of growing market share, which ignores short-term profitability, would be in the UK or the USA. Nevertheless, these constraints are open to manipulation and avoidance. The move by many British companies – Dyson, GKN, etc. – to manufacture outside the UK and/or to form international alliances is an example of this, as is the Japanese trend to establish manufacturing plants in the USA and Europe in order to avoid high production costs on the one hand and import quotas on the other. Another example is the lobbying of governments and national and international bodies for changes in laws and regulations that particular organisations or industries see as operating against their interests.

Industry and sector practices and norms

This section follows from Child and Smith's (1987) firm-in-sector perspective. As discussed earlier, they believe that the objective conditions operating in a sector, managers' understanding of the dynamics of the sector, and the nature and degree of inter-firm collaboration all combine to determine the path a firm must take for its future success. This is especially the case where the sector is highly competitive. In effect, Child and Smith's argument is that firms must stick to the rules of engagement in their sector or perish. They do concede that, where competition is less intense, then managers have a greater degree of freedom with regard to the selection of strategy. Indeed, the low level of competition may explain how Japanese companies were able to change the rules of engagement to their advantage in many industries in the 1960s and 1970s (Hamel and Prahalad, 1989), although it is also the case that Japanese companies pay less attention to today's sectoral constraints than to reshaping the rules of the game to create competitive conditions more favourable to themselves (Turner, 1990). Another method of overcoming sectoral constraints and conditions is, as illustrated by Allaire and Firsirotu (1989), by diversifying into new products and different sectors.

Business environment

For nearly all the approaches to strategy that we have discussed, their proponents assume, explicitly or implicitly, that they are operating in a particular type of environment. The Classical approach to strategy is clearly predicated on the existence of a relatively stable and predictable environment. If this exists, then predicting the future and planning accordingly is a much less hazardous exercise than would otherwise be the case. The Systemic view also seems to assume a degree of environmental stability. As the history of Japan and Germany shows, however, stability needs to be actively promoted by government–industry cooperation rather than relying on the invisible, and often volatile, hand of the market. For Processualists, and even more so for Evolutionists, the environment is a hostile, unpredictable and uncertain place. Planning is almost impossible, and success comes either from continuously adapting to changes in the environment, or from being in the right place at the right time.

For three of these perspectives, the environment is a given, even if they disagree about exactly what is given. However, for those advocating a Systemic approach, the environment is not a given: it can be changed. As this chapter and Part 1 have shown, there are strong supporters of this view (Hatch and Cunliffe, 2006; Morgan, 1997; Stacey, 2003). Shapiro (1989) utilises the tools of game theory to show how firms influence the behaviour and actions of their competitors, and in so doing change the environment in which they operate. In a similar way, Teece *et al* (1997) argue that investments in production capacity, R&D and advertising can all be used to alter an organisation's environment favourably. Weick (1979) takes a different perspective. He argues that the world is so complex and ambiguous that an organisation cannot possibly 'know' its environment. Instead, organisations have to 'enact' their environment; that is to say, they have to develop and act upon their own interpretation of their environment. This is very similar to the learning organisation and postmodernist perspectives, as discussed in Chapters 3 and 4, that organisations have the ability to 'invent' their own reality. The implication from these different perspectives is that though many companies may have to adjust their strategic approach to environmental conditions, some companies may be able to do the reverse. The UK National Health Service is a good example of this. Burnes and Salauroo (1995) relate that the NHS operated prior to 1990 as a typical government bureaucracy. The government allocated resources and gave policy direction, whilst the NHS centrally planned how resources would be allocated and policies operationalised (i.e. the Classical approach to strategy). This meant that there was considerable stability and predictability in its environment. However, the government of the day wanted the NHS to operate in a more cost-conscious and entrepreneurial mode. To facilitate and encourage this, it changed the way funds were provided and distributed. Rather than funds being given as of right to service providers (e.g. hospitals), they were reallocated to service purchasers (e.g. local doctors) who could decide what to buy and from whom. This creation of a market for the provision of medical services destabilised the environment and made planning and prediction very hazardous exercises (thus making an Evolutionary or Processual approach to strategy more relevant). However, with a change of government in 1997, the pendulum began to swing back. Whilst wishing to retain some of the perceived benefits of a market system, the new government announced that it would modify the purchaser–provider system to create greater stability (Salauroo and Burnes, 1998). Since then, of course, the government has once again swung the pendulum back towards market forces, something which has not always been wholeheartedly welcomed by staff in the NHS (Roberts, 2008).

Normally, however, attempts at manipulating the environment aim to reduce uncertainty, or at least cope with it rather than increase it. Allaire and Firsirotu (1989) identified three ways of coping with uncertainty:

- The first of these is through predicting and planning (the Classical approach).
- The second is to restructure for flexibility (the Contingency approach).
- The third, however, is to manipulate or control the environment.

In terms of the latter, Allaire and Firsirotu cite the examples of Boeing and IBM, which created and subsequently dominated their environments. Another major approach they identify is the use of cooperative strategies – collusion, market-sharing and other methods of reducing competition. An example of this in the UK was the agreement in the early 1990s by the main companies in the milk industry to 'carve up the country so they stop competing with each other' for doorstep sales (Cowe, 1995: 40). However, perhaps the most famous recent example is Microsoft's attempt to dominate the market for Internet products by providing its web browser 'free' to everyone who bought its Windows operating system.

Therefore, as can be seen, there is certainly sufficient evidence to show that it is possible to change, control or manipulate the environment in which an organisation operates, and thus either necessitate or make possible a particular approach to strategy.

Organisation characteristics

Obviously, there are many organisation characteristics that act to constrain or facilitate managerial choice. There appear to be four that have particular importance: structure, culture, politics and managerial style. Apart from the last, these have been reviewed extensively in Chapters 3 and 4 and can be discussed relatively briefly. An organisation's structure and culture have clear implications for managerial choice in the area of strategy. Organisations with organic structures and task cultures are likely to be resistant to or incapable of operating a Classical form of strategy. Similarly, organisations with mechanistic structures and role cultures are likely to have a somewhat hostile attitude towards Processual or Evolutionary approaches to strategy. Moving on to the issue of organisational politics: where decisions are heavily influenced by individual and/or group self-interest, as opposed to organisational objectives, it is unlikely that a Classical or Systemic approach to strategy would be successful. A Processual or Evolutionary approach, though, would have clear applicability.

There remains the subject of managerial or leadership style. There has been considerable interest in applying Burns's (1978) pioneering work on political leadership to leadership in organisations (Barker, 2001; Bass, 1995; Beatty and Lee, 1992; Burnes and James, 1995; Gibbons, 1992; Price, 2003; Storey, 2004; Yukl, 2006). Burns identified two basic organisational states:

- *Convergent* – a stable state.
- *Divergent* – where predictability and stability are absent.

For each of these states, he argued, there is an appropriate managerial style.

- *Convergent* states require managers with a *transactional style* – ones who are good at optimising the performance of the organisation within the confines of existing policy.
- *Divergent* states, however, require managers with a *transformational style* – ones who challenge the status quo and create new visions.

It follows from this that transactional managers will prefer approaches to strategy that stress continuity and predictability (i.e. the Classical or, in some circumstances, Systemic approach), whilst transformational managers will be more comfortable with a Processual or Evolutionary type of approach. Managerial style will be further discussed in Chapter 12.

As was the case with the other three forms of constraint, organisational characteristics can be amended. The debate on structure and culture has been well covered already, but the level of political behaviour is also open to change. As Pfeffer (1981, 1992) showed, though political behaviour is never absent from organisations, there are situations where it is likely to be more prevalent. In particular, political behaviour is likely to be most evident where major structural changes are taking place that affect the power distribution in organisations. By recognising that this is the case, by taking steps to reduce ambiguity and by trying to increase the transparency and openness of the decision-making process, the ability of individuals to pursue their own interests can be reduced. This is demonstrated by the Japanese *ringi* system, which promotes extensive and open debate over decisions in order to ensure that they fit in with the company's objectives rather than those of sectional interests. As far as changing managerial styles is concerned, although there is evidence that these are shaped and changed by the organisations in which managers work, there is also considerable evidence that senior managers tend to change organisations to fit their style (Morgan, 1986; Yukl, 2002).

Choices and constraints: summary

It should be borne in mind that the particular mix of these four forms of constraint will vary from organisation to organisation, even where these operate in the same country and industry. Also, it needs to be recognised that these constraints are as likely to conflict with each other as they are to complement each other: for example, car companies operating in the UK may find that the culture of the UK's financial institutions favours short-term profit maximisation, whilst the car industry appears to require long-term investment in building market share. This may be one reason why the UK motor industry is now mostly foreign-owned. In addition, it should be noted that whilst managers are not obliged to take account of the constraints they face, they may well pay a price for this in terms of the performance of their organisation. Successful firms are likely to be ones whose managers are aware of, and can balance, the various constraints they face. This obviously raises the issue of managerial ability and competence, an issue we shall explore in some depth in Chapter 12.

Therefore, the key point to recognise from the above review is that the type of strategic approach adopted is a matter of managerial choice, but that choice is constrained by a variety of organisational, environmental, sectoral and national factors, as are the outcomes which flow from it. As was argued in Part 1, organisations and managers may be able to influence or change the constraints they face. Therefore, by recognising, as Figure 6.4 shows, that there are real constraints on managerial choice, one is acknowledging that both the realist and complexity perspectives on organisations have much to offer. However, by recognising that some constraints can be consciously manipulated or influenced and changed, one is also acknowledging that the postmodernists' arguments should not be lightly dismissed.

Even so, both the case for managerial choice and the argument for manipulating constraints need to be taken with a pinch of salt. The fact of the matter is that in the West, as noted by many writers, the Classical approach to strategy, latterly through the work of the Positioning school, is still dominant (Joyce and Woods, 2001; Rigby and Gillies, 2000; Teece *et al*, 1997; Whittington, 1993). Also, as noted in Chapter 5, there is a tendency for decision-makers to 'satisfice'. That is to say, rather than undertaking an extensive examination of the issues involved and searching for all the possible solutions, decision-makers tend to accept the first satisfactory solution to a problem (Butler, 1997). This equates to Argyris and Schön's (1978) concept of single-loop learning (*see* Chapter 3). It is also similar to Cohen *et al*'s (1972) comment that decisions are often not taken but happen. They suggest that decisions occur when four independent streams meet: problems, solutions, participants and choice opportunities – the so-called Garbage Can model of decision-making (*see* Figure 6.5).

Cohen *et al* argue that when a problem becomes severe it demands attention. Solutions, on the other hand, are answers looking for a problem. Participants are the people in the organisation possessing problems and/or solutions, while choice opportunities are

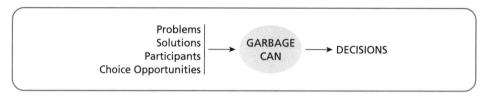

Figure 6.5 The garbage can model of decision-making

occasions when organisations are required to make a decision. When these four elements come together, decisions occur. Seen in this way, decision-making is not conscious, rational or systematic; on the contrary, decisions are haphazard, accidental and unplanned. From a slightly different perspective, Nelson and Winter (1982) argue that in many cases decision-making is an unconscious and automatic process, based on a repertoire that individuals develop over time of responses to particular situations. This is similar to Ashforth and Fried's (1988) observation that there is a tendency in some organisations for behaviour to become almost mindless – employees and managers, as a result of organisational socialisation and experience, respond automatically to events in a programmed way. Consequently, though the potential for choice exists, the reality is that many managers appear not to exercise it, preferring instead to stick to tried-and-tested, routine, orthodox, textbook approaches – regardless of their suitability.

Yet, it is important to note that, in the academic world, the weight of the argument appears to be shifting from seeing strategy as a rational, mathematical process, to seeing it as the outcome of the ability of an organisation's management to utilise its strengths and competences in the competitive pursuit of success. There are some writers, however, who believe the reverse is true of the business world, and that more and more firms are opting for rational decision-making approaches to strategy based on value-maximising financial techniques and quantitative analysis of market positions (Grant, 1991b; Teece *et al*, 1997). As Kay (1993: 357) maintains:

> To observe [as the proponents of the Descriptive stream of strategy do] that organizations are complex, that change is inevitably incremental, and that strategy is inevitably adaptive, however true, helps very little in deciding what to do. Managers wish to be told of a process which they can at least partially control and, whatever its weaknesses, that is what rationalist [Prescriptive] strategy appears to offer.

Whatever the validity or otherwise of this view, the main strategies favoured by organisations – as the following chapter will show – are still, though no longer exclusively, market- and quantitatively-orientated, and certainly give greater credence to rational decision-making than to more qualitative approaches.

Conclusions

Strategic planning or management has moved in and out of fashion over the years and is once again firmly back in fashion (Galagan, 1997; Hill and Jones, 2006; Johnson *et al*, 2006; Joyce and Woods, 2001; Kay, 1993; Rigby and Gillies, 2000). It has developed (and fragmented) considerably since it began to be widely used in America in the 1950s and 1960s (Brews, 2003; Hambrick and Frederickson, 2001). No longer is strategy purely about the external world, no longer is it solely seen as a rational, quantitative process. Neither is it any longer seen as a process that is geared towards predicting the future, but instead it seeks to shape or create the future (Joyce and Woods, 2001). Indeed, writers and practitioners from different backgrounds and countries, such as Hamel and Prahalad (1994), Mintzberg *et al* (1998b), Ohmae (1986) and Stacey (2003), have argued that it is not a process at all, but the outcome of a process: an outcome that is shaped not by mathematical models but by human creativity.

The move towards this new, more emergent, perspective on strategy has been brought about by the mounting criticisms against the Classical or Prescriptive approach to strategy. The main criticisms are that it is mechanistic, inflexible, and reliant on quantitative tools and techniques of dubious validity. The result is that organisations that attempt to construct strategies using the Classical approach fall foul of what Peters and Waterman (1982) described as 'Paralysis Through Analysis' and 'Irrational Rationality'. In effect, organisations contort themselves in a vain attempt to make the real world fit the constraints and limitations of their mathematical models, rather than vice versa.

The alternative view, and one that is gaining adherents, is that organisations should move away from exclusive reliance on mathematical models. Instead, human creativity should be brought into play. Senior managers should create a vision of the organisation's future – establish its strategic intent. This should then be pursued relentlessly by the organisation. In the process of doing so, the strategy emerges from the decisions that are taken with regard to resource allocation, organisation structure and the other key areas of operation. From different perspectives, a number of writers have come to the same conclusion. For successful companies, strategy does not appear to be a preconceived and detailed set of steps for achieving a coherent package of concrete goals within a given timescale. Neither does it seem to be a rational process that is amenable to mathematical modelling. Rather, it is the outcome of a process of decision-making and resource allocation that is embarked upon in pursuit of a vision (though even here there is disagreement about how conscious this process is). Such an approach is inherently irrational, inherently unplannable – it cannot be modelled or quantified, though it can and must be pursued with rigour and determination. Needless to say, just as the rational approach to strategy sat easily with a modernist perspective, so the irrational approach sits better with the postmodernist view of the world.

The problem is that, though we can identify two major perspectives on strategy, within and between them there are a great number of variants which, as Khalifa (2008) notes, serve to confuse managers rather than help them. In the face of this confusion, the tendency is for managers to limit their strategic domain and to focus on the use of one particular strategic tool (such as the Boston Consulting Group's Growth Share Matrix) regardless of the drawbacks and limited applicability of such tools (Coyne and Subramaniam, 1996; Hambrick and Frederickson, 2001; Mintzberg and Lampel, 1999).

In this chapter, we have suggested a third approach to strategy, one which sides with neither the quantitative nor the qualitative schools of thought but which instead seeks to promote (rather than reduce) managerial choice. It has been argued in this chapter that the approach to strategy that organisations adopt is or can be the outcome of managerial choice and preference. However, choice in this respect, as in most others, is constrained. The key constraints identified were societal, sectoral, environmental and organisational. Whilst on the face of it this appears to impose severe limitations on the degree of freedom managers have with regard to the choice of strategy, it was also argued that managers can influence or manipulate the constraints they face in order to create their own preferred organisational reality. Therefore, though being very much in the realist and complexity camps, it does not totally reject the postmodernist view either.

This follows on from Part 1, where it was claimed that managers are not the passive creatures portrayed by much of organisation theory. Instead of having to adapt their organisations to the circumstances in which they find themselves, they can attempt to amend or even reinvent the circumstances. So, managers in organisations faced by a dynamic and unpredictable environment could seek to change markets and/or products, influence the behaviour of competitors, or change customers' perceptions, in order to reduce uncertainty and increase predictability. By so doing, an organisation could still function efficiently at the more mechanistic end of the mechanistic–organic spectrum, if that was the type of structure preferred by its managers.

This argument would seem equally applicable to the constraints managers face when choosing an approach to strategy. Some managers might prefer an Evolutionary or Processual approach to strategy, either because it suits their own temperament or because they believe that a hostile and turbulent environment suits them better than their competitors (the move by Rupert Murdoch's newspapers in the UK in the 1990s to start a price-cutting war was an example of this). On the other hand, constraints might be manipulated or changed for ideological reasons, such as the attempt by most Western governments to privatise or introduce market forces into the public sector (Burnes, 2009). The point is that the possibility does exist for managers to choose not only their approach to strategy but also, to an extent at least, the constraints they face.

To choose an approach to strategy is one thing; to apply it is an entirely different matter. As Mintzberg *et al* (1998a, 1998b) observe, whether one takes the view that strategy drives change or that it emerges from the changes an organisation makes, the two are inseparable. Therefore, just as this chapter has reviewed the main arguments with regard to strategy, so the remaining chapters in Part 2 will review the strengths and weaknesses of the main approaches to applying strategy and implementing change.

Test your learning

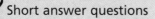

Short answer questions

1. What does Hoskin (1990) see as being the origins of modern business strategy?

2. Define long-range planning.

3. What technique did the Design school develop for assessing an organisation's potential?

4. How do Johnson and Scholes (1993) define strategy?

5. What is the Prescriptive school of strategy?

6. What is the Analytical school of strategy?

7. What is emergent strategy?

8. What is an umbrella strategy?

9. What are the main constraints on organisational choice?

10. Describe the relationship between organisational strategy and organisational change.

Essay questions

1. How do Whittington's four generic approaches to strategy relate to the Prescriptive and Analytical schools of strategy?

2. Discuss the following statement: strategy development and implementation can never be a rational process.

Suggested further reading

1. Mintzberg, H, Ahlstrand, B and Lampel, J (1998) *Strategy Safari*. Prentice Hall: Hemel Hempstead.

   Almost anything with Henry Mintzberg's name on it is worth reading and this book is no exception. It provides a succinct and pertinent review of the main perspectives on strategy.

2. Whittington, R (2001) *What Is Strategy and Does it Matter*? (2nd edition). Thomson Learning: London.

   In this short and eminently readable book, Richard Whittington challenges much of the orthodox thinking on strategy.

CASE STUDY 6

The rise and fall of Marconi[1]

BACKGROUND

There can be few who are not aware of the spectacular crash of Marconi, which, in the space of two years, went from a share value of £12.50 to under 2p, a stock market valuation of £35bn to just a few million pounds, and a profit of £750m to a loss of some £5.6bn, one of the biggest in UK corporate history.

Marconi grew out of GEC, the giant industrial conglomerate built by Arnold Weinstock. In a period when the UK's industrial competitiveness, and its base, declined, GEC was one of the UK's leading and most successful industrial enterprises. Weinstock, who died in 2002 at the age of 77, created GEC and was the UK's leading industrialist for over 30 years.

Weinstock graduated from the London School of Economics in 1944. He worked for the Admiralty for three years before moving into property development. In 1954, he joined his father-in-law's firm, Radio and Allied Industries, where he built a strong reputation for his managerial abilities. In 1961, the firm made a reverse takeover of the larger but struggling GEC. Weinstock became GEC's Managing Director, a post he held for over 30 years until he retired in 1996. In his period as Managing Director, he turned GEC into one of the great British success stories, through a combination of acquisition and organic growth. In 1961, GEC took over AEI, and in 1968 they bought English Electric, the owners of Marconi. GEC's acquisitions continued into the 1970s and 1980s. Under Weinstock, GEC acquired a portfolio of solid, well-regarded and profitable companies, including Hotpoint, Avery,

Metropolitan Vickers, Yarrow Shipbuilders and Marconi. GEC's last purchase under Weinstock was the VSEL shipyard at Jarrow, reflecting its commitment to maintaining the strength of its defence businesses, which accounted for some 50 per cent of sales and profits.

Weinstock had a knack for running businesses profitably where others had failed. This was down to his famously intimidating management style, which produced profits and, in the early years at least, gained him much praise from financial markets. For their time, his methods were revolutionary, at least in the UK. He was legendary for tight control of cash and focus on financial measures. He moved cash out of the separate GEC businesses and held it in the centre. He drove and monitored each business on its financial performance. Budgets became key growth mechanisms that put managers under enormous pressure to deliver on their forecasts. By ruthlessly cutting out overheads, introducing tight financial controls and forcing managers to think intelligently about their businesses, GEC grew in size and increased shareholder value.

Throughout his period in charge, GEC profits grew. Indeed, in 1990–2, when the UK economy was undergoing one of its worst recessions, GEC broke the £1bn profit barrier. Despite this, however, in the 1990s, GEC and particularly Weinstock became increasingly unpopular with investors in the City of London. GEC was a massive, sprawling industrial conglomerate when these were hugely unfashionable. Driven by academics and consultants such as Tom Peters and Rosabeth Moss Kanter, and break-up specialists such as Lord Hanson,

[1] I am very grateful for the comments and suggestions made by Brian Wolf, a former Director of GEC-Marconi.

managers were told that they had to identify their core business, 'stick to the knitting' and sell off non-core activities to release shareholder value. This went against Weinstock's business philosophy. He was not particularly interested in whether there was synergy between the various GEC businesses. In GEC, he had created a company composed of businesses that were leaders in their fields, made steady and consistent profits and which were, to an extent, insulated from wilder economic fluctuations. It was anathema to him to sell a business that had a profitable future or to buy one that was overpriced or unlikely to perform. In the early 1990s, he looked at many companies, but bought few. This approach did not please the markets, which seemed enamoured of companies that sold, spent and borrowed. However, the performance of the companies he turned down appeared to justify Weinstock's parsimonious approach (Owen, 2002). It also enabled the company to build up a cash stockpile of over £2bn, but strangely enough, this also attracted criticism.

Two of the City of London's main ways of making money are to lend it or to charge for their services in mergers and takeovers. GEC's stockpile of cash meant it did not need to borrow money, and Weinstock's insistence that he would not buy companies that were either overpriced or did not fit into GEC's portfolio appeared to enrage the City money men. There was also a common view in the City that GEC had missed the high-tech boat and that it was stuck in the 'old economy' when the smart money was moving into the 'new economy'. Certainly, as Heller (2002) commented, there was a downside to Weinstock's tough financial, risk-averse regime in that it appeared to discourage inter-company working in the GEC empire. Though GEC had a toehold, and sometimes a lot more, in the various technologies and markets that would allow companies such as Nokia, Intel and Dell to become giants of

the Internet era, it never quite managed to link them together or develop them enough to establish itself in the new economy.

Having passed the age of 70, Weinstock was finally pressured into resigning as GEC's Managing Director in 1996 and became its President Emeritus. Under pressure, he recruited George Simpson as a replacement. However, he saw this as an interim measure until his son Simon was ready to take over. Simon Weinstock's sudden death in late 1996 changed these plans and George Simpson became undisputed head of GEC. Simpson had run and sold both Rover and Lucas, was much admired in the City of London, and was considered to have the entrepreneurial qualities needed to reinvigorate GEC.

Whatever criticisms there were of Weinstock in his later years, his legacy was huge. Not only had he built an enormously successful industrial conglomerate in a period when British industry was in decline but also, as Brummer (2002: 1) commented:

> The fact that Britain is still a leading player in the global power industry, and has a world-class research-based defence industry, can largely be attributed to his precocious skills.

THE RISE OF MARCONI

Simpson bought into the popular view that GEC needed to get out of the old economy, characterised by its involvement in defence and heavy engineering, and into the new, high-tech world of telecoms and the Internet. He believed it also needed to stop being a UK/European company and become a global player. As he later said:

> What else were we going to do? The old GEC had had it and everyone told us that focus was what was needed. Telecoms was the obvious industry to expand into.
> (Quoted in M Harrison, 2002: 24)

He began to bring in his own people, notably John Mayo as Finance Director. Mayo had been an investment banker before moving to Zeneca as Finance Director, from where he was recruited by Simpson. It was Simpson and Mayo who charted GEC's push into the new dotcom economy through a whirlwind series of sales and acquisitions. The crucial period was 1999 to 2001. In 1999, GEC divested itself of its defence business to BAe. This halved the size of GEC and sold off its most consistently profitable elements. To mark this momentous step, GEC was renamed Marconi to signal its intention to become a leading telecoms company, and began a process of acquiring new businesses in the then growing international market for high-capacity telecoms networks. Simpson and Mayo believed, like many more, that the future lay with dotcom companies, and they wanted a big share of it. Not only did they spend the proceeds from selling businesses they did not want and the money that Weinstock bequeathed them, but they borrowed over £4bn as well. In the three years up to the middle of 2001, they sold off almost all of Marconi's non-telecoms business, i.e. the vast majority of the old GEC, and purchased over 20 telecoms businesses, for prices ranging from a few hundred million to a few billion pounds. Mayo stated that:

> The common theme between our [new] core businesses is the ability to securely capture, manage and communicate enormous amounts of data. The 'data wave' is turning into a tidal wave and we have positioned ourselves to ride the wave.
>
> (Quoted in Gow, 1999c: 25)

At another time, the speed of Marconi's transformation into a rapidly growing telecoms equipment provider might have been a cause for concern. But this was taking place at the height of the dotcom bubble. It seemed that everyone wanted to have a slice of the telecoms/Internet cake and was not too concerned how much they paid. Rather than worrying the financial markets, Marconi's splurge of buying, selling and borrowing seemed to please them enormously. The share price soared to £12.50 and Marconi was the darling of the financial markets.

THE FALL OF MARCONI

Marconi's popularity with the stock market was to prove short-lived. By late 2000, whilst Simpson and Mayo were still issuing optimistic forecasts of what was to come, other telecoms companies such as Nortel, Alcatel, Nokia and Ericsson began issuing sales and profit warnings as the telecoms recession, and the dotcom collapse, began to bite. Almost to the last, Marconi denied there were any problems, but in July 2001 it asked for its shares to be suspended ahead of a profits warning, a highly unusual move for a FTSE 100 company.

Though Marconi's profits warning was clearly going to damage the company's standing, the lateness and severity of the warning led to a disastrous fall in the share price, a rapid exit from the Board of senior staff and the virtual destruction of the company. Indeed, such was the concern for the way the Board handled the profits warning that the UK's financial watchdog, the Financial Services Authority (FSA), conducted a lengthy investigation into it. Its report was issued in April 2003. The FSA pointed out that the company had a legal obligation to keep the market informed of price-sensitive information in a timely manner, and that in this instance it had not, and had therefore broken the FSA's rules. Treanor and Wray (2003) reconstructed the events leading up to and just after the profits warning:

17 May 2001	Marconi says the first six months of 2001 are unlikely to show an improvement on the previous year's figures.
12 June	Trading figures show a 10 per cent decline for April and May. No public statement is made.
21 June	Accounts for April and May show a loss of £180m, £156m more than the previous year. No public statement is made.
26 June	The financial forecast for the six months to September 2001 show a loss of £47m, as opposed to the £320m profits that analysts had predicted. The forecast also shows that profits for the year to March 2002 will be £491m as against the predicted £807m. The Board disputes these figures and asks for them to be recalculated. No public statement is made.
28 June	A Board meeting is called for 4 July.
30 June	The revised financial forecasts are even worse than those presented to the Board on June 26. Full-year profits are projected to be only £272m, and half-year losses have risen to £121m. No public statement is made.
4 July	At 7.40 am, Marconi asks for its shares to be suspended pending a meeting of the Board at 4 pm. At 6.41 pm, the Board issues a statement saying that profits are likely to halve, with sales down 15 per cent.
5 July	When the markets open, Marconi's shares fall by nearly 50 per cent. John Mayo tells investors that business will

recover in 2002 when the telecom networks 'will be running so hot they'll fall over' and that there will be no change in Marconi's management. Marconi's share price continues to collapse. At 9.40 pm John Mayo resigns.

Two months later, George Simpson also resigned. Both men received substantial pay-offs. As a Leader in the *Financial Times* (2003: 20) stated, 'we can only speculate whether more could have been saved had directors been quicker to acknowledge that their headlong rush into telecoms oblivion was flawed'. Regardless of this, the events of June and July meant that, for Marconi, the dotcom bubble had burst with a vengeance. From then on, it was downhill all the way. In May 2002, Marconi announced one of the biggest yearly losses in UK corporate history: some £5.6bn. Its share price plunged to below 2p, making the company in effect bankrupt and its shares worthless. It then began a long process of trying to stay alive by negotiating with its creditors. In May 2003, Marconi finally agreed a debt restructuring deal with its creditors. In return for writing off over 90 per cent of the approximately £4.5bn they were owed, Marconi's creditors received 99.5 per cent of the company's equity. The refinanced company would be valued at just over £600m. The previous shareholders would own just 0.5 per cent, thus reducing the value of their holding to £3m from £35bn at its peak, always assuming that anyone would want to buy the shares.

SUMMARY

Simpson and Mayo argued that they were taking GEC through a much-overdue reinvention. However, there is a world of difference between reinventing a company around its

▶

279

core business and spending billions to construct a new one from scratch. What Simpson and Mayo did was to sell off most of what was GEC and to use the money from the sale, and much more besides, to create a new telecoms company that could rival established companies such as Alcatel, Siemens and Lucent. Unfortunately for them, their vision of creating a leading telecoms company came at a time when the dotcom bubble was about to burst. Even taking this into account, they made three classic business mistakes.

Firstly, they bought at the top of the market. In the space of three years they bought some two dozen companies for billions of pounds that very quickly became almost worthless as their markets collapsed. The US company Fore Industries is a prime example of this. Marconi bought the company for £2.8bn in 1999. In 2002, a financial analyst commented that: 'The business has very little value. If Marconi tried to dispose of it, there may even be costs associated with it' (quoted in Hirst, 2002: 1). Marconi was brought low by the combination of massive overcapacity in the industry, a worldwide economic slowdown and the enormous financial drain on telecom operators of paying for third-generation mobile phone licences. This led Marconi's customers, especially its biggest customer, BT, to cut their purchasing of telecoms equipment quickly and savagely. In effect, Marconi's market collapsed.

Secondly, Simpson and Mayo knew little of the businesses they were buying or the industry they were moving into. Simpson had made his reputation on running, and selling, Rover and Lucas, both firmly established in the 'old economy'. Mayo was an investment banker turned finance director. They were both dealmakers who had never worked in the telecoms

industry. As Weinstock commented, 'They knew nothing about the business they were in, and nothing about the businesses they were buying' (quoted in Aris, 2002: 8).

Lastly, they lost financial control of the business. GEC under Weinstock was legendary for its tight financial controls. The cornerstone of these controls was Weinstock's Eight Business Ratios which formed the framework of the monthly reports that had to be submitted to Weinstock by the Managing Director of each of the GEC businesses. These financial controls were discarded under the new regime with an almost fanatical belief that they constituted old-fashioned thinking. The result was that, as the events of June and July 2001 show, the Marconi Board seemed unaware until the very last minute that the company was in deep financial trouble.

It is difficult to exaggerate the disaster that happened at Marconi. Whatever the criticisms of the old GEC, when Weinstock handed over power in 1996, it was a strong and profitable company. The parts that were sold off by Simpson and Mayo still appeared profitable. On the other hand, by 2002, the new Marconi was bankrupt and worthless. When he stepped down, Weinstock was the biggest private investor in GEC, with some 45 million shares valued at over £400m. At the time of his death in 2002, these were practically worthless. Simpson and Mayo, who were both forced out, received handsome payoffs, and appeared not to accept that they bore any personal responsibility for the Marconi debacle, preferring to cite bad luck, poor timing and other people for the collapse of Marconi (M Harrison, 2002; Hirst, 2002). Hardly surprising, therefore, that Weinstock commented: 'I'd like to string them up from a high tree and let them swing there for a long time' (quoted in Aris, 2002: 8).

Questions

1. Analyse the Marconi case study from both the rational and emergent perspectives on strategy. What does Marconi tell us about these two perspectives?

2. Imagine you are Michael Porter. What advice would you have offered to George Simpson when he took over GEC-Marconi in 1996? How would his advice have changed the fate of Marconi when the dotcom bubble burst in 2000?

3. Imagine you are Henry Mintzberg. What advice would you have offered to George Simpson when he took over GEC-Marconi in 1996? How would his advice have changed the fate of Marconi when the dotcom bubble burst in 2000?

CHAPTER 7

Applying strategy

Models, levels and tools

Learning objectives

After studying this chapter, you should be able to:

- describe the three basic approaches to strategy that organisations can adopt;
- discuss the three levels of strategic decision-making in organisations;
- list the main strategic planning tools;
- state the strengths and weaknesses of quantitative tools;
- list the advantages and disadvantages of qualitative tools;
- understand why quantitative tools have tended to be preferred to more qualitative ones;
- appreciate the growing interest in vision-building techniques;
- identify the implications for organisational change of both quantitative and qualitative tools and techniques.

Ideas and perspectives 7.1
Strategic management tools

Bain's global 2007 Management Tools and Trends Survey

Overall tool use and satisfaction

> *Today, executives around the world are using more tools than when last surveyed in 2004. They averaged 15 tools in 2006, up from 13 in 2004. This increase was especially prevalent among small and midsize companies, both of which had significantly reduced tool usage in 2004. But while companies are employing more tools, they appear to be finding them less effective. Usage increased, yet the average overall satisfaction rating dropped to 3.75 from 3.89 in 2004, as measured on a one-to-five satisfaction scale.*

Recommendations

On the basis of our research to date, we offer four suggestions for the use of tools:

1. Get the facts. Every tool has its own strengths and weaknesses. To succeed, you must understand the effects (and side effects) of each tool, then combine the right tools in the right ways at the right times. Use the research. Talk to other tool users. Don't naively accept hyperbole and simplistic solutions.
2. Champion enduring strategies, not fleeting fads. Managers who promote fads undermine employees' confidence that they can create the change that is needed. Executives are better served by championing realistic strategic directions – and viewing the specific tools they use to get there as subordinate to the strategy.
3. Choose the best tools for the job. Managers need a rational system for selecting, implementing and integrating the tools that are appropriate for their companies. A tool will improve results only to the extent that it helps discover unmet customer needs, helps build distinctive capabilities and helps exploit the vulnerabilities of competitors – or a combination of all three.
4. Adapt tools to your business system (not vice versa). No tool comes with prepackaged instructions and a guarantee. Every tool must be adapted to a company's particular circumstance.

Source: Rigby and Bilodeau (2007: 5–7)

Introduction

This chapter begins where the previous one ended. Chapter 6 reviewed the main perspectives on strategy. In seeking to understand and define strategy formulation, it identified two streams of thought, the Prescriptive and the Analytical. As the name implies, the Prescriptive stream comprises approaches that seek to 'prescribe' how organisations should undertake strategy but, in so doing, tends to ignore or downplay the irrational and highly convoluted nature of organisational life. The Analytical stream, on the other hand, rather than telling organisations how they should build strategy, seeks to analyse – to understand and describe – the complexity and range of forces that affect how organisations actually do build strategy. This divergence is reflected in their respective views of strategy.

The Prescriptive stream, which was the first on the scene and is very much practitioner-orientated, sees strategy formulation as an economic–rational process based on mathematical models. The Analytical stream, which began to appear in the 1970s, represents the more reflexive and more academically-orientated face of strategy. It views strategy not as a process, but as an outcome of a process. Its proponents' emphasis is not on the construction of detailed plans, which in any case they believe to be an unworkable approach, but on the organisational, social and political aspects of strategy formulation. The two streams represent markedly different perspectives on strategy formulation, and whilst the Analytical stream has tended to win the academic arguments over the last 20 years, the Prescriptive one has had considerably more impact and influence on the practice of strategy.

Nevertheless, this may be changing. As the survey by Bain & Company (Ideas and perspectives 7.1) shows, the use of strategic planning tools is growing, especially amongst small- and medium-sized companies but, as Ideas and perspectives 7.1 also shows, 'while companies are employing more tools, they appear to be finding them less effective'. This would appear to bear out the arguments of the Analytical school regarding the efficacy of quantitative tools. It may also account for why the Survey's authors found an increase in the use of more qualitative tools such as vision-building and scenario-planning, and why 91% of respondents rated culture as important as strategy for business success (Rigby and Bilodeau, 2007).

This chapter begins by examining the three basic types or models of strategy that organisations can adopt: the Competitive Forces model; the Resource-Based model; and the Strategic Conflict model. The chapter then moves on to look at the three levels of strategic decision-making in organisations: corporate, business and functional. This is followed by a review of the main strategic planning tools.

The chapter ends by arguing that one of the principal reasons for the dominance of prescriptive approaches to strategy has been the alliance between leading consultancies and business schools in America to develop, market and update these. In so doing, the Prescriptive school has established itself as the orthodox, safe and practical approach to strategy formulation. However, with the take-up of more analytically based types of strategy, this is beginning to change. As Chapter 6 maintained, the model or type of strategy an organisation should adopt, and the associated planning tools that accompany it, are dependent upon the constraints the organisation faces. However, organisations do not have to fit themselves and their strategies to these constraints. Rather, they have a choice; they can seek to influence or mould the constraints they face in order to make them more amenable to the type or model of strategy they wish to pursue. Therefore, the approach to strategy an organisation adopts may have less to do with the merits of the different models on offer and more to do with the type of organisation it is and the orientation of its managers.

Types of strategy

As the previous chapter demonstrated, there is a wide, and often confusing, variety of approaches to strategy development that organisations can adopt. It follows that the same comment can be made with regard to the types of strategy that organisations do actually adopt in order to achieve competitive advantage over their rivals (Johnson *et al*, 2006; Joyce and Woods, 2001). However, Teece *et al* (1997) argue that, in the main, there are only three basic types or models of strategy that organisations do adopt in practice, which are as follows.

The Competitive Forces model

This stems from the Positioning school and, since its inception in the 1980s, has become the dominant approach to strategy. The central tenet of this approach is the need to align the organisation with its environment, the key aspect of which is the industry or industries in which it competes. Proponents of this view believe that industry structure

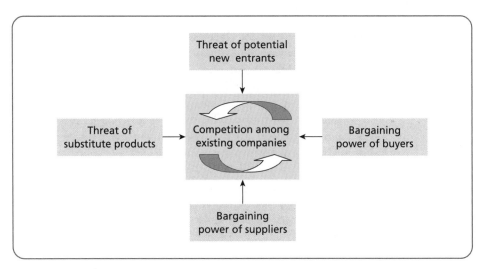

Figure 7.1 Porter's five competitive forces
Source: Porter (1980)

strongly influences the competitive rules of the game as well as the range of strategies open to the organisation. This model is most closely associated with the work of Michael Porter (1980, 1985) and his 'five forces' framework (*see* Figure 7.1).

Porter argues that it is these five industry-level competitive forces, the bargaining power of buyers and sellers, the threat of potential substitute products and new entrants, and rivalry among existing competitors, that determine the inherent profit potential of an industry. Consequently, he argues, these are the main factors which an organisation needs to take into account when developing its strategy. For Porter (1985: 47), strategy is concerned with 'positioning a business to maximize the value of the capabilities that distinguish it from its competitors'. Porter (1980) maintains that there are only three basic generic strategies a firm can adopt in order to outperform competitors: *cost leadership*, *product differentiation* and *specialisation by focus* (these are discussed in more detail below). Porter believes that a firm's ability to increase its profits is dependent on its ability to influence the competitive forces in the industry or to change its market position in relation to competitors and suppliers. This approach obviously has links to Contingency Theory (*see* Chapter 2), given that it is based on a systematic empirical search for relationships between external conditions and internal strategies. In addition, because of its focus on the importance of sector and industry factors, it has an affinity with Child and Smith's (1987) firm-in-sector perspective discussed in Chapter 6.

There is little doubt that the Positioning school in general, and Porter's work in particular, has had a huge influence on the practice of strategy within organisations (Hussey and Jenster, 1999; Johnson and Scholes, 2002). However, as one would expect, it has also attracted considerable criticism. Perhaps the most serious is that the choice of forces in the model appears to be arbitrary and without justification; nor is there any indication as to how to assess the relative power of the forces or how they interact (O'Shaughnessy, 1984; Speed, 1996). In terms of more specific charges, Miller (1992) criticised the model as too narrow and inflexible, and thus likely to leave organisations vulnerable if social, technological or economic developments lead, as can happen, to rapid changes in the marketplace. Ghemawat (2008) argues that rather than organisations focusing on a single variable, such as cost or differentiation, they need to be able to be competitive on a range of variables. Mintzberg *et al* (1998a) note that the Positioning school's assumption of rationality ignores the political nature of organisations; that it is biased towards big business, where market power is greatest, and therefore has little to say to small and medium-sized enterprises; and that its dependence on analysis and calculation impedes both learning and creativity. For Fleisher and Bensoussan (2003), the key weaknesses of Porter's approach are its lack of explicit recognition of the importance of socio-political factors, its lack of a longitudinal focus and that it underestimates the importance of core competences. A further and telling criticism is that the big competitive battles of the last 30 years, especially between Japanese and American firms, tend not to have been won by those who have identified and defended their market position, such as General Motors and Xerox, but by those, such as Toyota and Cannon, who have used their unique resources to change the rules of the game itself (Hamel and Prahalad, 1989, 1994). For these reasons, the last decade has seen a growing interest in both the Resource-Based and Strategic Conflict models of strategy.

The Resource-Based model

The focus of the Resource-Based model of competitive advantage is on the relationship between an organisation's resources and its performance (Furrer *et al*, 2008). The Resource-Based view sees above-average profitability as coming from the effective deployment of superior or unique resources that allow firms to have lower costs or better products, rather than from tactical manoeuvring or product market positioning (Fahy, 2000). Such resources include tangible assets, such as plant and equipment; intangible assets, such as patents and brands; and capabilities, such as the skills, knowledge and aptitudes of individuals and groups (Amit and Schoemaker, 1993; Hall, 1993; Wernerfelt, 1995). Resources such as these are not free-standing assets that a firm can obtain or dispose of easily or quickly, but are deeply embedded in an organisation's processes and as such are very difficult for others to replicate (Ordanini and Rubera, 2008).

The Resource-Based view grew from the work of economists who, in seeking to identify the factors which gave rise to imperfect competition and super-normal profits, drew attention to differences between firms in terms of technical know-how, patents, trademarks, brand awareness and managerial ability (Chamberlin, 1933; Learned *et al*, 1965; Penrose, 1959; Wernerfelt, 1984). Consequently, proponents of the Resource-Based view see firms as being heterogeneous in respect of their resources, i.e. no two firms possess exactly the same combination of these. In relation to strategic management, this view really came to the fore in the 1980s and 1990s initially through the work of Wernerfelt (1984), who asserted that an organisation's competitiveness stemmed from the possession and ability to exploit resources, but it attracted attention mainly as an explanation for the rise of corporate Japan.

It was out of research into the competitiveness of Japanese firms that Prahalad and Hamel (1990) produced their article 'The core competence of the corporation'. In it, they argued that real competitive advantage comes from the ability to build, at lower cost and more speedily than competitors, those core competences that spawn unanticipated products. They also argued that senior managers should spend a significant proportion of their time developing a corporation-wide architecture for establishing objectives for competence-building. The influential study of the car industry by Womack *et al* (1990), *The Machine that Changed the World*, came to a similar view of Japanese competitiveness. Support for this perspective has also come from a number of studies of Western firms. Cool and Schendel (1988) showed that there are systematic and significant performance differences among firms in the same industry sectors. Rumelt (1991) showed that intra-industry profit differentials are greater than inter-industry differentials. Kay's (1993) work on strategy also comes to the conclusion that an organisation's success comes from developing distinctive capabilities.

Hax and Majluf (1996: 10) stated that:

> *The essence of the resource-based model . . . [is] that competitive advantage is created when resources and capabilities that are owned exclusively by the firm are applied to developing unique competencies. Moreover, the resulting advantage can be sustained due to the lack of substitution and imitation capabilities by the firm's competitors.*

The influence of the Resource-Based view has grown considerably over the last two decades (Fahy, 2000; Ordanini and Rubera, 2008). It is now the received wisdom that organisations should, in Peters and Waterman's (1982) phrase, 'stick to the knitting' and discard activities that are not part of their core business and which do not build on their core competences (Hax and Majluf, 1996). Therefore, the advent of the Resource-Based view of the firm challenges the view of Porter and earlier writers on strategy that competitive advantage arises mainly from environmental factors. Instead, the Resource-Based view maintains that the possession of valuable, rare, inimitable and non-substitutable resources may result in sustained superior performance (Furrer *et al*, 2008).

Even so, there are criticisms which have been raised against this view of strategy, including the lack of empirical support, complex and ambiguous definitions of resources, and that it is merely a rehash of the SWOT analysis (Fleisher and Bensoussan, 2003). A further criticism is that the concept of what constitutes a valuable resource is based on a tautology. As Priem and Butler (2001) noted, the main method for identifying a valuable resource is that it already has value. In addition, because resources cannot easily or quickly be acquired or developed, in the short run firms are stuck with the ones they possess. Therefore, depending on the circumstances, and how they change, these firm-specific assets can be either a boon or a curse. Perhaps the main criticism of this approach comes from population ecologists who argue that, because these competences take so long to develop and environments change so quickly, any beneficial match between an organisation's competences and its environment is likely to be accidental or fortuitous rather than the result of deliberate or foresightful actions by managers (Hannan and Freeman, 1988). This is perhaps why there has also been a growing interest in the Strategic Conflict model, which draws attention to the dynamic nature of organisational strategy.

The Strategic Conflict model

This model harks back to the military metaphor, and portrays competition as war between rival firms. In particular, there is a tendency to draw on the work of military strategists such as von Clausewitz (von Clausewitz *et al*, 2001) and Sun Tzu (Michaelson, 2001) and attempt to apply their military aphorisms to modern business organisations (Mintzberg *et al*, 1998a). Sayings such as, 'No battle plan ever survived the first encounter with the enemy' are used to illustrate not just the dynamic nature of strategy but also the need to respond to competitors who do not always behave as anticipated. In its current manifestation, it came to prominence with the publication of Carl Shapiro's (1989) article 'The theory of business strategy'. Central to this approach is the view that a firm can achieve increased profits by influencing the actions and behaviour of its rivals and thus, in effect, manipulate the market environment. This can be done in a number of ways, such as by investment in capacity (Dixit, 1980), R&D (Gilbert and Newbery, 1982) and advertising (Schmalensee, 1983). However, such moves will have little impact if they can be easily undone; therefore, to be effective, they require irreversible commitment.

Furthermore, it is argued, these various manoeuvres are crucially dependent on what one firm thinks another firm will do in a particular situation. Therefore, the model incorporates the role of strategic signalling as an important mechanism for influencing or intimidating rivals. This includes such practices as predatory pricing (Kreps and Wilson, 1982) and limit pricing (Milgrom and Roberts, 1982). In addition, more recently, the model has come to embrace issues relating to the role of commitment and reputation (Ghemawat, 1991) and the simultaneous use of competition and cooperation (Brandenburger and Nalebuff, 1996).

Therefore, from the Strategic Conflict perspective, an organisation's ability to increase its profits is dependent on its ability to outwit, out-bluff and out-manoeuvre its rivals. This approach also draws on game theory to understand the nature of competitive interaction between rival firms. Game theory has allowed established intuitive arguments concerning various types of business tactics and strategy (e.g. predatory pricing) to be explained and formalised. In terms of the Prescriptive and Analytical streams of strategy, although Porter (1980) acknowledges the benefits of strategic manoeuvring, it does not fit in with his or the rest of the Positioning school's work. Instead, its emphasis on quick-wittedness, gut instinct and the more emotional elements of decision-making means it sits better with the Analytical stream.

Given that conflict-based strategies do not take account of the wide range of external and internal factors which also contribute to an organisation's competitiveness, its usefulness may well be limited. As Teece *et al* (1997) noted, strategic conflict is likely to be more appropriate in situations where there is an even balance between rivals in an industry (e.g. Coca-Cola and Pepsi) rather than in situations where one organisation has a substantial competitive advantage over its rivals (e.g. Microsoft). In these latter situations, it is perhaps the Resource-Based model of strategy that is of most interest.

These three types or models of strategy are all currently fashionable, though Porter and the Positioning school are the more dominant. They are, however, very different in their emphasis and timescales:

- The Strategic Conflict model is outward-facing and very much about out-manoeuvring the opposition. It tends to have a short-term focus, although a number of its tactics do have longer-term implications.
- The Competitive Forces model is also outward-facing but is concerned with identifying and occupying a defensible market position, and thereby achieving higher profits than others in the industry. This tends to have a medium-term focus.

- The Resource-Based model is the only one which has an internal focus; it also has a much longer-term focus than either of the other two. Its proponents believe that organisations need to build strategic competences that, almost through a process of serendipity, will allow it to meet future and unanticipated market needs.

There are, of course, as Mintzberg *et al* (1998a) and others have shown, many more strategies than these three. However, the popularity of these three tends to emphasise the point made by a number of writers that many managers tend to have a preferred approach to strategy which they stick to regardless (or perhaps because) of the fact that it tends to narrow their perspective and limit their options (Khalifa, 2008; Hambrick and Frederickson, 2001; Mintzberg and Lampel, 1999).

Nevertheless, just because managers have preferred approaches to strategy and just because the proponents of particular strategies put theirs forward as the 'one best way', that does not prevent organisations from drawing on a combination of strategies which can be deployed as the circumstances warrant.

In 2007, a very bitter and public row broke out between the satellite broadcaster BSkyB and the cable company Virgin Media (*see* Mini Case Study 7.1). The flashpoint for the battle between the two companies was BSkyB's steep increase in the price it charged Virgin Media to carry its channels. However, underlying this was Virgin Media's manoeuvring to challenge BSkyB's dominance on the UK satellite market and the latter's attempt to maintain its position. Therefore, on the surface, this appears to be a prime example of the Strategic Conflict model in action. Both organisations are seeking to gain an advantage over the other through, in this case, some very public tactics. It also has to be remembered that BSkyB is part of Rupert Murdoch's News International empire and that Virgin Media is part of Richard Branson's Virgin empire, and that both men have form as corporate warriors. In Murdoch's case, a good example is his long-running battles with his UK newspaper rivals. In Branson's case, the prime example is the long-running battle between his Virgin Atlantic and British Airways.

Therefore, both Murdoch and Branson appear to give support to the case for the Strategic Conflict model. However, it also needs to be acknowledged that both men have built their empires on strong brands – in Branson's case, it is Virgin; in Murdoch's case, it is newspapers such as the *Times* and *Sun* and broadcasters such as BSkyB. The possession and development of strong brands is a key element of the Resource-Based model of strategy. Beyond that, of course, both men have sought to achieve strong positions in their market by, in Murdoch's case, being the lowest-cost producer, or in Branson's case the use of product/service differentiation or specialisation by focus. Consequently, they can be seen to offer support for the Competitive Forces model. This illustrates clearly that successful organisations such as Virgin and News International rarely limit themselves to one approach to strategy. They tend to be pragmatists – using the approach which offers the best chance of success in their particular circumstance. Sometimes this will be to battle it out with their rivals, sometimes it will be to achieve a particular market position by differentiation, focus or low cost, but in pursuing these strategies they are unlikely to forget the need to develop unique resources which their rivals cannot copy.

The key points to remember are that all types of strategies have weaknesses as well as strengths, and that whilst they are applicable to some situations, there will be many

Mini Case Study 7.1
Row between Virgin and Sky is reignited

Virgin Media and British Sky Broadcasting traded more accusations as an exchange of letters between the two rivals' chief executives prompted claims on both sides of bad faith and negotiation through the media. The long-running argument about the price Virgin Media pays to carry channels such as Sky One and Sky News flared again yesterday, after the satellite group released letters claiming that its cable rival had rejected a compromise offer. Sky shows such as Lost and 24 have not been aired on Virgin Media's rebranded service since February 28 after the cable group refused to meet BSkyB's demand for an increase in its carriage fees. The two sides have since disputed each other's claims on the prices demanded and offered. Yesterday, BSkyB released a letter sent on May 10 by James Murdoch, its chief executive, to Steve Burch, his opposite number at Virgin Media. Mr Murdoch offered to split what he claimed was a £10m difference between the offers made by the two companies in February. Virgin Media disputed the figures as it released Mr Burch's response, faxed to BSkyB on May 17. Mr Burch said he was 'fully prepared to negotiate' but claimed the new proposal would simply reduce 'an excessive and anti-competitive price' by 15 per cent. The fax also highlighted a shift in the cable group's negotiating position, arguing that any new offer should reflect 'the damage inflicted on Virgin Media' by the loss of the channels. 'Most of the damage has been to the Virgin Media customers who continue to pay for something they no longer get', BSkyB said. Mr Burch had given 'no indication of the terms he would be prepared to accept', added Jeremy Darroch, BSkyB finance director. In a second letter, sent yesterday, Mr Murdoch claimed BSkyB had 'no choice' but to publish the correspondence, citing 'consumer interest' in the issue and highlighting Virgin Media's own use of the media in the dispute. Virgin Media accused its rival of 'a crude attempt to exert undue pressure by putting negotiations under the public spotlight'.

Source: Andrew Edgecliffe-Johnson, *Financial Times*, 19 May 2007, p. 14.

others where their applicability will be limited. Therefore, as Coyne and Subramaniam (1996) maintain, and Murdoch and Branson have demonstrated, managers need to be familiar with the available range of strategic approaches and tools, and use the ones best suited to their circumstances. Sometimes they might engage in strategic conflict; sometimes they might concentrate on their market position and at other times on resource-building. Consequently, rather than being viewed as mutually exclusive, the three approaches to strategy discussed in this section might be seen as complementary.

Levels of strategy

It is easier to see how the three types of strategy above are applied in practice by examining the three levels of strategic decision-making in organisations: corporate, business and functional (*see* Ideas and perspectives 7.2).

Ideas and perspectives 7.2
Levels of strategic decision-making

- **The corporate level.** Strategy at this level concerns the direction, composition and coordination of the various businesses and activities that comprise a large and diversified organisation, such as Rupert Murdoch's News International or Richard Branson's Virgin empire.
- **The business level.** Strategy at this level relates to the operation and direction of each of the individual businesses within a group of companies, such as Nissan's car assembly plant at Sunderland.
- **The functional level.** Strategy at this level concerns individual business functions and processes such as finance, marketing, manufacturing, technology and human resources.

Each of these three levels has its own distinct strategic concerns and each can draw on a different battery of strategic tools, techniques and approaches to aid them. Nevertheless, it is important to remember that they are interrelated. Traditionally, it has been assumed that the corporate level sets the direction for each of its constituent businesses and, in turn, these set the direction for their various functions. Though this is true for some organisations, it is now recognised that these three levels interact in an iterative and dynamic fashion (Johnson and Scholes, 2002; Lynch, 1997). Therefore, Mintzberg (1994) argues, just as business-level and functional-level strategy can be seen as being imposed or driven by corporate-level decisions, so corporate-level strategy can be seen as emerging from, or being shaped by, functional-level and business-level decisions and actions. Consequently, it follows that although there are strategies at the corporate level that have their counterparts at the business and the functional levels, it would be wrong to assume that this is always a product of a top-down rather than a bottom-up process.

When running a diversified enterprise whose activities cut across a number of different areas of business, there is a tendency for senior managers to focus on corporate-level strategy, what Fleisher and Bensoussan (2003) refer to as the corporate 'game plan', and ignore or consider less strategic the concerns of the individual businesses and the functions within them. However, as Ideas and perspectives 7.3 shows, each level of an organisation has its own strategic concerns.

Given the different concerns of these three levels, it becomes easier to appreciate the need to integrate the strategies and structures at all three levels. Otherwise, for example, the corporate level may pursue a strategy of diversification whilst the individual businesses are busy concentrating their efforts on fewer products and markets. However, it is also easy to appreciate why in practice it is so difficult for large diversified organisations to identify and pursue a consistent strategy through all areas of their activities (Joyce and Woods, 2001; Lynch, 1997). As argued in the last chapter, strategy formulation and implementation is not a mechanical process that begins at the corporate level and moves in a linear and logical fashion through to the functional level. Strategy formulation is inherently iterative, and aims to optimise the operation of the organisation in its

Ideas and perspectives 7.3
Strategic questions

Corporate strategy is concerned with questions such as:

- What is the mission of the organisation?
- What are its unique attributes?
- How should the business portfolio be managed?
- Which existing businesses should be disposed of and which new ones acquired?
- What priority and role should be given to each of the businesses in the current portfolio?

The central strategic concerns at the individual business level are:

- How should the firm position itself to compete in distinct, identifiable and strategically relevant markets?
- Which types of products should it offer to which groups of customers?
- How should the firm structure and manage the internal aspects of the business in support of its chosen competitive approach?

Functional-level strategy concerns itself with the following issues:

- How can the strategies formulated at the corporate and business levels be translated into concrete operational terms in such a way that the individual organisational functions and processes (marketing, R&D, manufacturing, personnel, finance, etc.) can pursue and achieve them?
- How should the individual functions and processes of the business organise themselves in order not only to achieve their own aims, but also to ensure that they integrate with the rest of the business to create synergy?

entirety rather than maximising the product of any one particular part. These issues, and the main differences in scope and focus of the individual levels, can clearly be seen by a brief examination of the types of strategy that are pursued at the corporate, business and functional levels.

Corporate-level strategy

Large corporations by their nature tend to comprise a wide range of businesses operating increasingly on a global basis and offering a diverse range of products and services. The purpose of corporate strategy is to decide on the composition of and overall direction for such organisations. As Mini Case Study 7.2 shows, even well-established and well-resourced companies such as Philips find this a very difficult job.

Broadly speaking, there are six basic forms of strategy that organisations pursue at the corporate level:

- **Stability strategy** (also known as maintenance strategy). As its name implies, strategies under this heading are designed to keep organisations quiet and stable. They are most

Mini Case Study 7.2
Stewardship of a sprawling empire

If Philips did not exist, it is unlikely anyone would invent it. The great survivor of European industry has weathered innumerable crises and restructurings in the past quarter of a century, and its battered history shows up in the diverse range of operations that come under its stewardship. In spite of this, the Dutch electronics business that makes products from coffee machines to medical scanners has entered a calmer period, which is in no small part down to Gerard Kleisterlee, its chief executive since 2001. Yet the challenges he still faces underline the difficulty of bringing order to a sprawling collection of businesses with a long and illustrious past.

Under Mr Kleisterlee, the 114-year-old company has closed down underperforming factories and some surplus operations. Operating profit trebled last year to €1.6bn (£1.08bn) on sales of €30.3bn and, with steady progress during 2005, Mr Kleisterlee says the company is on course to hit its target of operating margins of 7 to 10 per cent by 2007. But Mr Kleisterlee still has to convince onlookers that he can knit together Philips' operations into a rational business capable of steady performance across all its divisions. One possible strategy is to sell off two of the company's five business groups – semiconductors and consumer electronics – even though these represent a considerable part of its heritage. That would leave Philips with three main divisions – medical equipment; lighting; and small electric appliances, such as shavers – in each of which the company appears capable of generating reasonable profits over the next decade. While Mr Kleisterlee gives few hints that he may want to do this in the near future, many see such a strategy as being high on his list of options.

'You must credit Mr Kleisterlee with making Philips a smoother running company', says Janardan Menon, an analyst at Dresdner Kleinwort Wasserstein. 'But Philips still comprises a bunch of parts that seem to have little link with each other. Mr Kleisterlee has got to show he has a vision for what to do with them.'

The chief executive of a large US capital goods company, who has followed Philips' progress for more than 20 years, is somewhat more unkind. 'They have had their ass kicked so many times I have lost count. But in spite of all the restructurings, they are still stuck with high-volume, low-margin businesses that they would be better off out of.'

Source: Ian Bickerton and Peter Marsh, *Financial Times*, 18 November 2005, p. 13.

frequently found in successful organisations, operating in medium-attractiveness industries, which are faced with unpredictable circumstances outside the range of their normal business experience. Because of their markets and products, such organisations believe they have no need to make sudden changes and have the time and position to allow events to unfold before making any response (Wheelen and Hunger, 1989). A typical example would be an established mortgage lender whose business would both necessitate and allow it to take a longer-term perspective.

- **Growth strategy.** This is possibly the most common form of all corporate strategies, and involves either concentrating on dominating one industry (e.g. Vodafone) or growing by diversification across a number of industries (e.g. Virgin). As a number of writers have suggested (*see* Argenti, 1974; Byars, 1984), its basic attraction is twofold. Firstly, it is claimed that there is a strong and proportional correlation between increased turnover and increased profit. Secondly, the performance of senior managers tends to be measured in terms of the annual increase in turnover and profit. There are those, however, who point out that increases in turnover are not necessarily matched by increases in profits and that, given the need to invest to achieve growth in turnover, growth may actually weaken a company's financial health (Byars, 1984; Drucker, 1974).

- **Portfolio extension**. This is another variant of the growth strategy, but is achieved through mergers, joint ventures or acquisitions, rather than through internally generated organic growth. The first two of these, mergers and joint ventures, allow growth or development to take place, without the organisations involved having to invest the level of resources that would be necessary if they were operating in isolation. The third variant, acquisition, is usually resource-intensive but brings immediate gains in the form of an established and, hopefully, profitable business (Byars, 1984; Little, 1984; Leontiades, 1986).

- **Retrenchment strategy**. This strategy is usually only embarked upon when an organisation is in trouble or, because of adverse market conditions, sees trouble ahead. It usually involves a process of downsizing, i.e. cutting back on numbers employed and activities undertaken, or even selling off the entire enterprise. The general aim is to cut back in order to match expenditure to projected income, and refocus the organisation so as to be able once again to attain prosperity in the future (Bowman and Asch, 1985; Thompson and Strickland, 1983). In the wake of the 2007 credit crunch, most financial service companies appear to be pursuing a retrenchment strategy.

- **Harvesting strategy**. This involves reducing investment in a business or area of activity in order to reduce costs, improve cash flow and capitalise on whatever residual competences or areas of advantage still remain. This approach can be implemented at different rates depending on the urgency of the situation. Slow harvesting means to reduce financial support at such a slow rate that it almost appears to be a maintenance strategy; at the other extreme, fast harvesting can result in budgets being cut at such a rate that it seems almost indistinguishable from liquidation (Harrigan, 1980; Kotler, 1978; Porter, 1980).

- **Combination strategy**. The above strategies are not mutually exclusive, and can be linked together in whatever combination seems appropriate given the circumstances of the organisation in question. Combination strategies, however, are clearly more appropriate, or at least more necessary, in large multi-divisional organisations where the circumstances faced by the different activities are likely to vary. Therefore, in such situations, organisations may experience a constant flurry of change, where some parts are being run down and/or disposed of whilst new units are being acquired and other areas of the business rapidly expanded (Glueck, 1978; Pearson, 1977).

The above list is not exhaustive, nor can it be, given that each organisation is free to develop its own strategic variant in relation to its own circumstances. As argued in Chapter 6, it is the circumstances of the particular organisation in question that should dictate the type of strategy adopted by its managers, rather than any attempt to copy what has been successful elsewhere. Though Porter's Competitive Forces model can be applicable to all these forms of strategy, the Strategic Conflict and Resource-Based models appear to be more applicable to situations where growth is being pursued or where companies have a strong market position. Yet it needs to be remembered that it is the precepts and assumptions of Porter and the Positioning school which still dominate the practice of strategy. A further point to note is that all except the first, stability strategy, imply fundamental restructuring of the internal operations of the organisation. In such situations, there are likely to be winners and losers, and managers may be more concerned with preserving their jobs and power than choosing the best strategy for the organisation (Mintzberg, 1994).

Nevertheless, in both America and Europe, over the last 25 years, the tide has been turning against corporate strategy, or rather against the large corporate centres responsible for developing corporate strategy and which wielded so much power in the 1970s and 1980s. The case against them is summed up by Koch (1995: 78), who maintains that:

> *Anything other than a minimal [corporate] Centre can only be justified if the Centre adds more value than it costs and subtracts from the business. . . . Yet it should be clear that . . . independent of their cost, most corporate Centres destroy more value than they add.*

This negative view of corporate strategy has, perhaps, been most vociferously championed by Peters and Waterman (1982), but has also received strong support from academic researchers (Goold *et al*, 1994). The result of this is that there has been an increasing tendency to devolve responsibility for strategy from the corporate to the business level.

Business-level strategy

Whilst corporate-level strategies are mainly concerned with managing diversified enterprises whose activities span a number of different areas, business-level strategies relate to the different ways that an individual business unit can compete in its chosen market(s). This does not mean that the strategies are necessarily determined by the individual businesses; they may be set at the corporate level. For example, Marks and Spencer comprises a range of different businesses – clothing, food, furniture, financial services, etc. The strategies for each of these businesses is set at corporate level and not the level of the individual business, though the responsibility for enacting the strategy lies at the business level. Therefore, it must be remembered that business-level strategies are chosen and deployed within the framework of an overall corporate strategy and not in isolation from it, though the degree of freedom allowed to individual business units in this respect will vary from organisation to organisation (Johnson *et al*, 2006). To this end, the strategic concerns of managers at the business level tend to be, according to Hax and Majluf (1996: 46):

> *. . . the mission of the business, the attractiveness of the industry in which the business belongs, and the competitive position of the business unit within the industry. These are the inputs that determine the strategic agenda of a business and lead to the formulation and implementation of its strategy.*

As was the case at the corporate level, the strategies available at the business level are many and varied. Rather than attempt to describe them all, we shall examine the main variants by addressing Porter's (1980, 1985) work in this area.

As mentioned earlier, Porter (1985: 11) argues that there are only two basic types of competitive advantage a firm can possess: low cost or differentiation. He adds to these the 'scope' of the business (i.e. the range of its markets) to create 'three generic strategies for achieving above average performance': cost leadership, product differentiation and specialisation by focus. As Figure 7.2 shows, the first two of these are strategies for achieving competitive advantage across an entire industry whilst the third, specialisation by focus, relates to achieving competitive advantage in a particular segment of an industry only.

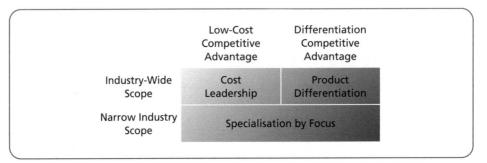

Figure 7.2 Porter's three generic strategies
Source: Porter (1980)

Cost leadership

The aim of this strategy is to achieve overall lower costs than one's competitors, without reducing comparable product quality. To do this requires a high volume of sales in order to allow organisations to structure themselves in such a way that they can achieve economies of scale. In the UK, the epitome of this strategy is the supermarket Tesco, which takes £1 in every £7 spent on the high street (*Observer*, 2008). With a market share twice that of its nearest rival, its sales volumes allow it to strike better deals with suppliers and offer customers lower prices whilst still maintaining better margins than its rivals. To achieve such a competitive advantage, as Porter (1980: 15) states, requires the:

> . . . *aggressive construction of efficient scale facilities, vigorous pursuit of cost reductions from experience, tight cost and overhead control, avoidance of marginal customer accounts, and cost minimization in areas like R&D, services, sales force and so on.*

Product differentiation

This strategy attempts to achieve industry-wide recognition of different and superior products and services compared to those of other suppliers. This recognition can be accomplished through the design of special brand images, technology features, customer service or higher quality, all of which have implications for the structure and operation of companies. Achieving differentiation is likely to result in insulation against competitive rivalry due to securing customer loyalty. The resultant competitive advantage also leads to increased returns, sometimes through making customers less sensitive to high product price. Perhaps the pre-eminent example of product differentiation is Apple Computers. It has never been the biggest company in the market but it has always had the most loyal, not to say fanatical, customers. There are hundreds, if not thousands, of computers on the market but there has only ever been one Mac – nobody else does anything like it. There are many, many MP3 players but the iPod is the player of choice for the discerning, fashion-conscious consumer. Similarly, as Mini Case Study 7.3 demonstrates, for all its limitations, there are few people who would not want to own an iPhone.

Mini Case Study 7.3
Shoppers in clamour for Apple's 3G iPhone

FT

Huge queues form in 22 countries
Fears over supplies disregarded

Excited customers queued in cities around the world for the global launch of Apple's 3G iPhone yesterday, undeterred by concerns that there might not be enough handsets. With a co-ordinated launch in 22 countries, some analysts were worried that the limited initial stock, estimated at 1.5m handsets, would be insufficient. Some Japanese iPhone fans had queued since Tuesday with collapsible chairs and energy drinks. Their reward was a place near the front of a queue of more than 1,500 people. SoftBank started sales of the iPhone at 7am at its Omote Sando store in central Tokyo.

While the iPhone lacks some of the functions such as television reception and e-payment that are popular in Japan, the phone is likely to be popular among Mac fans and customers drawn to the touch screen and pc-like internet usage. The first 3G iPhone customer was in New Zealand, where Jonny Gladwell, 22, a student, waited for 60 hours in freezing temperatures. 'I'm going to put this on charge and have a nice long sleep', he said. In the UK about 100 people queued at the flagship Apple store on London's Regent Street. Many had queued overnight, but were kept waiting inside the store by delays in activating the phones. At the front of the queue was David Suen, from Australia, who bought his place on online auction site Ebay for 'less than £50' to avoid waiting. The second-placed person had queued since 2pm on Thursday. Some customers said that they were looking forward to ditching their BlackBerrys. One technology consultant called his BlackBerry 'damned ugly' and said that having a 3G iPhone would be beneficial with clients. In New York the queue began forming outside the flagship Apple store on Fifth Avenue before midnight. Most people were young adults who said they believed the new 3G iPhone was the best device on the market for accessing the mobile internet.

Some of those still queuing complained that the in-store activation process mandated by AT&T and Apple appeared to be slow. In San Francisco, the scene outside the local Apple store was reminiscent of iPhone's original US launch last year, as an eclectic early-morning crowd drank coffee and ate doughnuts from a local bakery in a queue that stretched for two blocks.

Source: Rob Minto, *Financial Times*, 12 July 2008, p. 10.

Specialisation by focus

In this case the strategy is concerned with selecting (focusing upon) only certain markets, products or geographical areas in which to compete. As Mini Case Study 7.4 shows, the US retailer Best Buy chose to adopt a business strategy whereby each of its stores would focus on a particular segment of the market. Therefore, whilst some stores would focus on the affluent professional, others would focus on the needs of the small-business customers.

Porter argues that by focusing in this way, it becomes feasible for a firm to dominate its chosen area(s). The method of achieving domination could either be through cost advantage or product differentiation. According to Porter (1980: 15), however, such niche markets must have certain characteristics which separate them out from the market in general:

> *. . . the target segment must either have buyers with unusual needs or else the production and delivery system that best serves the target must differ from that of the other industry segments.*

If the niche market grows, or is incorporated, into a larger market, then market dominance is unlikely to be retained. In such circumstances, the previously dominant organisation will find itself having to compete for market share with others. In effect, the rules of the game will have changed and a different strategy is required – either attempting to gain cost leadership across the entire market, or adopting a product differentiation policy that neutralises other competitors' cost advantage.

Mini Case Study 7.4
Divide and conquer: Best Buy's strategy

Best Buy, the largest US consumer electronics retailer, has set out to customise its stores and staff training to focus stores on one or more of five customer groups:

- The affluent professional who is prepared to spend money on top-quality home entertainment and who wants the service and installation advice to go with it.
- The younger male 'early adopter', interested in the latest in personal wireless and digital technology and computer games, who wants to test out new games and technology at the store.
- The family man who wants practical technology and entertainment.
- The busy suburban mum who will buy technology and entertainment for her children, but who wants expert advice and reassurance when making a purchase.
- The small business customer – a new target for the retailer – who can use products such as web cameras or computer servers to enhance profitability, and who will seek technical support from the retailer's service teams.

The retailer plans to have half of its 700 or so US stores converted to its new segmented model by February next year. Best Buy is spending money on new store fittings and on staff training, as well as on managing and supplying a more complex network. But the retailer says higher sales and profit margins justify the expenditure.

Source: *Financial Times*, 31 October 2005, p. 10.

Porter's assertion concerning these three strategies is that they are distinct and cannot be mixed. That is to say, it is not possible to pursue successfully a cost leadership strategy and a product differentiation strategy at the same time, because each requires different organisational arrangements to be successful. Also, if a firm does not achieve cost leadership, product differentiation or specialisation in its products, services or market, it is bound to produce low profitability and have below-average performance. Porter (1980: 41) refers to these sorts of firms as 'stuck in the middle' because they lack:

. . . the market share, capital investment, and resolve to play the low cost game, the industry-wide differentiation necessary to obviate the need for a low cost position, or the focus to create differentiation or low cost in a more limited sphere.

Influential though Porter's work is, there are many who disagree with him on this point (Mintzberg *et al*, 1998a). Hlavacka *et al* (2001), in a study of public and private hospitals in the Slovak Republic, found that those which pursued a 'stuck in the middle' strategy had the best performance. An earlier study by Dess and Davis (1984) also questioned Porter's view. They found evidence to show that businesses with both a low cost and a high differentiation position can be very successful.

Miller (1992) challenged Porter's assertion that firms should pursue only one strategy. He points out that such strategic specialisation can lead to inflexibility and narrow an organisation's vision. In addition, Gilbert and Strebel (1992) point to the success of 'outpacing' strategies. This is where firms enter a market as low-cost producers and then, once established, differentiate to capture a larger slice of the market. This was the approach, i.e. moving from one successful form of strategy to another, used by Japanese companies to capture Western markets in the 1970s and 1980s (Johnson and Scholes, 2002). In so doing, Japanese firms used a Strategic Conflict approach, but this was underpinned by their commitment to building and developing their core competences. Therefore, though Porter's work has tended to dominate the practice of strategic management in Western firms, both the Resource-Based and Strategic Conflict models have shown their worth, as mentioned above.

Regardless of which business-level approach to strategy organisations have followed, prompted by the success of Japanese companies, there has been a growing interest in the importance of functional-level strategy (Hax and Majluf, 1996; Schonberger, 1982).

Functional-level strategies

Organisations can construct good corporate strategies and good business strategies but in order to achieve their objectives, they need good functional strategies as well. For example, Dyer's (1996) study of the reason why Toyota outperformed its American and Japanese rivals found that the key to its success was a better supply chain strategy. Similarly, as Mini Case Study 7.5 shows, in responding to the recent rise in world commodity prices, coupled with stagnant or falling demand, Toyota did not change its corporate or business strategy but instead changed its product design strategy to take cost out of its vehicles (which is also likely to lead to changes to its supply chain and manufacturing strategies). This emphasises the crucial role that functional strategies play in achieving and maintaining competitive advantage.

Mini Case Study 7.5
Thin times for lean car production

FT

Presenting its annual earnings in Tokyo yesterday, the world's most profitable carmaker [Toyota] also briefed investors on some new wrinkles in its much-studied manufacturing process. Alongside its financial results and market-share statistics, Toyota outlined measures it was taking to reduce the thickness of resins it uses in its cars by more than 30 per cent, and to cut its use of sheet steel by 20 per cent. The carmaker suffered a 25 per cent rise in the price of rolled steel charged by Japanese producers last month, and said that 'soaring raw material costs', alongside the stronger yen and other factors, presented a major challenge to its global operations.

'The business environment is extremely tough', said Katsuaki Watanabe, the company's president. Toyota said it was looking to reduce materials costs starting at the development phase, for example by reducing the number of costly electronic control units it designs into its vehicles. The company is regarded as an industry leader in lean production, and its competitors will have been listening closely as they too struggle with rising prices for virtually all the raw materials that go into their cars.

Source: John Reed and Jonathan Soble, *Financial Times*, 9 May 2008, p. 16.

The main functional-level strategies concern marketing, finance, R&D, technology, human resources, manufacturing/operations and supply chain. Of the three levels of strategic decision-making, the functional level has probably been the most neglected by Western organisations. This is for three reasons:

- Firstly, the concentration at both the corporate and business levels on the external world, i.e. the market, led to a lack of interest in the internal operation of organisations. The assumption was that the internal world was malleable, and could and should adjust to the priorities set by corporate and business strategists (Schonberger, 1982).
- Secondly, key elements of functional-level strategy, especially concerning finance, marketing, R&D and technology, were in effect determined and constrained by corporate strategists. Indeed, in many organisations, even the human resource strategy was determined at the corporate level.
- Finally, even though the 1980s saw a renewed interest in functional-level strategy, this tended to be one-sided, stressing soft, personnel-type issues.

As discussed in Chapter 3, in seeking to understand and emulate Japanese success, Western researchers created the 7 S Framework: strategy, structure, systems, staff, style, shared values and skills (Peters and Waterman, 1982; Pascale and Athos, 1982). Though acknowledging that the Japanese were strong in and integrated all the seven Ss, the tendency in the West was to stress the so-called soft Ss: staff, style, shared values and skills. This not only continued to neglect areas such as manufacturing/operations and supply chain, but also, in so doing, failed to produce the sort of integrated corporate, business- and functional-level strategies that were seen as lying at the core of Japanese competitiveness. Once again, this highlights the difficulty that Western strategy practitioners, consultants and theorists have with creating an approach to strategy that goes beyond focusing on particular aspects to take an all-encompassing view (Mintzberg *et al*, 1998a).

In examining the corporate, business and functional levels, it can be seen that there are only a limited number of forms of strategy that organisations tend to adopt and which flow from the Competitive Forces, Strategic Conflict and Resource-Based models of strategy discussed earlier. The appropriateness of any of these for a particular organisation is, as maintained in Chapter 6, related to the nature of the societal, sector, environmental and organisational constraints it faces. These include the stage of product–market evolution, the competitive position the firm has, the competitive position it seeks, the business strategies being used by rival firms, the internal resources and distinctive competences at a firm's disposal, the prevailing market threats and opportunities, the type and vigour of competition, customer needs, and the conditions that financial institutions place on capital availability, to mention only the more obvious ones (Hax and Majluf, 1996; Hill and Jones, 2006; Johnson *et al*, 2006; Koch, 1995; Thompson and Strickland, 1983). In addition, it must be acknowledged that generic strategies will always give rise to a host of variants and, therefore, at any one time, the choice of the most suitable strategy will be a highly complex task. Indeed, this is what one would expect. If choosing and implementing strategy was easy, then all firms would be successful. But, given that success is usually measured in relative terms, by definition not everyone can be successful; therefore, strategy formulation will and must remain fraught with danger and difficulty.

A major point to note, though, is that almost without exception, whatever form of strategy is adopted, it will require the organisation to achieve a fit between its external environment and internal structures, culture and practices. Contrary to the views of earlier writers on strategy (such as Ansoff, 1965), if organisations are driven by their external environment, internal arrangements may, and usually do, need to change, often radically, in order to achieve the desired marketplace objectives. This once again emphasises the importance of functional-level strategy and shows why it should not be treated as a lesser issue. On the other hand, it should also be borne in mind, as argued in previous chapters, that the possibility does exist for organisations to shape their external environment to fit in with their internal arrangements. The fact that many do not do so may say more about the type of organisation they are than the constraints they face.

Types of organisation

Miles and Snow (1978) developed an important variant of the argument on types of strategy. Rather than attempting to classify the types or levels of strategy that organisations can adopt, they classify the organisations themselves as strategic types, based on the rate at which an organisation changes its products or markets. Miles and Snow identified four strategic types (*see* Ideas and perspectives 7.4).

Though Miles and Snow's classification has received empirical support from some researchers (e.g. Shortell and Zajac, 1990), others have questioned its applicability across industries (e.g. Hambrick, 1983). Notwithstanding this, as Waldersee and Sheather (1996) point out, there are some similarities between Miles and Snow's work and Porter's work. They argue that successful firms pursue one of two basic types of strategy – innovative or stability.

Ideas and perspectives 7.4
Miles and Snow's classification of strategic types

- **Defenders**. These seek internal stability and efficiency by producing only a limited set of products, directed at a narrow but relatively stable segment of the overall market, which they defend aggressively. Such organisations are characterised by tight control, extensive division of labour and a high degree of formalisation and centralisation.
- **Prospectors**. These are almost the opposite of defenders. They aim for internal flexibility in order to develop and exploit new products and markets. To operate effectively in a dynamic environment they have a loose structure, low division of labour and formalisation, and a high degree of decentralisation.
- **Analysers**. These types of organisation seek to capitalise on the best of both the preceding types. They aim to minimise risk and maximise profit. They move into new markets only after viability has been proved by prospectors. Their internal arrangements are characterised by moderately centralised control; with tight control over current activities but looser controls over new undertakings.
- **Reactors**. This is a residual strategy. These types of organisation exhibit inconsistent and unstable patterns caused by pursuing one of the other three strategies erratically. In general, reactors respond inappropriately, perform poorly, and lack the confidence to commit themselves fully to a specific strategy for the future.

Source: Miles and Snow (1978)

Organisations pursuing innovative strategies, which embrace both Porter's product differentiators and Miles and Snow's prospectors, seek to achieve success through reducing price competition by offering products and services that are considered unique in terms of their design, brand image and features. On the other hand, organisations pursuing stability strategies, which embrace Porter's cost leaders and Miles and Snow's defenders, seek to achieve success by locating and maintaining secured niches in stable product areas where they can produce higher-quality or lower-price products than their competitors.

Covin (1991) agrees with the proposition that successful organisations pursue one of two forms of strategy, though he labels them 'entrepreneurial' and 'conservative'. The former falls within Waldersee and Sheather's innovative category, whilst the latter falls within their stability category. Covin argues that the strategy an organisation adopts reflects its basic nature (i.e. its culture). Therefore, for Covin, the selection and pursuit of strategy is driven by managerial style and organisational culture. However, Waldersee and Sheather dispute this. Their work sought to examine the relationship between strategy and managerial style, and whether one drove the other. Their conclusion, which was tentative, was that different types of strategy may predispose managers to act in different ways (i.e. managerial style follows strategy type) rather than managers' styles predisposing them to a particular type of strategy. Yet, recalling Chapter 6's discussion of strategy and the constraints on managerial choice, it could be argued that these writers are taking too narrow and deterministic a view. It might well be that, depending on the constraints faced by managers and their perceptions of these, in some situations strategy does require managers to adopt a particular style of working, whilst in other situations managerial style does influence the nature of the strategy adopted. This discussion of the relationship between managerial style and organisational context will be returned to in the concluding chapter of this book.

Before moving on to examine the strategic tools that organisations have at their disposal, it is important to remember that the concept of strategy (whether at the functional, business or corporate level) is contentious. There are many influential writers who do not believe in strategy as a conscious and planned process (e.g. Mintzberg, 1994; Pettigrew, 1985; and Stacey, 2003). This does not invalidate corporate, business or functional strategies *per se*, but it does mean that they occupy a problematic and contested terrain.

Strategic planning tools

This section briefly reviews the main tools that organisations use to select and construct their strategies. By and large, these tools tend to have either a quantitative or a qualitative bias. In the past, and to a major extent even now, it was the quantitative tools (mathematical models) that tended to dominate. This is largely a reflection of the types of strategy organisations adopt, and a (not unrelated) preference for quantification, especially in the financial arena, in the USA, where many of the leading tools of and approaches to strategy originated (Grant, 1991b; Hax and Majluf, 1996; Moore, 1992). It should be noted, though, that other leading industrial nations, especially Germany and Japan, place less reliance on financial and other quantitative measures in determining strategy (Carr *et al*, 1991; Whittington, 1993). For example, the Japanese electronics giant, NEC, never uses discounted cash flow; and though Toyota does calculate cash flows, it does not take account of them for decision-making purposes (Williams *et al*, 1991).

Beginning in the 1990s, even in the USA and the UK where financial considerations appear paramount, there has been a movement away from the sole reliance on quantitative techniques, and a growing interest in softer, qualitative tools such as scenario- or vision-building (Fleisher and Bensoussan, 2003; Joyce and Woods, 2001; Rigby, 2001; Rigby and Bilodeau, 2007). In part, this interest in more qualitative techniques is a result of the perceived failure, especially in the face of Japanese competition, of more quantitative approaches favoured by proponents of the Positioning school to deliver a genuine and sustainable competitive advantage. This interest in qualitative techniques has also received a boost from the growing interest in the Strategic Conflict and Resource-Based approaches to strategy. In addition, it forms part of, and has been given impetus by, the move away from quantification and towards the use of more qualitative techniques in organisation theory in general.

As one would expect, there are an enormous range and number of tools and techniques available to the strategist. However, perhaps the ones that have attracted most attention are, in chronological order:

1. the PIMS (Profit Impact on Marketing Strategy) model;
2. the Growth-Share Matrix;
3. the Scenario- or Vision-Building approach.

The first two focus on corporate and business-level strategies and are biased towards large organisations that have an established and significant presence in the markets they serve. The third, though, has no such restrictions or biases and can be applied to a wide range of situations.

PIMS

The PIMS (Profit Impact on Marketing Strategy) programme was launched in 1972 and derived from research by Sidney Schoeffler. This was put into practice by General Electric, who wanted to analyse their operations with the aim of identifying those factors determining business success (Schoeffler, 1980). In 1975, Schoeffler founded the Strategic Planning Institute (SPI), which is linked to Harvard Business School, to provide a permanent base for the PIMS work. Since then, PIMS has grown to become the largest privately owned database in the world, comprising over 200 major corporations and some 2,600 individual business units (McNamee, 1985; Moore, 1992).

The rationale underlying the PIMS model is that certain characteristics of a business and its markets determine profitability. Consequently, understanding these characteristics and acting upon them will aid a company to become more profitable. The model is based upon the belief that there are three major factors which determine a business unit's performance: its strategy, its competitive position, and the market or industry characteristics of the field in which it competes (Moore, 1992). Underpinning the model are two key assumptions. The first is that all business situations are basically alike and obey the same laws of the marketplace (Schoeffler, 1980). The second is that the future will resemble the past, i.e. if certain linkages between strategy and performance resulted in profitability in the past, they will do so again in the future (Buzzell and Gale, 1987).

PIMS operates as a form of club. It collects information from its member companies relating to such factors as market share, profitability, product quality and investment. This information is fed into the PIMS database and is then used to provide individual members with answers to questions such as:

- What profit rate is 'normal' for a given business?
- What strategic changes are likely to improve performance?
- What are the likely effects on profitability, cash flow, etc., of adopting a particular strategy?

There has been much discussion as to the success of the PIMS. Certainly, some of its users, as well as academic observers, regard it as having only a limited use (Ford, 1981; Mitroff and Mason, 1981). The main criticisms levelled against PIMS are as follows:

- It is flawed because it uses historic data, without consideration for future changes. The argument is that, as organisations operate in a dynamic environment, to use the past to predict the future can be a dangerous exercise. Indeed, PIMS seems to be useful only in a stable environment, where companies stick to doing what they know best. It is even questioned whether PIMS can be regarded as a tool for policy in a strategic sense, since it can be argued that the 'variables' it so relies on, such as market share, are performance variables, not strategic ones (Abell, 1977).

- It is highly analytical, but very limited in solving problems. In addition, because PIMS has to use a very large database for its analysis, it is argued that this creates a major problem for managers in terms of absorbing all the data generated. In turn, since the statistical errors in its output are rarely openly discussed, there is a tendency for managers not to question its findings because 'the computer is always right' (Andrews, 1980).

- Its most famous, and contentious, assertion, that profitability is closely linked to market share, and that an improvement in market share can be associated with a proportionate increase in return on investment, is of dubious validity. As Smith (1985) maintains, it could equally be argued that both are due to common factors, such as low costs and good management. It is also said to be responsible for inculcating in managers and consultants a belief that low-market-share businesses are bad and must either increase their market share or withdraw from the industry in question, regardless of profitability (McKiernan, 1992).

- Most of the factors that govern the forecasts of the model are beyond the control of individual companies. Therefore, since PIMS relies heavily on these data, whatever conclusions it reaches about the fate of a company are final. It is neither comforting nor particularly useful to be told that you cannot do anything to turn a negative forecast around, because the factors responsible are out of your hands (Anderson and Paine, 1978).

- It assumes that a rather large set of quantitative variables, primarily of a financial nature, are sufficient to capture the state of a business and from this determine a realistic strategy (Naylor, 1981). Also, as Mintzberg *et al* (1998a: 99) comment, 'finding a correlation between variables . . . is one thing; assuming a causation, and turning that into an imperative, is quite another'.

- It is based on the premise that business problems are orderly or well-structured. PIMS thus assumes that the determination or classification of the level of the organisation or business unit, the customer group, the competition, the market and the product line to which the analysis applies are all either well-known or well-specified. It is, therefore, not equipped to handle imprecise, let alone conflicting, definitions of business problems (Koch, 1995; Naylor, 1981).

In summary, the main criticisms of PIMS are that it is too mechanistic, overly complex, based on unreliable data, and cannot cope adequately with dynamic and unpredictable environments. Yet, despite the criticisms levelled against it, many researchers still believe that PIMS is a useful tool (Chang, 1997; Johnson and Scholes, 2002; Thompson, 1996). The PIMS method has also been praised for the insight it has given into the true nature of the relationships between strategic variables such as profit and market share. Obviously, managers deal with these variables and their relationships on a daily basis, but attempts at conceptualising these relationships had been lacking until the advent of the PIMS research programme (Anderson and Paine, 1978; Ford, 1981; Mitroff and Mason, 1981).

This is not, however, to minimise the shortcomings of the PIMS model. It is biased towards, and contains data almost exclusively provided by, large and well-established corporations that already occupy significant positions in their markets. Therefore, as Mintzberg *et al* (1998a: 99) observe, its emphasis is on 'being there' or 'staying there' rather than 'getting there'. It follows that its prescriptions may have little relevance for new, small or innovative businesses seeking to enter new markets.

The Growth-Share Matrix

This was the brainchild of the Boston Consulting Group (BCG) in the USA and is arguably the most famous strategic tool ever developed (Koch, 1995). BCG was formed in 1963 by Bruce Henderson, and it is generally considered to be the pioneer of business strategy analysis. The Growth-Share Matrix, or 'Boston Box' as it is colloquially referred to, arose from two concepts developed by BCG: the experience curve and the sustainable growth formula (McKiernan, 1992).

The experience curve, which Henderson claims to have discovered in the 1960s, suggests that 'as the cumulative production of a product doubles, the cost of producing it seems to decrease by a constant percentage (usually 10 to 30 per cent)' (Mintzberg *et al*, 1998a: 97). From this, BCG concluded that if costs fall in relation to production volume (i.e. experience), then cost must also be a function of market share. Therefore, the company with the largest market share should also have the greatest competitive advantage and, it follows, the highest profit margin.

The sustainable growth formula, which was developed by BCG in the early 1970s, is based on the relationship between growth, investment and returns. It maintains that companies with the highest rate of returns on investments can, theoretically, grow the fastest (McKiernan, 1992).

It was bringing together these two concepts (that the company with the highest returns can grow the fastest and that the company with the highest market share should have the highest profit margin) that created the basis for the Growth-Share Matrix. The matrix is based on the assumption that all except the smallest and simplest organisations are composed of more than one business. The collection of businesses within an organisation is termed its business portfolio. Using pictorial analogies (*see* Figure 7.3), it posits that businesses in an organisation's portfolio can be classified into stars, cash-cows, dogs and problem children (Smith, 1985).

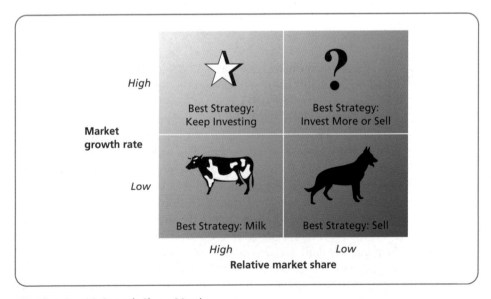

Figure 7.3 BCG Growth-Share Matrix

- **Stars** are business units, industries or products with high growth and high market share. Because of this, stars are assumed to use and generate large amounts of cash. It is argued that as they, generally, represent the best profit and investment opportunities, then the best strategy for stars, usually, is to make the necessary investments to maintain or improve their competitive position.
- **Cash-cows** are defined as former stars whose rate of market growth is in decline. They were once market leaders, during the early days when the market was rapidly growing, and have maintained that position as the growth tapered off. They are regarded as businesses with low growth but high market share. Because they are entrenched in the market, they have lower costs and make higher profits than their competitors. These businesses are cash-rich; therefore the appropriate strategy for such businesses is to 'milk' them in order to develop the rest of the organisation's portfolio.
- **Dogs** are businesses that have low market share and which operate in markets with low growth potential. Low market share normally implies poor profit, and because the market growth is low, investment to increase market share is frequently prohibitive. Also, in such situations, the cash required to maintain a competitive position often exceeds the cash generated. Thus, dogs often become cash traps. It follows from this that, generally, the best strategy is for dogs to be sold off.
- **Problem children** or **question marks**, as they are sometimes labelled, are regarded as having a high growth rate and low market share. They have high cash requirements to keep them on course, but their profitability is low because of their low market share. They are so named because, most of the time, the appropriate strategy to adopt is not clear. With their high growth rate, it might be possible to turn them into stars, by further investment. On the other hand, because of the uncertainty that surrounds this type of business, the best strategy might be to sell them off altogether.

The originators of the Growth-Share Matrix see it as a dynamic tool for assessing and planning market and business developments. For example, the matrix predicts that as growth in their industries slows down, the original stars will move into the position of cash-cows, as long as they keep maintaining their high market share; otherwise they will become dogs. It also claims to predict how cash-cows and dogs will develop as their markets change. Therefore, the Growth-Share Matrix can be used to forecast the development of a business portfolio over a period of time. There are two basic assumptions underlying the matrix:

- Firstly, that those industries, products or businesses that have a high growth rate can be differentiated from those that have a low growth rate.
- Secondly, that those that have a high competitive position or market share can be differentiated from those that have a low competitive position or market share.

Based on these assumptions, the matrix classifies business units or activities according to the growth rate of the industry of which they are part and by their market share (Koch, 1995; McKiernan, 1992; Moore, 1992).

The matrix was widely and rapidly adopted by American corporations in the 1970s. This was for two reasons: firstly, the matrix's simplicity and ease of construction; and secondly, because most large corporations were busy splitting their organisation into strategic business units focusing on particular industries and products. The corporate centres were looking for a simple means of categorising and directing the activities of these units, and the matrix was seen by them as an ideal tool for this purpose. McKiernan (1992), however, argues that its advantages go far beyond merely its simplicity and ease of construction. He maintains that it aids strategic planning, balancing cash flow between businesses, investment decisions and competitive benchmarking.

Nevertheless, as many commentators note, over the years, the Growth-Share Matrix has attracted its fair share of criticisms as well as praise (Koch, 1995; McKiernan, 1992; Mintzberg *et al*, 1998a). One of the obvious objections to the matrix is the labels it employs for the classification of businesses. Andrews (1980) described these labels as a 'vulgar and destructive vocabulary'. There are, however, other more substantial criticisms concerning the assumptions underlying, and the operation of, the 'Boston Box' (Johnson and Scholes, 2002). The main one is that the uniqueness of an organisation and its problems may not be adequately captured by this or any other tight classification scheme (Hax and Majluf, 1996). This is reflected in the views of Mitroff and Mason (1981), who argue that the critical assumptions underlying the matrix are tautologous and simplistic, e.g. the classification scheme applies to all businesses, because all businesses can be classified as one of the four basic types, or the classification scheme is relevant to all businesses, meaning that all businesses should be able to be classified as one of the four types.

Researchers have also drawn attention to the difficulty in defining and measuring the major variables, such as growth, market share and profitability, on which the matrix relies (Hax and Majluf, 1982; Hax and Nicholson, 1983; Johnson and Scholes, 2002). Hax and Nicholson (1983) also question whether market share really is the major factor determining profitability, and whether industry growth is really the only variable that fully explains growth opportunities. These reservations are echoed by Smith (1985). A further concern is that the matrix assumes that a good portfolio analysis should identify the competitive strengths and the industry attractiveness of each business unit. Alternatives to the Growth-Share Matrix, however, reject this assertion. Instead they start by assuming that these two dimensions cannot be revealed by a single measurement, but require a wider set of critical factors for reliable position-ing of the business units (Hax and Majluf, 1982; Hofer and Schendel, 1978). Another reservation, expressed by Fawn and Cox (1985), is the difficulty of defining what con-stitutes a single business.

One of the most telling criticisms is that many of the companies that have used the matrix found, to their alarm, that all their component businesses were classed as dogs even though these businesses were actually profitable!

Perhaps the key and most common criticism relates to the way the matrix, and other similar tools, have been used. As Hax and Majluf (1996: 313) observe:

> ... *matrices tend to trivialize strategic thinking by converting it into simplistic and mechanistic exercises, whose final message is dubious at best. Also the matrix methodology has tended to take strategic analysis and, subsequently, strategic think-ing away from managers and into the realms of planning departments.*

In the face of such criticisms, a number of alternatives were developed to BCG's original portfolio matrix. Hax and Majluf (1996) identified the following as the most popular:

- The Industry Attractiveness–Business Strength Matrix developed by General Electric in association with management consultants McKinsey (Hax and Nicholson, 1983). (A similar system called the Directional Policy Matrix (DPM) was also developed by Shell Chemicals in the UK (Hussey, 1978).)
- The Life-Cycle Matrix developed by the consultants Arthur D Little. As well as identifying the appropriate strategy for each business in a portfolio, this also provides detailed guidance on action programmes to implement the strategies.
- The Alternative BCG Matrix developed by the Boston Consulting Group to update the original matrix.
- The Profitability Matrix developed by the consultants Marakon Associates. This seeks to identify the profitability, growth and cash-generating capabilities of each business in a portfolio.

Figure 7.4 shows the main external and internal factors which each of these matrices seeks to identify. It also needs to be noted that many other organisations have developed or employed similar schemes to meet their organisational needs (Koch, 1995; McKiernan, 1992; Patel and Younger, 1978). Nevertheless, portfolio models all seem to attract similar criticisms to those levelled at the Growth-Share Matrix (Fleisher and Bensoussan, 2003; Mintzberg *et al*, 1998a; Turner, 1990).

Regardless of the merits of these criticisms, even its proponents would not dispute that, like PIMS, the Growth-Share Matrix is primarily suited to well-structured planning problems in which the basic definition of a business unit, product or competition is not an issue (Bowman and Asch, 1985). Unfortunately, because of the uncertain and rapidly changing nature of business today, such situations are becoming less and less common. This, to an extent, may account for the increase in the popularity of the next approach.

Matrices	External Factors	Internal Factors
Original BCG Matrix	Market growth	Relative market share
Industry Attractiveness– Business Strength Matrix	Overall industry attractiveness: • Critical structural factors • Five-forces model	Sources of competitive advantage: • Critical success factors • Value chain
Life-Cycle Matrix	Industry maturity	Overall measurement of business position
Alternative BCG Matrix	Ways to compete (opportunities for differentiation)	Size (sustainability) of competitive advantage
Profitability Matrix developed	Market growth potential Cost of capital	Profitability Cash generation

Figure 7.4 Main external and internal factors of matrices (adapted from Hax and Majluf, 1996: 302)

The scenario- or vision-building approach

As a way of overcoming some of the criticisms of the above quantitative approaches, scenario-building techniques emerged in the 1970s. The use of scenarios is based on the assumption that, in a rapidly changing and uncertain world, if you cannot predict the future, then by considering a range of possible futures, an organisation's strategic horizons can be broadened, managers can be opened up to new ideas and, perhaps, the right future can even be identified (Ringland, 1998). Scenarios allow organisations to exercise strategic choice in terms of whether to try shaping the future, adapting to the future or keeping their options open by investing in a range of products, technologies and markets (Courtney *et al*, 1997). Johnson and Scholes (2002: 107) define a scenario as:

> . . . *a detailed and plausible view of how the business environment of an organisation might develop in the future based on groupings of key environmental influences and drivers of change about which there is a high level of uncertainty.*

The rationale for the scenario approach is that it allows an organisation to carry out an intensive examination of its own unique and complex circumstances and needs, rather than attempting to fit itself to standard strategic planning tools such as PIMS and the Growth-Share Matrix (Linneman and Klein, 1979).

Kahn and Weiner (1978) defined a scenario as a hypothetical sequence of events constructed for the purpose of focusing attention on causal processes and decision points. For them, the purpose of scenarios is to display, in as dramatic and persuasive a fashion as possible, a number of possibilities for the future. To Norse (1979), scenarios are a means of improving our understanding of the long-term global, regional or national consequences of existing or potential trends or policies and their interaction. Essentially, therefore, building scenarios can be regarded as making different pictures of an uncertain future (business or otherwise) through the construction of case studies, either quantitatively or qualitatively (McNulty, 1977). The quantitative variant of scenario-building, sometimes called the hard method, uses mathematics, models and computers to make pictures of the future, through the production of a vast array of numbers and figures. The main approach, however, is the qualitative, or soft, method, which is essentially intuitive and descriptive; it is based on the resources of the human mind and derived from the methods of psychology and sociology (Joyce and Woods, 2001; Ringland, 1998).

The two main scenario-building approaches that have become well-established are the *Delphi method* and the *Cross Impact method*. However, in recent years, a third approach has become increasingly influential: *vision-building*. Though this bears some relation to other scenario-building techniques, it comes from a different tradition. The scenario approach and especially vision-building have some similarities with the postmodernist view that organisations exist in and represent multiple realities which compete with each other for supremacy (Joyce and Woods, 2001). From the postmodernist perspective, organisations have the ability to create their own reality and, therefore, both scenario- and vision-building can be viewed as processes that assist organisations, or the dominant group within an organisation, to select or construct the reality that most suits their needs. However, scenario- and vision-building are also compatible with the realist and complexity approaches described in Chapter 4. For realists, scenarios could provide a way of separating real constraints from the plethora of different perspectives that surround them; whereas for adherents of complexity, they can be used to locate the 'edge of chaos' and the order-generating rules necessary to maintain an organisation in this position.

One of the main functions of scenario-type approaches is that they enable organisations to question the very foundations of their existence, to examine the usefulness of their values and norms. Instead of asking how they can improve what they are doing, they begin to ask: Why are we doing this at all? What alternatives are there? This questioning of basic assumptions is something that is alien to the quantitative tools discussed above, especially given that most managers do not understand the assumptions built into such models in the first place. Indeed, quantitative models appear to remove the necessity for managers to think by providing them with 'answers' rather than information on which to base their own decisions (Hax and Majluf, 1996). The three main qualitative approaches, on the other hand, are designed specifically to make managers think radically about their organisation, its purpose and its future.

The Delphi method

This uses a panel of experts, who are interrogated about a number of future issues within their area of expertise. In the classic application, the interrogation is conducted under conditions where each respondent is unknown to the others, in order to avoid effects of authority and the development of a consensual bandwagon. After the initial round of interrogations, the results are reported to the panel and another round of interrogations is conducted. Several rounds may be carried out in this manner.

Results produced from these interrogations may be amenable to statistical treatment with a view to yielding numbers, dates and ranges from them. At the end of the process, depending on whether a quantitative or qualitative approach is taken, either a detailed numerical forecast of the future is obtained, or a more descriptive and richer picture. In both cases, the central tendencies of majority opinion and the range of minority disagreements will also be included (McNulty, 1977; Zentner, 1982).

The Cross Impact method

This is a variation to the Delphi method. It uses essentially the same interrogation method as the Delphi, i.e. a panel of experts; the difference, however, lies in what they are asked to do. The Delphi requires the experts to identify a number of future issues that they think will affect the organisation or business within their area of expertise. The Cross Impact method, on the other hand, asks its panel of experts to assign subjective probabilities and time priorities to a list of potential future events and developments supplied by the organisation. The emphasis is on identifying reinforcing or inhibiting events and trends, to uncover relationships and to indicate the importance of specific events. The accruing data from this exercise are used to create yield curves of the probabilities for each event as a function of time (Lanford, 1972).

Vision-building

As regular surveys by Bain & Co have shown, over the last decade or so, vision-building established itself as one of the key management tools (Rigby, 2001; Rigby and Bilodeau, 2007). Whilst it certainly bears a resemblance to the other scenario-building techniques, it is influenced more by Japanese management practices than by those in the West (Collins and Porras, 1991; Hamel and Prahalad, 1989). Though it is one of the most popular management tools, it is perhaps also one of the least understood and idiosyncratic (Cummings and Worley, 2001; Stacey, 1992). This is perhaps because it is a much less structured approach than the other two scenario-building techniques, and relies more on a company's own management. According to research by Collins and Porras (1997), compelling visions have two components:

- A core ideology which describes the organisation's core values and purpose; and
- A strong and bold vision of the organisation's future which identifies specific goals and changes.

The major elements of vision-building are as follows:

- The conception by a company's senior management team of an 'ideal' future state for their organisation;
- The identification of the organisation's mission, its rationale for existence;
- A clear statement of desired outcomes and the desired conditions and competences needed to achieve these.

Vision-building is an iterative process that is designed to move from the general (the vision) to the specific (desired outcomes and conditions), and back again. By going round the loop in this manner, according to Cummings and Huse (1989), an ambitious yet attainable future can be constructed and pursued. This owes much to the Japanese, who pioneered the concept of strategic intent on which vision-building is based. The work of Hamel and Prahalad (1989) is of particular importance in this respect. They argued that the strategic approach of Japanese companies is markedly different from that of their Western counterparts. Rather than attempting to lay down a detailed plan in advance, Japanese companies operate within a long-term framework of strategic intent. They create a vision of their desired future – their 'intent' – which they then pursue in a relentless but flexible manner. Hamel and Prahalad quote examples of leading Japanese companies who, in the 1960s, when they were insignificant in world terms, set out to dominate their markets:

- Honda's strategic intent was to be the 'Second Ford'.
- Komatsu's was to 'Encircle Caterpillar'.
- Canon's was to 'Beat Xerox'.

These companies then mobilised their resources towards achieving their individual strategic intent. In this, the prime resource they deployed was the commitment, ingenuity and flexibility of their workforces.

Like all approaches to strategic planning, these scenario-/vision-building approaches have many criticisms (Cummings and Worley, 2001; Fleisher and Bensoussan, 2003; Joyce and Woods, 2001; Keshavan and Rakesh, 1979; Porter, 1985; Wack, 1985; Whittington, 1993), the main ones being:

- They are prone to subjectivity and bias. The fact that any five management specialists can interpret the same situation in totally different ways is an oft-quoted example of this type of criticism.
- They can encourage retrospection. People's ideas of the future are informed by their knowledge and experience of the past. Since experience is not always the best teacher, scenarios and visions may be based on false assumptions.
- Participants can be strongly influenced in their preference of scenario by their own sectional and personal interests.
- The process cannot be carried out by novices and can, therefore, be time-consuming and expensive in terms of senior management time and outside experts.
- There is much debate about how many scenarios to construct and how they should be used.
- The more radical the vision or scenario, the more difficult it will be to get managers and others to commit to it.
- Visions often require strong visionary leaders, which are in short supply.

Despite these criticisms, the use of scenarios and visions now forms an important part of the managerial toolbox (Collins and Porras, 1997; Cummings and Worley, 2005; Hamel, 2007; Leemhuis, 1990; Rigby and Bilodeau, 2007).

In describing and discussing the main strategic planning tools, it is sometimes difficult to get a sense of how important businesses consider them to be. However, as Mini Case Study 7.6 shows, for those who run companies such as General Electric, buying and selling businesses, reviewing and renewing their portfolios, trying to assess future trends and when to move into and out of markets, lie at the core of what they do. It is not a once-a-year event but a continuous process of shaping and reshaping their organisations. They are not unaware of the weaknesses of strategic planning tools but they are reliant on them to aid decision-making. This is why organisations such as General Electric invest in the development and refinement of such tools. It is also why, despite the continuing popularity of quantitative tools and quantitative strategies, there has been a growth in more qualitative tools and techniques to match the increasing popularity of less prescriptive and more qualitative models of strategy (Rigby and Bilodeau, 2007).

Conclusions

Just as the aim of Chapter 6 was to examine the main approaches to understanding strategy, the aim of this chapter has been to examine the main approaches to applying strategy. The chapter began by describing the three main models of strategy which organisations have tended to utilise over the last 25 years: the Competitive Forces model, the Resource-Based model and the Strategic Conflict model. This was followed by an examination of the different organisational levels at which strategy is applied and the main forms of strategic planning tools on offer.

What the examination of these areas has shown is that, in the West at least, it is the approaches, tools and techniques of the Prescriptive stream of strategy that organisations have tended to favour. The continuing prominence of the Positioning school, through

Mini Case Study 7.6
Shaping and reshaping businesses

When some of the parts don't add up; conglomerates that thrive are ruthless in their scrutiny of when to shed beloved but worn-out assets

As Chris Zook, head of the global strategy practice at Bain, the management consultancy, says: 'Conglomerates tend to have around a third of their divisions in businesses they have no long-term logical reason to be in.'

Every month, the slide presentations arrive in Pam Daley's e-mail inbox. They come from each of General Electric's business leaders, offering updated lists of their leading candidates for acquisitions and partnerships. Initiated in 2001 by Jeffrey Immelt, chief executive, the process requires division heads to submit five of each, says Ms Daley, GE's senior vice-president of corporate business development. 'None of these guys can count to five', Ms Daley says. 'You get lists of 20 from some, which is exactly what you want if the opportunities are there.'

At GE, the process of adding to its portfolio of businesses is as stringent as the one that determines what is subtracted. The similarities reflect the fact that any company, even one with pockets as deep as GE, has only so much capital to invest. The business heads then travel to GE's Fairfield, Connecticut, headquarters for a meeting with the company's senior executives to discuss changes to their so-called pipeline list and, when necessary, seek Mr Immelt's blessing to enter negotiations or make a bid. Very few items escape Mr Immelt's radar, Ms Daley notes; managers need their boss's approval to pursue any deal worth more than $3m.

Then, after the business heads have made their pitches and left the room, Mr Immelt, Ms Daley and other corporate officers stay behind to discuss the other pipeline – those businesses GE thinks might be better off owned by another company. In his seven years at the helm, Mr Immelt has jettisoned more than $50bn in businesses. Gone are insurance, plastics and industrial supply, among others. 'This is a 130-year-old company, and it does evolve', Ms Daley says.

Source: Adapted from Justin Baer and Francesco Guerrera, *Financial Times*, 7 August 2008, p. 10.

---

the work of Michael Porter, clearly demonstrates the enduring influence of the Prescriptive stream. This of course should not be surprising. After all, the livelihood of those who make up the Prescriptive stream, whether they be consultants, consultancies, business schools or individual academics, is dependent to a large extent upon creating a market for its strategic planning products. It is also, probably, the case that when leading consultancies, business schools and large corporations are all arguing for a particular approach, there is enormous pressure on managers elsewhere to follow. To paraphrase the old slogan that 'no one ever got fired for buying IBM', one could also say, 'no one ever got fired for calling in the Boston Consultancy Group or Michael Porter'.

Yet, as this chapter has also shown, the Resource-Based model and the Strategic Conflict model have been growing in importance in the last two decades. Both tend to be located in and draw support from the Analytical stream of strategy. The Strategic Conflict model has its roots in the perspective of strategy as a battle between warring organisations. As explained, however, its renewed prominence has come both from practical concerns about the applicability of the Competitive Forces model, and from new theoretical insights from areas such as game theory. The Resource-Based approach, on the other hand, owes much to those, such as Prahalad and Hamel (1990), who have sought to understand and explain the Japanese approach to strategy. In both cases it can be seen that strategy is conceived of as an emergent rather than a planned process. Therefore, though the Prescriptive stream of strategy is still extremely influential in determining how managers develop and implement strategies, the influence of the Analytical stream is also growing.

To return, however, to the argument developed in Chapter 6, it would be wrong to fall into the trap of seeing the Analytical stream as being the 'right' way to apply strategy and the Prescriptive as the 'wrong' way, or vice versa. Instead, it may be that approaches from both the Prescriptive and Analytical streams have much to offer organisations, depending on their circumstances or constraints. For organisations with a dominant position in a relatively stable market, an approach from the Prescriptive stream, such as the Competitive Forces model, may be suitable. Likewise for organisations seeking to enter new markets or grow their business over a long time-frame, an approach from the Analytical stream, such as the Resource-Based model, has much to commend it. Similarly, in evenly balanced competitive situations, the Strategic Conflict model may be more appropriate. This is not, though, to propose a Contingency model of strategy. Rather, as was argued in Chapter 6, what is being suggested is that organisations have a choice; they can seek to influence or mould the constraints they face in order to make them more amenable to the type or model of strategy they wish to pursue. Therefore, as indicated earlier in this chapter when looking at the work of Miles and Snow (1978), the approach to strategy an organisation adopts may have less to do with the merits of the different models on offer and more to do with the type of organisation it is and the orientation of its managers.

Nevertheless, choosing the type or model of strategy to pursue is one thing; implementing it is an entirely different matter. This is especially so if one recognises that the Prescriptive and Analytical streams of strategy have distinctly different, indeed almost opposite, perspectives on implementation. For the former, implementation flows from the organisation's strategic plan. For the latter, the strategy emerges from and is given shape by the actions and decisions organisations make on a day-to-day basis to change and adapt themselves to their circumstances. But no matter which model of strategy one subscribes to, it is only when organisations implement changes that strategies come alive. This highlights the crucial importance of organisational change. Consequently, just as this chapter and the previous one have reviewed the main arguments with regard to strategy, so the next two chapters will review the strengths, weaknesses and implications of the main approaches to change management.

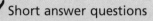

Test your learning

Short answer questions

1. What is the Competitive Forces model of strategy?

2. Define the Strategic Conflict model of strategy.

3. Briefly discuss the case for the Resource-Based model of strategy.

4. What are the three levels of strategic decision-making in organisations?

5. Give Miles and Snow's four strategic types of organisations.

6. Describe the BCG Growth-Share Matrix (Figure 7.3) and identify a company for each of the four squares.

7. What is the Scenario-/Vision-Building approach?

8. Briefly discuss the implications for organisational change of the following: (a) the PIMS model and (b) vision-building.

Essay questions

1. Contrast and compare the strengths and weaknesses of quantitative and qualitative strategic planning tools.

2. To what extent can vision-building be seen as a realist approach?

Suggested further reading

There are a vast number of books on strategy but, unfortunately, no one book covers all the main tools and techniques. However, the following three books, whilst leaning towards the Prescriptive approach, do cover the main strategic planning methods, techniques and processes.

1. Bensoussan, BE and Fleisher, CS (2008) *Analysis without Paralysis: 10 Tools to Make Better Strategic Decisions*. Financial Times Prentice Hall: Harlow.

2. Grant, RM (2007) *Contemporary Strategy Analysis: Concepts, Techniques and Applications* (4th edition). Blackwell: Oxford.

3. Joyce, P and Woods, A (2001) *Strategic Management: A Fresh Approach to Developing Skills, Knowledge and Creativity*. Kogan Page: London.

Process Control Inc.

BACKGROUND

Process Control Inc (PCI) is the European manufacturing arm of an American conglomerate. Its present operation came into being in 1979, through a merger with a subsidiary of a British-owned electronics company. PCI specialises in the assembly of printed circuit boards (PCBs) and process control equipment. It produces over 95 per cent of the conglomerate's total PCB needs, and has a staff of 395.

In recent years, with a rapid expansion of PCB assembly, the company began to experience major operational problems relating to quality and delivery. This in turn caused increasing difficulties for the parent company in the USA, which found its own deliveries and quality suffering as a consequence. Despite efforts by PCI, its performance was worsened rather than improved and a large proportion of its target completion dates could not be met. Similarly, its quality problems worsened.

As a consequence, the parent company sacked the plant's British CEO and replaced him with an American who was to be seconded to PCI for a one- to two-year period. This came as a shock not only to the CEO but also to the entire workforce. There was widespread feeling, at all levels in the company, that he had been treated shabbily, especially given that he had been with the company, in its various forms, for 25 years. This shock was compounded by the character of the new CEO. He was a colourful and flamboyant person who wore a Mickey Mouse watch, dressed as Father Christmas and the Easter Bunny at the appropriate time of the year, and was given to public soul-searching.

In his first three months, the Chief Executive flattened the management hierarchy. The previous CEO had only three managers reporting directly to him, with a further tier of eight managers reporting to them. The new CEO combined these two layers and created a new 11-person management team responsible to him. This levelling-up created some resentment amongst the original three team members, which was compounded when two of them were told to switch jobs with their former subordinates. Indeed, at one point there was talk that these managers might resign.

DEVELOPING A STRATEGY

After six months, when these changes had failed to improve the company's performance, the CEO In organised a weekend-long, off-site management seminar. This was led by an outside facilitator and was, the CEO said, about soul-searching and team-building. At the end of this, he felt that the weekend was a turning-point in the organisation's fortunes. Not only did they emerge as a more coherent and committed team, but they also came up with the bones of a Strategic Plan which they saw as the solution necessary to pull the organisation out of its predicament. According to the CEO, who introduced the concept and continued to be its main champion, the initial reaction of the management team to the idea of developing a manufacturing strategy was: 'Yes, we need to do planning but Jesus!, we are in a deep mess, we don't have time to do it'. The CEO said that, 'in the end, I had to force the idea of strategic planning on the organisation'. The vision produced by the management team was:

▶

CASE STUDY 7 CONT.

To empower the organisation to be a world-class manufacturing unit and thereby achieve customer delight.

Throughout the summer, the management team and various sub-groups met to develop and approve the elements of the manufacturing strategy. However, whilst some maintained their original enthusiasm, others became more sceptical. Some managers felt the process was being rushed, and that as a consequence the time available for thinking through and discussing the proposals was limited. The sub-groups did not have the time to meet and the chairman of each group wrote the plans with little input from others. Notwithstanding this, by September, the complete strategy was agreed by the management team, along with the priorities and timetables for the next 12 months.

The CEO then organised a meeting of all supervisory and middle management staff to brief them on the strategy and to attempt to involve them. This was not particularly successful. The main reason for this was the sheer volume of information presented. Therefore, a second meeting was organised. The problem, however, with both meetings was that because the organisation was under pressure for quick results to turn its fortunes around, much of the time was spent on the action required to achieve the plan, rather than taking enough time to explain the rationale underlying the plan and what the outcomes would mean for the workforce. It was left to the members of the management team to explain these to their own subordinates. However, some of the managers themselves were unclear or in need of convincing of the merits of the proposed changes. Consequently, rather than giving reassurance, these briefings had the opposite effect – especially when staff compared what different managers were saying. Also, the trade union, usually very supportive of the company, complained about 'the looming prospects of redundancy'. There was also a fear among the supervisors and middle managers about their future in the plant, because the plans involved structural changes which would result in the removal of some of their posts.

The management team's response was to introduce a series of weekend and lunch-break meetings aimed at educating the workforce. These were able to calm some of the fears but, overall, they could not fully come to grips with people's worries, because most of the meetings (especially the plant-wide monthly lunch-break meetings) were too large, and so personal concerns and sensitive questions were not even asked, let alone discussed in the open.

Nevertheless, by December elements of the strategy were being implemented. However, there was still much to do both in implementing what had been decided and in clarifying what the new organisational structure should look like. Indeed, the question of structure emerged as the main issue of uncertainty and contention in the management team. Though the CEO said he was clear about the new structure, the rest of his team were not. Despite this, the CEO pushed ahead with a plan to create 'mini' factories within a new matrix-type structure. This clearly demonstrated the growing gap between the CEO and his team – even those who supported him. The gap was particularly obvious amongst those managers who controlled support functions such as quality, purchasing and production control, because they felt their specialism would be dismembered and career prospects threatened.

ALL CHANGE

In the week before Christmas, all this was thrown into confusion when the CEO announced he was leaving. He had been offered, and had accepted the chance to take over a more important plant in the company's portfolio in the USA. It was not clear who would take over – though there had been an undercurrent of fighting for succession in the management team all along, especially between the Production Manager and the Materials Manager. It was announced that there would be a delay before a new, permanent, CEO could be appointed and that an interim, part-time CEO would take over. However, he could only make intermittent visits to PCI and the management team were mainly left to their own devices. Most of the management team were content to await the appointment of the permanent CEO rather than continuing with the more controversial elements of the strategy. However, the Production Manager, who had been won over by the previous CEO's ideas, and who saw himself as a potential successor, began to push the strategy very strongly. This was quickly put down by the rest of the team through non-cooperation. Most managers reverted to their former state of dealing with the day-to-day running of the plant, and the strategy, which was of top priority a few weeks previously, now came to play a secondary role.

After 12 months without an on-site or full-time CEO, it was announced the Materials Manager would be the new CEO. This news was welcomed by most people, though the Production Manager was extremely upset at being passed over. The new CEO surprised most of his colleagues by declaring that he wanted to resuscitate the strategy. This was partly as an olive branch to the Production Manager and partly because he recognised that the company was still underperforming in major areas. The CEO decided to present the strategic plan to his superiors in the USA in order to get their backing and improve its chances of being

accepted in PCI. However, the outcome was not what he expected. His superiors liked the plan but were doubtful of PCI's ability to implement it. Instead, they gave the CEO three months to evaluate the following options and make a recommendation of which one to adopt:

1. Close the plant entirely and contract out all the work to the Far East.
2. Subcontract out the manufacture of PCBs to the Far East and leave a much-reduced PCI responsible for some managerial functions and the assembly of certain larger systems.
3. Convince his superiors that PCI could overcome its difficulties.

The CEO was left in no doubt that his superiors were sceptical about the third option or that his own future with the company would depend not only on which option he recommended but also on whether it was successful in achieving the company's targets. However, they did concede that they had no hard evidence that firms in the Far East were equipped to do a better job than PCI.

Questions

1. Analyse the case study from the perspectives of the Prescriptive and Analytical streams of strategy. Which perspective, if any, offers the best insight into PCI's failure to implement its strategy?

2. Imagine that you are consultant for Prescriptive Strategy Inc. What advice would you offer the CEO in terms of how he should evaluate and decide upon the three options?

3. Imagine that you are consultant for Analytical Strategy Inc. What advice would you offer the CEO in terms of how he should evaluate and decide upon the three options?

CHAPTER 8

Approaches to change management

Mini Case Study 8.1
The importance of people

Culture is key to CPA professional development

A notable culture of development at Plante and Moran, one of the largest US accountancy and business advice firms, is a result of the degree in philosophy held by Frank Moran, one of the firm's founders. He spent a lot of time in the 1950s in conversation with Professor Harry Levinson, Harvard Business School's groundbreaking management psychologist. 'He brought a real understanding of human psychology in the workplace', says Richard Brehler, the firm's training and education director. Mr Moran had a vision of a firm renowned for its service to clients, and for the working environment it could offer certified public accountants. He introduced the team concept, where each partner is responsible for the professional development and retention of six to 10 professionals, who may never work on an audit for them. The partner keeps them on track, gives them feedback where they need to improve, makes sure they get the right experiences and supervises their progress through professional development.

New joiners are also assigned a 'buddy' who has been at the firm a year or two and is responsible for their introduction to the firm. 'They teach them the ropes in getting on in engagements and make sure they are introduced to the right people', says Mr Brehler. 'They also provide informal "off-the-job" training and advice.'

The firm's investment of time and energy in its staff raises their morale, reduces turnover and improves teamwork. This makes for happier clients and an improved bottom line, which allows the company to further invest in its staff. 'We believe in "tending the orchard" by paying attention to the growth and long-term legacy of the firm, not just immediate profitability', says Mr Brehler. 'We average a 12 per cent staff turnover rate, against 25–30 per cent in our industry. Clients like to see the same faces turning up to do their audit each year.'

The biggest challenge is the impact on staff development of automated paperless audit procedures and review. These reduce much of the human contact. 'Years ago audit teams sat across the table around the ledger sheets and had a lot of time for informal discussions, question and dialogue', says Mr Brehler, 'but these inherent learning opportunities have disappeared. If people are not free to ask the dumb question, to expose their ignorance or to enquire, then their development is at risk.' Mr Brehler says that all CPA firms he talks to are facing the same challenges. 'We have an advantage', he says, 'because we don't have to engender a culture of learning and professional exchange, as we have always focused on it.'

Source: Rod Newing, *Financial Times*, 12 November 2007, p. 2.

Introduction

This chapter follows on from the discussion of strategy in the two previous chapters. Chapters 6 and 7 were essentially concerned with approaches to determining and charting an organisation's strategic direction. Underpinning both chapters was the division between the Prescriptive stream of strategy, whose members seek to tell organisations how they should formulate strategy, and the Analytical stream of strategy, whose members seek to understand what organisations actually do to formulate strategy. The former tend to see strategy as a formal, rational and pre-planned process. The latter tend to see strategy as a more messy, less rational, emergent process. Therefore, for the Prescriptive stream, organisational change flows from, and is concerned with implementing, an organisation's predetermined strategy. For the Analytical stream, organisational change is not an outcome of strategy but the process by which it is created and given form. For both streams, change management is vitally important, whether it be for strategy implementation or development.

Consequently, this and the next two chapters will focus on understanding and categorising the main approaches to planning and implementing the changes required to achieve, or shape, strategic objectives. As has been shown in previous chapters, there is now a wide recognition that this is not a technical or quantitative exercise but that successful change is dependent on what Douglas McGregor (1960) referred to, in the title of his famous book, as *The Human Side of Enterprise*. This was something that Plante and Moran recognised over 50 years ago (*see* Mini Case Study 8.1). From its foundation, the company began to apply 'human psychology to the workplace'. This is why they are not only a financially successful company but also regularly appear in the *Fortune* list of 100 best companies to work for. As *Fortune* (2007) commented, what makes Plante and Moran such a great company is '[An] Extraordinary employee-centric culture [which] goes back more than 50 years'.

The core of this chapter is the exploration of Planned change, which focuses on developing the human side of organisations, and whose founder, Kurt Lewin, was a key influence on McGregor's work. The chapter begins by describing the theoretical foundations of change management. In particular, it is shown that the three main schools of thought that underpin approaches to change management can be distinguished by their respective concentration on individual, group and organisation-wide issues. This leads on to the examination of the Planned approach to change. It is shown how, from its development by Kurt Lewin in the 1940s, this approach, under the umbrella of Organization Development, dominated both the theory and practice of change management from then until the 1980s. From the early 1980s onwards, it met with increasing levels of criticism, from both those questioning its suitability for organisations operating in dynamic and unpredictable environments, and those who believed that Organization Development had lost its sense of direction and purpose.

The review of Planned change and Organization Development is followed by a description of the Incremental, Punctuated Equilibrium and Continuous Transformation models of change. The chapter concludes by arguing that, though some of the criticism may be unjustified, the Planned approach does appear to be more suited to incremental change than larger-scale and more radical change initiatives.

Theoretical foundations

Change management is not a distinct discipline with rigid and clearly defined boundaries. Rather, the theory and practice of change management draw on a number of social science disciplines and traditions. Though this is one of its strengths, it does make the task of tracing its origins and defining its core concepts more difficult than might otherwise be the case.

The task is complicated further by the simple fact that the social sciences themselves are interwoven. As an example, theories of management education and learning, which help us to understand the behaviour of those who manage change, cannot be fully discussed without reference to theories of child and adult psychology. Neither can these be discussed without touching on theories of knowledge (epistemology), which is itself a veritable philosophical minefield.

The challenge, then, is to range wide enough to capture the theoretical foundations of change management, without straying so far into its related disciplines that clarity and understanding suffer. In order to achieve this delicate balance, the examination will be limited to the three schools of thought that form the central planks on which change management theory stands:

- the Individual Perspective school;
- the Group Dynamics school;
- the Open Systems school.

The Individual Perspective school

The supporters of this school are split into two camps: the Behaviourists and the Gestalt-Field psychologists. The former view behaviour as resulting from an individual's interaction with their environment. Gestalt-Field psychologists, on the other hand, believe that this is only a partial explanation. Instead, they argue that an individual's behaviour is the product of environment and reason.

In Behaviourist theory, all behaviour is learned; the individual is the passive recipient of external and objective data. Among the earliest to work in the field of conditioning of behaviour was Pavlov (1927). In an experiment that has now passed into folklore, he discovered that a dog could be 'taught' to salivate at the ringing of a bell, by conditioning the dog to associate the sound of the bell with food. Arising from this, one of the basic principles of the Behaviourists is that human actions are conditioned by their expected consequences. Behaviour that is rewarded tends to be repeated, and behaviour that is ignored tends not to be. Therefore, in order to change behaviour, it is necessary to change the conditions that cause it (Skinner, 1974).

In practice, behaviour modification involves the manipulation of reinforcing stimuli so as to reward desired activity. The aim is to reward immediately all instances of the wanted behaviour, but to ignore all instances of the unwanted behaviour (because even negative recognition can act as a reinforcer). This is based on the principle of extinction; a behaviour will stop eventually if it is not rewarded (Lovell, 1980). Not surprisingly, given the period when it emerged, the Behaviourist approach mirrors in many respects that of the Classical school, portraying humans as cogs in a machine, who respond solely to external stimuli.

For Gestalt-Field theorists, learning is a process of gaining or changing insights, outlooks, expectations or thought patterns. In explaining an individual's behaviour, this group takes into account not only a person's actions and the responses these elicit, but also the interpretation the individual places on these. As French and Bell (1984: 140) explain:

> Gestalt therapy is based on the belief that persons function as whole, total organisms. And each person possesses positive and negative characteristics that must be 'owned up to' and permitted expression. People get into trouble when they get fragmented, when they do not accept their total selves . . . Basically, one must come to terms with oneself, . . . must stop blocking off awareness, authenticity, and the like by dysfunctional behaviours.

Therefore, from the Gestalt-Field perspective, behaviour is not just a product of external stimuli; rather it arises from how the individual uses reason to interpret these stimuli. Consequently, the Gestalt-Field proponents seek to help individual members of an organisation change their understanding of themselves and the situation in question, which in turn, they believe, will lead to changes in behaviour (Smith *et al*, 1982). The Behaviourists, on the other hand, seek to achieve organisational change solely by modifying the external stimuli acting upon the individual.

Both groups in the Individual Perspective school have proved influential in the management of change; indeed, some writers even advocate using them in tandem. This is certainly the case with advocates of the Culture–Excellence school, who recommend the use of both strong individual incentives (external stimuli) and discussion, involvement and debate (internal reflection) in order to bring about organisational change (*see* Chapter 3).

This combining of extrinsic and intrinsic motivators owes much to the work of the Human Relations movement, which (especially through the work of Maslow, 1943) stresses the need for both forms of stimuli in order to influence human behaviour. Though acknowledging the role of the individual, however, the Human Relations movement also draws attention to the importance of social groups in organisations, as do the Group Dynamics school.

The Group Dynamics school

As a component of change theory, this school has the longest history (Schein, 1969) and, as will be shown later in this chapter, it originated with the work of Kurt Lewin. Its emphasis is on bringing about organisational change through teams or work groups, rather than individuals (Bernstein, 1968). The rationale behind this, according to Lewin (1947a, 1947b), is that because people in organisations work in groups, individual behaviour must be seen, modified or changed in the light of groups' prevailing practices and norms.

Lewin (1947a, 1947b) postulated that group behaviour is an intricate set of symbolic interactions and forces that not only affect group structures, but also modify individual behaviour. Therefore, he argued that individual behaviour is a function of the group environment or 'field', as he termed it. This field produces forces, tensions, emanating from group pressures on each of its members. An individual's behaviour at any given time, according to Lewin, is an interplay between the intensity and valence (whether the force is positive or negative) of the forces impinging on the person. Because of this, he asserted that a group is never in a 'steady state of equilibrium', but is in a continuous process of mutual adaptation which he termed 'quasi-stationary equilibrium'.

To bring about change, therefore, it is useless to concentrate on changing the behaviour of individuals, according to the Group Dynamics school. The individual in isolation is constrained by group pressures to conform. The focus of change must be at the group level and should concentrate on influencing and changing the group's norms, roles and values (Cummings and Worley, 2005; French and Bell, 1999; Smith *et al*, 1982).

Norms are rules or standards that define what people should do, think or feel in a given situation. For the Group Dynamics school, what is important in analysing group norms is the difference between implicit and explicit norms. Explicit norms are formal, written rules which are known by, and applicable to, all. Implicit norms are informal and unwritten, and individuals may not even be consciously aware of them. Nevertheless, implicit norms have been identified as playing a vital role in dictating the actions of group members.

Roles are patterns of behaviour to which individuals and groups are expected to conform. In organisational terms, roles are formally defined by job descriptions and performance targets, though in practice they are also strongly influenced by norms and values as well. Even in their work life, individuals rarely have only one role. For example, a production manager may also be secretary of the company's social club, a clerical officer may also be a shop steward, and a supervisor may also be the company's safety representative. A similar situation exists for groups. A group's main role may be to perform a particular activity or service, but it might also be expected to pursue continuous development, maintain and develop its skills, and act as a repository of expert knowledge for others in the organisation. Clearly, where members of a group and the group itself are required to conform to a number of different roles, the scope for role conflict or role ambiguity is ever-present. Unless roles are both clearly defined and compatible, the result can be sub-optimal for the individual (in terms of stress) and for the group (in terms of lack of cohesion and poor performance).

Values are ideas and beliefs that individuals and groups hold about what is right and wrong. Values refer not so much to what people do or think or feel in a given situation; instead they relate to the broader principles that lie behind these. Values are a more problematic concept than either norms or roles. Norms and roles can, with diligence, be more or less accurately determined. Values, on the other hand, are more difficult to determine because group members are not always consciously aware of, or can easily articulate, the values that influence their behaviour. Therefore, questioning people and observing their actions is unlikely to produce a true picture of group values. Nevertheless, the concept itself is seen as very important in determining, and changing, patterns of behaviour.

The Group Dynamics school has proved to be very influential in developing both the theory and practice of change management. This can be seen by the very fact that it is now usual for organisations to view themselves as comprising groups and teams, rather than merely collections of individuals (Mullins, 1989).

As French and Bell (1984: 127–9) pointed out, the importance given to teams is reflected in the fact that:

> . . . *the most important single group of interventions in OD [Organization Development] are team-building activities, the goals of which are the improved and increased effectiveness of various teams within the organization. . . . The . . . team-building meeting has the goal of improving the team's effectiveness through better management of task demands, relationship demands, and group processes. . . . [The team] analyzes its way of doing things, and attempts to develop strategies to improve its operation.*

In so doing, norms, roles and values are examined, challenged and, where necessary, changed.

Nevertheless, despite the emphasis that many place on groups within organisations, others argue that the correct approach is one that deals with an organisation as a whole.

The Open Systems school

Having examined approaches to change that emphasise the importance of groups and individuals, we now come to one whose primary point of reference is the organisation in its entirety. The Open Systems school (as mentioned in Chapter 2) sees organisations as composed of a number of interconnected sub-systems. It follows that any change to one part of the system will have an impact on other parts of the system, and, in turn, on its overall performance (Scott, 1987). The Open Systems school's approach to change is based on a method of describing and evaluating these sub-systems, in order to determine how they need to be changed so as to improve the overall functioning of the organisation.

This school does not just see organisations as systems in isolation, however; they are 'open' systems. Organisations are seen as open in two respects. Firstly, they are open to, and interact with, their external environment. Secondly, they are open internally: the various sub-systems interact with each other. Therefore, internal changes in one area affect other areas, and in turn have an impact on the external environment, and vice versa (Buckley, 1968).

The objective of the Open Systems approach is to structure the functions of a business in such a manner that, through clearly defined lines of coordination and interdependence, the overall business objectives are collectively pursued. The emphasis is on achieving overall synergy, rather than on optimising the performance of any one individual part *per se* (Mullins, 1989).

Miller (1967) argues that there are four principal organisational sub-systems:

- **The organisational goals and values sub-system.** This comprises the organisation's stated objectives and the values it wishes to promote in order to attain them. To operate effectively, the organisation has to ensure that its goals and values are compatible not only with each other, but also with its external and internal environments.
- **The technical sub-system.** This is the specific combination of knowledge, techniques and technologies which an organisation requires in order to function. Once again, the concern here is with the compatibility and appropriateness of these in relation to an organisation's particular circumstances.
- **The psychosocial sub-system.** This is also variously referred to as organisational climate and organisational culture. In essence, it is the fabric of role relationships, values and norms that binds people together and makes them citizens of a particular miniature society (the organisation). It is influenced by an organisation's environment, history and employees, as well as its tasks, technology and structures. If the psychosocial sub-system is weak, fragmented or inappropriate, then instead of binding the organisation together, it may have the opposite effect.
- **The managerial sub-system.** This spans the entire organisation. It is responsible for relating an organisation to its environment, setting goals, determining values, developing comprehensive strategic and operational plans, designing structure and establishing control processes. It is this sub-system that has the responsibility for consciously directing an organisation and ensuring that it attains its objectives. If the managerial sub-system fails, so does the rest of an organisation.

The Open Systems school is concerned with understanding organisations in their entirety; therefore, it attempts to take a holistic rather than a particularistic perspective. This is reflected in its approach to change. According to Burke (1980), this is informed by three factors:

1. Sub-systems are interdependent. If alterations are made to one part of an organisation without taking account of its dependence or impact on the rest of the organisation, the outcome may be sub-optimal.

2. Training, as a mechanism for change, is unlikely to succeed on its own. This is because it concentrates on the individual and not the organisational level. As Burke (1980: 75) argues, 'although training may lead to individual change and in some cases to small group change, there is scant evidence that attempting to change the individual will in turn change the organisation'.

3. In order to be successful, organisations have to tap and direct the energy and talent of their workforce. This requires the removal of obstacles which prevent this, and the provision of positive reinforcement which promotes it. Given that this is likely to require changes to such things as norms, reward systems and work structures, it must be approached from an organisational, rather than an individual or group, perspective.

Though the Open Systems perspective has attracted much praise, attention has also been drawn to its alleged shortcomings. Butler (1985: 345), for example, while hailing it as a major step forward in understanding organisational change, points out that, 'Social systems are extremely dynamic and complex entities that often defy descriptions and analysis. Therefore, one can easily get lost in attempting to sort out all the cause-and-effect relationships.' Beach (1980: 138), in a similar vein, argues that Open Systems theory:

> . . . does not comprise a consistent, articulated, coherent theory. Much of it constitutes a high level of abstraction. To be really useful to the professional practice of management, its spokesmen and leaders must move to a more concrete and operationally useful range.

Despite these criticisms, the level of support for this approach, from eminent theorists such as Burns and Stalker (1961), Joan Woodward (1965) and Lawrence and Lorsch (1967), is formidable. This is why, as explained in Chapter 2, it has proved so influential.

Summary

In looking at the three schools that form the central planks of change management theory, four major points stand out:

- Firstly, with the exception of the Behaviourists, not only do these schools of thought stand, generally, in sharp contrast to the mechanistic approach of the Classical school towards organisations and people, but also, in their approach to individuals, groups and organisations as a whole, form a link to the emerging organisational paradigms that were discussed in Chapter 3. Indeed, it might be possible to go further and say that these three schools provide many of the core concepts of the new paradigms, especially in respect to teamwork and organisational learning. If this is so, the claim (by Kanter, 1989; Senge, 1990; and others) that these new forms of organisation are a radical break with the past may have to be reconsidered.
- Secondly, the three theoretical perspectives on change focus on different aspects of organisational life and, therefore, each has different implications for what type of change takes place and how it is managed. It follows that any approach to managing change should be judged by whether or not it is applicable to all or only some of the types of change covered by the Individual Perspective, Group Dynamics and Open Systems schools.

- Thirdly, though each school puts itself forward as the most effective, if not the only, approach to change, they are not necessarily in conflict or competition. Indeed, it could well be argued that they are complementary approaches. The key task, which will be examined in more detail later in this and the next two chapters, is to identify the circumstances in which each is appropriate: does the problem or the objective of change lie at the level of the organisation, group or individual? Can any of these levels be tackled in isolation from the others?

- Lastly, the Open Systems perspective has a valid point in claiming that change at one level or in one area should take into account the effect it will have elsewhere in the organisation, and vice versa. However, whether the perspective adopted is organisation-wide, or limited to groups and individuals, in the final analysis, what is it that is being changed? The answer, surely, is the behaviour of individuals and groups, because organisations are, as the proponents of these perspectives admit, social systems. To change anything requires the cooperation and consent, or at least acquiescence, of the groups and individuals that make up an organisation, for it is only through their behaviour that the structures, technologies, systems and procedures of an organisation move from being abstract concepts to concrete realities. This is made even plainer in the remainder of this chapter and in the next two chapters, where we examine the main approaches to managing organisational change.

The Planned approach: from Lewin to Organization Development (OD)

Change has always been a feature of organisational life, though many argue that the frequency and magnitude of change are greater now than ever before (IBM, 2008). Planned change is a term first coined by Kurt Lewin to distinguish change that was consciously embarked upon by an organisation, as opposed to unintended changes such as those that might come about by accident, by impulse, by misunderstanding or that might be forced on an unwilling organisation (Marrow, 1969). Therefore, 'Planned', in this case, does not mean that someone sits down in advance and writes a plan detailing what will take place, when and how. Rather, it means that the organisation identifies an area where it believes change is required and undertakes a process to evaluate and, if necessary, bring about change.

Just as the practice of change management is dependent on a number of factors, not least the particular school of thought involved, so, not surprisingly, even amongst those advocating Planned change, a variety of different models of change management have arisen over the years. Though these were devised to meet the needs of particular organisations, or arose from a specific school of thought, the Planned approach to change is now most closely associated with the practice of Organization Development (OD) and indeed lies at its core. According to French and Bell (1995: 1–2):

Organization development is a unique organizational improvement strategy that emerged in the late 1950s and early 1960s. . . . [It] has evolved into an integrated framework of theories and practices capable of solving or helping to solve most of the important problems confronting the human side of organizations. Organization development is about people and organizations and people in organizations and how they function. OD is also about planned change, that is getting individuals, teams and organizations to function better. Planned change involves common sense, hard work applied diligently over time, a systematic, goal-oriented approach, and valid knowledge about organizational dynamics and how to change them. Valid knowledge derives from the behavioral sciences such as psychology, social psychology, sociology, anthropology, systems theory, and the practice of management.

As Cummings and Worley (2005) observe, OD evolved from five main developments:

- The growth of the National Training Laboratory (NTL);
- Action Research/Survey Feedback;
- Participative Management;
- Quality of Working Life;
- Strategic Change.

Cummings and Worley state that the first three developments derived from work by Kurt Lewin on Planned change in the 1940s, whilst the last two did not emerge until the 1960s and 1970s. Therefore, as Burnes (2007) points out, the foundations of OD clearly rest on Lewin's work on Planned change. However, Lewin did not just provide OD with a range of tools, techniques and approaches; he also imbued it with his democratic–humanist values. Underpinning OD is a set of values, assumptions and ethics that emphasise its humanistic orientation and its commitment to organisational effectiveness. These values have been articulated by many writers over the years (Conner, 1977; French and Bell, 1999; Gellerman *et al*, 1990; Warwick and Thompson, 1980). One of the earliest attempts was by French and Bell (1973), who proposed four core values for OD (*see* Ideas and perspectives 8.1).

In a survey of OD practitioners, Hurley *et al* (1992) found these values were clearly reflected in the five main approaches they used in their work:

1. empowering employees to act;
2. creating openness in communications;
3. facilitating ownership of the change process and its outcomes;
4. the promotion of a culture of collaboration; and
5. the promotion of continuous learning.

Ideas and perspectives 8.1
French and Bell's core values of OD

- The belief that the needs and aspirations of human beings provide the prime reasons for the existence of organisations within society.
- Change agents believe that organisational prioritisation is a legitimate part of organisational culture.
- Change agents are committed to increased organisational effectiveness.
- OD places a high value on the democratisation of organisations through power equalisation.

Source: French and Bell (1973)

Within the OD field, there are a number of major theorists and practitioners who have contributed their own models and techniques to its advancement (e.g. Argyris, 1962; Beckhard, 1969; Blake and Mouton, 1976; French and Bell, 1973). OD also shares some concepts with, and sits easily alongside, the Human Relations movement. Indeed, Douglas McGregor, a key figure in the Human Relations movement, also played a significant role in the early stages of OD (*see* McGregor, 1967). However, despite this, there is general agreement that the OD movement grew out of, and became the standard bearer for, Kurt Lewin's pioneering work on behavioural science in general, and his development of Planned change in particular (Burnes, 2007; Cummings and Worley, 1997).

Kurt Lewin and Planned change

Though there has been a tendency since the 1980s to play down the significance of his work for contemporary organisations, few social scientists can have received the level of praise and admiration that has been heaped upon Kurt Lewin (Ash, 1992; Bargal *et al*, 1992; Dent and Goldberg, 1999; Dickens and Watkins, 1999; Tobach, 1994). As Edgar Schein (1988: 239) enthusiastically commented:

> *There is little question that the intellectual father of contemporary theories of applied behavioral science, action research and planned change is Kurt Lewin. His seminal work on leadership style and the experiments on planned change which took place in World War II in an effort to change consumer behavior launched a whole generation of research in group dynamics and the implementation of change programs.*

For most of his life, Lewin's main preoccupation was the resolution of social conflict and, in particular, the problems of minority or disadvantaged groups. Underpinning this preoccupation was a strong belief that only the permeation of democratic values into all facets of society could prevent the worst extremes of social conflict. As his wife wrote in the Preface to a volume of his collected work published after his death:

> *Kurt Lewin was so constantly and predominantly preoccupied with the task of advancing the conceptual representation of the social-psychological world, and at the same time he was so filled with the urgent desire to use his theoretical insight for the building of a better world, that it is difficult to decide which of these two sources of motivation flowed with greater energy or vigour.* (GW Lewin, 1948b)

To a large extent, his interests and beliefs stemmed from his background as a German Jew. Lewin was born in 1890 and, for a Jew growing up in Germany, at this time, officially approved anti-Semitism was a fact of life. Few Jews could expect to achieve a responsible post in the civil service or universities. Despite this, Lewin was awarded a doctorate at the University of Berlin in 1916 and went on to teach there. Though he was never awarded tenured status, Lewin achieved a growing international reputation in the 1920s as a leader in his field (Lewin, 1992). However, with the rise of the Nazi Party, Lewin recognised that the position of Jews in Germany was increasingly threatened. The election of Hitler as Chancellor in 1933 was the final straw for him; he resigned from the University and moved to America (Marrow, 1969).

In America, Lewin found a job first as a 'refugee scholar' at Cornell University and then, from 1935 to 1945, at the University of Iowa. Here he was to embark on an ambitious programme of research, which covered topics such as child–parent relations, conflict in marriage, styles of leadership, worker motivation and performance, conflict in industry, group problem-solving, communication and attitude change, racism, anti-Semitism, anti-racism, discrimination and prejudice, integration–segregation, peace, war and poverty (Bargal *et al*, 1992; Cartwright, 1952; Lewin, 1948a). As Cooke (1999) notes, given the prevalence of racism and anti-Semitism in America at the time, much of this work, especially his increasingly public advocacy in support of disadvantaged groups, put Lewin on the political left.

During the years of the Second World War, Lewin did much work for the American war effort. This included studies of the morale of front-line troops and psychological warfare, and his famous study aimed at persuading American housewives to buy cheaper cuts of meat (Lewin, 1943a; Marrow, 1969). He was also much in demand as a speaker on minority and inter-group relations (Smith, 2001). These activities chimed with one of his central preoccupations, which was how Germany's authoritarian and racist culture could be replaced with one imbued with democratic values. He saw democracy, and the spread of democratic values throughout society, as the central bastion against authoritarianism and despotism. That he viewed the establishment of democracy as a major task, and avoided simplistic and structural recipes, can be gleaned from the following extracts from his article on 'The special case of Germany' (Lewin, 1943b):

> *. . . Nazi culture . . . is deeply rooted, particularly in the youth on whom the future depends. It is a culture which is centred around power as the supreme value and which denounces justice and equality . . .* (p. 43)

> *To be stable, a cultural change has to penetrate all aspects of a nation's life. The change must, in short, be a change in the 'cultural atmosphere', not merely a change of a single item.* (p. 46)

> *Change in culture requires the change of leadership forms in every walk of life. At the start, particularly important is leadership in those social areas which are fundamental from the point of view of power.* (p. 55)

With the end of the War, Lewin established the Research Center for Group Dynamics at the Massachusetts Institute of Technology. The aim of the Center was to investigate all aspects of group behaviour, especially how it could be changed. At the same time, he was also chief architect of the Commission on Community Interrelations (CCI). Founded and funded by the American Jewish Congress, its aim was the eradication of discrimination against all minority groups. As Lewin wrote at the time:

> *We Jews will have to fight for ourselves and we will do so strongly and with good conscience. We also know that the fight of the Jews is part of the fight of all minorities for democratic equality of rights and opportunities . . .*
>
> (Quoted in Marrow, 1969: 175)

In pursuing this objective, Lewin believed that his work on Group Dynamics and Action Research would provide the key tools for the CCI.

Lewin also had links with and provided part of the intellectual basis for the Tavistock Institute in the UK and its journal, *Human Relations* (Jaques, 1998; Marrow, 1969). In addition, in 1946, the Connecticut State Inter-Racial Commission asked Lewin to help train leaders and conduct research on the most effective means of combating racial and religious prejudice in communities. This led to the development of sensitivity training and the creation, in 1947, of the now famous National Training Laboratories. However, his huge workload took its toll on his health, and on 11 February 1947 he died of a heart attack (Lewin, 1992).

The key projects and events which contributed to the development of Planned change and laid the foundations of OD can be seen in Ideas and perspectives 8.2. What this shows is not just the range of studies that Lewin was involved in, but also the importance of his work with the Harwood Manufacturing Corporation. As Dent (2002) commented on the work conducted at Harwood:

> . . . although this comprehensive effort is much less well-known than the Hawthorne studies, the research which came out of it has perhaps had a greater impact on group decision-making processes, self-management, leadership development, meeting management, stereotyping and resistance to change, among others.

Burnes (2007) also shows that the Harwood studies constitute a milestone in the study of organisational change. Harwood (in Marion, Virginia) became the arena where Lewin developed, tested and proved Planned change, and as such laid the foundations of OD.

Lewin and Planned change

Lewin was a humanitarian who believed that only by resolving social conflict, whether it be religious, racial, marital or industrial, could the human condition be improved. Lewin believed that the key to resolving social conflict was to facilitate learning and so enable individuals to understand and restructure their perceptions of the world around them. In this he was much influenced by the Gestalt psychologists he had worked with in Berlin (Smith, 2001). A central theme of much of his work is the view that 'the group to which an individual belongs is the ground for his perceptions, his feelings and his actions' (Allport, 1948: vii). Also, despite the fact that his work covered many subjects and fields, as Gold (1999: 295) states, 'It is quite clear that Lewin thought of his professional activities as a piece, seamless and integrated.' Therefore, though Planned change has four individual elements – Field Theory, Group Dynamics, Action Research and the Three-Step model – and though they are often treated as separate themes of his work, Lewin saw them as a unified whole with each element supporting and reinforcing the others, and all of them necessary to understand and bring about Planned change, whether it be at the level of the individual, group, organisation or even society (Bargal and Bar, 1992; Kippenberger, 1998a, 1998b; Smith, 2001). Allport (1948: ix) states that:

> All of his concepts, whatever root-metaphor they employ, comprise a single well-integrated system.

This can be seen from examining these four elements of his work in turn.

Field Theory

Lewin believed that for group behaviour to change, it was necessary to 'unfreeze' the forces restraining change, such as personal defences or group norms (Weick and Quinn,

Ideas and perspectives 8.2
Lewin – key projects and events 1939–47

Date	Study/Event	Location	Focus	Concepts	Citation
1938/9	Autocracy–Democracy	Iowa	The effects of different leadership styles on children's behaviour	Participation and group decision-making	Lewin *et al* (1939)
1939	Employee Turnover	Harwood	Employee retention	Changing supervisory behaviour	Marrow (1969)
1940/1	Group Decision-Making	Harwood	Democratic participation and productivity	Participation and group decision-making	Marrow (1969)
1941	Training in Democratic Leadership	Iowa	Improving leadership behaviours and techniques	Sensitivity training	Bavelas and Lewin (1942)
1942	Food Habits	Iowa	Changing the food-buying habits of housewives	Participation and group decision-making	Lewin (1943a)
1942	Self-Management	Harwood	Increasing workers' control over the pace of work	Group decision-making	Marrow (1969)
1944/5	Leadership Training	Harwood	Improving the interpersonal skills and effectiveness of supervisors	Role play	French (1945)
1944/5	Commission on Community Interrelations (CCI)	New York	The problems and conflicts of group and community life	Action Research	Marrow (1969)
1945	Research Center for Group Dynamics	MIT	Understanding and changing group behaviour	Action Research	Marrow (1969)
1946	Changing Stereotypes	Harwood	Changing attitudes to older workers	Information gathering, discussion and reflection	Marrow (1957 & 1972)
1946	Connecticut State Inter-Racial Commission	New Britain, Connecticut	Leadership training	Sensitivity training/Role play	Marrow (1969)
1947	National Training Laboratory	Bethel, Maine	Leadership training	T-groups (sensitivity training/role play)	Marrow (1967 & 1969)
1947	Overcoming Resistance to Change	Harwood	The impact of different approaches to change on productivity	Participative change/force field analysis	Coch and French (1948)

Source: Adapted from Burnes (2007)

1999). In order to achieve this, it is first necessary to identify the restraining forces. Field Theory is an approach to understanding group behaviour by identifying and mapping the totality and complexity of the field in which the behaviour takes place (Back, 1992). Lewin maintained that to understand any situation it was necessary that: 'One should view the present situation – the *status quo* – as being maintained by certain conditions or forces' (Lewin, 1943a: 172). As Figure 8.1 shows, the status quo is maintained because forces driving change are in balance with the forces restraining change. Lewin (1947b) postulated that group behaviour is an intricate set of symbolic interactions and forces that not only affect group structures, but also modify individual behaviour. Therefore, individual behaviour is a function of the group environment or 'field', as he termed it. Consequently, any changes in behaviour stem from changes, be they small or large, in the forces within the field, i.e. either an increase in the driving forces or a decrease in the restraining forces (Lewin, 1947a). Lewin defined a field as 'a totality of coexisting facts which are conceived of as mutually interdependent' (Lewin, 1946: 240). Lewin believed that a field was in a continuous state of adaptation and that 'Change and constancy are relative concepts; group life is never without change, merely differences in the amount and type of change exist' (Lewin, 1947a: 199). This is why Lewin used the term 'quasi-stationary equilibrium' to indicate that, whilst there might be a rhythm and pattern to the behaviour and processes of a group, these tended to fluctuate constantly owing to changes in the forces or circumstances that impinge on the group.

Lewin's view was that if one could identify, plot and establish the potency of these forces, then it would be possible not only to understand why individuals, groups and organisations behave as they do, but also what forces would need to be diminished or strengthened in order to bring about change. In the main, Lewin saw behavioural change as a slow process; however, he did recognise that under certain circumstances, such as a personal, organisational or societal crisis, the various forces in the field can shift quickly and radically. In such situations, established routines and behaviours break down and the status quo is no longer viable; new patterns of activity can rapidly emerge and a new equilibrium (or quasi-stationary equilibrium) is formed (Lewin, 1947a; Kippenberger, 1998a).

With Lewin's death, the interest in field theory waned (Back, 1992; Gold, 1992; Hendry, 1996). However, in the past two decades, it has once again begun to attract interest,

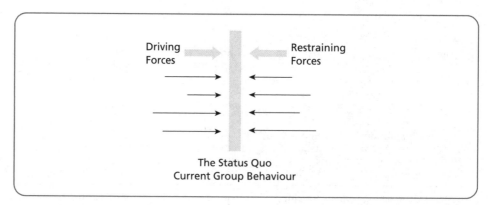

Figure 8.1 Force Field analysis

especially in terms of understanding and overcoming resistance to change (Argyris, 1990; Hirschhorn, 1988). According to Hendry (1996), even critics of Lewin's work have drawn on field theory to develop their own models of change (*see* Pettigrew *et al*, 1989, 1992). Indeed, parallels have even been drawn between Lewin's work on field theory and the work of complexity theorists (Back, 1992; Kippenberger, 1998a). Nevertheless, field theory is now probably the least understood element of Lewin's work, yet, because of its potential to map the forces impinging on an individual, group or organisation, it underpinned the other elements of his work.

Group Dynamics

> ... *the word 'dynamics'* ... *comes from a Greek word meaning force*. ... *'group dynamics' refers to the forces operating in groups*. ... *it is a study of these forces: what gives rise to them, what conditions modify them, what consequences they have, etc.*
> (Cartwright, 1951: 382)

Lewin was the first psychologist to write about 'group dynamics' and the importance of the group in shaping the behaviour of its members (Allport, 1948; Bargal *et al*, 1992). Indeed, Lewin's (1939: 165) definition of a 'group' is still generally accepted: 'it is not the similarity or dissimilarity of individuals that constitutes a group, but interdependence of fate.' As Kippenberger (1998a) notes, Lewin was addressing two questions:

- What is it about the nature and characteristics of a particular group that causes it to respond (behave) as it does to the forces which impinge on it?
- How can these forces be changed in order to elicit a more desirable form of behaviour?

It was to address these questions that Lewin began to develop the concept of Group Dynamics. Group Dynamics stresses that group behaviour, rather than that of individuals, should be the main focus of change (Bernstein, 1968; Dent and Goldberg, 1999). Lewin (1947b) maintained that it is fruitless to concentrate on changing the behaviour of individuals because the individual in isolation is constrained by group pressures to conform. Consequently, the focus of change must be at the group level and should concentrate on factors such as group norms, roles, interactions and socialisation processes to create 'disequilibrium' and change (Schein, 1988).

Lewin's pioneering work on Group Dynamics not only laid the foundations for our understanding of groups (Dent and Goldberg, 1999; Cooke, 1999; French and Bell, 1984; Marrow, 1969; Schein, 1988) but has also been linked to complexity theories by researchers examining self-organising theory and non-linear systems (Tschacher and Brunner, 1995). Since Lewin's day, much has been written about the nature of groups. Perhaps the best-known work is Belbin's work on team roles and Tuckman's work on the stages of team development. Belbin's (1996) work on team roles has been highly influential in the construction and development of groups. Belbin maintains that individuals in groups fall into one of nine team roles – Plant, Resource Investigator, Co-ordinator, Shaper, Monitor Evaluator, Teamworker, Implementer, Completer Finisher and Specialist. Tuckman (1965) identified four stages which a team must go through in order to grow and develop its effectiveness – Forming, Storming, Norming and Performing. He later added a fifth stage – adjourning – in recognition that the original objectives and tasks of a group may have been achieved or may no longer be required and, therefore, the group is no longer required (Tuckman and Jensen, 1977).

Lewin was perhaps the first to recognise the need to study and understand the internal dynamics of a group – the different roles people play and how groups need to change over time. However, for him, this understanding was not sufficient by itself to bring about change. Lewin also recognised the need to provide a process whereby group members could be engaged in and committed to changing their behaviour. This led Lewin to develop Action Research and the Three-Step model of change.

Action Research

This term was coined by Lewin (1946) in an article entitled 'Action Research and Minority Problems'. Lewin stated in the article:

> In the last year and a half I have had occasion to have contact with a great variety of organizations, institutions, and individuals who came for help in the field of group relations.
> (Lewin, 1946: 201)

However, though these people exhibited . . .

> . . . a great amount of good-will, of readiness to face the problem squarely and really do something about it. . . . These eager people feel themselves to be in a fog. They feel in a fog on three counts: 1. What is the present situation? 2. What are the dangers? 3. And most importantly of all, what shall we do?
> (Lewin, 1946: 201)

Lewin conceived of Action Research as a two-pronged process which would allow groups to address these three questions:

- Firstly, it emphasises that change requires action, and is directed at achieving this.
- Secondly, it recognises that successful action is based on analysing the situation correctly, identifying all the possible alternative solutions and choosing the one most appropriate to the situation at hand (Bennett, 1983).

To be successful, though, there has also to be a 'felt-need'. Felt-need is an individual's inner realisation that change is necessary. If felt-need is low in the group or organisation, introducing change becomes problematic. The theoretical foundations of Action Research lie in Gestalt psychology, which stresses that change can only successfully be achieved by helping individuals to reflect on and gain new insights into the totality of their situation. Lewin (1946: 206) stated that Action Research 'proceeds in a spiral of steps each of which is composed of a circle of planning, action, and fact-finding about the results of the action'. As Figure 8.2 shows, it is an iterative process whereby research leads to action, and action leads to evaluation and further research. As Schein (1996: 35) comments, it was Lewin's view that 'one cannot understand an organization without trying to change it'. Indeed, Lewin's view was very much that the understanding and learning that this process produces for the individuals and groups concerned, which then feeds into changed behaviour, is more important than any resulting change as such (Lewin, 1946).

To this end, Action Research draws on Lewin's work on field theory to identify the forces that focus on the group to which the individual belongs. It also draws on Group Dynamics to understand why group members behave in the way they do when subjected

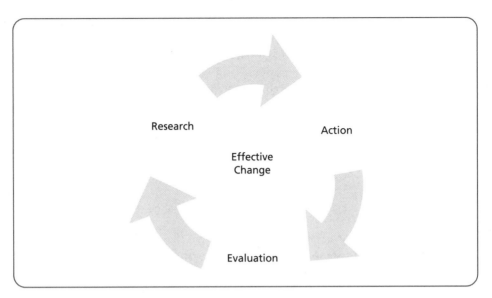

Figure 8.2 Action Research

to these forces. Lewin stressed that the routines and patterns of behaviour in a group are more than just the outcome of opposing forces. They have a value in themselves and have a positive role to play in enforcing group norms (Lewin, 1947a). Action Research stresses that for change to be effective, it must take place at the group level, and must be a participative and collaborative process which involves all of those concerned (Allport, 1948; Bargal *et al*, 1992; Darwin *et al*, 2002; Dickens and Watkins, 1999; French and Bell, 1984; Lewin, 1947b; McNiff, 2000).

Lewin's first Action Research project was to investigate and reduce violence between Catholic and Jewish teenage gangs. This was quickly followed by a project to integrate black and white sales staff in New York department stores (Marrow, 1969). However, Action Research was also adopted by the Tavistock Institute in Britain, and used to improve managerial competence and efficiency in the newly nationalised coal industry. Since then it has acquired strong adherents throughout the world (Dickens and Watkins, 1999; Eden and Huxham, 1996; Elden and Chisholm, 1993). However, Lewin (1947a: 228) was concerned that:

> *A change towards a higher level of group performance is frequently short lived; after a 'shot in the arm', group life soon returns to the previous level. This indicates that it does not suffice to define the objective of a planned change in group performance as the reaching of a different level. Permanency at the new level, or permanency for a desired period, should be included in the objective.*

It was for this reason that he developed his Three-Step model of change.

Three-Step model

This is often cited as Lewin's key contribution to organisational change. It needs to be recognised, however, that when he developed his Three-Step model, Lewin was not thinking only of organisational issues. Nor did he intend it to be seen separately from the other three elements which make up his Planned approach to change (i.e. Field Theory, Group Dynamics and Action Research). Rather Lewin saw the four concepts as forming an integrated approach to analysing, understanding and bringing about change at the group, organisational and societal levels. A successful change project, Lewin (1947a) argued, involved three steps (*see* Figure 8.3).

Figure 8.3 Lewin's Three-Step model of change

Step 1: Unfreezing. Lewin believed that the stability of human behaviour was based on a quasi-stationary equilibrium supported by a complex field of driving and restraining forces (*see* Figure 8.1). Others refer to this as inertia – the inability of organisations or groups to change as fast as the environment in which they operate (Pfeffer, 1997). D Miller (1993, 1994) argues that the more successful an organisation or group has been, the greater the inertia. This is because success tends to make organisations focus on those factors which are seen as having brought success and to discard those which are seen as peripheral. Successful organisations also tend to ignore signals which might indicate the need for change. The result is that they sacrifice adaptability and increase inertia. This is why Lewin argued that the equilibrium (the forces of inertia) needs to be destabilised (unfrozen) before old behaviour can be discarded (unlearnt) and new behaviour successfully adopted. Given the type of issues that Lewin was addressing, as one would expect, he did not believe that change would be easy or that the same approach could be applied in all situations:

> The 'unfreezing' of the present level may involve quite different problems in different cases. Allport . . . has described the 'catharsis' which seems necessary before prejudice can be removed. To break open the shell of complacency and self-righteousness it is sometimes necessary to bring about an emotional stir up.
>
> (Lewin, 1947a: 229)

Enlarging on Lewin's ideas, Schein (1996: 28) comments that the key to unfreezing:

> . . . was to see that human change, whether at the individual or group level, was a profound psychological dynamic process that involved painful unlearning without loss of ego identity and difficult relearning as one cognitively attempted to restructure one's thoughts, perceptions, feelings, and attitudes.

Schein (1996) identifies three processes necessary to achieve unfreezing: disconfirmation of the validity of the status quo, the induction of guilt or survival anxiety, and creating psychological safety. He argued that: 'unless sufficient psychological safety is created, the disconfirming information will be denied or in other ways defended against, no survival anxiety will be felt, and consequently, no change will take place' (Schein, 1996: 30). In other words, those concerned have to feel safe from loss and humiliation before they can accept the new information and reject old behaviours.

Step 2: Moving. As Schein (1996: 32) notes, unfreezing is not an end in itself; it 'creates motivation to learn but does not necessarily control or predict the direction of learning'. This echoes Lewin's view that any attempt to predict or identify a specific outcome from Planned change is very difficult because of the complexity of the forces concerned. Instead, one should seek to take into account all the forces at work and identify and evaluate, on a trial and error basis, all the available options (Lewin, 1947a). This is, of course, the learning approach promoted by Action Research. It is this iterative approach of research, action and more research that enables groups and individuals to move from a less acceptable to a more acceptable set of behaviours. However, as noted above, Lewin (1947a) recognised that, without reinforcement, change could be short-lived.

Step 3: Refreezing. This is the final step in the Three-Step model. Refreezing seeks to stabilise the group at a new quasi-stationary equilibrium in order to ensure that the new behaviours are relatively safe from regression. The main point about refreezing is that new behaviour must be, to some degree, congruent with the rest of the behaviour, personality and environment of the learner or it will simply lead to a new round of disconfirmation (Schein, 1996). This is why Lewin saw successful change as a group activity, because unless group norms and routines are also transformed, changes to individual behaviour will not be sustained. In organisational terms, refreezing often requires changes to organisational culture, norms, policies and practices (Cummings and Huse, 1989).

Like other aspects of Lewin's work, his Three-Step model of change has become unfashionable since the 1980s (Dawson, 1994; Hatch, 1997; Kanter *et al*, 1992). Nevertheless, such is its continuing influence that, as Hendry (1996: 624) commented:

> *Scratch any account of creating and managing change and the idea that change is a three-stage process which necessarily begins with a process of unfreezing will not be far below the surface.*

Hendry's view is supported by the work of Elrod and Tippett (2002), who reviewed a wide range of change models. They found that most approaches to organisational change were strikingly similar to Lewin's Three-Step model. When they extended their research to other forms of human and organisational change, Elrod and Tippett (2002: 273) also found that:

> *Models of the change process, as perceived by diverse and seemingly unrelated disciplines [such as bereavement theory, personal transition theory, creative processes, cultural revolutions and scientific revolutions] . . . follow Lewin's . . . three-phase model of change . . .*

Others support this view (Zell, 2003). Carnall (2003) draws on these various models of change to develop the Coping Cycle (*see* Figure 8.4) which shows how people react and adjust when faced with change.

The Coping Cycle comprises five stages:

Stage 1 – Denial: When faced with the need to make or accept significant changes, the first reaction by many people or groups is to deny there is a need for change.

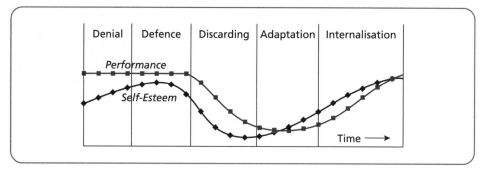

Figure 8.4 The Coping Cycle

Stage 2 – Defence:	Once people realise that change is taking place and they cannot stop it, they may feel rejected and depressed. This can turn into defensive behaviour whereby people will defend their past practices and behaviours and deny that the new ways are suitable to them and their job.
Stage 3 – Discarding:	If people realise that the change will take place whether they like it or not, and that it does affect them and that they need to adjust to the new situation, they begin the process of discarding past behaviour – recognising that what was suitable in the past is no longer suitable for the current situation.
Stage 4 – Adaptation:	No proposed change is ever likely to be 100 per cent suitable at the outset. Therefore, for change to be successful, not only must those affected by it adapt to the new ways, but the new ways must also be adapted to fit in with the existing people and circumstances.
Stage 5 – Internalisation:	The is the stage of the Coping Cycle where change becomes fully operational, and new ways of working and behaving have been developed. People reach the point where, psychologically, they see the changes not as *new* but as *normal* – the way things should be.

There are four points to note about the Coping Cycle:

- Firstly, individuals will often react differently when faced with the same situation, even though they may be members of the same group. Some will move from Denial to Internalisation very quickly whilst others may stick at the Denial or Defence stages and never accept the legitimacy of the changes.
- Secondly, as Figure 8.4 shows, people's self-esteem and performance can fluctuate wildly as they move through the Coping Cycle. To use a somewhat hackneyed phrase, people can experience an emotional rollercoaster.
- Thirdly, the point between Stage 3, Discarding, and Stage 4, Adaptation, where people are beginning to accept the need for change and embarking on a process of mutual accommodation, is the point where their self-esteem and performance are likely to be at their lowest. It is at this point, when success is almost within reach, that those

driving and sponsoring change and those experiencing it may begin to feel that they have chosen the wrong course of action and should abandon it. It is important, therefore, at the outset of any change process to recognise the truth of the old adage that: *Things will get worse before they get better!*

- Lastly, following Elrod and Tippet's (2002) argument, if we superimpose Lewin's Three-Step model of change onto the Coping Cycle (*see* Figure 8.5), the remarkable applicability and appropriateness of Lewin's approach to change stands out. Step 1 of Lewin's Model – Unfreezing – aligns with Stages 1 to 3 of Carnall's Coping Cycle and provides the insights and tools necessary to address the issues of Denial, Defence and Discarding. Step 2 – Moving – aligns with Stage 4 and once again provides the means of dealing with the issues and obstacles that arise from Adaptation. Finally, Step 3 of Lewin's model, Refreezing, aligns with Stage 5 of the Coping Cycle and provides an approach to and the mechanisms for achieving Internalisation.

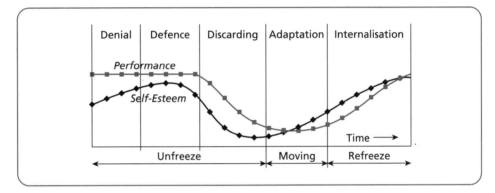

Figure 8.5 Three-Step model and the Coping Cycle

As can be seen, therefore, though Lewin's Planned approach to change was developed over 60 years ago, it still appears to have much to recommend it as an approach to changing the behaviour of individuals and groups.

Lewin and change: a summary

Lewin was primarily interested in resolving social conflict through behavioural change, whether this be within organisations or in the wider society. He identified two requirements for success:

1. To analyse and understand how social groupings were formed, motivated and maintained. To do this, he developed both Field Theory and Group Dynamics.
2. To change the behaviour of social groups. The primary methods he developed for achieving this were Action Research and the Three-Step model of change.

Underpinning Lewin's work was a strong moral and ethical belief in the importance of democratic institutions and democratic values in society. Lewin believed that only by strengthening democratic participation in all aspects of life and being able to resolve social conflicts could the scourge of despotism, authoritarianism and racism be effectively countered. Since his death, Lewin's wider social agenda has been mainly pursued under the umbrella of Action Research. For example, Bargal and Bar (1992) described how, over a number of years, they used Lewin's approach to address the conflict between Arab-Palestinian and Jewish youths in Israel through the development of inter-group workshops. The workshops were developed around six principles based on Lewin's work:

> *(a) a recursive process of data collection to determine goals, action to implement goals and assessment of the action; (b) feedback of research results to trainers; (c) cooperation between researchers and practitioners; (d) research based on the laws of the group's social life, on three stages of change – 'unfreezing,' 'moving,' and 'refreezing' – and on the principles of group decision making; (e) consideration of the values, goals and power structures of change agents and clients; and (f) use of research to create knowledge and/or solve problems.* (Bargal and Bar, 1992: 146)

As mentioned earlier, in terms of organisational change, Lewin and his associates had a long and fruitful relationship with the Harwood Manufacturing Corporation, where his approach to change was developed, applied and refined (Burnes, 2007). Coch and French (1948: 512) observed that, at Harwood: 'From the point of view of factory management, there were two purposes to the research: (1) Why do people resist change so strongly? and (2) What can be done to overcome this resistance?' Therefore, in both his wider social agenda and his narrower organisational agenda, Lewin sought to address similar issues and apply similar concepts. Since his death, it is the organisational side of his work that has been given greater prominence by his followers and successors, mainly through the creation of the Organization Development (OD) movement (Cummings and Worley, 1997; French and Bell, 1999). However, whilst attempting to remain true to his participatory philosophy, and being greatly influenced by Lewin's work on group dynamics, OD tends to equate Planned change with Lewin's Three-Step model, rather than treating it as an integrated package that also requires the use of Field Theory, Group Dynamics and Action Research. As a stand-alone approach to change, the Three-Step model is rather underdeveloped, so OD practitioners have sought to develop it further.

Phases of Planned change

As Armenakis and Bedeian (1999) have shown, there have been many attempts to elaborate upon Lewin's Three-Step model. In so doing, writers have expanded the number of steps or phases. For example, Lippitt *et al* (1958) developed a seven-phase model of Planned change, whilst Cummings and Huse (1989), not to be outdone, produced an eight-phase model and Galpin (1996) proposed a model comprising nine wedges that form a wheel. As Cummings and Huse (1989: 51) point out, however, 'the concept of planned change implies that an organization exists in different states at different times and that planned movement can occur from one state to another'. Therefore, in order to understand Planned change, it is not sufficient merely to understand the processes that bring about change; there must also be an appreciation of the states that an organisation must pass through in order to move from an unsatisfactory present state to a more desired future state.

Bullock and Batten (1985) developed an integrated, four-phase model of Planned change based on a review and synthesis of over 30 models of Planned change (*see* Ideas and perspectives 8.3). Their model describes Planned change in terms of two major

Ideas and perspectives 8.3
Bullock and Batten's four-phase model of planned change

1. **Exploration phase.** In this state an organisation has to explore and decide whether it wants to make specific changes in its operations and, if so, commit resources to planning the changes. The change processes involved in this phase are becoming aware of the need for change; searching for outside assistance (a consultant/facilitator) to assist with planning and implementing the changes; and establishing a contract with the consultant which defines each party's responsibilities.

2. **Planning phase.** Once the consultant and the organisation have established a contract, then the next state, which involves understanding the organisation's problem or concern, begins. The change processes involved in this are collecting information in order to establish a correct diagnosis of the problem; establishing change goals and designing the appropriate actions to achieve these goals; and persuading key decision-makers to approve and support the proposed changes.

3. **Action phase.** In this state, an organisation implements the changes derived from the planning. The change processes involved are designed to move an organisation from its current state to a desired future state, and include establishing appropriate arrangements to manage the change process and gaining support for the actions to be taken; and evaluating the implementation activities and feeding back the results so that any necessary adjustments or refinements can be made.

4. **Integration phase.** This state commences once the changes have been successfully implemented. It is concerned with consolidating and stabilising the changes so that they become part of an organisation's normal, everyday operation and do not require special arrangements or encouragement to maintain them. The change processes involved are reinforcing new behaviours through feedback and reward systems and gradually decreasing reliance on the consultant; diffusing the successful aspects of the change process throughout the organisation; and training managers and employees to monitor the changes constantly and to seek to improve upon them.

Source: Bullock and Batten (1985)

dimensions: change phases, which are distinct states an organisation moves through as it undertakes Planned change; and change processes, which are the methods used to move an organisation from one state to another.

According to Cummings and Huse (1989), this model has broad applicability to most change situations. It clearly incorporates key aspects of many other change models and, especially, it overcomes any confusion between the processes (methods) of change and the phases of change – the sequential states that organisations must go through to achieve successful change.

The focus of Bullock and Batten's model, just as with Lewin's, is change at individual and group level. However, OD practitioners have recognised, as many others have, that 'Organizations are being reinvented; work tasks are being reengineered; the rules of the marketplace are being rewritten; the fundamental nature of organizations is changing', and, therefore, Organization Development has had to adapt to these new conditions and broaden its focus out beyond individual and group behaviour (French and Bell, 1995: 3–4).

The changing nature of Organization Development

Though founded in the USA, OD has expanded across the globe (Fagenson-Eland *et al*, 2004). In the USA at least, it has taken on the characteristics of a profession with its own professional associations, such as the NTL Institute and the Organization Development Network, to which most OD practitioners belong. Amongst other things, these bodies offer accreditation, training in OD tools and techniques, and promote their own ethical codes of practice (Cummings and Worley, 1997). OD practitioners, whether employed in academic institutions, consultancy practices or private and public organisations, exist to provide consultancy services. As with any profession or trade, unless they provide their customers with what they want, they will soon go out of business. Therefore, to appreciate the current role and approach of Planned change, it is necessary to say something of how OD has responded to the changing needs of its customers.

As stated earlier, Organization Development is a process that applies behavioural science knowledge and practices to help organisations achieve greater effectiveness. The original focus of OD was on work groups within an organisational setting rather than organisations in their entirety, and it was primarily concerned with the human processes and systems within organisations. However, even in the 1960s, there were those who saw the need for a more organisation-wide approach to change. Greiner (1967: 119) for example, observed:

> *Whereas only a few years ago the target of organization change was limited to a small work group or a single department, especially at lower levels, the focus is now converging on the organization as a whole, reaching out to include many divisions and levels at once, and even the top managers themselves.*

By the 1970s, the economic, technological, organisational and workforce conditions were vastly different from those in the 1940s and 1950s. As a consequence serious questions were being raised about the suitability of OD for the needs of contemporary organisations. In particular, Greiner's (1972b) article 'Red flags in organization development' was seen as a wake-up call for the movement as whole (*see* Ideas and perspectives 8.4).

From the 1970s onwards, the OD movement experienced a major shift of focus from the group to the organisation setting, and even beyond, in response to the changing organisational landscape (Armenakis and Bedeian, 1999; Pasmore and Fagans, 1992; Sashkin and Burke, 1987; Woodman, 1989). Three developments in particular caused it to broaden out its perspective:

- With the rise of the Job Design movement in the 1960s (*see* Chapter 2), and particularly the advent of Socio-Technical Systems theory, OD practitioners came to recognise that they could not solely concentrate on the work of groups and individuals in organisations but that they needed to look at other systems. Gradually, OD has adopted an Open Systems perspective which allows it to look at organisations in their totality and within their environments.

Ideas and perspectives 8.4
Greiner's red flags

Flag 1: Putting the individual before the organization. The obsession of OD with individual behavior change caused less focus on the formal organization – its strategy, structure, controls, and so on. As a result, OD neglected to address potential sources of environmental support and reinforcement for behavior change.

Flag 2: Informal before formal organization. There was also an overemphasis on interpersonal values (e.g., openness, trust, etc.) in an attempt to change the informal culture of organizations, often at the expense of the design of the formal organization and its values of efficiency, hierarchy, and accountability. Again, an opportunity was missed to produce a wider impact.

Flag 3: Behavior before diagnosis. OD was preoccupied with behavior change along the lines of OD's core values, not on diagnosing whether the existing behavior was compatible with the strategic thrust or culture of the organization. Thus, OD's goal of promoting more open and trusting relationships became the normative model for change; it was taken for granted without questioning its applicability to particular situations.

Flag 4: Process before task. With its emphasis on how one person should relate to others, OD became enamored with the human dynamics of working together, assuming that team building was the preferred alternative. In doing so, it neglected the realities of technology and the substantive problems in front of people. Contingency theory revealed that some jobs were inherently mechanistic and programmable; therefore, they did not require much teamwork and openness for effective performance.

Flag 5: Experts before the manager. OD programs were designed and conducted by expert consultants. NTL had become an elitist organization of trained experts. Their target of change was the manager in organizations. Unfortunately, managers were relatively uninvolved in the planning and conducting of consultant-led OD programs. They were simply supposed to be the recipients of change and conform to the model being advocated by the consultants.

Flag 6: Package before the situation. Potential clients for OD activities usually preferred packaged change programs – formal activities that were structured, tangible, and easy to explain to employees. Many OD consultants also welcomed this approach because structured programs were easier to sell and administer than open-ended and evolving efforts. The unfortunate result was that organizations were frequently shoehorned to fit the OD program's characteristics rather than customizing the program to fit the uniqueness of the client organization.

Source: Greiner and Cummings (2004: 378–9)

- This organisation-wide perspective caused OD practitioners to broaden out their perspective in two interrelated ways. Firstly, and not surprisingly, they developed an interest in managing organisational culture. Given that, when working with groups, OD consultants have always recognised the importance of group norms and values, it is a natural progression to translate this into an interest in organisational culture in general. Secondly, they developed an interest in the concept of organisational learning. Once again, as derived from Lewin's work, OD practitioners tend to stress that their interventions are as much about learning as change. Therefore, it is a natural extension to move from group learning to organisational learning. In both cases, these developments have tended to reflect and follow on from a general interest in such issues by organisations and academics rather than necessarily being generated by the OD profession itself.

- The increasing use of organisation-wide approaches to change (e.g. culture change programmes), coupled with increasing turbulence in the environment in which organisations operate, drew attention to the need for OD practitioners to become involved in transforming organisations in their totality rather than only focusing on changes to their constituent parts.

Therefore, as can be seen, OD has had to move considerably away from its roots in group-based and Planned change and now takes a far more organisation- and system-wide perspective on change. This has created something of a dilemma for proponents of OD. As Krell (1981) pointed out, much of what can be conceived of as traditional OD (e.g. Action Research, t-groups, etc.) had become accepted practice in many organisations by the early 1980s. Even some of the newer approaches, such as Job Design and self-managed work teams, had become mainstream practices in many organisations (Beer and Walton, 1987). By and large, these tried-and-tested approaches still tend to focus on the group level rather than on the wider organisation level. However, the more organisation-wide transformational approaches, which are seen as crucial to maintaining OD's relevance for organisations, are less clear, less well-developed and less well-accepted (Cummings and Worley, 1997; French and Bell, 1995). In addition, the more that OD becomes focused on macro issues, the less it can keep in touch with and involve all the individuals affected by its change programmes and the less able it is to promote its core humanist and democratic values. Indeed, quite a number of leading writers on the subject have begun to argue that OD has lost its sense of direction and purpose to the extent that it is no longer clear what constitutes OD (Bradford and Burke, 2004; Greiner and Cummings, 2004; Worley and Feyerhern, 2003).

It would indeed be an irony if at this time, in pursuit of what is perceived as continued relevance, OD lost sight of its core values. This is because, as Wooten and White (1999) argue, the core values of OD – equality, empowerment, consensus-building and horizontal relationships – are ones that are particularly relevant to the postmodern organisation. If this is the case, rather than loosening its ties with its traditional values in order to retain its relevance, OD should be strengthening them in order to create the 'framework for a postmodern OD science and practice' (Wooten and White, 1999: 17).

Planned change: summary and criticisms

Planned change, as developed by Kurt Lewin, comprised four elements: Field Theory, Group Dynamics, Action Research and the Three-Step model. It is an iterative, cyclical, process involving diagnosis, action and evaluation, and further action and evaluation. It is an approach that recognises that once change has taken place, it must be self-sustaining (i.e. safe from regression). The original purpose of Planned change was to resolve social conflict in society, including conflict within organisations. In organisational terms, its original purpose was to focus on improving the effectiveness of the human side of the organisation. Central to Planned change in organisations is the emphasis placed on the collaborative nature of the change effort: the organisation, both managers and recipients of change, and the consultant jointly diagnose the organisation's problem, and jointly plan and design the specific changes. Underpinning Planned change and indeed the OD movement is a strong humanist and democratic orientation and an emphasis on organisational effectiveness. Marching hand in hand with this humanist and democratic orientation was the development of a host of tried-and-tested tools and techniques for promoting group participation and change.

Nevertheless, as OD practitioners have developed Planned change over the years, and moved their focus from group behaviour change to organisational transformation initiatives, two fundamental dilemmas have arisen (*see* Ideas and perspectives 8.5).

The first dilemma is that whilst OD practitioners are well equipped to bring about change in group behaviour, they are far less well equipped to achieve the same in terms of organisational transformation. The former is well understood, OD practitioners find it relatively easy to gain the support of those involved, and Planned change, with its host of tried-and-tested tools and techniques, is ideally suited to this kind of initiative. On the other hand, OD practitioners have found it more difficult to apply their skills and expertise to organisational transformational initiatives. The process of diagnosing the need for and specifying what is required in terms of transformational change at the organisational level is much less clear than it is at the group level. Also, the tools and techniques for bringing about transformational change are less developed, and the process tends to be more contentious and conflict-ridden.

Ideas and perspectives 8.5
OD dilemmas

Over the years, OD practitioners have sought to focus more on organisational transformation initiatives and less on group behaviour change. This has led to two fundamental dilemmas:

Dilemma One: OD Expertise

- The group behaviour focus is well-understood, accepted and supported by tried and tested tools and techniques.
- The organisational transformation focus is unclear, less developed and more contentious.

Dilemma Two: OD Values

- The group behaviour focus promotes humanistic and democratic values through participative learning.
- The organisational transformation focus is more autocratic, less participative and less about individual and group learning.

The second dilemma concerns the values which underpin OD. As OD has moved more to address large-scale organisational transformation issues, though the emphasis on organisational effectiveness has remained, a difference has emerged with regard to the participatory and democratic nature of its approach. Though this is partly due to the numbers of people involved in such changes, it is largely driven by the approach of top management. As French and Bell (1995: 351) observed, from the 1980s onwards, there has been a growing tendency for top managers to focus less on people-orientated values and more on 'the bottom line and/or the price of stock . . . [consequently] some executives have a "slash and burn" mentality'. Clearly, this tendency is not conducive to the promotion of democratic and humanistic values. This 'slash and burn' mentality has impacted on the role of the change consultant. Lewin stressed the need to solve problems through social action (dialogue). He believed that successful change could only be achieved through the active participation of the change adopter (the subject) in understanding the problem, selecting a solution and implementing it. Lewin, and the early OD practitioners, saw the change agent as a facilitator, not a director or a doer. More important even than the solution to the problem, Lewin believed that the consultant's real task was to develop those involved, and to create a learning environment that would allow them to gain new insights into themselves and their circumstances. Only through this learning process could people willingly come to see the need for and accept change.

Bullock and Batten's model, as with other more recent variants of Planned change, gives the consultant a more directive and less developmental role. Their model seems to place a greater emphasis on the consultant as an equal (or even senior) partner rather than as a facilitator; the consultant is as free to direct and do as the others involved. Those involved are more dependent on the change agent, not just for his or her skills of analysis but also for providing solutions and helping to implement them. Therefore, the focus is on what the change agent can do for those involved, rather than on seeking to enable the subjects to change themselves. This tendency for consultants to have a more directive role, and for employees to have a less participatory one, has become even more pronounced as OD practitioners have shifted their focus from individuals and groups to organisations in their entirety.

Lewin's approach to change was greatly influenced by the work of the Gestalt-Field theorists, who believe that successful change requires a process of learning. This allows those involved to gain or change insights, outlooks, expectations and thought patterns. This approach seeks to provide change adopters with an opportunity to 'reason out' their situation and develop their own solutions (Bigge, 1982). The danger with Bullock and Batten's approach, and certainly with organisational transformation initiatives, is that they appear to be moving more in the Behaviourist direction. The emphasis is on the consultant as a provider of expertise that the organisation lacks. The consultant's task is less to facilitate participative change and more to provide solutions which can be imposed in a rapid fashion. The danger in this situation is that the learner (the change adopter) becomes a passive recipient of external and, supposedly, objective data: one who has to be directed to the 'correct' solution. Reason and choice do not enter into this particular equation; those involved are shown the solution and motivated, through the application of positive reinforcement, to adopt it on a permanent basis (Skinner, 1974). This appears to be especially the case with the newer, organisation-wide and transformational approaches about which even supporters of OD admit there is some confusion (Bradford and Burke, 2004; Greiner and Cummings, 2004; Worley and Feyerhern, 2003).

Therefore, the move away from its original focus and area of expertise, i.e. the human processes involved in the functioning of individuals and groups in organisations, coupled with a more hostile business environment, appear to be eroding the values which Lewin and the early pioneers of OD saw as being central to successful change.

Though many proponents of OD see its broadening out as necessary and appropriate (Armenakis and Bedeian, 1999; Pasmore and Fagans, 1992; Sashkin and Burke, 1987; Woodman, 1989), not everyone shares this view. These developments in OD, as well as newer perspectives on organisations, have led many to question not only particular aspects of the Planned approach to change, but also the utility and practicality of the approach as a whole. The main criticisms levelled against the Planned approach to change, according to Burnes and Salauroo (1995), are as follows.

Firstly, as Wooten and White (1999: 8) observe, 'Much of the existing OD technology was developed specifically for, and in response to, top-down, autocratic, rigid, rule-based organizations operating in a somewhat predictable and controlled environment.' Arising from this is the assumption that, as Cummings and Huse (1989: 51) pointed out, 'an organization exists in different states at different times and that planned movement can occur from one state to another'. An increasing number of writers, however, especially from the complexity perspective, argue that, in the turbulent and chaotic world in which we live, such assumptions are increasingly tenuous and that organisational change is more a continuous and open-ended process than a set of discrete and self-contained events (Arndt and Bigelow, 2000; Bechtold, 1997; Black, 2000; Brown and Eisenhardt, 1997; Garvin, 1993; IBM, 2008; Kanter *et al*, 1997; Peters, 1997a; Stacey, 2003).

Secondly, and on a similar note, a number of writers have criticised the Planned approach for its emphasis on incremental and isolated change and its inability to incorporate radical, transformational change (Dawson, 1994; Dunphy and Stace, 1993; Harris, 1985; Miller and Friesen, 1984; Schein, 1985; Pettigrew, 1990a, 1990b).

Thirdly, the Planned change approach is seen as being based on the assumption that common agreement can be reached, and that all the parties involved in a particular change project have a willingness and interest in doing so (Dawson, 1994; Hatch, 1997; Wilson, 1992). This assumption appears to ignore organisational conflict and politics, or at least assumes that problem issues can be easily identified and resolved. Given what was said of organisational power, politics and vested interests in Chapter 5, such a view is difficult to substantiate. Also, as Stace and Dunphy (1994) have shown, there is a wide spectrum of change situations, ranging from fine-tuning to corporate transformation, and an equally wide range of ways of managing these, ranging from collaborative to coercive. Though Planned change may be suitable to some of these situations, it is clearly much less applicable to situations where more directive approaches may be required, such as when a crisis, requiring rapid and major change, does not allow scope for widespread involvement or consultation.

Fourthly, it assumes that one type of approach to change is suitable for all organisations, all situations and all times. Dunphy and Stace (1993: 905), on the other hand, argue that:

Turbulent times demand different responses in varied circumstances. So managers and consultants need a model of change that is essentially a 'situational' or 'contingency model', one that indicates how to vary change strategies to achieve 'optimum fit' with the changing environment.

In supporting and adding to this list of criticisms, many writers have drawn attention to the increasing frequency and magnitude of change and, whilst the Planned approach may be applicable to incremental change, it is less relevant to larger-scale and more radical transformational changes that many organisations have undergone or are experiencing (Brown and Eisenhardt, 1997; Hayes, 2002). The same can be said in relation to the three schools of thought which provide the theoretical underpinnings of organisational change that were discussed at the beginning of this chapter. Planned change is certainly applicable to the individual and group contexts, but seems less appropriate for system-wide change.

Leading OD advocates, as might be predicted, dispute these criticisms and point to the way that Planned change has tried to incorporate issues such as power and politics and the need for organisational transformation (Cummings and Worley, 2005; French and Bell, 1999). Also, as Burnes (1998b) argues, there is a need to draw a distinction between Lewin's original analytical approach to Planned change and the more prescriptive and practitioner-orientated variants that have been developed by the OD profession subsequently. In defence of Lewin, Burnes (2004c) points out that Lewin did not ignore the importance of power and politics, nor did he fail to recognise that change could be fast and dramatic. In particular, Burnes argues that whilst Lewin saw human behaviour, both at the individual and group level, as being relatively stable over time (*see* the earlier section on Field Theory), he did not see organisations as stable and changeless entities. In this respect, his view was not dissimilar to that of many of his critics. As already mentioned, a number of proponents of complexity theory have also made similar observations. This is a point which will be revisited towards the end of the next chapter. Furthermore, it has to be recognised that Lewin never saw Planned change as being applicable to all change situations, and it was certainly never meant to be used in situations where rapid, coercive and/or wholesale change was required. However, from the 1970s onwards, the incremental, small-group view of change favoured by Lewin and his supporters began to be replaced by one which saw change as being more frequent and of greater magnitude.

The frequency and magnitude of organisational change

As has been mentioned often in this book, the view which many leading commentators take is that organisations are changing at a faster pace and in a more fundamental way than ever before (Greiner and Cummings, 2004; IBM, 2008; Kanter, 2008; Kotter and Rathgeber, 2006; Peters, 2006). These commentators judge the present level of organisational change to be unprecedented, although – as Chapters 1 and 6 noted – the history of the past 200 years could well be characterised as successive periods of unprecedented change. Obviously, an appreciation of whether organisational change is to be a continuing feature or a one-off event, whether it is on a small or large scale, and whether change is fast or slow, plays a key role in judging the appropriateness of particular approaches to managing change. It is, therefore, important to go beyond the tabloid-like headlines thrown up by writers such as Tom Peters and to examine the main models of organisational change that are currently being promoted and, also, to recognise that there are strong disagreements about the nature and pace of change that organisations experience. In this respect, there are three current models that are prominent in the literature.

The incremental model of change

See Figure 8.6. Advocates of this view see change as being a process whereby individual parts of an organisation deal incrementally and separately with one problem and one goal at a time. By managers responding to pressures in their local internal and external environments in this way, over time, their organisations become transformed. Miller and Friesen (1984: 222) explain that:

> *The incrementalist perspective on change has been around a, relatively, long time. It stems from the work of Lindblom (1959) and Cyert and March (1963), and was further developed by Hedberg et al (1976) and especially Quinn (1980b and 1982). Quinn argues that strategic change is best viewed as 'muddling through with purpose,' using a continuous, evolving and consensus building approach.*

Pettigrew *et al* (1992: 14) add that: 'The received wisdom therefore is that change will take place through successive, limited and negotiated shifts.' Though Quinn (1980b, 1982) and others have marshalled considerable support for the incrementalist perspective from Western sources, and though Planned change sits very comfortably with this view, the pre-eminent exemplars of incremental change have been Japanese companies (Hamel and Prahalad, 1989). As described in Chapter 3, Japanese companies have an enviable track record of achieving fierce competitiveness through pursuing incremental change year in, year out. Dunphy and Stace (1992) also advocated this approach for Western companies, arguing for a form of managed incrementalism that avoids both the stagnation engendered by fine-tuning and the brutality associated with rapid corporate transformations. However, Mintzberg (1978) argued that though organisations do go

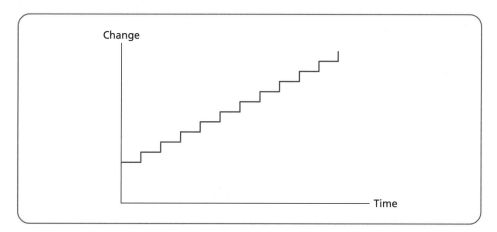

Figure 8.6 Incremental change

through long periods of incremental change, these are often interspersed with brief periods of rapid and revolutionary change. Indeed, given the turbulence of the last 20 years, some writers have argued that it is now the periods of stability which are brief and the revolutionary change periods which are long, at least in Western firms (Pettigrew *et al*, 2001; Weick and Quinn, 1999). Not surprisingly, this has led to an increased interest in how organisations move between periods of stability and instability.

The punctuated equilibrium model of organisational transformation

See Figure 8.7. This somewhat inelegantly titled approach to change:

> . . . *depicts organizations as evolving through relatively long periods of stability (equilibrium periods) in their basic patterns of activity that are punctuated by relatively short bursts of fundamental change (revolutionary periods). Revolutionary periods substantively disrupt established activity patterns and install the basis for new equilibrium periods.*   (Romanelli and Tushman, 1994: 1141)

The punctuated equilibrium model is associated with the work of Miller and Friesen (1984), Tushman and Romanelli (1985) and Gersick (1991). The inspiration for this model arises from two sources: firstly, from the challenge to Charles Darwin's gradualist model of evolution in the natural sciences: Steven Jay Gould (1989), in particular, mounted a case for a punctuated equilibrium model of evolution; and secondly, from the assertion that whilst most organisations do appear to fit the incrementalist model of change for a period of time, there does come a point when they go through a period of rapid and fundamental change (Gersick, 1991). Orlikowski (1996: 64) notes that:

> *Punctuated discontinuities are typically triggered by modifications in environmental or internal conditions, for example, new technology, process redesign, or industry deregulation.*

Though this view began to take hold in the 1980s, it is by no means new. In the 1970s, Greiner (1972a) observed that as organisations grow, they go through long periods of evolutionary change and short, sharp bursts of revolutionary change. Indeed, Lewin made

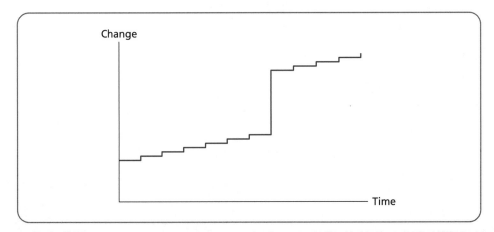

Figure 8.7 Punctuated Equilibrium

a similar observation in the 1940s (Lewin, 1947a; Kippenberger, 1998a). However, as even Romanelli and Tushman (1994: 1142) admit, 'Despite the growing prominence and pervasiveness of punctuated equilibrium theory, little research has explored the empirical validity of the model's basic arguments.' In addition, just as the incremental model is criticised for assuming that organisations operate in or go through periods of stability, so too is the punctuated model. The assumption of both is that stability is the natural or preferred state for organisations (Orlikowski, 1996). However, there are some who believe that continuous change is or should be the norm and this has led them to reject both the incremental and punctuated models of change (Brown and Eisenhardt, 1997).

The continuous transformation model of change

See Figure 8.8. The argument put forward by proponents of this model is that, in order to survive, organisations must develop the ability to change themselves continuously in a fundamental manner. From this perspective, Weick and Quinn (1999: 366) argue that:

> *Change is a pattern of endless modifications in work processes and social practice. It is driven by organizational instability and alert reactions to daily contingencies. Numerous small accommodations accumulate and amplify.*

This is particularly the case in fast-moving sectors such as retail where, as Greenwald (1996: 54) notes, 'If you look at the best retailers out there, they are constantly reinventing themselves.' Brown and Eisenhardt (1997: 1) maintain that:

> *For firms such as Intel, Wal-Mart, 3M, Hewlett-Packard and Gillette, the ability to change rapidly and continuously, especially by developing new products, is not only a core competence, it is also at the heart of their cultures. For these firms, change is not the rare, episodic phenomenon described by the punctuated equilibrium model but, rather, it is endemic to the way these organizations compete. Moreover, in high-velocity industries with short product cycles and rapidly-shifting competitive landscapes, the ability to engage in rapid and relentless continuous change is a crucial capability for survival . . .*

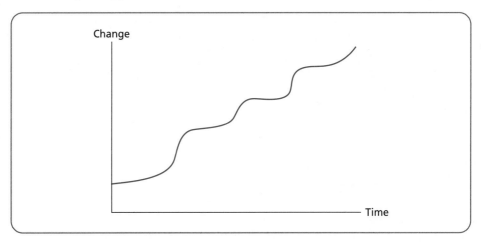

Figure 8.8 Continuous Change

The underpinning rationale for the continuous transformation model is that the environment in which organisations operate is changing, and will continue to change, rapidly, radically and unpredictably. Only by continuous change and adaptation will organisations be able to keep aligned with their environment and thus survive. Though this view has many adherents, there are two groups that are its main promoters. The first is the Culture–Excellence school. This group, especially Tom Peters (1997a, 1997b) and Rosabeth Moss Kanter *et al* (1997), have been arguing for a continuous transformation model of change since the early 1980s. However, as noted in Chapter 3, they provide little solid empirical evidence to support their view. The second group are those who seek to apply complexity theories to organisations (Wheatley, 1992b). As described in Chapter 4, complexity theories are concerned with the emergence of order in dynamic non-linear systems operating at the edge of chaos: in other words, systems that are constantly changing and where the laws of cause and effect appear not to apply (Beeson and Davis, 2000; Haigh, 2002; Wheatley, 1992b). Order in such systems manifests itself in a largely unpredictable fashion, in which patterns of behaviour emerge in irregular but similar forms through a process of self-organisation, which is governed by a small number of simple order-generating rules (Black, 2000; MacIntosh and MacLean, 2001; Tetenbaum, 1998). Many writers have argued that organisations are also complex systems which, to survive, need to operate at the edge of chaos and have to respond continuously to changes in their environments through just such a process of spontaneous self-organising change (Hayles, 2000; Lewis, 1994; Macbeth, 2002; MacIntosh and MacLean, 1999, 2001; Stacey, 2003; Stickland, 1998). In applying this perspective to the computer industry, Brown and Eisenhardt (1997: 28) found that:

> The rate and scale of innovation . . . was such that the term 'incremental' seemed, in retrospect, stretched. Yet it was not radical innovation such as DNA cloning, either. . . . Similarly, managers described 'constantly reinventing' themselves. This too seemed more than incremental (i.e., unlike replacing top managers here and there) but also not the massive, rare, and risky change of the organizational and strategy literatures. And so we realized that we were probably looking at a third kind of process that is neither incremental nor radical and that does not fit the punctuated equilibrium model . . .

The problems with this perspective, as Stickland (1998) shows, are that (a) it is not clear that one can readily apply theories from the physical sciences to the social sciences, as is demonstrated by the fact that even proponents of its use in the social sciences are equivocal on this point; and (b) there have been few empirical studies which provide strong evidence to support the complexity view.

Nevertheless, as the next chapter will show, there is growing support for the continuous transformation model. In turn this has led to a search for what are seen as more appropriate approaches to change than the one offered by Lewin and the OD movement.

Conclusions

This chapter began by examining the theoretical foundations of change management and it was argued that in judging the applicability of approaches to managing change, one should assess whether they apply to individual, group or system-wide change.

The chapter then proceeded to examine the origins and development of the Planned approach to change, which dominated the theory and practice of change management from the 1940s to the 1980s. It was shown that the foundations of Planned change were laid by Kurt Lewin. After his death, however, it was taken up, and over time significantly modified, by the Organization Development movement in the USA. In terms of organisational change, the Planned approach focused upon resolving group conflicts and improving group performance by bringing together managers, employees and a change consultant. Through a process of learning, those involved gain new insights into their situation and are thus able to identify more effective ways of working together. Advocates of Planned change, especially the earlier ones, believe that group learning and individual development are at least as important as the actual change process itself. This, in part, arises from the humanist and democratic values that underpin Planned change and which derive from Kurt Lewin's background and beliefs.

Under the auspices of Organization Development, however, the influence of these values has lessened. The focus of Planned change has moved from conflict resolution to performance enhancement, as Organization Development has grown into a consultancy industry aimed almost exclusively at resolving problems within client organisations. Therefore, as was the case with the approaches to strategy discussed in Chapters 6 and 7, it is possible to draw a distinction between those proponents of Planned change, especially Lewin and early OD pioneers, who take an analytical approach, and those who take a more prescriptive approach, especially those whose livelihood depends upon their selling their services as change consultants.

In the 1960s and 1970s, Planned change, with its increasing array of tools, techniques and practitioners, became the dominant approach to managing organisational change. From the 1980s onwards, however, Planned change has faced increasing levels of criticism, the main ones relating to its perceived inability to cope with radical, coercive change situations or ones where power and politics are dominant. In its defence, as described earlier, there are proponents of Planned change who would argue that these criticisms are not valid, that it is a more flexible and holistic approach than its detractors would acknowledge, and that it is capable of incorporating transformational change (Bradford and Burke, 2004; French and Bell, 1999; Greiner and Cummings, 2004; McLennan, 1989; Mirvis, 1990; Worley and Feyerhern, 2003). However, they would acknowledge that OD as a whole does have serious issues which need to be addressed. There are also those who believe that many of the criticisms of Lewin's work are misplaced (Burnes, 2004b, 2004c, 2007). Nevertheless, partly as a consequence of these criticisms of the Planned approach, and partly in the context of newer perspectives on change such as the punctuated-equilibrium and continuous transformation models, new approaches to change have been gaining ground in recent years, one of which in particular has come to dominate the literature. Though aspects of it have been given a number of different labels, such as continuous improvement or organisational learning, it is more often referred to as the *Emergent* approach to change. The Emergent approach tends to see change as driven from the bottom up rather than from the top down; it stresses that change is an open-ended and continuous process of adaptation to changing conditions and circumstances; and it also sees the process of change as a process of learning, and not just a method of changing organisational structures and practices (Dawson, 1994; Mabey and Mayon-White, 1993; Wilson, 1992). Therefore, the next chapter will examine the principles and merits of the Emergent approach to change.

Test your learning

Short answer questions

1. What are the main theoretical foundations of change management?

2. What are the key differences between the main theoretical foundations of change management?

3. How did Kurt Lewin define the term 'Planned change'?

4. How do contemporary OD practitioners define Planned change?

5. How has OD developed since the 1960s?

6. What are the ethical principles which underpin Planned change and OD?

7. What are the main criticisms of the Planned approach?

8. What are the main criticisms of OD?

9. Evaluate the validity of the main criticisms of Planned change and OD.

10. Discuss the implications of the Planned approach for managerial behaviour.

Essay questions

1. What was Kurt Lewin's main contribution to change management and how relevant is it for contemporary organisations?

2. How has the OD movement sought to update its approach to organisational change? To what extent has it been successful?

Suggested further reading

1. Burnes, B (2004c) Kurt Lewin and the planned approach to change: a re-appraisal. *Journal of Management Studies*, **41**(6), 977–1002.

   Burnes, B (2007) Kurt Lewin and the Harwood studies: the foundations of OD. *Journal of Applied Behavioral Science*, **43**(2), 213–31.

   Marrow, AJ (1969) *The Practical Theorist: The Life and Work of Kurt Lewin*. Teachers College Press (1977 edition): New York, USA.

   Taken together, the articles and the book provide a comprehensive examination of Lewin's life and work.

2. Cummings, TG and Worley, CG (2005) *Organization Development and Change* (8th edition). South-Western College Publishing: Mason, OH, USA.

   French, WL and Bell, CH (1999) *Organization Development* (6th edition). Prentice-Hall: Upper Saddle River, NJ, USA.

   These two books provide a comprehensive guide to the origins and practices of OD.

The transformation of XYZ Construction:
Phase 2 – change of structure

BACKGROUND

XYZ Construction employs 500 staff and is part of a European-based multinational enterprise. Its main business is the provision of specialist services to major construction projects. As is typical for the construction industry, XYZ operates in a highly competitive and at times hostile and aggressive environment. In 1996 a new Managing Director was appointed. He spent much of the next three years developing a more participative culture in the organisation (see Case Study 3, Chapter 3). In 1999, XYZ decided it was time to change its structure to reflect its new ways of working and its developing culture.

TOWARDS TEAM XYZ

By 1999, the company was a much more cohesive, open and efficient organisation. However, its basic structure remained the same as when the new Managing Director had taken over. There was Head Office, which dealt with large, national projects, and five regional offices that dealt with smaller, local projects. Each of these offices was organised on a functional basis; they each had separate departments for Finance, Estimation, Design and Engineering. In addition, the Head Office had a Human Resources function which covered the entire company. This structure gave rise to a number of problems: rivalry between the Head Office and the regional offices; and rivalry and lack of communication within the various offices between departments and functions. A particular problem was the relationship between Estimation and Design in the Head Office.

The former was responsible for dealing with customers and setting the price for a job. The cost of a job, however, was based on the design provided by the Design Office. Though based in the same building, there was friction between the two functions, with each seeking to second-guess the other. The large jobs were often very complex, and even within the two functions of Estimation and Design there could be disputes about the best way to carry out a job. However, there was much more dispute between the two functions. Estimation felt that Design sometimes made jobs too complex and costly, and Design felt that Estimation did not understand the technical aspects of what they were suggesting to customers. This caused problems for Engineering, which was responsible for the actual construction process. The engineers sometimes found themselves starting jobs where there were still disagreements between Estimation and Design over what had been quoted for and what was required. Nevertheless, the general view was that the company was more efficient, better-run and a friendlier place than it had been three years earlier.

In 1999, the Managing Director and his Deputy began to have discussions in the company over restructuring. Their basic aim was to remove functional barriers and create a more teamwork-based, process-focused organisation. However, they did not underestimate how difficult this would be. It would need a complete reorganisation within and between the offices. It would reduce the power of the regional managers and amalgamate the Head Office empires of some directors. The Managing Director recognised that such changes

▶

could and probably would create friction and resistance. He also recognised that XYZ lacked the skills to plan and implement such a change. He, therefore, brought in a change consultant to assist with the exercise. After discussions with the consultant, a five-stage change process was agreed comprising the following activities:

1. Change readiness audit
2. Evaluation and planning workshops
3. Communication
4. Implementation and team-building
5. Evaluation

STAGE 1

The consultant undertook a change readiness audit to identify key issues and concerns which needed to be addressed. This consisted of face-to-face interviews with all senior managers, and interviews and discussions with other staff from all levels of the company. It also involved a SWOT exercise to assess the company's competitive position. Some 70 people, at all levels, were involved in the SWOT. The interviews showed that there was a general recognition of the problems brought about by the existing structure, but little agreement about any new structure, and some concern over potential loss of status and career opportunities if a flatter, less functional structure was adopted. However, the audit also showed that managers and staff alike had faith in and respect for the Managing Director. They also felt that the changes that had taken place over the previous three years had been positive. In addition, there was a strong sense of self-belief in the company that whatever the changes required, they could achieve them. Nevertheless, there was also concern by some individuals that changes in structure would affect their career progres-

sion or status, especially if the new structure involved multi-function teams and reduced the number of departments. The SWOT exercise showed that there was considerable agreement that the company had a strong technical base but concerns about lack of teamworking and entrepreneurial flair. In particular, staff in the regional offices felt that opportunities for new business were being missed. They also felt that their skills were under-utilised by being devoted to mainly small jobs rather than having an opportunity to participate in the larger contracts. The findings from the change audit were used to structure and begin the second stage of the change process, the evaluation and planning workshops.

STAGE 2

There were five one-day workshops spread over a two-month period. The purpose of these workshops was to establish a set of criteria for evaluating alternative structures, identify what alternatives existed, test these against the evaluation criteria, select a preferred structure and develop plans for implementing it. This was seen as an iterative process. Even when the evaluation criteria had been agreed, it was expected that further discussions about alternative structures and planning would lead to some of these being questioned, challenged and amended. Similarly, once a preferred structure had been agreed, it could still be amended if the planning process threw up issues that had not been considered. At the end of each workshop, participants had an agreed set of actions which they had to undertake, a key one being to go out and discuss what had emerged from the workshops with their colleagues in the rest of the company. A newsletter was also issued from each workshop.

The first two workshops were for the senior management team (SMT) only and the remaining three for the SMT plus the next layer of managers down, an additional 15 to 20 people. The results of the audit were presented to the first workshop, which began the process of developing a set of evaluation criteria and generating alternative structures. At the end of Workshop 1, a consensus seemed to be emerging with regard to a preferred structure. At the end of Workshop 2, it was agreed that the new structure should be built around the three core activities of the company, which were labelled: Get Work; Do Work; and Get Paid. It was also agreed that whilst it was important to keep the regional offices, their staff should be merged into the new structure. In effect, what emerged was a process-orientated flat, matrix structure with staff in the regional offices being responsible both to the Regional Manager and the Process Manager in Head Office. For the Head Office staff, in the main, their line manager and process manager would be the same person. As might be expected, this new structure did not emerge without much discussion, debate and in some cases soul-searching. The SMT also recognised that this was probably the most radical of the proposals they had looked at, and the one likely to meet the most resistance both from regional managers, whose power would be much reduced, and functional specialists in Estimation and Design who would have to be merged to create the 'Get Work' group. In addition, it was clear that some Directors were not happy to see their own department dismantled and their own position threatened.

Workshop 3 was devoted to presenting the proposed structure to the new participants, testing it and in some cases agreeing to amend it. Workshops 4 and 5 concentrated on the details of implementing the new structure. This covered everything from where people would sit, to whom they would report, new job descriptions, communication and team-building. This last exercise was seen as vital to ensuring that staff in the reorganised

structure worked as teams and cooperated with other teams rather than merely creating another set of functional barriers. It was at this point that it was agreed that the new structure be named 'Team XYZ' to emphasise that the intention was to create a company where everyone felt they were members of one team. There was also much discussion and consultation between the Workshops with staff in the rest of the company. At the end of Stage 2, almost all managers and supervisors in the company and a great number of the workforce had been involved in the process and by November 1999, the company was ready to communicate the new structure both internally and externally (to their parent company and customers).

STAGE 3

The communication stage was both short and intense. Members of the SMT were given the task of visiting all areas of the company and briefing them on the new structure and how it would impact on them. Though there were also newsletters and information on the company's intranet, it was these face-to-face briefings with small groups of staff which generated the most debate. They also raised some questions, mainly of a detailed nature, which had not been addressed. In general, however, the new structure received a positive welcome and the implementation stage then began.

STAGE 4

The new structure was rolled out over a three-month period. Ideally everything would have changed overnight, but the logistics of moving staff around from one group to another, physically altering office accommodation, and training managers for their new roles took time. Also, the intention was to ensure that all managers and supervisors, including those on

(CASE STUDY 8 CONT.)

sites, went through Team XYZ team-building workshops. Although, as expected, there were some hiccups and some unanticipated problems, by the end of March 2000 the new structure was fully up and running with remarkably little difficulty.

STAGE 5

In April, a two-day meeting of all the company's senior and middle managers was held to evaluate the change that had taken place, identify issues that needed to be addressed, and ensure that the momentum was maintained and that staff did not fall back into old ways of working. As part of this process, each manager was asked to identify two steps that they personally would take to develop the new structure further and promote teamworking. These were all written on flip charts and pinned to the walls for everyone to see. At the beginning of the two days, there was something of an air of exhaustion about the managers; they had been through a period of major upheaval and, as one said, 'We need a period of consolidation'. At the end of the two days, they left not only having agreed that the new structure was working remarkably well, but also with a whole host of new changes they wanted to make to improve the structure further.

SUMMARY

Though the development and implementation of a new structure at XYZ was not without its difficulties, it was achieved remarkably quickly and with relatively little disruption. There was significant potential for those who might lose out from the changes to try to prevent, or at least slow down, their implementation. All the regional managers and a

number of the directors saw their areas of responsibility, and thus power, reduced. Many of the functional specialists found themselves operating in multi-function teams where their promotion prospects depended less on their technical abilities *per se* and more on their ability to work and manage as a team player. There was also the fact that people who did not like each other suddenly found that they were working side by side. One explanation as to why the potential dangers to the change process did not emerge is clearly a result of the way it was managed. It was an open process that involved a great number of people either directly or indirectly. At some point, all the issues that needed to be considered, even personality issues, were brought out on the table and discussed, sometimes quite often. There was also a tenacity and momentum to the process. It was clear from the start that the Managing Director wanted to see a new structure and would not be fobbed off with a sub-optimal compromise. It was also clear from the change audit that many other people in the company recognised that its structure needed changing, even if they were nervous about such a change. In essence, the company was ready for such a change, even if some were uncomfortable with the outcome.

Questions

1. Compare and discuss XYZ's approach to change with Lewin's Three-Step model.

2. Undertake a Force Field Analysis (Figure 8.1) of XYZ prior to the change of structure. Identify and discuss which of the forces were changed, why they needed to be changed and how the changes were achieved.

3. Use the Coping Cycle, Figure 8.4, to analyse and discuss why the change of structure appeared to be accepted with such little resistance.

CHAPTER 9

Developments in change management

The Emergent approach and beyond

Learning objectives

After studying this chapter, you should be able to:

- list the reasons for the decline in popularity of the Planned approach to change;
- discuss the main elements of the Emergent approach to change;
- describe the processualist approach to change;
- explain the implications of complexity theories for organisational change;
- state the strengths and weaknesses of the Emergent approach;
- understand how Emergent change can be applied in practice;
- appreciate the role of the change agent.

Ideas and perspectives 9.1
Continuous change

The Enterprise of the Future

What will the Enterprise of the Future look like? To answer that question, we spoke with more than 1,000 CEOs from around the world. These conversations, together with our statistical and financial analyses, provide a unique perspective on the future of the enterprise. CEOs are rapidly positioning their businesses to capture the growth opportunities they see. Our discussions about their plans and challenges revealed several striking findings:

Organizations are bombarded by change, and many are struggling to keep up.
Eight out of ten CEOs see significant change ahead, and yet the gap between expected change and the ability to manage it has almost tripled since our last Global CEO Study in 2006.

CEOs view more demanding customers not as a threat, but as an opportunity to differentiate. CEOs are spending more to attract and retain increasingly prosperous, informed and socially aware customers.

▶

Nearly all CEOs are adapting their business models – two-thirds are implementing extensive innovations. More than 40 percent are changing their enterprise models to be more collaborative.

CEOs are moving aggressively toward global business designs, deeply changing capabilities and partnering more extensively. CEOs have moved beyond the cliché of globalization, and organizations of all sizes are reconfiguring to take advantage of global integration opportunities.

Financial outperformers are making bolder plays. These companies anticipate more change, and manage it better. They are also more global in their business designs, partner more extensively and choose more disruptive forms of business model innovation.

These findings – across industries, geographies and organizations of different sizes – paint a surprisingly similar view of the traits that we believe will be needed for future success. At its core, the Enterprise of the Future is . . .

- *Hungry for change.*
- *Innovative beyond customer imagination.*
- *Globally integrated.*
- *Disruptive by nature.*
- *Genuine, not just generous.*

Source: IBM (2008) *The Enterprise of the Future: IBM Global CEO Study*, pp. 7–8.

Introduction

As the IBM Study shows (*see* Ideas and perspectives 9.1), organisations today view themselves less and less as stable and enduring institutions, and more and more as 'work in progress' subject to continuing and continuous change. Chapter 8 described how the Planned approach to change dominated the theory and practice of change management from the late 1940s to the early 1980s. Since then, the Emergent approach has taken over from the Planned approach as the dominant approach to change. This approach starts from the assumption that change is not a linear process or a one-off isolated event but is a continuous, open-ended, cumulative and unpredictable process of aligning and re-aligning an organisation to its changing environment (Falconer, 2002). Weick (2000: 225) comments as follows on studies of Emergent change:

> *The recurring story is one of autonomous initiatives that bubble up internally; continuous emergent change; steady learning from both failure and success; strategy implementation that is replaced by strategy making; the appearance of innovations that are unplanned, unforeseen and unexpected; and small actions that have surprisingly large consequences.*

Advocates of Emergent change argue that it is more suitable to the turbulent and continually changing environment in which firms now operate. They reject both the incremental approach of Planned change, which they characterise as individually separate and distinct change-events, and the large-scale, unexpected, discontinuous and reactive approach of those who espouse the punctuated equilibrium model. Instead, they argue that organisations must continually and synergistically adapt their internal practices and behaviour in real time to changing external conditions (Beer and Nohria, 2000). Consequently, 'The art of leadership in the management field would seem to lie in the ability to shape the process [of change] in the long term rather than direct single episodes' (Pettigrew and Whipp, 1991: 143). As Orlikowski (1996: 65–6) maintains:

> *In this perspective, organizational transformation is not portrayed as a drama staged by deliberate directors with predefined scripts and choreographed moves, or the inevitable outcome of a technological logic, or a sudden discontinuity that fundamentally invalidates the status quo. Rather, organizational transformation is seen here to be an ongoing improvisation enacted by organizational actors trying to make sense of and act coherently in the world. . . . Each variation of a given form is not an abrupt or discrete event, neither is it, by itself, discontinuous. Rather, through a series of ongoing and situated accommodations, adaptations, and alterations (that draw on previous variations and mediate future ones), sufficient modifications may be enacted over time that fundamental changes are achieved. There is no deliberate orchestration of change here, no technological inevitability, no dramatic discontinuity, just recurrent and reciprocal variations in practice over time. Each shift in practice creates the conditions for further breakdowns, unanticipated outcomes, and innovations, which in their turn are responded to with more variations. And such variations are ongoing; there is no beginning or end point in this change process.*

In a similar vein, Caldwell (2006: 77) refers to Emergent change as 'a long-term complex and incremental process of shaping how change unfolds over time'. For Brown and Eisenhardt (1997: 28) change is 'neither incremental nor radical' but 'a third kind of process' that lies somewhere in between. Though they may disagree with Caldwell about the 'size' of change, all three would agree to view change as occurring continuously and synergistically with each change initiative being linked to the critical path of the organisation rather than being a separate or rare event. This is why the advocates of Emergent change argue that it needs to be viewed holistically and contextually (Mintzberg and Westley, 1992). Furthermore, and just as importantly, proponents of Emergent change recognise that organisations are power systems and, consequently, change is a political process whereby different groups in an organisation struggle to protect or enhance their own interests (Orlikowski and Yates, 2006).

To understand the nature of Emergent change, this chapter begins by presenting the case against the Planned approach and the rise of the Emergent perspective on change. It then goes on to examine the main arguments for, and characteristics of, Emergent change, including those put forward by complexity theorists. This will show that, although they do not always agree with each other, the advocates of Emergent change are united by the emphasis they place on organisational structure, culture and learning, and their perspective on managerial behaviour and the role of power and politics in the change process. Following this, the chapter presents the recipes for change put forward by proponents of Emergent change. It then goes on to examine the different perspectives on change agents and their role. In summarising the Emergent approach, it is argued that, though it has a number of distinct strengths, like Planned change it is a flawed and partial approach to change. In conclusion, it is argued that despite the large body of literature devoted to the topic of change management, and the many tools and techniques available to change agents, there is considerable debate and little agreement regarding the most appropriate approach. One thing is clear: neither the Emergent approach nor the Planned approach is suitable for all situations and circumstances.

From Planned to Emergent change

As was shown in Chapter 8, the Planned approach to change has been, and remains, highly influential, not just in the USA but across the world (Fagenson-Eland *et al*, 2004). It is still far and away the best developed, documented and supported approach to change. This is because of the custodianship of the Organization Development (OD) movement in the USA. OD has taken Kurt Lewin's original concept of Planned change and turned it into a thriving consultancy industry with its own standards, accreditation procedures and membership (Cummings and Worley, 1997). In doing so, Lewin's conception of Planned change as applying to small-group, human-centred change has been extended to include organisation-wide change initiatives. This has led to some confusion between Planned (participative) change as promoted by the OD movement and Planned (directive–transformational) change as promoted by some elements of the strategic planning movement (Beer and Nohria, 2000; Mintzberg *et al*, 1998a, 1998b).

This section, following on from the previous chapter, is concerned with the Planned approach to change as promoted by Lewin and the OD movement and which, from the late 1940s to the early 1980s, was the dominant approach to change, especially in the USA. As was discussed in Chapter 8, from the early 1980s onwards, it has faced increasing levels of criticism as to its appropriateness and efficacy, especially in terms of its ability to cope with continuous change, its emphasis on incremental change, its neglect of organisational conflict and politics, and its advocacy of a 'one best way' approach to change.

It was the rise of Japanese competitiveness and the apparent eclipse of Western industry in the late 1970s that precipitated the questioning of existing approaches to structuring, managing and changing organisations (e.g. Pascale and Athos, 1982; Peters and Waterman, 1982). Weick (2000: 226–7) states that the main drawbacks of Planned change were seen as:

> . . . *a high probability of relapse; uneven diffusion among units; large short-term losses that are difficult to recover; less suitability for opportunity-driven than for threat-driven alterations; unanticipated consequences due to limited foresight; temptations towards hypocrisy (when people talk the talk of revolution but walk the talk of resistance); adoption of best practices that work best elsewhere because of a different context; ignorance among top management regarding key contingencies and capabilities at the front line; and lags in implementation that make the change outdated before it's even finished.*

For Wilson (1992), it is the increasingly dynamic and uncertain nature of the business environment that undermines the case for Planned change and underlines the appropriateness of the Emergent approach. He also believes that the Planned approach, by attempting to lay down timetables, objectives and methods in advance, is too heavily reliant on the role of managers, and assumes (rashly) that they can have a full understanding of the consequences of their actions and that their plans will be understood and accepted and can be implemented. Similarly, Buchanan and Storey (1997: 127) maintain that the main criticism of those who advocate Planned change is:

> . . . *their attempt to impose an order and a linear sequence to processes that are in reality messy and untidy, and which unfold in an iterative fashion with much back-tracking and omission.*

The proponents of Culture–Excellence were perhaps the most vociferous and scathing critics of Planned change, arguing that:

> *Lewin's model was a simple one, with organizational change involving three stages; unfreezing, changing and refreezing . . . This quaintly linear and static conception – the organization as an ice cube – is so wildly inappropriate that it is difficult to see why it has not only survived but prospered. . . . Suffice it to say here, first, that organizations are never frozen, much less refrozen, but are fluid entities with many 'personalities'. Second, to the extent that there are stages, they overlap and inter-penetrate one another in important ways.* (Kanter *et al*, 1992: 10)

The advocates of Culture–Excellence, as described in Chapter 3, argued that Western organisations were bureaucratic, inflexible and stifled innovation. In place of Lewin's 'wildly inappropriate' model of change, the advocates of Culture–Excellence called for organisations to adopt cultures that promote innovation and entrepreneurship and encourage bottom-up, flexible, continuous and cooperative change. However, they also recognised that top-down coercion, and rapid transformation, might be necessary to create the conditions in which this type of approach could flourish.

At the same time, other new perspectives on organisations, especially concerning the role of power and politics in decision-making, were also coming to the fore (*see* Chapter 5). Writers such as Jeffrey Pfeffer (1981, 1992) maintained that the objectives, and outcomes, of change programmes were more likely to be determined by power struggles than by any process of consensus-building or rational decision-making. This paved the way for the development of a processual approach to organisational change (see next section), which highlights the continuous, unpredictable and political nature of change (Dawson, 1994; Pettigrew, 1985, 1997; Wilson, 1992). Looking at Planned change versus a processual approach, Dawson (1994: 3–4) comments that:

> *Although this [Lewin's] theory has proved useful in understanding planned change under relatively stable conditions, with the continuing and dynamic nature of change in today's business world, it no longer makes sense to implement a planned process for 'freezing' changed behaviours. Implementing stability and reinforcing behaviour which conforms to a rigid set of procedures for new work arrangements does not meet the growing requirements for employee flexibility and structural adaptation to the unfolding and complex nature of ongoing change processes. . . . The processual framework . . . adopts the view that change is a complex and dynamic process which should not be solidified or treated as a series of linear events. . . . central to the development of a processual approach is the need to incorporate an analysis of the politics of managing change.*

For the postmodernists (*see* Alvesson and Deetz, 1996; Foucault, 1983; Gergen, 1992), power is also a central feature of change, but it arises from the socially constructed nature of organisational life:

In a socially-constructed world, responsibility for environmental conditions lies with those who do the constructing. . . . This suggests at least two competing scenarios for organizational change. First, organization change can be a vehicle of domination for those who conspire to enact the world for others . . . An alternative use of social constructionism is to create a democracy of enactment in which the process is made open and available to all . . . such that we create opportunities for freedom and innovation rather than simply for further domination. (Hatch, 1997: 367–8)

Thus, from the early 1980s, a powerful consensus built up against the Planned approach to change. It is a consensus, however, that criticises Planned change from very different perspectives: ranging from the free market neo-liberalism of Tom Peters to the neo-Marxism of some of the postmodernists. Therefore, they are certainly a much less coherent group than the advocates of Planned change and, rather than being united by a shared belief, they tend to be distinguished by a common disbelief in the efficacy of Planned change. Nevertheless, they do share at least two beliefs: firstly, instead of seeing change as a phenomenon that can be pre-planned and has a finite end point, they see change as an 'emerging' and ongoing process of organisational adaptation and transformation. Secondly, they adopt an open systems perspective. That is, they see individual organisations as interdependent parts or sub-systems of a much larger environment, though they disagree about whether the environment is a concrete reality or a socially constructed phenomenon. The environment impacts upon and affects the actions and decisions of organisations, but they also impact on the environment. Proponents of the Emergent approach see change as emerging from the day-to-day actions and decisions of members of an organisation. In this sense, change can emerge from attempts by members of organisations to align the organisation with its environment, or as the result of different groups battling for domination, or even from attempts to construct a new, or challenge an old, social reality.

Having identified what separates it from the Planned approach to change, we can now move on to examine the Emergent approach in more detail.

The Emergent approach to change

For proponents of the Emergent approach, change is a continuous, dynamic and contested process that emerges in an unpredictable and unplanned fashion. For Weick (2000: 227), the advantages of Emergent change include:

. . . sensitivity to local contingencies; suitability for on-line real-time experimentation, learning, and sensemaking; comprehensibility and manageability; likelihood of satisfying needs for autonomy, control, and expression; proneness to swift implementation; resistance to unravelling; ability to exploit existing tacit knowledge; and tightened and shortened feedback loops from results to action.

The rationale for the Emergent approach stems, according to Hayes (2002: 37), from the belief that:

. . . the key decisions about matching the organisation's resources with opportunities, constraints and demands in the environment evolve over time and are the outcome of cultural and political processes in organisations.

One of the main strands of the Emergent approach is provided by processual analysts, deriving from the work of Andrew Pettigrew (1973, 1979, 1985, 1990a, 1990b, 1997, 2000, *et al*, 2001). Processualists, as the name implies, conduct process research in organisations. They define a process as 'a sequence of individual and collective events, actions, and activities unfolding over time in context' (Pettigrew, 1997: 338). Therefore, process research in organisations is the study of organisational change over time and in context. Processualists reject prescriptive, recipe-driven approaches to change and are suspicious of single causes or simple explanations of events. Instead, when studying change, they focus on the interrelatedness of individuals, groups, organisations and society (Dawson, 2003; Pettigrew and Whipp, 1993). In particular, they claim that the process of change is a complex and untidy cocktail of rational decision processes, individual perceptions, political struggles and coalition-building (Huczynski and Buchanan, 2001). Within this complex and untidy cocktail, processualists recognise 'the importance of planning for change' and the presence of 'processes of continuity'; they also recognise, however, that these are constrained and influenced by 'the complex untidy and messy nature of change' (Dawson, 2003: 25). Nevertheless, Pettigrew and Whipp (1991: 165) observed:

Leading change calls for the resolution of not so much great single issues but rather a pattern of interwoven problems.

The elaborateness of the processualist view of change is shown by Pettigrew (1997: 340), who states that processualists pursue their work through five internally consistent guiding principles (*see* Ideas and perspectives 9.2).

Ideas and perspectives 9.2
Pettigrew's five guiding principles of processual research

The irreducible purpose of a processual analysis remains to account for and explain the what, why and how of the links between context, processes and outcomes. I would like to conclude this statement of theory of method for conducting processual research by reaffirming five internally consistent guiding assumptions. They are:

1. *embeddedness, studying processes across a number of levels of analysis;*
2. *temporal interconnectedness, studying processes in past, present and future time;*
3. *a role in explanation for context and action;*
4. *a search for holistic rather than linear explanations of process; and*
5. *a need to link process analysis to the location and explanation of outcomes.*

Source: Pettigrew (1997: 340)

For Pettigrew, change is never a one-off or isolated event. For him, it cuts across functions, spans hierarchical divisions, and has no neat starting or finishing point; instead it is a 'complex analytical, political, and cultural process of challenging and changing the core beliefs, structure and strategy of the firm' (Pettigrew, 1987: 650).

Therefore, advocates of Emergent change tend to stress the developing and unpredictable nature of change. They view change as a process that unfolds through the interplay of multiple variables within an organisation, especially context, consultation and political behaviour (Dawson, 2003).

Power and politics

Dawson (1994: 180–2) states that:

> *In managing these transitions practitioners need to be aware of: the importance of power politics within organizations as a determinant of the speed, direction and character of change; the enabling and constraining properties of the type and scale of change being introduced; and the influence of the internal and external context on the pathways and outcomes of change on new work arrangement. . . . [Also] . . . the management of these changes cannot be characterized as being composed of a linear series of phases, nor do the outcomes represent the results of objective rational decision-making on the part of managers. . . . [nor] as a single reaction to adverse contingent circumstances.*

Therefore, successful change is less dependent on detailed plans and projections than on reaching an understanding of the intricacy of the issues concerned, including the central role played by power and politics in initiating and managing change, and in identifying the range of available options (Pettigrew, 1997). The political dimension of change is further emphasised by the postmodernists, for whom the struggle for power and domination is the central feature of change in organisations (Hassard, 1993; Hatch, 1997). As Finstad (1998) notes, however, the difference is that, for the processualists, the political nature of change tends to close off options, whereas for the postmodernists, the presence of conflicting interests gives people a range of new possibilities and ideas to choose from.

Despite their difference in emphasis, proponents of the Emergent approach do agree that power and politics play an important role in the process of organisational change. This is a major point of departure between them and proponents of Planned change. In commenting on the failure to incorporate the political nature of change into the traditional and more prescriptive literature on change, Hardy (1996) argues that this 'aversion' to discussing power has restricted our understanding of change and impeded our ability to manage it effectively. Pugh (1993) makes a similar point about the political nature of organisational life in Principle Two of his analysis of organisational change (*see* Ideas and perspectives 9.3). However, he also argues, in Principle Three, that rational and occupational systems need to be considered alongside, and not subordinate to, the political system. This clearly conflicts with the processualists, who see the political system as being paramount.

Ideas and perspectives 9.3
Pugh's four principles for understanding change

Principle One: Organizations are organisms. They are not mechanisms which can be taken apart and reassembled differently as required. They can be changed, but the change must be approached carefully with the implications for the various groupings thought out and the participants convinced of the worthwhileness of their point of view.

Principle Two: Organizations are political and occupational systems as well as rational resource allocation ones. Every reaction to a change proposal must be interpreted not only in terms of rational arguments of what is best for the firm . . . The reaction must also be understood in relation to the occupational system . . . and the political system (how will it affect the power, status, prestige of the group?).

Principle Three: All members of an organization operate simultaneously in all three systems – the rational, the occupational and the political ones. Do not make the mistake of becoming cynical and thinking that the occupational and the political aspects are all that matter, and that rational arguments are merely rationalizations to defend a particular position.

Principle Four: Change is most likely to be acceptable and effective in those people or departments who are successful in their tasks but who are experiencing tensions or failure in some particular part of their work. . . . They will have the two basic ingredients [for successful change] of confidence in their ability and motivation to change.

Source: Pugh (1993: 109–10)

The change process

Moving on to examine the change process itself, the Emergent perspective rejects both simple taxonomies of change, and approaches such as Total Quality Management and Business Process Re-engineering, which promise success through following a series of laid-down steps and stages (Beer and Nohria, 2000; Collins, 1998). According to Stace and Dunphy (2001: 5):

> *The appealing aspect of the promises held out for these change technologies is that they can absolve the manager from the onerous task of critically reviewing the full range of other competing approaches or devising a custom-made program. They cut through complexity. However, the offer is often illusory, for particular change approaches usually apply to particular situations, and simple solutions sometimes ignore the complexity of real life.*

Dawson (2003) sees change as:

. . . a complex ongoing dynamic in which the politics, substance and context of change all interlock and overlap, and in which our understanding of the present and expectations of the future can influence our interpretation of past events, which may in turn shape our experience of change.

From this perspective, even when changes are operational, they will need to be constantly refined and developed in order to maintain their relevance. Genus (1998: 51) uses an 'interpretive' perspective to explain the messy nature of organisational change, arguing that the 'various political, symbolic and structural factors [involved in the change process] condition the perceptions of individuals or groups'. Finstad's (1998) view of organisational change, whilst being consistent with the perspectives of Dawson and Genus, appears to adopt a realist perspective on change by drawing an important distinction between the concrete elements of change, such as structures and practices, and the more symbolic elements, such as people's basic understandings and assumptions about their organisations. He maintains, though, that it is the symbolic aspects that dominate the change process rather than the more concrete changes. The importance of symbolism and ritual in the change process is also emphasised by Schuyt and Schuijt (1998), who argue that the management of these is not only central to achieving successful change, but also plays a crucial role in reducing the uncertainty which change generates.

The role of managers

It is because change is so complex and multifaceted that Carnall (2003) suggests that mastering the challenge of change is not a specialist activity to be facilitated or driven by an expert, but an increasingly important part of every manager's role. Carnall (2003: 125–6) proposes four core managerial competences that are essential for the effective management of change:

- **Decision-making:** this includes intuition and vision, the ability to gather and utilise information, understanding the practical and political consequences of decisions, the ability to overcome resistance, the skill to understand and synthesise conflicting views and to be able to empathise with different groups.
- **Coalition-building:** this comprises the skills necessary to gain the support and resources necessary to implement decisions. These include checking the feasibility of ideas, gaining supporters, bargaining with other stakeholders and presenting new ideas and concepts in a way that wins support.
- **Achieving action:** this includes handling opposition, motivating people, providing support and building self-esteem.
- **Maintaining momentum and effort:** this involves team-building, generating ownership, sharing information and problems, providing feedback, trusting people and energising staff.

Stace and Dunphy (2001) take a more contextual view of managerial competences. Their Change Matrix identifies a spectrum of change situations, ranging from fine-tuning to corporate transformation, and a matching spectrum of styles of change management, ranging from cooperative to coercive. The Matrix identifies at least 16 combinations of change situations and styles of management, each of which requires a different set of managerial competences (*see* Figure 9.1).

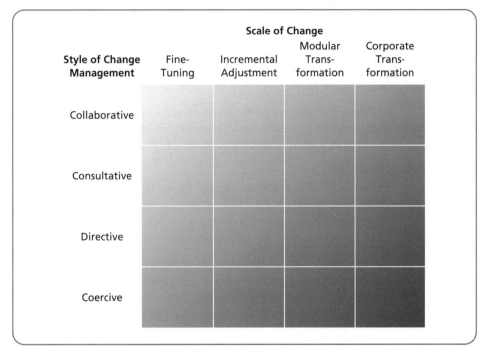

Figure 9.1 The Dunphy–Stace change matrix
Source: Stace and Dunphy (2001: 107)

Contingency

This view tallies with that of McCalman and Paton (1992) who suggest that, to be effective in creating sustainable change, managers need an extensive and systemic understanding of their organisation's environment, in order to identify the pressures for change and to ensure that, by mobilising the necessary internal resources, their organisation responds in a timely and appropriate manner. Similarly, Dawson (1994) claims that change must be linked to developments in markets, work organisation, systems of management control and the shifting nature of organisational boundaries and relationships. He emphasises that, in a dynamic business environment, one-dimensional change interventions are likely to generate only short-term results and heighten instability rather than reduce it. This is a point emphasised by many other writers (Beer and Nohria, 2000; Graetz *et al*, 2002; Hartley *et al*, 1997; Senior, 2002).

As can be seen, though not all state it openly, advocates of Emergent change tend to adopt a Contingency perspective, arguing that approaches to change need to be tailored to the situation of the individual organisation and the type of change it is undertaking (Weick, 2000). This is a point that is central to Pettigrew's contextualist approach to change:

> . . . *context and action are inseparable.* (Pettigrew, 2000: 243)

Leadership [of change] requires action appropriate to its context.

(Pettigrew and Whipp, 1991: 165)

Therefore, Pettigrew offers a very particularistic view of change whereby each change situation is different and must be approached and managed differently. It follows from this that implicit in the case for Emergent change is the assumption that if organisations operated in more stable and predictable environments, the need for change would be less and it might be possible to conceive of it as a process of moving from one relatively stable state to another. As Dawson (1994: 3) observes:

Although [Lewin's] theory has proven to be useful in understanding planned change under relatively stable conditions, with the continuing and dynamic nature of change in today's business world, it no longer makes sense to implement a planned process of 'refreezing' changed behaviours.

For advocates of Emergent change, therefore, it is the uncertainty of the environment that makes Planned change inappropriate and Emergent change more pertinent. This is a point emphasised by Stickland (1998: 14), who draws on systems theory to emphasise the way that organisations are separate from but connected to their environment:

A system has an identity that sets it apart from its environment and is capable of preserving that identity within a given range of environmental scenarios. Systems exist within a hierarchy of other systems. They contain subsystems and exist within some wider system. All are interconnected . . .

From this systems perspective, Stickland (1998: 76) raises a question that many of those studying organisational change appear not to acknowledge:

To what extent does the environment drive changes within a system [i.e. an organisation] and to what extent is the system in control of its own change processes?

Finstad (1998: 721) puts this issue in a wider context by arguing that 'the organization is . . . the creator of its environment and the environment is the creator of the organization'. Though this has a postmodernist sound to it, realists would also recognise that organisations do contribute to the creation or the maintenance of their environment, but they see this as a long-term and largely unconscious process. This reciprocal relationship between an organisation and its environment clearly has profound implications for how organisations conceptualise and manage change. It also serves to emphasise that a key competence for organisations is the ability to scan the external environment in order to identify and assess the impact on them of trends and discontinuities and also to understand how their actions might affect the environment (Graetz *et al*, 2002; McCalman and Paton, 1992; Pettigrew and Whipp, 1993). This involves exploring the full range of external variables, including markets and customers, shareholders, legal requirements, the economy, suppliers, technology and social trends. This activity is made more difficult by the changing and arbitrary nature of organisation boundaries: customers can also be competitors; suppliers may become partners; and employees can be transformed into customers, suppliers or even competitors for scarce resources.

To cope with these complications and uncertainties, Pettigrew and Whipp (1993) maintain that organisations need to become open learning systems, with strategy development and change emerging from the way the company as a whole acquires, interprets and processes information about its environment. Carnall (2003) and Hayes (2002) take a similar view, arguing that an organisation's survival and growth depend on identifying environmental and market changes quickly, and responding opportunistically. This is in line with the discussion on organisational learning covered in Chapter 3. However, as Benjamin and Mabey (1993: 181) point out:

> . . . *while the primary stimulus for change remains those forces in the external environment, the primary motivator for how change is accomplished resides with the people within the organization.*

Bottom-up, not top-down

Consequently, actual or potential changes in the external environment require organisations to make choices over how and when to respond. Such responses, the supporters of the Emergent approach state, should promote, throughout the organisation, an extensive and deep understanding of strategy, structure, systems, people, style and culture, and how these can function either as sources of inertia that can block change, or alternatively, as levers to encourage an effective change process (Dawson, 2003; Pettigrew, 1997; Wilson, 1992). A concomitant development is the adoption of a 'bottom-up' rather than 'top-down' approach to initiating and implementing change. After all, there is little point in encouraging staff to identify change opportunities unless they are also encouraged to implement them. The case in favour of this move is based on the view that the pace of environmental change is so rapid and complex that it is impossible for a small number of senior managers effectively to identify, plan and implement the necessary organisational responses. The responsibility for organisational change is therefore of necessity becoming more devolved. As described in Chapter 2, this is very much what the advocates of Contingency Theory would expect in such a situation.

Nevertheless, the need for a bottom-up approach does not just arise from external pressures. As Stickland (1998: 93) notes, organisations are continually experiencing 'natural changes', i.e. the unintended consequences of deliberate decisions and actions:

> *Within any organisation at a given point in time there are a number of continual shifts and changes playing out at various levels. These are not planned changes with a defined beginning and end, but rather reflect the natural dynamics which take place internally.*

Such events may present organisations with unexpected and unlooked-for opportunities, such as new product ideas, but may also present unwelcome threats, such as the departure of key staff. Given that such changes are continually happening at all levels and across all functions, organisations would quickly become paralysed if it was left solely to senior managers to identify and resolve them. Therefore, if they are to be dealt with speedily, these local problems or opportunities have to be dealt with locally. As Senior (2002) comments, this requires organisations to empower their employees to make changes at a local level. This follows from Mintzberg's (1994) assertion that it is from these local and bottom-up actions that the direction of the organisation emerges and is given shape. This view is also supported by advocates of the complexity approach (*see* below).

In many ways, this is the crux of the Emergent argument – top-down, senior-management-imposed change does not work. What is required is managers and employees, on a day-to-day basis, to have the authority to be able to shape and reshape their part of the organisation to deal with the threats and opportunities presented by an ever-changing environment. However, as these changes emerge from a host of local responses, if they are to have a synergistic and positive effect on the organisation, as opposed to tearing it apart, such changes must be guided by a common vision of the future and a shared understanding of the organisation's priorities and situation.

Therefore, a bottom-up approach requires a major change in the role of senior managers. Instead of controlling employees, they have to empower people. Instead of directing and controlling change, they have to ensure that the organisation's members are receptive to the change process, and have the necessary skills, motivation and power to take charge of it. There is a distinction here between those who take a narrow view of empowerment, seeing it mainly as devolving some limited managerial responsibility, and those, *à la* Lewin, who see it as an emancipatory process that aims to create genuine organisational democracy, though it must be pointed out that even the former have a poor track record of success (Eccles, 1993; Foegen, 1999; Graetz *et al*, 2002; Huczynski and Buchanan, 2001; Lawler *et al*, 1998; Lee, 1999; Pfeffer, 1996; Stohl and Cheney, 2001; Wetlaufer, 1999). Nor is this just an issue of managers changing. Wilson (1992) believes that to achieve effective empowerment, senior managers must not only change the way they perceive and interpret the world, but achieve a similar transformation amongst everyone else in the organisation as well. Pettigrew and Whipp (1993: 17–18) contend that the degree to which organisations can achieve such a difficult task, and create a climate receptive to change, is dependent on four conditioning factors:

1. the extent to which there are key actors within the firm who are prepared to champion assessment techniques which increase the openness of the organisation;
2. the structural and cultural characteristics of the company;
3. the extent to which environmental pressures are recognised and their associated dramas developed; and
4. the degree to which assessment occurs as a multi-function activity which is not pursued as an end in itself but is then linked to the central operation of the business.

The complexity approach

As was described in Chapter 4, a wide range of organisational theorists and practitioners have argued that organisations are complex, non-linear systems in which change emerges through a process of spontaneous self-organisation, which is underpinned by a set of simple order-generating rules (Arndt and Bigelow, 2000; Bechtold, 1997; Black, 2000; Fitzgerald, 2002a; MacIntosh and MacLean, 2001; Stacey, 2003). The concept of self-organisation, as well as its implications for organisations, is very similar to the concept of Emergent change, especially in terms of the link between the emergent or self-organising nature of change and the need for greater organisational democracy (Burnes, 2005).

Complexity theorists argue that the best-run companies survive because they operate at the edge of chaos by relentlessly pursuing a path of continuous innovation brought about by a process that resembles self-organisation in nature (Brown and Eisenhardt,

1997; Frederick, 1998; Jenner, 1998). However, Beeson and Davis (2000) make the point that whilst it might be fruitful to see organisations as non-linear systems, to do so will require a fundamental shift in the role of management. Like many others (e.g. Boje, 2000; Stacey *et al*, 2002; Sullivan, 1999; Tetenbaum, 1998; Wheatley, 1992b), they point out that self-organising principles explicitly reject cause-and-effect, top-down, command-and-control styles of management. Brodbeck (2002) suggests that the belief by managers that order and control are essential to achieve their objectives should be rejected. For Tetenbaum (1998), the move to self-organisation will require managers to destabilise their organisations and develop the skill of managing order and disorder at the same time. Managers will need to encourage experimentation, divergent views, even allow rule-breaking, and recognise that 'people need the freedom to own their own power, think innovatively, and operate in new patterns' (Bechtold, 1997: 198). Beeson and Davis (2000) echo this point and argue that, in such situations, change becomes an everyday event undertaken by all in the organisation.

The implication of this for Bechtold (1997) is that organisations seeking to adopt a complexity approach will need to have a balanced distribution of power, strong customer focus, a strategy of continuous learning and an orientation towards community service. A further strand in this argument is provided by Kiel (1994), who claims that because small actions can have large and unpredictable consequences, individual human activity assumes great importance. Similarly, Jenner (1998) claims that for self-organisation to work, authority must be delegated to those who have access to the broadest channels of information that relate to the issue or problem concerned. Therefore, to all intents and purposes, the complexity approach to change, as it has been applied to organisations, lies firmly within the Emergent approach to change, and provides some of the rationale for it.

As can be seen, the advocates of Emergent change come from a wide variety of backgrounds and each offers their own distinct view on how organisations should and should not manage change. As the following section will show, however, there are some core similarities which link them.

The Emergent approach to successful change

Though the proponents of the Emergent approach reject the concept of universally applicable rules for change, the guidance they do provide tends to stress five features of organisations that either promote or obstruct success (see Figure 9.2).

Organisational structure

This is seen as playing a crucial role in determining where power lies, in defining how people relate to each other and in influencing the momentum for change (Carnall, 2003; Dawson, 2003; Hatch, 1997; Huczynski and Buchanan, 2001; Kotter, 1996). Crucially, as Galbraith (2000: 154) notes: 'The theory of organization has always identified some types of [organisational structures] as being more easily changeable than others.' As Morgan (1988) noted, there are really only four basic forms of structure which range from the very rigid to the very flexible, as follows: bureaucracy, matrix, project and loosely coupled organic network. Therefore, an appropriate organisational structure, in both its formal and informal elements, can be an important facilitator of change.

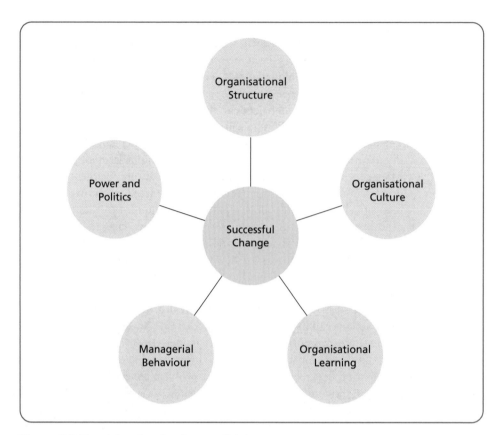

Figure 9.2 The determinants of successful change

The case for developing more appropriate organisational structures in order to facilitate change very much follows the arguments of the Contingency theorists (discussed in Chapter 2) and the Culture–Excellence school (discussed in Chapter 3), i.e. that dynamic and chaotic environments require organisations to adopt more flexible, less hierarchical structures. Those favouring an Emergent approach to change point out that the 1990s witnessed a general tendency to create flatter organisational structures in order to increase responsiveness by devolving authority and responsibility (Senior, 2002). As Kotter (1996: 169) remarks, the case for such structural changes is that:

An organization with more delegation, which means a flat hierarchy, is in a far superior position to maneuver than one with a big, change-resistant lump in the middle.

A similar point is made by proponents of the complexity approach. For Jenner (1998: 402), the key issue is that:

. . . enterprise must be organized into flexible basic units that permit new organizational structures to be identified and to emerge, and which promote efficient exchanges of information.

In studying innovating organisations, Brown and Eisenhardt (1997: 29) refer to such flexible structures as 'semistructures', which they claim:

. . . are sufficiently rigid so that change can be organized, but not so rigid that it cannot occur. . . . sustaining this semistructured state is challenging because it is a dissipative equilibrium and so requires constant managerial vigilance to avoid slipping into pure chaos or pure structure.

A like point is made by Galbraith (2000: 155), who refers to the 'reconfigurable' organisation, which:

. . . consists of a stable part and a variable part. The stable part consists of 'homes' for specialists in functions, which also host generalists on rotating assignments. . . . The variable part of the structure consists of integrating mechanisms and networks across the functions.

Brown and Eisenhardt (1997) claim that such structures are essential for ensuring organisational survival in highly competitive environments because they facilitate continuous innovation and improvisation and allow intensive, real-time communication within a structure of a few, very specific rules.

A common aspect of these new structures is the move to create customer-centred organisations with structures that reflect, and are responsive to, different markets rather than different functions (Galbraith, 2000; Hamel and Prahalad, 1994; Stace and Dunphy, 2001). Customer responsiveness places greater emphasis on effective horizontal processes and embodies the concept that, whether one is looking internally or externally, everyone is someone else's customer (Dale, 2003; Jenner, 1998).

One result of attempts to respond rapidly to changing conditions by breaking down internal and external barriers, disseminating knowledge and developing synergy across functions is the emergence of network organisations (Morgan, 1997; Wisdom, 2001). Network organisations have been defined in a number of ways and given a number of names – Handy (1989) refers to them as 'federal organisations', Robbins (1997) uses the term 'virtual organisation', after the Internet on which many of them either rely or are based, and Senge (2000: 77) writes of 'living human communities'. For Cummings and Worley (2001: 291), the purpose of a network-based structure is that it:

. . . manages the diverse, complex, and dynamic relationships among multiple organizations or units, each specializing in a particular business function or task.

Birchall and Lyons (1995) stress that networks can be in a constant state of flux as they adjust to the changing needs of their dynamic customer base. They also comment that in some cases, customers are even part of the network. For Snow *et al* (1993), a major benefit of network structures is that the semi-autonomous nature of each part of a network reduces the need for and erodes the power of centrally managed bureaucracies, which, in turn, leads to change and adaptation being driven from the bottom up rather than from the top down. They further argue that the specialisation and flexibility required to cope with globalisation, intense competition and rapid technological change, especially the challenge of the Internet, can only be achieved by loosening the central ties and controls that have characterised organisations in the past (Genus, 1998; Hardaker and Graham, 2001; Kanter *et al*, 1997; Kotter, 1996; Wisdom, 2001). However, is it clear that every organisation will have to adopt such structural changes in order to survive? The premise that this is necessary is based on the assumption that all organisations experience similar levels of environmental turbulence and cannot do anything other than adapt their internal arrangements to these external conditions. As argued in previous chapters, there are three flaws to this argument. Firstly, environmental instability is not uniform; it varies from industry to industry and organisation to organisation. Secondly, even where instability is present, organisations can choose to take action to reduce it rather than merely having to adapt to it. Lastly, as Child's concept of equifinality discussed in Chapter 6 suggests, there are a range of internal arrangements that are compatible with external turbulence, of which flattened hierarchies are only one.

A further point which needs to be recognised is that structures do not stand in isolation from the other elements of an organisation (Mintzberg and Westley, 1992). As Hannan *et al* (2003: 401) comment:

> *Organizational analysts commonly distinguish between formal architectural and informal cultural features. Architecture refers to the formal (official) specifications of an organization and its governance. Architectural choices are reflected in the formal structures for assigning work, that is, constructing the units that undertake the sub-transactions. The choices also specify the means of coordinating members and units, monitoring them, and allocating resources and rewards. Culture governs how work actually gets completed, how members interact, how decisions are actually made, which units defer to others, and so forth.*

Therefore, as argued in Chapter 5, it is not sufficient to have an appropriate structure; it must be matched with an appropriate culture if it is to be effective.

Organisational culture

There can be few people who now doubt the important role culture plays in the life of organisations, especially when it comes to change (Allaire and Firsirotu, 1984; Brown, 1995; De Witte and van Muijen, 1999; Hirschhorn, 2000). Johnson (1993: 64) suggested that the strategic management of change is 'essentially a cultural and cognitive phenomenon' rather than an analytical, rational exercise. Clarke (1994) states that the essence of sustainable change is to understand the culture of the organisation that is to be changed. If proposed changes contradict cultural biases and traditions, it is inevitable that they will be difficult to embed in the organisation. Kotter (1996) takes a similar view, arguing that for change to be successful it must be anchored in the organisation's culture.

Dawson (2003) echoes this theme. He suggests that attempts to realign internal behaviours with external conditions require change strategies that are culturally sensitive. Organisations, he points out, must be aware that the process is lengthy, potentially dangerous, and demands considerable reinforcement if culture change is to be sustained against the inevitable tendency to regress to old behaviours. Pointing to Pirelli's attempt to implement TQM in two of its Australian plants, Dawson (2003: 33) comments that:

> *Management had a plan and a timeframe for the 'successful' management of change, but they were not prepared for the very different contextual conditions and local operating cultures of the two adjacent plants in South Australia. The cultural socio-political aspects of change turned out to be far more important and influential than had been anticipated, or could be accommodated for, in planning the process of change.*

Likewise, Pettigrew (1997) stresses that organisational processes are embedded in an organisation's context, of which culture forms an important part. Pettigrew also points out that, because of this embeddedness, change can be slow. From the complexity perspective, Stacey (2003) similarly points to the importance of having an appropriate culture and the difficulty involved in changing an existing one. Cummings and Worley (2001) likewise recognise that culture can hinder the speed of change, especially when it is the culture that needs to change. In such cases, they point out, it is necessary to challenge mechanisms that reinforce old or inappropriate behaviour, such as reward, recruitment and promotion structures – all areas where resistance can be expected. In addition, if these reinforcement mechanisms are complemented by managerial behaviour which promotes risk aversion and fear of failure, it is unlikely to create a climate where people are willing to propose or undertake change. Accordingly, as Clarke (1994: 94) suggests, 'Creating a culture for change means that change has to be part of the way we do things around here, it cannot be bolted on as an extra.'

Therefore, for many proponents of the Emergent approach, an essential factor in successful change is for organisations to possess or to be able to develop an appropriate organisational culture. However, Senior (2002) notes that many writers and researchers take a different view. Beer *et al* (1993), for example, suggest that the most effective way to promote change is not by directly attempting to influence organisational behaviour or culture. Instead, they advocate restructuring organisations in order to place people in a new organisational context which imposes new roles, relationships and responsibilities upon them. This, they believe, forces new attitudes and behaviours upon people. This view, as discussed in Chapter 3, is also shared by Tom Peters (1993), who advocates rapid and complete destruction of existing hierarchical organisation structures as a precursor to behavioural change.

In Chapter 5, we discussed the difficulty and relevance of achieving cultural change, by whatever means. This discussion found some support for the Beer *et al* and Peters position. It noted that what many proponents of cultural change appear to advocate are changes to structure, policies and norms rather than attempts to change the deeper elements of culture. It was argued that many writers are highly sceptical about seeing culture as a promoter of change. This view is, perhaps, best summed up by Wilson (1992: 91), who claims that:

> ... to effect change in an organization simply by attempting to change its culture assumes an unwarranted linear connection between something called organizational culture and performance. Not only is this concept of organizational culture multi-faceted, it is also not always clear precisely how culture and change are related, if at all, and, if so, in which direction.

Organisational learning

This was examined in Chapter 3. For advocates of the Emergent approach, learning plays a key role in preparing people for, and allowing them to cope with, change (Bechtold, 1997; Senge, 2000). Put simply, learning means:

> ... the capacity of members of an organization to detect and correct errors and to seek new insights that would enable them to make choices that better produce outcomes that they seek. (Martin, 2000: 463)

A willingness to change often only stems from the feeling that there is no other option (Argyris, 1999; Pettigrew *et al*, 1992). Therefore, as Wilson (1992) suggests, change can be precipitated by encouraging dissatisfaction with current systems and procedures or making impending crises real to everyone in the organisation. Kotter (1996) even advocates engineering a crisis in order to build the momentum for change. Whatever the spur for change, however, staff are unlikely to recognise the need for change unless managers create mechanisms which allow them to become familiar with the company's performance, marketplace, customers, competitors, legal requirements, etc. (Fiol and Lyles, 1985; Probst and Buchel, 1997). Pettigrew and Whipp (1993: 18) also contended that 'collective learning' is one of the main preconditions for sustainable change. They argue that 'collective learning' ensures that the full implications of an organisation's view of its environment can then inform subsequent actions over the long term and, in turn, the way in which future shifts in the environment are tackled.

Clarke (1994) and Nadler (1993) suggest that individual and organisational learning stem from effective top-down communication and the promotion of self-development and confidence. In turn, this encourages the commitment to, and shared ownership of, the organisation's vision, actions and decisions that are necessary to respond to the external environment and take advantage of the opportunities it offers. Additionally, as Pugh (1993) points out, in order to generate the need and climate for change, people within organisations need to be involved in the diagnosis of problems and the development of solutions. Carnall (2003) takes this argument further, arguing that:

> *The effective organization is one which encourages and supports learning from change. This means that an open management style, encouraging initiative and risk, is needed.*

Likewise, Clarke (1994: 156) maintains that involving staff in change management decisions has the effect of 'stimulating habits of criticism and open debate', which enables them to challenge existing norms and question established practices.

Clarke goes on to say that although this can create the opportunity for innovation and radical change, challenging the status quo is also akin to challenging managerial judgement and authority. As Benjamin and Mabey (1993) maintain, though the questioning of the status quo is the essence of bottom-up change, it also leads to a form of role reversal whereby, rather than managers' pressuring staff to change, the reverse occurs. Therefore, a new, open management style can result in staff putting pressure on managers to address fundamental questions about the purpose and direction of the organisation which previously they might have preferred to avoid. Consequently, as Easterby-Smith *et al* (2000) and Tsang (1997) suggest, organisational learning is neither an easy nor an uncontentious option for organisations. There is also a great diversity of opinion as to what it is and how it can be promoted, which makes organisational learning a more difficult concept to apply than many of its supporters acknowledge (Burnes *et al*, 2003).

Managerial behaviour

Chapter 1 showed that the traditional view of managers sees them as directing and controlling staff, resources and information. It sees managers as being the only ones with the expertise, knowledge and legitimate authority to decide how and when change should take place. However, the Emergent approach to change, as with the Culture–Excellence approach to managing organisations, requires a radical change in the role of managers (Dawson, 2003; Kanter, 2008; Kotter and Cohen, 2002; Peters, 2006; Weick, 2000). Instead of directing change from the top, managers are expected to operate as facilitators and coaches who, through their ability to span hierarchical, functional and organisational boundaries, can bring together and empower teams and groups to identify the need for, and achieve, change (Bennis, 2000; Carnall, 2003; Mabey and Mayon-White, 1993; Weick, 2000). Crucial to this, according to Kotter (1996), is for managers to develop leadership skills. Drawing on the work of Burns (1978 – *see* Chapter 12), Kotter (1996: 25) argued that

> *Management is a set of processes that can keep a complicated system of people and technology running smoothly. The most important aspects of management include planning, budgeting, organizing, staffing, controlling, and problem solving. Leadership is a set of processes that creates organizations in the first place or adapts them to significantly changing circumstances. Leadership defines what the future should look like, aligns people with that vision, and inspires them to make it happen despite the obstacles.*

Therefore, in order to be effective, managers must become leaders, they require knowledge of and expertise in strategy formulation, human resource management, marketing and sales and negotiation and conflict resolution, and much more (Beer and Nohria, 2000; Clarke, 1994; Hayes, 2002). But the key to success, the decisive factor in creating a focused agenda for organisational change is, according to many observers, managers' own behaviour (Graetz *et al*, 2002; Kanter, 1989; Kotter, 1999; Pfeffer, 1996). If managers are to gain the commitment of others to change, they must first be prepared to challenge their own assumptions, attitudes and mindsets so that they develop an understanding of the emotional and intellectual processes involved (Buchanan and Boddy, 1992; Burns, 1978; Harrison, R, 2002; Sosik and Megerian, 1999).

For supporters of the Emergent approach, the essence of change is the move from the familiar to the unknown, from the certain to the uncertain (Jones *et al*, 2000). In this situation, it is essential for managers to be able to tolerate risk and cope with paradox and ambiguity (Weick, 2000; Stacey *et al*, 2002). Pugh (1993) takes the view that, in a dynamic environment, open and active communication with those participating in the change process is the key to coping with risk and ambiguity. This very much follows the view expressed by many that top-down, unilaterally imposed change doesn't work and that bottom-up change, based on devolved responsibility and genuine empowerment, is the way forward (Brown and Eisenhardt, 1997; Clarke, 1999; Falconer, 2002; Harung *et al*, 1999; Styhre, 2002). This in turn requires managers to facilitate open, organisation-wide communication via groups, individuals, and formal and informal channels (Hayes, 2002; Kanter *et al*, 1992; Senior, 2002).

An organisation's ability to gather, disseminate, analyse and discuss information is crucial for successful change, from the perspective of the Emergent approach. The reason for this, as Wilson (1992) argues, is that to effect change successfully, organisations need consciously and proactively to move forward incrementally. Large-scale change and more formal and integrated approaches to change (such as Total Quality Management) can quickly lose their sense of purpose and relevance for organisations operating in dynamic and uncertain environments (Hodge and Coronado, 2007). However, if organisations move towards their strategic vision by means of Emergent, continuous, localised and relatively small-scale change efforts, managers must ensure that those concerned, which could potentially be the entire workforce, have access to and are able to act on all the available information. Also, by encouraging a collective pooling of knowledge and information in this way, a better understanding of the pressures and possibilities for change can be achieved, which should enable managers to improve the quality of strategic decisions (Boddy and Buchanan, 1992; Quinn, 1993).

Proponents of complexity take a slightly different view. They reject both small-scale change and large-scale radical-transformational change in favour of 'a third kind' which lies between these two, and which is continuous and based on self-organisation at the team or group level (Brodbeck, 2002; Brown and Eisenhardt, 1997). To a certain extent, part of this difference is about terminology: how big is incremental change? Perhaps the two issues to concentrate on are as follows. Firstly, there is general agreement among proponents of Emergent change that large-scale, top-down change programmes, whilst sometimes being necessary, rarely succeed (Beer and Nohria, 2000). Secondly, Emergent change, whether incremental or 'a third kind', is not concerned with isolated change events (whether big or small) but sees change as a pattern of interwoven and continuous events which play out over the long term (Pettigrew and Whipp, 1991). This does not mean that there is not a crucial role for managers in identifying issues to be addressed or in developing an organisational vision which can guide Emergent change (Bennis, 2000; Dunphy, 2000). It does mean, however, that successful change is seen as coming from bottom-up initiatives which emerge from local responses to issues, threats or opportunities in the environment (Bennis, 2000; Pettigrew, 2000). It follows that the size of such responses will vary but, because they are local responses, they can never be large-scale.

Whatever the scale of the change, however, the potential for resistance will always be present. Resistance to change can arise from a number of sources, including middle and senior managers, and for a number of reasons ranging from different perspectives on what is best for the organisation to sectional or individual self-interest (Hayes, 2002; Huczynski and Buchanan, 2001). To cope effectively with resistance, managers will need to acquire and develop a range of interpersonal skills that enable them to deal with individuals and groups who seek to block or manipulate change for their own benefit (Boddy and Buchanan, 1992; Kotter, 1996). Promoting openness, reducing uncertainty and encouraging experimentation can be powerful mechanisms for overcoming resistance and promoting change (Mabey and Mayon-White, 1993). In this respect, Coghlan (1993) and McCalman and Paton (1992) advocated the use of Organization Development (OD) tools and techniques (such as transactional analysis, teamwork, group problem-solving, role-playing, etc.), which have long been used in Planned change programmes. However, there is an enormous and potentially confusing array of these; Mayon-White (1993) and Buchanan and Boddy (1992) argue that managers have a crucial role to play in terms of identifying and applying the appropriate ones. The main objective in deploying such tools and techniques is to encourage shared learning through teamwork and cooperation. It is this that provides the framework and support for the emergence of creative and innovative solutions and encourages a sense of involvement, commitment and ownership of the change process (Carnall, 2003; Kanter *et al*, 1997; McCalman and Paton, 1992; Peters, 1997a).

Nevertheless, it would be naïve to assume that everyone will want to work, or be able to function effectively, in such situations. The cognitive and behavioural changes necessary for organisational survival may be too large for many people, especially managers (Ghoshal and Bartlett, 2000). An important managerial task will, therefore, be to identify sources of inertia, assess the skill mix within their organisation and, most of all, consider whether their own managerial attitudes and styles are appropriate. It needs also to be recognised that there are different types of change, and that these often require different approaches (Stace and Dunphy, 2001). Proponents of Emergent change tend to see the world from one perspective but, as will be discussed in Chapter 10, there are other ways of viewing change and other ways of bringing it about (Beer and Nohria, 2000).

Power and politics

Change and politics are inexorably linked . . . This means that at the top, middle, and lower reaches of the organization, campaigning, lobbying, coalition building, and the sharing of information, rewards, and recognition are all fateful for change through all the various unpredictable stages and loops of the innovation journey.

(Pettigrew, 2000: 250)

The importance of power and politics in organisational life, especially change situations, was explored in Chapter 5. Though the advocates of Emergent change tend to view power and politics from differing perspectives, they recognise their importance and that they have to be managed if change is to be effective. Dawson (1994: 176), for example, concluded that:

The central argument is that it is important to try and gain the support of senior management, local management, supervisors, trade unions and workplace employees.

According to Weick (2000: 236) gaining support requires 'considerable linguistic skills to capture and label the flow of events [and] resequence and relabel that sequence'. The postmodernists also argue that managers manipulate and use language and symbols to create a new organisational reality (Hatch, 1997). Pettigrew *et al* (1992: 293) take a similar view, stating that:

The significance of political language at the front end of change processes needs emphasizing. Closures can be labelled as redevelopments. Problems can be re-coded into opportunities with . . . broad positive visions being articulated to build early coalitions . . .

Kanter *et al* (1992: 508) argued that the first step to implementing change is coalition-building: 'involve those whose involvement really matters . . . Specifically, seek support from two general groups: (1) power sources and (2) stakeholders.' In a similar vein, Nadler (1993) advocates the need to shape the political dynamics of change so that power centres develop that support the change rather than block it. Senior (2002), drawing on the work of Nadler (1988), proposes four steps that organisations need to take to manage the political dynamics of change (*see* Ideas and perspectives 9.4).

Ideas and perspectives 9.4
Managing the political dynamics of change

Step 1 Ensure or develop the support of key power groups.
Step 2 Use leader behaviour to generate support for the proposed change.
Step 3 Use symbols and language to encourage and show support for the change.
Step 4 Build in stability by using power to ensure that some things remain the same.

Source: Senior (2002)

Important though power and politics are in the change process, Hendry (1996) and Pugh (1993) remind us that they are not the be-all and end-all of change and that it is important not to focus on these to the exclusion of other factors. Nevertheless, the focus placed on the political dynamics of change does serve to highlight the need for those who manage change to be aware of and control this dimension of the change process. To this end, Carnall (2003: 133) offers a model of the political skills that can be utilised to manage change (*see* Table 9.1). As Table 9.1 shows, Carnall identifies three basic types of political skill: the ability to utilise resources, such as formal authority and information; the aptitude to understand and manage political processes, such as negotiation and mobilising support; and the capacity to recognise and engage in the various forms of political activity, such as battles over budgets and organisational structures. Carnall's argument is not that one individual will possess all these skills, but that those managing change will have to gain the support of those who do.

As can be seen, therefore, there are a number of core issues on which the advocates of Emergent change share similar views. Having identified the beliefs which distinguish them as a group, it is equally important to understand what advice they offer for putting their approach into practice.

Table 9.1 Political skills and the management of change (Carnall, 2003: 133)

Resources	Process	Form
Formal authority	Negotiation	Politics of:
Control of resources	Influencing	Budgets
Control of information	Mobilising support	Careers
Control of agenda	Mobilising bias	Succession
Control of access symbols	Use of emotion	Information
	Ceremony and rituals	Organisational structures
	Professional 'mystery'	Appraisal

The five features of organisations discussed above – structure, culture, learning, managerial behaviour, and power and politics – help explain why the advocates of the Emergent approach see change as an enormously complex process. However, in the main, they do not show how change should be managed in organisations. The next section will address this issue.

Recipes for Emergent change

Pettigrew and Whipp (1993: 6) maintain that there are no universal rules with regard to leading change; rather it involves 'linking action by people at all levels of the business'. However, this has not prevented most of the advocates of Emergent change from suggesting sequences of actions which organisations should follow. Pettigrew and Whipp (1993), for example, propose a model for successfully managing strategic and operational change that involves five interrelated factors (*see* Ideas and perspectives 9.5).

Ideas and perspectives 9.5
Pettigrew and Whipp's five central factors for managing change

- **Environmental assessment** – organisations, at all levels, need to develop the ability to collect and utilise information about their external and internal environments.
- **Leading change** – this requires the creation of a positive climate for change, the identification of future directions and the linking together of action by people at all levels in the organisation.
- **Linking strategic and operational change** – this is a two-way process of ensuring that intentional strategic decisions lead to operational changes and that emergent operational changes influence strategic decisions.
- **Human resources as assets and liabilities** – just as the pool of knowledge, skills and attitudes possessed by an organisation is crucial to its success, it can also be a threat to the organisation's success if the combination is inappropriate or managed poorly.
- **Coherence of purpose** – this concerns the need to ensure that the decisions and actions that flow from the above four factors complement and reinforce each other.

Source: Pettigrew and Whipp (1993)

For his part, not to be outdone by Pettigrew and Whipp's five factors, Dawson (1994: 179) puts forward fifteen 'major practical guidelines which can be drawn from a processual analysis of managing organizational transitions'. These guidelines range from the need to maintain an overview of the dynamics and long-term process of change, to the need to take a total organisational approach to managing transitions. On the way, he makes the case for understanding and communicating the context and objectives of change, and ensuring managerial and employee commitment. Wilson (1992: 122) also draws attention to the complex and long-term nature of change, writing that:

This book has deliberately taken a particular stance towards the question of organizational change. The argument has largely been against skill-based approaches, ready-made models of good organizational practice (for example, the 'excellence' models) and reliance upon analysing change as primarily the outcome-oriented pursuit of great and charismatic individuals. The arguments have, rather, favoured the potency of organizational structures, of economic determinism, of institutionalization within which the manager must operate. To operate successfully (and in the long term) he or she must understand and learn from the wider context or organization. This is not to say that individual skills are unimportant, only that they cannot be considered in isolation from the wider factors of strategic change.

Unfortunately, the problem with much of the advice for managing change offered by advocates of the Emergent approach, or at least those who come from the more processualist–analytical camp, is that it tends to be too general or cursory in nature and thus difficult to apply. It can sometimes also appear almost as an afterthought (Caldwell, 2006). However, those from the more prescriptive camp do offer much more substantial guidance to managers. Unlike the analytical camp, they are more concerned with telling organisations what they should do than in providing detailed analyses of what they do do. The two leading exponents of change in this respect are Rosabeth Moss Kanter and John P Kotter. Kanter's work has already been discussed extensively in Chapter 3, but to recap briefly, as shown in Ideas and perspectives 9.6, she proposes 'Ten Commandments for Executing Change' (Kanter *et al*, 1992).

Ideas and perspectives 9.6
Ten Commandments for Executing Change

1. Analyse the organisation and its need for change.
2. Create a shared vision and a common direction.
3. Separate from the past.
4. Create a sense of urgency.
5. Support a strong leader role.
6. Line up political sponsorship.
7. Craft an implementation plan.
8. Develop enabling structures.
9. Communicate, involve people and be honest.
10. Reinforce and institutionalise change.

Source: Kanter *et al* (1992: 382–3)

Looking at approaches to change, Kanter *et al* (1992) distinguished between 'Bold Strokes' and 'Long Marches'. The former relate to major strategic decisions or economic initiatives, usually of a structural or technological nature. These, they argue, can have a clear and rapid impact on an organisation, but they rarely lead to any long-term change in habits or culture. The Long March approach, on the other hand, favours a host of relatively small-scale and operationally focused initiatives, each of which can be quickly implemented but whose full benefits are achieved in the long term rather than the short term. However, the Long March approach can, over time, lead to a change of culture. Bold Strokes are initiatives taken by a few senior managers, sometimes only one; they do not rely on the support of the rest of the organisation for their success. In contrast, the Long March approach requires widespread commitment throughout an organisation. Without the involvement and commitment of the majority of the workforce, Kanter *et al* argue, such initiatives cannot succeed. They do maintain that Bold Strokes and Long Marches can be complementary, rather than alternative, approaches to change; though in practice companies appear to favour one or the other. Companies may need both if they are to succeed in transforming themselves. Therefore, though Kanter appears to prefer the Emergent approach of the Long March, she does see situations where Bold Strokes may be a necessary precursor, or adjunct, to the Long March.

Like Kanter, Kotter is a professor at the Harvard Business School and runs his own highly successful consultancy – Kotter Associates. He is the author of a wide range of books and articles on management and change, including his highly influential 1995 *Harvard Business Review* article, 'Leading change: why transformation efforts fail'. This article immediately jumped to first place among the thousands of reprints sold by the *Review*, which, considering the quality of the articles in its reprint base, is a considerable achievement. Spurred on by the reception of his views on change, Kotter went on to write his 1996 book, *Leading Change*. This elaborates and expands on the ideas in his *Harvard Business Review* article. The book begins by identifying eight key errors that Kotter believes cause transformation efforts to fail (*see* Ideas and perspectives 9.7).

Ideas and perspectives 9.7
Why change initiatives fail

Error 1 Allowing too much complacency.
Error 2 Failing to create a sufficiently powerful guiding coalition.
Error 3 Underestimating the power of vision.
Error 4 Undercommunicating the vision by a factor of 10 (or 100 or even 1000).
Error 5 Permitting obstacles to block the new vision.
Error 6 Failing to create short-term wins.
Error 7 Declaring victory too soon.
Error 8 Neglecting to anchor changes firmly in the corporate culture.

Source: Kotter (1996)

Kotter (1996: 16) maintains that the consequences of these errors are that:

- *New strategies aren't implemented well.*
- *Acquisitions don't achieve expected synergies.*
- *Reengineering takes too long and costs too much.*
- *Downsizing doesn't get costs under control.*
- *Quality programs don't deliver hoped-for results.*

Ideas and perspectives 9.8
Kotter's eight steps to successful change

Step 1 Establishing a sense of urgency.
Step 2 Creating a guiding coalition.
Step 3 Developing a vision and strategy.
Step 4 Communicating the change vision.
Step 5 Empowering broad-based action.
Step 6 Generating short-term wins.
Step 7 Consolidating gains and producing more change.
Step 8 Anchoring new approaches in the culture.

Source: Kotter (1996)

In order to eliminate these errors and their consequences, the book then proceeds to present Kotter's Eight-Stage Process for successful organisational transformation (*see* Ideas and perspectives 9.8).

Kotter (1996: 23) stresses that his eight stages are a process and not a checklist, and that 'Successful change of any magnitude goes through all eight stages . . . skipping even a single step or getting too far ahead without a solid base almost always creates problems.' He also points out that most major change efforts comprise a host of small and medium-sized change projects which, at any one point in time, can be at different points in the process. Kotter (1996: 24–5) cites the example of a telecommunications company where:

The overall effort, designed to significantly increase the firm's competitive position, took six years. By the third year, the transformation was centered in steps 5, 6 and 7. One relatively small reengineering project was nearing the end of stage 8. A restructuring of corporate staff groups was just beginning with most of the effort in steps 1 and 2. A quality program was moving along, but behind schedule, while a few small initiatives hadn't even been launched yet. Early results were visible at six to twelve months, but the biggest payoff didn't come until near the end of the overall effort.

As can be seen, there is a reassuring similarity between Kanter *et al*'s Ten Commandments and Kotter's Eight-Stage Process. Taken together, they provide detailed guidance for implementing change. However, there is one area where both they and the other advocates of the Emergent approach seem strangely imprecise. Though advocates of Emergent change place a great deal of emphasis on leadership and the ability to manage change, what most of them put to one side is the role of the change agent. But, as Dawson (2003: 25) notes from his own studies of change:

. . . the role of the change agent is identified as a central element in the power plays and political manoeuvring of individuals and groups during programmes of change.

As the next section will show, though there are a number of different models of change agency identified in the literature, there is a tendency to assume there is a 'one best' model or set of skills or competences which fits all situations (Caldwell, 2001, 2003, 2006).

The role of the change agent

Whether one is dealing with change at the individual, group or organisational level, whether one perceives change as incremental, punctuated or continuous, or whether one is viewing it from a Planned or Emergent perspective, change has to be managed; someone has to take responsibility for ensuring that change takes place. Whether this person is a team leader, facilitator, coach or even a dictator, there is usually one individual who bears the responsibility of being the change agent. Such people are referred to by a variety of titles – change consultant, change practitioner, project manager, etc. For simplicity's sake, we shall use the title 'change agent'. The previous chapter showed that the concept of the change agent originated with Kurt Lewin and has been extensively developed by the OD movement. However, over the last two decades, as different perceptions of change have emerged, so different views of the role of the change agent can also be perceived. As Caldwell (2003) notes, we have seen eulogies to the 'heroic' change leader capable of transforming organisations, calls for line managers and functional specialists to become change agents, and the increased popularity of internal and external management consultants as 'catalysts' for change. However, rather than clarifying the role and competences of the change agent, these developments appear to have made the picture more confused.

One of the strengths of the Planned approach is that it not only offers a well-developed change process, but it also provides a blueprint for the behaviour and attributes of change agents who, in turn, are buttressed and supported by a host of tools and techniques for analysing organisations and managing change (Cummings and Worley, 2005). The Emergent approach, whilst stressing the issue of process, takes the view that change is not a specialist activity driven by an expert, but an increasingly important part of every manager's role (Clarke, 1994). The drawback with this perspective is that it deflects attention from or even ignores the specialist skills necessary to manage the different types of change, whether this is being done by a manager or by a change specialist. It may also be one reason why, as Hartley *et al* (1997) observe, there has been relatively little empirical research on the roles played by change agents. Buchanan and Boddy (1992: 27) sought to redress the balance by analysing the skills needed to be a successful change agent and, in particular, by drawing attention to the change agent's need to:

> . . . *support the 'public performance' of rationally considered and logically phased and visibly participative change with 'backstage activity' in the recruitment and maintenance of support and in seeking and blocking resistance. . . . 'Backstaging' is concerned with the exercise of 'power skills', with 'intervening in political and cultural systems', with influencing and negotiating and selling, and with 'managing meaning'.*

Buchanan and Boddy suggest a model of the expertise of the change agent which identifies the skills and competences necessary to achieve successful change. Their model begins by listing the diagnostic skills required to identify the organisation type; change category; personal vulnerability; agenda priorities; and public performance and backstage skills. The model then goes on to list 15 competences under five clusters: goals; roles;

communication; negotiation; and managing up. The last two elements of their model relate to process outcomes and personal and organisational outcomes. What emerges from their work is a picture of the change agent as a highly skilled and well-trained political operator who has not only an in-depth knowledge of change processes and tools, but also the personal qualities and experience to use them both in the open and, especially, behind the scenes. In contrast to this, the Planned approach sees the change agent's role as being mainly an up-front 'public performance' activity and working with a transparent agenda to help those involved to identify the options and make their own choices (French and Bell, 1995).

Weick and Quinn (1999) contrast the role of the change agent under Planned change and under Emergent change. Under the former, they see the change agent as the prime mover – the person who makes the change happen. Though traditionally focused on small-group change, agents of Planned change are increasingly involved in large-scale change projects, such as culture change, where they:

> . . . *abandon several traditional organizational development (OD) assumptions. Large-scale interventions rely less on action theory and discrepancy theory and more on systems theory; less on closely held, internal data generation and more on gathering data from the environment and sharing it widely; . . . less on individual unit learning and more on learning about the whole organization; . . . less incremental and more fundamental in terms of the depth of change.*

> (Weick and Quinn, 1999: 374)

Consequently, new types of Planned change interventions require new skills. In particular, Weick and Quinn (1999: 374) argue that the quality of the change agent's argument becomes less important than the language they use: 'Language interventions are becoming a crucial means for agents to create change.'

They go on to argue that the use of language by change agents is even more important when dealing with Emergent change. Weick and Quinn (1999: 381) maintain that:

> . . . *the role of the change agent becomes one of managing language, dialogue, and identity . . . and . . . the most powerful change interventions occur at the level of everyday conversations.*

Drawing on the work of Ford and Ford (1995), Weick and Quinn (1999: 381) assert that agents of Emergent change bring about change through a combination of five forms of language or speech acts: 'assertives or claims, directives or requests, commissives or promises, expressives that convey affective states, and declarations that announce a new operational reality'.

It follows that under Emergent change, the change agent is not a neutral facilitator, but an active manager of the change process with his or her own agenda which they seek to promote or impose by managing and shaping the perceptions of those concerned (Pettigrew, 2000; Weick, 2000). Buchanan and Boddy (1992: 123) also draw attention to the social construction of the process of change which, they argue, is a creative activity:

> *Expertise does not simply involve the mechanical deployment of diagnostic tools, competences and stereotyped solutions, but involves also the innovative and opportunistic exploitation of other dimensions of the organizational context.*

Mirvis (1988) is another who focuses on the crucial role played by innovative and creative skills of change agents in achieving successful change. In an article entitled 'Grace, magic and miracles', Lichtenstein (1997) investigated this side of the change agent's role further by examining the work of three leading change practitioners: Peter Senge, William Torbert and Ellen Wingard. In the article, the three consultants each described their approach to change and the theories which underpin it. They also described how, in applying their approaches, it was insufficient just to follow the steps laid down. Success required the consultants to overcome major obstacles, and, in so doing, to adopt novel and experimental methods. Senge, Torbert and Wingard use terms such as 'grace', 'magic' and 'miracles' to describe the moment of breakthrough; the point where serious obstacles were overcome and genuine progress made. In fact, what they describe is the ability of the change agent to recognise the need to depart from the 'script' and to experiment with the unknown in order to make progress. Just as Buchanan and Boddy (1992) identified the need for change agents to be able to present and utilise the rational face of change, whilst being adept at the less rational 'backstage' skills, so Lichtenstein (1997: 407) also concludes that:

> . . . there is a logical framework that produces rational actions in the first stages of an intervention effort. However, at a critical threshold it is non-linear logic and spontaneous felt action – grace, magic and miracles – that actually supports organizational (and personal) transformation.

Drawing on the work of cultural anthropologists, Schuyt and Schuijt (1998) use the analogy of the change agent as a magician. They point out that magicians, witch doctors and medicine men in non-Western cultures use symbols and rituals to smooth the various transitions in life cycles: birth, puberty, marriage and death. In the same way, Schuyt and Schuijt (1998: 399) pose the following question: are not consultants and change agents 'also, in a certain sense, magicians who guide and structure important transitions through the use of rituals and symbols?' These rituals and symbols have a number of key functions: to establish the change agent's credentials, to prepare the participants mentally for change, to guide them through the transition, and to reinforce the 'participants' feeling that they are taking part in a controlled and well-managed process of change . . . but ultimately the crux is to reduce the client's uncertainty' (Schuyt and Schuijt, 1998: 405).

The argument of many in the Emergent school is that the multifaceted and multi-level nature of change mean that it cannot be left to a few experts or a few managers but is the responsibility of everyone in the organisation. However, if this is so, what skills and competences do they need and how are they to get them? What the work of Buchanan and Boddy, Lichtenstein, Schuyt and Schuijt, and, indeed, the Organization Development movement, would seem to argue is that the more complex the change process, the more difficult it is to achieve, and the greater the need to utilise the skills and experience of a specialist change agent. The conclusion they draw from this is that there is a 'one best' type of change agent who possesses a generic set of high-level competences that can be employed in any situation.

Caldwell (2003) takes issue with Buchanan and Boddy *et al.* Just as Dunphy and Stace (1993: 905) called for a 'situational' or 'contingency model' of change, so Caldwell calls for a contingency model of change agency which recognises that different change situations require different types of change agent. From an extensive literature review, Caldwell

Ideas and perspectives 9.9
Caldwell's models of change agent

- Leadership models where change agents are senior managers responsible for identifying and delivering strategic/tranformational change.
- Management models where change agents are seen as middle-level managers/functional specialists who have responsibility for delivering or supporting specific elements of strategic change programmes or projects.
- Consultancy models where change agents are external or internal consultants who can be called on to operate at any level.
- Team models where change agents are seen as teams that operate at various levels in an organisation and which are composed of the requisite managers, employees and consultants necessary to accomplish the particular change project set them.

Source: Caldwell (2003)

identifies four groups of models of change agent (*see* Ideas and perspectives 9.9). These four different types of change models highlight the difficulty, not to say impossibility, of attempting to construct a generic change agent who can operate in any situation.

The type of change agent identified by Buchanan and Boddy may fit into some of these models but not all of them. Similarly, the OD type of change agent may fit into some of these models, but not all of them. What Caldwell has done is to direct academics and practitioners away from both the 'it's everyone's responsibility' and the 'one best way' schools and towards identifying the behaviours and competences necessary for each type of change situation.

Emergent change: summary and criticisms

The proponents of Emergent change are a somewhat broad group who may seem to be united more by their scepticism regarding Planned change than by a well-focused and commonly agreed alternative. Indeed, some might argue that any label which spans the prescriptive, consultant-orientated views of Kotter and Kanter and the analytical–processual views of Pettigrew and Dawson is too broad; certainly this is Dawson's (2003) view. Nevertheless, this would ignore two crucial points. Firstly, Planned change is an equally broad church. It ranges from those who see it as only applicable to behavioural change in small groups to those who see it as an approach for transforming entire organisations (Armenakis and Bedeian, 1999; Burnes, 2004c; Greiner and Cummings, 2004; Worley and Feyerhern, 2003). Secondly, any approach to change which seeks to be applicable beyond the classroom or have validity wider than the management consultancy needs to incorporate both the prescriptive practitioner and the analytical academic. The issue is not how broad the church is but whether what unites them is greater than what divides them. In the former respect, there does seem to be some agreement regarding the main tenets of Emergent change, which are as follows:

- Organisational change is not a linear process or a one-off isolated event but is a continuous, open-ended, cumulative and unpredictable process of experimentation and adaptation aimed at matching an organisation's resources and capabilities to the opportunities, constraints and demands of a dynamic and uncertain environment.
- This is best achieved through an interwoven pattern of (mainly) small- to medium-scale continual changes which, over time, can lead to a major re-configuration and transformation of an organisation.
- Change is a multi-level, cross-organisation process that unfolds in an iterative and messy fashion over a period of years and comprises a series of interlocking projects.
- Change is not an analytical–rational process. Instead, key change decisions evolve over time and are the outcome of political and cultural processes in organisations.
- The role of managers is not to plan or implement change *per se*, but to shape the long-term process of change by creating or fostering an organisational structure and climate which encourages and sustains experimentation, learning and risk-taking, and to develop a workforce that has the freedom and motivation to take responsibility for identifying the need for change and implementing it.
- Though managers are expected to become facilitators rather than doers, they also have the prime responsibility for developing a collective vision or common purpose that gives direction to their organisation, and within which the appropriateness of any proposed change can be judged.
- The key organisational activities that allow these elements to operate successfully are:
  - Information-gathering – about the external environment and internal objectives and capabilities.
  - Communication – the transmission, analysis and discussion of information.
  - Learning – the ability individually and collectively to develop new skills, identify appropriate responses and draw knowledge from their own and others' past and present actions.

Though not always stated openly, the case for the Emergent approach to change is based on the assumption that the environment in which organisations operate is changing rapidly, radically and unpredictably, and will continue to do so. Just as advocates of Planned change assume that stability is the *natural* or *preferred* state for organisations, so proponents of Emergent change assume the *natural* or *preferred* state for organisations is turbulence and unpredictability (Brown and Eisenhardt, 1997; Orlikowski, 1996). Consequently, if the external world is changing in a rapid, uncertain and continuous way, organisations need to change in a continuous, appropriate and timely manner if they are to remain competitive. It is because they view change as a continuous and open-ended process that proponents of Emergent change see the Planned approach to change is inappropriate. To be successful, changes need to emerge locally and (relatively) incrementally in order to counter environmental threats and take advantage of opportunities.

Presented in this manner, there is an apparent coherence and validity to the Emergent approach. However, it is a fragile coherence and a challengeable validity. As far as coherence is concerned, some proponents of Emergent change, especially Pettigrew (1997) and Dawson (2003), clearly approach it from the processual perspective on organisations. However, it is not clear that Buchanan and Boddy (1992) and Wilson (1992) would fully subscribe to this view. In the case of Carnall (2003), Clarke (1994), Kanter *et al* (1992) and Kotter (1996), it is clear that they do not take a processual perspective. They do not doubt the importance of power and politics in the change process, but for them the issue is one of legitimacy and pragmatism. Managers and change agents have the legitimate right to introduce changes, but to do so they must use political skills in a pragmatic way to build support and overcome or avoid resistance. For the processualists, like the postmodernists, change is about dominant coalitions, and smaller groupings, trying to impose their will on all or part of an organisation in order to maintain or improve their position. Partly, this is explained by the fact that some of these writers (especially Dawson, 2003; Pettigrew, 1997; Wilson, 1992) are attempting to understand and analyse change from a critical perspective, whilst others (notably Kanter *et al*, 1992; Kotter, 1996) are more concerned with prescribing recipes and checklists for successful change. In addition to these apparent tensions, as Caldwell (2006) notes, there are some open disagreements amongst advocates of the Emergent approach. For example, Pettigrew's processual stance has been criticised from both the practitioner wing and processual wing for its lack of practicality (Buchanan and Boddy, 1992; Dawson, 2003). Therefore, though the advocates of Emergent change have a number of common bonds, their differing objectives and perspectives do put a question mark against the coherence of their approach. Nevertheless, it is debatable whether these differences are any greater or any more significant than those among advocates of Planned change.

In terms of the validity or general applicability of the Emergent approach to change, this depends to a large extent on whether or not one subscribes to the twin assumptions that (a) environmental instability and unpredictability is the *natural* or *preferred* state for organisations and that (b) the best way for organisations to cope with this is through a continuous process of small-to-medium-sized changes which emerge from the bottom up and not the top down. As a recent IBM (2008) report shows, there is much evidence that organisations face an increasingly hostile, rapidly changing and unpredictable environment. However, it is not clear that the environment impacts on all organisations in the same way or that they should respond with the same approach, a point that Pettigrew and Whipp (1991: 165) acknowledge when they state that: 'Leadership [of change] requires action appropriate to its context.' If one considers the history of organisations over the last hundred years, there have been many disruptive economic, political and military events which have required rapid, major responses by organisations which could not be coped with or anticipated by the Emergent approach. Indeed, since the year 2000 there have been three major global shocks which have disrupted organisations in a significant fashion and which have required immediate and disruptive responses – the dotcom collapse, 9/11 and the recent credit crunch. Therefore, whilst one might accept that the *preferred* environmental state, at least for advocates of Emergent change, is one that is amenable to being dealt with by Emergent change, it is difficult to accept that this is necessarily the *natural* state of affairs, or at least not for all organisations.

This viewpoint reinforces the discussion of the nature and uniformity of the organisational environment which took place in previous chapters. The conclusion reached was that not all organisations experience the same degree of turbulence or need to respond to it in the same way. For example, though they operate in the same industry and, to a degree, serve the same customers, Apple and Microsoft tend to respond to environmental turbulence differently. In addition, for some organisations, it may be possible to manipulate or change environmental constraints to allow them more scope for manoeuvre. None of this invalidates the Emergent approach, but it does indicate that organisations may need to have a range of change responses available to them in order to cope with the challenges they face, of which the Emergent approach is just one. Therefore, for some, Emergent change may be appropriate, for others, the Planned approach may be more appropriate, whilst in some organisations and in some situations, directive or coercive change may be used.

Obviously, the above raises questions over the universal applicability of the Emergent approach; even without reservations regarding its coherence and validity, however, there would still be serious criticisms of this approach. For example, many of its supporters seem to advocate the same approach to organisations as the Culture–Excellence school and are, therefore, open to the same criticisms (*see* Chapter 3). Given this link to Culture–Excellence, not surprisingly, a great deal of emphasis is placed on the need for appropriate organisational cultures. But, as the writers on Emergent change seem to sway between advocating the need for culture change (Kanter *et al*, 1992) and advocating the need to work with existing cultures (Pettigrew, 1997), it is not clear what they perceive the role of culture to be. In any case, as was noted in Chapter 5, the whole issue of the role and the manipulability of organisational culture is a veritable minefield. Indeed, as also mentioned in Chapter 5, even Wilson (1992), who supports the Emergent perspective, was sceptical about the case for culture change. Similar points can be made regarding the 'learning organisation' approach. As Whittington (1993: 130) comments:

> The danger of the purely 'learning' approach to change, therefore, is that . . . managers [and others] may actually recognize the need for change, yet still refuse to 'learn' because they understand perfectly well the implications for their power and status. Resistance to change may not be 'stupid' . . . but based on a very shrewd appreciation of the personal consequences.

A variant of this criticism relates to the impact of success on managerial learning. Miller (1993: 119) observes that, whilst managers generally start out by attempting to learn all they can about their organisation's environment, over time, as they gain experience, they 'form quite definite opinions of what works and why' and as a consequence tend to limit their search for information and knowledge. So experience, especially where it is based on success, may actually be a barrier to learning, in that it shapes the cognitive structures by which managers, and everyone else, see and interpret the world. Nystrom and Starbuck (1984: 55) observe that:

> What people see, predict, understand, depends on their cognitive structures . . . [which] manifest themselves in perceptual frameworks, expectations, world views, plans, goals . . . myths, rituals, symbols . . . and jargon.

This brings us neatly to the topic of the role of managers. Though this will be discussed extensively in Chapter 12, for now it should be noted that managers are the people who appear to have to make the greatest change in their behaviour. As the above quotations indicate, however, they may neither welcome nor accept such a change, especially where it requires them to challenge and change their own beliefs, and where it runs counter to their experience of 'what works and why'. Also, if the possibility exists (as mentioned above) to manipulate environmental variables and constraints rather than having to change their behaviour, managers may perceive this as a more attractive or viable option.

Though the above reservations regarding the validity of the Emergent approach are fairly significant, there are three further criticisms that are equally serious. The first relates to the difference between that approach and the Planned approach. The Planned approach is attacked because of its reliance on Lewin's Three-Step model of unfreezing, moving and refreezing. It is argued that in a turbulent environment, organisations are in a constant state of change and that, therefore, to speak of unfreezing and refreezing is nonsense (Kanter *et al*, 1992). However, if one examines the process of change advocated by, for example, Dawson (1994), Kotter (1996) and Pettigrew *et al* (1992), though they argue to the contrary, they do speak of change as a 'transition' process with a beginning, middle and end. Indeed, it is important to remember Hendry's (1996: 624) comment which was quoted in Chapter 8:

> *Scratch any account of creating and managing change and the idea that change is a three-stage process which necessarily begins with a process of unfreezing will not be far below the surface.*

There are others who strongly support Hendry's view that the Three-Step model has greater validity and wider usage than its critics acknowledge (Burnes, 2004b, 2004c; Elrod and Tippett, 2002). It should also be noted that there are a number of Lewin supporters amongst proponents of the complexity approach to change (Back, 1992; Tschacher and Brunner, 1995) and that MacIntosh and MacLean (2001) advocate the use of the Three-Step approach to identify and change order-generating rules.

The second criticism concerns the emphasis placed on the political and cultural aspects of change. Advocates of the Emergent approach have undoubtedly provided a valuable contribution to our understanding of change by highlighting the neglect of these important issues in the past. However, they have also been criticised from a number of perspectives for perhaps going too far the other way. Hendry (1996: 621) argues that 'The management of change has become . . . overfocused on the political aspects of change', whilst Collins (1998: 100), voicing concerns of his own and of other researchers, argues that:

> *. . . in reacting to the problems and critiques of [the Planned approach], managers and practitioners have swung from a dependence on under-socialized models and explanations of change and instead have become committed to the arguments of, what might be called, over-socialized models of change.*

This very much fits in with those who take a realist perspective on organisations; they argue that whilst the social world, including organisations, is a product of human action, it is not necessarily a product of conscious human design but exists independently of human beings (Connelly, 2000; Easton, 2000).

Lastly, though the Emergent approach undoubtedly raises key issues, and offers valuable insights and guidance, it does not appear to be as universally applicable as its advocates imply. As Dawson (2003) notes, it is clear that there are many situations where managers find it more appropriate to push change through in a rapid and confrontational manner (*see* Stace and Dunphy, 2001; Edwardes, 1983; Franklin, 1997; Grinyer *et al*, 1988). In Chapter 8, we identified three different perspectives on change: the individual, group and system perspectives, and three categories of change: incremental, punctuated equilibrium and continuous transformation. The Emergent approach is specifically founded on the assumption that organisations operate in a dynamic environment where they have to transform themselves continuously in order to survive. The focus of Emergent change is continuous, synergistic, interconnected change which, though small- or medium-sized in nature, affects the organisation and its major sub-systems. Consequently, it is by its own definition not applicable to organisations operating in environments which require isolated incremental change at the individual and/or group levels, or punctuated equilibrium change initiatives at the organisation level.

It is also the case that advocates of the Emergent approach seem unclear regarding the degree to which change should be viewed as cooperative and voluntary. On the one hand, great play is made of change being driven from the bottom up by motivated and empowered employees. On the other hand, change is seen as a battle for power, and change agents are expected to have the political skills to manipulate those involved.

Therefore, in examining Emergent change, two things are clear. Firstly, like Planned change, Emergent change has much to recommend it but it also has a number of significant shortcomings. Secondly, even taking Planned change and Emergent change together, they do not appear to cover or be applicable to all change situations.

Conclusions

Organisations come in all shapes and sizes, provide a vast variety of products and services, and face an enormous array of challenges. Perhaps the only factor common to all organisations is change. Organisations never stand still, though the speed and magnitude of change does vary from organisation to organisation and over time. It is now generally accepted that the ability to manage change effectively is a crucial component of an organisation's ability to compete successfully. As Chapter 8 demonstrated, for many years, the Planned approach was considered to be the best way of managing change. However, as was shown at the beginning of this chapter, from the early 1980s onwards, the Planned approach has faced a torrent of criticisms as to its suitability in a world of rapid and unpredictable change. In particular, its detractors claim that the notion that organisations operate in stable environments and can move from one fixed state to another is, to quote Kanter *et al* (1992: 10), a 'quaintly linear and static conception . . . [and] . . . wildly inappropriate'.

In the light of these criticisms of the Planned approach, the chapter went on to examine the Emergent approach and its claim to being the best way to manage change. The Emergent approach sees organisational change as an ongoing process of adaptation to an unpredictable and ever-changing environment. For proponents of this view, change is a messy, unpredictable, open-ended and political affair. In such a situation, it is impossible for a few managers at the top of an organisation to identify and implement all the changes necessary to keep the organisation aligned with its environment. Consequently, successful change is a bottom-up, emergent, response to events. However, just as the Planned approach to change can be criticised as limited and flawed, similar criticisms can be made of the Emergent approach. In particular, it may be less a coherent approach to change and more a label for a collection of approaches critical of Planned change. In addition, questions have been raised about key elements of Emergent change such as its perception of culture, organisational learning and the role of managers. The Emergent approach has also been criticised for its over-emphasis on the political dimension of change and its view that all organisations operate in a dynamic and unpredictable environment. From this it is clear that Emergent change is limited in terms of both the types of organisational change to which it can be applied, and how it can be applied. Therefore, though it has apparent advantages over the Planned approach, or rather it is applicable to situations for which Planned change is not suitable, an examination of the Emergent approach reveals that there are serious question marks over its coherence, validity and general applicability.

From this and the previous chapter, it is clear that, even taken together, neither the Planned nor the Emergent approach covers the full extent of the broad spectrum of change events organisations encounter. Though both Planned and Emergent change have important theoretical and practical benefits, their dominance of the change literature appears to have led to a neglect of other approaches to change. In order to address this neglect, the next chapter will examine the change situations faced by organisations, and will construct *A Framework for Change* that identifies the range of change situations and a matching range of approaches to change.

Test your learning

Short answer questions

1. Briefly discuss the Processual approach to change.

2. List the main attributes of the Emergent approach to change.

3. How do proponents of the Emergent approach view the nature of the environment in which organisations operate?

4. What are the reasons for considering the complexity approach to change as part of the Emergent approach?

5. From the Emergent perspective, what are the five features of organisations that promote or hinder successful change?

6. List the main criticisms of the Emergent approach.

7. What are the implications of the Emergent approach for managerial behaviour?

Essay questions

1. Discuss and evaluate the following statement: Emergent change does not offer a coherent alternative to Planned change but merely provides an umbrella for those who oppose it.

2. To what extent and how do Caldwell's four models of the change agent undermine Buchanan and Boddy's generic model of the expertise of the change agent?

Suggested further reading

1. Dawson, P (2003) *Organizational Change: A Processual Approach*. Routledge: London.

   Patrick Dawson's book is an excellent guide to the processual approach to change which raises some important questions about both Planned and Emergent change.

2. Kotter, JP (1996) *Leading Change*. Harvard Business School Press: Boston, MA, USA.

   John Kotter's work represents the more prescriptive and pragmatic wing of Emergent change.

CASE STUDY 9

Midshires College of Midwifery and Nursing

BACKGROUND

This case study describes the attempt to merge five colleges of midwifery and nursing to form the new Midshires College of Midwifery and Nursing. The existing colleges, between them, serviced hospitals in ten different Health Authorities. The Health Authorities, in consultation with the Regional Health Authority, appointed a Steering Group of senior managers, drawn from the Boards of Governors of the five colleges, to oversee the merger. The Steering Group comprised General Managers from NHS Hospital Trusts within the Health Authorities, Chief Nursing Officers, and representatives from the Regional Health Authority, some 24 members in all.

The remit of the Steering Group was fairly straightforward:

To oversee the amalgamation of the five colleges.

In the past, such mergers had been relatively straightforward with everyone keeping their jobs and, for managers at least, an increase in pay to reflect the increased size of the new college. However, there were three issues which made this process significantly different and potentially more complicated than past amalgamations:

Firstly, there was uncertainty over the demand for nurse education in the future (both in terms of numbers and function). Therefore, there was a threat to jobs.

Secondly, a potential conflict of interest existed between the General Managers on the Steering Group on the one hand and the new college on the other. This was owing to the fact that in the past NHS policy had tied hospitals to a particular college of nursing, whether they liked it or not. This policy had changed and, in future, the General Managers would be able to choose which college of nursing would educate their trainee nurses. They could, if they so wished, put their requirements for training new nurses out to open tender to any college in the country, as one Trust elsewhere in the UK had already done. In addition, and in the short term more probably, they could seek alternative suppliers for post-experience courses (i.e. courses for already trained nurses who needed to upgrade their skill), or even provide these courses themselves in competition with the new college. Indeed, two of the Health Authorities had already established their own organisation for delivering post-experience

▶

nurse education in competition with the new college. This is perhaps why some members of the Steering Group suggested that the new college should not have in its remit the provision of post-experience courses (with implications for the jobs of some 30 per cent of existing staff in the five colleges to be amalgamated). Therefore, key players in establishing the college found themselves placed in a somewhat ambiguous position with regard to its purpose and remit.

Lastly, it was expected that qualifications gained at the new college would be validated by a higher education institution and that eventually, as similar colleges were doing, it would actually merge into the university sector.

There seems to have been no formal acknowledgement of these potential problems or that this amalgamation was in any way different from previous ones. It might have been expected that the Steering Group would seek to clarify these key issues before proceeding to resolve the structure and organisation of the new college. After all, how could decisions regarding its structure and functioning be resolved in advance of key decisions on student numbers, course content, areas of operation, and whether or not it would merge with a higher education institution? Nevertheless, the Steering Group avoided consciously tackling these issues prior to commencing the merger process.

DEVELOPING THE STRATEGY

The Steering Group decided that merging the five colleges could and should be managed as a straightforward and uncomplicated, almost mechanical, process. They established a 24-month timetable for merging the colleges and appointed a Project Leader, on a fixed-term contract of 24 months, to accomplish the task.

The appointee was the principal of one of the colleges being merged. He had no direct experience of merging colleges, but had only two years' service left prior to retirement. This meant that, unlike the other four college principals, he would not be a potential candidate for the principal's post in the new college. Surprisingly, the Project Leader was given no budget or support, not even a secretary. He could, though, call on the resources of the five colleges, providing that the principals agreed.

Within forty-eight hours of his appointment, the Project Leader contacted the principals of the other colleges, by fax, and announced both the formation of a Project Board and its membership. The membership included the Project Leader and the principals of the five colleges, including the acting principal from his own college. There were also three external members brought in as advisors to the project group. These were a Finance Manager and a Personnel Manager from the Regional Health Authority and the Education Officer from the English National Board for Nursing.

By the time of the Project Board's first meeting, the Project Leader had produced a plan which, amongst other objectives, proposed the immediate integration of some administrative processes and the centralisation of student recruitment. The core of the plan was the establishment of four sub-projects aimed at integrating the major functions of the five colleges: pre-registration courses for nursing; post-registration courses for nursing; midwifery education; and education support services.

The first meeting of the Project Board discussed its own membership, the Project Leader's project plan, the roles of the Project Board members, communications, the development of new courses, and the accountability of the Project Board to the Steering Group. The Project Leader stated that he had been given clear instructions by the Steering Group, and that the task of the Project Board was to get on with the job of integrating the five colleges as laid down in his project plan. This first meeting set the pattern for the future; the Project Leader would act as the only conduit between the Steering Group and the Project Board, and questions relating to the pace, purpose and form of the proposed merger were not part of the Board's remit. Within these constraints, scope for questions and initiatives existed, but the Project Leader had the final say on all matters.

TIME FOR A RETHINK

In month five of the merger timetable, a one-day staff conference was organised for everyone employed at the five colleges. The purpose of the day was to brief staff on developments and get feedback from them. It was apparent as the day progressed that, although staff in the colleges were enthusiastic about the change, and indeed appeared to have more enthusiasm and ideas than the Project Board itself, there were key issues which were not being addressed and which were causing increasing concern. The main concern for staff was that no one seemed to have a clue as to how many staff would retain their posts in the new college, or what mix of skills would be required. However, staff were just as concerned, if not more so, by the lack of any clear direction for the new college: What was its mission? What products and services would it provide? How would it be structured? Who would make these decisions, when and on what basis? What seemed to shock and dismay many of the staff was that the Project Leader seemed as uncertain and powerless as themselves regarding these issues.

The conference brought home to the Project Leader the lack of progress made towards amalgamation. The sub-groups had met frequently and produced extremely detailed plans; but the ability to turn these plans into actions seemed to elude them, partly because key issues had still not been resolved.

For the Project Leader, the conference had crystallised a number of his concerns regarding both the pace of the amalgamation and the effectiveness of the Project Board system. He also, privately, expressed the view that he had become a 'piggy in the middle' between the Project Board and the Steering Group, having critics in both camps but supporters in neither. In addition, some members of the Project Board were meeting informally but regularly to discuss and promote alternative ideas to those of the Project Leader, though whether he was aware of this was unclear. Similarly, Board members were seeing members of the Steering Group informally as well. So a great deal of behind-the-scenes lobbying and jockeying for position was taking place. This was hardly surprising, given the uncertainty – particularly over jobs – which was present.

Shortly after the staff conference, the Project Leader called a one-day Project Board meeting to discuss progress, and he invited the Chair of the Steering Group to part of the meeting. Though members were told that the meeting was to examine the situation and discuss options, they were in effect presented with a *fait accompli* by the Project Leader. He made a number of major announcements at this meeting which in effect tore up the previous four months' work:

- The Project Board was to be disbanded and replaced by an interim Management Committee for the new college.
- The four existing principals would become part of the Management Committee with specific areas of responsibility.
- The role of the existing principals in the five individual colleges would be replaced by the appointment of heads of sites.

- The sub-projects were to be abandoned; in their place, the Project Leader announced a structure for the new college which would, he stated, be fully operational by month 12 of the merger timetable.

Despite these changes, decisions had still not been taken regarding the number of students the new college would have in the future, whether it would be allowed to offer post-registration courses, or whether it would be moving into higher education. Without this information, it was almost impossible to determine staffing levels and the skill mix for the new college, or judge the appropriateness of the proposed structure. In such a situation, inevitably, staff morale continued to decline, especially amongst staff on short-term contracts. One example of this was the high number of staff, especially in managerial positions, who were on long-term sick leave with stress-related illnesses.

TIME FOR A ANOTHER RETHINK

The creation of the Management Committee appeared to have had little positive impact upon the new college. The new structure still only existed on paper. The reports from the Management Committee were vague, irregular and fragmented. However, in month 9 of the merger timetable, a new Chair of the Steering Group was appointed. The new Chair came in with a sense of urgency to resolve staffing issues because it had been decided by the Regional Health Authority that his Trust would take over formal responsibility for the college by month 18 of the merger timetable. This meant that any redundancies that might arise, and any associated costs, would be borne by his Trust.

Questions

1. Imagine that you are the new Chair of the Steering Committee. You have decided to take direct charge of the merger process yourself without the aid of any outside assistance:
   a. What is your analysis of what has gone wrong so far and who is to blame?
   b. What are the main steps you need to take to merge the colleges successfully?
   c. What obstacles might you expect to encounter and how might you overcome these?

2. Imagine that you are an outside consultant brought in to advise the new Chair of the Steering Committee:
   a. What are the key issues he needs to address and resolve?
   b. What are the main steps he needs to take to merge the colleges successfully?
   c. What obstacles might he expect to encounter and how might he overcome these?

3. Imagine that you are the Project Leader. The new Chair of the Steering Committee has asked you to produce a report on the current state of the merger and plans for successfully completing the merger within the 24-month timetable. The report should include:
   a. An analysis and explanation of the slow progress to date.
   b. The main steps that need to be taken to complete the merger on time.
   c. The main obstacles to achieving the merger and how they can be overcome.

CHAPTER 10

A framework for change

Approaches and choices

Learning objectives

After studying this chapter, you should be able to:

- recognise that, even taken together, the Planned and Emergent approaches do not cover all change situations;
- list the range of change situations that organisations face;
- appreciate the variety of approaches to change;
- understand the situations in which the various approaches to change are most appropriately used;
- describe how organisations can increase their degree of choice when undertaking change.

**Mini Case Study 10.1
Learning to innovate** **FT**

Public-sector innovation will take you by surprise

The stereotypical image of public services is familiar. Slow, grudging and inefficient, the public sector is usually contrasted with an idealised private sector that is nimble and innovative, and focused with laser-like intensity on its individual customers' needs.

Critics say that public-sector services have for too long been delivered on the principle that one size must fit all. Even that verb, to deliver, is revealing. Citizens are supposed to wait, as supplicants, by their letter boxes, hoping that the state might, in its generosity and wisdom, post essential services through the door.

Time has moved on. Expectations have risen. And the now more affluent public, marketed and sold to for decades by commercial enterprises, is used to having its individual desires catered for. Even those of modest means do not see, rightly, why they should have to put up with impersonal, mediocre public services.

So why am I bothering the (largely) private-sector readership of this column with this potted history of the public sector? Because, happily, there are now many impressive examples of innovation in the public sector. And, perhaps more surprisingly, the public sector is arguably learning things about innovation that many in the private sector have not yet fully grasped.

Healthcare in the UK has traditionally been provided either by a massive yet remote state organisation or by expensive and often inefficient private-sector companies. But in Sheffield in the north of England a new not-for-profit company called Patient Opinion (www.patientopinion.org.uk) has challenged the old model.

The Patient Opinion website is filled with 'user-generated content' – comments from patients about the quality of care they have received from general practitioners and local hospitals. One hospital manager says: 'The positive comments are nice to get. But it's the critical ones that are really useful because they are the ones that make staff sit up and notice . . . they know everyone can see them.' How energetically do businesses seek the uncensored feedback of their customers? How happy are they for these comments to go on public display?

Elsewhere, Irene Lucas, chief executive of South Tyneside Council, says that 'people will innovate, if they are allowed to'. Her employees are charged with making day-to-day repairs to public property and facilities. Cutting out unnecessary tiers of management speeded up the team's work, and helped them build a better relationship with local residents.

Change is coming from below. As Su Maddock, innovation adviser for the UK's National School of Government, has written: 'Innovative responses do not usually come from executives, research or policy thinkers. They come from those most in contact with social problems.' Spoken like a true devotee of open-source innovation.

Whether in the public or private sectors, top-down imposed change is just so last-century.

Source: Adapted from Stefan Stern, *Financial Times*, 6 November 2007, p. 14.

Introduction

Since the Industrial Revolution, the conventional wisdom has been that the private sector is the leader in terms of customer responsiveness and the public sector is the laggard. This view is based on the belief that only free-market competition will drive organisations and individuals to innovate and change. Consequently, if the public sector is to improve, it needs to learn from the private sector; certainly, this was the view in the 1980s and 1990, when not just ideas and techniques were imported from the private sector but many managers as well. However, as Mini Case Study 10.1 shows, the public sector has gone beyond copying the private sector. Over the last decade or so, the public sector has put much effort into developing its own approaches to innovation and change which suit the particular circumstances and many challenges it faces (Buchanan *et al*, 2006; By and Macleod, 2009). This should come as no surprise: successive governments in the UK and elsewhere have put considerable pressure on their respective public sectors to deliver more cost-effective and more customer-responsive services (Burnes, 2009).

Therefore, the notion that the private sector is always the leader and the other sectors always the followers when it comes to managing and changing organisations is something of a misconception. All the same, though the public sector may have something to teach the private sector when it comes to innovation and change, the real lesson is that whilst different sectors and different organisations can learn from each other, they can also face widely differing challenges, and what is appropriate for one organisation or sector is not necessarily appropriate for another. Consequently, a 'one-size-fits-all' approach is unlikely to work, whether it be based on private- or public-sector experiences. This is particularly the case when considering organisational change. As Stickland (1998: 14) remarks:

> . . . the problem with studying change is that it parades across many subject domains under numerous guises, such as transformation, development, metamorphosis, trans-mutation, evolution, regeneration, innovation, revolution and transition to name but a few.

The last two chapters have reviewed the two dominant approaches to managing change, identifying their strengths and weaknesses and the situations they are designed to address. It has become clear that, even taken together, neither the Planned nor Emergent approach covers the broad spectrum of change events that organisations encounter. Pettigrew (2000: 245–6) observes that:

> There is a long tradition in the social sciences and in management and organization theory of using bipolar modes of thinking: dichotomies, paradoxes, contradictions and dualities. . . . The duality of planned versus emergent change has served us well as an attention director but may well now be ready for retirement.

Though both Planned and Emergent change have important theoretical and practical benefits, their dominance of the change literature has led to a neglect of other approaches. In order to address this neglect, this chapter will seek to identify the range of change situations organisations face and match these to a wider group of approaches. This will enable the construction of a framework that will allow different change situations to be matched to appropriate approaches to managing change. It will then be argued that, by manipulating key variables in this framework, it is possible for organisations to have genuine choices in what to change, how to change and when to change.

Varieties of change

As noted in Chapter 8, types of change can be categorised as to whether their primary focus applies to individuals, groups, or systems and sub-systems. As far as models of change are concerned, once again as noted in Chapter 8, the three main ones are the Incremental model; the Punctuated Equilibrium model; and the Continuous Transformation model. Figure 10.1 brings these together to create a change matrix that, as the examples illustrate, appears to cover most situations.

However, there are other types, models and forms of change that expand on, cut across or are not included in this matrix. Senior (2002), drawing on the work of Grundy (1993), identifies three categories of change:

	Incremental	Punctuated	Continuous
Individuals	IT Training	Promotion Dismissal	Career Development
Groups	*Kaizen*	Forming, Storming, Norming, Performing and Adjourning	Changes in Composition and Tasks
Systems	Fine-Tuning	BPR, Organisation Restructuring	Culture

Figure 10.1 Varieties of change

- *smooth incremental*, covering slow, systematic, evolutionary change;
- *bumpy incremental*, pertaining to periods where the smooth flow of change accelerates;
- *discontinuous change*, which is similar to the punctuated equilibrium model.

As discussed in Chapter 9, Kanter *et al* (1992), in addressing the issue of transformational change, argued that it can be achieved either by:

- a *Bold Stroke* approach – rapid overall change; or
- a *Long March* approach – incremental change leading to transformation over an extended period of time.

In a similar vein, Beer and Nohria (2000) identify two basic archetypes, or theories of change:

- *Theory E*: This is similar to Kanter *et al*'s Bold Stroke. The main objective of this approach is to maximise shareholder value. It is applied in situations where an organisation's performance has diminished to such an extent that its main shareholders demand major and rapid change to improve the organisation's financial performance. Typically this is a 'hard' approach based on downsizing, divestment of non-core or low-performing businesses, and the heavy use of financial incentives.
- *Theory O*: This is similar to Kanter *et al*'s Long March. Theory O is also aimed at improving an organisation's performance, but this is more a 'soft' approach based on a slow incremental development of the organisation's culture and its human capabilities, and promoting organisational learning.

Beer and Nohria (2000) believe that both of these are valid models of change but that both have their flaws. Theory E can achieve short-term financial gains but at the cost of denuding an organisation of the human capabilities and organisational culture necessary for long-term survival. Theory O, whilst focusing on people and culture, falls into the trap of not restructuring to concentrate on core activities, thus failing to deliver shareholder value. To achieve the gains of both these approaches, whilst avoiding the pitfalls,

Beer and Nohria advocate using these in tandem by focusing on the rapid restructuring elements of Theory E but following this with the slow human capability development offered by Theory O.

Cummings and Worley (2001: 30) identify a 'continuum ranging from incremental changes that involve fine-tuning the organization to quantum changes that entail fundamentally altering how it operates'. Stace and Dunphy (2001), in a similar but more detailed way, identify a four-stage change continuum that comprises the following: fine-tuning, incremental adjustment, modular transformation and corporate transformation (*see* Figure 9.1 in Chapter 9). Looking at the last of these, Stace and Dunphy argue that corporate transformations can take four forms: developmental transitions; task-focused transitions; charismatic transformations; and turnarounds. For Peters (1989), rapid, disruptive and continuous change is the only appropriate form of change there is. With echoes of Peters, Quinn (1996) differentiates between incremental change, which he sees as leading to slow death, and deep, radical change leading to irreversible transformation. Pettigrew *et al* (1992) distinguish between types of change by their scale and importance. Their change continuum spans:

- Operational change – small-scale, relatively unimportant.
- Strategic change – major and important structural changes.

Buchanan and Boddy's (1992) classification is almost the same as Pettigrew *et al*'s, but they use two dimensions:

- Incremental change to radical change.
- Changes that are of central importance to the organisation to those that are peripheral to its purpose.

Kotter (1996) ignores the notion of a continuum of change as such and, instead, argues that organisations need to be continuously transforming themselves through a series of large and small interlinked change projects spanning different levels and functions and having different timescales.

One could of course extend this review further by including other writers (e.g. Dawson, 2003; Stickland, 1998; Wilson, 1992); however, the end product would be the same: change can be viewed as running along a continuum from incremental to transformational. Incremental or fine-tuning forms of change are geared more to changing the activities, performance, behaviour and/or attitudes of individuals and groups, whereas transformational change is geared towards the processes, structures and culture of the entire organisation. Obviously, there are differences in how these writers construe these concepts. Some writers see fine-tuning or incremental change as being relatively isolated and/or relatively unimportant (i.e. Stace and Dunphy, 2001; Pettigrew *et al*, 1992), whilst others see it as being part of an overall plan to transform an organisation (e.g. Kanter *et al*, 1992; Senior, 2002). In contrast, all seem to view transformational change as being strategic and important; though there are those who see it as being a relatively slow process (Kotter, 1996), those who see it as being a relatively rapid one (Peters, 1989), and those who argue that it can take both forms (Kanter *et al*, 1992; Stace and Dunphy, 2001).

Regardless of these differences, the overall view as shown by Figure 10.2 is that change can be seen as running along a continuum from small-scale incremental change

Figure 10.2 Change continuum

to large-scale transformational change. This of course is no surprise; intuitively, one would expect change to range from small-scale to large-scale and from operational to strategic. The important consideration is perhaps not the type of change but how it should be conceived and managed. Implicit in the arguments of the Emergent approach is the view that Planned change stands at the left-hand end of this spectrum and Emergent change at the right-hand end, and that what separates them is the nature of the environment (*see* Figure 10.3).

Figure 10.3 Approaches to change

As argued in Chapter 8, Lewin saw Planned change as being appropriate for changing the behaviour of a group, which does tend to be relatively stable over time. On the other hand, Emergent change, as argued in Chapter 9, is better suited to more turbulent, organisation-wide environments. However, Chapters 8 and 9 also showed that these two approaches to change are more limited than their advocates claim. In particular, both the Planned and Emergent approaches tend to stress the collaborative and consultative approach to managing change. In contrast Stace and Dunphy (2001) identify four approaches to managing change based on the degree to which employees are involved in planning and executing change, as follows: collaborative, consultative, directive and coercive. They argue that consultative and directive approaches tend to dominate, except where rapid organisational transformations are required, when more coercive approaches come into play. Kotter (1996) takes a different view, seeing the overall direction of change as being decided by senior managers, but its implementation being the responsibility of empowered managers and employees at all levels. Boddy and Buchanan (1992) believe that the way in which a change should be managed will be viewed differently, depending on whether it is central or peripheral to the organisation's purpose. Davenport (1993) expands on these two issues by constructing a list of five principal factors that influence how a project will be managed: the scale of change; the level of uncertainty about the outcome; the breadth of change across the organisation; the magnitude of change in terms of attitudes and behaviour; and the timescale for implementation. Storey (1992), taking a slightly different tack, begins by identifying two key dimensions:

- The degree of collaboration between the parties concerned: varying from change that is unilaterally constructed by management, to change brought about by some form of joint agreement with those involved.
- The form that change takes: ranging from change that is introduced as a complete package, to change comprising a sequence of individual initiatives.

From these two dimensions, Storey constructs a fourfold typology of change:

1. **Top-down systemic change** aimed at transforming the organisation.
2. **Piecemeal initiatives** devised and implemented by departments or sections in an unconnected fashion.
3. **Bargaining for change** where a series of targets are jointly agreed between managers and workers, but are pursued in a piecemeal fashion.
4. **Systemic jointism** where managers and workers agree a total package of changes designed to achieve organisational transformation.

As with the earlier review of the types of change, to make sense of this review of the nature of change and how it should be managed, we need to find a way of categorising and tabulating the various viewpoints. However, this is a far-from-straightforward exercise. Stace and Dunphy's (2001) fourfold categorisation of approaches to change, ranging from cooperative to coercive, is useful in that it appears to cover most of the managerial approaches on offer. However, it is the circumstances in which each of these might best be used that is perhaps of most concern. Boddy and Buchanan's categorisation of central–peripheral is interesting but, in most instances, this appears to boil down to an issue of project size. Almost by definition, all major projects can be considered as central by virtue of their size and, for a similar reason, most smaller projects are, relatively speaking, peripheral. Davenport's five factors are perhaps more useful in helping us to categorise change, especially those concerning uncertainty, behaviour and attitudes, and timescale. As we have noted frequently in this book, uncertainty tends to be present when the environment is changing in a rapid and unpredictable fashion. This requires organisations to respond quickly; advocates of the Emergent approach believe this is best done by small- to medium-scale local or cross-functional or process changes. The ability to do this, however, is dependent on having appropriate structures, attitudes and cultures in place. If this is not the case, then change will be delayed or not quick enough and, as Stace and Dunphy (2001) showed, will be likely to require rapid transformational change undertaken in a directive or coercive fashion. Nevertheless, both Kanter *et al* (1992) and Beer and Nohria (2000), as well as the review of culture in Chapter 5, argue that changes in attitudes and culture cannot be achieved in a rapid and coercive manner. That type of approach tends to be effective in changing structures and processes, but achieving attitudinal and/or cultural change is a much slower process.

A framework for change

If we summarise the above views, we can create yet another change continuum (*see* Figure 10.4). At one end is slow change, where the focus is on behavioural and cultural change. At the other end of the continuum is rapid change, where the focus is on major changes in structures and processes.

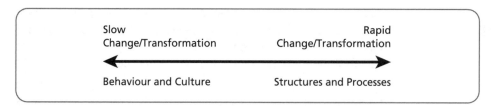

Figure 10.4 Speed and focus of change

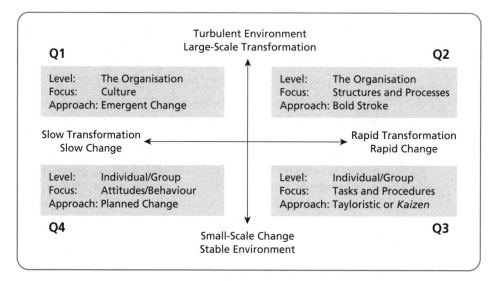

Figure 10.5 A framework for change

If we merge Figure 10.4 (putting it along the horizontal axis) with Figures 10.2 and 10.3 (putting them along the vertical axis), what we get, as Figure 10.5 shows, are four quadrants, each of which has a distinct focus in terms of change.

The top half of Figure 10.5, Quadrants 1 and 2, represents situations where organisations need to make large-scale, organisation-wide changes to either their culture or structure. These changes may be required because the organisation's structure/culture, though appropriate in the past, is inappropriate for the turbulent environment in which it finds itself operating. The bottom half of the figure, Quadrants 3 and 4, represents situations where organisations need to make relatively small-scale, localised adjustments to the attitudes and behaviours or tasks and procedures of individuals and groups. Such changes must be sustained and, therefore, it is crucial to ensure that the post-change environment is stable.

As can be seen, the left-hand side of the figure, Quadrants 1 and 4, represents situations where the main focus of change is the human side of the organisation, i.e. cultural and attitudinal and/or behavioural change. As argued above, these sorts of changes are likely to be best achieved through a relatively slow, participative approach, rather than a rapid and directive or coercive one. The right-hand side of Figure 10.5, Quadrants 2 and 3, represents situations where the primary focus is on achieving changes to the technical side of the organisation, i.e. structures, processes, tasks and procedures. These types of changes tend to be less participative in nature and relatively rapid in their execution.

Taking each of the quadrants in turn: Quadrant 1 identifies situations where the culture of an organisation operating in a turbulent environment is no longer appropriate. For such relatively large-scale initiatives, where the main focus is culture change at the level of the entire organisation or large parts of it, the Emergent approach (e.g. Kanter *et al*'s Long March), which emphasises both the collaborative and political dimensions of change, is likely to be most appropriate. As argued in Chapter 5, attempts to change culture through top-down, directive or coercive initiatives are liable to fail. Therefore, where they are to be successful, such forms of change are less likely to be consciously embarked on and more likely to 'emerge' from a host of initiatives that arise in response to changes in the environment, though this does not necessarily exclude some elements of deliberation and guidance from senior managers. Although the organisation may be operating in a turbulent environment and, therefore, individual elements of the cultural change may be rapid, the overall cultural transformation is likely to be a slow process.

Quadrant 2 relates to situations where the focus is on achieving major changes in structures and processes at the level of the entire organisation (e.g. Kanter *et al*'s Bold Stroke). Situations where such changes are required arise for a variety of reasons. It may be that an organisation finds itself in serious trouble and needs to respond quickly to realign itself with its environment (e.g. financial institutions responding to the credit crunch). Alternatively, it may be that an organisation is not experiencing a crisis, but that it perceives that it will face one unless it restructures itself to achieve a better fit with its environment. In such cases, it may not be possible or advisable to change the structure slowly or on a piecemeal basis and, therefore, a major and rapid reorganisation is necessary. Because it involves the entire organisation or major components of it, this is likely to be driven by the centre and to be the focus of a political struggle, given that major structural changes are usually accompanied by major shifts in the distribution of power. Therefore, the new structure will be imposed from the top in a directive or even coercive way, depending on the balance between winners and losers.

Quadrant 3 presents a different picture. This represents situations where change is aimed at the individual and group level rather than at the level of the entire organisation. The aim is to improve the performance of the areas involved through changes to the technical side of the organisation. Such changes tend to be relatively small-scale and piecemeal and with few (if any) implications for behaviour and attitudes. A key objective is to ensure the predictability and stability of the performance of the areas involved but at a higher level. How these changes are managed will depend on the culture of the organisation. In a traditional, bureaucratic organisation, a Tayloristic approach may be adopted, i.e. specialist managers and engineers will identify the 'best way of working' and impose it. In a more participative culture, such as a Japanese company, a more collaborative approach may be appropriate, such as a *Kaizen* initiative that brings together a team comprising workers and specialists. But either is possible and both can be achieved in a relatively speedy fashion.

Finally, Quadrant 4 covers relatively small-scale initiatives whose main objective is performance improvement through attitudinal and behavioural change at the individual and group level. As in the case of Quadrant 3, a key objective is to ensure the predictability and stability of the performance of the people involved but at a higher level. In such situations, Planned change, with its emphasis on collaboration and participation, is likely to be the more appropriate approach. However, because of the focus on behavioural and attitudinal change, the process may be relatively slow.

Of course, it could be argued that, at the organisational level, it is difficult to identify situations that involve solely cultural changes or solely structural changes. A similar comment could be made with regard to attitudinal and/or behavioural change and changes to tasks and procedures at the individual or group level. Such comments are valid to an extent, but the real issue is to identify the main focus of the change. Chapter 3 examined the work of the Culture–Excellence approach. Here it was shown that writers such as Tom Peters and Rosabeth Moss Kanter were arguing for structural change in order to promote the values and behaviours necessary for organisations to survive in an increasingly complex world. Therefore, though significant structural changes were recommended, these were part of the process of culture change and not an end in themselves. John Kotter, as noted in the previous chapter, advocates the need for organisations to restructure themselves on a continuous basis in order to meet the challenges of the future. At different times and in different areas, he believes that this can involve all of the types of change shown in Figure 10.1. There are also many cases, as Kotter argues, where an organisation already has an appropriate culture and where changes to its overall structure, and piecemeal changes to its component parts, are seen as working with and reinforcing the existing organisational culture rather than leading to its replacement.

Therefore, the question of whether changes can be labelled as mainly structure-orientated or mainly people-orientated is partly a matter of sequencing: what does the organisation need to do first? It is also partly concerned with the extent to which environmental turbulence has a uniform effect across an organisation. As shown in Chapter 2, in the 1960s, James Thompson (1967) identified that different sections of an organisation, by accident or design, could experience different levels of uncertainty. On this basis, it would be perfectly feasible for some parts of an organisation to be experiencing relatively low levels of uncertainty and concentrating on small-scale, piecemeal changes whilst at the same time the overall organisation was going through a process of rapid transformation.

Where does this leave us? Drawing on the work of Davenport (1993), we need to distinguish between initiatives that focus on fundamental attitudinal change and those aimed at fundamental structural change. As mentioned by Allaire and Firsirotu (1984) and as argued in Chapter 5, there is a strong relationship between organisational structures and organisational cultures, and so changes in one may require corresponding changes in the other. As was also argued earlier, however, it is much easier and quicker to change structures than to change cultures. Consequently, we need to take into account the timescale for change. Culture change, to be effective, is likely to be slow and involves incremental changes to the human side of the organisation. Also, because of its nature, it is likely to be participative and collaborative. Rapid change is only likely to be effective or necessary where the main changes are to structure, or where the organisation is in such trouble that delay is not an option (e.g. the recent takeover of HBOS by Lloyds TSB). In the case of structural change, this may involve some consultation but is likely to have a large element of direction from the centre. In the latter case, where the organisation is in trouble because of the urgency of the situation, change is likely to be directive and, probably, coercive.

There is one further point that needs to be noted, and that relates to how these various approaches can be used in combination. In a manner reminiscent of Mintzberg's (1994) definition of 'umbrella' strategies, Pettigrew *et al* (1992: 297) write of instances where change is both 'intentional and emergent'. Storey (1992) identifies the need for change projects whose outlines are decided at corporate level with little or no consultation, but whose implementation comprises an interrelated series of change initiatives, some or all of which could be the product of local cooperation and consultation. Kotter (1996) takes a similar perspective. He sees strategic change as comprising a series of large and small projects aimed at achieving the same overall objectives but which are begun at different times, which can be managed differently and which vary in nature. Buchanan and Storey (1997) also hint at this when criticising Planned change for attempting to impose order and a linear sequence to processes that are untidy, messy, multi-level and multi-function, and that develop in an iterative and backtracking manner. This is also identified by Kanter *et al* (1992) when speaking of Long Marches and Bold Strokes. They argue that Bold Strokes often have to be followed by a whole series of smaller-scale changes over a more extended timescale in order to embed the changes brought about by the Bold Stroke. Beer and Nohria (2000) are even more explicit in arguing for the use of Theory E and Theory O in tandem. Similarly, Burnes (2004a) also shows that major change projects that involve both structural and cultural change can successfully utilise both Planned and Emergent approaches. Consequently, when considering major change projects, one should not see them as being managed solely in a cooperative fashion or solely in a coercive fashion. Instead, they may have elements of both but at different levels, at different times and managed by different people. They may also, indeed probably will, unfold in an unexpected way which will require rethinking and backtracking from time to time.

A framework for employee involvement

The received wisdom in the literature on organisational change is that employee involvement is crucial to successful change, especially in situations that require attitudinal and cultural change. The discussion around Figure 10.5 supported this view, arguing that cultural and behavioural change would require greater levels of employee involvement than those that focused on restructuring tasks or even entire organisations. The implication of this is that rapid organisational transformations can only be successful if they focus on structural as opposed to cultural change. This is a conclusion that can certainly be drawn from the literature on both Planned and Emergent change. It is also something stressed by Kanter *et al* (1992), who believe that an organisation's structure can be changed relatively quickly through a 'Bold Stroke' but that cultural change can only be achieved by a 'Long March' requiring extensive participation over time. However, as the case study of Oticon at the end of this chapter shows, this is not always the case. Sometimes, cultural change can be relatively swift and employee involvement relatively low. To understand why this should be so, it is necessary to examine three theories which underpin many of the arguments for employee involvement.

Theory 1 – The Depth of Intervention. In addressing the question of why cultural or behavioural change can sometimes be achieved more quickly than conventional wisdom would deem acceptable, the work of Schmuck and Miles (1971) is particularly useful. They argue that the level of involvement required in any change project is dependent on the impact of the change on the people concerned. Huse (1980) developed this distinction further. Incorporating earlier work by Harrison (1970), Huse categorised change interventions along a continuum based on the 'depth' of intervention, ranging from the 'shallow level' to the 'deepest level'. The greater the depth of the intervention, Huse argues, the more it becomes concerned with the psychological make-up and personality of the individual, and the greater the need for the full involvement of individuals if they are to accept the changes.

The argument, therefore, is that it is necessary to link levels of involvement to the types of change proposed. The key is that the greater the effect on the individual in terms of psychological constructs and values, the deeper the level of involvement required if successful behaviour change is to be achieved. This appears to explain why in some cases, involvement can be dispensed with or minimised, i.e. in cases where the psychological impact is shallow, whilst in others it is vital. It does not, though, explain why major and rapid attitudinal changes can be achieved without a great deal of employee involvement.

Theory 2 – Cognitive Dissonance. In seeking to understand and explain such apparent contradictions, Burnes and James (1995) draw on the theory of cognitive dissonance. This theory states that people try to be consistent in both their attitudes and behaviour. When they sense an inconsistency either between two or more attitudes or between their attitudes and behaviour, people experience dissonance; that is, they feel frustrated and uncomfortable with the situation, sometimes extremely so (Jones, 1990). Therefore, individuals will seek a stable state where there is minimum dissonance. This latter point is important. It is unlikely that dissonance can ever be totally avoided, but where the elements creating the dissonance are relatively unimportant, the pressure to correct them will be low. Where the issues involved are perceived by the individual to be significant, however, the presence of such dissonance will motivate the person concerned to try to reduce the dissonance and achieve consonance, by changing either their attitudes or behaviour to bring them into line (Robbins, 1986; Smith *et al*, 1982). This may involve a process of cognitive restructuring, which is unlikely to be free from difficulties for the individual concerned (Mahoney, 1974). However, as Festinger (1957), one of the originators of the concept, pointed out, in addition to trying to reduce the dissonance, people will actively avoid situations and information that would be likely to increase the dissonance. Since the emergence of the theory of cognitive dissonance in the 1950s, it has been developed and refined (*see* Cooper and Fazio, 1984; Fazio *et al*, 1977; Jones, 1990).

Applying principles of cognitive dissonance to organisational change, it can be seen that, if an organisation embarks on a change project that is decisively out of step with the attitudes of those concerned, it will meet with resistance unless those concerned change their attitudes. On the other hand, where the level of dissonance occasioned by proposed changes is low, attitudinal adjustments will be minor and potential resistance negligible. Therefore, the level and type of involvement should be geared to the level of dissonance that any proposed changes may provoke.

Up to this point, cognitive dissonance supports the work of Schmuck and Miles (1971) and Huse (1980). However, if we apply the theory to situations where old certainties have lost their legitimacy and the very survival of the organisation is at stake, a different picture emerges. The crisis (or potential crisis) raises the level of dissonance in the organisation as it becomes apparent that existing practices are no longer viable and change is required. Not only does this make individuals and groups more receptive to radical change, but, in addition, change can be one of the main ways of reducing dissonance. In such situations, fundamental attitudinal change can be achieved relatively quickly and without a great deal of employee involvement, because management and employees recognise the need for (and indeed want) major change and see the creation and implementation of a new vision as their only hope for the company's survival. Therefore, in such instances, the dissonance is occasioned not by the change, but by the condition of the organisation leading up to the change. However, in many other situations, the absence of a sense of deep crisis prevents existing certainties being successfully challenged. Only when more severe threats arise are these old certainties challenged, and those involved become more prepared to accept and promote radical solutions that may have previously been rejected.

Theory 3 – The Psychological Contract. A similar and complementary explanation for the involvement or non-involvement of employees is offered by the notion of the psychological contract. Though this concept has been around since the 1950s (*see* for example Argyris, 1960), it was only in the 1980s and 1990s that it became widely used by organisation theorists, especially in America (Arnold *et al*, 1998). As Schein (1988: 22–3) explains:

> *The notion of a psychological contract implies that there is an unwritten set of expectations operating at all times between every member of an organization and the various managers and others in that organization. . . . The psychological contract implies further that each role player, that is, employee, also has expectations about such things as salary or pay rate, working hours, benefits and privileges . . . and so on. Many of these expectations are implicit and involve the person's sense of dignity and worth. . . . Some of the strongest feelings leading to labor unrest, strikes, and employee turnover have to do with violations of these aspects of the psychological contract, even though the public negotiations are often over the more explicit issues of pay, working hours, job security, and so on.*

We can certainly see why, for, example, the employees of a public-sector organisation with a public-sector ethos might feel as though their psychological contract had been violated if they were suddenly told they were to be transferred to the private sector – particularly as such a change might represent a considerable threat to their job security. However, in other instances, similarly radical change might not produce a significantly adverse reaction from staff. The reason offered by proponents of the psychological contract for this would be that in these cases staff recognised the need and justification for the changes and therefore the legitimacy of the need to change their psychological contracts.

Consequently, it is necessary to treat the employee involvement/non-involvement issue with some caution. In general, we can say that cultural and behavioural changes, i.e. the left-hand side of Figure 10.5, are likely to require greater levels of employee involvement than the more structural changes of the right-hand side of Figure 10.5. However, if we draw on the complementary ideas of levels of involvement, cognitive dissonance and the psychological contract, we see that this general rule of involvement has to take account of the context of the change situation and not just the type of change being proposed. In many cases where change is proposed it will be necessary to convince staff, through a process of constructive engagement, of the need to challenge their existing beliefs, behaviours and expectations and to renegotiate their 'contracts' with the organisation. However, in some instances, the legitimacy of existing beliefs, behaviours and expectations may already have been undermined because the organisation is going through a crisis (the restructuring of many financial institutions owing to the credit crunch may be a good example). In such situations, it might be that cultural and behavioural change can be quickly achieved without the need for elaborate involvement techniques, because those concerned can see that the old attitudes and ways of behaving have had their day and, unless major or radical changes are made, their jobs or even the entire organisation may cease to exist. Of course, the reverse may also be the case. Organisations seeking to bring about small changes to structures or tasks might find they meet greater resistance than they expected because they underestimate the psychological importance employees attach to these existing arrangements. Therefore, approaches to change, including the level of employee involvement, have to be tailored to the change context rather than being applied in an unthinking fashion. As will be argued next, it might be possible to influence the change context to make it more amenable to particular approaches to change.

A framework for choice

As can be seen from Figure 10.5, what appears to be on offer is a menu approach to change whereby organisations, or more accurately those who manage them, can choose the approach which fits their circumstances. This conception of a multiplicity of approaches is in line with the call by Dunphy and Stace (1993: 905) for 'a model of change that is essentially a "situational" or "contingency model", one that indicates how to vary strategies to achieve "optimum fit" with the changing environment'. If we were to stop at this point, it might be considered that we had indeed made significant progress in our understanding of change; yet there would still be one essential question outstanding: what about choice? We have identified situations where these various approaches seem appropriate or not, but does that mean they cannot be used in other situations and does that mean that the context cannot be changed? Supposing organisations, whose management prefers a cooperative approach, find themselves seriously out of alignment with their environment: is their only option rapid and coercive structural change? Or, alternatively, where managers prefer a more directive, less participative style, are they compelled to adopt a more participative style and culture?

These questions revolve around two issues. The first issue concerns the extent to which an organisation can influence the forces driving it to change in one direction or another. If we accept that the speed and nature of the changes that organisations are required to make are dependent upon the nature of the environment in which they are operating, then choice will relate to the extent that organisations can influence, manipulate or recreate their environment to suit their preferred way of working. This is a subject that has been examined a number of times so far, especially in Chapters 5 and 6, and will be touched on again in Chapters 11 and 12. The conclusion reached was that organisations could influence their environment, either to stabilise or to destabilise it. If this is the case, then the important question is not just how organisations can do this, but whether, finding themselves in trouble, they have the time to influence their environment.

This leads on to the second issue: to what extent and for how long can an organisation operate with structures, practices and cultures that are out of line with its environment? The answer to this question revolves around Child's (1972) concept of equifinality. As discussed in Chapter 6, equifinality 'quite simply means that different sorts of internal arrangements are perfectly compatible with identical contextual or environmental states' (Sorge, 1997: 13). This does not imply that any structure is suitable for any environment. What it does suggest, though, is that total alignment between structure and environment is not always necessary. The duration for which this non-alignment is sustainable will clearly vary with the degree of non-alignment and the circumstances of the organisation in question; at the very least, however, it does offer organisations the potential to stave off realignment for some time during which they can influence or change their circumstances. It follows that Figure 10.5 depicts not only a framework for change but also a framework for choice.

In summary, therefore, what we can see, as Pettigrew (2000) suggested, is that the debate between Planned change and Emergent change is too narrow. It is too narrow in the sense that there are other approaches to change that organisations have available to them; in particular, it tends to ignore the more coercive and directive approaches to change that, in many organisations, may be more prevalent than more cooperative ones. It is also too narrow in the sense that it assumes that change is unidirectional, i.e. is driven by the environment. Organisations do have the opportunity to make choices about what to change, how to change and when to change. This does not mean that all organisations will exercise such choices or that those which do will be successful. Nor, as Chapter 6 argued, does it mean that choice is not severely constrained. What it does mean is that those that do not recognise that choice exists may be putting themselves in a worse competitive position than those that do.

Conclusions

The previous two chapters examined the Planned and Emergent approaches to change, which have successively dominated the theory and, to a large extent, the practice of organisational change over the past 50 years. Chapter 8 was devoted to the Planned approach to change. It was argued that, though still appropriate for changing the behaviour of groups in organisations, attempts by OD practitioners to apply it to organisation-wide change initiatives have led to confusion and a loss of direction. In the increasingly dynamic and unpredictable business environment of the 1980s, writers began to question the appropriateness of a top-down approach that saw the process of change primarily in terms of a 'beginning, middle and end' framework. In place of the Planned approach, as was shown in Chapter 9, the Emergent approach began to gain support. With its emphasis on bottom-up and open-ended change, it appeared to offer a more appropriate method of accomplishing the stream of adaptations organisations believed they needed to make in order to bring themselves back into line with their environment. However, Chapter 9 also showed that Emergent change may have as many shortcomings as Planned change.

Nevertheless, the two approaches appear to have some striking similarities, especially the emphasis they place on change as being a learning process. They also share a common, and major, difficulty, which is that whilst both claim to be universally applicable, they were developed with particular change situations, organisation types and environments in mind. Originally, the Planned approach was developed to focus on behaviour change in small groups. It is based on the assumption that group behaviour is relatively stable and predictable. It also assumes that managers can identify where change is required and that change is about moving from one fixed point to another fixed point, and that the steps or phases in between are relatively clear and realisable. Later elaborations have sought to apply this approach to entire organisations. The Planned approach also appears to assume that organisations, managers and employees are open and frank, they welcome involvement, and are willing to change, or that these attributes can be achieved with the application of the appropriate tools and techniques.

The Emergent approach, on the other hand, assumes that organisations are open and fluid systems that operate in unpredictable and uncertain conditions over which they have little control. It further assumes that change is a continuous process of adaptation and transformation which, because of its speed and frequency, managers can neither fully identify nor effectively control centrally. Therefore, from the Emergent perspective, identifying and managing change has to be the responsibility of everyone in the organisation. This view portrays managers, who are seen as highly competent and adaptable, as capable of changing themselves from outmoded controllers and coordinators to new-style facilitators and partners; and employees are seen as willing to take responsibility for identifying deficiencies and implementing change. Above all, and perhaps somewhat contradictorily, change is seen as being a political process whereby different groups and individuals strive to protect or enhance their power and position. As mentioned earlier, it is on this last point – the overriding importance of power and politics in the change process – that postmodernists are most in agreement with the Emergent approach and realists most in disagreement.

As Chapter 8 showed, the Planned approach has had a considerable impact on organisation practice since its inception in the 1940s. However, despite its undoubted merits, as argued earlier, it does appear limited in terms of the situations in which it can successfully be applied. In particular, the Planned approach has been criticised for its lack of suitability to situations requiring large-scale change and/or ones where political and power considerations are prevalent. However, as was demonstrated in Chapter 9, the Emergent approach also has drawbacks in terms of its applicability to large-scale and abrupt change programmes, preferring a continuous programme of small- to medium-sized changes. In addition, criticisms have been raised over its heavy emphasis on the political dimension of change and its contradictory tendency, both implicitly and explicitly, to characterise change as a slow and cooperative process. Consequently, even taken together, the Planned and Emergent approaches do not cover all change situations. In particular, neither approach seems suitable for situations where the primary focus is rapid and radical structural change.

Instead of portraying the argument regarding the most appropriate approach to change as a contest between the merits of the Planned and Emergent approaches, the Framework for Change (Figure 10.5) provides an overview of the range of change situations organisations face, and the approaches they are offered and the types of situations in which they can best be applied.

Though this Contingency-type approach to change appears to have some merit, it is subject to the same sort of criticisms levelled at Contingency Theory in Chapter 2. However, this chapter has also argued that, if we adopt the perspective developed in previous chapters and see the environment and other organisational constraints as potentially manipulable or subject to managerial choice, many of these criticisms can be answered and new possibilities opened up. It has to be recognised that there is dispute between the realists and postmodernists as to what can be manipulated and the degree of choice which exists. However, this is a matter of degree; both acknowledge the existence of choice. Therefore, some organisations will find that the organisational adjustments required to accommodate their position on the environmental continuum coincide with the dominant view in the organisation of how it should operate. In that case, whether the approach to change adopted is Planned or Emergent, directive or cooperative, it will fit in with both how the organisation wishes to operate and the needs of the environment. Some organisations will, obviously, find that the dominant view internally of how they should operate is out of step with what is required to align or realign them with their environment. Such organisations face a number of choices ranging from whether to attempt to change their structure, culture or style of management to accommodate the environment, or whether to attempt to manipulate the environment and other constraints so as to align them more closely with the dominant view within the organisation of how it should operate. Still further, there will be other organisations who face severe problems either because they failed to respond quickly enough or in an appropriate manner to changes in their environment, or because the environment moved too rapidly for an incremental approach to respond adequately. Nevertheless, by showing that a more conducive environment can be brought about, the framework also provides those who wish to promote more cooperative approaches to change with the means to argue their case in situations where previously more directive and coercive measures appeared to be the only option.

The concept of a Framework for Change that allows approaches to change to be matched to environmental conditions and organisational constraints is clearly attractive. The fact that it incorporates the potential for managers, and others, to exercise some choice or influence over their environment and other constraints allows the model to move beyond the limitations of mechanistic and rational perspectives on organisations, and into the heartland of organisational reality. In addition, though not by accident, it is in harmony with the approach to strategy developed in Chapters 6 and 7.

Nevertheless, though such a model of change has its attractions, its usefulness depends on how well it accommodates the reality of organisational life. This will be addressed in the remaining chapters of the book.

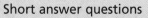

Test your learning

Short answer questions

1. To what extent can we say that Kanter *et al*'s (1992) 'Bold Stroke' and 'Long March' approaches to change are the same as Beer and Nohria's (2000) 'Theory E' and 'Theory O' approaches?

2. Using the headings in Figure 10.1, identify your own 'varieties of change'.

3. Describe Storey's (1992) fourfold typology of change. Give a real-life example of each type of change.

4. What are the main components of the Framework for Change shown in Figure 10.5?

5. Evaluate the following statement: At the organisation level, change can either be structure-orientated or culture-orientated but it cannot be both at the same time.

6. To what extent and how does Child's (1972) concept of 'equifinality' indicate that organisations may be able to control the pace at which they change?

7. Summarise the case presented in Chapters 5 and 6 that organisations can manipulate or change the contingencies they face.

Essay questions

1. What are the arguments for and against Pettigrew's (2000: 245–6) comment that: 'The duality of planned versus emergent change has served us well as an attention director but may well now be ready for retirement'?

2. Use the Framework for Change, Figure 10.5, to analyse change in one of the case studies which appear at the end of each chapter in this book or for a case of your own choosing. In particular, identify the type of change or changes involved, the selection and suitability of the approach to change and the degree to which the approach was aligned with the management style of the organisation.

Suggested further reading

Beer, M and Nohria, N (eds) (2000) *Breaking the Code of Change*. Harvard Business School Press: Boston, MA, USA.

This edited collection contains contributions by many of the leading thinkers on organisational change. It covers the main approaches to change, including the Planned and Emergent.

Oticon – the Disorganised Organisation

BACKGROUND

Oticon, a Danish company founded in 1904, was the first hearing instrument company in the world. In the 1970s, it was the world's number one manufacturer of 'behind-the-ear' hearing aids. However, as the market for 'in-the-ear' products grew in the 1970s and 1980s, its fortunes plummeted and it lost money and market share. However, its fortunes began to change with the appointment of Lars Kolind as President of the company in 1988. In order to revitalise the company, Kolind resolved to 'think the unthinkable':

Maybe we could design a new way of running a business that could be significantly more creative, faster, and more cost-effective than the big players, and maybe that could compensate for our lack of technological excellence, our lack of capital, and our general lack of resources.

The vision – a knowledge-based organisation Kolind realised that the industry was totally technology-focused, but he thought this was short-sighted. He believed Oticon was not in the hearing-aid business *per se*; they were in the business of 'making people smile' – restoring the enjoyment of life that hearing impairment can destroy. To this end, the company adopted a new mission statement:

To help people with hearing difficulties to live life as they wish, with the hearing they have.

Kolind had the vision for Oticon's role in meeting customers' needs, but he still had to find a way of implementing it. He believed the key lay in the mix of expertise necessary to provide each customer with an effective hearing aid: micro-mechanics, microchip design, audiology, psychology, marketing, manufacturing, logistics, and all-round service capability. If Oticon were to move away from merely making hearing aids and instead provide a total package of support for people with hearing difficulties, it would have to develop a whole new concept in hearing-aid service. In short, they would have to move from being a technology-based manufacturing company to a knowledge-based service business. They had to build a learning organisation where experts put aside their expertise and work as a team to 'make people smile'.

For Kolind, a knowledge-based or learning organisation:

. . . should not work like a machine, it should work like a brain. Brains do not know hierarchies – no boxes – no job descriptions; what there is is a very chaotic set of thousands of relationships tangled in with each other based on certain knowledge centres, with an interaction which may seem chaotic. It is the reflection of the brain into the organisation that creates companies that are able to manage that knowledge process.

Kolind began by redefining his role as CEO. Instead of seeing himself as the captain that steers the ship, he saw himself as the naval architect who designs it. He believed that it was more important to design the organisation to act in a clever and responsible way than to control every action. On this basis, he drafted plans for the company's future which

▶

he first presented in April 1990. He wanted to create 'the spaghetti organisation' – a chaotic tangle of relationships and interactions that would force the abandonment of preconceived ideas and barriers to innovation and competitiveness.

The strategy: Having identified the vision for the organisation, the next step was to set about fleshing out and implementing his strategy for change. Beginning with the Head Office, which comprised the finance, management, marketing and product development functions, he decided to abandon the concept of a formal organisation; instead he wanted to create a 'disorganised organisation'. Formal structures, job descriptions and policies were seen as creating barriers to cooperation, innovation and teamwork rather than facilitating it. Kolind's new disorganised organisation would be founded on four principles:

- Departments and job titles would disappear and all activities would become projects initiated and pursued informally by groupings of interested people.
- Jobs would be redesigned into fluid and unique combinations of functions to suit each employee's needs and capabilities.
- All vestiges of the formal office would be eradicated and replaced by open space filled with workstations that anyone could use.
- Informal, face-to-face dialogue would replace memos as the acceptable mode of communication.

Therefore, Oticon got rid of departments, departmental heads and other managerial and supervisory positions. Job descriptions and titles and anything else that created a barrier between one member of staff and another were also eliminated. The company wanted to get rid of everything associated with traditional organisations, including budgets. The intent was to see what happened when staff were 'liberated' to do what they thought best. Kolind wanted everyone in the organisation, from secretaries to technical experts, to work much more closely together to make things happen more creatively, faster and more cost-effectively.

Implementing the strategy: Oticon now operates on a project basis. Anyone can start a project, provided they have the permission of one of five senior managers. Some projects are also initiated by management. Whomsoever the idea comes from, the main criterion for acceptance is that a project is customer-focused. Anyone can join a project, provided they have the agreement of the project leader. The basic idea, going back to the concept that Oticon treats everyone as an adult, is that it is the individual's responsibility to fill their day usefully. If people do not have anything to do, it is their job to find something useful to do – either by starting a project or by joining one.

Kolind's view of Oticon would send shivers down the spine of most traditional CEOs: 'Hearing aids are not the core of what this company is about. It's about something more fundamental. It's about the way people perceive work. We give people the freedom to do what they want.' This is perhaps why, as well as the 100 or so 'authorised' projects, as Kolind comments, 'We have a lot of skunk work going on that's not in any official priority.' There is a saying in Oticon that 'It's easier to be forgiven than to get permission.' Basically, this means, 'If in doubt do it. If it works, fine. If it doesn't, we forgive you.'

The physical embodiment of this new 'structureless' structure is the workplace. Gone are individual offices, gone are corridors – all the walls were taken out and everyone works in the same open-plan office. Staff gather where they wish to work. Instead of individual offices, everyone has a little filing cabinet on wheels. Staff come in each morning, pick up their mobile office and trundle it to where they are working that day. Oticon is also a genuinely 'paperless office'. All incoming mail is scanned into the computer and then shredded. The reason for this is simple: Oticon wants staff to move around from project group to project group as work requires. It does not want this process hindered by staff having to transport masses of paper as happens in most offices – the solution is to get rid of the paper.

This requires everyone to have access to and to be able to use a computer. However, the emphasis at Oticon is on face-to-face, informal communication (although, for example, e-mail is used but not extensively). This is why the office is littered with stand-up coffee bars to encourage small, informal (but short) meetings. Three or four people will meet to discuss an issue or exchange ideas and information and then return to where they are working that day and follow up ideas and suggestions. These are usually fed straight into the computer and are available to everybody else. There is also an expectation not only that all information is open to staff in this manner, but that staff actually want to know the information. Therefore, rather than putting up barriers or operating on a need-to-know basis, Oticon tries to be transparent about all aspects of its business, whether it be new products, staff salaries or finance in general. The view is that the more a person knows, the more valuable they are to the company.

Staff did not take to this radically new way of working overnight. This is perhaps not surprising. Staff were not originally recruited for their teamworking and project management skills, and some found it hard to come to terms with these new arrangements. Nor did they welcome the loss of routine and clear authority relationships or find the resultant uncertainty easy to adjust to. This was especially the case with managers for whom the loss of their power base, information monopoly and status symbols was difficult to accept.

In addition, under the new arrangement, managers were reclassified as project leaders and had to compete for the best staff, rather than having their own dedicated subordinates. Some groups of staff also found it difficult to find a role in the project team environment; for some time, receptionists, for instance, still answered the telephone.

The biggest boost to the new arrangements came when staff could see they actually worked better than the old ones. One immediate benefit was that Oticon 'found' that it had already developed the industry's first automatic, self-adjusting hearing aid in the 1980s. However, owing to technical problems (the solution to which was given a very low priority), lack of communication between the R&D and sales staff, and a lack of imagination, nobody seemed to have realised that they had developed a potentially world-beating product. In the transformed Oticon, this new type of hearing aid quickly resurfaced, the technical problems were rapidly ironed out, and the MultiFocus hearing aid, as it became known, was launched in late 1991. In the next two years, three more powerful variants of the MultiFocus were developed and its size reduced by half.

Where next?: The changes to – or rather the transformation of – Oticon started at 8 am on 8 August 1991. At the beginning, all was chaos. It took months before everyone understood their new roles, and for the organisation to cast off its old ways and begin to operate in the manner Kolind had envisaged. By 1994, however, the results were impressive:

▶

CASE STUDY 10 CONT.

- 15 new products had been launched (twice as many as the company had previously);
- new product lead time had been halved;
- the company's sales were growing at 20 per cent per year, after a period of 10 years without real growth and at a time when the market had begun shrinking by 5 per cent per year;
- Oticon's market share increased from 8 per cent to 12 per cent in the two years following the changes.

Nor did the progress stop there. In 1995, Oticon launched the world's first digital hearing aid, the DigiFocus. This is, in effect, a four-gram computer that fits in the ear but has the processing power of a desk-top machine. Not only was this a technological breakthrough for which Oticon has won a number of major innovation awards, but it also allowed Oticon to regain its position as one of the world's top three hearing aid producers. Also, by 1995 turnover had increased by 100 per cent on 1990 and profits had increased tenfold.

For some, this would have been a time to sit back and feel satisfied. Yet Kolind was becoming increasingly dissatisfied. The launch of the DigiFocus had dominated 1995 and the long-standing project teams created to develop and launch the product had taken on an air of permanency. He believed the company was in danger of slipping back into a traditional departmental organisational form.

Questions

1. Imagine that you are Lars Kolind. The changes you have made have been far more successful than you could have imagined. The company is profitable, producing innovative products and the workforce is pleased with the new arrangements.
   a. What are the advantages and disadvantages of allowing the company to regain a more formalised structure?
   b. What are the advantages and disadvantages of once again 'disorganising' the company?
   c. Which course of action do you intend to take and why?

2. Imagine that you were formerly a senior manager with Oticon and are now one of its most successful project leaders. Lars Kolind has shared his concerns with you and asked you to produce a report on the options for future organisation of the company from your perspective. In particular, he wishes you to address the following questions:
   a. What are the advantages and disadvantages of allowing the company to regain a more formalised structure?
   b. What are the advantages and disadvantages of once again 'disorganising' the company?
   c. Which course of action would you recommend and why?

3. Imagine that you are an outside consultant brought in to advise Lars Kolind. He wishes you to address the following questions:
   a. What are the advantages and disadvantages of allowing the company to regain a more formalised structure?
   b. What are the advantages and disadvantages of once again 'disorganising' the company?
   c. Which course of action would you recommend and why?

Managing choice

CHAPTER 11

Organisational change and managerial choice

Mini Case Study 11.1
BA struggles to escape T5 twilight zone

The events that have turned BA's self-proclaimed 'new dawn' into a public-relations twilight zone were caused by a blend of incompetence and hubris, an FT investigation suggests.

Problems had begun to develop even before the first passengers left the inaugural flight from Hong Kong. Staff arriving for work at 4 am had found queues for the car parks that were filling up with people arriving to witness the debut of the £4.3bn ($8.6bn) project. When would-be travellers started arriving, there were problems with lifts and an escalator, and check-in staff had to wait for computer systems to spring to life.

Many of these teething troubles were quickly dealt with [but] . . . The real chaos began when the new baggage-handling system started up. Many of the 400 handlers – who are BA staff – were not only unable to find their work stations but were also unfamiliar with the new system.

▶

Despite a senior manager's warning more than a year earlier that previous airport openings had been marred by the failure to familiarise staff with the terminal building, only 50 or so of 400 baggage-handlers had been fully trained when the terminal opened on March 27, the FT has been told. Even they had taken part only in trials that never ran the system at full capacity for lengthy periods. Many of the others had visited the new terminal, but most had had little more than a walk around and were expected to respond to instructions via hand-held computers known as PDAs. 'The other 350 [handlers] got lost in the terminal', said one executive involved in the project. 'When they were given instructions on where to go through the PDAs they did not know where to go. And given the size of T5, it takes a long time to get from A to B.'

Baggage distributed along the 18 km of conveyor belts quickly started to pile up at the bottom of the chutes, where staff were supposed to put them in containers for loading on to the aircraft. That brought the whole system to a halt. BA then prioritised loading baggage on to departing flights, but that meant the bags from incoming flights were not fed into the system.

Yet people involved in the project insist . . . 'The root cause was not having enough baggage handlers there and trained', said one.

According to Jonathon Counsell, head of T5 development, who had identified the need to familiarise more than 10,000 people with the building before it opened as key to avoiding confusion, BA's 6,700 Heathrow customer service staff were supposed to have four 'familiarisation' days. But union leaders have questioned whether all materialised, while industry executives queried whether staff knew what was expected of them.

Others familiar with BA say the company's management culture was also poor at checking that instructions had been fully implemented. Time and again, in the interviews carried out by the FT, the blame for this was laid principally at the door of Mr Walsh [BA's CEO]. A number of insiders said that he expected to be brought solutions rather than problems. 'He will have been told what he wanted to hear', said a Heathrow executive with long experience of dealing with BA. 'He is a terrier. He knows this culture. He will have looked people in the eye, but people will have told him it was ready.' Mr Walsh, who declined to be interviewed for the FT investigation, has reportedly been asking why he had not been warned of the difficulties building up.

Source: Adapted from Kevin Done and John Willman, *Financial Times*, 5 April 2008, p. 5.

Introduction

Many, many change projects fail but, as Mini Case Study 11.1 shows, few fail quite as spectacularly and with so much attendant publicity as BA's move to Terminal 5 at Heathrow. As with most failures, the causes were both simple and complex:

- In simple terms, BA and Heathrow's owners, BAA, failed to prepare and train staff sufficiently or to test equipment fully.
- On a more complex level, these issues were never raised at the level where action could be taken because the BA CEO wanted 'solutions and not problems' and was only told 'what he wanted to hear'.

This is indicative of a culture and leadership style where failure and perceived weakness are not tolerated. Whilst this approach may be successful in some situations, for change it can be fatal. As this chapter will show, central to the change process is the choice process – what to change, when to change, how to change. In BA's case, crucial choices were never consciously made because they were never raised. In effect, they were made by default, and in this case the default option was to do nothing.

As previous chapters have shown, whilst organisational change can be a complex, ambiguous and open-ended phenomenon, it can also be relatively straightforward with understandable and limited objectives. This in itself is not a new or radical finding – anyone who works in or studies organisations will have noted that change comes in a wide variety of shapes and sizes. It was argued in Chapter 10, however, that in order to cope with the wide variety of types of change, there is a need for a corresponding variety of approaches to strategy development and change management.

This point, the need to match types of change with appropriate approaches to managing change, is not as prominent in the literature on organisational change and behaviour as one might expect. As Part 2 showed, despite the widespread influence of Contingency Theory, the majority of writers and practitioners are committed to a 'one best way' approach to strategy and change. The call by Dunphy and Stace (1993) for a situational or contextual approach to these issues has been taken up by few others. Though there are writers on strategy, such as Mintzberg *et al* (1998a) and Whittington (1993), who identify the various approaches to strategy, in most cases they tend, eventually, to opt for one as their preferred approach. This is even more pronounced in the change literature, where there is a clear distinction between those who support the Planned approach (such as Cummings and Worley, 1997; French and Bell, 1995) and those who adhere to a more Emergent approach (such as Kotter, 1996; Pettigrew, 1997; Weick, 2000; Wilson, 1992).

Many of those arguing for their own favoured approach to strategy and change do so, either explicitly or implicitly, on the basis of their perception of the nature of the environment in which organisations operate. Those arguing for a Planned approach to strategy and/or change appear to assume that the environment is relatively stable, predictable and controllable. Those who take a more Emergent approach to both seem to operate on the assumption that the environment is turbulent, unpredictable and uncontrollable.

Furthermore, most writers seem to assume that the principal role of managers and the ultimate objective of strategy and change is to align or realign an organisation with its environment. In the preceding chapters, a case has been built for rejecting this argument and adopting a different stance. Rather than accepting the view that managers are prisoners of the circumstances in which their organisations operate or find themselves, it was argued that managers can and do exercise a considerable degree of choice. It was further argued, however, that the scope and nature of the choices managers face and make are constrained by a range of external factors (national characteristics, the business environment and industry norms) and internal organisational characteristics (especially structure, culture, politics and managerial style). This argument goes much further than many by challenging the assumption that managers are in some way the passive agents of forces beyond their control, but it still leaves them as prisoners of circumstances – although the prison in this case is much roomier than many of the writers we have discussed would acknowledge.

The arguments in Chapters 5, 6 and 10 challenged even this definition of managerial choice. It was suggested that many of the constraints on choice are themselves amenable to managerial actions – in effect, organisations can influence or change the constraints under which they operate. This possibility was first suggested when examining Contingency Theory in Chapter 2; it was further developed in subsequent chapters and shown to be more than a possibility. In particular, some managers are even capable of reinventing their organisations or, as the postmodernists would have it, creating a preferable reality for them. As the case studies at the end of the preceding chapters have shown, though organisations do try to align and realign themselves with their environment, they also attempt to influence and restructure the environment and other constraints in their favour. Sometimes, by accident or design, this results in a reconfiguration of the accepted rules by which the industry in which they operate competes; whilst in other instances, it prevents organisations being forced to undertake more radical internal upheavals.

In the case of Nissan (Chapter 1), it sought to change the adversarial relationships that had existed between car companies and their suppliers in Europe to make it more amenable to its preferred way of working. In the case of Oticon (Chapter 10), it can be seen that the company deliberately set out to change the basis on which it competed by reinventing itself as a service-based rather than a technology-driven organisation. Lacking the technological strength of its competitors, which was the accepted cornerstone of competition in its industry, it proposed to offer a superior level of service instead. By changing the rules of the game in its industry, Oticon hoped to steal a march on its competitors. In the case of XYZ (Chapters 3 and 8), the new Managing Director sought to change the internal constraints in the company, in terms of its culture, management style and structure, in order to improve its performance and align it with the changing nature of the construction industry and the desires of its parent company. In essence, the new Managing Director was attempting to reinvent the company, based on more cooperative internal relationships, in order to create more stable relationships with customers and establish a less uncertain external environment.

So, as the case studies show, organisations can and do influence and change the constraints under which they operate. On the other hand, though, the case studies give some support to those, such as proponents of the realist perspective discussed in Chapter 4, that there are some types of constraint that are not amenable to change. This can be seen from the Marconi example (Chapter 6), where no amount of effort on behalf of its management could alter the situation that they had borrowed too much money to buy overpriced assets at the top of the dotcom boom that, when the demand for telecoms equipment went into freefall, were found to be virtually worthless.

Therefore, we can see that organisations do have considerable scope for changing or influencing the constraints they face but that, despite what the postmodernists may claim, there are some constraints that appear beyond the scope of individual organisations to change. Nevertheless, this still leaves most organisations with considerably more freedom of choice than many commentators on strategy and change would acknowledge. The implications of this wider perspective on managerial choice for the nature and focus of change management are, as the above shows, significant. Change management need not be seen as a mechanism for achieving a specified and predicted outcome (the Planned approach). Nor need it be conceived of as a continuing process of aligning and realigning the organisation with its environment (the Emergent approach). Instead, as this chapter will show, by linking managerial choice to the management of change, organisations can open up a much wider spectrum of options. These range from focusing on achieving radical internal change to align an organisation with its external constraints, doing the same in an attempt to restructure such constraints, to influencing or changing external constraints in order to avoid internal upheavals. In such a situation, not only are managers trying to make sense of their situation for themselves and others, but they are also seeking to construct a more favourable environment as well.

Building on this insight into managerial choice, the next section in this chapter will present an overview of the Choice Management–Change Management model for understanding and implementing organisational change. This is followed by a detailed description of the three components of the model: the choice process, the trajectory process and the change process. The chapter concludes by maintaining that though organisations may choose to restructure their internal operations and practices in order to align them with the external circumstances they face, they can also choose to change or modify external and internal conditions and constraints in order to avoid extensive internal upheaval and/or to bring the constraints into line with their preferred *modus operandi*. Whatever choices are made, it is the role of managers consciously to explore and identify all the available options, however improbable they seem, rather than assuming that they have no, or only limited, choice in the matter.

The Choice Management–Change Management model

As the Choice Management–Change Management model in Figure 11.1 shows, organisational change can be viewed as the product of three interdependent organisational processes:

- **The choice process** – which is concerned with the nature, scope and focus of organisational decision-making.
- **The trajectory process** – which relates to an organisation's past and future direction and is seen as the outcome of its vision, purpose and future objectives.
- **The change process** – which covers approaches to, mechanisms for achieving, and outcomes of change.

These processes are interdependent because, as Figure 11.1 shows, the change process is itself an integral part of the trajectory process and this, in turn, is a vital part of the choice process. Within each of these processes there are a group of elements, or forces, which interact, clash with and influence each other in subtle and complex ways. It is this interaction of elements or forces which prevents decision-making and change management

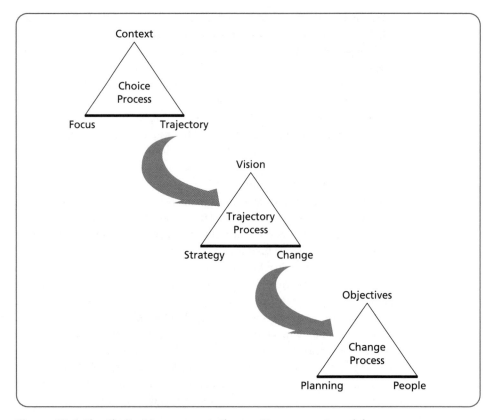

Figure 11.1 The Choice Management–Change Management model

from being a totally, or even predominantly, rational–mechanical process, and ensures that they are based on subjective and imperfect judgement.

Each of these three processes will now be described, not only to show their complexity and interdependence, but also to provide a guide to putting the Choice Management–Change Management model into practice. For this latter reason, the description of the change process, in particular, will dwell on the steps necessary to accomplish change successfully.

The choice process

As can be seen from Figure 11.2, the choice process comprises three elements:

- Organisational context
- Focus of choice
- Organisational trajectory.

Organisational context

One of the standard prescriptions for successful organisations is that they should know their own strengths and weaknesses, their customers' needs and the nature of the

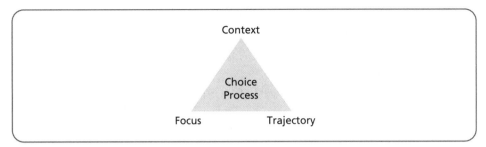

Figure 11.2 The choice process

environment in which they operate. As the case studies show, however, many organisations appear only to begin collecting this sort of information when they are in trouble. Yet how can organisations hope to understand and appreciate the options open to them unless they develop mechanisms for collecting and analysing information on their performance and general situation?

No one would suggest that assembling information on past, present and anticipated future performance is easy or that understanding the nature of the constraints faced by an organisation is simple. However, there are relatively well-established methods for benchmarking an organisation's performance against a range of internal and external comparators (Camp, 1989). There are also a number of tried-and-tested tools that organisations can use for gathering information on and evaluating the main internal constraints, such as structure, culture, politics and management style, and the main external constraints, such as national characteristics, industry and sector norms, and the business environment. Ideas and perspectives 11.1 and 11.2 show two of the tools most widely used by organisations for this purpose, the SWOT analysis and the PESTEL framework (Johnson and Scholes, 2002; Lynch, 1997).

Ideas and perspectives 11.1
SWOT analysis

What is a SWOT analysis?	What does it do?
SWOT stands for: **S**trengths (internal) **W**eaknesses (internal) **O**pportunities (external) **T**hreats (external)	A SWOT analysis enables managers to identify the key internal and external issues they need to take into account in order to understand the context in which the organisation operates. Also, by identifying key issues, it begins to focus managers on the areas where they need to make choices, and helps to identify some of the constraints and risks involved.

Ideas and perspectives 11.2
PESTEL framework

What is the PESTEL framework?	What does it do?
PESTEL stands for: Political Economic Sociocultural Technological Environmental Legal	The PESTEL framework is a rigorous approach to identifying and understanding the main external environmental factors which affect an organisation. As with the SWOT analysis, it also plays a role in focusing organisations on the choices open to them and the constraints and risks involved in these choices.

As in Phase 2 of the XYZ case study (Chapter 8), one advantage of adopting such well-understood tools, which are easily explained and do not require expert assistance, is that organisations can use them to promote openness and reduce, though probably not eliminate, political behaviour and conflict. Nevertheless, some organisations will find that owing to the context in which they operate, teamwork, cooperation and openness are very difficult to achieve without first changing those factors which hinder or prevent these. Perhaps the prime consideration in this respect is the prevalent style of management. The issue of management style will be discussed in Chapter 12; however, as Ideas and perspectives 11.3 shows, different styles of management can have significantly different implications for the way managers see, run and change their organisations.

Though others can exert pressure, managers are really the only group who can initiate change and will rarely (as a group) voluntarily adopt changes which adversely affect them (Pfeffer, 1992). It follows that, faced with a mismatch between their organisation and its environment, some managers will seek to achieve realignment by influencing the environment rather than pursuing an internal upheaval that may involve changes in management style and personnel.

An organisation's management style will also influence how and by whom information is gathered and discussed. If an accurate picture of an organisation's context is to be constructed, it will require the involvement of a wide range of people. Not only should this provide a robust basis for decision-making, it can also develop a sense of teamwork, cooperation and mutual understanding amongst those concerned. If only a few managers are involved, however, it is likely to result in a skewed and biased picture of the organisation. Nevertheless, it should also be recognised that no matter how rigorously information is collected, analysed and argued over, there will always be a large element of subjectivity in this process. This is why, as a number of writers have commented, one of the key tasks managers perform is 'sensemaking' (Weick, 1995). As Weick (1995: 13) commented:

> . . . sensemaking is about the ways people generate what they interpret. Jury deliberations, for example, result in a verdict. Once jurors have that verdict in hand, they look back to construct a plausible account of how they got there.

**Ideas and perspectives 11.3
Styles of management**

Strengths	Weaknesses
Traditionalist management	
• Practical common sense	• Makes snap decisions
• Attentive to facts	• Lacks responsibility for change
• Systems focus	• Poor at relationships
• Steady worker	• Concerned with difficulties
• Super-dependable	
• Realistic about timescales	
Catalyst management	
• Charisma and commitment to staff	• Can be drawn into pleasing others
• Communicates well	• Has difficulties with rules and conventions
• Comfortable with changing environment	• May spend too long on issues
• Comfortable with diversity	• Takes over problems and responsibilities
Visionary management	
• Strong on intellectual vision	• May be insensitive to others
• Creative and progressive	• Devalues others who are not intellectual
• Enjoys problem-solving	• Expects too much of people
• Outspoken	• Restless and easily bored

Source: From Maddock (1999: 40), based on Vinnecombe (1987)

For managers in organisations, sensemaking is about understanding, interpreting and explaining, making sense of, their organisation's world for themselves and others in such a way that it provides a rationale and justification for past, present and future actions. Sensemaking is also the process by which managers attempt or can attempt to impose their view of reality on others. The Oticon case study (Chapter 10) is a prime example of where a CEO first made sense of the world for himself and then imposed this sense on others in such a way that it allowed the organisation to move successfully forward. Marconi (Chapter 6) is another example where a senior manager attempted to impose his 'sense' on others in order to justify and guide actions. In this case, however, the outcome was far from successful. Grint (2005: 1470–1) remarked that:

> . . . I suggest that . . . the context or situation is actively constructed by the leader, leaders, and/or decision-makers. In effect, leadership involves the social construction of the context that both legitimates a particular form of action and constitutes the world in the process. If that rendering of the context is successful – for there are usually contending and competing renditions – the newly constituted context then limits the alternatives available such that those involved begin to act differently.

Focus of choice

Many organisations can find themselves in a situation where they appear to be constantly reacting to events and indulging in 'fire-fighting' rather than being proactive. Certainly, this seems to be the current position in the music industry, as the case study in Chapter 4 shows. One of the characteristics of successful sensemaking (i.e. context construction) is that, as Grint remarked, it 'limits the alternatives available' and focuses managers' attention on a narrow range of short-, medium- and long-term issues. Some of these will relate to the organisation's performance, whilst others may be more concerned with building or developing particular competences or technologies. In some instances, the issues may be of passing interest only, whilst in other instances they may be fundamental to the organisation's survival. Certainly, in most situations, organisations will in one way or another focus on aligning themselves with or even influencing or changing the constraints under which they operate.

How an organisation decides upon which issues to focus, and whether this is done in a concerted way (as in the case of Volvo in Chapter 2), or in a way which allows different groups and individuals to pursue their own agenda (as in the case of Midshires in Chapter 9), is a fundamental factor in any organisation's decision-making process. Certainly, the received wisdom is that a concerted and coordinated approach, which focuses upon a small number of issues at any one time, is more effective than a fragmented one (Kay, 1993; Senge, 1990). It is interesting to note that Weick (1995) appears to consider the Japanese approach to decision-making as an example of sensemaking in action. This may explain why Japanese organisations are particularly good at identifying the key aspects of their strategy on which they need to focus. The particular technique many Japanese companies use is called *Hoshin Kanri* (*see* Ideas and perspectives 11.4). *Hoshin Kanri*, or Policy Deployment as it is often termed in the West, was developed in Japan to communicate a company's policy, goals and objectives throughout its hierarchy in a structured and consistent fashion (Lee and Dale, 2003). Its main benefit is that it focuses attention on key activities for success. It is a process that is undertaken annually to ensure that everyone in the company is conscious of and addressing the same objectives and that these inform actions and decision-making at all levels in the organisation (Akao, 1991).

Ideas and perspectives 11.4
Hoshin Kanri

The word *hoshin* can be broken into two parts. The literal translation of *ho* is *direction*. The literal translation of *shin* is *needle*, so the word *hoshin* could translate into *direction needle* or the English equivalent of *compass*. The word *kanri* can also be broken into two parts. The first part, *kan*, translates into control or channeling. The second part, *ri*, translates into reason or logic. Taken altogether, *hoshin kanri* means management and control of the organization's direction needle or focus.

Source: Total Quality Engineering Inc (2003)

Organisational trajectory

An organisation's trajectory or direction is shaped by its past actions and future objectives and strategies. As such it provides a guide or framework within which to judge the acceptability, relevance or urgency of issues, concerns and proposed actions. The trajectory process encompasses the determination of and interplay between an organisation's vision, strategies and approach to change. This can be seen from Volvo's strong commitment to Job Design, which has arisen from the interplay of events over more than 30 years (*see* Chapter 2). Any attempt by Ford to reverse this commitment would surely face strong opposition at all levels in Volvo.

The concept of trajectory comprises not only an organisation's 'memory' of past events but also its intent in terms of future ones. For some organisations, such as Nissan (Chapter 1) with its commitment to partnership working, the trajectory will be clear and unambiguous, unless there is some major disturbance which throws into question past practice. In others, as the Marconi example shows (Chapter 6), making sense of past events and agreeing proposals for future actions can be the subject of much dispute, uncertainty and bitterness. Certainly, after its crash, one would assume that there was much rewriting of history in the Marconi boardroom, especially with regard to the supposed failure of GEC and the attractiveness of telecoms. Also, in the light of the 2008 banking crisis, one might assume that many financial service organisations, and their shareholders, have encountered a great deal of trouble and disagreement in trying to make sense of their past, present and future direction.

Some organisations will deliberately and consciously attempt to plot their trajectory in minute detail, such as PCI (Chapter 7), whilst others, such as Oticon (Chapter 10), may adopt a more global and distant set of objectives from which their trajectory emerges. Whatever the approach, as Mintzberg (1994: 25) observes:

> . . . *few, if any, strategies can be purely deliberate, and few can be purely emergent. One suggests no learning, the other, no control. All real-world strategies need to mix these in some way – to attempt to control without stopping the learning.*

Therefore, an organisation's trajectory can be seen as a blend of, or clash between, the deliberate and emergent elements of its strategy (*see* Figure 11.3). Whether or not this blend or clash produces the intended or expected outcomes for the organisation appears to depend partly on the quality of its sensemaking and partly on the degree of control it can exert, or chooses to exert, over events. Furthermore, as the case studies show, it is also dependent on an organisation's ability to learn from, deal with and take advantage of unexpected events as they emerge. For Oticon, XYZ and above all Volvo, the ability to learn and successfully move on was crucial. For Marconi, the inability to do so was disastrous. Therefore, it is the interplay between the interpretation of past actions and future intent coupled to the ability of organisations to shape developing events to their advantage that makes decision-making so complex.

Each of the three elements of the choice process, context, focus and trajectory, is complex in itself, but they also interact with each other in an intricate and unpredictable way. An organisation's trajectory, whether it is seen as successful or not, can influence both the focus of its decision-making, and the context within which the organisation operates. Likewise, the context provides a framework within which the trajectory is

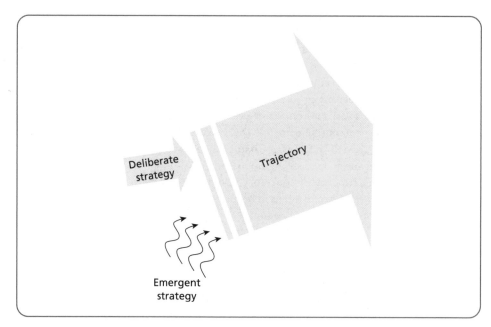

Figure 11.3 Organisational trajectory
Source: Adapted from Mintzberg (1978: 13)

developed. Similarly, the focus of choice will influence which aspect of the organisa-tion's context its trajectory will be directed towards, not only in the short term but also in the medium and long term.

The case studies show that decision-making is a complex and multifaceted process. One reason for this is the type of decisions that have to be addressed when organisations deal with major questions. Rollinson (2002) maintains that decisions can be classed on a spectrum that runs from 'bounded' to 'unbounded' (see Figure 11.4). Bounded decisions are usually small, have relatively easily defined parameters, and tend to be relatively separable from the environment or context in which they arise. A typical example might be the purchase of a laptop computer. With a degree of exactitude and relatively speedily, the purchaser can determine what they want from a computer, calculate how much they can afford to spend, gather information on competing products and choose the one that best meets their needs for the price they are prepared to pay. Unbounded decisions usually concern large and important issues, have difficult-to-define parameters, are ambiguous and are intertwined with other issues and factors in the environment or con-text in which they arise. An obvious example of an unbounded decision is the question of global warming. Even getting key stakeholders such as the US government to admit that there is a question to be addressed has been a major problem. More problematic still is getting agreement on what causes it, how to tackle it, what the priorities are, what the timescale for action is and who should pay. Though most of the major strategic issues facing an organisation are not on the same scale as global warming, nevertheless, they do tend to lie at the unbounded rather than bounded end of the spectrum.

Given the unbounded nature of strategic decisions, it is not surprising, as models of decision-making described in Ideas and perspectives 11.5 illustrate, that managers tend

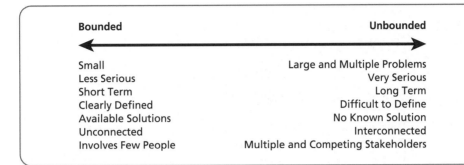

Bounded	**Unbounded**

Small | Large and Multiple Problems
Less Serious | Very Serious
Short Term | Long Term
Clearly Defined | Difficult to Define
Available Solutions | No Known Solution
Unconnected | Interconnected
Involves Few People | Multiple and Competing Stakeholders

Figure 11.4 Types of decision
Source: Adapted from Rollinson (2002: 254)

to adopt a less rational and more haphazard approach to decision-making than they themselves would often openly acknowledge. However, as the case studies in this book show, and as writers have pointed out for many years, there is a tendency for managers to 'muddle through' rather than attempt an exhaustive and exhausting examination of all the available options (Lindblom, 1968). Nor is it surprising that some managers prefer 'fire-fighting' to tackling fundamental issues (Burnes, 1991) – at least the objective is immediate and clear, and a favourable outcome can be achieved (though it is usually short-lived).

Appreciating the complexity of decision-making also casts the Japanese *ringi* system (discussed in Chapter 3) in a favourable light. Only by an exhaustive analysis of the issue concerned and the options available is the most appropriate decision likely to be arrived at. Moreover, the *ringi* system is usually aided by and carried out within the framework of a strong corporate vision and clear strategies for its pursuit, which make it easier to identify which decisions and actions are appropriate. By embracing decisions within such a framework, Japanese companies ensure that they do not have to explore all the available possibilities when taking decisions – merely those that are in harmony with their vision, strategy and intent. In this way, the entire choice process is simplified and made more achievable. Japanese companies have shown themselves to be masters of developing visions and strategies that not only make them successful but also, and not incidentally, reduce the uncertainty in their environment, alter the basis of competition in their favour, and narrow the focus of decision-making (Hamel and Prahalad, 1989). The result is that though the choice process remains complex, not only does it have a greater degree of consistency between the elements and people involved, but it is also more focused in the range of issues and decisions required.

Therefore, what can be seen is that whilst the choice process is uncertain, complex and time-consuming, there are approaches that do reduce these factors and can make the process more transparent and effective. Even so, the degree of transparency and the efficacy of the choice process are heavily influenced by an organisation's ability to turn choices into workable strategies and to turn strategies into successful actions. The success of these, in their turn, will influence future choices. In order to understand the choice process further, we shall now examine the trajectory process, followed by the change process.

Ideas and perspectives 11.5
Decision-making models

Model	Assumptions
The Rational Choice model of decision-making	• Decision-makers have knowledge of all possible alternative solutions. • They have complete knowledge of the consequences of all these alternatives. • They have a robust set of criteria for evaluating these alternatives. • They have unlimited resources, including time, money and abilities. • They follow a systematic and orderly sequence of decision steps.
The Bounded Rationality model of decision-making	• Decision-makers do not have complete knowledge. They rely on hunches and intuition. • Decision-makers do not have fixed and consistent preferences. • Decision-makers do not have unlimited resources. • An optimal solution may not exist or even be necessary. • Decision-makers do not optimise or seek a solution that maximises the expected benefits. • They 'satisfice' – seek a solution or decision option which is 'good enough' rather than ideal. • They do follow a systematic and orderly sequence of steps.
The Garbage Can model of decision-making	• Decisions involve four elements: problems, solutions, participants and choice opportunities. • Some decisions will only be made when all four elements come together. • Political motives can lead to these elements being manipulated. • Decision-making is volume-sensitive – managers cannot be everywhere at once or deal with all issues at once. • As the number of problems increases, decision opportunities decrease. • Novel problems are likely to attract more attention than mundane ones. • Decision-makers do not follow an orderly sequence of steps. • Chance plays a large part in what decisions get made and when.

Source: Adapted from Rollinson (2002)

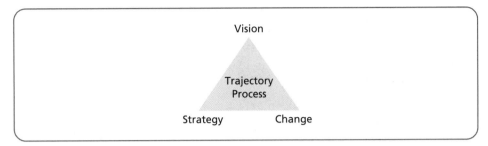

Figure 11.5 The trajectory process

The trajectory process

As shown by Figure 11.5, like the choice process, the trajectory process comprises three elements:

- Organisational Vision
- Organisational Strategy
- Organisational Change.

Vision

As described in Chapter 7, many organisations now use scenario-building and 'visioning' techniques. The purpose of these techniques is to generate different organisational futures, or realities, in order to select the one that seems most favourable or appropriate. The cases of Midshires (Chapter 9) and FI (Chapter 11) show that not all organisations have visions, and the case of Marconi (Chapter 6) shows that not all visions lead to success. Nevertheless, the concept of organisations driving themselves forward by creating an ambitious vision (or intent or scenario) of where they wish to be in the long term has become increasingly influential over the last 20 years (Cummings and Worley, 2005; Johnson and Scholes, 2006; Rigby and Bilodeau, 2007), though it has also generated increasing levels of cynicism (Collins, 1998; Watson, 1994). The argument, in brief, for this approach is that previous attempts to plan the future have either fallen foul of the difficulty of accurately translating past trends into future projections, or have not been ambitious enough because they have allowed future plans to be constrained by present resources (Hamel and Prahalad, 1989). The process of developing an organisation's vision attempts to overcome this by encouraging senior managers to think freely, without considering present resource constraints, about possible futures for their organisation in the long term.

This can produce very ambitious objectives, such as Honda's declaration in the 1960s (when it was barely more than a motorcycle producer little known outside Japan) that it wanted 'to become the second Ford'. As the Marconi case shows, however, the possession of an ambitious vision is, by itself, no guarantee of success, though the rigour with which a vision is developed may help to overcome or avoid some of the more obvious pitfalls. Cummings and Huse (1989), Ideas and perspectives 11.6, maintain that visions comprise four elements: *mission*; *valued outcomes*; *valued conditions*; and *mid-point goals*.

Ideas and perspectives 11.6
Constructing a vision

The four elements of a vision

1. **Mission**. This states the organisation's major strategic purpose or reason for existing. It can indicate such factors as products, markets and core competencies.
2. **Valued outcomes**. Visions about desired futures often include specific performance and human outcomes the organisation would like to achieve. These can include types of behaviour and levels of skill as well as more traditional outcomes such as turnover and profit. These valued outcomes can serve as goals for the change process and standards for assessing progress.
3. **Valued conditions**. This element of creating a vision involves specifying what the organisation should look like to achieve the valued outcomes. These valued conditions help to define a desired future state towards which change activity should move. Valued conditions can include issues relating to structure, culture, openness and managerial style as well as external issues such as relations with customers and suppliers.
4. **Mid-point goals**. Mission and vision statements are by nature quite general and usually need to be fleshed out by identifying more concrete mid-point goals. These represent desirable organisational conditions but lie between the current state and the desired future state. Mid-point goals are clearer and more detailed than desired future states, and thus, they provide more concrete and manageable steps and benchmarks for change.

Source: Cummings and Huse (1989)

The creation of visions should be an iterative process whereby options are identified, an initial vision is created, and the gap between this and the present circumstances is identified. Then the organisation considers its strategic options to bridge the gap, and in so doing refines the vision itself. This refining process serves partly to ensure that the vision is discussed widely within the organisation, and to gain employees' commitment to its objectives, thus using the vision as a motivating and guiding force for the organisation. Over time, by this process of revisiting and refining the vision, loose and intangible ideas become transformed into achievable medium-term goals that people can relate to and pursue. The process can, and in some cases does, eventually encompass everyone in the organisation. Nevertheless, as in the case of Oticon (Chapter 10), the vision is usually driven, not to say created by, one or two senior managers who use the power of their position and strength of their personalities to get others to accept the vision as a beneficial and achievable reality.

The organisational vision can best be described as a beacon shining from a faraway hillside at night that guides travellers to their destination. Travellers can usually only see a few feet ahead but are prevented from getting lost by the beacon. Occasionally the traveller will have to make a detour, or sometimes even reverse course, but this is done in the certain knowledge that they still know where it is that they are travelling to. The concept of the beacon is a useful analogy, in that it highlights one of the main differences between vision-building and other forms of long-range planning. Normally it is only the leadership of an organisation that has a clear view of where the organisation is going in the long term. The vision, like the beacon, should shine clearly for everyone in the organisation to see, however, so that they can all know where they are heading for, and use it to judge the appropriateness of their actions.

By constructing a vision in this manner, the organisation not only has a picture of what it wishes to become but also some concrete targets to aim for. In the case of Oticon, its vision of becoming a knowledge-based organisation sprang from the mind of its CEO, Lars Kolind. However, to give it flesh and to be able to construct his 'disorganised organisation' required the involvement of everyone else in the organisation. It was an iterative process of trial and error. Above all, it was a process of experimentation. He and they knew how they wanted to operate, what they wanted to achieve, but the actual details had to be worked out.

The Marconi vision, on the other hand, seemed both to start and end with two senior managers. The extent to which they required the commitment and understanding of others, as opposed to their compliance, appears to be small. Also, unlike Kolind, they seemed unable to adapt their strategy to save their vision. When the downturn in demand for telecoms equipment became evident to other companies, which took action to protect themselves, Marconi did not. Instead, it continued its strategy of selling profitable companies and borrowing money to buy ones which fitted its vision but whose viability declined with the decline in demand for telecoms equipment. The point is that visions (and components of visions) identify the intent, and mid-point goals are then needed to help identify a way forward. As the vision is implemented, these goals will periodically have to be renewed and revisited in the light of changing circumstances, usually within the context of the vision, as was the case with Oticon. As the Marconi example shows, however, the possibility always exists that changing circumstances, or the process of implementation, can raise serious questions about the viability of the vision itself. It is through the development of strategy that visions are implemented, brought to life and, if necessary, changed.

Strategy

In the context of a vision, strategy can be defined as a coherent or consistent stream of actions which an organisation takes or has taken to move towards its vision. This stream of actions can be centrally planned and driven, they can be delegated and distributed throughout the organisation, and they can be either conscious actions in pursuit of the vision, or unconscious or emergent ones resulting from past patterns of decisions or resource allocations, or from current responses to problems and opportunities. In reality, as Figure 11.3 illustrates, an organisation's strategy tends to be a combination of, and be pursued through, a mixture of formal and informal plans and planned and unplanned actions.

Chapter 7 showed that formal strategies usually cover marketing, product development, manufacturing, personnel, purchasing, finance, information technology and quality. The characteristics of conscious strategies are that they generally look 5 years or more ahead, but only contain firm and detailed plans for the next 12 to 18 months (this is because changing circumstances usually prevent most companies from being firm about their intentions for any longer than this). These strategies are put together in one strategic plan that is, usually, formally reviewed annually, but is frequently reviewed informally and when major and unexpected events occur. Because the strategies are not ends in themselves, but means to an end (the vision), they should by necessity be both flexible and pragmatic. They should be constructed and pursued only to the extent that they facilitate the pursuit of the vision. Indeed, even when their strategies appear to fail, the more successful organisations seem to have an innate ability to turn failure into success, as the Microsoft example in Mini Case Study 11.2 shows. Microsoft established MSN in 1995 in order to become an Internet content provider. It quickly saw that this was not where its core competences lay, but what it also saw was that MSN gave it a direct link to an enormous customer base. The original strategy of adding content provision to its software activities was abandoned in favour of a much more ambitious strategy of delivering its services over the Internet directly to customers, something on which Bill Gates stated he had 'bet the company'. It is also something that contributes directly to Microsoft's vision of remaining the world's dominant software company.

Mini Case Study 11.2
The development of MSN

FT

Microsoft's direct connection to the customer

Sometimes it seems that even when Microsoft loses, it wins. . . . take MSN, the company's internet portal. This unit of Microsoft has lost money ever since it was set up . . . But to Microsoft that does not really matter. The real point of MSN is not to make money at all. Instead, the division serves a peculiar mixture of purposes including research and development, testing the company's software, advertising its services and even product distribution. What is more, these capabilities set Microsoft apart from its rivals.

In the next phase of Microsoft's plans, its .Net vision, in which software becomes a service delivered over the internet – a vision on which Bill Gates admits he has 'bet the company' – the site will become even more vital. MSN is quietly emerging as the centrepiece of the whole .Net strategy. This is a far cry from the original MSN, named for the Microsoft Network. The website was initially set up as a media play in 1995, the early days of the dotcom boom. It produced content including news and sport, horoscopes, and e-commerce offers. For a while it looked as if Microsoft had serious ambitions in media . . .

That phase did not last long. The career of Geoff Sutton, now Managing Director of MSN in the UK, illustrates the change of heart. Mr Sutton was originally brought into the company in 1997 to run a team of journalists writing news for the portal. In 1998, the news team was scrapped and Mr Sutton found himself working in a software company.

'It quickly became apparent that Microsoft shouldn't try to be a content player', he says. Judy Gibbons, vice-president of MSN for EMEA [Europe, the Middle East and Africa], agrees: 'Microsoft is a software company, that's what we do, and we shouldn't stray away from our core competences.'

With its foray into content, however, Microsoft had managed to gather up something very useful: an audience. Through MSN, Microsoft found it had a direct line with consumers that it had never experienced before. People visited the site regularly, . . . in the process being exposed to Microsoft branding and services.

Today, MSN is one of the world's top three internet destinations, along with Yahoo and AOL, receiving some 270m visitors a month, while its Hotmail has 110m users.

Once this kind of connection with customers was in place, all kinds of things became possible. Microsoft could start marketing services to its customers direct. It could even start giving them software direct, over the internet.

This interactive and instant relationship with customers even gave Microsoft a testing ground for new software products, as people could be asked to download beta software, software still in the process of development, from the site for comments and suggestions.

The .Net strategy neatly takes advantage of all these aspects of Microsoft's portal. . . . Users will plug into a web of services running across a wide variety of devices, including PCs, handheld computers, phones, television sets, and even games consoles.

'MSN will provide the entry point for consumers to .Net services, as you will be able to go up to the site and sign on and get access to all the pieces you want', says Ms Gibbons.

Microsoft estimates that the market for such services could run into trillions of dollars by 2010, in what it terms the 'digital decade'.

No other internet portal can yet offer anything similar. And no other software company boasts its own internet portal through which to dispense rival versions of these web services. The huge MSN user base forms a ready-made audience to which Microsoft can market its services with ease. The fact that all the visitors attracted to the portal by this range of services can be 'monetised' by charging advertisers to market them is just the icing on the cake. If MSN can reach break-even from these advertising dollars, so much the better, if not, it scarcely matters.

Source: Fiona Harvey, *Financial Times*, 31 December 2001, p. 7.

Therefore, in pursuit of its vision, an organisation can have a central strategy and a number of sub-strategies and, influenced by the vision and circumstances, a general awareness of the need to act or respond in a particular way to opportunities and threats, or successes and failures. From this perspective, one way of viewing strategy is to see it as a series of links in a chain which stretch from the present to the indeterminate future where the vision lies. Each link in the chain represents particular strategies or groups of decisions that organisations pursue to move themselves forward, in the light of both their eventual target and the prevailing circumstances of the time. The links (strategies) are continually having to be forged and reforged (or to use Mintzberg's (1987) term, 'crafted') over time as events develop and circumstances change. For Microsoft, MSN was a link forged for one purpose which became reforged for another purpose but with the same end in sight: to bolster Microsoft's dominance of the software market. So an organisation's strategy is likely to comprise both deliberate (planned) and emergent (unplanned) elements – the exact balance being determined by the circumstances of the particular organisation in question rather than any intrinsic merit of either the deliberate or emergent approaches to strategy.

One final point: it follows from this that organisations do not need to be able to see all the links in the strategic chain: merely those that will guide them over the next few years. Nor do they need to dictate centrally or identify in detail what should be done and when. Instead, they need to establish both a climate of understanding and a general willingness to pursue certain courses of action, as the opportunity arises or circumstances necessitate. It is only when a course of action is pursued, however, that organisations begin to change and move towards their vision.

Change

Just as an organisation's trajectory is both an important element of the choice process and a process in its own right, the same applies to change. The change process will be discussed below, but in the context of the trajectory process it is necessary to note that, though visions and strategies can be crucial in shaping the life of organisations, it is only when some facet of the organisation is changed or changes that visions and strategies advance from being mere possibilities to become reality. This is also a two-way street. On the one hand, visions and strategies shape and direct change. They indicate what needs to change and where. They also create the conditions and climate within which change takes place. On the other hand, because visions and strategies only become reality through the actions of the organisation, it is these changes, these actions, which shape visions and strategies.

In summary, we can see that the trajectory process, whilst playing a key role in shaping choice, is also itself a complex process comprising vision, strategy and change. Though it is difficult to conceive of any organisation that does not possess some elements of all three, the degree to which they are held in common or are consistent with each other or are part of a conscious effort clearly varies. Partly this relates to the circumstances of the organisation. Under conditions of stability and predictability, even without prompting from senior managers, it is much easier for people to make sense of their situation and develop a common view of how their organisation should operate, what its future should be and what changes need to be made. In rapidly changing circumstances, however, where certainties and fixed points of reference are few and far between, a common understanding is unlikely to arise automatically. Even if a common understanding does exist in such situations, it is likely to be outmoded and inappropriate. In such cases, one of the key roles of senior managers is to make sense of the situation for themselves and others by constructing a new vision which can unite the organisation in a common cause. Such a vision should reduce uncertainty, make sense of what is happening, and create a broad understanding of what needs doing, and how. For many organisations, the merit of this approach is not only that it makes change easier, but that it also allows staff to judge for themselves what changes need to be made and what approach to adopt. In order to explore this further, we can now examine the change process itself.

The change process

Change can be viewed as a one-off event, an exception to the normal running of an organisation and, therefore, something to be dealt with on an issue-by-issue basis as it arises. On the other hand, some organisations see change not as an exception but as the norm, a continuous process that forms part of the organisation's day-to-day activities. As the case studies in this book have shown, where change is seen as the exception, such as in GK (Chapter 5), organisations tend to have difficulty in choosing the most appropriate approach and there also tends to be no structured, or even informal, procedure for capturing the lessons from one change project and making them available for future projects. Each change is seen as a unique event, and seems to involve an element of reinventing the wheel as the organisation struggles to determine how best to deal with it. However, in organisations where change is seen as a continuous process, such as Volvo (Chapter 2), they appear to be able not only to treat each project as a learning opportunity, but to capture this learning and pass it on. This allows them to select the most appropriate approach for each situation. In such organisations, not only is change seen as an everyday event, but the management of it is also seen as a core capability that needs to be developed and in which all staff need to become competent.

As Figure 11.6 shows, the change process itself, like the choice and trajectory processes, comprises three interlinked elements:

- Objectives and outcomes
- Planning the change
- People.

Figure 11.6 The change process

Objectives and outcomes

There is now much evidence and a general acceptance, at least amongst those studying it, that a high proportion of change efforts end in failure (Beer and Nohria, 2000; Burnes, 2003; Rogers *et al*, 2006; Senturia *et al*, 2008). The reasons for such a high level of failure include complacency, poor communication, weak leadership, inappropriate culture and political infighting (Huczynski and Buchanan, 2001; Hoag *et al*, 2002; Kotter, 1996). In terms of this last point, the detrimental effect of political behaviour was highlighted in Chapter 5. Because change often affects the distribution of power and resources in an organisation, it is, therefore, an inherently political process which can be undermined by sectional interests rather than driven by organisational needs.

Though it is difficult to envisage a situation where political interests are not present, Burnes (1988) suggested an approach to assessing the need for and type of change that attempts to make the process of establishing objectives and outcomes more rigorous and open. Openness and rigour not only make it harder to disguise political considerations, they also allow assumptions regarding the merits (or lack of them) of particular options to be tested. Burnes's approach has four elements – the trigger, the remit, the assessment team and the assessment.

The trigger

Organisations should only investigate change (other than relatively minor projects that can be easily accommodated) for one of the following reasons:

- The company's vision or strategy highlights the need for change or improved performance.
- Current performance or operation indicates that severe problems or concerns exist.
- Suggestions or opportunities arise (either from the area concerned or elsewhere) that potentially offer significant benefits to the organisation.

If one or more of the above arises, then this should trigger the organisation to assess the case for change, which leads to the next phase.

The remit

This should state clearly the reasons for the assessment, its objectives and timescale, and who should be involved and consulted. The remit should stress the need to focus as much on the people aspects as the technical considerations involved. In addition, it must make clear that those who will carry out the assessment must look at all options rather than merely considering one or two alternatives. Organisations need to be clear who draws up such remits and who has the final say on the assessment team's recommendations. As was shown by Burnes and Weekes (1989), this responsibility is often unclear. In traditional organisations, this responsibility would lie with senior managers. In many of today's organisations, the responsibility for such activities is devolved. There is usually a requirement to inform senior managers of change, however, and certain types of major change remain the responsibility of senior managers. Also, where change affects more than one area or activity, coordination between areas will be essential. The important point is that there must be clarity and agreement about who has the responsibility and authority to initiate change before an assessment begins.

The assessment team

This is the body that will assess the need for change. In most cases, this should be a multi-disciplinary team consisting of representatives from the area affected (both managers and staff), specialist staff (e.g. finance, technical and personnel), and, where appropriate, a change specialist, either an internal facilitator or an external consultant who is a specialist in organisational change. It may also require the involvement of senior managers.

The assessment

The first task of the assessment team is to review and if necessary clarify or amend its remit. Only then can it begin the assessment, which should comprise the following four steps:

1. **Clarification of the problem or opportunity.** This is achieved by gathering information, especially from those involved. In some situations it might be found that the problem or opportunity is redefined, or does not exist, or can be dealt with easily by those most closely concerned. If so, this is reported back and probably no further action needs to be taken. If the clarification reveals that a significant problem or opportunity does exist, however, then the remaining steps need to be completed.

2. **Investigate alternative solutions.** A wide-ranging examination should take place to establish the range of possible solutions. These should be tested against an agreed list of criteria covering costs and benefits, in order to eliminate those solutions that are clearly inapplicable and to highlight those that appear to offer the greatest benefit. Companies will usually seek to define benefits in monetary terms. It should be recognised, however, that not all changes, particularly those of a behavioural or strategic nature, can be assessed on purely financial criteria, e.g. Oticon's restructuring and XYZ's move to teamworking. In any case, changes rarely have single benefits. For example, a change in technology that brings financial benefits may also offer opportunities to increase teamworking and to develop the skill and knowledge base of the organisation. Therefore, organisations need to develop ways of defining and assessing non-monetary benefits. Also, where there are benefits there are usually disbenefits. Where new skills are gained, old ones are discarded. For example, Nissan's partnership approach to customer–supplier relations has many benefits but it can also lead to a loss of negotiating and bargaining skills; moves to greater teamworking, such as at XYZ, can undermine the authority of line managers and middle managers. If such disbenefits are to result from change, it is better to recognise this in advance and prepare for them rather than finding out later when the damage is done. This then leads on to the next step.

3. **Feedback.** The definition of the problem or opportunity and the range of possible solutions should be discussed with interested or affected parties, particularly those from whom information was collected in the first place. This helps to counter the tendency to fit solutions to problems, i.e. it makes it more difficult for people to promote their favoured solution regardless of its suitability. It also helps to prepare people for any changes that do take place. In addition, the response to feedback can provide an important source of information on the advantages and disadvantages of the possible solutions on offer and, thus, it helps to establish the criteria for selecting the preferred solution or solutions.

4. **Recommendations and decision.** The team should present their recommendations in a form that clearly defines the problem or opportunity, identifies the range of solutions, establishes the criteria for selection and makes recommendations. These recommendations should include not only the type of change, but also the mechanics and timescale for making such changes and the resource implications, as well as performance targets for the new operation.

This then leaves those responsible for making the final decision in a position to assess, modify, defer or reject the assessment team's recommendations in the light of the vision and strategic objectives of the organisation. Indeed, some change programmes and projects are so complex that it is only possible to judge their worth in relation to an organisation's long-term intent. For example, in the 1990s, one of the UK's largest biscuit makers established an assessment team to determine whether the company should build a new factory solely dedicated to the production of chocolate biscuits (the biggest growth area for the company). The team recommended that one should be built next door to an existing factory in the north of England. The Board accepted the recommendation for the new factory but decided, because of its long-term ambitions to develop in Europe, to locate the new factory in France. This decision could be justified as being in the long-term interests of the company, but even so, such decisions are more an act of faith than a racing certainty, though managers may choose to present them as closer to the latter in order to garner support. Nevertheless, if the decision is to proceed with the proposed changes, then it becomes necessary to begin planning the implementation process.

Planning the change

Whether the need for change is driven by an organisation's strategy or emerges from its day-to-day activities, once it has been established that it should take place and what form it should take, it is then necessary to plan how this will be achieved and then to implement the plan. Chapter 10 showed that there are many different approaches to change and that their appropriateness depends on what is to be changed. Small-scale and relatively technical or structural changes can usually be planned and executed relatively quickly, and may not require extensive consultation with or the involvement of the staff affected. Similarly, changes which are isolated to one part of the organisation and seen as 'inevitable' may also be relatively straightforward. However, unless the need for radical change is already accepted, as it was at Oticon, to adopt a rapid-change, low-involvement approach to larger-scale changes, particularly where people's attitudes and behaviours are the prime object of the change process, can bring with it a high risk of failure. Therefore, as the two XYZ examples show, planning and execution, and consequent development, in such cases can be extensive, span hierarchical levels and horizontal processes and include a high degree of involvement. For these reasons, the success of large-scale changes will depend, to a significant extent, on the involvement and commitment of all those concerned with and affected by them. The range of change situations and approaches, therefore, needs to be borne in mind when considering the following six interrelated activities that make up the planning and change process:

1. **Establishing a change management team.** To maintain continuity, the team should include some, if not all, of those responsible for the original assessment of the need for change. However, it will usually also have a greater user input, especially at the implementation stage. When the Labour government was first elected in the UK in 1997, the Inland Revenue was asked to undertake a review as to whether the Contributions Agency, then a semi-autonomous body, should become part of the Inland Revenue. The man who led the assessment team, and who recommended that the Contributions Agency should become part of the Inland Revenue, was also made responsible for leading the change management team that had to implement his recommendation. In the case of Phase 2 of the changes at XYZ, all the original assessment team became members of the change management team, along with a much wider spectrum of middle and line managers. For large change projects, it is usual to establish sub-groups responsible for discrete elements of the change programme. These

will generally comprise those most closely affected by the changes, both managers and staff. Their role is to handle the day-to-day implementation issues. It must be recognised that all the people in the change management team, and its sub-groups, are in effect 'change agents'. Nevertheless, as was the case at XYZ, change specialists should also be involved, i.e. people whose primary input is their experience in managing change. As was discussed in Chapter 9, the role of change agents is not just a technical one concerned with establishing plans and ordering their implementation. Change agents need a wide range of skills, not least of which is what Buchanan and Boddy (1992: 27) refer to as the ability to deploy 'backstage activity':

> 'Backstaging' is concerned with the exercise of 'power skills', with 'intervening in political and cultural systems', with influencing and negotiating and selling, and with 'managing meaning'.

Change agents also need the ability to deal with the unexpected. 'Expect the unexpected' might well be the motto of most change agents. In discussing the role of change agents in Chapter 9, the article on 'Grace, magic and miracles' by Lichtenstein (1997) was cited. This showed that whilst a structured approach to change is necessary, it is often, by itself, not sufficient to ensure success. Success, Lichtenstein (1997: 393) argued, also requires change agents to have the ability and experience to recognise and take advantage of 'intuitive, unexpected, and serendipitous' situations. Therefore in choosing members of the change management team, it is necessary to have the right blend of skills for the change being undertaken, including the ability to deal with the unexpected.

2. **Management structures**. Because larger change projects, especially organisational transitions, are wide-ranging, have multiple objectives and can involve a high degree of uncertainty, existing control and reporting systems are unlikely to be adequate for managing them. For example, the more that a change project challenges existing power relations and resource allocation procedures, the more it is likely to encounter managerial resistance. In such cases, unless the change management team has a direct line to senior managers or the CEO, and their public support, the change process is likely to become bogged down or even abandoned. For example, one of the main reasons why Regional Managers did not block the organisational changes at XYZ was because the Managing Director was closely involved in the change process. He was aware that the Regional Managers might try to block changes that threatened their interests and standing, and he was prepared to take action if they did so, and he made sure the Regional Managers knew this. Where senior managers are less directly involved, effective reporting and management structures need to be put in place in advance in order to provide direction, support, resources, and where necessary decisive interventions. The case of FI, described at the end of this chapter, shows what can happen when a project manager is in effect abandoned by senior managers.

3. **Activity planning**. Beckhard and Harris (1987: 70–1) refer to this as a process of 'getting from here to there'. They state that: 'The activity plan is the road map for the change effort, so it is critical that it is realistic, effective and clear.' Ideas and perspectives 11.7 describes Beckhard and Harris's five key characteristics of an effective activity plan. Activity planning involves constructing a schedule for the change programme, citing the main activities and events that must occur if the transition is

Ideas and perspectives 11.7
Beckhard and Harris's approach to activity planning

The five characteristics of an effective activity plan

- **Relevance** – activities are clearly linked to the change goals and priorities
- **Specificity** – activities are clearly identified rather than broadly generalized
- **Integration** – the parts are closely connected
- **Chronology** – there is a logical sequence of events
- **Adaptability** – there are contingency plans for adjusting to unexpected forces

Source: Beckhard and Harris (1987: 72)

to be successful. It must be recognised, however, that not all the elements of a large change programme can be planned in detail in advance. Such programmes are by their nature multi-level, multi-stage, can stretch over an extended time-frame, and can involve elements of backtracking and rethinking. However, as a change programme proceeds, it becomes possible for successive levels and stages to become clearer and for plans to become more detailed. It follows that, in order to stay on course, activity planning should clearly identify and integrate key change events and stages and ensure they are linked to the organisation's change goals and priorities. Activity planning should also gain top-management approval, should be cost-effective, and should remain adaptable as feedback is received during the change process. Activity planning therefore comprises the final and intermediate objectives, and ensures that where and when possible these are tied to a specific timetable in order to avoid uncertainty amongst those who have to carry out the changes.

4. **Commitment planning**. This activity involves identifying key people and groups whose commitment is needed, and deciding how to gain their support. Beckhard and Harris (1987: 92) observe that:

> . . . *in any complex change process, there is a* critical mass *of individuals or groups whose active commitment is necessary to provide the energy for change to occur.*

Designating someone as a key person is concerned less with their nominal position or level of authority in an organisation than with their ability to block or promote particular changes. This may be because they have power to dispense or withhold specific resources or information, or because, as Mini Case Study 11.3 shows, others look to them for guidance or leadership, even though they may have no formal role in this respect.

The case of FI at the end of this chapter is an extreme example of lack of commitment – no one other than the senior engineer responsible for the project showed any commitment to make it work. Most of the Board of Directors stood back from it and the Finance Director appeared positively hostile to the project. On the other hand, the case of XYZ (Chapters 3 and 8) is an example of where the company recognised it needed to gain the commitment of key staff in planning and implementing change.

Ideas and perspectives 11.8 shows the main steps in developing a commitment plan. Beckhard and Harris (1987) note, however, that even where the commitment of an individual or group is necessary, it is not necessary to gain the same level of commitment from all. They identify three kinds of commitment:

Let it happen – i.e. do not obstruct the change.
Help it happen – i.e. participate in the change process.
Make it happen – i.e. drive the change.

For most kinds of change, success depends on winning the commitment of key staff. Without this support, it will be impossible to mobilise the energy necessary to start the change process and keep it moving to a successful conclusion. However, whilst

---

Mini Case Study 11.3
The importance of commitment

Getting rid of the bonus

Northern Engineering is a very efficient and progressive manufacturing company which has successfully introduced many Japanese techniques for improving its business. However, it did operate a shopfloor bonus system based on individual output. It recognised that this was detrimental to quality but felt that the workforce would strongly resist any effort to change it. Eventually though, the company decided it would offer the workforce a very tempting financial package to buy out the bonus. The Operations Director was the man responsible for selling the idea to the workforce. He did this through a series of presentations, to each of the company's three shifts.

The group he was most concerned about were the night shift. These were the people he seldom met and who had shown the least commitment to change in the past. The Operations Director described his experience with the night shift:

They work ten to six, four nights a week. I went to brief them at the beginning of their shift. The presentation took about 20 minutes and then I opened it up for questions. All through my presentation, this big bloke on the front row had been staring at me with a disgruntled look on his face. When I finished he stood up and everybody looked at him in an expectant fashion. When he began talking, I thought, 'I'm sunk'. He said, 'It's the same as usual. You only see the bosses when they want to take something off you.' Others on the shift nodded in agreement at this. He then went on, 'Once they take the bonus off us, we won't get it back. Some might be OK, but others'll lose money. But, this is not a bad company, so I think we should give them a chance.' He sat down, nobody else said anything, and it was agreed, the bonus would go. I was totally flummoxed. The bloke's body language, his tone, his first words, all indicated that he was against it. I was very, very lucky; if he'd gone against the idea, I could see that everybody would have gone with him. What I learned that night was a very valuable lesson. The next time I have to talk to the night shift, I'll get hold of that bloke first and win him over.

Ideas and perspectives 11.8
Beckhard and Harris's approach to commitment planning

A *commitment plan* is a strategy, described in a series of action steps, devised to secure the support of those [individuals and groups] which are vital to the change effort. The steps in developing a commitment plan are:

1. Identify target individuals or groups whose commitment is necessary.
2. Define the critical mass needed to ensure the effectiveness of the change.
3. Develop a plan for getting the commitment of the critical mass.
4. Develop a monitoring system to assess the progress.

Source: Beckhard and Harris (1987: 93)

most managers, with some encouragement, might be able to identify the critical mass, many would lack the skills and motivation to win them over. This is why the participation of experienced change agents, with the necessary 'backstage' expertise, is crucial to the change process.

5. **Audits and post-audits**. It is important to monitor progress and see to what extent objectives are being met. This allows plans to be modified in the light of experience. It also allows for opportunities to improve on the original objective to be identified or created. The more uncertain and unclear the change process, the greater the need for periodic review. After the change, or when a particular milestone has been passed, a post-audit should be carried out (a) to establish that the objectives have really been met, and (b) to ascertain what lessons can be learned for future projects. In addition, periodic reviews give senior managers the chance to praise, support and encourage those carrying out the change.

Though the auditing process sounds straightforward, it rarely is. Large projects, in particular, are collections of a number of relatively smaller sub-projects and, as Kotter (1996: 25) remarks, 'Because we are talking about multiple steps and multiple projects, the end result is often complex, dynamic, messy, and scary.' These 'multiple projects' start at different times and operate at different levels and in different areas of an organisation. Some of these sub-projects will run concurrently, some consecutively and a few may even be largely free-standing. By their nature, they will also be geared to different sub-objectives, which may need to be monitored and measured in different ways. Seen in this way, it becomes easier to understand why conducting audits and post-audits, and even day-to-day monitoring of progress, can be exceedingly difficult but is also exceedingly necessary. However, as the FI case shows at the end of this chapter, if you do not monitor progress, the end result can come as a very nasty shock. Even when a change programme has been completed, the post-audit should not be treated as the end of the line: a chance for people to rest on their laurels. It can be another opportunity for improvement. The post-audit at XYZ (Chapter 8) was turned into an opportunity for continuing to drive the change process forward, by the simple expedient of asking each manager to identify two initiatives they would personally take to reinforce and enhance the benefits from the company's new organisational structure. This is an example of what Kotter (1996: 21) refers to as 'consolidating gains and producing more change'.

6. **Training and development**. This is a key part of any change project and takes a number of forms. The obvious one is in relation to new skills and competences that might be necessary. Furthermore, as the case studies in this book show, training and development can have a number of other purposes. They may aim to give staff the skills to undertake the change themselves. It may be the intention to leave them with the ability to pursue continuous improvement, once the change has been substantially achieved, or training and development may be intended to make them aware of the need for change and to win them over. Also, there is a need to give general awareness training to those in the organisation who might be indirectly affected. Even where the primary objective is to enhance skills, training can also contribute to other objectives, such as culture change, by structuring it in such a way that training promotes teamworking or inter-departmental cooperation. To ensure that the various types of training are targeted at the right people or groups, a training programme – starting before implementation and continuing after completion – should be established, showing who needs training, the form of the training and when it will take place.

7. Looking wider than just individual change projects and programmes, as Burnes (2003) argues, there are many benefits to linking an organisation's overall management and staff development programme formally with its various change initiatives. Burnes comments that many of the skills and competences that organisations wish to develop in staff and managers are the same ones necessary for bringing about successful change. Therefore, management and staff development programmes can provide the human resources necessary for managing change, and change projects can provide the real learning opportunities that staff and managers need to develop their skills and competences. The link between management development and change will be returned to in Chapter 12.

There is often a tendency to portray the planning element of change as a technical exercise involved with timetabling and resource allocation. Though planning change is in some ways a 'technical' issue, as the above six activities show, it is also very much a people issue. The success of any change effort is always likely to hinge on an organisation's ability to involve and motivate the people concerned and those whose support is necessary.

People

Chapter 10 showed that organisational change takes many forms. It can be of a predominantly structural or technical nature which requires little of individuals in terms of behavioural or attitudinal change. On the other hand, as the case studies in this book show, increasingly the objective of change is to modify the attitudes and behaviours of individuals and groups, sometimes radically so. People are being required to reconsider their attitudes towards how work is performed, how they behave towards their colleagues internally, and their attitudes to their counterparts externally. Whatever form it takes, however, if it is to be successful, there are three people-related activities that need to be undertaken: creating willingness to change; involving people; and sustaining the momentum.

Creating a willingness to change

Even where change is purely of a technical or structural form, there has to be willingness amongst those concerned to change: to accept the new arrangements. In an ideal world, organisations would want everyone to buy into a change project. However, as mentioned above, the important issue is to win over what Beckhard and Harris (1987: 92) refer to as the '*critical mass* of individuals or groups whose active commitment is necessary to provide the energy for change to occur'. There are organisations that have put, and are continuing to put, a great deal of effort into creating a climate where change is accepted as the norm and the critical mass is already present or needs little effort to assemble. The cases of Oticon and XYZ are examples of this. Most organisations, however, are still at the stage where they have to convince staff of the need for change. This is especially the case in those organisations, such as GK (Chapter 5), where each change project is perceived to be a one-off event, almost an exception to the 'normal' flow of organisational life.

For many people, organisational change involves moving from the known to the unknown, with the possibility of loss as well as gain. In such situations, it is often the case that those who fear they will lose out will vociferously oppose any change, whilst those who believe they will gain from the change will keep quiet for fear of antagonising the losers. This was a point most famously made by Niccolo Machiavelli (1515, Chapter VI, p. 1):

> *And it ought to be remembered that there is nothing more difficult to take in hand, more perilous to conduct, or more uncertain in its success, than to take the lead in the introduction of a new order of things. Because the innovator has for enemies all those who have done well under the old conditions, and lukewarm defenders in those who may do well under the new.*

Organisations, therefore, in seeking to create a willingness and a readiness for change, need to be aware that stressing the positive aspects of any proposed change may have much less impact than they might imagine. This point was recognised by Lewin (1947a) when he argued that the *status quo* needs to be destabilised before old behaviour can be discarded (unlearnt) and new behaviour successfully adopted. He referred to this process as 'unfreezing' (*see* Chapter 8). Drawing on his work on Field Theory, Lewin recognised that the *status quo* (what he referred to as the quasi-stationary equilibrium) occurred when the forces driving change and the forces resisting were equal (*see* Figure 11.7). To bring about change, one had to increase the strength of the former and reduce that of the latter. Like Machiavelli, however, he also recognised that making proposed changes seem attractive had less effect on increasing the pressure for change than making the current situation less attractive, i.e. it is often easier to create a readiness for change by making people dissatisfied with their current situation, and thus prepared to consider alternatives, than to try to paint a rosy picture of the future. Kotter (1996: 36) echoed this point when he stated that: 'Establishing a sense of urgency is crucial to gaining needed cooperation.' For Kotter (1996: 42):

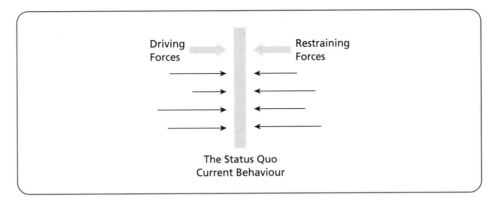

Figure 11.7 Force Field analysis

Increasing urgency demands that you remove sources of complacency or minimize their impact: for instance, eliminating such signs of excess as a big corporate air force; setting higher standards both formally in the planning process and informally in day-to-day interactions; changing internal measurement systems that focus on the wrong indexes; vastly increasing the amount of external performance feedback everyone gets; rewarding both honest talk in meetings and people who are willing to confront problems; and stopping baseless happy talk from the top.

In order to create a willingness for change, a sense of urgency, a feeling of dissatisfaction with the present, there are four steps an organisation needs to take:

1. **Make people aware of the pressures for change.** The organisation should inform employees on a continuous basis of its plans for the future, the competitive and/or market pressures it faces, customer requirements and the performance of its key competitors. This should be a participative process where staff have opportunity to question, make comments and make suggestions. Many companies now encourage staff at all levels to spend time meeting and working with customers. Customers are also increasingly being invited to come and give direct feedback to staff and managers. The aim is to make staff aware of what customers want and do not want and, particularly, to highlight the organisation's shortcomings. This seems to be a development that is common to both private- and public-sector organisations (Crawford *et al*, 2003; Kotter, 1996). Obviously, promoting the vision and explaining the strategic plan are also vital components in this. Through this approach, members of the organisation come to appreciate that change is not only inevitable, but is being undertaken to safeguard rather than threaten their future. It is also necessary to use informal as well as formal channels of communication. In any organisation, department or team there are individuals who are opinion-formers: people to whom others look for guidance. They may not hold any position of power or authority in the organisation's management structure but, as Mini Case Study 11.3 shows, they do have influence. Therefore, to get the message across successfully, managers must identify who these people are and seek to ensure that they not only understand the message being transmitted, but will also pass a favourable judgement on it.

2. **Give regular feedback on the performance of individual processes and areas of activity within the organisation.** This allows a company to draw attention to any discrepancy between actual performance and desired present and future performance. The feedback has to be in a form that people can relate to and act on. Telling a team that it is losing money is less useful than giving them feedback on productivity and quality. Feedback also has to be timely. Discussing yesterday's performance is useful in getting staff to identify and address problems; discussing last year's performance is rarely so. Also, giving people the skills and authority to undertake improvement activities, as XYZ did with its *Kaizen* initiatives (Chapter 3), is likely to make people more receptive to feedback because they can do something to improve the situation. In addition, it makes a difference who provides and delivers the feedback. A quarterly or annual meeting led by the CEO may have little impact. However, as mentioned above, direct and timely feedback from customers and product and service users, whether internal or external, is likely to have a much greater impact. Once again, the form of this and the recipient's ability to act upon it is also important. Feedback can encourage those concerned to begin to think about how their performance can be improved, and prepare them for the need for change. In looking at the case study companies in this book, it is noticeable that there was a greater readiness to change in those organisations where management was open about its objectives and the company's or function's current performance than in those organisations where information was guarded. This can clearly be seen in the Nissan, Volvo, Oticon and XYZ cases. Conversely, in the Midshires case (Chapter 9) suspicion over and opposition to the Project Leader's plans, and political behaviour by members of the Steering Committee and Project Board, led to confusion over and resistance to change. In GK, suspicion over the objectives of the Marketing and Design Manager led to resistance to change. Therefore, openness helps people to understand the need for change, which is an essential step on the road to achieving change.

3. **Understand people's fears and concerns.** One of the major mistakes companies can make when introducing change is to fail to recognise, and deal with, the real and legitimate fears of the managers and staff. Though people's concerns tend to focus on the proposed change, they will also be strongly influenced by the outcome of previous change initiatives. In the company in Mini Case Study 11.3, the success of past changes appeared to act to reduce concerns over its move to a new bonus system. On the other hand, given that the majority of change initiatives appear to fail (Beer and Nohria, 2000), the past experience of change for many people is not a positive one. Therefore, organisations need to recognise that change does create uncertainty and that some individuals and groups may resist, or may not fully cooperate with it, if they fear the consequences or if their views and concerns are ignored. In this respect, resistance can be seen as a signal that there is something wrong with the change process or its objectives rather than with those who are opposing or questioning it. From this perspective, resistance can be viewed as positive: it reminds the organisation that it has not considered all the consequences of its actions, and forces it to review its plans. It follows that those championing change need to pay special attention to the potential for resistance, both in terms of the adverse consequences it can bring and the underlying problems it may indicate. They also need to pay close

attention to the organisation's past history of change and the extent to which this reduces or enhances people's fears and concerns.

4. **Publicise successful change**. In order to reduce fears and create a positive attitude towards change, companies should publicise the projects that are seen as models of how to undertake change, and the positive effects change can have for employees. This does not mean that mistakes should be hidden or poor outcomes ignored; these should be examined and explained and lessons should be learned. Staff should, however, be encouraged to expect and set credible and positive outcomes for change programmes. Once again, the experience of the case study companies illustrates this point. At Volvo, there have now been over three decades of successful change, which have produced a positive attitude amongst employees and managers alike. It is also change that has been well publicised both inside and outside the company, and has been praised by independent academics who have examined it. Staff and managers can see the effects of Volvo's commitment to Job Design; they can see that Job Design has led to improvements for all concerned. Therefore, the wide publicity given to its past Job Design initiatives, and the rigorous examination of them have helped Volvo to reduce their employees' fears of future changes. Similarly, Nissan's SDT has now been operating for over two decades and have overcome the suspicion by suppliers that they were some sort of spies for Nissan rather than a group intent on helping suppliers to develop their potential.

As the above four steps show, in order to create a willingness for change, an effective two-way flow of information is vital. Even where this is the case, however, organisations should not take for granted the willingness of staff and managers to undertake every change that is proposed. It is noticeable that even after XYZ had spent a number of years creating a willingness and readiness for change, it undertook a change readiness audit before embarking on the project to change its organisation structure. Not only did this allow it to estimate the degree of readiness for change, but it also formed part of the second people-related activity, involving people in the change project.

Involving people

Chapter 10 reviewed the three main theories that underpin our understanding of employee involvement, i.e. cognitive dissonance, the 'depth' of intervention and the psychological contract. In summary, the argument from these theories is that the more a change challenges a person or group's existing norms of behaviour, beliefs or assumptions, the more resistance it is likely to meet. It follows from this that the appropriateness of an involvement strategy needs to be judged less by the type of change being considered and more by how people will react to it. Changes that may readily be accepted in some organisations may be strongly resisted in others. Likewise, some major changes may meet with much less reaction than much smaller ones. For example, over the last decade it has become the norm for staff in public services to give their name on the telephone and wear name badges when meeting members of the public. Previously, staff were not encouraged to give their name or to wear a name badge. When this was first introduced, it met with a level of hostility from staff that appeared to be greatly out of proportion to what was being suggested. The reason for this was that many staff felt threatened, exposed to public scrutiny, by having to give their name.

In developing an involvement strategy, it is also important to remember Beckhard and Harris's (1987) advice regarding levels of commitment. They argued that the key objective was for organisations to gain the active support of the *critical mass* of people necessary to bring about the change. This is not all, or even necessarily a majority, of those affected. Nor is the same level of support necessary from all of the *critical mass*. Instead it can be split into three groups: those who let it happen, those who help it to happen and those who make it happen. Though it can sometimes be difficult to win over key groups and individuals, it can sometimes be surprisingly easy – as Mini Case Study 11.4 shows, an occasional cup of tea may be all that's necessity to create an ally.

An involvement strategy needs to take account of the size and duration of the proposed change project. Though some change projects can be short-lived and, possibly, easily achieved, many are not. In some cases, achieving a successful change can be a long and complex task. There will be difficult obstacles to overcome, not all of which can be anticipated in advance. To gain and maintain the active involvement of the *critical mass*, and to develop the momentum necessary to ensure that the project is successful, is not a one-off occurrence but an ongoing activity stretching over the lifetime of the change project. There are two main activities that help secure and maintain this level of involvement:

- **Communication**. As well as being key to gaining people's involvement, communication is an essential element of all the above change activities. In terms of involvement, the establishment of a regular and effective communications process can significantly reduce people's levels of uncertainty. In turn, this eliminates one of the major obstacles to people's willingness to get involved in the change process. The purpose of communication is not just to inform staff that change is being considered, but by drawing them into the discussions and debates about the need for and form of the change, and allowing them the freedom to discuss the issues involved openly, to get them to convince themselves of the need for change. The evidence that this is one of the most effective ways of gaining support goes back to the work of Kurt Lewin in the 1940s (Lewin, 1999a). During the Second World War, he was asked by the American government to find an effective way of getting people to change their eating habits. Through a series of now classic experiments, he demonstrated that the most effective method of convincing people to change their behaviour was by providing groups with information for them to evaluate and discuss, and letting the group come to its own decision. Once the decision had been made by the group, it exerted a strong pressure on all the individuals concerned to adhere to the group's decision. However, merely telling people they should change had very little effect at all.

    Communication should be a regular rather than a one-off exercise. Nor should it be pursued through one or two channels, such as newsletters or team briefings. As mentioned above when discussing the need to make people aware of the need for change, organisations have a wide range of formal and informal channels for communication. They should consciously use all of these. As a rule of thumb, it should be recognised that, whilst people are often willing to believe the wildest rumour from unofficial sources, anything from management has to be stated at least six times in six different ways before people start giving it credence.

Mini Case Study 11.4
Gaining commitment

Tea with the Convenor

Mary Davenport is the Trade Union Convenor for a large NHS Hospital Trust in the north of England. This is a full-time post. The hospital site is very big and sprawling and, as she says, 'my office is about as far as you can get from the Trust Headquarters'. She believes that this is deliberate. The Trust has tended to see the trade unions as an obstacle to change rather than a partner in the same undertaking. This was reflected in the relationship between Mary and the Chief Executive of the Trust. She could never get to see him but when he wanted to see her, she was summoned to his office, usually at short notice, whereupon he would either announce a change programme and demand the unions agree to it or complain that the unions were being obstructive in blocking earlier changes he had announced. Not surprisingly, the Trust found it difficult to implement change. Sometimes this was due to poor planning but often it was due to lack of staff commitment.

One day it was suddenly announced that the Chief Executive was leaving and that a new Chief Executive had been appointed. It appeared that his superiors in the NHS and key supporters in the Trust Board had lost patience with the slow pace of change and the Chief Executive's excuses. The trade unions were as surprised by the sudden change as everyone else but not optimistic that the new man would be any different. As Mary stated, 'We assumed that he had been given the remit to sort us all out and to do it quickly.' Mary expected that at some point she and her colleagues would be summoned to meet the new Chief Executive and, as she put it, 'read the riot act'. However, on the day the new Chief Executive took up his post, there was a knock on Mary's door and a man she had never seen before walked in and introduced himself as the new Chief Executive and asked if she 'fancied a cup of tea'. 'We had a long chat over the tea in the canteen where everybody could see me chatting to him. Most of the chat was about our families, he hardly mentioned work. He then said that we ought to do this more often and we now have a cup of tea together in the canteen at least once a month. As well as that, I can see him whenever I like and, as often as not, he'll come to my office.'

After that first meeting, relations between the unions and the management were transformed. Changes which had previously been seen as impossible suddenly became very possible. Now the unions are always consulted and always involved in change. However, the changed relationship stems from that first meeting between Mary and the Chief Executive. As Mary put it, 'He had the courtesy, on his first day on the job, to come to me and treat me as a valued colleague rather than a despised opponent.'

In some cases, where all those concerned become directly involved in the change process, as with Nissan's SDT initiatives, communication is less of an issue. However, in most cases, it is impractical to give everyone this level of involvement; therefore, as at XYZ and Volvo, it is important to communicate proposals from the outset. This involves not only providing information, but also listening to the response and taking it seriously. This has a number of benefits. The change management team will very quickly pick up any worries and concerns and can respond to these; they will also be made aware of aspects that need to be taken into consideration which have been overlooked; and assumptions that have been made will be tested and sometimes challenged. In addition, this will assist in identifying issues, individuals and groups who might obstruct change. In terms of the three target groups for commitment, i.e. those who let it happen, those who help it to happen and those who make it happen, communication can secure the commitment of the first but, by itself, is unlikely to secure the commitment of the other two groups. Their commitment will come through (and be tested by) their direct involvement in the change process.

- **Getting people involved**. One of the most vital initiatives an organisation can take with staff is not to treat them as objects of change, or obstacles to it, but to involve them in it and make them responsible for it. There are good examples of this in Oticon, XYZ and Nissan. Particularly where large-scale projects are concerned, not everyone can be involved in all aspects of planning and execution. However, as mentioned above, it is important to identify and enrol those whose assistance is necessary and those who are essential to make change happen. This should be the main criterion for selecting who will be involved. Obviously, where it is possible, it is a good idea to ensure that all those most closely affected are involved in some, if not all, aspects. Similarly, again where possible, responsibility for aspects of the change project should be given to those who will be directly affected by the result. In many cases, however, the numbers involved will prevent all those affected being involved and, consequently, managers will need to select those to involve. Sometimes, volunteers will be asked for. Sometimes, people who are perceived to have 'the right attitude' will be chosen. On the other hand, the presence of sceptics, people prepared to challenge assumptions and ask awkward questions, can be useful. This not only ensures that awkward questions are asked but can also, if the sceptic is won over, create a powerful advocate for the change. Likewise, it is useful to consider involving key opinion-formers: people to whom their colleagues look for guidance.

As the above shows, communication and involvement are essential to gaining people's understanding of the need for change. Change can be a slow and difficult process, however, and commitment can diminish unless steps are taken to maintain it. This leads on to the third and last people-related activity, sustaining the momentum.

Sustaining the momentum

Even in the best-run organisations, it sometimes happens that initial enthusiasm and momentum for change wanes and, in the face of the normal day-to-day pressures to meet customer needs, progress becomes slower and can grind to a halt. Indeed, in PCI and Midshires, the enthusiasm waned very early. In some cases, the enthusiasm for change may not even be present in the beginning. In such situations, people will return to the methods and types of behaviour with which they are familiar and comfortable. Given that momentum for change does not arise of itself or continue without encouragement, organisations need to consider how to build and sustain it. The points already made above regarding planning and implementation, and especially involvement, are clearly part of this. In addition, organisations should also:

- **Provide resources for change.** Kotter (1996: 35) states that:

  In an organization with 100 employees, at least two dozen must go far beyond the normal call of duty to produce a significant change. In a firm of 100,000 employees, the same might require 15,000 or more.

  For a one-off change project of short duration, it might be acceptable to ask staff to 'go far beyond the normal course of duty'. However, for many organisations, as the case studies in this book demonstrate, change is a way of life. Also, in many organisations, staff and managers have to work long hours merely to get their normal work done. In situations such as these, and indeed in most situations, it is probably difficult, and certainly unwise, to ask staff to undertake change initiatives without some additional resources, whether these be financial or human. In cases where staff are required to keep up the same level of output during the transition phase, it may require considerable additional resources to achieve this. The 1999 case of the UK's Passport Agency, which failed to provide sufficient extra staff to cope with the introduction of a new computer system, is a case in point. Not only did this result in inexcusable delays in issuing passports, but the Passport Agency eventually had to provide 300 extra staff anyway. In all, the additional cost of the measures necessary to deal with the situation was around £12.6m (NAO, 1999). It is important, therefore, that the need for any extra resources is identified and extra resources are allocated, whether for the provision of temporary staff, the training of existing staff, senior management time or whatever. As the example of the Passport Office showed, nothing is guaranteed to be more demoralising than having to make changes without some additional resources or support.

- **Give support to the change agents.** As Buchanan and Boddy (1992) noted, an enormous responsibility falls upon the change management team. They have not only to plan and oversee the change project, but also to motivate others and deal with difficulties, sometimes very personal problems. However, just as they have to support others, so too must they receive support themselves. Otherwise they may be the ones who become demoralised and lose their ability to motivate others. The examples of Midshires (Chapter 9) and FI (at the end of this chapter) are cases where the change agents were not given support, with serious consequences for themselves and the projects they were managing.

  Sometimes change agents can be encouraged by offering them financial rewards, sometimes by the promise of future advancement, but often the most effective method is through public and private praise of the individuals concerned. In Chapter 2, we drew attention to Chester Barnard's (1938) observation that monetary rewards are often less effective than non-monetary ones, such as praise. This does not mean that monetary rewards should be avoided, but it does mean that too great a reliance on them may be counter-productive.

- **Develop new competences and skills.** This reiterates the point made when discussing 'planning the change' above. Change frequently demands new knowledge, skills and competences. Increasingly, managers are having to learn new leadership styles, staff are having to learn to work as teams, and all are expected to be innovators and improvers. This requires more than just training and re-training. It may also include on-the-job counselling and coaching. Consequently, organisations need to consider what is required, who requires it and – the difficult part – how to deliver it in a way that encourages rather than threatens staff. XYZ is a good example of a company that recognised that managerial and staff development go hand in hand with organisational change. This can be an expensive process, however, both in terms of staff time and the cost of training and development. This, once again, emphasises the need to provide additional resources for change.

- **Reinforce desired behaviour.** In organisations, people generally do those things that bring rewards or avoid criticism. Consequently, one of the most effective ways of sustaining the momentum for change is to reinforce the kinds of behaviour required to make it successful. Sometimes this may be monetary, such as increased pay or bonuses for particular types of activity or progress. Sometimes it may be symbolic, such as Oticon's tearing down of walls and elimination of personal desks. Sometimes it may be through recognition, whereby senior managers openly or privately single out individuals or groups for special praise. Such activities are particularly important during the early stages of change, when achieving an identifiable and openly recognised success helps participants develop a positive attitude about the change project. In XYZ, it could be argued that the change in organisational structure was a method of reinforcing the behavioural changes that had already taken place. Alternatively, it could be said that they reinforced the new organisational structure. However one views XYZ, the key point is that the behavioural changes might have been difficult to sustain without the new structure and, certainly, the new structure would have been much less effective without the prior behavioural changes.

In looking at the three interlinked elements that make up the change process – objectives and outcomes, planning the change, and people – we can see why change is so complex and why so many initiatives fail. Though there are technical aspects that must be accomplished, no matter what type of change is involved, it can never be a purely technical exercise. Establishing objectives involves testing assumptions and challenging preconceived ideas. It also involves gathering both fact and opinion, and making judgements about which is the most important. Similarly, planning change often involves an impressive and daunting array of challenges and activities, some of which are amenable to straightforward techniques of analysis and decision, many of which are not. The final element, though, is the most complex: people. People are not just important because they are often the 'object' of change, but also because they are the ones who have to carry it out. In a real sense, they are the glue that holds it together. They can influence the choice of objectives and the way change is planned. In turn, objectives and planning can also affect their willingness to accept or become involved in change.

One final point: even after a change project has been 'completed', the story does not end there. As the Japanese have shown, even when change has resulted in a stable state being achieved, there always remains scope for improvement. Furthermore, as is clear from the case studies, many change projects are open-ended. Change will continue to take place. Therefore, both in planning a project and evaluating its outcomes, it is necessary to identify the open-endedness of it, and the degree to which the final outcome will require a continuous improvement approach or a continuing change approach. As mentioned earlier, there is a marked difference, however, between organisations where change is seen as an everyday occurrence and those where it is seen as a one-off event. In the latter, it is very difficult to develop the capabilities and commitment necessary to achieve continuous improvement, whereas in the former, continuous improvement and continuous change, and the capabilities, skills and commitment required of both, go hand in hand.

Conclusions

This chapter has sought to merge the theory and practice of strategy development and change management as presented in Chapters 6–10. In doing so, it has also drawn on many of the arguments and insights into the behaviour, operation and rationality of organisations presented in Chapters 1–5. Based on these ten chapters, this chapter introduced and elaborated on the Choice Management–Change Management model for understanding and managing organisational change. This comprised three interrelated organisational processes: the choice process, the trajectory process and the change process (*see* Figure 11.1). It was argued that not only does this model incorporate and go beyond both the Planned and Emergent approaches to strategy and change, but it also demonstrates how managers could attempt to change their organisation's circumstances to fit them to the approach that best suited them and their organisation.

It was asserted that the Choice Management–Change Management model incorporates the full scope of the various approaches to strategy and change, including the Planned and Emergent approaches, and that it also accommodates and explains the use of more directive approaches. However, one of the fundamental differences between this model and many other approaches to strategy and change is that it recognises that managers are active players rather than passive spectators in the development of their own organisations. The model is based on the assumption that not only can managers choose to align their organisation with the external conditions and constraints it faces, but they can also do the reverse and align these external conditions and constraints to their preferred way of structuring and running their organisation. Whether they choose to attempt to influence or alter the circumstances their organisation faces or to align it with them will depend on a range of issues, not least their own views about whether they or the organisation is better suited by a stable, planned situation or whether more turbulent, emergent conditions are preferable.

Though the Choice Management–Change Management model appears to offer significant theoretical avenues for understanding how organisations and managers operate, it also offers considerable practical benefits. In Chapter 3, we examined the Culture–Excellence perspective on organisations. The proponents of this view, especially Tom Peters, argue that organisations have no choice but to change radically if they are to survive. The Culture–Excellence theory is based on a particular view of the environment and other constraints organisations face. Assuming that this view is accurate, the Choice Management–Change Management model indicates that organisations need not radically restructure themselves, but could seek to influence the constraints they face to bring them more in line with their existing organisational arrangements. Even if, in the long term, organisations did have to structure themselves along the lines advocated by Peters, Kanter and Handy, they could still seek to influence the conditions under which they operated to achieve this over a longer timescale than might otherwise be assumed. Indeed, as Chapter 3 revealed, this is just the approach the Japanese take. Between the 1950s and the 1980s, Japan's leading organisations transformed themselves. This was achieved by slow and gradual transformation rather than by rapid shock tactics. Japanese companies achieved this gradual transformation by a combination of long-term vision allied to the ability to influence and restructure the constraints under which they operate, especially, as argued by Hamel and Prahalad (1989), their ability to change the rules of competition in their particular industries. In so doing, they provide much support for Kanter *et al*'s (1992) view that a Long March is more effective than a Bold Stroke for building competitive organisations.

Therefore, the Choice Management–Change Management model, in conjunction with the Framework for Change presented in Chapter 10, potentially at least, resolves the dispute between proponents of Planned and Emergent approaches to strategy development and change. It also raises fundamental questions, however, about what managers *can* do and what they *do* do in terms of running and shaping their organisations. In particular, it raises questions about the way that managers can make sense of their situation for themselves and others and, in so doing, construct alternative scenarios or realities for their organisation's future. Many writers, especially from the Culture–Excellence perspective, have made a case for visionary leadership being the key to an organisation's success. Certainly, the transactional, steady-as-she-goes type of manager appears very much out of favour (Grint, 2005; Kotter and Rathgeber, 2006; Peters, 2006). The case for transforming managers, as well as organisations, however, tends to be based on a partial view of what managers need to do and, often, only a shallow understanding of what they actually do. In order to come to grips with the nature of managerial work and the extent to which the Choice Management–Change Management model requires a rethink of how managers operate, the concluding chapter of this book will examine the role of managers, management and leadership, and the differences between them.

Test your learning

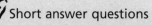

Short answer questions

1. Briefly describe the choice process.

2. How might a SWOT or PESTEL analysis help an organisation to understand better the context in which it operates?

3. What are the key features of the trajectory process?

4. Describe how an organisation might construct a vision for itself.

5. List the key components of the change process.

6. What does commitment planning involve?

7. Discuss the role of the change agent in planning and implementing change.

Essay questions

1. Critically evaluate the key linkages between the three processes that make up the Choice Management–Change Management model.

2. Use the Choice–Change model to assess one of the case studies in this book or another organisation of your choice.

Fabrication International (FI) Plc

BACKGROUND

FI is a multinational company which specialises in the fabrication of relatively small but very complex structures. In the past, assembling complex fabrications had been a very labour-intensive activity, but this is changing and the industry is becoming more computerised and automated. FI had been the leading company in its field but in recent years it had been overtaken by a number of its more innovative competitors, which had been quicker and more adept at introducing more computerised equipment in their design, fabrication and business systems areas. Therefore, FI was in the position of trying to catch up with its competitors in this area. Because such equipment is expensive and the company is risk-averse when it comes to borrowing money for new investments, FI has developed a four-step investment-appraisal process for assessing bids for new equipment and other investment decisions to ensure that it makes the right purchases and gets value for money. Despite this, FI has found that such investments have not always proved successful.

THE APPRAISAL PROCESS

The four steps in the appraisal process are as follows:

Step 1: At the beginning of each financial year, each departmental head is asked to generate a wish list of investments it would like to make. At this stage, they are not asked to provide a financial case for the investment (though they are asked to give a ball-park figure). The main rationale at this stage is to identify how the investment would address a strategic issue faced by the organisation.

Step 2: The Head of Department then discusses the wish list with a member of the Board of Directors not connected with his or her department. The purpose of this is to reduce the wish list to five items which are seen as central for investments.

Step 3: A detailed financial case is then put together for each item and they are put in priority order.

Step 4: The Board meets over a two-day period and each departmental head is cross-examined over their investment proposals. At the end of the two days, the Board decides which cases to support.

Though the investment procedure appears to be a rational strategy-driven process, there are three rules which drive it:

- The company has an overall limit on how much it will invest each year. Therefore, this provides the cut-off point for how many investment projects it will support. Even after the pruning of the wish lists at Step 2, there are always many more projects than can be accommodated in the financial limits.
- The company will only support projects with a two- to three-year investment payback.
- Each department will get one of its projects (though not necessarily its number one project).

In public, the Board and departmental heads are openly supportive of this process, however, privately some of them are highly critical of it. The main criticisms are that:

▶

- Short payback periods can militate against some forms of investment which may need longer than three years before the full benefits come on-stream.
- This type of departmental bidding process can cause conflict between departments that are bidding for the same resources and thus encourages a silo mentality rather than encouraging cooperation. It also tends to increase friction between the accountants, who police the system, and those who are bidding for money.
- Direct cost savings, which are what the company focuses on, are not the only benefits of introducing new equipment. Reduced lead times, improved quality and reliability, and greater flexibility can also be achieved. However, these tend to be classed as 'intangibles' and not counted.
- As departments know they will always get something, there is a tendency to overbid in the hope that the more you ask for, the more you will get. This makes the Board's job more difficult as they have many bids to decide upon. It can also result in departments being allocated money for something that is not a priority and being turned down for something that is.
- Some investments which may be crucial to the company are not made because they fall between or across departments.
- Once the Board has allocated money, the responsibility for introducing new equipment lies with the department, even if the Board has made significant changes to the original proposal which make it difficult to achieve. As one departmental head commented, 'The Board take the credit for successes and we take the blame for any failures.'

The following is an example of how FI's approach to the purchase of new equipment works in practice.

THE COMPUTERISED WELDING SYSTEM (CWS)

After failing to win orders from old clients which FI had expected to win, the senior engineer in the Small Fabrications Department concluded that it could not meet customer demands for reduced cost, and improved quality and reliability using traditional welding methods. Their competitors, which had invested heavily in automated and computerised systems, were now able to offer lower prices, better quality and shorter lead times.

Faced with the loss of business in this area, the senior engineer began to examine how best to automate the Department's processes in order to regain competitiveness. After studying what FI's competitors had done and after visits to equipment suppliers, he recommended the purchase of a Computerised Welding System (CWS). Such a system was not available on the open market but would have to be tailor-made for FI's specific needs. After much investigation of equipment and suppliers, the senior engineer persuaded the Department to put a CWS on its capital investment wish list. The senior engineer proposed that the CWS should be purpose-built for the company by a reputable supplier who would act as the turnkey contractor for the project, i.e. they would take responsibility for designing the system, purchasing and integrating the separate parts, and ensuring that the final product met FI's performance criteria.

Consequently, the CWS appeared on the Department's wish list at Step 1 of the investment appraisal process. The ball-park figure for the CWS was around £1m to £1.2m, though the senior engineer was privately sure that the cost would be nearer the former rather than the latter price. The Head of Department had been taken aback by the projected cost but accepted that the main issue at this stage was that it was a strategic necessity if the Department was to regain its competitiveness.

At Step 2, the Director charged with assessing the Department's wish list was also wary of the cost but accepted the strategic case for the CWS, and it went forward to Step 3, where a very detailed case for the CWS was compiled. The bottom line was that the CWS would cost £1,025,000; it would take nine months from placing the order to being fully up and running; and it would be four years before the company achieved payback on its investment. A fundamental element of the case was that a turnkey contractor be appointed to oversee the design and installation of the CWS.

At Step 4, the Board of Directors spent more time debating the purchase of the CWS than any other item. There was significant opposition from the Finance Director but strong support from the Marketing Director and the Design and Engineering Director. Eventually, the Managing Director suggested a compromise. They would agree to the CWS but it would have to achieve a three-year payback. In order to do this, the cost would be reduced by £200k. The savings were to be achieved by dispensing with a turnkey contractor; the company's own engineers were to be given the task of integrating the separate elements of the CWS. The equipment cost was to be reduced by purchasing lower-specification components.

INSTALLING THE CWS

The Small Fabrications Department's senior engineer was given responsibility for project-managing the CWS. Not surprisingly, he was somewhat disgruntled that there was no turn-key contractor and that savings would also have to be made on equipment. However, he did think that the CWS could be made to work, though not to the level originally anticipated. Even so, the situation proved far worse than he anticipated. The equipment prices and delivery times quoted by the original turnkey contractor were prices and times available only to them – they dealt regularly with the suppliers who were prepared to offer them favourable terms for repeat business. FI, on the other hand, found that it had to pay the going rate and accept the normal delivery times. Not only did this mean that the equipment specification had to be further lowered to keep the cost down, but it took FI nine months before all the equipment was delivered and it could begin to assemble the CWS. The turnkey contractor had promised that the CWS would be fully up and running by this time.

The senior engineer had assembled a team of engineers, maintenance staff and shop-floor workers to assemble and test-run the CWS. However, most of them seemed to think that being involved in the project was something of a poisoned chalice – only the senior engineer seemed to think that it could be made to work. After a further six months of intense effort, the senior engineer had to concede that the CWS was something of a disaster. The various components of the CWS were not compatible or of the necessary quality, and the system only ran in a limited and unsatisfactory manner. In the main, the Board of Directors had kept their distance from the project, other than the Finance Director who remained hostile to the project and was determined that the project engineer stick to the agreed budget. Even the Head of Department kept his distance; he had no intention of being connected with what he saw as a major disaster.

In essence, the senior engineer was left to his own devices and it was unclear who, if anyone, he could report to or seek assistance from. As a last resort, he prepared a report for the Board asking for more money to replace the inadequate equipment and to bring in the original turnkey contractor. He pointed out that if they did not they would have wasted over £800k and 15 months and still be unable to compete effectively. He also made it clear that he considered that the problems stemmed from the Board's decision to try to reduce the cost of the CWS. The Managing Director was furious when he received the report, as were the rest of the Directors. However, neither he nor they could see an alternative. To have wasted £800k and 18 months and to have achieved nothing was even more unacceptable than spending more money. The result was that FI brought in the original turnkey contractor to sort out the problem. It cost another £450k and six months' hard work before the CWS was working as originally expected. It also cost the senior engineer his job. The Managing Director's view was that 'heads must roll'. Given that the Board was the body which had to decide whose head it would be, it clearly was not going to sack itself. The Head of Department, knowing a disaster when he saw one, had distanced himself from the project. That only left the senior engineer who, in any case, had had the temerity to point the finger of accusation at the Board. A further consequence was that the Board became even more risk-averse when it came to investing in new equipment.

SUMMARY

FI is an old-established business that expected to continue to win orders from what it saw as loyal customers and to do business much as it always had. It found the new world of automation and computerisation difficult to get to grips with. In addition, it had always prided itself on balancing its books and keeping borrowing low. It found it difficult to accept the need to invest heavily in new equipment and, concomitantly, to reduce its skilled workforce. The investment-appraisal process was designed, as the Finance Director put it, 'as both a strategic tool to guide investment and a financial tool to instil financial prudence'. As the CWS showed, it may be that it is unfit to achieve either of these aims; though whether this is due to a fault in the investment-appraisal process, or to the way that the Board uses it, is open to debate.

Questions

Using the Choice Management–Change Management model, address the following questions:

1. Critically evaluate the extent to which FI's investment-appraisal process aids it in making strategic investment decisions.

2. What went wrong with the CWS introduction and how could it have been avoided?

3. Imagine that you are the senior engineer. What would you have done to make the CWS a success when faced with the decision by the Board to cut the original budget?

CHAPTER 12

Management – roles and responsibilities

Learning objectives

After studying this chapter, you should be able to:

- define globalisation and understand the importance of sustainability, workforce diversity and business ethics;
- list the key duties of managers;
- understand that much of what managers do is reactive and driven by expediency;
- describe the three main perspectives on leadership;
- identify the primary approaches to managerial development and education;
- appreciate the differences between management and leadership and the different skills required for each;
- explain the relationships between management, leadership and organisational change;
- appreciate the need for managers to identify and examine the full range of choices facing them;
- understand the impact of managers' decisions on society as a whole, and their wider and longer-term responsibilities.

Mini Case Study 12.1
A lesson in leadership

FT

Manage with mother

As a lesson in leadership, the residential course I have been on for the last four months has been quite something. Requiring 24-hour commitment seven days a week, it has been more gruelling than the toughest Outward Bound exercise. There has been no 'facilitator' to show the way, nor any schedule at all. Instead, I have been assigned a group of four young people to manage, and left to get on with it.

My group is aged between nought and seven, but despite their young age they have much in common with top executives. Each is equipped with a towering ego, an agenda all of their own and a disturbing mixture of friendliness and outright hostility towards each other. They have awesome will-power, yet are strikingly incompetent at everyday tasks, needing help with eating, sleeping, crossing roads and so forth. Rational behaviour is also a problem for most of them; indeed the youngest shows scant sign of rationality at all. My task, then, has been similar to that facing every leader: how to get a group of difficult people to work happily together.

A little time spent with my four team members and you start to understand why senior managers behave as they do. When you have witnessed a seven and a five-year-old fighting over the sharing of a bedroom, the failure of the merger between Glaxo Wellcome and SmithKline Beecham becomes a lot easier to comprehend. Sir Richard Sykes and Jan Leschly could not agree on who was going to have control of the bedside light nor on where their favourite teddies were going to go, so it turned out to be impossible for them to share a bedroom after all.

My course had hardly begun before I realised that command and control was the only way forward. In the corporate world this model has sadly fallen from favour. But in my company rules and rigid structures are essential. As chief executive I make sure that everyone knows that 7pm is bedtime. I have also come to see that choice is my enemy. To start the day by offering Cheerios, Coco Pops, Frosties or Honey Nuts is to ask for trouble. I offer Bran Flakes or nothing, and breakfast is faster and smoother as a result.

A second problem is the non-executive director I have been saddled with. Periodically he will pop in, flagrantly disregard all the rules and then have the cheek to offer advice in the fond belief that he understands the business.

I have also discovered that both rewards and punishments are poor motivational tools. Give a strawberry Chewit to one team member and before you know it you find inflation has taken hold and you are handing out Chewits as a reward for getting dressed. Punishments are even worse.

The first time you lose your temper you get results; but to achieve the same effect on subsequent occasions requires ever increasing quantities of violence. Understanding this is one thing. Living by it is another. On bad days I do nothing other than bribing and bollocking.

Like most chief executives, I have found that I get little feedback, and what I do get is inadequate. 'I hate you, you're poo', is not exactly constructive. I am at the top, and it can be lonely up here. Not to say stressful. The boss of a big company may lay awake fretting about his share price – being woken up every three hours by the youngest member may be nearly as bad.

So what is the answer? Surprise, surprise, it turns out to be complicated, exhausting and quite impossible to bring off. You have to be firm, but also nice and approachable. You need to keep your temper and motivate people by making them want to do the job in hand.

Source: Lucy Kellaway, *Financial Times*, 2 March 1998, p. 14.

Introduction

Lucy Kellaway's article, Mini Case Study 12.1, on the similarities between managing children and managing organisations will strike a chord with most parents and managers. Though written in a way that amuses, it raises serious questions concerning the nature of management: How can we control organisations? How can we motivate staff? How can we win over colleagues? The answer, as Kellaway states, 'turns out to be complicated, exhausting and quite impossible to bring off'. Not all people have the same needs or can be motivated in the same way. Also, people's needs change over time; what motivates them one day may have little effect the next. Neither do organisations, or their customers, suppliers and competitors, stand still. Faced with the vast array of present challenges, organisations must also look to the future. The challenges of the new millennium seem to have inspired many writers and commentators to provide us with their views on the future. Sometimes these have a postmodern rosy glow about them, whilst often, in the throes of the credit crunch, they present a gloomy, doomsday picture of the future. As Kellaway's article indicates, it is unlikely that the challenges facing managers in the future will get any easier, but one thing we do know about attempts to predict the future, as Ideas and perspectives 12.1 shows, is that they usually fall very short of the mark. Nor, as Ideas and perspectives 12.2 illustrates, is this anything new.

Ideas and perspectives 12.1
Predicting inflation

Mervyn King is the Governor of the Bank of England. He has an army of highly trained economists and advisors who work for him. He can also draw upon a vast array of public- and private-sector knowledge both in the UK and abroad. Yet even his economic forecasts can be spectacularly wrong, as the following two quotations show.

August 2008:

'Price increases will continue to enter the measure of CPI inflation for 12 months, so inflation is likely to remain markedly above the target until well into next year.'

November 2008:

'Although CPI inflation did rise above 5% its expected future path has fallen significantly . . . There is obviously a risk that [deflation] could happen.'

Source: The two quotes are from Elliott and Seager (2008: 1)

Ideas and perspectives 12.2
Predicting the future

This 'telephone' has too many shortcomings to be seriously considered as a means of communication.　(Western Union internal memo, 1876)

Airplanes are interesting toys, but of no military value.　(Marshal Foch, 1911)

Who the hell wants to hear actors talk?
(HM Warner of Warner Brothers, 1927)

I think there is a world market for maybe five computers.
(Thomas Watson, Chairman IBM, 1943)

This is unfortunately no excuse for ignoring the many serious and daunting challenges that organisations and those who manage them, not to mention the world at large, have to face in the coming decades. The globalisation of world trade may open up new markets and create new opportunities, but it also brings with it new competitors and new uncertainties. The same holds true for scientific advances. The beneficial effects of computers are there for all to see, with the range of applications expanding daily. However, advances such as genetically modified crops and even genetically modified human beings are much more controversial and unpredictable. For most of the developed world, the spectre of an increasingly ageing population looms large. Then there is the reality of global warming, the dwindling of natural resources, the growing gap between rich and poor countries, and the threat to the natural world of indiscriminate industrialisation; we are reminded of these almost daily (Becker, 2008; Dunphy *et al*, 2007; Newman, 2008).

Nevertheless, nothing is inevitable until it actually happens, and even then it may be reversed. Individual consumers and pressure groups have some influence, and governments can pass laws; but in an age where organisations dominate our lives, where they appear to be more powerful then ever before, the role and performance of managers will be crucial. Managers will need to recognise that in the future, as in the past, regardless of the particular issues involved, the environment in which their organisations operate will continue to change. They will also have to recognise that the appropriateness of their decisions will be judged by a wider set of criteria and a wider range of stakeholders than in the past. At the same time, managers will continue to have to find ways of ensuring that their organisation and its environment, and the other constraints under which it operates, are, as far as possible, kept aligned. As pointed out in previous chapters, this does not mean that each and every organisation has to change rapidly and radically, though many will. Instead, managers can seek to influence the constraints under which their organisation operates, and the pace and timing of change, to make them more favourable to their preferred way of working.

The case studies in this book show that change is neither easy nor necessarily always successful – something that most people's everyday experiences will confirm. Regardless of this, organisations do change, either by design or default, and managers do play a crucial role in determining whether the outcome is success or failure. Managers are the ones who have the responsibility for ensuring that options are identified, choices made and actions taken. They are also the ones who have the responsibility for making sense, presenting a coherent picture, of the events and developments that make up an organisation's past, present and potential future. Therefore, in concluding this book, it is only right that we look at how well or not managers are equipped, or can be equipped, for this task.

The chapter begins by examining the implications of globalisation, especially in terms of sustainability, workforce diversity and business ethics. This highlights the need for managers not just to acquire appropriate skills and competences but also to adopt appropriate behaviours. This leads on to a review of the literature on what managers are supposed to do and what they really do. This shows that, despite what leading thinkers such as Fayol and Weber believed and advocated, most managers are driven by expediency and operate in a responsive mode. The chapter then moves on to discuss the importance and nature of leadership in organisations. In particular, it seeks to identify the characteristics and contexts that make for effective leadership. Arising from this, the leadership role played by managers in the case studies is explored. This is followed by an examination of the education and development of managers, which leads on to a discussion of the relationships between management, leadership and change. The chapter and the book conclude by arguing that managers have an important responsibility to identify and exercise choice, when faced with situations which require change. Though choice can be determined on a very narrow basis of short-term financial return, increasingly managers will have to take into account wider organisational and societal factors. Especially important in this respect is that managers should be prepared to question trends and advice that seem designed to increase organisational and societal instability and fragmentation. The interests of society in general and their own organisations in particular may be better served by seeking stability rather than promoting instability.

Globalisation and the challenge of change

Arguably, the biggest single challenge facing managers today is globalisation: the creation of a unified world marketplace (Dunphy *et al*, 2007). Allied to globalisation, however, are three other challenges: how to achieve sustainability in a world of dwindling natural resources and increasing environmental pollution; how to manage an increasingly diverse workforce; and, at a time when business leaders are considered less trustworthy than ever before, how to manage ethically.

Trade between different parts of the world has been taking place for thousands of years. In the last 20 to 30 years, however, and particularly since the fall of communism in Eastern Europe, the integration of the global economy appears to have gone through a step change. Whereas in the 1970s and 1980s it was common to talk about international brands such as Coca-Cola and McDonald's, it is now equally common to speak of global, transnational corporations that dominate their industries and gobble up the smaller companies. Perhaps not surprisingly, in 2008, six of the world's top global corporations were oil companies (*see* Ideas and perspectives 12.3).

Ideas and perspectives 12.3
The world's 10 biggest companies

1. Wal-Mart
2. Exxon Mobil
3. Royal Dutch Shell
4. BP
5. Toyota
6. Chevron
7. ING Group
8. Total
9. General Motors
10. ConocoPhillips

Source: Fortune (2008) www.cnnmoney.com/magazines/fortune/global500/2008

One obvious manifestation of globalisation is that, in the developed world, we take for granted that our supermarkets will be stocked with our favourite foods from every part of the world all year round. Even so, it is perhaps still surprising that the top global corporation in 2008 was Wal-Mart. Nor is globalisation merely an issue for large companies; it is affecting smaller organisations as well, whether through the threat of increased competition and takeover, or the promise of new markets.

Like many hot topics that attract a great deal of attention, it is difficult to find an agreed definition of globalisation. For some, it is primarily an economic phenomenon, concerned with the integration and convergence of economic systems through the growth in international trade, investment and capital flows (Jones, 1995; Deresky, 2000). Others, though, see it as a much wider phenomenon involving social, cultural and technological exchanges that will 'transform our world into the beginnings of a global civilization, a new civilization of civilizations, that will blossom through the coming century' (Schwartz and Leyden, 1997: 1). For Giddens (2002), the advent of new communications technologies is leading to the 'death of distance' and making it possible to share knowledge and culture across the globe instantaneously and simultaneously. Some argue that globalisation may also be sounding the death knell of the nation state, as large trading blocks, based on Europe, North America and Asia and overseen by the World Trade Organization, take over (Deresky, 2000). Reich (1998), in an attempt to make sense of these differing perspectives, identifies the four main definitions of globalisation: a historical epoch; a confluence of economic phenomena; the hegemony of American values; and a technological and social revolution.

Despite these different views as to what globalisation is, as Reich (1998) shows, there is some agreement amongst commentators as to what is driving it: the intensification of international competition, the fall of communism, economic liberalisation, the removal of trade barriers, and the advent of new communication technologies such as the Internet. It is these very real developments which make globalisation a key issue for managers rather than a passing fad. Globalisation is also a highly contentious issue which has given rise to a great deal of bitter conflict between those who see it as a force for global good and those who see it as the oppression of poor nations by rich ones (*Economist*, 2002; Hobsbawm, 2008; Klein, 2001; Stiglitz, 2007). To a great extent, much of the pro-and-anti argument revolves around the size and behaviour of the large, transnational corporations that are coming to dominate the global economy. For example, in 2003:

- more than half of the 100 largest economies in the world were private corporations;
- the sales of Ford and General Motors combined were greater than the combined GDP of sub-Saharan Africa;
- the combined turnover of the six largest Japanese trading companies was almost as big as the national incomes of all the nations in Latin America (GlobalisationGuide.org, 2003).

For the pro-globalisation camp, this provides the rationale for the creation of global institutions such as the World Trade Organization (WTO) and the World Bank that can set the rules for such organisations and police them. For the 'antis', this shows that big business is the dominant force in globalisation, and the WTO and the World Bank exist to do their bidding.

Regardless of whether one sees globalisation as a force for good or ill, organisations have to come to terms with the changing nature of domestic and international trade. They have to live with a situation where the rules that govern their behaviour are set by supra-national bodies such as the EU and WTO. In addition, as mentioned above, they need to come to terms with three other issues whose importance has been intensified by globalisation, namely sustainability, workforce diversity and business ethics.

Sustainability

Globalisation both derives from and is driving economic development across the globe; the greater the level of economic integration across the planet, the greater the level of consumption. As we are reminded every day, however, the result of this rush for ever-greater levels of economic growth and consumption is the dwindling and depredation of natural resources, increasing levels of pollution and rapid global warming. The surge in oil prices in recent years reflects both the increased demand for oil brought about by globalisation, especially the growth of the Chinese economy, and dwindling reserves of oil (Strahan, 2008). Nor is it just a case of oil running out. As Lines (2002: 126–7) argues:

> *The regenerative and assimilative capacities of the biosphere cannot support even the current levels of consumption, much less the manifold increase required to generalize to higher standards of living worldwide. Still less can the planet afford an ever-growing human population striving to consume more per-capita.*

It would be good to think that with the election of President Obama in the USA, the sustainability of the planet will move to the top of the political agenda. However, as was shown by the failure of the USA to sign up to the Kyoto Protocol on achieving reductions in the emissions of greenhouse gases, governments have tended to put short-term economic benefits ahead of long-term environmental survival. As the then UN Secretary General, Kofi Annan, stated in 2006:

The world remains locked into short-term thinking, from election cycles in politics to profit-taking in the business world. Sustainable development cries out for a long-term perspective. The world remains captive to the old idea that we face a choice between economic growth and conservation. One of two jobs worldwide – in agriculture, forestry and fisheries – depends on the sustainability of ecosystems.

(quoted in Dunphy *et al*, 2007: 30)

Even if governments can reach an accord over action on climate change, we also know that organisations, driven by market forces, will have a major influence on how such actions are formulated and will have the major responsibility for their implementation. As Dunphy and Griffiths (1998: 183) argued in their book, *The Sustainable Corporation*:

There is a widespread view that governments must solve environmental problems. However, the major multinationals outstrip many of the world's national economies in terms of wealth and power, and their global coverage allows them to escape the requirements of particular governments seeking to place severe environmental restrictions on them. They can simply move their operations across national borders. The world's multinationals are in fact more powerful than most national governments.

Nevertheless, Dunphy and Griffiths do believe that it is possible for these large organisations to change their ways. They point out that those who run organisations live in the same world as the rest of us, and, to a large extent, experience the consequences of their actions in the same way everyone else does. Therefore, they argue, managers cannot divorce their actions from the wider impact they have on society; nor can they ignore the fact that a sustainable future for their organisations requires a sustainable future for the world. This presents a major challenge for managers, particularly at the senior level. Whilst operating in competitive and hostile markets, they have to marry the desire of their shareholders for increased profit with the need to act in the wider and longer-term interests of society as a whole. They will not achieve this without pressure and support from governments and the force of public opinion. Nor, as Dunphy *et al* (2007) show, will managers be able to create sustainable organisations unless they have the change management skills to do so. Dunphy *et al* argue that both incremental and transformational approaches can be used to create sustainable organisations. However, the appropriateness of either depends on the circumstances of the organisation in question. Therefore, the role of managers is not just to lead change, but to develop the skills necessary to identify which approach to change is suitable for their organisation.

Furthermore, as Docherty *et al* (2002: 12) maintain, sustainability is not just about the relationship of organisations to their environment, or the depletion of natural resources:

Sustainability . . . encompasses three levels: the individual, the organizational and the societal. Sustainability at one level cannot be built on the exploitation of the others. These levels are intimately related to the organization's key stakeholders: personnel, customers, owners and society. An organization cannot be sustainable by prioritizing the goals and needs of some stakeholders at the expense of others . . . Thus sustainability has a value basis in the due considerations and balancing of different stakeholders' legitimate needs and goals.

Therefore, as Dunphy *et al* (2007) argue, life cannot be sustained on earth unless we create sustainable organisations. However, Docherty *et al* (2002) claim that creating sustainable organisations cannot be achieved unless all stakeholders, including the organisation's own members, are treated in an equitable and ethical manner. This is why the issues of workforce diversity and business ethics are so important.

Workforce diversity

Jones *et al* (2000: 166–7) observe that:

> *Diversity is dissimilarities – differences – among people due to age, gender, race, ethnicity, religion, sexual orientation, socioeconomic background, and capabilities/ disabilities . . . Diversity raises important ethical issues and social responsibility issues as well. It is also a critical issue for organizations, one that if not handled well can surely bring an organization to its knees, especially in our increasingly global environment.*

Ever since the Industrial Revolution ushered in the age of the organisation, the workforce has become increasingly diverse, though faster in some industries and countries than others. Globalisation is intensifying workforce diversity in three key ways.

The first and most obvious is that the growth of the transnational corporations means that, increasingly, companies are being owned and managed by people from different countries and cultures. The fact that Ford Motors operates its own plants in most major markets and owns Volvo in Sweden, has a partnership with Mazda in Japan and a partnership with Volkswagen in Brazil is a typical example. There are also many examples of Japanese and South Korean companies, such as Honda and Hyundai, establishing factories in Europe and the USA. Indeed, the famous MG sports car is now manufactured in the UK by the Nanjing Automobile Corporation (NAC). Companies are also increasingly buying products and services from overseas. The epitome of German manufacturing, Mercedes-Benz, now purchases car components from India, and many big UK companies, such as BT and Aviva, have relocated call centres to India.

The second effect of globalisation concerns the migration and recruitment of workers from other countries. Richer countries have always been a magnet for workers from poorer countries. The emigration from Europe to the USA in the nineteenth century is a case in point. It offered the potential for a better life for immigrants and met the severe shortage of workers the USA was experiencing. The last 50 years has seen the mass migration of people from South America to the USA. In some American cities, Hispanics are now the largest ethnic grouping and by 2050 will make up some 25 per cent of the population of the USA (Hitt *et al*, 2009). The transportation and communications infrastructures that have made globalisation possible also make it easier to move from one country to another, whether legally or illegally, to seek a better life. Also, with globalisation, the need to move skilled labour from where it is plentiful to where it is scarce, or where it can be better rewarded, is an increasingly important factor of competitiveness. In recent years, for example, the UK government has sought to recruit medical staff from across the world to compensate for staff shortages in the National Health Service.

The third effect of globalisation on diversity has been to increase the participation rate of women and minority groups in the workforce. As economies develop, they require greater amounts of labour. The tendency is first of all to recruit male workers, and often to give preference to ones from particular groups, whether these be based on grounds of race, tribe, religion, age or sexual orientation. As demand for labour grows, other groups are drawn into the workforce. In the twentieth century, for example, the participation of women in the workforce of most developed countries probably accounted for the biggest increase in diversity.

It has always been the case that the USA tends to exemplify workforce diversity. Hitt *et al* (2009: 41) recommend their readers to consider the following:

> *Over the past decade, more than one-third of people entering the US workforce have been members of racial or ethnic minority groups. Moreover, the proportion of racial and ethnic minorities in the workforce is expected to increase indefinitely. The situation is similar in some European countries.*

Cummings and Worley (2001: 429–30) echo this point, stating that:

> *. . . contemporary workforce characteristics are radically different from what they were just twenty years ago. Employees represent every ethnic background and color; range from highly educated to illiterate; vary in age from eighteen to eighty; may appear perfectly healthy or may have terminal illness; may be single parents or part of dual-income, divorced, same-sex or traditional families; and may be physically or mentally challenged.*

Diversity would not be an issue if we all reacted to the same things in the same ways and treated everybody else as we would wish to be treated ourselves. In his entertaining and enlightening book *Blunders in International Business*, Ricks (1999) catalogues the blunders made by businesses in trying to sell their products in other countries or trying to establish businesses in other countries. He points out (Ricks, 1999: 4) that:

> *Cultural differences are the most significant and troublesome variables encountered by the multinational company. The failure of managers to comprehend fully these disparities has led to most international business blunders.*

Hofstede (1980, 1990) sought to identify the similarities and differences between national cultures and the implications of these for the management of different groups (*see* Chapter 5). From the work of Hofstede and that of other researchers (*see* Trompenaars, 1993, for example) it is clear that approaches which might be effective when managing, say, Japanese workers might be considerably less effective when managing employees from the USA. Jones *et al* (2000: 175) comment that:

> *When American and Japanese managers interact, for example, the Americans often feel frustrated by what they view as indecisiveness in the Japanese, and the Japanese are often frustrated by what they perceive as hasty, shortsighted decision making by the Americans.*

Managing diversity is not just about how to manage effectively relationships between people with different national cultures. Managing diversity is also concerned with developing appropriate approaches to managing differences in gender, age, abilities, sexuality, ethnicity, etc. For instance, in the West, it is argued that male and female workers have different strengths and weaknesses and different preferences in how they prefer to manage and be managed (Maddock, 1999; Thomas, 2003). Alimo-Metcalfe (1995a, 1995b) maintains that women tend to be more motivated by organisational goals than their male counterparts and more amenable to change. Women also appear to have different work–life balance priorities, especially in terms of childcare, as BA found to its cost in 2003. An attempt by the airline to impose a new clocking-on arrangement on its check-in staff at Heathrow Airport turned out disastrously when the predominantly female workforce went on unofficial strike. This cost BA some £40 million in lost revenues and an incalculable amount in bad publicity (Harrison, 2003). The company failed to understand its staff's priorities and concerns, as Phillips (2003: 17) relates:

Currently, shifts are organised three months at a time and women can arrange childcare around their working hours. What they fear is a system in which a computer will decide on a day-to-day, or hour-to-hour, basis when they should come into work. . . . BA, and the unions too, have been caught on the hop because they failed to understand that, for these relatively low-paid, often part-time, women workers, the welfare of children comes first – above money.

Despite the evidence that women have different preferences and priorities to men, studies have shown that if women are to progress up the managerial hierarchy, they are expected to conform to male characteristics such as decisiveness, competitiveness and playing by the rules (Schein and Mueller, 1992). Workforce diversity is not just about sexual, however, or even cultural or ethnic differences, as Cummings and Worley (2001: 429–30) point out:

Such a definition is too narrow and focuses attention away from the broad range of issues that a diverse workforce poses. Diversity results from people who bring different resources and perspectives to the workplace and who have distinctive needs, preferences, expectations and lifestyles. Organizations must design human resource systems that account for these differences if they are to attract and retain a productive workforce and if they want to turn diversity into a competitive advantage.

That people who are different are treated less well than those who conform to whatever the prevailing stereotype is in organisations and society is well known. Most countries now have laws that seek to prevent or punish discrimination. This of course can provide a powerful incentive for organisations to recognise and manage workforce diversity. In raising the issue of competitive advantage, however, Cummings and Worley draw attention to the positive side of diversity. In a fiercely competitive world where markets are expanding and customers are increasingly rejecting standardised products and services in favour of ones tailored to their needs, workforce diversity can bring substantial benefits. It offers the possibility of more creativity, innovation and flexibility, and it provides a heightened sensitivity to different customer groupings and a wider pool of talent to draw from. This is certainly the view taken by Google (2008):

Diversity and inclusion are fundamental to Google's way of doing things. We strive to be a local company in every country that we operate and we understand that our users all have different cultures, languages and traditions. It drives the projects we work on, the people we hire and the goals we set ourselves. We go to great lengths to create products that are useful to our user wherever they are and we've found that this commitment to diversity and to our users has been key to our success.

Google aspires to be an organization that reflects the globally diverse audience that our search engine and tools serve. We believe that in addition to hiring the best talent, the diversity of perspectives, ideas, and cultures leads to the creation of better products and services. The diversity of our employees and partners serves as the foundation for us to better serve our diverse customers and stakeholders all over the world.

Only by attracting, retaining and motivating workers effectively, including recognising and promoting the benefits of diversity, can organisations expect to prosper or even survive in an increasingly competitive global economy. This means that organisations have to achieve the difficult but essential task of treating workers differently because of their diversity but treating them all fairly. This is a task that can only be achieved if those in positions of power and authority in organisations are also prepared to manage ethically. However, for some companies, as the next section shows, this appears to go against their normal business practices.

Business ethics

It is commonplace, as the following quotations show, for most books on organisations and management to make some reference to business ethics:

Ethics are moral principles or beliefs about what is right or wrong. These beliefs guide people in their dealings with other individuals and groups (stakeholders) and provide a basis for deciding whether behavior is right and proper.

(Jones *et al*, 2000: 183)

Three issues are prominent in discussions of proper conduct in developed nations: (1) corruption . . . the chief issues involve bribing foreign public officials in order to win business. . . . (2) exploitation of labor . . . [this] involves the employment of children, the forced use of prison labor, unreasonably low wages and poor working conditions. . . . (3) environmental impact . . . [this] relates to pollution and overuse of scarce resources.

(Hitt *et al*, 2009: 95–6)

Managers today are usually quite sensitive to issues of social responsibility and ethical behavior because of pressure from the public, from interest groups, from legal and government concerns, and from media coverage. It is less clear where to draw the line between socially responsible behavior and the corporation's other concerns, or between the conflicting expectations of ethical behavior among different countries.

(Deresky, 2000: 56)

There is certainly no shortage of advice about what ethics are or how they should be applied to business. The problem, as the last quotation shows, is that, in an increasingly complex, diverse and competitive world, applying an ethical approach to business is not straightforward. This is why many companies and governments, even those that profess to have ethical policies, have difficulty bridging the gap between rhetoric and reality, as the following extracts show:

The arms company BAe secretly paid Prince Bandar of Saudi Arabia more than £1bn in connection with Britain's biggest ever weapons contract, it is alleged today. A series of payments from the British firm was allegedly channelled through a US bank in Washington to an account controlled by one of the most colourful members of the Saudi ruling clan, who spent 20 years as their ambassador in the US. It is claimed that payments of £30m were paid to Prince Bandar every quarter for at least 10 years. It is alleged by insider legal sources that the money was paid to Prince Bandar with the knowledge and authorisation of Ministry of Defence officials under the Blair government and its predecessors. For more than 20 years, ministers have claimed they knew nothing of secret commissions, which were outlawed by Britain in 2002.

(Leigh and Evans, 2007)

Swiss investigators have joined the US in the biggest bribery investigation ever into foreign deals where millions of pounds of apparently legitimate payments by BP, Shell and others allegedly ended up in the hands of Kazakhstan officials.

(Macalister, 2003: 1)

Tin hats will be all the rage this morning at their [Primark's] Reading-based head offices. After watching last night's Panorama, which revealed that the retailer has been using sub-contracted child labour in India to produce its cheap-enough-to-chuck clothing, employees – and customers – might be wondering what the future holds for the company.   (Hickman, 2008)

A chill must have swept through many a City [of London] boardroom yesterday after Louise Barton won her appeal in a high-profile sex discrimination case. The case has shone a spotlight on the secretive pay structures of investment banks, which are known for paying large discretionary bonuses. . . . Statistics show that women earn on average 19 per cent less per hour than men across all professions. But for women working in the City, the disparity can be even greater. Typically, those on six-figure salaries earn an average of almost 60 per cent less than their male counterparts.

(Saigol, 2003: 8)

Though these ethical shortcomings can be viewed as examples of corporate management valuing the interests of one group of stakeholders above those of other groups, that is not the end of the story. The last decade has also shown that in many instances, senior and even junior managers have put their own personal interests above those of everybody else, even to the extent of breaking the law. There can be few people unaware of the Enron scandal, where a number of senior managers conspired to line their own pockets at the expense of everyone else and, in the process, ruined the company and destroyed its accountants, Arthur Andersen (Bryce, 2002). Furthermore, as Partnoy (2003: 1) observed, this was not an isolated incident:

The 1990s were a decade of persistently rising markets – 10 years of economic expansion, with investors pouring record amounts into stocks and pocketing double-digit returns year after year. . . . The decade was peppered with financial debacles, but these faded quickly from memory even as they increased in size and complexity. The billion dollar-plus scandals included Robert Citron of Orange County, Nick Leeson of Barings and John Meriwether of Long-Term Capital Management, but the markets merely hiccoughed and then started going up again. When Enron collapsed in late 2001, it shattered some investors' beliefs and took a few other stocks down with it. Then Global Crossing and WorldCom declared bankruptcy, and dozens of corporate

*scandals materialised as the leading stock indices lost a quarter of their value. . . .
Companies' reported earnings were a fiction and financial reports chock-full of disclosures that would shock the average investor if they ever even glanced at them – not that anybody ever did.*

In the USA, the finger has been pointing very sharply at the practices of Wall Street analysts who aggressively oversold shares, as Tran (2003: 1) observed:

. . . analysts hoodwinked investors by hyping up the prospects of internet and other hi-tech companies, while privately dismissing them. Former star internet analyst Henry Blodget once privately described as a 'piece of shit' a stock he was publicly touting, according to previously disclosed emails.

According to Teather (2002), the hyping or 'ramping' of shares was central to the operation of Wall Street's financial institutions and not just limited to a few rogue analysts. In May 2003, in an attempt to draw a line under the crimes of the boom years, leading Wall Street financial institutions agreed to pay fines totalling $1.4 billion (Tran, 2003).

Even so, neither the jailing of a few brokers and Enron executives nor the levying of billion-dollar fines appears to have changed the behaviour of the financial institutions. Indeed, the behaviour appears to have worsened in the last decade, as the sub-prime mortgage scandal has shown:

A pair of Bear Stearns executives were arrested and charged with fraud yesterday over the collapse of two hedge funds. In early-morning raids, the FBI arrested Ralph Cioffi and Matthew Tannin at their homes in New Jersey and New York. The pair were handcuffed and escorted, grim faced, into court in front of a battery of television cameras. According to the US government, the duo concocted a web of lies to persuade investors to keep funds in two mortgage-heavy funds that evaporated in value in June last year, losing more than $1.4bn (£710m) of clients' money. Among the biggest victims was Barclays Bank, which had pumped in $400m. Benton Campbell, a federal prosecutor, said: 'They lied in the futile hope that the funds would turn around and that their income and reputations would remain intact.'

(Clark, 2008)

Nor was this a case of a few corrupt executives. As Ideas and perspectives 12.4 shows, the sub-prime scandal stretched from the top to the bottom of the mortgage industry and was as blatant as it was illegal.

In public at least, there are two aspects of business ethics that business leaders agree upon: all businesses should have them, and all businesses have difficulty abiding by them. Difficult though they are to implement and maintain, if organisations fail to adopt an ethical approach, the result can be disastrous, as the sub-prime scandal and the ensuing credit crunch have shown. Managers – like those at Enron – can put their own interests above those of shareholders, staff and the law. The sub-prime example demonstrates that entire industries can become corrupt, even threatening the entire world economy.

Globalisation is often couched in terms of the competitive challenge it poses for individual organisations, i.e. how can an organisation, whether in the public, private or voluntary sector, survive and prosper in a borderless world that is increasingly dominated by a few giant, transnational corporations? However, the discussion of sustainability,

Ideas and perspectives 12.4
Broker's clients detail web of dashed dreams

When Marcia Neilson couldn't qualify for a home loan in early 2006 because of poor credit, her mortgage broker, Nicole Lyder, had an unusual solution: Add Neilson's daughter to the loan application. Neilson's 21-year-old daughter had just lost her job, but Lyder remained undeterred. 'That wasn't a problem', Neilson recalled her broker saying.

Neilson's real estate agent said Lyder enlisted him to drive Neilson and her daughter to Brockton City Hall. The pair filled out a business certificate that claimed they owned a hair salon in Brockton. The Neilsons qualified for a mortgage and bought a Dorchester house in June 2006 for $565,000. Last fall, Marcia Neilson learned from state investigators looking into Lyder's business practices that her loan application was padded in other ways: a statement for a $25,000 bank account in Neilson's name that she had no knowledge of.

Fake documents, a phantom borrower, and other irregularities were common features of five subprime mortgages brokered by Lyder between November 2005 and June 2006 that were examined by the Boston Globe. Lyder's clients ranged from the barely employed to struggling working-class couples; one had just left a homeless shelter and two others gave up government-subsidized housing to buy homes. They said Lyder arranged loans that they later realized had monthly payments that far exceeded their means. All five loans are now in foreclosure.

Source: Blanton (2008: 1)

diversity and ethics shows globalisation also raises crucial questions about the role and impact of organisations in and on a global society. These questions go beyond traditional business concerns such as profit and loss, value for money or market share; they are concerned with fundamental issues of the role of organisations in sustaining life on Earth, respect for human diversity and dignity, and the ethical rules by which we live. These issues are not new, but globalisation has accentuated and brought them to the fore as never before. Governments, international bodies and individual organisations have responded by adopting policies that supposedly promote responsible and ethical behaviour. All big organisations, including the financial institutions involved in the sub-prime scandal, and many smaller companies, have policies on minimising their environmental impact, promoting and managing diversity, and on behaving in an ethical fashion. Yet, the gap between ethical rhetoric and the reality of unethical behaviour seems to be getting wider rather than narrower. The real challenge for organisations is to change managerial behaviour so that business ethics become business practices. Policies, skills and good intentions are clearly not enough. The fundamental point is that managers need to behave differently. They need to put the policies and skills into practice. Therefore, in examining the role and development of managers in the rest of this chapter, one of the key issues to be addressed will be what determines managerial behaviour and how can we change it.

The manager's role

It is generally accepted that serious attempts to define the role of managers began in 1916 with the publication of Henri Fayol's (1949) book *General and Industrial Management* (Hales, 1999; Lamond, 2004). In this book, Fayol stated that the key functions of managers were: forecasting and planning, organising, commanding, coordinating and controlling (*see* Chapter 1). Since then, there have been a great number of other attempts to define the manager's role (*see* Barnard, 1938; Brewer and Tomlinson, 1964; Carlson, 1951; Constable and McCormick, 1987; Golding and Currie, 2000; Griffin, 2002; Handy *et al*, 1987; Horne and Lupton, 1965; Kotter, 1982, 1990; Mintzberg, 1973; Nahavandi, 2000; Silverman and Jones, 1976; Sjöstrand, 1997; Stewart, 1976; Yukl, 2006). As Hales (1986, 1999) found when he reviewed many of these studies, the information available presents the reader with a confusing and conflicting picture of what managers should do and how they should do it. All the same, Fayol's work still attracts support (Lamond, 2004; Duncan, 1999; Wren, 1994) and many textbooks still take a recognisably Fayolian approach when defining the role of managers. For example, Dakin and Hamilton (1990: 32) maintain that:

> [The manager] plans, organises, directs and controls, on proprietors' or own behalf, an industrial, commercial or other undertaking, establishment or organisation, and co-ordinates the work of departmental managers or other immediate subordinates.

Others, though, have taken a distinctly different approach. Peter Drucker (1985: 53), often referred to as the 'father of modern management', argues that the essence of the manager's role is the:

> . . . task of creating a true whole that is larger than the sum of its parts, a productive entity that turns out more than the sum of the resources put into it.

Drucker also likened the manager to the conductor of a symphony orchestra. As conductor, the manager is the one through whose effort, vision and leadership the various instrumental parts, that are so much noise by themselves, become the living whole of music. In this instance, the manager is also the composer as well as the conductor.

Charles Handy (1986: 365–6), whose work was examined in Chapter 3, likened the manager to a doctor:

> The manager, like the GP, is the first recipient of problems. However he may deal with them, whatever role he may choose to assume, he must first (just like the doctor) decide whether it is a problem and if so, what sort of problem it is, before he proceeds to act. He must, in other words:
>
> Identify the symptoms in any situation;
> Diagnose the disease or cause of the trouble;
> Decide how it might be dealt with – a strategy for health;
> Start the treatment.

Such analogies are useful in that they create a concrete picture of the manager's role, but they can also be misleading. Conducting is an art form; is management an art form? Or, as Handy's analogy implies, is it a science in the same way that medicine is a science? As Part 1 of this book showed, the clash between those who see management as a rational, science-based process, and those who believe it to be more intuitive and less rational, is not new.

Duncan (1975) tries to resolve this conflict by taking a holistic view of the job of the manager. He identifies three distinct levels of management activity:

Philosophical – goal formation.
Scientific – goal accomplishment and evaluation.
Art – implementation of decisions.

At the philosophical level in forming goals, the manager – Duncan argues – is mainly concerned with the effects of the actions and reactions of other individuals and groups within the wider economic and social context within which the organisation is set. At this level, managers and their associates formulate clear and precise strategies that will encompass all envisaged effects that can result from the set goals, not only on the various pressure groups within its internal and external environment, but also on competitors and regulatory agencies. It is also at this level that the ethics of managerial behaviour, values and priorities of the organisation are formulated and established.

At the scientific level, management develops plans, methods and techniques for achieving set goals, and establishes procedures for monitoring and evaluating progress.

The art level is concerned with the implementation of decisions; this is the level at which tactical and administrative decisions are made to deploy the organisation's resources and attain the optimum degree of operational efficiency. This level is an 'art' because, according to Duncan, there appears to be a particular talent necessary to persuade others that management-generated goals and decisions should be accepted.

Whilst one might not necessarily agree with his definitions, especially in terms of strategy formulation, Duncan's three-level approach is extremely useful in that it shows that management is both a science and an art. By its very nature, management is forced to deal with both rational, science-based activities, such as the design and operation of manufacturing and administrative systems, and less rational, more intuitive activities, especially those concerning managing and motivating people. The extent to which a manager is involved in any of these activities will depend on the kind of organisation the manager works for, the type of job the manager has, and – crucially – the manager's level in the organisation's hierarchy (Hales, 1986). Position in the hierarchy, formally at least, is likely to exert the greatest influence on the role given to and expected of a manager. The three main hierarchical levels are as follows:

- **Top management** – the policy-making group responsible for the overall direction of the company.
- **Middle management** – responsible for the execution and interpretation of policies throughout the organisation and for the successful operation of assigned divisions or departments.
- **First-level or supervisory management** – directly responsible to the middle management group for ensuring the execution of policies by their subordinates. They are also responsible for the attainment of objectives by the units they control, through practices and procedures approved and issued by top or middle management.

Superficially, at least, these three hierarchical levels of management appear to mirror Duncan's three levels of management activity. On a closer examination, however, it becomes more difficult to match them because each hierarchical level of management can encompass philosophical, scientific and art activities, though not necessarily to the same extent. This can be seen more clearly by examining what it is that managers actually do, as opposed to what academics say they should do.

There have been a number of important studies conducted to determine how managers spend their time (*see* for example Brewer and Tomlinson, 1964; Child and Ellis, 1973; Kotter, 1982). Hales (1999) claims that the most widely known and replicated work in this area is by Mintzberg (1973, 1975).

Mintzberg (1973), in his book *The Nature of Managerial Work*, argued that management is not about functions but about what managers actually do. His aim was to replace the 'folklore' about what managers do with the 'fact' of what they actually do:

If you ask a manager what he does, he will most likely tell you that he plans, organizes, coordinates and controls. Then watch what he does. Don't be surprised if you can't relate what you see to these four words. . . . The fact is that these four words, which have dominated management vocabulary since the French industrialist Henri Fayol first introduced them in 1916, tell us little about what managers actually do. At the best, they indicate some vague objectives managers have when they work.

(Mintzberg, 1975: 49)

Synthesising his results (Mintzberg, 1973) and the previous research on the role of managers, he concluded as follows:

- Although much managerial work is unprogrammed, all managers do have regular, ordinary duties to perform.
- Rather than being systematic, reflective thinkers and planners, managers simply respond to the pressures or demands of their jobs.
- Managerial activities are characterised by brevity, variety and discontinuity.

Some 30 years after Mintzberg's work, Yukl (2002), in reviewing the literature on management, came to similar conclusions:

- The content of managerial work is varied and fragmented.
- Many activities are reactive.
- Interactions often involve peers and outsiders.
- Many interactions involve oral communications.
- Decision processes are disorderly and political.
- Most planning is informal and adaptive.

Yukl (2002: 22) also found that the pace of managerial work was hectic and unrelenting:

During the typical workday there is seldom a break in the workload. Managers receive almost continuous requests for information, assistance, direction, and authorization from a large number of people, such as subordinates, peers, superiors, and people outside the organization.

Yukl's work confirms Mintzberg's (1973) finding that managers' jobs are remarkably similar, and that their work can be described in terms of ten very important roles that could be categorised under three headings: interpersonal, informational and decision-making.

Interpersonal roles

One of the most time-consuming and important aspects of most managerial jobs is to work with, direct and represent people. The three key roles in this respect are as follows:

- **figurehead** – as the formal representative of the organisation;
- **liaison** – forming connections with other organisations;
- **leader** – in relation to members of a group within the organisation.

Informational roles

Those in managerial positions have unique opportunities to obtain and disseminate information. The three key roles involved are given below:

- **monitor** – as monitors, managers seek, receive and store information that can be used to the advantage of the company;
- **disseminator** – the manager must broadcast this useful information to the organisation;
- **spokesperson** – on behalf of the organisation, the manager communicates information to other relevant groups and bodies, both internal and external.

Decision-making roles

One of the main parts of any manager's job is to take decisions. In this respect, there are four key roles involved:

- **entrepreneur** – looking for ways to improve the operation of the organisation or for new product or market opportunities;
- **disturbance-handler** – managers must handle crises effectively;
- **resource-allocator** – responsible for constructing budgets and allocating resources;
- **negotiator** – according to Mintzberg, managers spend a great deal of their time as negotiators, because only they have the necessary information and the authority to carry out this role.

As Yukl (2002) notes, though these roles are common to most managerial jobs, the emphasis and importance of these roles varies between managers depending on a range of factors such as organisation size, level of management, level of managerial independence, and the stage the organisation had reached in its life cycle. Mintzberg (1973) argued that the lack of uniformity within managerial jobs can be accounted for by hierarchical and functional differentiation. He contended that chief executives, for example, focus considerable attention on external roles, such as liaison, spokesperson and figurehead, which link the organisation to its environment. At lower levels, work is more focused, more short-term in outlook, and the characteristics of brevity and fragmentation are more pronounced. As a result of this, the external managerial roles are less important, and real-time internal roles (disturbance-handler and negotiator) concerned with daily operating problems and maintaining the workflow become relatively more important. Furthermore, he argued that interpersonal roles are more important to sales managers, that staff managers give more attention to informational roles, and production managers focus on decisional roles. Mintzberg's observations have been supported by a number of other studies (Kotter, 1982; Silverman and Jones, 1976).

Stewart (1976, 1982) drew particular attention to demands, constraints and choices in shaping managerial roles:

- **Demands** – these are the expectations that those in positions of power have for a role holder.
- **Constraints** – these are factors peculiar to the organisation and its environment that limit a manager's freedom of manoeuvre.
- **Choices** – though managers are limited in what they can do by the demands and constraints of their jobs, all managers have a degree of discretion (choice) in what to do and when to do it.

One key area where managers are called on to make choices is when faced with role conflicts. For example, managers are often caught between subordinates' expectations that managers will protect their interests and provide resources, and superiors' expectations that managers will act in the best interests of the organisation and minimise costs. Another example of conflict between roles is where managers are expected to spend considerable time, in their figurehead role, dealing with the external world whilst at the same time colleagues expect them to be present internally carrying out their leadership role.

Nevertheless, despite the presence of conflicts and choices, Hales (1986: 102), in reviewing the research on the manager's role, concluded that:

Much of what managers do is, of necessity, an unreflective response to circumstances. The manager is less a slow and methodical decision maker, more a 'doer' who has to react rapidly to problems as they arise, 'think on his feet', take decisions in situ and develop a preference for concrete activities. This shows in the pace of managerial work and the short time span of most activities . . .

Therefore, in examining the role of managers, there appears to be a discrepancy between what the literature says managers should do (as epitomised by Fayol) and what the managers actually do (as shown by Mintzberg). However, Lamond (2004: 353) takes a different view:

It is neither Fayol (1949) nor Mintzberg (1973) who captures 'management', but together they encapsulate in a pair of overlapping Venn diagrams some, but not all, of the concerns and behaviours of those charged with executing managerial functions in organizations, whether they are called 'managers' or not. Those with managerial responsibilities may prefer the sense of rationality and sense of purpose that infuses Fayol's (1949) characterisation, but they act in different ways, reflecting the day-to-day exigencies faced by Mintzberg's (1973) managers.

Lamond's argument is that the difference is not between Fayol's view of management and Mintzberg's view but between managers' preferred style of behaviour and their actual style of behaviour. He maintains that, in seeking to be effective, managers' behaviour is shaped by the day-to-day circumstances they face rather than how they would prefer to behave. Therefore, important as it is to understand the manager's role, it is just as important to understand what constitutes effectiveness.

Despite the very many books and articles on management and the role of the managers, most writers seem to shy away from defining either organisational or managerial effectiveness. Part 1 of this book reviewed organisation theory and behaviour.

What this showed is that the promoters of these theories, either implicitly or explicitly, state that effectiveness is defined by the extent to which managers adopt the theorists' 'one best way'. From this perspective, however, effectiveness is something of a moving target; the 'best way' for Frederick Taylor is not the best way for Douglas McGregor or Tom Peters or Peter Senge. Nahavandi (2000: 5) made a similar point when commenting that 'leadership effectiveness depends on the point of view of the person who is evaluating the leader'. In an attempt to cut through the idea that effectiveness is defined by adherence to a particular approach or theory, or lies solely in the eye of the beholder, Burnes (1998a: 101) defined effectiveness as 'the ability or power to have a desired effect'. In terms of managerial effectiveness, this means that an effective manager is one who achieves what is required of them, whether that be to transform an organisation or merely to ensure that services continue to be delivered on time, at the right cost and to the right quality. If this is the definition of managerial effectiveness, the next question is: 'What determines managerial effectiveness?' Are there key attributes, skills or competences that managers need to possess in order to 'have a desired effect'? As the next section will show, there are three main perspectives on what makes an effective manager.

Management and leadership

Regardless of the difficulty in identifying what managers do or how they should do it, there has been a long-held belief that the major factor which distinguishes successful organisations from their less successful counterparts is the presence of dynamic and effective leadership (Jones *et al*, 2000). However, as Yukl (2002: 5) observes, 'there is a continuing controversy about the difference between leadership and management'. Bennis and Nanus (1985: 21), for example, associate management and leadership with different types of people: 'managers are people who do things right and leaders are people who do the right thing'. In a similar vein, Nahavandi (2000) views management and leadership as being distinctly different activities (*see* Table 12.1).

Table 12.1 Management v leadership

Managers	Leaders
Focus on the present	Focus on the future
Maintain status quo and stability	Create change
Implement policies and procedures	Create a culture based on shared values
Remain aloof to maintain objectivity	Establish an emotional link with followers
Use the power of their position	Use personal power

Source: Adapted from Nahavandi (2000)

Nahavandi contends that the process of management is essentially concerned with achieving stability. On the other hand, he sees leadership as essentially being concerned with bringing about change. Nahavandi (2000: 13) comments that:

Whereas leaders have long-term and future-oriented perspectives and provide a vision for their followers that looks beyond their immediate surroundings, managers have short-term perspectives and focus on routine issues within their own immediate departments or groups.

Though it is conceptually appealing to separate people into one of two mutually exclusive types, managers or leaders, there is little empirical evidence for this view (Yukl, 2006). It is also a view that, in a rapidly changing world, tends to imply that visionary leaders are superior to their stick-in-the-mud managerial counterparts.

On the other hand, there are many writers who, whilst distinguishing between management processes and leadership processes (as in Table 12.1), do not assume that leaders and managers are different types of people (Bass, 1990; Hickman, 1990; Mintzberg, 1973; Rost, 1991; Yukl, 2002). Indeed, Vroom and Jago (1988) specifically argue that managers can and do possess both managerial and leadership skills, which they swap between depending on the situation.

Though the topic of leadership, its definition, promotion and difference from management, has dominated the management literature for over 50 years, it still remains an elusive concept. Even in the 1950s, when there had been much less research on the subject than now, Bennis (1959: 259) commented:

Always it seems that the concept of leadership eludes us or turns up in another form to taunt us again with its slipperiness and complexity. So we have invented a proliferation of terms to deal with it . . . and still the concept is not sufficiently defined.

Now, at the beginning of the third millennium, we are faced with a greater proliferation of articles and books on the subject than ever before, yet the topic appears more fragmented and confusing than ever whilst the recipes for success 'do not show much deviation from convention' (Barker, 2001: 481). As Thomas (2003: 25) comments in relation to the question 'What is management?':

The inquisitive reader seeking an answer to this question will find not only differences but complete contradictions and may well be inclined to beat a hasty retreat . . .

Thomas may have had Yukl and Van Fleet (1992: 149) in mind when he made the above statement, given their take on the issue of defining leadership:

Definitions are somewhat arbitrary, and controversies about the best way to define leadership usually cause confusion and animosity rather than providing new insights into the nature of the process. At this point in the development of the field, it is not necessary to resolve the controversy over the appropriate definition of leadership.

Whilst it may be difficult to define leadership, it is possible to divide researchers on leadership and management into three main groups:

- Those who primarily focus on the personal characteristics–traits of the leader.
- Those who concentrate on the leader–follower situation, especially the characteristics of the follower.

- Those who take a contextual approach by relating leadership and management styles to the overall organisation context and climate.

The personal characteristics–traits approach to effective leadership

The trait approach to leadership maintains that leaders are effective or ineffective owing to their personal characteristics. It is based on the assumption that some people are natural or born leaders who possess unique personal qualities (intelligence, age, experience) or personality traits (extroversion, dominance) not possessed by other people (Yukl, 2006). This is sometimes known as the 'great man' approach because its proponents tend to use historical figures such as Napoleon, Churchill, Roosevelt, Gandhi, Henry Ford, etc., to support their arguments. Consequently, regardless of the task or situation, if a person possesses the appropriate traits, it is argued that they will be a good or great leader and if they do not possess the appropriate personal attributes, then they will be unlikely to be a good leader.

Unfortunately, the numerous studies of leadership failed to reveal any consistent pattern of traits or characteristics related to leadership, and the theory has been effectively demolished (Arnold *et al*, 2005; Gibb, 1969; Grint, 2005; Stogdill, 1948, 1974; Yukl, 2006). Nevertheless, it does attempt to make a comeback from time to time. For example, Kirkpatrick and Locke (1991) identify six traits which they maintain characterise good leaders. These are as follows: drive, motivation, honesty and integrity, self-confidence, cognitive ability, and knowledge of business. However, not only is it difficult to differentiate these 'good leadership' traits from those that define an effective manager (Rost, 1993), but it is also the case that many great leaders, such as Roosevelt and Gandhi, do not appear to have possessed all of these traits (Barker, 2001).

In an effort to breathe new life into this approach, attempts were made to view leadership as a process, and the focus moved to examining the interaction between leaders and followers (i.e. subordinates), and how leaders influence individuals and groups to pursue the achievement of a given goal. This view, that leadership behaviour rather than attributes may more effectively predict leadership success, has been advanced in a variety of approaches. Fleishman (1953, 1969) identified two separate classes of behaviour as important in determining effective leadership:

1. **Consideration** – the quality of the interpersonal relationship between the leader and his or her subordinates, and in particular the degree to which a leader shows trust of subordinates, respect for their ideas and consideration for their feelings.
2. **Initiating structure** – the degree to which leaders define and structure their own and their subordinates' roles towards achieving set goals. It also covers the extent to which a leader directs group activities through planning, communication, information, scheduling, trying out new ideas, and praise and criticism.

Another related dimension of leadership behaviour that received much attention in the 1950s and 1960s was participation – whether the leader leans towards an autocratic or democratic style of management. As was noted in Chapters 2 and 8, both the Human Relations school and proponents of Planned change believed that, in the aftermath of the Second World War, participation and democracy would prove to be essential components of organisational effectiveness. It was not a coincidence that those studying leadership and those studying organisational change should develop similar views on participation and democracy. Much of the work on leadership at this time was influenced by a series of ground-breaking studies into leadership styles by Kurt Lewin, Ronald Lippitt and Ralph White (Marrow, 1969). These studied three styles of leadership – democratic, autocratic and laissez-faire, and found that democratic leadership produced the best results (Burnes, 2007; Lewin *et al*, 1939; Lewin, 1999b; Lippitt and White, 1960). According to Gastil (1994), there are three key elements of democratic leadership:

- maximising participation and involvement of group members;
- empowerment;
- facilitating group decision-making.

In the 1950s and 1960s, this emphasis on leadership characteristics gave rise to a number of 'universal theories' of effective leader behaviour – which is to say, researchers began to argue for a 'one best way' approach to leadership (*see* for example Argyris, 1964; Likert, 1967; McGregor, 1960). These theories postulated that the same style of leadership is optimal in all situations (Yukl, 1994).

Perhaps the best known and most influential of these 'universal theories' is Blake and Mouton's (1969, 1985) Managerial Grid – later re-named the Leadership Grid (Blake and McCanse, 1991). The Grid has two critical dimensions: *concern for people* – similar to *consideration*; and *concern for production* – similar to *initiating structure*. By examining how these two dimensions interact, in both their strong and weak states, Blake and Mouton identified five different styles of management, which they labelled as follows:

- **Team management.** This arises from a high concern for people and a high concern for production. The objectives are to achieve high levels of both performance and job satisfaction by gaining subordinates' willing commitment to achieving their assigned tasks.
- **Country club management.** This occurs when concern for production is low but concern for people is high. The main concern of this approach is to achieve the harmony and well-being of the group in question by satisfying people's social and relationship needs.
- **Middle-of-the-road management.** This situation comes about where there is moderate concern for production and moderate concern for people. Managers who follow this approach tend to have a 'live and let live' philosophy and tend to avoid difficult or contentious issues.
- **Task management.** This can be defined as a high concern for production but a low concern for people. The objective is to achieve high productivity by planning, organising and directing work in such a way that human considerations are kept to a minimum.
- **Impoverished management.** This ensues from a low concern for both production and people. This form of managerial behaviour centres on exacting the minimum effort from subordinates in order to achieve the required result.

Though Blake and Mouton (1985) identify these five styles of management, for them the most effective is team management, where leaders are both task- and people-orientated – the so-called 'high–high' leader (i.e. their aim is to ensure subordinates achieve high levels of performance and high levels of job satisfaction). They also argue that whilst managers have a dominant or preferred style of leadership, many managers are capable of switching from one style to another or of combining styles if they encounter a situation where their preferred style does not work. In a significant departure from other adherents of the personal characteristics approach, Blake and Mouton also argue that a person's dominant style is influenced not only by their personal values and personal history but by the nature of the organisation in which they are operating, and chance – the types of management situations and styles they have encountered in their career.

Despite the wide number of studies seeking to test and elaborate the Managerial Grid approach, however, the evidence in support of it, or for any of the universal theories, is limited (Evans, 1970; Filley *et al*, 1976; Larson *et al*, 1976; Wagner, 1994; Yukl, 2006). Because of the difficulty of relating leadership traits and behaviours to effectiveness, many writers turned to investigate the characteristics of subordinates (followers) and how these interacted with the characteristics of leaders.

The leader–follower situation approach to effective leadership

In response to the inability of researchers to make a convincing case for a 'one best way' approach to leadership, attention began to focus on identifying the situations in which leaders were effective. In particular, researchers began to examine subordinates' behaviour and how a leader's behaviour varies from subordinate to subordinate. This leader–follower approach, or leader–member exchange as it is sometimes called, is concerned with how the two parties develop an interpersonal relationship over time. It focuses on how the leader and the follower influence each other and negotiate the subordinate's role in the organisation. The basic premise of the theory is that a leader develops a different relationship with each subordinate and that this will be based on the behaviour (or expected behaviour) of each party. These relationships take one of two forms: the leader will develop a close and trusting relationship with a small number of people, and a much more distant and formal relationship with the rest. In the first type of relationship, both parties have high expectations of each other. The leader expects loyalty and commitment and the follower expects preferment and advancement. In the more distant types of relationship, both parties have relatively low expectations. The leader expects the subordinate to comply with rules and perform their allocated duties. In turn, the subordinate expects to receive the rate for the job and be treated fairly (Graen and Cashman, 1975; Yukl, 2006).

In examining leader–follower relations, Kerr *et al* (1974) took the two forms of leadership behaviour identified by Fleishman (1969) – consideration and initiating structure – and applied these to a framework that included three situational variables or contingencies:

1. **Subordinate considerations** – such as the subordinates' experience and abilities, and their expectations of the leader.
2. **Superior considerations** – in particular, the amount of influence subordinates have over the behaviour of their superiors.
3. **Task considerations** – including factors such as time urgency, amount of physical danger, permissible error rate, presence of external stress, degree of autonomy and scope, importance and meaningfulness of work, and degree of ambiguity.

Kerr *et al* (1974) argued that the effectiveness of the two forms of leadership beha-viour (consideration and initiating structure) in promoting high levels of performance from subordinates is moderated by the above three situational variables. For example, if the task to be performed is characterised by time pressure, subordinates will be more amenable to a higher level of initiating structure (i.e. direction by superiors) and there will be a stronger relationship between job satisfaction, performance and initiating struc-ture. Alternatively, when a task is seen as intrinsically very satisfying to a subordinate, a leadership style with high consideration will not significantly increase satisfaction or performance. Support for the central premises of Kerr *et al*'s (1974) model has been limited. Research by Schriesheim and Murphy (1976) produced mixed results. There was evidence that high levels of initiating structure did increase performance in high-pressure situations and reduce it under low levels of pressure. Different levels of pressure, however, did not appear to impact on subordinates' satisfaction with their superiors. Nor, where tasks were viewed as having higher clarity, were either consideration-based or initiating-structure-based styles significantly related to satisfaction.

The most influential situational theory of leadership has been Fiedler's (1967) Least Preferred Co-worker (LPC) model. Based on a decade of research, Fiedler argued that leaders have relatively stable personal characteristics that, in turn, leave them with a particular set of leadership behaviours which they cannot change. Therefore, there is no point in trying to train or educate managers to adopt different behaviours towards their subordinates. Instead, both they and their subordinates have to learn to live with the leader's behaviour. For Fiedler, the key personal characteristics involved in leadership concern how positively or not the leader views his or her Least Preferred Co-worker. Fiedler developed a questionnaire to determine a leader's LPC measure. The questionnaire is built around a scale of 16 bipolar adjectives (e.g. pleasant–unpleasant, distant–close, efficient–inefficient) that attempts to measure whether a person is 'task'- or 'relationship'-orientated. As Arnold *et al* (2005) note, there is some dispute about exactly what a leader's LPC score means and how it relates to other leadership dimensions such as consideration and structure. In general, leaders with a high LPC are often seen as being people- or relationship-orientated, whilst those with a low LPC are seen as being task-orientated. From his work, Fiedler concluded that the effectiveness of particular leadership traits or behaviours, as measured by a high or low LPC score, are moderated by the situation in which they are deployed. Therefore, it is important to match the leader to the situation (Fiedler and Chemers, 1984). Fiedler identified three key aspects of a work situation, which taken together, he argued, deter-mined the effectiveness or not of particular leadership characteristics. In descending order of importance, these are as follows:

1. **The leader–follower relationship** – friendliness and loyalty from subordinates increases the leader's influence over them.
2. **Task structure** – the greater the degree of standardisation, detailed instructions and objective measures of performance, the more favourable the situation for the leader.
3. **The leader's formal position and power** – the more discretion and authority the leader has regarding the reward and punishment of subordinates, the more influence he or she will be able to exert.

By attributing a high or low score to each of these three aspects, Fielder constructed eight (i.e. $2 \times 2 \times 2$) types of work situation. He maintained that the most favourable situation is where leader–follower relations are good, the task is well-defined and highly structured, and the leader has a high level of formal authority. In contrast, the least favourable situation is where leader–follower relations are poor, the task structure is ill-defined, and the leader has only a low level of formal authority.

Although (or perhaps because) it is the most influential and widely utilised situational theory of leadership, it is also the most widely criticised. The main criticisms are that it lacks empirical support, that it fails to explain how particular leadership behaviour affects subordinates' performance, and that the measures used by Fiedler are arbitrary and lack any explicit rationale (Ashour, 1973; Shiflett, 1973; Vecchio, 1983). Fiedler's model has also been subjected to the same type of criticism as other contingency–situational approaches (*see* Chapter 2). In particular, critics maintain that it ignores a manager's ability to change or influence factors such as task structure to favour their style of leadership. In this respect, a number of writers have pointed out that Fiedler treats structure, an important component of his model, as a given, whereas in many instances, determining and changing organisation and job structures is a major component of a manager's role (O'Brien and Kabanoff, 1981). In response to these criticisms, Fiedler (1995) moved away from LPC to develope cognitive resource theory (CRT) which examines how the cognitive resources of leaders and subordinates affect group performance. This approach has also attracted criticism (Arnold *et al*, 2005). In any case, as the following shows, there are those who believe that managers, rather than having fixed behaviours, can and do change their leadership behaviours to accommodate changing circumstances (Vroom and Jago, 1988).

The contextual approach to effective leadership

One of the weaknesses of the leadership literature, as was demonstrated above, is that it tends to concentrate on the traits of individual managers and their followers and the relation between the two groups. The assumption, both explicit and implicit, is that effectiveness is an attribute of the individual manager, moderated by the leader–subordinate situation; a good manager in one organisation will be a good manager in all organisations. Yet, as many writers have observed, a manager's effectiveness may be determined as much by the nature of the organisation in which he or she operates as by the qualities of the individual manager (*see* Arnold *et al*, 2005; Burnes, 1991; Griffin, 2002; Hales, 1986; Nahavandi, 2000; Sjöstrand, 1997; Yukl, 2006).

It is out of and in response to such observations that the contextual approach to leadership developed. This approach is a variant of the leader–follower approach to leadership; however, instead of concentrating on leadership behaviour, it focuses on leadership style, and instead of the narrow leader–follower situation, it focuses on the overall organisation context and climate. In addition, it is the only one of the three approaches to leadership that incorporates change as a variable.

One of the most influential contingency approaches to leadership was developed by Vroom and Yetton (1973) and later extended by Vroom and Jago (1988). In contrast to Fiedler, this approach suggests that leaders can and do change their behaviour from situation to situation. The theory identifies five styles of leader decision-making, ranging from the most autocratic to the most democratic. To complement these, Vroom and Jago (1988) also identified some key features of problem situations that leaders have to take into account, such as the need to resolve conflict or achieve goal congruence. By combining leadership styles with problem situations, Vroom and Jago developed a computer package to help managers to identify how suitable or not their style is for particular situations. Unfortunately, the package proved to be of limited value as it was very complex to use. Nevertheless, Vroom and Jago have expressed the hope that knowledge of its general principles may be sufficient for most situations. To this end, as Arnold *et al* (2005) note, Vroom and Jago's model has been used to provide some general 'rules of thumb' for leaders, including advice such as:

- Where subordinates' commitment is important, a more participative style of leadership is better.
- Where subordinates do not share the organisation's goals, group decision-making should be avoided.

However, advice couched in such broad terms is usually too general to be of much use. Even if they were not so general, these rules of thumb are still subject to being overridden by factors such as time constraints, organisational policies and the ability and preferences of managers and subordinates. This is perhaps why other contextual approaches have also been put forward.

One of the most interesting and influential of these was developed not by a social scientist but by a political scientist, James MacGregor Burns, in his 1978 Pulitzer Prize-winning book, *Leadership*. Burns's book combines biography, history and political theory to produce a major study of the nature of leadership. Primarily, he identifies two basic organisation states or contexts, convergent and divergent; and two matching management–leadership styles, transactional management and transformational leadership (*see* Figure 12.1). Most writers tend to use the terms management and leadership interchangeably. Burns was the first to draw a distinction between what he called transactional management (which focuses on maintaining the status quo) and transformational leadership (which focuses on overthrowing the status quo). However, Burns was primarily concerned with management and leadership in the political context. Bass (1985, 1995) refined Burns's concepts and applied them to organisations.

A *convergent* state occurs when an organisation is operating under stable conditions; where there are established and accepted goals and a predictable external and internal

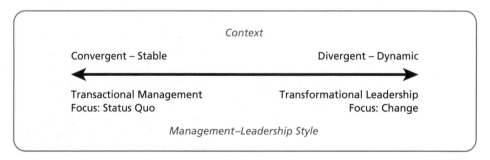

Figure 12.1 Burns's contextual approach to leadership

environment. The most appropriate style of management in such a situation, it is contended, is *transactional*. The concept of transactional management stems from the notion that the manager–subordinate relationship is based on a transaction between the two, whereby managers exchange rewards for subordinates' performance. Transactional managers focus on task completion, goal clarification and optimising the performance of the organisation through incremental changes within the confines of existing policy, structures and practices – basically, they seek to work within and maintain the status quo (*see* Table 12.2). Transactional managers motivate followers to perform the tasks expected of them by appealing to their self-interest through the use of incentives and rewards such as pay and promotion.

Table 12.2 Management v leadership

	Transactional management	Transformational leadership
Creating the agenda	Planning and budgeting: developing a detailed plan of how to achieve the results.	Establishing direction: developing a vision that describes a future state along with a strategy for getting there.
People	Organising and staffing: which individual best fits each job and what part of the plan fits each individual.	Aligning people: a major communication challenge in getting people to understand and believe the vision.
Execution	Controlling and problem-solving: monitoring results, identifying deviations from the plan and solving the problems.	Motivating and inspiring: satisfying basic human needs for achievement, belonging, recognition, self-esteem, a sense of control.
Outcomes	Produces a degree of predictability and order.	Produces changes – often to a dramatic degree.

Source: Adapted from Kotter (1990)

A *divergent* state occurs when environmental changes challenge the efficiency and appropriateness of an organisation's established goals, structures and ways of working. The Oticon case study – Chapter 10 – is an example of an organisation operating in a divergent state. The most appropriate style of leadership in this situation, it is argued, is *transformational*. Transformational leaders are often portrayed as charismatic or visionary individuals who seek to overturn the status quo and bring about radical change (*see* Table 12.2). Transformational leaders use the force of their personality to motivate followers to identify with the leader's vision and to sacrifice their self-interest in favour of that of the group or organisation. Transformational leaders seek to gain the trust and emotional commitment of their followers by appealing to higher moral and ethical values.

The compatibility between organisational state and leadership style is seen as essential for successful leadership. Where the organisation is required to face new challenges and develop new ways of adapting to these for the sake of survival, then a purely transactional approach would be counter-productive – the phrase 'fiddling while Rome burns' springs to mind. However, transformational leadership is just as likely to be counter-productive during periods where maintenance of the current operational systems would be most appropriate.

Since its publication in 1978, Burns's work has been taken up and cited by a wide range of organisation theorists who subscribe to the view that managers need to, and can, match or adapt their style and approach to the circumstances of the organisation in which they operate (Arnold *et al*, 2005; Bass, 1985, 1995; Beatty and Lee, 1992; Burnes and James, 1995; French and Bell, 1995; Gibbons, 1992; Yukl, 2006). However, the late 1970s and early 1980s, the period when Burns's book was published, were a time of crisis for many Western organisations. It was a period when organisations and entire industries and sectors were going through massive changes. Not surprisingly, therefore, there was a tendency for those in the leadership field to focus on transformational leadership, and downplay or even denigrate transactional management (Yukl, 2002). Bass (1985, 1995), whilst seeking to develop the concept of the transformational leader, nevertheless argued that transformational leadership and transactional management are distinct but not mutually exclusive processes. Transformational leaders may be more effective at motivating their followers but, Bass maintains, effective leaders need to have both transformational and transactional tools in their armouries.

All the same, in situations where radical change is required, as Alimo-Metcalfe and Alban-Metcalfe (2000: 27) found when studying leadership in the UK National Health Service (NHS), 'the transactional competencies of managers, while crucial, are simply not sufficient on their own'. The argument from Bass (1985, 1995) and Alimo-Metcalfe and Alban-Metcalfe (2000) is that someone with purely transactional skills would struggle to deal effectively with the many changes that are an ever-present part of organisational life. On the other hand, someone with purely transformational skills would not be able to cope with the day-to-day, routine activities that need to be accomplished even where radical change is taking place. The key issue, therefore, is to identify the optimum balance of transactional–transformational skills in any given circumstances.

Kanter (1989) offers a different perspective on the balance issue by maintaining that good leaders need to incorporate both transactional and transformational characteristics. She argues that archetypal images of managers tend to derive from two basic models: the 'corpocrat' (i.e. the transactional manager) and the 'cowboy' (i.e. the transformational leader). The former is the corporate bureaucrat, the conservative resource-preserver who lives by, and controls the organisation through, established and detailed rules. The latter, the 'cowboy', is a maverick who challenges the established order, who wants to seize every opportunity and question every rule, and who motivates and controls through personal loyalty. However, instead of seeking to relate the balance of these two sets of characteristics to their appropriate organisational setting, Kanter (1989: 361) argues that modern organisations require managers who combine the best of both corpocrat and cowboy:

Without the bold impulses of the take-action entrepreneurs and their constant questioning of the rules, we would miss one of the most potent sources of business revitalization and development. But without the discipline and coordination of conventional management, we could find waste instead of growth, unnecessary risk instead of revitalization. . . . Our new heroic model [of leadership] should be the athlete who can manage the amazing feat of doing more with less, who can juggle the need to both conserve resources and pursue growth opportunities. This new kind of business hero avoids the excesses of both the corpocrat and the cowboy. . . . the business athlete has the strength to balance somewhere in the middle, taking the best of the corpocrat's discipline and the cowboy's entrepreneurial zeal.

Ideas and perspectives 12.5
Kanter's characteristics of the business hero

Skills and sensibilities of the business athlete

1. Learn to operate without the might of the hierarchy.
2. Compete in a way that enhances rather than undercuts cooperation.
3. Operate with the highest ethical standards.
4. Have a dose of humility.
5. Develop a process focus.
6. Be multifaceted and ambidextrous.
7. Gain satisfaction from results.

Source: Kanter 1989: 361–4.

As Ideas and perspectives 12.5 shows, Kanter maintains that there are seven skills and sensibilities that this 'new heroic' type of leader needs to possess. Kanter's model avoids the issue of how to determine the optimum balance of transactional and transformational skills in a given set of circumstances. Instead, she argues that there is a basic set of transactional and transformational skills or characteristics that all effective leaders need to possess and which can be applied successfully in any situation. In effect, she is attempting to return to the trait approach to leadership, arguing that good leaders are those who possess the requisite set of skills and sensibilities.

Kanter's argument, as mentioned in Chapter 3, is basically that all organisations operate in the same turbulent context, face the same challenges and, consequently, require the same style of leadership. Whilst not necessarily challenging her description of the skills required of transformational leaders, most proponents of the contextual school tend to take the view that there are a wider range of organisational contexts than acknowledged by Kanter and, therefore, manager–leaders need to be able to change their approach from transactional to transformational and vice versa as the situation dictates (Hitt *et al*, 2009: 268). However, this still leaves the issue of managerial choice – the degree to which managers and leaders have to adapt their approach to the context, as opposed to the degree to which they can influence the context to bring it into line with their preferred way of working. It has been argued in previous chapters that managers do have the ability to adapt the organisational context to make it more amenable to the way they wish to run their organisations. In terms of leadership, Grint (2005: 1467) argues that 'decision-makers are much more active in the constitution of the context than conventional contingency theories allow'.

Taking a social-constructionist view (*see* Chapter 4), Grint (2005) argues:

Leadership theories that eschew the dominant and proactive role of the individual leader in favour of more social or structural accounts tend to assume that the context or situation should determine how leaders respond . . . However, I suggest that this is a naïve assumption because it underestimates the extent to which the context or situation is actively constructed by the leader, leaders, and/or decision-makers. In effect, leadership involves the social construction of the context that both legitimates a particular form of action and constitutes the world in the process. (pp. 1470–1)

Hence, CEOs should not be assessed against their ability to 'read' the environment but rather their ability to render that environment suitable for their intended strategies. (pp. 1491–2)

Grint's criticism of the contextual approach to leadership does not invalidate the view that particular situations require a particular set of leadership skills. His argument is that managers have the ability to choose whether to adapt their skills and behaviours to the situation or adapt the situation to their preferred skills and behaviours.

Though there are different perspectives on the contextual approach to leadership, taken as a whole, the approach does not seek to invalidate either the characteristics or situational approaches; rather it tries to incorporate them within and link them to the wider organisational context. It explicitly recognises that a manager's personal characteristics are an important component of leadership style, and consequently, effectiveness. In addition, it acknowledges the crucial importance not just of the relationship between leaders and followers, but also of the overall context within which this takes place (Yukl, 2006). In particular, as Gibbons (1992: 5) remarked, 'organizational survival and success are dependent on the ability of leader–follower relations to resolve the problems of internal integration and external adaptation'. Many writers argue, however, that (despite its attractiveness) there is little evidence to support the case for the contextual approach to leadership or to show that is a more suitable approach to running organisations than either the personal characteristics or leader–follower models (Arnold *et al*, 2005; Hinkin and Tracey, 1999; Yukl, 2006).

Leadership research – a note of caution

Just as a review of the role of managers produced a confusing and conflicting picture, so too does an examination of the three approaches to leadership. Nevertheless, the idea of considering context and style together does fit in, partly at least, with the argument developed in the previous parts of this book: namely that there is a need to match the approach to change to the context of the organisation. That argument was developed further to include the possibility that managers could reverse this process and match the organisation's context to their preferred style of working. However, one major factor needs to be remembered when considering approaches to management: most of the research and writing on leadership is set in Western, and particularly American, organisations, and addresses their concerns from their cultural perspective (Alimo-Metcalfe and Alban-Metcalfe, 2000; Barker, 2001). Also, the majority of research studies have tended to focus on male managers and their characteristics (Maddock, 1999; Thomas, 2003). Therefore, before moving on, we need to return to the issue of diversity raised earlier when discussing globalisation.

To recap, Jones *et al* (2000: 166–7) explain that:

Diversity is dissimilarities – differences – among people due to age, gender, race, ethnicity, religion, sexual orientation, socioeconomic background, and capabilities/ disabilities . . .

Diversity is not just about differences within groups of people but also between groups of people, however, it is also about differences between people. According to Ricks (1999: 4):

Cultural differences are the most significant and troublesome variables encountered by the multinational company.

In terms of differences between people, the posited differences in managerial style between men and women have attracted a great deal of attention (Loden, 1986; Macdonald *et al*, 1999; Maddock, 1999; Mullins, 2002; Thomas, 2003). Davies (1995), for example, found significant differences between masculine and feminine approaches to management. In particular, she found that the masculine approach valued self-esteem, abstract thinking, control and loyalty to superiors. The feminine approach, on the other hand, valued selflessness, contextual thinking, experience and accommodation. It is findings like these that have led writers such as Alimo-Metcalfe (1995a, 1995b) to argue that women prefer to use a more transformational style of leadership whilst men tend to be more transactionally orientated. Furthermore, differences in management style are not just gender-related; they can also arise due to age, ethnicity, religion or simple differences in personality (Deresky, 2000; Jones *et al*, 2000).

To complicate the picture, these preferences are not stable between countries and cultures. Much of the work on gender and management has tended to focus on the USA and Europe. It is not clear, however, that men and women managers in, for example, Japan and China have the same style preferences as their Western counterparts. Indeed, as Trompenaars' (1993) ten-year study of management in 28 countries covering 47 national cultures showed, the differences between countries are as great as the differences within. His work showed, for example, that managers as a whole, male and female, in Japan and China tended to fit the characteristics attributed to women managers in the West. For example, they favoured relationships as against rules, they promoted interpersonal trust as against contracts, and they tended to avoid rather than welcome confrontation. This, of course, confirms Hofstede's (1980, 1990) earlier work on cultural differences, which showed that organisational culture, and the values and behaviours of managers, do vary from country to country. Arnold *et al* (1998) maintain that there is also sufficient evidence to show that leader behaviour is interpreted differently in different cultures. Consequently, managerial behaviour that might be considered supportive in one society may be seen as threatening in another. Therefore, we have to be very wary of taking work on managerial styles and behaviour developed in one setting, and assuming it applies to all organisations and all societies.

The implications of these findings for management and leadership are significant.

Firstly, there are no universal rules as to what is an effective manager or leader. An effective manager in one country, company or situation may be less so in others.

Secondly, therefore, effectiveness is situation-dependent. In judging what is or is not an effective approach, managers and leaders need to take into account the nature of the organisation and the diversity of its workforce.

Lastly, in training and developing managers, there is a need to recognise that whilst there are some essential generic skills, competences and behaviours, there will also be a need to tailor development programmes to the person and their situation. The issue of management development will be examined next.

Management development

Learning and flexibility

The literature on management and leadership gives support for the notion that different situations require different approaches to change. They also show that managers are, sometimes at least, able to change their style of management or leadership, and even exhibit different styles to different parts of their organisations at the same time. This is consistent with the arguments in Chapter 11 that managers can and do adopt both the Planned and Emergent approaches to change management either alternatively or simultaneously as the situation requires. In addition, as Grint (2005) and others argue, managers can choose to change, or redefine, the context in which their organisations operate to suit their preferred or existing approach to both management and change (see for example the Nissan and Volvo case studies in Chapters 1 and 2). As argued in Chapters 10 and 11, changing the situational context can be very important; yet in terms of leadership roles and managerial expectations, one of the main findings from the contextual perspective is the need for managers not only to adapt their style to the particular situation, but also to adopt transactional and transformational approaches at the same time (Alimo-Metcalfe and Alban-Metcalfe, 2000; Bass, 1985, 1995).

In part at least, the argument that there are managers who can change their style of leadership runs counter to some of the literature on managerial learning discussed in Chapter 9. D Miller (1993: 119) argued that as they gain experience, managers 'form quite definite opinions of what works and why'. Miller (1994) maintained that this was particularly the case with managers in successful organisations who were highly resistant to changing a 'winning formula'. This view was supported by earlier work from Nystrom and Starbuck (1984), who maintained that managers interpret the world through their own perceptions and expectations, which are built up over time. Yet, as the Oticon case study illustrated (*see* Chapter 10), some managers do seem capable under certain conditions – especially when faced with a crisis – of restructuring their mental models of how the world is and how they should respond. In Chapter 10, the concepts of Cognitive Dissonance, Depth of Intervention and the Psychological Contract were used to explain why it was that people could, in crisis situations, change deeply held attitudes very quickly. This 'crisis mode' only partly helps to explain, however, how some managers, when faced with change situations, appear capable of switching from a transactional approach to a transformational one as the circumstances demand or, indeed, become capable of adopting both at the same time.

The work of Mintzberg (1976) offers some clues as to how managers might accomplish this mental juggling act. In studying brain functions and successful managers, he concluded that effective and proficient managers are 'whole thinkers' – they use both the left and the right hemispheres of their brain. That is, they can combine a rational–analytical approach to management with creativity and lateral thinking. Mintzberg argued, however, that, in general, Western managers tend to think on the left side of their brain – they tend to adopt a rational–analytical approach. Interestingly, this is compatible not only with a transactional approach to management, but also with a rational–planned approach to strategy and the directive approach to change.

In contrast, Nonaka (1991) argued that one of the great strengths of Japanese companies is their belief that creating new knowledge depends more on tapping the tacit and often subjective insights and intuitions of all their employees, whether managers or not. He maintains that traditional Western management, on the other hand, sees organisations as information processing machines with the only useful knowledge being formal, scientific, quantifiable and rational. He contends that such a perspective limits the creation of new knowledge which, in turn, makes it difficult for organisations to respond to changing and new situations. Nonaka argues that new knowledge always begins with the individual. One of the main foundations of the success of Japanese companies is, he states, managers' ability to gather and combine the insights and intuitions of individual employees and use them for the benefit of the entire organisation. The tendency of Japanese managers to use softer, more creative approaches and to involve staff in decision-making was also noted in Chapters 3, 6 and 7 when discussing approaches to management and strategy.

The success of many Western firms, particularly those concerned with creative processes (such as software development) and the performing arts (such as film-making), show that it is not inevitable that Western managers should operate solely in a rational–analytical mode. Even so, as Hofstede's (1980, 1990) and Trompenaars' (1993) work on national cultures reveals, there is a predisposition in Western societies towards more rational–analytical ways of working, whereas in Japan and China managers tend to use more subjective decision-making processes. Also, as D Miller (1993, 1994) points out, a manager's view of the world and what works is shaped by his or her previous work experience. If this has been in organisations that have operated on traditional Western principles, which are structured in a Classical way and give credence primarily to formal and scientific knowledge, then they undoubtedly will tend to operate on the left side of the brain. This does not mean that such managers cannot develop or access the right side of their brain, but it does mean it is unlikely to come about accidentally or without strong encouragement from the organisations in which they work. To this end, many organisations are seeking to construct management development programmes designed to broaden the outlook and develop the creative, inductive and questioning side of their managers' personalities (Harrison, 2005). However, this is unlikely to be achieved through traditional management development programmes, which offer standard packages delivered in classroom situations, because of their low success rate (Burnes, 2003; Lessem, 1998; Mullins, 2002; Mumford et al, 2000). If management development programmes are to be effective, in future, as Harrison (2005) contends on behalf of the UK's Chartered

Institute of Personnel and Development (CIPD), they will have to be tailored to both the needs of the individual manager and the strategic objectives of their organisation.

In respect of developing managers' creativity, Kirton's (1989) Adaptation–Innovation theory, and subsequent work by Talbot (1993, 1997), provide useful insights. Kirton maintains that not only do people exhibit different degrees of creativity, but that they also express their creativity in different ways, along a spectrum which runs from *adaptors* to *innovators*. Those who tend towards the adaptor end of the spectrum prefer to work within the existing system to improve things. Adaptors are efficient, tend to conform to existing norms and like to deal with only a few ideas at a time. Innovators tend to ignore or challenge the system and to come up with radical proposals for change. Figure 12.2 shows how Kirton's ideas relate to transactional management and transformational leadership. As can be seen, it follows from Kirton's work that transactional managers will tend to need lower levels of creativity because they are dealing with changes at the group level, whereas transformational leaders need higher levels of creativity because they are involved in transformational activities at the organisation level.

However, as Figure 12.2 also shows, even within the transformational dimension of leadership, there will be situations which require a more adaptive approach, such as structural rather than cultural change. Similarly, transactional managers may be faced with situations where more innovative than adaptive solutions are required, such as when dealing with behavioural issues as opposed to technical ones. Regardless of their levels of creativity, some managers may find it easier than others to switch between innovative and adaptive behaviour. There may also be many managers who can exhibit varying levels of creativity as the situation demands. This may be the reason why some people, as demonstrated by our case studies and the leadership literature, can change their style of leadership or even adopt different styles at the same time. The story does not end there. Talbot (1997) demonstrated that, regardless of the level of creativity a person possesses or where they are located on the adaptor–innovator spectrum, there are proven tools and techniques for increasing their level of creativity and flexibility. By so doing, transactional managers may find it easier to operate in a more transformational and innovative mode, or move between both as circumstances necessitate. Talbot (1993) also points out, though, that such tools and techniques can only overcome barriers to

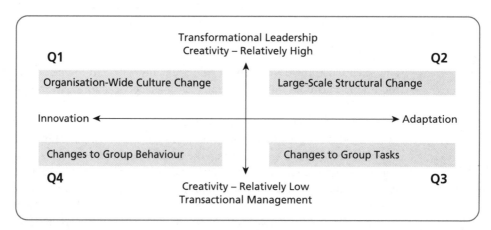

Figure 12.2 Leadership, management and change

creativity that lie within the individual. Other barriers, he argues, such as the attitudes and behaviours of superiors and colleagues, and the way the organisation operates, can also block individual creativity. Therefore, in management development, as with so many other aspects of organisational life, we cannot consider the individual in isolation from the rest of the organisation.

The management development process

Under different names, management training and education have been around since the Industrial Revolution. In the nineteenth century, they tended to be geared towards giving managers specific skill, such as engineering or production control, through either on-the-job training or self-help societies. In the twentieth century, more and more, employers took on the job of specifying and providing formal management training, but it still tended to be geared towards giving managers specific skills. Over the last 30 years or so, there has been a significant change in emphasis. Management development programmes are increasingly seeking to change managerial behaviour, especially to promote leadership and creativity, and to align managers' behaviour with the longer-term strategic objectives of their organisations and with society's wider social and ethical considerations (Harrison, 2005). Though management development is big business in all advanced countries, there is no universally agreed definition of what it is. The following quotations give a flavour of the range of definitions on offer:

> . . . a conscious and systematic decision-action process to control the development of managerial resources in the organisation for the achievement of organisational goals and strategies. (Ashton *et al*, 1975: 5)

> . . . that function which from deep understanding of business goals and organisational requirements, undertakes: (a) to forecast needs, skill mixes and profiles for many positions and levels; (b) to design and recommend the professional, career and personal development programmes necessary to ensure competence; (c) to move from the concept of 'management' to the concept of 'managing'. (Beckhard, 1985: 22)

> . . . an attempt to improve managerial effectiveness through a planned and deliberate learning process. (Quoted in Mumford, 1987: 29)

> *Management development is concerned not only with improving the effectiveness of individual managers but also with an improvement in management performance as a whole and organisational effectiveness.* Mullins (2002: 845)

In an age where organisations are often required to change rapidly and radically, management education and development are taken seriously in most advanced countries and entry into a managerial job often requires formal, university-level qualifications (Arnold *et al*, 2005; Jones *et al*, 2000; Lippitt, 1982; Marsh, 1986; Morgan, 1988; Mullins, 2002; Pearson, 1987; Storey, 1989). The nature of management development varies between countries, however (Keuning, 1998). In Japan, for example, it tends to be a very competitive process which begins by recruiting elite cohorts who have usually studied law or engineering at a top university. In Germany, there is a greater emphasis on a formal apprenticeship system which develops managers through a career path that often involves the attainment of higher degrees. France, like Japan, tends to be very elitist and managers are expected to have studied for a degree in business or law at one of the Grandes Ecoles (R Harrison, 2002).

In the UK, management education tends to be more *ad hoc* and less well-regarded, even in large organisations. UK companies also spend a much lower percentage of their turnover promoting education and training than their counterparts in France, Germany, Japan and the USA (R Harrison, 2002; Keuning, 1998). This is probably why a number of studies revealed in the 1980s that the UK was particularly poor at providing the type of formal and structured education necessary for nurturing managerial creativity (Constable and McCormick, 1987). Partly in response to these findings, the 1980s and 1990s saw a growing interest in management development by government and organisations (OECD, 1996; Sissons and Storey, 1988; Storey, 1989, 1990; Worrall and Cooper, 1997, 1998). However, a 1997 survey of 258 chief executives carried out for the *Sunday Times* found that UK managers did not have the skills to obtain the full potential from their businesses (Hannagan, 2002). Likewise, the government has seen poor management as the reason why UK productivity lags behind that of the US by 42 per cent, France by 14 per cent and Germany by 7 per cent (Paton, 2003). This continuing lack of management skills appears to be the main reason why the UK government has abandoned most of the management training and development schemes its predecessors launched in the 1980s and 1990s, such as the Management Charter Initiative, and in 2002 established a new body, the Council for Excellence in Management and Leadership. Certainly, the Council itself has concluded that most management and business leadership programmes are 'dysfunctional' and that the lack of appropriate leadership skills is detrimental to the UK's economic performance (Paton, 2003).

Regardless of the encouragement (or not) of governments, it is individual organisations that initiate such programmes. Given that organisations are different and face different challenges, if management development programmes are to be successful in producing effective managers and improving the performance of organisations, then it is self-evident not only that they will vary from company to company, but also that they will need to vary from individual to individual. R Harrison (2002: 348) claims that, despite the differences between organisations, an effective management development process (MDP) has six basic features:

- a clear MDP mission, linked to the organisation's business strategy;
- specific programme objectives that relate to the external challenges that the organisation is facing;
- a focus on major internal organisational issues;
- programmes tailored to organisational and individual needs;
- the systematic assessment of management development needs, aims and outputs;
- a professional business-led approach to MDP.

Harrison's six basic features of an effective MDP represent a clear break with the standard management development programmes of the past that companies required all their managers to pursue, regardless of their individual needs, and which appear to have served them and their managers poorly (Arnold *et al*, 2005; Burnes, 2003; Mangham Working Party, 1987; Sissons, 1989; Storey, 1989; Thornberry, 1987; Yukl, 2002). The two main problems with such standard offerings is that, firstly, they tend to develop managers within an existing behaviour pattern and set of expectations. Therefore, traditional organisations will tend to continue to produce transactional managers, regardless of the presence or absence of formal training and education programmes. The second problem is that they fail to address the needs of individual managers. Whilst they might meet a manager's training requirements in terms of technical skills (such as accountancy or engineering), they rarely address how they could develop the attitudes and behaviours necessary to be an effective manager.

Though formal, classroom-based qualifications such as Management Diplomas and MBAs are still seen as having an important role in most management development programmes, they are now being balanced with more individual and experientially based approaches. These approaches include the use of assessment and assessment centres, coaching and mentoring, self-development and, increasingly, Action Learning. Though such approaches have been around for a long time, their potential contribution to management development has been ignored (Burgoyne and Germaine, 1984; Harrison, 2005; Long, 1986; Mullins, 2002; Newstrom, 1985; Pedler, 1996; Stuart, 1986; Wilkinson and Orth, 1986; Willbur, 1987). More recently, with a greater emphasis being placed on individual development, especially in terms of aligning behaviour with the needs of the organisation and society, these techniques are finding increasing favour.

Changing managerial behaviour

In terms of challenging and changing managerial attitudes and behaviours, the use of Action Learning is particularly interesting. It was developed in the 1940s in the UK by Reg Revans and is based on small groups of managers tackling a set problem or case study. As Pedler (1996: 9) states:

> *Action Learning is a method of problem solving and learning in groups to bring about change for individuals, teams and organisations. It works to build relationships which help any organisation improve existing operations and learn and innovate for the future.*

The aim is not only that managers learn how to approach problems together, but also that they learn about themselves and challenge the appropriateness of their own attitudes and behaviours. As Revans commented:

> *The central idea of this approach . . . is today that of the set, or small group of comrades in adversity, striving to learn with and from each other as they confess failures and expand on victories.* (Quoted in Crainer, 1996: 195)

Though Revans's ideas were out of fashion for many years, his emphasis on teamworking and the power of groups to solve their own problems, linked with the potential for self-reflection and development, is making it an increasingly popular approach (Mullins, 2002). Contemporary approaches to Action Learning tend to be based on Kolb's cycle of experiential learning (Experience–Understanding–Planning–Action) with sets or groups being guided by a facilitator who acts as a catalyst for ideas (Darwin *et al*, 2002). Also, as its name implies, Action Learning has strong similarities to and can be seen as a derivation of Lewin's Action Research (McLaughlin and Thorpe, 1993). Action Research is one of the four elements of Lewin's Planned approach to change (*see* Chapter 8). Like

Action Research, Action Learning places a heavy emphasis on self-reflection, behavioural change and learning. Whilst the latter tends to focus on developing the individual, however, Action Research focuses more on change at the group level. Nevertheless, Revans's statement that 'there is no learning without action and no (sober and deliberate) action without learning' (quoted in Pedler, 1996: 15) could have been written by Lewin.

Burnes (2003) links Action Learning with organisational change. He argues that change projects can double as Action Learning projects, and vice versa. Burnes maintains that there are clearly situations and times when organisational change and management development go hand-in-hand. These are not situations where it is either necessary or desirable for the objectives of one to become subservient to the other, or to be compromised by the needs of the other. Rather these are genuinely situations where the need to change an organisation and the need to develop managers are mutually supportive. Unfortunately, as Crainer (1998: 259) comments, though Action Learning is attracting much attention, its complexity makes it a 'daunting prospect'. Given that organisational change projects can, in themselves, be a 'daunting prospect', it is perhaps not surprising that many organisations choose not to link them to management development initiatives. Nevertheless, the benefits, Burnes argues, may be considerable.

As with all general developments, this move away from formal, off-the-job training programmes to more personalised and experiential, on-the-job programmes needs to be viewed critically. Storey (1989), in a major review of the management development literature, argued that drawing a distinction between on-the-job and off-the-job training may miss the main issue. This is the requirement to assess the development and training needs of individual managers accurately and to provide programmes that allow managers to develop a much more critical and intuitive approach to their situation. Argyris (1991) argues, however, that one of the main barriers to developing more critical and intuitive approaches is that, within the narrow confines of transactional behaviour, many managers do operate effectively, even though, looking at the wider picture, their organisation may be in trouble. This is akin to Peters and Waterman's (1982) concept of 'irrational rationality' – managers applying the 'right' solution even when the situation means that it is no longer appropriate. Argyris believes that managers need to experience failure or recognise the inappropriateness of their behaviour before they can begin questioning their assumptions and practices, and develop their ability to be critical and creative. Senge (1990) contends that the most important factor in developing such a questioning approach and achieving organisational success is the ability to comprehend in a critical way the overall organisational context. This takes us back to the point made by Talbot (1993, 1997), cited earlier, that it is insufficient to develop managers if the organisation as a whole – people, values and systems – does not also change, or perceive the need for change. The case studies of XYZ and Oticon (Chapters 3, 8 and 10) support this argument. It was the need for transformational change that forced or enabled managers in both companies to break out of their transactional mould and think critically and creatively about solutions to the problems their organisations faced.

Therefore, whilst management development has increasingly come to be seen as a process that must address the needs of the individual managers, it must not lose sight of the need to develop management as a whole in organisations. Nowhere is this more apparent than when we look at the areas discussed earlier in this chapter covering sustainability, diversity and ethics. These are areas where organisations have failed significantly in the past, whether it be in terms of environmental depredations, racial and sexual discrimination and stereotyping, or the recent sub-prime mortgage scandal. Organisations often put such transgressions down to the failure of an individual or group to follow the organisation's guidelines and policies. The regular occurrence of illegal and unethical practices in business, especially the sub-prime mortgage scandal, reveals that these are a failure of management as a group in organisations, however, rather than the failure of individual managers.

Though it is necessary for individual managers to address issues of sustainability, diversity and ethics as part of their personal development, by itself this is not sufficient. If organisations and those in them are to behave differently, it is also necessary that the management of an organisation as a whole should address these issues as part of its development. The question, of course, is how this can be done. If organisations are capable of systematically side-stepping the policies and guidelines that they have developed, how can a management development programme make them face up to the issues? One answer might be to utilise Action Learning, where managers 'learn with and from each other as they confess failures'. Yet Action Learning has a number of drawbacks, not least that its focus is on developing individual managers, albeit in a group setting (McGill and Beaty, 1995). It does not appear to be appropriate to situations where behavioural change and reflection need to take place at the group rather than the individual level. Nor does it appear suitable for situations where the issue is the effectiveness of management at the organisational level, rather than the individual level.

There is an approach that was specifically established to enable groups to address the appropriateness of their behaviour, especially in terms of discriminatory activity, and which also has a strong ethical basis. It is, of course, Planned change, as formulated by Kurt Lewin. Planned change was designed to enable groups, in this case management groups in an organisation, to understand the factors which make them act as they do, and to develop effective ways to change them and then 'freeze' or institutionalise those changes. As described in Chapter 8, Planned change has four elements: Field Theory, Group Dynamics, Action Research and the Three-Step approach to change. Lewin's critics maintain that Lewin's approach is not suitable for large-scale, rapid and coercive change situations, or situations where the focus is on structural rather than behavioural change. However, both Lewin's own work, and that of his successors, have shown that it is a highly effective process for achieving sustained behavioural changes in groups. It has been applied to a wide variety of situations, including the food habits of American housewives, teenage inter-racial gang warfare in American cities, conflict between Palestinians and Israelis, and management behaviour in organisations (Bargal and Bar, 1992; Burnes, 2004c, 2007; Cummings and Worley, 2001; Gold, 1999; Lewin, 1947a; Marrow, 1969). Lewin's approach to change was specifically developed to bring about changes in group behaviour, and it has had considerable success in achieving this in the years since his death (Day et al, 2002; French and Bell, 1995; Harvey and Brown, 2001; McNiff, 2000; Wheelan et al, 1990). Therefore, as an approach to tackling the failures of management as a group in an organisation, Planned change has a lot to recommend it. This does not undermine the case for other approaches which address the needs of managers as individuals, but does recognise that individual behaviour and effectiveness cannot be separated from group behaviour and effectiveness. Indeed, it may be one of the ironies of management development that, in order to equip managers to meet the challenges of the twenty-first century, it has to look back to the work of Kurt Lewin.

Summary

From the above examination of managerial learning, seven factors can be discerned as important in the ability of managers to operate effectively:

1. The manager's past experience, and whether this has reinforced their beliefs or, instead, led them to question their appropriateness.
2. The level of creativity of the manager. Does the manager have a preference for trans-actional management or transformational leadership, and to what degree can they move between the two?
3. His or her cognitive style: are they adaptors or innovators? Are they 'whole thinkers', or are they more left-hemisphere–rational thinkers or right-hemisphere–creative thinkers?
4. The manager's ability to perceive the whole picture. Can they see the organisation in its context? In particular, do they understand the choices available in terms of changing the organisation itself, its context, and their own approach to leadership, strategy and change?
5. The organisational context: is it amenable, or can it be made amenable, to a more critical, creative and ethical style of leadership?
6. The organisation's management team: does it have a commitment to promoting sus-tainability, diversity and ethical behaviour, and are the senior managers committed to ensuring that its statement and policies in these areas are implemented through the day-to-day actions of all its members?
7. The organisation's management development process: is it effective? Is it geared to developing individual managers and the management cadre of the organisation as a whole?

As far as the UK is concerned, as surveys by Worrall and Cooper (1997, 1998) found, the 1990s saw a considerable increase in the provision of education and training for managers. This was driven by a number of factors: individuals seeing the need to main-tain their employability; organisations recognising the importance to them of well-trained managers; and successive governments identifying the link between good management and the overall health of the UK economy. Even so, Worrall and Cooper also found that some 20 per cent of managers still receive no formal training for their role. Furthermore, they found that many managers question the appropriateness of the training they do receive and feel the quantity is insufficient; in addition, the increasing pressure of work, and their longer working hours, are reducing their ability to take advantage of and apply the training and education that is available.

Management, leadership and change

The literature on management and leadership goes back many hundreds of years. Indeed, if one takes the view of some writers that *The Art of Warfare* by Sun Tzu, which was written in China around 400 BC, is pertinent to managing today's organisations, then the study of management goes back thousands of years (Michaelson, 2001). As was shown in Chapter 1, however, to all intents and purposes the systematic study of management in Western cultures can be said to have begun with the work of Frederick Taylor at the beginning of the twentieth century. Since then, there have been more books and articles on management than anyone can possibly count. These have thrown up a plethora of theories, studies and terminology which, as Thomas (2003) comments, has probably caused more confusion than clarification. In this chapter, we have tried, as Weick (*see* Chapter 11) might put it, to make sense of the literature on management. This 'sensemaking' began with an examination of the challenges posed to management by globalisation, especially in terms of sustainability, diversity and ethics. This was followed by a review of the literature on the manager's role which drew attention to the three main theories on leadership, i.e. the personal characteristics approach, the leader–follower approach, and the contextual approach. Finally, we investigated the role played by, or that could be played by, management development in shaping the behaviour of managers and leaders at both the individual and group levels. This attempt to make sense of management and the literature on management has shown the following:

- The incredible variety and complexity of the role of people who hold the title 'manager'. The title is applied to people in a wide range of hierarchical levels and functional specialisms. These 'managers' are presented with a myriad of responsibilities and challenges, ranging from the mundane, but vital, everyday tasks required to ensure that organisations operate efficiently, to the rarer and far more spectacular need to transform and reinvent organisations.
- The wide range of factors that impinge on managerial effectiveness, including managers' own personalities, those of their followers, superiors and peers, and the wider organisational context and objectives in which they operate.
- The ability or potential of managers to increase their level of creativity and change their style of management from transactional to transformational, and back, as situations require.
- The recognition that management development has a key role to play not only in developing individual creativity but also in changing the ethical behaviour of management as a group in organisations.

What conclusions can we draw from this review for the relationship between management, leadership and change in organisations? The first is that there does seem to be some terminological agreement, as shown in Tables 12.1 and 12.2, as to the differences between management and leadership. Management is about the present, it is about maintaining the *status quo*, and it is about objectivity and aloofness. Leadership is about the future, it is about change and it is about values and emotions. However, whilst management and leadership may be different, this does not mean that managers and leaders are or should be different people. This chapter has argued that most management and leadership roles require a mixture of transactional and transformational skills. In an ideal world, managers would be able to adjust the balance of transactional and transformational skills they deploy to match the organisation's requirements at any one time. In our less-than-ideal world, the balance is likely to be static rather than dynamic, and usually determined by the background, experience and personality of the individual manager. Nevertheless, it would be difficult to think of a manager who never had to deal with organisational change, even on a small scale, and who, therefore, did not need to possess some transformational skills. Similarly, it would also be difficult to think of a leader who, regardless of the size of the changes they were responsible for, did not have to possess some of the transactional skills necessary for ensuring that an organisation continued to satisfy its stakeholders. Therefore, the balance of management–leadership and transactional–transformational skills an individual needs to possess at any one time is related to the degree of change or stability they encounter.

The second conclusion we can draw, as Figure 12.2 showed, is that management and leadership focus on different types of change. Management tends to focus on small-scale, localised changes, whilst leadership tends to focus on more radical, organisation-wide changes. The former tend to require only relatively low levels of creativity, whilst the latter require relatively high levels. Even within these different types of change, however, there are some forms of change that appear to be more innovative and others more adaptive. Consequently, the ability of managers and leaders to deal effectively with different change situations will be related to the level of creativity they possess and the degree to which their creativity expresses itself in an innovative or adaptive manner.

Having drawn these two conclusions, we are now in a position to relate approaches to management and leadership to approaches to managing change. In Chapter 10, we developed a *Framework for Change* (*see* Figure 10.5). This related the types of changes organisations experienced, such as cultural or structural change, to the most appropriate approach to change, such as Emergent or Planned. If we merge Figure 10.5 from Chapter 10 with Figure 12.2 from this chapter, we can construct a *Framework for Management, Leadership and Change* (*see* Figure 12.3).

The four quadrants in Figure 12.3 show what form of management or leadership is best suited to each form of change and each approach to change management.

For example, quadrant 3 shows that where changes to tasks and procedures are concerned, these can be achieved by either a Tayloristic or *Kaizen* approach and managed in a transactional manner which requires only a low level of adaptive creativity.

Quadrant 1, on the other hand, presents a much more complex picture. It shows that where an organisation wishes to change its culture, this is best achieved by an Emergent approach to change led by someone with a transformational approach to leadership and who exhibits a high degree of innovation. Remembering, however, that Emergent change can encompass a wide range of change initiatives spread over a period of time, which can include Planned change and Bold Strokes, such transformational leaders may also need to possess adaptive and transactional skills, or be able to call on others who possess such skills.

Figure 12.3 also allows us to understand better the obstacles and approaches to dealing effectively with issues of sustainability, diversity and ethics. As was shown in examining globalisation earlier in this chapter, these are issues that organisations are aware of and, at least in large organisations, have policies and procedures to address. Possessing the ability to put these policies and procedures into practice is a different matter. These are issues that, for most organisations, require a major change of culture, especially by management and leadership at all levels. If sustainability, diversity and ethics are treated merely as structural or policy issues, as in quadrant 2, this is unlikely

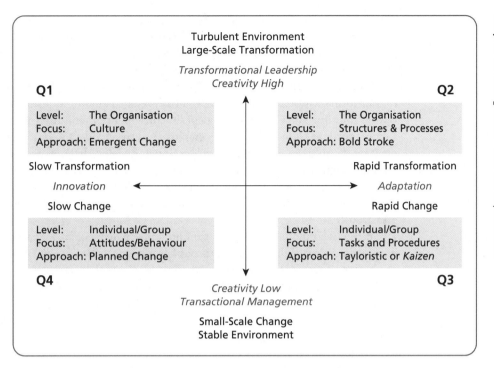

Figure 12.3 A Framework for Management, Leadership and Change

to lead to any permanent or sustained changes in attitudes and behaviour. Similarly, if they are seen as issues that are primarily about individual behaviour and attitudes, as in quadrant 4, there is unlikely to be an organisation-wide and lasting change to the way that managers and leaders behave. If ethics, diversity and sustainability are treated as issues that need to be embedded in an organisation's culture, however, and if the required changes are managed and led as shown in quadrant 1, then changes in attitudes and behaviour at the overall level are likely to be achieved and maintained.

Summary and conclusions

In reading some of the literature on strategy and change, one might be forgiven for asking whether managers and what they do matter at all. If strategy is Emergent, often unrelated to conscious decisions, does an important role exist for managers? Or if, as the evolutionary perspective on strategy would have it, luck plays a greater part in success than conscious action, does the quality of the manager matter? However, as this chapter has shown, the way an organisation is managed and led can have profound implications not only for the organisation and its members but for society as a whole.

On the negative side, managers can act to hold back organisations, prevent beneficial change and create a climate of blame and wrong-doing where infighting and discrimination are tolerated or even promoted. On the positive side, managers can identify opportunities for progress, promote ethical behaviour, recognise the opportunities that diversity brings, and create sustainable organisations which achieve harmony with their environment. Good managers and leaders can create the conditions for growth and prosperity. Effective managers are, therefore, for very positive reasons, important to an organisation. However, they do not operate in isolation or have a totally free rein.

The Chief Executives of Oticon (Chapter 10) and Marconi (Chapter 6) both wanted to transform their organisations. They both developed ambitious visions for their organisation's future. The Chief Executive of Oticon sought organisation-wide approval and support for his vision. All Oticon's employees were involved in developing and implementing the strategy to realise the vision. It was a vision that was seen as benefiting all Oticon's employees. It was a vision which succeeded. The vision for the new Marconi, on the other hand, was not seen as benefiting its employees, nor were they involved in developing or implementing it. With hindsight, the vision was badly flawed and it failed disastrously.

There is a strand in the management literature which equates organisational success with strong, clear-sighted and charismatic leadership (Thomas, 2003). Certainly, there are leaders, such as Jack Welch in his time at General Electric, Pehr Gyllenhammar before his departure from Volvo, Richard Branson at Virgin, Bill Gates when at Microsoft or Rupert Murdoch at News International, who through sheer force of personality dominated and transformed organisations. There are also others who have ruined their organisations. The successful charismatic leader appears to be in the minority. In any case, as the Arnold Weinstock example at GEC-Marconi shows, successful leaders may outstay their welcome, or radical surgery to fit their organisations for the future may become overdue.

Most managers, even of very large corporations, have to rely far less on their personality, important though this may be, and far more on their business knowledge, skills, creativity and experience. They are also called upon to perform a wide range of duties and activities. Though the theories and approaches to strategy and change appear to paint managers as either directing change or facilitating it, and the leadership literature tends to dwell on whether they are transactional or transformational managers, the reality is that they are often required to be all of these things, depending on the circumstances. As Figure 12.3 shows, in bringing about organisational change, there will be occasions when managers and leaders will need to devolve responsibility to subordinates; sometimes, though, they will need to encourage and support change projects; and, in other instances, they will have to lead the process themselves. Although the approach adopted will depend to a certain extent upon the size and importance of the change project, the timescale involved and the state of the organisation, in the final analysis it will rely on managerial judgement to make the appropriate choice. Changing organisations is a complex process fraught with more opportunities for failure than success. If managers are to accomplish and keep accomplishing this task, as this book has argued, they have to be aware of the choices and approaches available and be willing themselves to change their beliefs and attitudes.

Despite the views of some writers, there can never be any general recipes or formulas for organisational success. The vast variety of organisations, each with its own differing constraints and pressures, makes that impossible. What there is, however, is a large body of theories and associated advice which organisations can draw upon to assist them. As the quotation by George Box at the beginning of this book states: 'All models are wrong, some models are useful'. This book has shown that there is no such thing as an uncontested theory – all have their drawbacks. In particular, most tend to be situation-specific, even if they do not acknowledge this. Managers and organisations need to treat theories with a degree of scepticism. They also need to realise, however, that if they can identify the main theories for running and changing organisations, and they do understand the context in which they operate, they are in a position to identify choices and make changes.

Sometimes managers may choose or be required by circumstances to change their organisations radically and quickly; sometimes they may choose to influence the context to promote or reduce the need for such changes. In other cases, change may take place more slowly and over a long period, as both organisation and context are shaped and changed. The key factor in all this is to make conscious decisions rather than rely on untested assumptions. This will require those who manage and lead organisations to question and challenge their own and other people's assumptions. It will also require them to gather and be open to a wide variety of information – as Chapter 3 showed, the experience of more and more successful companies is that learning should be an organisation-wide and continuous process, rather than one limited to a few like-minded individuals at one point in time.

Even where choices are identified, managers should not assume that exercising choice is easy or that the results will be beneficial for all concerned, including themselves. For this reason, managers have a responsibility in making and implementing choices to consider the implications in the widest context: not just for themselves, not just for their organisation, but for society as well. In the West, especially the UK and the USA, there is a tendency to think mainly in terms of short-term profitability, and ignore the longer-term organisational and social consequences of actions. We can see this in the context of the Classical school, whose concentration on narrow issues of control and efficiency leads to the creation of jobs that are both physically strenuous and mind-numbingly boring. The adverse consequences of organisation theory are not limited to the Classical school, however; in many ways, the policies and approaches advocated by the Culture–Excellence school could be considered even worse. Though both Handy (2007b) and, to a lesser extent, Kanter (1997) are concerned about the impact of fragmented organisations and insecure jobs on society at large and family life in particular, neither appears to believe that these can be avoided.

Yet the consequences of this approach in creating instability and unpredictability in the job market are disastrous. As was noted in Chapter 3, the 1990s saw the UK become more socially divided than at any time since the Second World War, with some 60 per cent of the population either marginalised or living in very insecure circumstances (Hutton, 1995; Saul, 1997; White, 1999). Increasingly, the rich are choosing to live behind security fences in elite communities (Arnot, 2002). The situation is even worse in the USA, where the tendency for the better-off to retreat into walled compounds patrolled by armed guards is widespread and long-established (Dunphy and Griffiths, 1998; Elliott, 1997; Reich, 1997). Nevertheless, as the discussion on globalisation showed, in a borderless world, it will be impossible to escape the consequences of environmental depredation, a lack of business ethics and discriminatory behaviour merely by building walls. If this seems a somewhat apocalyptic vision, then bear in mind the reality of global warming. Bear in mind the millions of people who lost their savings and pensions in the dotcom boom, and the millions more who lost their jobs and homes in the sub-prime mortgage scandal. Also bear in mind that one of the most fashionable American gurus of the late 1990s, William Bridges, advocates the jobless organisation. He believes that there should no longer be any permanent jobs, not even for managers. Instead, he wants to see the labour force form one enormous pool of labour waiting for temporary employment – the Just-in-Time workforce to complement the Just-in-Time organisation (Bridges, 1996, 1998; Golzen, 1995). In support of his view that jobless organisations are the future, he points out that in the 1990s General Motors ceased to be the largest employer in the USA; instead, it was overtaken by the temporary employment agency, Manpower.

Some would argue that these developments are only the inevitable consequence of capitalism (Collins, 1998). However, as Crouch and Streeck (1997) and Whitley (1998) demonstrated, capitalism comes in many forms and guises. The fragmentation and insecurity of the labour market that was a growing characteristic of the USA and the UK in the 1980s and 1990s was much less pronounced in some other countries. This was especially the case in those nations that, historically, had seen the objectives of individual organisations as subservient to national interests. In the 1990s for example, despite economic problems associated with reunification, Germany still had an enviable record of attempting to prevent job losses and reduce job insecurity, as did the Scandinavian states and Japan.

This, of course, emphasises that national governments as well as individual organisations have a major contribution to make when considering the wider context and implications of managers' decisions. In the West, led by the USA and the UK, the last 20 years have seen an increasing move towards deregulation, privatisation and the introduction of market forces into the operation of the public sector. Whatever the merits of these policies in terms of efficiency, and they are debatable (Flynn, 1993; Ferlie et al, 1996), no one can doubt that they acted to increase instability both in the economy at large and in public-sector bodies. Whether such changes will eventually lead to a better deal for consumers or not is obviously an issue, but so is the effect on the social fabric. Post-1945, all Western governments used their public sectors both to provide services and as a means of creating employment and maintaining economic and social stability. These latter functions have now been abandoned in many countries, and the resulting insecurity is evident for all to see.

The point of mentioning this is not merely to show concern, but to argue that it need not be the case. The Culture–Excellence concept is only one of many approaches to running organisations. All have their downside, but not all result in job cuts and labour market instability. One alternative is for managers to choose to adopt approaches that reduce instability in their environment, rather than to implement policies that increase the use of short-term contracts and part-time and casual working. If followed widely, this would have two effects. Firstly, the result of many organisations seeking stability would be to reduce the overall level of turbulence in the environment. This is because, as Stickland (1998) maintains, organisations and their environment are not separate entities, but part of the same system. If organisations become more stable, so too does the environment. If organisations become more sustainable, so does the planet. Similarly, if, as recommended by Tom Peters, organisations adopt internal chaos to cope with external chaos, this merely acts to increase the overall turbulence in the system; in effect, a vicious spiral of increasing chaos is created which, instead of poising an organisation at the 'edge of chaos', may tear it apart. Also, if organisations focus solely on narrow profitability, environmental and ethical problems will grow. The second consequence of organisations seeking stability is that it increases the stability in society – jobs and communities become more stable and more sustainable.

Therefore, as a final note: organisations face many challenges and choices. Some organisations will find that their room for manoeuvre is very limited. Others may find that there is considerable scope for discretion. It is the role of managers and leaders to ensure that all available options and choices are identified, and that the choices made take account of both the short- and long-term interests of all their stakeholders – whether these be shareholders, employees, the managers themselves or the community at large. The worst managers may not be those who make poor choices; they may be those who fail to recognise that there are choices to be made.

Test your learning

Short answer questions

1. What is globalisation?

2. What is the link between sustainability, workforce diversity and ethics?

3. Describe Duncan's (1975) three levels of management.

4. Briefly discuss Mintzberg's (1973, 1975) description of managerial roles.

5. What is the personal characteristics approach to leadership?

6. State the key features of the leader–follower approach to leadership.

7. Describe the contextual approach to leadership.

8. How does Kirton's (1989) Adaptation–Innovation theory help us to understand managerial behaviour?

9. Describe two approaches to managerial development.

10. What is the difference between management and leadership?

11. How do management and leadership relate to organisational change?

12. List three ways in which managers' decisions can have a wider impact on society.

Essay questions

1. How can the Framework for Management, Leadership and Change (Figure 12.3) be used to guide organisational change? Illustrate your answer with reference to one of the case studies in this book or by using an organisation of your choice.

2. How can the concept of managerial choice help managers to reconcile the needs of their organisation with the wider needs of society?

Suggested further reading

1. Yukl, G (2006) *Leadership in Organizations* (6th edition). Prentice Hall: London.

   Gary Yukl's book is an excellent guide to the literature and research on management and leadership.

2. Deresky, H (2000) *International Management: Managing across Borders and Culture* (3rd edition). Prentice-Hall: Upper Saddle River, NJ, USA.

   This book provides a well-researched and well-written guide to international management. It is especially strong in the areas of culture, diversity and ethics.

3. Dunphy, D, Griffiths, A and Benn, S (2007) *Organizational Change for Corporate Sustainability* (2nd edition). Routledge: London.

   This is an important book which does not just make the case for creating sustainable organisations but also provides illustrations of and guidance on managing the changes necessary to achieve this.

CASE STUDY 12

Jobs International (India) Ltd[1]

BACKGROUND

Jobs International (India) Ltd is based in New Delhi and is a subsidiary of Jobs International (UK) Ltd. It is a family-owned company whose Managing Director and major shareholder is David Jacobs. He established the company in India in 1998 to provide advice to Indian nationals wanting to work in the UK and for UK companies wanting to recruit staff from India. It is now one of the largest job consultancies in India and represents over 100 major UK public- and private-sector employers. Its Indian Head Office is in New Delhi and there is a network of nine regional offices spread throughout India.

JI (UK) is based in London and its workload is quite light compared with the Indian operation. When JI was first set up, Mr Jacobs spent most of his time in India developing the business there. Once JI (India) was firmly established, he moved back to run the London office.

In 2005, Mr Jacobs became concerned that JI's fortunes were based too much on the success of the Indian operation, and began to look for opportunities to expand the London office. He came to the following conclusions:

1. The expansion of the EU into Eastern Europe and concomitant changes to UK immigration rules could lead to a reduced demand for Indian nationals by UK organisations.

2. There was a growing demand by UK organisations, including JI's main customers, for Eastern European workers and a reciprocal demand by them for UK jobs.

3. Though the UK market for Indian nationals might decline, the same did not appear to be the case in Australia and North America.

[1] This case study is based on research conducted by Ambika Nagar. I am very grateful for her permission to draw on her own work.

After much discussion with his parents, who were the other shareholders, Mr Jacobs decided upon a two-pronged expansion programme:

- JI would open offices in Eastern Europe, the first one being in Poland. These would operate on a similar basis to the Indian operation. Over the next three years, the London office would concentrate most of its time on building this business.
- The activities of JI (India) would be expanded and refocused on North America and Australia. This would involve recruiting an Australian and a North American to lead the two new activities in India. However, both would be responsible to the Indian Managing Director who would still have overall control.

Mr Jacobs had little doubt that he could make the Eastern European operation a success. However, he was more concerned with the changes to the Indian operation. He had established the business in India and had worked there full-time for the first three years of its existence. He then made his deputy Managing Director, an English man who had spent most of his adult life in India. This had worked well until 2004 when the Managing Director of JI (India) announced he was going to retire and move his family back to the UK. There was no obvious successor and eventually Mr Jacobs appointed his cousin, an English woman, to take over. She had no direct experience of India and had not worked for JI before but she had worked as a recruitment consultant with a number of major international companies and she was a very experienced manager. The fact that she was also a family member meant that she was unlikely to use the job to learn about JI and then set up a rival business in India, which was always one of Mr Jacobs' fears. However, in the year since she had taken over,

Mr Jacobs had begun to have doubts about the appointment. She often complained about the staff in the Indian offices, especially New Delhi, and he had heard that they were less than impressed with her. Therefore, before proceeding with the expansion of the Indian operation, he decided to carry out a change readiness audit.

THE CHANGE READINESS AUDIT

Mr Jacobs contacted a consultant he knew in India who was experienced at carrying out such audits. The consultant was English but had worked in India for some 30 years. Mr Jacobs was aware that he had to be very sensitive in dealing with his cousin, the Managing Director of JI (India). He knew that if he upset her she would contact her parents who would contact his parents and things could become quite fraught. As he said to a colleague, 'I'm now finding out the downside of employing family'. Therefore, Mr Jacobs told his cousin that the audit was to help her sort out the problems she had encountered and prepare the way for the expansion of business. The consultant told the same story.

The consultant spent a month examining the Indian operation. He visited the nine regional offices but spent most of his time in New Delhi. The main findings from his audit were as follows.

Organisation and operation: Overall, the Indian operation is very profitable, though how profitable only the Indian Managing Director, her Finance Director and Mr Jacobs know. The managers of the individual offices do not know whether they make or lose money, though the new Managing Director has told all of them that they are less profitable than each other as an incentive to get them to change their ways and take more individual responsibility. This does not seem to have worked.

The consultant considered the organisational structure to be more traditional and hierarchical than many similar companies in India. This tended to be more in terms of attitudes rather than actual grade levels. Staff tend to wait to be told what to do and not to act on their own initiative. The consultant also thought there was lack of professionalism in how staff carried out their jobs and that the company seemed to work as separate units rather than an integrated whole. These issues were in many ways a hangover from when Mr Jacobs ran the Indian operation. He had appointed all the staff and had a paternal attachment to them. This was reflected in his style of management, which was both informal and highly centralised – he did not like to delegate. However, the operation was then much smaller. His successor tended to operate in the same way. He was also, as the consultant said, 'an old India hand and he knew how to get the best out of his staff'. Mr Jacobs' cousin, the new Managing Director, had a very different style. She had worked in large organisations where professionalism, teamwork and individual initiative were the order of the day. She told the staff that this was how she wanted to run JI (India). To this end, she tried to flatten the hierarchy and instill a more professional attitude amongst staff, but this had generated a great deal of resentment.

The consultant felt that slotting two new Divisions, one for Australia and one for North America, into the existing structure might make matters worse. He also felt that neither an Australian nor a North American would be prepared to be left in the dark as to financial performance.

Staff: The new Managing Director stated that she wanted to be open and honest and involve all staff in the business, especially middle managers. However, attempts at 'straight talking' by the Managing Director appeared to be counter-productive as this was construed as negative feedback rather than open dialogue. The consultant pointed out that 'straight talking' did not sit well with the Indian culture which tended to be more circumspect in terms of making or receiving criticism.

The staff were nervous about moves into new markets and the introduction of two new senior members of staff, neither of which would be Indians. They had felt very comfortable in promoting the UK brand but the proposed changes seemed to have a paralysing effect on staff. The consultant stated that 'staff are taking even less initiative than in the past and have stopped taking responsibility as they feel that they will be used as scapegoats if things go wrong'.

The staff blame the Managing Director for their low morale and lack of initiative. They claim that the two previous managing directors were more proactive and took a close interest in the well-being of the staff. As one employee stated, 'Mr Jacobs had his finger on the pulse of the organisation, the new Managing Director has no idea where the pulse is . . . We understand that each leader has different leadership styles, and it is not fair to compare but the earlier levels of professionalism, commitment, and service are not followed any more . . .'. Another middle manager stated that, '. . . we no longer feel it's our company . . . we're just used as target practice . . .'.

Leadership: The Managing Director believes that she has been given the remit to shake JI (India) 'out of its complacent and unprofessional ways'. She is openly critical about her immediate predecessor, who she feels let staff 'get away with murder'. For example, previously, farewell gifts were presented to staff who left after being with the company for five years. She discontinued this because 'we should not reward people for leaving'. Also, staff in financial hardship could ask for an advance on their salary. This was also discontinued because she felt that, 'if staff can't manage their own money, how can we trust them with the company's?' Employees interpret such changes as showing a lack of respect. In addition, they point out that the Managing Director takes time off in office hours to go swimming and to the movies.

A key initiative taken by the Managing Director was to create a team spirit among the New Delhi and regional managers. Previously, they had tended to go their own way, with the New Delhi staff feeling superior to the regional managers whom they see as subordinates rather than colleagues. She spoke to them individually and as a group, telling them they were being unprofessional and should work as a team. The result was that both groups felt they were being bullied and shown a lack of respect.

She initiated communication sessions with staff where she would discuss the company's and individual department's performance and areas for improvement. However, staff were very hostile to discussing such matters in an open forum, and the Managing Director tended to be the only person who spoke. She also expressed the need for a management development programme for the company to 'bring in modern ideas and develop new talent'. Once again, staff and managers tended to see this as criticism of their performance rather than as an opportunity to develop themselves or the organisation.

Despite her somewhat rough ride since taking over, the Managing Director stated that she did not foresee any problems with re-orientating the existing staff towards the new business opportunities in Australia and

North America. Indeed, she welcomes the idea of appointing an Australian and a North American to the company because it would give her the opportunity to bring in allies who would support her. The consultant took a much more pessimistic view of the introduction of new business and new people.

THE CONSULTANT'S VIEW

The consultant's view is that there are serious problems with JI (India) which make it unlikely that the introduction of the Australian and North American business will be successful. He believes that the problems stem from three sources:

1. The company has grown quickly since it was first established, but staff still see it as a small business and expect the Managing Director to operate as an 'owner–manager' responsible for its day-to-day operation.
2. Staff are nervous of the changes the Managing Director has been trying to introduce and of the proposed expansion of the business. There is also some resentment, especially among the managers, that a non-Indian and a woman was appointed as Managing Director. A number of the managers had hoped that they would be offered the job.
3. The Managing Director has been used to working in big organisations and believes that JI (India) should adopt the same standards of professionalism and teamwork she is used to. Her view is that she has made a big effort to create a team spirit but is not receiving the support and response she deserves. She is aware that some staff are resentful that she has not been prepared to adapt to Indian culture. However, she points out that it is a UK-owned company placing prospective

523

CASE STUDY 12 CONT.

employees with UK companies and, therefore, Indian staff need to adapt to UK ways of doing business. As to her taking time off in working hours, she pointed out that she is always the last to leave and often works weekends. Therefore, if she takes few hours off during the day, it is no one's business but her own.

Questions

1. Imagine you are the consultant:
   a. What would your recommendations be as to how Mr Jacobs should proceed?
   b. What obstacles would you expect Mr Jacobs to meet in implementing your recommendations and how should these be overcome?
2. Imagine you are Mr Jacobs and you have just received the consultant's report:
   a. What action would you take and why?
   b. What obstacles would you expect to meet and how would you overcome them?
3. Imagine you are the Managing Director of JI (India). Mr Jacobs has just informed you of the contents of the consultant's report. He has asked you to produce an action plan for turning the situation round within six months and preparing the ground for the introduction of the Australian and North American business:
   a. What actions would you propose and why?
   b. What obstacles would you expect to meet and how would you overcome them?

Bibliography

Abegglen, J (1958) *The Japanese Factory*. Free Press: Glencoe, IL, USA.

Abegglen, J and Stalk, G (1984) *Kaisha, the Japanese Corporation*. Basic Books: New York, USA.

Abell, DF (1977) *Using PIMS and Portfolio Analysis in Strategic Market Planning: A Comparative Analysis*. Intercollegiate Case Clearing House, Harvard Business School: Boston, MA, USA.

Abell, P (1975) Organisations as technically constrained bargaining and influence systems. In P Abell (ed): *Organisations as Bargaining and Influence Systems*. Heinemann: London.

Abodaher, D (1986) *Iacocca*. Star: London.

Ackroyd, S (2000) Connecting organisations and societies: a realist analysis of structures. In S Ackroyd and S Fleetwood (eds): *Realist Perspectives on Management and Organisations*. Routledge: London.

Ackroyd, S and Fleetwood, S (2000a) Realism in contemporary organisation and management studies. In S Ackroyd and S Fleetwood (eds): *Realist Perspectives on Management and Organisations*. Routledge: London.

Ackroyd, S and Fleetwood, S (eds) (2000b) *Realist Perspectives on Management and Organisations*. Routledge: London.

Ackroyd, S, Burrell, G, Hughes, M and Whitaker, A (1988) The Japanisation of British industry. *Industrial Relations Journal*, 19(1), 11–23.

Adams, C, Cavendish, W and Mistry, P (1996) *Adjusting Privatisation: Case Studies from Developing Countries*. Heinemann: London.

Addis, M and Podesta, S (2005) Long life to marketing research: a postmodern view. *European Journal of Marketing*, 39(3/4), 386–412.

AFL-CIO (2003) *Trends in Executive Pay*. Available at www.aflcio.org.

Aglietta, M (1979) *A Theory of Capitalist Regulation: The US Experience*. New Left Books: London.

Aguren, S, Bredbacka, C, Hansson, R, Ihregren, K and Karlsson, KG (1984) *Volvo/Kalmar Revisited: Ten Years of Experience*. The Development Council: Stockholm, Sweden.

Aitken, H (1960) *Taylorism at the Watertown Arsenal: Scientific Management in Action 1908–1915*. Harvard University Press: Cambridge, MA, USA.

Akao, Y (ed) (1991) *Hoshin Kanri: Policy Deployment for Successful TQM*. Productivity Press: Cambridge, MA, USA.

Albrow, M (1970) *Bureaucracy*. Pall Mall Press: London.

Albrow, M (1997) *Do Organizations Have Feelings?* Routledge: London.

Alderman, J (2001a) *Sonic Boom: Napster, P2P and the Battle for the Future of Music.* Fourth Estate: London.

Alderman, J (2001b) Free for all. *Guardian*, 4 August, available at www.guardian.co.uk.

Alimo-Metcalfe, B (1995a) Female and male constructs of leadership and empowerment. *Women in Management*, 10(2), 3–8.

Alimo-Metcalfe, B (1995b) Leadership and assessment. In S Vinnicombe and NL Colwill (eds): *The Essence of Women in Management.* Prentice-Hall: Englewood Cliffs, NJ, USA.

Alimo-Metcalfe, B and Alban-Metcalfe, R (2000) Heaven can wait. *Health Service Journal*, 12 October, 26–29.

Allaire, Y and Firsirotu, ME (1984) Theories of organizational culture. *Organization Studies*, 5(3), 193–226.

Allaire, Y and Firsirotu, ME (1989) Coping with strategic uncertainty. *Sloan Management Review*, 30(3), 7–16.

Allen, FR and Kraft, C (1982) *The Organizational Unconscious. How to Create the Corporate Culture You Want and Need.* Prentice-Hall: Englewood Cliffs, NJ, USA.

Allen, RW, Madison, DL, Porter, LW, Renwick, PA and Mayes, BT (1979) Organizational politics: tactics and characteristics of its actors. *California Management Review*, 22, 77–83.

Allport, GW (1948) Foreword. In GW Lewin and GW Allport (eds): *Resolving Social Conflict.* Harper & Row: London.

Alvesson, M and Deetz, S (1996) Critical theory and postmodern approaches to organizational studies. In SR Clegg, C Hardy and WR Nord (eds): *Handbook of Organization Studies.* Sage: London.

Amin, A and Robins, K (1990) The re-emergence of regional economics? The mythical geography of flexible accumulation. *Environment and Planning D: Society and Space*, 8, 7–34.

Amit, R and Schoemaker, PJ (1993) Strategic assets and organisational rents. *Journal of Management Studies*, 30, 31–49.

Anderson, C and Paine, F (1978) PIMS: a re-examination. *Academy of Management Review*, 3(3), 602–12.

Andrews, KR (1980) *The Concept of Corporate Strategy.* Irwin: Homewood, IL, USA.

Andrews, KR (1998) The concept of corporate strategy. In H Mintzberg, JB Quinn and S Ghoshal: *The Strategy Process.* Prentice Hall: London.

Ansoff, HI (1965) *Corporate Strategy.* McGraw-Hill: New York, USA.

Ansoff, HI (1987) *Corporate Strategy* (revised version). McGraw-Hill: New York, USA.

Antonacopoulou, E and Chiva, R (2007) The social complexity of organizational learning: the dynamics of learning and organizing. *Management Learning*, 38(3), 277–95.

Appignanesi, R and Garratt, C (1995) *Postmodernism for Beginners.* Icon Books: Cambridge.

Argenti, J (1974) *Systematic Corporate Planning.* Nelson: London.

Argyris, C (1960) *Understanding Organizational Behavior*. Dorsey: Homewood, IL, USA.

Argyris, C (1962) *Interpersonal Competence and Organizational Effectiveness*. Irwin: Homewood, IL, USA.

Argyris, C (1964) *Integrating the Individual and the Organization*. Wiley: London.

Argyris, C (1970) *Intervention Theory and Method*. Addison-Wesley: Reading, MA, USA.

Argyris, C (1973) Peter Blau. In G Salaman and K Thompson (eds): *People and Organizations*. Longman: London.

Argyris, C (1977) Double-loop learning in organizations. *Harvard Business Review*, September–October, 115–25.

Argyris, C (1980) *Inner Contradictions of Rigorous Research*. Academic Press: New York, USA.

Argyris, C (1990) *Overcoming Organizational Defenses: Facilitating Organizational Learning*. Allyn & Bacon: Boston, MA, USA.

Argyris, C (1991) Teaching smart people how to learn. *Harvard Business Review*, May–June, 99–109.

Argyris, C (1992) *On Organizational Learning*. Blackwell: Oxford.

Argyris, C (1999) *On Organizational Learning* (2nd edition). Blackwell: Oxford.

Argyris, C and Schön, D (1978) *Organizational Learning: A Theory of Action Perspective*. Addison-Wesley: Reading, MA, USA.

Argyris, C, Putnam, R and McLain-Smith, D (1985) *Action Science: Concepts, Methods and Skills for Research and Intervention*. Jossey-Bass: San Francisco, CA, USA.

Aris, S (2002) Weinstock: I wanted to string up Simpson. *The Sunday Times*, 28 July, 8.

Armenakis, AA and Bedeian, AG (1999) Organisational change: a review of theory and research in the 1990s. *Journal of Management*, 25(3), 293–315.

Arndt, M and Bigelow, B (2000) Commentary: the potential of chaos theory and complexity theory for health services management. *Health Care Management Review*, 25(1), 35–8.

Arnold, J, Cooper, CL and Robertson, IT (1998) *Work Psychology* (3rd edition). Pitman: London.

Arnold, J, Silvester, J, Patterson, F, Robertson, IT, Cooper, CL and Burnes, B (2005) *Work Psychology* (5th edition). Financial Times Prentice Hall: Harlow.

Arnot, C (2002) Laager toffs. *The Guardian*, 30 January, 2–3.

Aronowitz, S (1989) Postmodernism and politics. In A Ross (ed): *Universal Abandon: the Politics of Postmodernism*. Edinburgh University Press: Edinburgh.

Ash, MG (1992) Cultural contexts and scientific change in psychology – Lewin, Kurt in Iowa. *American Psychologist*, 47(2), 198–207.

Ashforth, BE and Fried, Y (1988) The mindlessness of organizational behaviours. *Human Relations*, 41(4), 305–29.

Ashley, J (2008) Equality is tricky, but women are in the workplace to stay. *The Guardian*, 21 July, available at www.guardian.co.uk.

Ashour, AS (1973) The contingency model of leadership effectiveness: an evaluation. *Organizational Behavior and Human Performance*, 9, 339–55.

Ashton, D, Easterby-Smith, M and Irvine, C (1975) *Management Development: Theory and Practice*. MCB: Bradford.

Ashton, TS (1948) *The Industrial Revolution 1760–1830*. Oxford University Press: Oxford.

Ashworth, W (1987) *A Short History of the International Economy since 1850*. Longman: London.

AT Kearney (1989) *Computer Integrated Manufacturing: Competitive Advantage or Technological Dead End?* Kearney: London.

AT Kearney (1992) *Total Quality: Time to Take off the Rose-Tinted Spectacles*. IFS: Kempston.

AT Kearney Ltd (1994) *Partnership or Powerplay?* AT Kearney: London.

Auer, P and Riegler, C (1990) *Post-Taylorism: The Enterprise as a Place of Learning Organizational Change – A Comprehensive Study on Work Organization Changes and its Context at Volvo*. The Swedish Work Environment Fund: Stockholm, Sweden.

Ayres, R (1995) Privatisation and distributional equity: the case of Brazil. *International Journal of Social Economics*, 22(12), 36–49.

Babbage, C (1835) *On the Economy of Machinery and Manufacture*. Knight: London.

Bachman, JG, Bowers, DG and Marcus, PM (1968) Bases of supervisory power: a comparative study in five organizational settings. In AS Tannenbaum (ed): *Control in Organizations*. McGraw-Hill: New York, USA.

Back, KW (1992) This business of topology. *Journal of Social Issues*, 48(2), 51–66.

Balakrishnan, A and Collinson, P (2007) Merrill Lynch: avoid risk but look for opportunities. *The Guardian*, 16 August, 28.

Bargal, D and Bar, H (1992) A Lewinian approach to intergroup workshops for Arab-Palestinian and Jewish youth. *Journal of Social Issues*, 48(2), 139–54.

Bargal, D, Gold, M and Lewin, M (1992) The heritage of Kurt Lewin – introduction. *Journal of Social Issues*, 48(2), 3–13.

Barker, RA (2001) The nature of leadership. *Human Relations*, 54(4), 469–94.

Barnard, C (1938) *The Functions of the Executive*. Harvard University Press: Cambridge, MA, USA.

Barnard, C and Scott, J (eds) (2002) *The Law of the Single European Market: Unpacking the Premises*. Hart Publishing: London.

Barratt, ES (1990) Human resource management: organisational culture. *Management Update*, 2(1), 21–32.

Barrie, C (1995) Saatchi loses accounts to new agency. *Guardian*, 16 February, 15.

Barrie, C (1999) It's a far cry from safe and secure. *Guardian* – Jobs Section, 2 January, 12–13.

Bass, BM (1985) *Leadership and Performance beyond Expectations*. Free Press: New York, NY, USA.

Bass, BM (1990) *Handbook of Leadership: A Survey of Theory and Research*. Free Press, New York, NY, USA.

Bass, BM (1995) Transformational leadership redux. *Leadership Quarterly*, 6, 463–78.

Bateson, G (1972) *Steps to an Ecology of the Mind*. Ballantine: New York, USA.

Batten, JD and Swab, JL (1965) How to crack down on company politics. *Personnel*, 42, 8–20.

Baudrillard, J (1983) *Simulations*. Semiotexte: New York, USA.

Bavelas, A and Lewin, K (1942) Training in democratic leadership. *Journal of Abnormal Psychology*, 37, 115–19.

Beach, SD (1980) *Personnel*. Macmillan: London.

Beatty, CA and Lee, GL (1992) Leadership among middle managers – an exploration in the context of technological change. *Human Relations*, 45(9), 957–89.

Bechtold, BL (1997) Chaos theory as a model for strategy development. *Empowerment in Organizations*, 5(4), 193–201.

Becker, WS (2008) *The 100 Day Action Plan to Save the Planet*. St Martin's Griffin: New York, NY, USA.

Beckhard, R (1969) *Organization Development: Strategies and Models*. Addison-Wesley: Reading, MA, USA.

Beckhard, R (1985) Whither management development? *Journal of Management Development*, 4(2).

Beckhard, R and Harris, RT (1987) *Organizational Transitions: Managing Complex Change* (2nd edition). Addison-Wesley: Reading, MA.

Beer, M and Nohria, N (eds) (2000) *Breaking the Code of Change*. Harvard Business School Press: Boston, MA, USA.

Beer, M and Walton, RE (1987) Organizational change and development. *Annual Review of Psychology*, 38, 339–68.

Beer, M, Eisenstadt, RA and Spector, B (1990) *The Critical Path to Corporate Renewal*. Harvard Business School Press: Boston, MA, USA.

Beer, M, Eisenstadt, RA and Spector, B (1993) Why change programmes don't produce change. In C Mabey and B Mayon-White (eds): *Managing Change* (2nd edition). The Open University/Paul Chapman Publishing: London.

Beesley, ME and Littlechild, SC (1983) Privatisation principles, problems and priorities. *Lloyds Bank Review*, 149, 1–20.

Beeson, I and Davis, C (2000) Emergence and accomplishment in organizational change. *Journal of Organizational Change Management*, 13(2), 178–89.

Belbin, M (1996) *Team Roles at Work*. Butterworth-Heinemann: London.

Bell, D (1973) *The Coming of Post-Industrial Society*. Basic Books: New York, USA.

Bell, RM (1973) *The Behaviour of Labour, Technical Change, and the Competitive Weakness of British Manufacturing*. Technical Change Centre: London.

Benjamin, G and Mabey, C (1993) Facilitating radical change. In C Mabey and B Mayon-White (eds): *Managing Change* (2nd edition). The Open University/Paul Chapman Publishing: London.

Bennett, J and Jayes, S (1995) *Trusting the Team: The Best Practice Guide to Partnering in Construction*. Reading University, Centre for Strategic Studies in Construction: Reading.

Bennett, R (1983) *Management Research. Management Development Series, 20*. International Labour Office: Geneva.

Bennis, WG (1959) Leadership theory and administrative behaviour. *Administrative Science Quarterly*, 4, 259–301.

Bennis, WG (1966) The coming death of bureaucracy. *Think*, November–December, 30–5.

Bennis, WG (2000) Leadership of change. In M Beer and N Nohria (eds): *Breaking the Code of Change*. Harvard Business School Press: Boston, MA, USA.

Bennis, WG and Nanus, B (1985) *Leaders: The Strategies for Taking Charge*. Harper & Row: New York, NY, USA.

Bensoussan, BE and Fleisher, CS (2008) *Analysis without Paralysis: 10 Tools to Make Better Strategic Decisions*. Financial Times Prentice Hall: Harlow.

Berggren, C (1992) *The Volvo Experience*. Macmillan: London.

Bernstein, L (1968) *Management Development*. Business Books: London.

Bessant, J (1983) Management and manufacturing innovation: the case of information technology. In G Winch (ed): *Information Technology in Manufacturing Processes*. Rossendale: London.

Bessant, J and Haywood, B (1985) *The Introduction of Flexible Manufacturing Systems as an Example of Computer Integrated Manufacture*. Brighton Polytechnic: Brighton.

Bhaskar, R (1979) *A Realist Theory of Science* (2nd edition). Harvester: Brighton.

Bhaskar, R (1986) *Scientific Realism and Human Emancipation*. Verso: London.

Bhaskar, R (1989) *Reclaiming Reality*. Verso: London.

Bhote, KR (1989) *Strategic Supply Management*. American Management Association: New York, NY, USA.

Biberman, J and Whitty, M (1997) A postmodern spiritual future for work. *Journal of Organizational Change*, 10(2), 130–8.

Bigge, LM (1982) *Learning Theories for Teachers*. Gower: Aldershot.

Birchall, D and Lyons, L (1995) *Creating Tomorrow's Organization: Unlocking the Benefits of Future Work*. Pitman: London.

Black, JA (2000) Fermenting change: capitalizing on the inherent change found in dynamic non-linear (or complex) systems. *Journal of Organizational Change Management*, 13(6), 520–5.

Blackler, F and Brown, C (1978) *Job Redesign and Management Control: Studies in British Leyland and Volvo*. Saxon House: Farnborough.

Blackler, F and Brown, C (1984) Alternative models to guide the design and introduction of new information technologies into work organisations. *Journal of Occupational Psychology*, 59(4), 287–314.

Blackler, F and McDonald, S (2000) Power, mastery and organisational learning. *Journal of Management Studies*, 37(6), 833–51.

Blake, RR and McCanse, AA (1991) *Leadership Dilemmas – Grid Solutions*. Gulf Publishing: Houston, TX, USA.

Blake, RR and Mouton, JS (1969) *Building a Dynamic Corporation through Grid Organization Development*. Addison-Wesley: Reading, MA, USA.

Blake, RR and Mouton, JS (1976) *Organizational Change by Design*. Scientific Methods: Austin, TX, USA.

Blake, RR and Mouton, JS (1985) *The Managerial Grid III*. Gulf Publishing: Houston, TX, USA.

Blanchard, K (1994) Changing role of executives. *Executive Excellence*, 11(4), 7.

Blanton, K (2008) Broker's Clients Detail Web of Dashed Dreams. *Boston Globe*, 20 January, 1.

Blau, PM (1970) The formal theory of differentiation in organizations. *American Sociological Review*, 35, 201–18.

Blau, PM and Schoenherr, RA (1971) *The Structure of Organizations*. Basic Books: New York, USA.

Block, P (1981) *Flawless Consulting: A Guide to Getting Your Expertise Used*. Learning Concepts: Austin, Texas, USA.

Boddy, D and Buchanan, D (1992) *Take the Lead: Interpersonal Skills for Change Agents*. Prentice Hall: London.

Boddy, D (2002) *Management: An Introduction*. Financial Times Prentice Hall: Harlow.

Boje, DM (2000) Phenomenal complexity theory and change at Disney: response to Letiche. *Journal of Organizational Change Management*, 13(6), 558–66.

Boje, DM (2006) What happened on the way to postmodern? *Qualitative Research in Organizations and Management: An International Journal*, 1(1), 22–40.

Borchardt, K (1973) Germany 1700–1914. In C Cipolla (ed): *The Fontana Economic History of Europe Vol. 4, The Emergence of Industrial Societies – Part 1*. Fontana: London.

Bower, T (1996) *Maxwell: The Final Verdict*. HarperCollins: London.

Bowers, DG, Franklin, JL and Pecorella, P (1975) Matching problems, precursors and interventions in OD: a systematic approach. *Journal of Applied Behavioural Science*, 11, 391–410.

Bowles, M (1989) Myth, meaning and work organisation. *Organization Studies*, 10(3), 405–23.

Bowman, C and Asch, D (1985) *Strategic Map*. Macmillan: London.

Bracker, J (1980) The historical development of the strategic management concept. *Academy of Management Review*, 5(2), 219–24.

Bradford, DL and Burke, WW (2004) Introduction: Is OD in crisis? *Journal of Applied Behavioral Science*, 40(4), 369–73.

Bradshaw-Camball, P and Murray, VV (1991) Illusions and other games: a trifocal view of organizational politics. *Organization Science*, 2(4), 379–98.

Brandenburger, AM and Nalebuff, BJ (1996) *Co-opetition*. Doubleday: New York, USA.

Bratton, J (1992) *Japanization at Work: Managerial Studies for the 1990s*. Macmillan: London.

Breslin, J and McGann, J (1998) *The Business Knowledge Repository: Consolidating and Accessing Your Ways of Working*. Quorum Books: Westport, CT, USA.

Brewer, E and Tomlinson, JWC (1964) The manager's working day. *Journal of Industrial Economics*, 12, 191–7.

Brews, PJ (2003) Star trek strategy: real strategy at work. *Business Strategy Review*, 14(3), 34–43.

Bridges, W (1996) *Jobshift: How to Prosper in a Workplace without Jobs*. Nicholas Brealey: London.

Bridges, W (1998) *Creating You & Co: Learn to Think Like the CEO of Your Own Career*. Perseus Books: New York, USA.

Brindle, D (1998a) Benefits payments in chaos: computer collapse wipes out records. *Guardian*, 10 September, 1.

Brindle, D (1998b) Gap between rich and poor widens again. *Guardian*, 16 October, 7.

Brindle, D (1999) Pensions computer upgrade hit by 1,900 bugs as deadline looms. *Guardian*, 26 January, 3.

Brodbeck, PW (2002) Implications for organization design: teams as pockets of excellence. *Team Performance Management: An International Journal*, 8(1/2), 21–38.

Brown, A (1995) *Organisational Culture*. Pitman: London.

Brown, A (1998) *Organisational Culture* (2nd edition). Financial Times Pitman: London.

Brown, DH and Jopling, D (1994) Some experiences of outsourcing: a systemic analysis of strategic and organisational issues. Paper presented to the British Academy of Management Annual Conference, University of Lancaster, September.

Brown, SL and Eisenhardt, KM (1997) The art of continuous change: linking complexity theory and time-paced evolution in relentlessly shifting organizations. *Administrative Science Quarterly*, 4(1), March, 1–34.

Bruland, K (1989) The transformation of work in European industrialization. In P Mathias and JA Davis (eds): *The First Industrial Revolutions*. Blackwell: Cambridge.

Brummer, A (1999) Weinstock's heirs look for an encore. *Guardian*, 20 January, 21.

Brummer, A (2002) Lord Weinstock. *Guardian*, 24 July, available at www.guardian.co.uk.

Brummer, A and Cowe, R (1998) *Weinstock*. HarperCollins: London.

Bryant, A (1998) Beyond BPR: confronting the organizational legacy. *Management Decision*, 36(1), 25–30.

Bryant, D (1979) The psychology of resistance to change. *Management Services*, March, 9–10.

Bryce, R (2002) *Pipe Dreams: Greed, Ego, Jealousy and the Death of Enron*. Public Affairs: London.

Buchanan, DA (1984) The impact of technical implications and managerial aspirations on the organization and control of the labour process. Paper presented to the Second Annual Conference on the Control and Organisation of the Labour Process, UMIST/Aston, 28–30 March.

Buchanan, DA and Badham, R (1999) *Power, Politics and Organizational Change: Winning the Turf Game*. Sage: London.

Buchanan, DA and Boddy, D (1992) *The Expertise of the Change Agent*. Prentice Hall: London.

Buchanan, DA and Storey, J (1997) Role-taking and role-switching in organizational change: the four pluralities. In I McLoughlin and M Harris (eds): *Innovation, Organizational Change and Technology*. International Thompson: London.

Buchanan, DA, Fitzgerald, L and Ketley, D (eds) (2006) *The Sustainability and Spread of Organizational Change: Modernizing Healthcare*. Routledge: London.

Buckingham, L and Finch, J (1999) SmithKline bows to revolt over directors' pay. *Guardian*, 24 April, 22.

Buckley, PJ and Mirza, H (1985) The wit and wisdom of Japanese management. *Management International Review*, 25, 16–32.

Buckley, W (1968) *Modern Systems and Research for the Behavioral Scientist*. Aldine Publishing: Chicago, USA.

Bullock, RJ and Batten, D (1985) It's just a phase we're going through: a review and synthesis of OD phase analysis. *Group and Organization Studies*, 10, December, 383–412.

Burawoy, M (1979) *Manufacturing Consent: Changes in the Labor Process under Monopoly Capital*. University of Chicago Press: Chicago, USA.

Burgoyne, J (1995) Feeding minds to grow the business. *People Management*, 1(19), 22–6.

Burgoyne, J and Germaine, C (1984) Self development and career planning: an exercise in mutual benefit. *Personnel Management*, 16(4), April, 21–3.

Burgoyne, J, Pedler, M and Boydell, T (1994) *Towards the Learning Company*. McGraw-Hill: London.

Burke, W (1980) *Organisation Development*. Little, Brown and Co: Toronto, Canada.

Burke, W, Michael, RS, Luthems, F, Odiorne, S and Hayden, S (1981) *Techniques of Organisational Change*. McGraw-Hill: London.

Burnes, B (1988) *Strategy for Success: Case Studies in Advanced Manufacturing Technologies*. EITB: Watford.

Burnes, B (1989) *New Technology in Context*. Gower: Aldershot.

Burnes, B (1991) Managerial competence and new technology: don't shoot the piano player – he's doing his best. *Behaviour and Information Technology*, 10(2), 91–109.

Burnes, B (1996) No such thing as . . . a 'one best way' to manage organizational change. *Management Decision*, 34(10), 11–18.

Burnes, B (1997) Organisational choice and organisational change. *Management Decision*, 35(10), 753–9.

Burnes, B (1998a) Recipes for organisational effectiveness: mad, bad, or just dangerous to know. *Career Development International*, 3(3), 100–6.

Burnes, B (1998b) The planned approach to change: come back Kurt Lewin – all is forgiven. Paper presented to the Second Maintaining Organizational Effectiveness Conference, Edge Hill University College, Ormskirk, June, 17.

Burnes, B (2003) Managing change and changing managers: from ABC to XYZ. *Journal of Management Development*, 22(7), 627–42.

Burnes, B (2004a) Emergent change and planned change – competitors or allies? The case of XYZ Construction. *International Journal of Operations and Production Management*, 24(9), 886–902.

Burnes, B (2004b) Kurt Lewin and complexity theories: back to the future? *Journal of Change Management*, 4(4), 309–25.

Burnes, B (2004c) Kurt Lewin and the planned approach to change: a re-appraisal. *Journal of Management Studies*, 41(6), 977–1002.

Burnes, B (2005) Complexity theories and organisational change. *International Journal of Management Reviews*, 7(2), 73–90.

Burnes, B (2007) Kurt Lewin and the Harwood studies: the foundations of OD. *Journal of Applied Behavioral Science*, 43(2), 213–31.

Burnes, B (2009) Organisational change in the public sector: The case for planned change. In RT By and C Macleod (eds): *Managing Organisational Change in Public Services: International Issues, Challenges and Cases*. Routledge: London.

Burnes, B and Coram, R (1999) Barriers to partnership in the public sector: the case of the UK construction industry. *Supply Chain Management*, 4(1), 43–50.

Burnes, B and Dale, B (eds) (1998) *Working in Partnership*. Gower: Aldershot.

Burnes, B and James, H (1995) Culture, cognitive dissonance and the management of change. *International Journal of Operations and Production Management*, 15(8), 14–33.

Burnes, B and New, S (1996) *Strategic Advantage and Supply Chain Collaboration*. AT Kearney: London.

Burnes, B and New, S (1997) Collaboration in customer–supplier relationships: strategy, operations and the function of rhetoric. *International Journal of Purchasing and Materials Management*, 33(4), 10–17.

Burnes, B and Salauroo, M (1995) The impact of the NHS internal market on the merger of colleges of midwifery and nursing: not just a case of putting the cart before the horse. *Journal of Management in Medicine*, 9(2), 14–29.

Burnes, B and Weekes, B (1989) *AMT: A Strategy for Success?* NEDO: London.

Burnes, B and Whittle, P (1995) Supplier development: getting started. *Logistics Focus*, February, 10–14.

Burnes, B, Cooper, C and West, P (2003) Organisational learning: the new management paradigm? *Management Decision*, 41(5), 443–51.

Burnes, B, Katsouros, M and Jones, T (2004) Privatisation and the European Union: the case of the Public Power Corporation of Greece. *International Journal of Public Sector Management*, 18(1).

Burns, JM (1978) *Leadership*. Harper & Row: New York, USA.

Burns, T and Stalker, GM (1961) *The Management of Innovation*. Tavistock: London.

Burrell, G (1988) Modernism, post modernism and organisational analysis 2: the contribution of Michel Foucault. *Organization Studies*, 9(2), 221–35.

Burrell, G (1997) Organization paradigms. In A Sorge and M Warner (eds): *The IEBM Handbook of Organizational Behaviour*. International Thompson Business Press: London.

Burt, T (2002) Divorcees with a difference: Volvo. *Financial Times*, 4 March, 13.

Burton, F, Yamin, M and Young, S (eds) (1996) *Europe in Transition*. Macmillan: London.

Business Notebook (2003) Old expressions. *Guardian*, 2 July, 16.

Butler, R (1997) Decision making. In A Sorge and M Warner (eds): *The IEBM Handbook of Organizational Behaviour*. International Thompson Business Press: London.

Butler, VG (1985) *Organisation and Management*. Prentice Hall: London.

Buzzell, RD and Gale, BT (1987) *The PIMS Principles – Linking Strategy to Performance*. Free Press: New York, USA.

By, RT and Macleod, C (eds) (2009) *Managing Organisational Change in Public Services: International Issues, Challenges and Cases*. Routledge: London.

Byars, LL (1984) *Strategic Management: Planning and Implementation*. Harper & Row: London.

Bywater PLC (1997) *Executive Briefings: The Executive Role in Sponsoring Change – Making It Happen*. Bywater PLC: Reading.

Caldwell, R (2001) Champions, adapters, consultants and synergists: the change agents in HRM. *Human Resource Management Journal*, 11(3), 39–52.

Caldwell, R (2003) Models of change agency: a fourfold classification. *British Journal of Management*, 14(2), 131–42.

Caldwell, R (2006) *Agency and Change*. Routledge: London.

Callinicos, A (1989) *Against Postmodernism*. Polity: Cambridge.

Camp, RC (1989) *Benchmarking*. ASQC Quality Press: Milwaukee, USA.

Campbell, A and Warner, M (1988) Organization of new forms of manufacturing operations. In M Wild (ed): *International Handbook of Production and Operations Management*. Cassell: London.

Cant, M and Jeynes, L (1998) What does outsourcing bring you that innovation cannot? How outsourcing is seen – and currently marketed – as a universal panacea. *Total Quality Management*, 9(2/3), 193–202.

Cao, G, Clarke, S and Lehaney, B (2000) A systemic view of organisational change and TQM. *The TQM Magazine*, 12(3), 186–93.

Cao, G, Clarke, S and Lehaney, B (2001) A critique of BPR from a holistic perspective. *Business Process Management Journal*, 7(4), 332–9.

Carew, A (1987) *Labour under the Marshall Plan: The Politics of Productivity and the Market*. Manchester University Press: Manchester.

Carlson, S (1951) *Executive Behaviour*. Strombergs: Stockholm.

Carnall, CA (1990) *Managing Change in Organizations*. Prentice Hall: London.

Carnall, CA (1995) *Managing Change in Organizations* (2nd edition). Prentice Hall: London.

Carnall, CA (2003) *Managing Change in Organizations* (4th edition). Financial Times Prentice Hall: Harlow.

Carr, C, Tomkins, C and Bayliss, B (1991) Strategic controllership – a case study approach. *Management Accounting Research*, 2, 89–107.

Carr, P and Donaldson, L (1993) Managing healthily: how an NHS region is managing change. *Personnel Management*, October, 48–51.

Carroll, DT (1983) A disappointing search for excellence. *Harvard Business Review*, November–December, 78–88.

Carroll, GR (ed) (1988) *Ecological Models of Organizations*. Ballinger: Cambridge, MA, USA.

Cartwright, D (1951) Achieving change in people: some applications of group dynamics theory. *Human Relations*, 6(4), 381–92.

Cartwright, D (ed) (1952) *Field Theory in Social Science*. Social Science Paperbacks: London.

Carvel, J (2002) Long working hours harming family life. *Guardian*, 25 September, 13.

Cassidy, J (2002) *Dot.con: The Greatest Story Ever Sold*. Allen Lane: London.

Caulkin, S (2003) The bosses we love to hate. *Observer*, 6 July, available at www.guardian.co.uk.

Caves, R (2001) *Creative Industries*. The Free Press: New York, USA.

Cellan-Jones, R (2003) *Dot.bomb: The Strange Death of Dot.com Britain*. Arum: London.

Chamberlin, EH (1933) *The Theory of Monopolistic Competition*. Harvard University Press: Cambridge, MA, USA.

Chandler, AD (1962) *Strategy and Structure: Chapters in the History of the American Industrial Enterprise*. MIT Press: Cambridge, MA, USA.

Chang, T-L (1997) Cultivating global experience curve advantage on technology and marketing capabilities. *Journal of Marketing Practice: Applied Marketing Science*, 3(4), 230–50.

Chapman, L (1978) *Your Disobedient Servant Published*. Chatto & Windus: London.

Chapman, SD and Chassagne, S (1981) *European Textile Printers in the Eighteenth Century. A Study of Peel and Oberkampf*. Heinemann: London.

Chatterjee, S (2007) Why is synergy so difficult in mergers of related businesses? *Strategy and Leadership*, 35(2), 46–52.

Chawla, S and Renesch, J (1995) *Learning Organizations: Developing Cultures for Tomorrow's Workplace*. Productivity Press: Portland, OR, USA.

Child, J (1972) Organizational structure, environment and performance: the role of strategic choice. *Sociology*, 6(1), 1–22.

Child, J (1984) *Organization*. Harper & Row: Cambridge.

Child, J and Ellis, T (1973) Predictors of variation in managerial roles. *Human Relations*, 26(2), 227–50.

Child, J and Smith, C (1987) The context and process of organisational transformation – Cadbury Limited in its sector. *Journal of Management Studies*, 24(6), 565–93.

Chin, R and Benne, KD (1976) General strategies for effecting changes in human systems. In WG Bennis, KD Benne, R Chin and KE Corey (eds): *The Planning of Change* (3rd edition). Holt, Rinehart and Winston: New York, USA.

Choi, TY, Dooley, KJ and Rungtusanatham, M (2001) Supply networks and complex adaptive systems: control versus emergence. *Journal of Operations Management*, 19(3), 351–66.

Christopher, M (1998) *Logistics and Supply Chain Management* (2nd edition). Pitman: London.

Chua, A and Lam, W (2005) Why KM projects fail: a multi-case analysis. *Journal of Knowledge Management*, 9(3), 6–17.

Cipolla, C (ed) (1973) *The Fontana Economic History of Europe, Vol. 4*. Fontana: London.

Clark, A (2008) Feds charge Bear pair with fraud over $1.4bn sub-prime collapse. *The Guardian*, 20 June, available at www.guardian.co.uk

Clark, P (1972) *Action Research and Organisational Change*. Harper & Row: London.

Clark, RC (1979) *The Japanese Company*. New Haven, CT, USA.

Clarke, L (1994) *The Essence of Change*. Prentice Hall: London.

Clarke, M (1999) Management development: a new role in social change. *Management Decision*, 37(10), 767–77.

Clegg, CW (1984) The derivation of Job Design. *Journal of Occupational Behaviour*, 5, 131–46.

Clegg, CW and Symon, G (1991) Technology-led change: a case study of the implementation of CADCAM. *Journal of Occupational Psychology*, 64(4), 273–90.

Clegg, S (1990) *Modern Organisation: Organisation Studies in the Postmodern World*. Sage: London.

Coch, L and French, JRP, Jr (1948) Overcoming resistance to change. *Human Relations*, 1(4), 512–32.

Coghlan, D (1993) In defence of process consultation. In C Mabey and B Mayon-White (eds): *Managing Change* (2nd edition). The Open University/Paul Chapman Publishing: London.

Cohen, MD, March, JG and Olsen, JP (1972) A garbage can model of organizational choice. *Administrative Science Quarterly*, 17, 1–25.

Cole, RE (1979) *Work, Mobility and Participation: A Comparative Study of Japanese and American Industry*. University of California Press: Los Angeles, USA.

Collier, A (1994) *Critical Realism*. Verso: London.

Collins, D (1998) *Organizational Change*. Routledge: London.

Collins, D (2000) *Management Fads and Buzzwords*. Routledge: London.

Collins, D (2008) Has Tom Peters lost the plot? A timely review of a celebrated management guru. *Journal of Organizational Change Management*, 21(3), 315–334.

Collins, JC and Porras, JI (1991) Organizational vision and visionary organizations. *California Management Review*, Fall, 30–52.

Collins, JC and Porras, JI (1997) *Built to Last: Successful Habits of Visionary Companies*. Harper Business: New York, USA.

Connelly, J (2000) A realistic theory of health sector management: the case for critical realism. *Journal of Management in Medicine*, 14(5/6), 262–71.

Conner, PE (1977) A critical enquiry into some assumptions and values characterizing OD. *Academy of Management Review*, 2(1), 635–44.

Constable, J and McCormick, R (1987) *The Making of British Managers*. British Institute of Management/Confederation of British Industry: London.

Cook, T (1998) New Labour, new NHS . . . new internal market? *Management Accounting*, 76(3), March, 24–6.

Cooke, B (1999) Writing the left out of management theory: the historiography of the management of change. *Organization*, 6(1), 81–105.

Cool, K and Schendel, D (1988) Performance differences among strategic group members. *Strategic Management Journal*, 9(3), 207–23.

Coombs, R and Hull, R (1994) The best or the worst of both worlds: BPR, cost reduction, and the strategic management of IT. Paper presented to the OASIG Seminar on Organisation Change through IT and BPR: Beyond the Hype, September, London.

Cooper, CL and Jackson, SE (eds) (1997) *Creating Tomorrow's Organizations*. Wiley: Chichester.

Cooper, J and Fazio, RH (1984) A new look at dissonance theory. In L Berkowitz (ed): *Advances in Experimental Social Psychology*, Vol. 17, 229–67. Academic Press: New York, USA.

Cooper, R and Burrell, G (1988) Modernism, postmodernism and organizational analysis: an introduction. *Organization Studies*, 9, 91–112.

Cooper, Z (2008) Faiths to faith. *The Guardian*, 7 June, available at www.guardian.co.uk

Coopey, J and Burgoyne, J (2000) Politics and organisational learning. *Journal of Management Studies*, 37(6), 869–85.

Copley, FB (1923) *Frederick Winslow Taylor: Father of Scientific Management*, Vol. 2. Harper & Row: New York, USA.

Coram, WR (1997) The privatisation of the Property Services Agency, Vols 1 and 2. Unpublished PhD Thesis. UMIST: Manchester.

Coram, R and Burnes, B (2001) Managing organizational change in the public sector: lessons from the privatisation of the Property Services Agency. *International Journal of Public Sector Management*, 14(2), 205–20.

Coulson-Thomas, C and Coe, T (1991) *The Flat Organization*. British Institute of Management: London.

Coupland, D (1995) *Microserfs*. Regan Books: New York, USA.

Courtney, H, Kirkland, J and Viguerie, P (1997) Strategy under uncertainty. *Harvard Business Review*, 75(6), 67–79.

Covin, JG (1991) Entrepreneurial versus conservative firms: a comparison of strategies and performance. *Journal of Management Studies*, 28, 439–62.

Cowe, R (1995) Compete carefully. *Guardian*, 25 March, 40.

Coyne, KP and Subramaniam, S (1996) Bringing discipline to strategy. *McKinsey Quarterly*, 4, 14–25.

Crainer, S (ed) (1995) *The Financial Times Handbook of Management*. Pitman: London.

Crainer, S (1996) *Key Management Ideas*. Financial Times Pitman: London.

Crawford, M, Rutter, D and Thelwall, S (2003) *User Involvement in Change Management: A Review of the Literature*. Department of Psychological Medicine, Imperial College: London.

Cressey, P (1996) Enriching production: perspectives on Volvo's Uddevalla plant as an alternative to lean production. *Industrial Relations Journal*, 27(1), 77–80.

Cringely, RX (1992) *Accidental Empires: How the Boys of Silicon Valley Make their Millions, Battle Foreign Competition, and Still Can't Get a Date*. Addison-Wesley: Reading, MA, USA.

Crosby, PB (1979) *Quality Is Free*. McGraw-Hill: New York, USA.

Crossan, MM and Guatto, T (1996) Organizational learning research profile. *Journal of Organizational Change Management*, 9(1), 107–12.

Crouch, C and Streeck, W (eds) (1997) *Political Economy of Modern Capitalism*. Sage: London.

Crozier, M (1964) *The Bureaucratic Phenomenon*. Tavistock: London.

Cruise O'Brien, R and Voss, C (1992) *In Search of Quality*. Working Paper, London Business School: London.

Cummings, TG and Huse, EF (1989) *Organization Development and Change* (4th edition). West: St Paul, MN, USA.

Cummings, TG and Worley, CG (1997) *Organization Development and Change* (6th edition). South-Western College Publishing: Cincinnati, OH, USA.

Cummings, TG and Worley, CG (2001) *Organization Development and Change* (7th edition). South-Western College Publishing: Mason, OH, USA.

Cummings, TG and Worley, CG (2005) *Organization Development and Change* (8th edition). South-Western College Publishing: Mason, OH, USA.

Cuthbert, N (1970) Readings from Henri Fayol, *General and Industrial Management*. In A Tillett, T Kempner and G Willis (eds): *Management Thinkers*. Pelican: Harmondsworth.

Cyert, RM and March, JG (1963) *A Behavioral Theory of the Firm*. Prentice-Hall: Englewood Cliffs, NJ, USA.

Daft, RL (1998) *Organizational Theory and Design* (6th edition). Southwestern: Cincinnati, OH, USA.

Dakin, SR and Hamilton, RT (1990) How 'general' are your general managers? *Management Decision*, 28(2), 32–7.

Dale, BG (ed) (1999) *Managing Quality* (3rd edition). Blackwell: Oxford.

Dale, BG (ed) (2003) *Managing Quality* (4th edition). Blackwell: Oxford.

Dale, BG and Cooper, CL (1992) *TQM and Human Resources: An Executive Guide*. Blackwell: Oxford.

Dale, PN (1986) *The Myth of Japanese Uniqueness*. Croom Helm: London.

Darwin, J, Johnson, P and McAuley, J (2002) *Developing Strategies for Change*. Financial Times Prentice Hall: Harlow.

Dastmalchian, A (1984) Environmental dependencies and company structure in Britain. *Organization Studies*, 5(3), 222–41.

Davenport, TH (1993) *Process Innovation: Re-engineering Work through IT*. Harvard Business School Press: Boston, MA, USA.

Davies, C (1995) *Gender and the Professional Predicament in Nursing*. Routledge: London.

Davis, E and Star, J (1993) The world's best performing companies. *Business Strategy Review*, 4(2), 1–16.

Davis, JA (1989) Industrialisation in Britain and Europe before 1850. In P Mathias and JA Davis (eds): *The First Industrial Revolutions*. Blackwell: Cambridge.

Davis, LE (1979) Job Design: historical overview. In LE Davis and JC Taylor (eds): *Design of Work*. Goodyear: Santa Monica, CA, USA.

Davis, LE and Canter, RR (1956) Job Design Research. *Journal of Industrial Engineering*, 7(6), 275.

Davis, LE, Canter, RR and Hoffman, J (1955) Current job design criteria. *Journal of Industrial Engineering*, 6(2), 5–11.

Davis, R (1928) *The Principles of Factory Organization and Management*. Harper & Row: New York, USA.

Davis, TRV (1985) Managing culture at the bottom. In R Kilmann, M Saxton, R Serpa and Associates (eds): *Gaining Control of the Corporate Culture*. Jossey-Bass: San Francisco, CA, USA.

Dawkins, W (1993) Costly burden of tradition. *Financial Times*, 1 December, 10.

Dawkins, W (1994) Loosening of the corporate web. *Financial Times*, 30 November, 15.

Dawson, P (1994) *Organizational Change: A Processual Approach*. Paul Chapman Publishing: London.

Dawson, P (2003) *Organizational Change: A Processual Approach*. Routledge: London.

Day, C, Elliott, J, Somekh, B and Winter, R (eds) (2002) *Theory and Practice in Action Research*. Symposium Books: Oxford.

Day, J, Reynolds, P and Lancaster, G (1998) A marketing strategy for public sector organisations compelled to operate in a compulsory competitive tendering environment. *International Journal of Public Sector Management*, 11(7), 583–95.

Deal, T and Kennedy, A (1982) Culture: a new look through old lenses. *Journal of Applied Behavioural Science*, 19(4), 497–507.

DeCarlo, S (2008) CEO compensation. *Forbes.Com*, 30 April. www.forbes.com

de Chernatony, L and Cottam, S (2008) Interactions between organisational cultures and corporate brands. *Journal of Product and Brand Management*, 17(1), 13–24.

Delbridge, R (2004) Working in teams: ethnographic evidence from two 'high performance' workplaces. In S Fleetwood and S Ackroyd (eds) *Critical Realist Applications in Organisation and Management Studies*. Routledge: London.

Deming, WE (1982) *Quality, Productivity and Competitive Position*. MIT Press: Boston, MA, USA.

Denegri-Knott, J, Zwick, D and Schroeder, JE (2006) Mapping consumer power: an integrative framework for marketing and consumer research. *European Journal of Marketing*, 40(9/10), 950–71.

Dent, EB (2002) The messy history of OB&D: How three strands came to be seen as one rope. *Management Decision*, 40, 266–80.

Dent, EB and Goldberg, SG (1999) Challenging resistance to change. *Journal of Applied Behavioral Science*, 35(1), 25–41.

Deresky, H (2000) *International Management: Managing across Borders and Cultures* (3rd edition). Prentice-Hall: Upper Saddle River, NY, USA.

Derrida, J (1978) *Writing and Difference*. Routledge and Kegan Paul: London.

Dess, GG and Davis, PS (1984) Porter's (1980) generic strategies as determinants of strategic group membership and original performance. *Academy of Management Journal*, 27(3), 467–88.

De Witte, K and van Muijen, JJ (1999) Organizational culture: critical questions for researchers and practitioners. *European Journal of Work and Organizational Psychology*, 8(4), 583–95.

Dickens, L and Watkins, K (1999) Action research: rethinking Lewin. *Management Learning*, 30(2), 127–40.

Dixit, A (1980) The role of investment in entry deterrence. *Economic Journal*, 90, 95–106.

Dobson, P (1988) Changing culture. *Employment Gazette*, December, 647–50.

Dobson, PJ (2001) The philosophy of critical realism – an opportunity for information systems research. *Information Systems Frontiers*, 3(2), 199–210.

Docherty, P, Forslin, J, Shani, AB and King, M (2002) Emerging work systems: from intensive to sustainable. In P Docherty, J Forslin, AB Shani and M King (eds): *Creating Sustainable Work Systems: Emerging Perspectives and Practices*. Routledge: London.

Doherty, TL and Horne, T (2002) *Managing Public Services: Implementing Change – A Thoughtful Approach*. Routledge: London.

Dolvik, JE and Stokland, D (1992) Norway: the 'Norwegian Model' in transition. In A Ferner and R Hyman (eds): *Industrial Relations in the New Europe*. Blackwell: Oxford.

Domberger, S (1998) *The Contracting Organization*. Oxford University Press: Oxford.

Done, K (1994) Up to strength once again: Volvo. *Financial Times*, 2 December.

Done, K and Willman, J (2008) BA struggles to escape T5 twilight zone. *Financial Times*, 5 April, 5.

Donkin, R (2002) How to preserve the soul of management: the increasing sophistication of measurement techniques threatens to reduce executives to robots. *Financial Times*, 19 Sept, 12.

Donovan, P (1995) Saatchis in row over share deal. *The Guardian*, 15 February, 22.

Doran, J (2008) Wall Street's collapse: who is next? *The Observer*, 20 July. www.guardian.co.uk

Dorling, D, Rigby, J, Wheeler, B, Ballas, D, Thomas, B, Fahmy, E, Gordon, D and Lupton, R (2007) *Poverty, Wealth and Place in Britain, 1968 to 2005*. Joseph Rowntree Foundation/Polity Press: Bristol.

Drennan, D (1992) *Transforming Company Culture*. McGraw-Hill: London.

Drory, A and Romm, T (1988) Politics in the organization and its perception within the organization. *Organization Studies*, 9(2), 165–79.

Drucker, PF (1974) *Management: Tasks, Responsibilities, Practices*. Harper & Row: London.

Drucker, PF (1985) *Innovation and Entrepreneurship*. Pan: London.

Dudley, G (1999) British Steel and the government since privatisation: policy 'framing' and the transformation of policy networks. *Public Administration*, 77(1), 51–71.

Dukakis, MS and Kanter, RM (1988) *Creating the Future*. Summit Books: New York, USA.

Duncan, WJ (1975) Organisations as political coalitions: a behavioral view of the goal function process. *Journal of Behavioral Economics*, 5, Summer, 25–44.

Duncan, WJ (1999) *Management: Ideas and Action*. Oxford University Press: Oxford.

Dunham, AL (1955) *The Industrial Revolution in France*. Exposition Press: New York, USA.

Dunphy, D (2000) Embracing paradox: top-down versus participative management of organizational change, A Commentary on Conger and Bennis. In M Beer and N Nohria (eds): *Breaking the Code of Change*. Harvard Business School Press: Boston, MA, USA.

Dunphy, DD and Griffiths, A (1998) *The Sustainable Corporation: Organisational Renewal in Australia*. Allen & Unwin: St Leonards, Australia.

Dunphy, DD and Stace, DA (1988) Transformational and coercive strategies for planned organizational change: beyond the OD model. *Organization Studies*, 9(3), 317–34.

Dunphy, DD and Stace, DA (1992) *Under New Management: Australian Organizations in Transition*. McGraw-Hill: Roseville, NSW, Australia.

Dunphy, DD and Stace, DA (1993) The strategic management of corporate change. *Human Relations*, 46(8), 905–18.

Dunphy, D, Griffiths, A and Benn, S (2003) *Organizational Change for Corporate Sustainability*. Routledge: London.

Dunphy, D, Griffiths, A and Benn, S (2007) *Organizational Change for Corporate Sustainability* (2nd edition). Routledge: London.

Dyer, H (1996) Specialized supplier networks as a source of competitive advantage: evidence from the auto industry. *Strategic Management Journal*, 17(4), 271–91.

Easterby-Smith, M (1997) Disciplines of organizational learning: contributions and critiques. *Human Relations*, 50(9), 1085–113.

Easterby-Smith, M, Crossan, M and Nicolini, D (2000) Organizational learning: debates past, present and future. *Journal of Management Studies*, 37(6), 783–96.

Easton, G (2000) Case research as a method for industrial networks: a realist apologia. In S Ackroyd and S Fleetwood (eds): *Realist Perspectives on Management and Organisations*. Routledge: London.

Eccles, T (1993) The deceptive allure of empowerment. *Long Range Planning*, 26(6), 13–21.

Economist (1998) All fall down. *Economist*, 28 February.

Economist (2002) *Globalisation: Reasons, Effects and Challenges*. Economist Books: London.

Economist (2008) Grossly distorted picture: If you look at GDP per head, the world is a different – and, by and large, a better – place. *Economist.com*, 13 March, www.economist.com

Economist Intelligence Unit (1992) *Making Quality Work – Lessons from Europe's Leading Companies*. Economist Intelligence Unit: London.

Eden, C and Huxham, C (1996) Action research for the study of organizations. In SR Clegg, C Hardy and WR Nord (eds): *Handbook of Organization Studies*. Sage: London.

Edwardes, M (1983) *Back from the Brink*. Collins: London.

Egan, G (1994) Cultivate your culture. *Management Today*, April, 39–42.

Elden, M and Chisholm, RF (1993) Emerging varieties of action research: introduction to the special issue. *Human Relations*, 46(20), 121–42.

Eldridge, JET and Crombie, AD (1974) *A Sociology of Organizations*. George Allen and Unwin: London.

Elliot, K and Lawrence, P (1985) *Introducing Management*. Penguin: Harmondsworth.

Elliott, L (1997) The weightless revolution. *Guardian*, 10 November, 17.

Elliott, L (2003) The lost decade. *Guardian*, 9 July, 1–2.

Elliott, L (2007) Cost of large mortgages hits post-9/11 high as credit squeeze ripples through economy. *The Guardian*, 2 October, 29.

Elliott, L (2008) Up. Up. Up. Child poverty, pensioner poverty, inequality. *The Guardian*, 11 June. www.guardian.co.uk

Elliott, L and Brittain, V (1998) The rich and poor grow further apart. *Guardian*, 9 September, 18.

Elliott, L and Seager, A (2008) Shape of things to come. *The Guardian*, 13 November, 1.

Elrod II, PD and Tippett, DD (2002) The 'death valley' of change. *Journal of Organizational Change Management*, 15(3), 273–91.

Erridge, A and Nondi, R (1994) Public procurement, competition and partnership. *European Journal of Purchasing and Supply Management*, 1(3), 169–79.

Etzioni, A (1975) *A Comparative Analysis of Complex Organizations*. Free Press: New York, USA.

Etzioni, A (2004) The post affluent society. *Review of Social Economy*, LXII(3), 404–20.

European Commission (1998) *Work Programme*. The Directorate General for Energy, DG XVII / 148 / 98–EN: Brussels.

Evans, MG (1970) The effects of supervisory behaviour on the path–goal relationship. *Organizational Behavior and Human Performance*, 5, 277–98.

Evans, R, Traynor, I, Harding, L and Carroll, R (2003) Web of state corruption dates back 40 years. *Guardian*, 13 June, available at www.guardian.co.uk.

EWERC (2007) The globalization of the temporary staffing industry. *EWERC Research News*, No 3, September, 2.

Ezzamel, M, Green, C, Lilley, S and Willmott, H (1994) *Change Management: Appendix 1 – A Review and Analysis of Recent Changes in UK Management Practices*. The Financial Services Research Centre, UMIST: Manchester.

Fagenson-Eland, E, Ensher, EA and Burke, WW (2004) Organization development and change interventions: a seven-nation comparison. *Journal of Applied Behavioral Science*, 40(4), 432–64.

Fahy, J (2000) The resource-based view of the firm: some stumbling-blocks on the road to understanding sustainable competitive advantage. *Journal of European Industrial Training*, 24(2–4), 94–104.

Falconer, J (2002) Emergence happens! Misguided paradigms regarding organizational change and the role of complexity and patterns in the change landscape. *Emergence*, 4(1/2), 117–30.

Fang, T (2005–6) From 'onion' to 'ocean': paradox and change in national cultures. *International Studies of Management and Organization*, 35(4), 71–90.

Farrell, D and Petersen, JC (1983) Patterns of political behaviour in organizations. *The Academy of Management Review*, 7, 403–12.

Fawn, J and Cox, B (1985) *Corporate Planning in Practice*. Strategic Planning Society: London.

Fayol, H (1949) *General and Industrial Management* (trans). Pitman: London.

Fazio, RH, Zanna, MP and Cooper, J (1977) Dissonance and self-perception: an integrative view of each theory's proper domain of application. *Journal of Experimental Social Psychology*, 13, 464–79.

Featherstone, M (1988a) In pursuit of postmodernism: an introduction. *Theory, Culture and Society*, 5, 195–215.

Featherstone, M (ed) (1988b) *Postmodernism*. Sage: Newbury Park, CA, USA.

Ferguson, CH (1988) From the people who brought you Voodoo Economics. *Harvard Business Review*, May–June, 55–62.

Ferlie, E, Ashburner, L, Fitzgerald, L and Pettigrew, A (1996) *The New Public Sector in Action*. Oxford University Press: Oxford.

Ferner, A and Hyman, R (eds) (1992) *Industrial Relations in the New Europe*. Blackwell: Oxford.

Festinger, L (1957) *The Theory of Cognitive Dissonance*. Stanford University Press: Stanford, CA, USA.

Fiedler, FE (1967) *A Theory of Leadership Effectiveness*. McGraw-Hill: New York, USA.

Fiedler, FE (1995) Cognitive resources and leadership performance. *Applied Psychology: An International Review*, 44, 5–28.

Fiedler, FE and Chemers, MM (1984) *Improving Leadership Effectiveness: The Leader Match Concept* (2nd edition). Wiley: New York, USA.

Filby, I and Willmott, H (1988) Ideologies and contradictions in a public relations department. *Organization Studies*, 9(3), 335–51.

Filley, AC, House, RJ and Kerr, S (1976) *Managerial Process and Organization Behavior*. Scott, Foresman and Company: Glenview, IL, USA.

Financial, The [of Greece] (2000) When would consumers get a better service: if service utilities were government- or privately-owned? *Financial, The* [of Greece], 6 October, 14–15.

Financial Times (2003) The madness in Marconi's fall: the FSA report obscures important lessons. *Financial Times*, 14 April, 20.

Financial Times (2007) Dreams are no basis for a sound corporate strategy. *Financial Times*, 20 March, 15.

Finch, J and Treanor, J (2003) Shares down 24%. Average earnings up 3%. Boardroom pay up 23%. *Guardian*, 31 July, 1.

Finstad, N (1998) The rhetoric of organizational change. *Human Relations*, 51(6), 717–40.

Fiol, MC and Lyles, MA (1985) Organizational learning. *Academy of Management Review*, 10(4), 803–13.

Fitton, R and Wadsworth, A (1958) *The Strutts and the Arkwrights 1758–1830*. Manchester University Press: Manchester.

Fitzgerald, LA (2002a) Chaos: the lens that transcends. *Journal of Organizational Change Management*, 15(4), 339–58.

Fitzgerald, LA (2002b) Chaos speak: a glossary of chaordic terms and phrases. *Journal of Organizational Change Management*, 15(4), 412–23.

Flamholtz, E (2001) Corporate culture and the bottom line. *European Management Journal*, 19(3), 268–75.

Fleetwood, S and Ackroyd, S (eds) (2004) *Critical Realist Applications in Organisation and Management Studies*. Routledge: London.

Fleisher, CS and Bensoussan, BE (2003) *Strategic and Competitive Analysis: Methods and Techniques for Analysing Business Competition*. Prentice-Hall: Upper Saddle River, NJ, USA.

Fleishman, EA (1953) The description of supervisory behaviour. *Personnel Psychology*, 37, 1–6.

Fleishman, EA (1969) *Manual for the Leadership Opinion Questionnaire*. Science Research Associates: USA.

Flynn, N (1993) *Public Sector Management* (2nd edition). Harvester Wheatsheaf: Hemel Hempstead.

Flynn, J, Dawley, H, Templeman, J and Bernier, L (1995) Suddenly British carmaking is burning rubber. *Business Week*, 3 April, 21.

Foegen, JH (1999) Why not empowerment? *Business and Economics Review*, 45(3), April–June, 31.

Fohlen, C (1973) France 1700–1914. In C Cipolla (ed): *The Fontana Economic History of Europe*, Vol. 4. Fontana: London.

Ford, JD and Ford, LW (1995) The role of conversations in producing intentional change in organizations. *Academy of Management Review*, 20(3), 541–70.

Ford, TM (1981) Strategic planning – myth or reality? A chief executive's view. *Long Range Planning*, 14, December, 9–11.

Fortune (1990) Global 500: the world's biggest industrial corporations. *Fortune*, 30 July.

Fortune (2007) 100 Best Companies to work for 2007. *Fortune*. Available at money.ccn.com/magazines/fortune/bestcompanies/2007.

Fortune (2008) Global 500: Our annual Ranking of the World's Largest Corporations. *Fortune*. Available at www.cnnmoney.com/magazines/fortune/global500/2008

Foster, R and Kaplan, S (2003) *Creative Destruction: Why Companies That Are Built to Last Underperform the Market – And How to Successfully Transform Them*. Doubleday: London.

Foucault, M (1977) *The Archaeology of Knowledge*. Tavistock: London.

Foucault, M (1983) The subject and power. In HL Dreyfus and P Rabinow (eds): *Michel Foucault: Beyond Structuralism and Hermeneutics* (2nd edition). University of Chicago Press: Chicago, USA.

Fox, JM (1975) Strategic planning: a case study. *Managerial Planning*, 23, May/June, 32–8.

Fox, M (1994) *The Reinvention of Work: A New Vision of Livelihood for Our Times*. Harper: San Francisco, USA.

Francks, P (1992) *Japanese Economic Development: Theory and Practice*. Routledge: London.

Franklin, B (1997) *Newszak and News Media*. Arnold: London.

Frederick, WC (1998) Creatures, corporations, communities, chaos, complexity: a naturo-logical view of the corporate social role. *Business and Society*, 37(4), 358–76.

Freeman, C (1988) The factory of the future: the productivity paradox, Japanese just-in-time and information technology. *ESRC PICT Policy Research Paper 3*. ESRC: Swindon.

French, JRP, Jr (1945) Role playing as a method of training foremen. *Sociometry*, 8, 410–25.

French, JRP, Jr and Raven, BH (1959) The bases of social power. In D Cartwright (ed): *Studies in Social Power*. Institute for Social Research: Ann Harbor, MI, USA.

French, WL and Bell, CH (1973) *Organization Development*. Prentice-Hall: Englewood Cliffs, NJ, USA.

French, WL and Bell, CH (1984) *Organization Development* (4th edition). Prentice-Hall: Englewood Cliffs, NJ, USA.

French, WL and Bell, CH (1995) *Organization Development* (5th edition). Prentice-Hall: Englewood Cliffs, NJ, USA.

French, WL and Bell, CH (1999) *Organization Development* (6th edition). Prentice-Hall: Upper Saddle River, NJ, USA.

Friedman, G (1961) *The Anatomy of Work*. Heinemann: London.

Frith, M (2003) Brain drain: the men who won't let jobs deprive them of fatherhood. *The Independent*, 14 June, 7.

Froebel, F, Heinrichs, J and Kreye, O (1980) *The New Industrial Division of Labour: Structural Unemployment in Industrialized Countries and Industrialization in Developing Countries*. Cambridge University Press: Cambridge.

Frost, PJ and Hayes, DC (1979) An exploration in two cultures of a model of political behaviour in organizations. In RW Allen and LW Porter (eds): *Organizational Influence Processes*. Scott, Foresman and Co: Glenview, IL, USA.

Frost, PJ, Moore, L, Louis, M, Lundberg, C and Martin, J (eds) (1991) *Reframing Organizational Culture*. Sage: Beverly Hills, CA, USA.

Fruin, WM (1992) *The Japanese Enterprise System*. Oxford University Press: Oxford.

Fukushige, A and Spicer, DP (2007) Leadership preferences in Japan: an exploratory study. *Leadership and Organization Development Journal*, 28(6), 508–30.

Fullerton, H and Price, C (1991) Culture change in the NHS. *Personnel Management*, March, 50–3.

Fulton, The Lord (1968) *The Civil Service: Report of the Committee Cmnd 3638*. HMSO: London.

Furrer, O, Thomas, H and Goussevskaia, A (2008) The structure and evolution of the strategic management field: a content analysis of 26 years of strategic management research. *International Journal of Management Reviews*, 10(1), 1–23.

Galagan, PA (1997) Strategic planning is back. *Training and Development*, 51, 32–8.

Galbraith, JR (2000) The role of formal structures and processes. In M Beer and N Nohria (eds): *Breaking the Code of Change*. Harvard Business School Press: Boston, MA, USA.

Galpin, T (1996) *The Human Side of Change: A Practical Guide to Organization Redesign*. Jossey-Bass: San Francisco, CA, USA.

Gandz, J and Murray, VV (1980) The experience of workplace politics. *Academy of Management Journal*, 23, 237–51.

Gardner, J (1990) *On Leadership*. Free Press: New York, USA.

Garratt, B (1987) *The Learning Organization*. Fontana: London.

Garratt, B (1999) The learning organisation 15 years on: some personal reflections. *The Learning Organization*, 6(5), 202–6.

Garvin, DA (1993) Building a learning organization. *Harvard Business Review*, 71(4), July–August, 78–91.

Gastil, J (1994) A definition and an illustration of democratic leadership. *Human Relations*, 47, 953–75.

Gay, CL and Essinger, J (2000) *Inside Outsourcing*. Nicholas Brealey Publishing: London.

Gellerman, W, Frankel, MS and Ladenson, RF (1990) *Values and Ethics in Organizational and Human Systems Development: Responding to Dilemmas in Professional Life*. Jossey-Bass: San Francisco, CA, USA.

Gell-Mann, M (1994) *The Quark and the Jaguar*. Freeman: New York, USA.

Genus, A (1998) *The Management of Change: Perspective and Practice*. International Thompson: London.

Gephart, RP, Thatchenkery, TJ and Boye, DM (1996) Reconstructing organizations for future survival. In DM Boye, RP Gephart and TJ Thatchenkery (eds): *Postmodern Management and Organizational Theory*. Sage: Thousand Oaks, CA, USA.

Gergen, KJ (1992) Organization theory in the postmodern era. In M Reed and M Hughes (eds): *Rethinking Organization: New Directions in Organization Theory and Analysis*. Sage: London.

Gersick, CJG (1991) Revolutionary change theories: a multilevel exploration of the punctuated equilibrium paradigm. *Academy of Management Review*, 16(1), 10–36.

Ghemawat, P (1991) *Commitment: The Dynamics of Strategy*. Free Press: New York, USA.

Ghemawat, P (2008) Reconceptualizing international strategy and organization. *Strategic Organization*, 6(2), 195–206.

Ghoshal, S and Bartlett, CA (2000) Rebuilding behavioral context: a blueprint for corporate renewal. In M Beer and N Nohria (eds): *Breaking the Code of Change*. Harvard Business School Press: Boston, MA, USA.

Gibb, CA (1969) Leadership. In G Lindzey and E Aronson (eds): *Handbook of Social Psychology*, Vol. 4 (2nd edition). Addison-Wesley: Reading, MA, USA.

Gibbons, PT (1992) Impacts of organisational evolution on leadership roles and behaviors. *Human Relations*, 45(1), 1–18.

Gibson, JL, Ivancevich, JM and Donnelly, JH (1988) *Organizations: Behavior–Structure–Processes*. Business Publications: Plano, TX, USA.

Gibson, O (2003a) Napster: hopes to relaunch before end of year. *Guardian*, 24 February, available at www.guardian.co.uk.

Gibson, O (2003b) Web piracy hits music sales. *Guardian*, 10 February, available at www.guardian.co.uk.

Gibson, O (2003c) EMI to sell music downloads. *Guardian*, 23 April, available at www.guardian.co.uk.

Giddens, A (1984) *The Constitution of Society*. Polity Press: Cambridge.

Giddens, A (2002) *Runaway World: How Globalisation Is Reshaping Our Lives*. Profile: London.

Gilbert, RJ and Newbery, DMG (1982) Preemptive patenting and the persistence of monopoly. *American Economic Review*, 72, 514–26.

Gilbert, X and Strebel, P (1992) Developing competitive advantage. In H Mintzberg and JB Quinn (eds): *The Strategy Process: Concepts, Contexts and Cases*. Prentice Hall: London.

Gilbreth, FB and Gilbreth, LM (1914) *Applied Motion Study*. Sturgis and Walton: New York, USA.

Gilchrist, A (2000) The well-connected community: networking to the edge of chaos. *Community Development Journal*, 3(3), 264–75.

Gillespie, R (1991) *Manufacturing Knowledge: A History of the Hawthorne Experiments*. Cambridge University Press: Cambridge.

Gillett, C (1996) *The Sound of the City: The Rise of Rock & Roll* (3rd edition). Souvenir Press: London.

Gilmore, T, Shea, G and Useem, M (1997) Side effects of corporate cultural transformations. *Journal of Applied Behavioral Science*, 33(2), 174–89.

Gittings, J (1998) Weakest pay the price for recession as African poverty comes to Asia. *Guardian*, 17 October, 16.

Gleick, J (1988) *Chaos: The Making of a New Science*. Heinemann: London.

Globalisation Guide.org (2003) Is globalisation shifting power from nation states to undemocratic organisations? Available at www.globalisationguide.org.

Glueck, WF (1978) *Business Policy and Strategic Management*. McGraw-Hill: New York, USA.

Gold, KA (1982) Managing for success: a comparison of the private and public sectors. *Public Administration Review*, November–December, 568–75.

Gold, M (1992) Metatheory and field theory in social psychology: relevance or elegance? *Journal of Social Issues*, 48(2), 67–78.

Gold, M (ed) (1999): *The Complete Social Scientist: A Kurt Lewin Reader*. American Psychological Association: Washington, DC, USA.

Golding, D and Currie, D (2000) *Thinking about Management: A Reflective Practice Approach*. Routledge: London.

Golzen, G (1995) Jobbing guru. *Human Resources*, 16, January/February, 42–8.

Goodwin, B (1994) *How the Leopard Changed its Spots*. Weidenfeld and Nicholson: London.

Google (2008) Google Jobs: Google Celebrates Diversity. www.google.co.uk/support/jobs.

Goold, M, Campbell, A and Alexander, M (1994) *Corporate-Level Strategy: Creating Value in the Multi-Business Company*. Wiley: Chichester.

Gordon, G (1985) The relationship of corporate culture to industry sector and corporate performance. In R Kilmann, M Saxton, R Serpa and Associates (eds): *Gaining Control of the Corporate Culture*. Jossey-Bass: San Francisco, CA, USA.

Gould, SJ (1989) Punctuated equilibrium in fact and theory. *Journal of Social Biological Structure*, 12, 117–36.

Goulielmos, M (2003) Outlining organisational failure in information systems development. *Disaster Prevention and Management*, 12(4), 319–27.

Gow, D (1999a) Vultures still circling Rover plant as BMW remains silent on investment. *Guardian*, 6 February, 11–12.

Gow, D (1999b) BMW to put £3bn into Rover car plants. *Guardian*, 24 June, 25.

Gow, D (1999c) Finance: EC plans global assault: Simpson pledges to double value within five years after Marconi defence sale. *Guardian*, 6 May, 25.

Gow, D and Traynor, I (1999) BMW split raises fears for Rover plant. *Guardian*, 2 February, 1.

Graen, GB and Cashman, JF (1975) A role making model of leadership in formal organizations: a developmental approach. In JG Hunt and LL Larson (eds): *Leadership Frontiers*. Kent State University Press: Kent, OH, USA.

Graetz, F, Rimmer, M, Lawrence, A and Smith, A (2002) *Managing Organisational Change*. Wiley: Milton, Queensland, Australia.

Graham, G, Burnes, B and Hardaker, G (2002) The peer-to-peer revolution: how the Internet is transforming the supply chain for music. *The International Journal of New Product Development and Innovation Management*, 4(2), June/July, 115–30.

Grant, A (1983) *Against the Clock*. Pluto: London.

Grant, L (2006) And the Brand Played On. *The Guardian Weekend*, 12 August, 18–25.

Grant, RM (1991a) *Contemporary Strategy Analysis*. Blackwell: Oxford.

Grant, RM (1991b) The resource-based theory of competitive advantage: implications for strategy formulation. *California Management Review*, 33(3), 114–22.

Grant, RM (2007) *Contemporary Strategy Analysis: Concepts, Techniques and Applications* (4th edition). Blackwell: Oxford.

Green, C (2008) Chief executives' pay rises by more than 30 per cent. *The Independent*, 24 May. www.independent.co.uk

Greenberg, P and Erios, L (2001) One year ago: MP3.com caves in to legal blow, *Ecommercetimes*, 1–3, 5 November, available at www.ecommercetimes.com.

Greenwald, J (1996) Reinventing Sears. *Time*, 23 December, 53–5.

Greiner, LE (1967) Patterns of organization change. *Harvard Business Review*, May–June, 119–30.

Greiner, LE (1972a) Evolution and revolution as organizations grow. *Harvard Business Review*, July–August, 37–46.

Greiner, LE (1972b) Red flags in organization development. *Business Horizons*, June.

Greiner, LE and Cummings, TG (2004) Wanted: OD more alive than dead! *Journal of Applied Behavioral Science*, 40(4), 374–91.

Grey, C (2003) The fetish of change. *Tamara: Journal of Critical Postmodern Organizational Science*, 2(2), 1–19.

Griffin, D (2002) *The Emergence of Leadership: Linking Self-Organisation and Ethics*. Routledge: London.

Grint, K (2005) Problems, problems, problems: the social construction of 'leadership'. *Human Relations*, 58(11), 1467–94.

Grinyer, PH, Mayes, DG and McKiermon, P (1988) *Sharpbenders: The Secrets of Unleashing Corporate Potential*. Blackwell: Oxford.

Grove, G (1998) The automotive industry – the customer's perspective: a study of Rover group. In B Burnes and B Dale (eds) (1998): *Working in Partnership*. Gower: Aldershot.

Grundy, T (1993) *Managing Strategic Change*. Kogan Page: London.

Guest, D (1992) Right enough to be dangerously wrong: an analysis of the *In Search of Excellence* phenomenon. In G Salaman (ed): *Human Resource Strategies*. Sage: London.

Guest, RH (1957) Job enlargement – revolution in Job Design. *Personnel Administration*, 20, 9–16.

Gyllenhammar, PG (1977) *People at Work*. Addison-Wesley: Reading, MA, USA.

Habakkuk, HJ and Postan, M (eds) (1965) *The Cambridge Economic History of Europe*, Vol. VI. Cambridge University Press: Cambridge.

Hackman, JR and Lawler, EE (1971) Employee relations and job characteristics. *Journal of Applied Psychology*, 55, 259–86.

Hackman, JR and Oldham, GR (1980) *Work Redesign*. Addison-Wesley: Reading, MA, USA.

Haggett, P. (1975) *Geography: A Modern Synthesis*. Harper & Row: New York: NY.

Haigh, C (2002) Using chaos theory: the implications for nursing. *Journal of Advanced Nursing*, 37(5), 462–9.

Hales, CP (1986) What do managers do?: a critical review of the evidence. *Journal of Management Studies*, 22(1), 88–115.

Hales, C (1999) Why do managers do what they do: reconciling evidence and theory in accounts of managerial work. *British Journal of Management*, 10, 335–50.

Hall, DT and Nougaim, KE (1968) An examination of Maslow's need hierarchy in an organizational setting. *Organizational Behaviour and Performance*, 3, February, 12–35.

Hall, R (1933) A framework linking intangible resources and capabilities to sustainable competitive advantage. *Strategic Management Journal*, 14, 607–18.

Hambrick, DC (1983) High profit strategies in mature capital goods industries: a contingency approach. *Academy of Management Journal*, 26, 687–707.

Hambrick, DC and Frederickson, JW (2001) Are you sure you have a strategy? *The Academy of Management Executive*, 15(4), 48–59.

Hamel, G (2007) *The Future of Management*. Harvard Business School Press: Boston, MA, USA.

Hamel, G and Prahalad, CK (1989) Strategic intent. *Harvard Business Review*, May–June, 63–76.

Hamel, G and Prahalad, CK (1994) *Competing for the Future*. Harvard Business School Press: Boston, MA, USA.

Hamilton, C (2003) Downshifting in Britain: A sea-change in the pursuit of happiness. Discussion Paper Number 58, November. The Australia Institute: Manuka, ACT, Australia.

Hammer, M and Champy, J (1993) *Re-engineering the Corporation*. Nicolas Brealey: London.

Hammersley, B (2002) Working the web: P2P technology. *Guardian*, 7 March, available at www.guardian.co.uk.

Handfield, RB and Nichols, EL Jr (1999) *Introduction to Supply Chain Management*. Prentice-Hall: Englewood Cliffs, NJ, USA.

Handy, C (1979) *Gods of Management*. Pan: London.

Handy, C (1984) *The Future of Work*. Blackwell: Oxford.

Handy, C (1986) *Understanding Organizations* (3rd edition). Penguin: Harmondsworth.

Handy, C (1989) *The Age of Unreason*. Arrow: London.

Handy, C (1993) *Understanding Organizations* (4th edition). Penguin: Harmondsworth.

Handy, C (1994) *The Empty Raincoat*. Hutchinson: London.

Handy, C (1997) *The Hungry Spirit*. Hutchinson: London.

Handy, C (2007a) *Myself and Other More Important Matters*. Arrow Books: London.

Handy, C (2007b) *The New Philanthropists*. Heinemann: London.

Handy, C, Gow, I, Gordon, C, Randlesome, C and Moloney, M (1987) *The Making of a Manager*. NEDO: London.

Hannagan, T (2002) *Management: Concepts and Practices* (3rd edition). Financial Times Pearson: Harlow.

Hannam, R (1993) *Kaizen for Europe*. IFS: Kempston.

Hannan, MT and Freeman, J (1977) The population ecology of organizations. *American Journal of Sociology*, 82, 929–64.

Hannan, MT and Freeman, J (1988) *Organizational Ecology*. Harvard University Press: Cambridge, MA, USA.

Hannan, MT, Pólos, L and Carroll, GR (2003) The fog of change: opacity and asperity in organizations. *Administrative Science Quarterly*, 8(3), 399–432.

Hanson, P (1993) Made in Britain – the true state of manufacturing industry. Paper presented at the Institution of Mechanical Engineers' Conference on Performance Measurement and Benchmarking, Birmingham, June.

Hardaker, G and Graham, G (2001) *Wired Marketing: Energizing Business for e-Commerce*. Wiley: Chichester.

Hardy, C (1996) Understanding power: bringing about strategic change. *British Journal of Management*, 7(Special Issue) March, S3–S16.

Harré, R (1972) *The Philosophies of Science*. Oxford University Press: Oxford.

Harré, R and Madden, EH (1975) *Causal Powers*. Blackwell: Oxford.

Harré, R and Secord, PF (1972) *The Explanation of Social Behaviour*. Blackwell: Oxford.

Harrigan, RK (1980) *Strategy for Declining Businesses*. Lexington Books: Lexington, MA, USA.

Harris, PR (1985) *Management in Transition*. Jossey-Bass: San Francisco, CA, USA.

Harrison, M (2002) Lord Simpson speaks out for the first time since leaving Marconi. *Independent*, 28 November, 24.

Harrison, M (2003) Swipe card strike wipes £40m off BA. *Independent*, 1 August, 19.

Harrison, R (1970) Choosing the depth of an organisational intervention. *Journal of Applied Behavioural Science*, 6, 181–202.

Harrison, R (1972) Understanding your organization's character. *Harvard Business Review*, 50(3), May/June, 119–28.

Harrison, R (2002) *Learning and Development* (3rd edition). CIPD: London.

Harrison, R (2005) *Learning and Development* (4th edition). CIPD: London.

Hartley, J, Bennington, J and Binns, P (1997) Researching the roles of internal-change agents in the management of organizational change. *British Journal of Management*, 8(1), 61–73.

Harukiyo, H and Hook, GD (eds) (1998) *Japanese Business Management: Restructuring for Low Growth and Globalization*. Routledge: London.

Harung, HS, Heaton, DP and Alexander, CN (1999) Evolution of organizations in the new millennium. *Leadership and Organization Development Journal*, 20(4), 198–207.

Harvey, D and Brown, DR (2001) *An Experiential Approach to Organization Development* (6th edition). Prentice-Hall: Upper Saddle River, NJ, USA.

Harvey, F (2001) Microsoft's direct connection to the customer. *Financial Times*, 31 December, 7.

Hassard, J (1990) An alternative to paradigm incommensurability in organization theory. In J Hassard and D Pym (eds): *The Theory and Philosophy of Organizations*. Routledge: London.

Hassard, J (1993) *Sociology and Organization Theory: Positivism, Paradigms and Postmodernity*. Cambridge University Press: Cambridge.

Hassard, J and Parker, M (eds) (1993) *Postmodernism and Organizations*. Sage: London.

Hassard, J and Sharifi, S (1989) Corporate culture and strategic change. *Journal of General Management*, 15(2), 4–19.

Hatch, MJ (1997) *Organization Theory: Modern, Symbolic and Postmodern Perspectives*. Oxford University Press: Oxford.

Hatch, MJ and Cunliffe, AL (2006) *Organization Theory: Modern, Symbolic and Postmodern Perspectives* (2nd edition). Oxford University Press: Oxford.

Hatvany, N and Pucik, V (1981) An integrated management system: lessons from the Japanese experience. *Academy of Management Review*, 6, 469–80.

Hax, CA and Majluf, NS (1982) Competitive cost dynamics. *Interfaces*, 12, October, 50–61.

Hax, CA and Majluf, NS (1996) *The Strategy Concept and Process* (2nd edition). Prentice-Hall: Upple Saddle River, NJ, USA.

Hax, CA and Nicholson, SM (1983) The use of the growth share matrix in strategic planning. *Interfaces*, 13, February, 46–60.

Hayes, J (2002) *The Theory and Practice of Change Management*. Palgrave: Basingstoke.

Hayles, KN (2000) From chaos to complexity: moving through metaphor to practice. *Complexity and Chaos in Nursing*, 4, available at www.southernct.edu/scsu/chaos-nursing/chaos4.htm.

Hedberg, B (1981) How organizations learn and unlearn. In PC Nystrom and WH Starbuck (eds): *Handbook of Organizational Design*. Oxford University Press: London.

Hedberg, B, Nystrom, P and Starbuck, W (1976) Camping on seesaws: prescriptions for a self-designing organization. *Administrative Science Quarterly*, 17, 371–81.

Hedlund, G and Nonaka, I (1993) Models of knowledge management in the West and Japan. In P Lorange (ed): *Implementing Strategic Processes*. Blackwell: Oxford.

Heller, F (1970) Group feed-back analysis as a change agent. *Human Relations*, 23(4), 319–33.

Heller, R (2002) A legacy turned to tragedy. *The Observer*, 18 August, available at www.observer.co.uk.

Hendry, C (1979) Contingency theory in practice, I. *Personnel Review*, 8(4), 39–44.

Hendry, C (1980) Contingency theory in practice, II. *Personnel Review*, 9(1), 5–11.

Hendry, C (1996) Understanding and creating whole organizational change through learning theory. *Human Relations*, 48(5), 621–41.

Herzberg, F (1968) One more time: how do you motivate employees? *Harvard Business Review*, 46, 53–62.

Herzberg, F, Mausner, B and Snyderman, B (1959) *The Motivation to Work*. John Wiley: New York, USA.

Hickman, CF (1990) *Mind of a Manager, Soul of a Leader*. John Wiley: New York, NY, USA.

Hickman, L (2008) Is this the end for Primark? *The Guardian*, 24 June, available from www.guardian.co.uk

Hickson, DJ and Butler, RJ (1982) Power and decision-making in the organisational coalition. Research report presented to the Social Science Research Council.

Hickson, DJ, Pugh, DS and Pheysey, DC (1969) Operations technology and organisation structure: an empirical reappraisal. *Administrative Science Quarterly*, 14, 378–97.

Hill, CWL and Jones, GR (2006) *Strategic Management: An Integrated Approach* (8th edition). Houghton Mifflin: Boston, MA.

Hines, P (1994) *Creating World Class Suppliers: Unlocking Mutual Competitive Advantage*. Pitman: London.

Hinkin, TR and Tracey, JB (1999) The relevance of charisma for transformational leadership in stable organizations. *Journal of Organizational Change Management*, 12(2), 105–19.

Hirschhorn, L (1988) *The Workplace Within*. MIT Press: Cambridge, MA, USA.

Hirschhorn, L (2000) Changing structure is not enough: the moral meaning of organizational design. In M Beer and N Nohria (eds): *Breaking the Code of Change*. Harvard Business School Press: Boston, MA, USA.

Hirst, C (2002) Marconi's £3bn debt lifeline. *Sunday Independent*, 7 April, 1.

Hitt, MA, Miller, CC and Colella, A (2009) *Organizational Behavior: A Strategic Approach* (2nd edition). Wiley: Hoboken, NJ, USA.

Hlavacka, S, Bacharova, L, Rusnakova, V and Wagner, R (2001) Performance implications of Porter's generic strategies in Slovak hospitals. *Journal of Management in Hospitals*, 15(1), 44–66.

HMSO (1989) *Working for Patients*, Cmnd 555. HMSO: London.

HMSO (1991) *Competing for Quality*, Cmnd 1730. HMSO: London.

Ho, DYF (1976) On the concept of face. *American Journal of Sociology*, 81(4), 867–84.

Hoag, BG, Ritschard, HV and Cooper, CL (2002) Obstacles to effective organization change: the underlying reasons. *Leadership and Organisation Development Journal*, 23(1), 6–15.

Hobsbawm, EJ (1968) *Industry and Empire*. Pelican: Harmondsworth.

Hobsbawm, EJ (1979) *The Age of Revolution*. Abacus: London.

Hobsbawm, EJ (2008) *Globalisation, Democracy and Terrorism*. Abacus: London.

Hock, D (1999) *Birth of the Chaordic Age*. Berrett-Koehler: San Francisco, CA, USA.

Hodge, B and Coronado, G (2007) Understanding change in organizations in a far-from-equilibrium world. *E:CO*, 9(3), 3–15.

Hofer, CH and Schendel, DE (1978) *Strategy Formulation: Analytical Concepts*. West: St Paul, MN, USA.

Hofstede, G (1980) *Culture's Consequences: International Differences in Work-Related Values*. Sage: London.

Hofstede, G (1990) The cultural relativity of organizational practices and theories. In DC Wilson and RH Rosenfeld (eds): *Managing Organizations: Text, Readings and Cases*. McGraw-Hill: London.

Hofstede, G (1993) Cultural constraints in management theories. *Academy of Management Executive*, 7(1), 81–94.

Hofstede, G (2001) *Culture's Consequences: Comparing Values, Behaviors, Institutions, and Organizations across Nations* (2nd edition). Sage: Thousand Oaks, CA, USA.

Holden, N and Burgess, M (1994) *Japanese-Led Companies*. McGraw-Hill: London.

Hoogerwerf, EC and Poorthuis, A-N (2002) The network multilogue: a chaos approach to organizational design. *Journal of Organizational Change Management*, 15(4), 382–90.

Horne, JH and Lupton, T (1965) The work activities of 'middle managers' – an exploratory study. *Journal of Management Studies*, 2(1), 14–33.

Horsley, W and Buckley, R (1990) *Nippon New Superpower; Japan since 1945*. BBC Books: London.

Horton, S (1996) The Civil Service. In D Farnham and S Horton (eds): *Managing the New Public Services* (2nd edition). Macmillan: Basingstoke.

Hoskin, K (1990) Using history to understand theory: a re-consideration of the historical genesis of 'strategy'. Paper prepared for the EIASM Workshop on Strategy, Accounting and Control, Venice, Italy.

Houchin, K and MacLean, D (2005) Complexity theory and strategic change: an empirically informed critique. *British Journal of Management*, 16, 149–66.

House, JS (1993) John R French, Jr: a Lewinian's Lewinian. *Journal of Social Issues*, 49(4), 221–6.

Howarth, C (1988) Report of the Joint Design of Technology, Organisation and People Growth Conference – Venice, 12–14, October. *Information Services News and Abstracts*, 95 November/December, Work Research Unit: London.

Huber, GP (1991) Organizational learning: the contributing processes and the literatures. *Organization Science*, February, 88–115.

Huczynski, AA (1993) *Management Gurus*. Routledge: London.

Huczynski, A and Buchanan, D (2001) *Organizational Behaviour* (4th edition). Financial Times Prentice Hall: Harlow.

Hughes, M (1995) Halifax and Leeds clear the courts. *Guardian*, 29 March, 15.

Hunter, A (2008) Parry's head on block as Americans escalate battle: Liverpool chief executive's rejection of Hicks demand highlights power vacuum in the Anfield boardroom. *The Guardian*, 11 April, available from www.guardian.co.uk

Hunter, JE (1989) *The Emergence of Modern Japan*. Longman: London.

Hurley, RF, Church, AH, Burke, WW and Van Eynde, DF (1992) Tension, change and values in OD. *OD Practitioner*, 29, 1–5.

Huse, EF (1980) *Organization Development and Change*. West: St Paul, MN, USA.

Hussey, DE (1978) Portfolio analysis: practical experience with the Directional Policy Matrix. *Long Range Planning*, 11, August, 2–8.

Hussey, DE and Jenster, P (1999) *Competitive Intelligence: Turning Analysis into Success*. John Wiley: Chichester.

Hutton, W (1995) *The State We're In*. Cape: London.

Hutton, W (2008a) This reckless greed of the few harms the future of the many. *The Observer*, 27 January, available at www.guardian.co.uk.

Hutton, W (2008b) A late call to account. *The Guardian*, 2 December, 30.

IBM (2008) *The Enterprise of the Future: IBM Global CEO Study*. IBM: Somers, NY, USA.

Inagami, T (1988) *Japanese Workplace Industrial Relations*. Japan Institute of Labour: Tokyo.

Inagami, T (1995) *Enterprise Unions in a Mature Society*. Japan Institute of Labour: Tokyo.

Industrial Society (1997) *Culture Change. Managing Best Practice 35*. Industrial Society: London.

Institute of Management (1995) *Finding the Time – A Survey of Managers' Attitudes to Using and Managing Time*. Institute of Management: London.

Ishikawa, K (1985) *What Is Total Quality Control? The Japanese Way*. Prentice-Hall: Englewood Cliffs, NJ, USA.

Ishizuna, Y (1990) The transformation of Nissan – the reform of corporate culture. *Long Range Planning*, 23(3), 9–15.

Ivancevich, J (1970) An analysis of control, bases of control, and satisfaction in an organizational setting. *Academy of Management Journal*, December, 427–32.

Jaques, E (1952) *The Changing Culture of a Factory*. Dryden Press: New York, USA.

Jaques, E (1998) On leaving the Tavistock Institute. *Human Relations*, 51(3), 251–7.

Jenner, RA (1998) Dissipative enterprises, chaos, and the principles of lean organizations. *Omega: International Journal of Management Science*, 26(3), 397–407.

Johnson, G (1987) *Strategic Change and the Management Process*. Blackwell: Oxford.

Johnson, G (1993) Processes of managing strategic change. In C Mabey and B Mayon-White (eds): *Managing Change* (2nd edition). The Open University/Paul Chapman Publishing: London.

Johnson, G and Scholes, K (1993) *Exploring Corporate Strategy*. Prentice Hall: London.

Johnson, G and Scholes, K (eds) (2001) *Exploring Public Sector Strategy*. Financial Times Prentice Hall: Harlow.

Johnson, G and Scholes, K (2002) *Exploring Corporate Strategy* (6th edition). Financial Times Prentice Hall: Harlow.

Johnson, G, Scholes, K and Whittington, R (2006) *Exploring Corporate Strategy* (7th edition). Financial Times Prentice Hall: Harlow.

Johnson, R and Ouchi, W (1974) Made in America (under Japanese management). *Harvard Business Review*, 52(5), 61–9.

Johnston, DC (2007) Income gap is widening, data shows. *The New York Times*, 29 March. www.truthout.org

Jones, EE (1990) *Interpersonal Perception*. Freeman: New York, USA.

Jones, GR, George, JM and Hill, CWL (2000) *Contemporary Management* (2nd edition). McGraw-Hill: Boston, MA, USA.

Jones, H (1989) Private property. *New Civil Engineer*, 29 June, 23.

Jones, RJB (1995) *Globalization and Interdependence in the International Political Economy: Reality and Rhetoric*. Pinter: London.

Jones, Q, Dunphy, D, Fishman, R, Larne, M and Canter, C (2006) *In Great Company: Unlocking the Secrets of Cultural Transformation*. Human Synergistics: Sydney, Australia.

Jorberg, L (1973) The Nordic countries 1850–1914. In C Cipolla (ed): *The Fontana Economic History of Europe* Vol. 4. Fontana: London.

Joyce, P and Woods, A (2001) *Strategic Management: A Fresh Approach to Developing Skills, Knowledge and Creativity*. Kogan Page: London.

Juran, JM (1988) *Quality Control Handbook*. McGraw-Hill: New York, USA.

Kahn, H and Weiner, A (1978) *The Year 2000*. Macmillan: London.

Kamata, S (1982) *Japan in the Passing Lane*. Pantheon: New York, USA.

Kanter, RM (1977) *Men and Women of the Corporation*. Basic Books: New York, USA.

Kanter, RM (1979) Power failure in management circuits. *Harvard Business Review*, 57(4), 65–75.

Kanter, RM (1983) *The Change Masters*. Simon & Schuster: New York, USA.

Kanter, RM (1989) *When Giants Learn to Dance: Mastering the Challenges of Strategy, Management, and Careers in the 1990s*. Unwin: London.

Kanter, RM (1997) *World Class: Thriving Locally in the Global Economy*. Simon & Schuster: New York, USA.

Kanter, RM (2006) Innovation: the classic traps. *Harvard Business Review* 84, November, 72–83.

Kanter, RM (2008). Transforming giants. *Harvard Business Review*, 86, January, 43–52.

Kanter, RM, Kao, J and Wiersema, F (eds) (1997) *Innovation: Breakthrough Thinking at 3M, DuPont, GE, Pfizer, and Rubbermaid*. HarperBusiness: New York, USA.

Kanter, RM, Stein, BA and Jick, TD (1992) *The Challenge of Organizational Change*. Free Press: New York, USA.

Kaplan, PJ (2002) *F'd Companies: Spectacular Dot-com Flameouts*. Simon & Schuster: New York, USA.

Karlsson, C (1996) Radically new production systems. *International Journal of Operations and Production Management*, 16(11), 8–19.

Karlsson, LE (1973) *Experiences in Employee Participation in Sweden: 1969–1972*. Mimeograph, Cornell University: New York, USA.

Kauffman, SA (1993) *Origins of Order: Self-Organisation and Selection in Evolution*. Oxford University Press: Oxford.

Kawakita, T (1997) Corporate strategy and human resource management. In M Sako and H Sato (eds): *Japanese Labour and Management in Transition*. Routledge: London.

Kay, J (1993) *Foundations of Corporate Success*. Oxford University Press: Oxford.

Kay, J, McKiernan, P and Faulkner, DO (2003) The history of strategy and some thoughts about the future. In DO Faulkner and A Campbell (eds): *The Handbook of Strategy*. Oxford University Press: Oxford.

Kazunori, O (1998) New trends in enterprise unions and the labour movement. In H Harukiyo and GD Hook (eds): *Japanese Business Management: Restructuring for Low Growth and Globalization*. Routledge: London.

Kellaway, L (1998) Manage with mother. *Financial Times*, 2 March, 14.

Kellaway, L (2001) A boast too far: Tom Peters' 'confession' that he faked the data for his most famous management book shows how attitudes have changed in 20 years. *Financial Times*, 3 December, 16.

Kelly, JE (1982a) Economic and structural analysis of Job Design. In JE Kelly and CW Clegg (eds): *Autonomy and Control at the Workplace*. Croom Helm: London.

Kelly, JE (1982b) *Scientific Management, Job Redesign and Work Performance*. Academic Press: London.

Kemp, T (1979) *Industrialization in Nineteenth Century Europe*. Longman: London.

Kempner, T (1970) Frederick Taylor and scientific management. In A Tillett, T Kempner and G Wills (eds): *Management Thinkers*. Pelican: Harmondsworth.

Kennedy, C (1994) *Managing with the Gurus*. Century Business Books: London.

Kerr, C and Fisher, L (1957) Plant sociology: the elite and the Aborigines. In M Komarovsky (ed): *Common Frontiers of the Social Sciences*. Greenwood: Westport, CT, USA.

Kerr, S, Schriesheim, CA, Murphy, CJ and Stogdill, RM (1974) Towards a contingency theory of leadership based upon the consideration and initiating structure literature. *Organizational Behavior and Human Performance*, 12, 62–82.

Keshavan, K and Rakesh, KS (1979) Generating future scenarios – their use in strategic planning. *Long Range Planning*, 12, June, 57–61.

Keuning, D (1998) *Management: A Contemporary Approach*. Pitman: London.

Keys, JB and Miller, TR (1984) The Japanese management theory jungle. *Academy of Management Review*, 9, 342–53.

Khalifa, AS (2008) The 'strategy frame' and the four Es of strategy drivers. *Management Decision*, 46(6), 894–917.

Kidd, P and Karwowski, W (eds) (1994) *Advances in Agile Manufacture*. IOS Press: Amsterdam.

Kiel, LD (1994) *Managing Chaos and Complexity in Government*. Jossey-Bass: San Francisco, CA, USA.

Kimberley, J and Miles, R (eds) (1980) *The Organizational Life Cycle*. Jossey-Bass: San Francisco, CA, USA.

Kipnis, D, Schmidt, SM and Wilkinson, I (1980) Intraorganizational influence tactics: explorations in getting one's way. *Journal of Applied Psychology*, August, 440–52.

Kipnis, D, Schmidt, SM, Swaffin-Smith, C and Wilkinson, I (1984) Patterns of managerial influence: shotgun managers, tacticians, and bystanders. *Organizational Dynamics*, Winter, 58–67.

Kippenberger, T (1998a) Planned change: Kurt Lewin's legacy. *The Antidote*, 3(4), 10–12.

Kippenberger, T (1998b) Managed learning: elaborating on Lewin's model. *The Antidote*, 3(4), 13.

Kirkpatrick, SA and Locke, EA (1991) Leadership: do traits matter? *The Executive*, 5, 48–60.

Kirton, MJ (1989) *Adaptors and Innovators: Styles of Creativity and Problem Solving*. Routledge: London.

Kjellberg, A (1992) Sweden: can the model survive. In A Ferner and R Hyman (eds): *Industrial Relations in the New Europe*. Blackwell: Oxford.

Klein, HK (2004) Seeking the new and the critical in critical realism: déjà vu? *Information and Organization*, 14, 123–44.

Klein, N (2001) *No Logo*. Flamingo: London.

Koch, R (1995) *The Financial Times Guide to Strategy*. Pitman: London.

Kodz, J, Davis, S, Lain, D, Sheppard, E, Rick, J, Strebler, M, Bates, P, Cummings, J, Meager, N, Anxon, D, Gineste, S and Trinczek, R (2003) *Working Long Hours in the UK: Excutive Summary*. Department of Trade and Industry: London, available at www.dtigor.uk/emar/longhours.htm.

Koji, O (1998) Small headquarters and the reorganisation of management. In H Harukiyo and GD Hook (eds): *Japanese Business Management: Restructuring for Low Growth and Globalization*. Routledge: London.

Kotler, P (1978) Harvesting strategies for weak products. *Business Horizons*, 21(4), August, 15–22.

Kotter, JP (1982) *The General Manager*. Free Press: New York, USA.

Kotter, JP (1990) *A Force for Change: How Leadership Differs from Management*. Free Press: New York, USA.

Kotter, JP (1995) Leading change: why transformation efforts fail. *Harvard Business Review*, March–April.

Kotter, JP (1996) *Leading Change*. Harvard Business School Press: Boston, MA, USA.

Kotter, JP (1999) What effective general managers really do. *Harvard Business Review*, 77(2), 145–59.

Kottter, JP and Cohen, DS (2002) *The Heart of Change: Real-Life Stories of How People Change Their Organizations*. Harvard Business School Press: Boston, MA, USA.

Kotter, JP and Heskett, JL (1992) *Corporate Culture and Performance*. Free Press: New York, USA.

Kotter, J and Rathgeber, K (2006). *Our Iceberg Is Melting*. Macmillan: London.

Krell, TC (1981) The marketing of organization development: past, present and future. *Journal of Applied Behavioral Science*, 10(2), 485–502.

Kreps, DM and Wilson, R (1982) Reputation and imperfect information. *Journal of Economic Theory*, 27, 253–79.

Kriedte, P, Medick, H and Schlumbohm, J (1981) *Industrialization before Industrialization*. Cambridge University Press: Cambridge.

Kuhn, TS (1962) *The Structure of Scientific Revolutions*. University of Chicago Press: Chicago, IL, USA.

Kumar, K (1995) *From Post-Industrial to Post-Modern: New Theories of the Contemporary World*. Blackwell: Oxford.

Laage-Hellman, J (1997) *Business Networks in Japan*. Routledge: London.

Lacey, R (1986) *Ford: The Men and the Machine*. Heinemann: London.

Laird, L (1998) Predators hover over Lonrho's African diamonds. *Guardian*, 14 November, 28.

Lamming, R (1993) *Beyond Partnership: Strategies for Innovation and Lean Supply*. Prentice Hall: Hemel Hempstead.

Lamming, R (1994) *A Review of the Relationships Between Vehicle Manufacturers and Suppliers*. DTI/SMMT: London.

Lamond, D (2004) A matter of style: reconciling Henri with Henry. *Management Decision*, 42(2), 330–56.

Landes, DS (1969) *The Unbound Prometheus*. Cambridge University Press: Cambridge.

Landsberger, HA (1958) *Hawthorne Revisited: 'Management and the Worker'. Its Critics and Developments in Human Relations in Industry*. Cornell University Press: New York, USA.

Lanford, HW (1972) *Technological Forecasting Methodologies: A Synthesis*. American Management Association: New York, USA.

Larson, LL, Hunt, JG and Osborne, RN (1976) The great hi-hi leader behavior myth: a lesson from Occam's razor. *Academy of Management Journal*, 19, 628–41.

Laudon, K and Starbuck, WH (1997) Organization information and knowledge. In A Sorge and M Warner (eds): *The IEBM Handbook of Organizational Behavior*. International Thompson Business Press: London.

Lawler, EE (1985) Challenging traditional research assumptions. In EE Lawler and Associates (eds): *Doing Research That Is Useful for Theory and Practice*. Jossey-Bass: San Francisco, CA, USA.

Lawler, EE and Suttle, JL (1972) A causal correlation of the need hierarchy concept in an organizational setting. *Organization Behaviour and Human Performance*, 7, April, 265–87.

Lawler, EE, Mohrman, SA and Ledford, GE (1998) *Strategies for High Performance Organizations*. Jossey-Bass: San Francisco, CA, USA.

Lawrence, PR (1973) How to deal with resistance to change. In GW Dalton, PR Lawrence and E Grenier (eds): *Organizational Change and Development*. Dorsey: Homewood, IL, USA.

Lawrence, PR and Lorsch, JW (1967) *Organization and Environment*. Harvard Business School: Boston, MA, USA.

Lawson, H (1985) *Reflexivity, the Post Modern Predicament*. Hutchinson: London.

Learned, EP, Christensen, CR, Andrews, KR and Guth, WD (1965) *Business Policy: Texts and Cases*. Irwin: Homewood, IL, USA.

Lee, J (1978) Labour in German industrialization. In P Mathias and M Postan (eds): *Cambridge Economic History of Europe*, Vol. VII. Cambridge University Press: Cambridge.

Lee, M (1999) The lie of power: empowerment as impotence. *Human Relations*, 52(2), 225–62.

Lee, RG and Dale, BG (2003) Policy deployment. In BG Dale: *Managing Quality* (4th edition). Blackwell: Oxford.

Leemhuis, JP (1990) Using scenario development strategies at Shell. In B Taylor and J Harrison (eds): *The Manager's Casebook of Business Strategy*. Butterworth-Heinemann: Oxford.

Left, S (2001) Nike. *Guardian Unlimited*, 23 February, available at www.guardian.co.uk.

Leifer, R and Huber, GP (1977) Relations amongst perceived environmental uncertainty, organisation structure and boundary-spanning behaviour. *Administrative Science Quarterly*, 22, 235–47.

Leigh, D and Evans, R (2007) BAE accused of secretly paying £1bn to Saudi prince. *The Guardian*, 7 June, available at www.guardian.co.uk.

Lenin, VI (1918) The immediate tasks of the Soviet government. Reprinted in: *On the Development of Heavy Industry and Electrification*. Progress Publishers: Moscow, Russia.

Leontiades, M (1986) *Managing the Unmanageable*. Addison-Wesley: Reading, MA, USA.

Leslie, K, Lindsay, V, Mullings, H and Salkeld, N (1999) Why companies have much to learn from charities. *The Financial Times*, 9 February, 16.

Lessem, R (1998) *Management Development through Cultural Diversity*. Routledge: London.

Leung, K, Bhagat, RS, Buchan, NR, Erez, M and Gibson, CB (2005) Culture and international business: recent advances and their implications for future research. *Journal of International Business Studies*, 36(4), 357–78.

Levine, AL (1967) *Industrial Retardation in Britain 1880–1914*. Basic Books: New York, USA.

Lewin GW (ed) (1948a) *Resolving Social Conflict*. Harper & Row: London.

Lewin, GW (1948b) Preface. In GW Lewin (ed) (1948): *Resolving Social Conflict*. Harper & Row: London.

Lewin, K (1939) When facing danger. In GW Lewin (ed) (1948): *Resolving Social Conflict*. Harper & Row: London.

Lewin, K (1943a) Psychological ecology. In D Cartwright (ed) (1952): *Field Theory in Social Science*. Social Science Paperbacks: London.

Lewin, K (1943b) The special case of Germany. In GW Lewin (ed) (1948): *Resolving Social Conflict*. Harper & Row: London.

Lewin, K (1943/4) Problems of research in social psychology. In D Cartwright (ed) (1952): *Field Theory in Social Science*. Social Science Paperbacks: London.

Lewin, K (1946) Action research and minority problems. In GW Lewin and GW Allport (eds) (1948): *Resolving Social Conflict*. Harper & Row: London.

Lewin, K (1947a) Frontiers in group dynamics. In D Cartwright (ed) (1952): *Field Theory in Social Science*. Social Science Paperbacks: London.

Lewin, K (1947b) Group decisions and social change. In TM Newcomb and EL Hartley (eds) (1959): *Readings in Social Psychology*. Henry Holt: New York, USA.

Lewin, K (1999a) Group decisions and social change. In M Gold (ed): *The Complete Social Scientist: A Kurt Lewin Reader*. American Psychological Association: Washington, DC, USA.

Lewin, K (1999b) The dynamics of group action. In M Gold (ed): *The Complete Social Scientist: A Kurt Lewin Reader*. American Psychological Association: Washington, DC, USA.

Lewin, K., Lippitt, R. and White, R. (1939). Patterns of aggressive behavior in experimentally created 'social climates'. *Journal of Social Psychology*, 10, 271–99.

Lewin, M (1992) The impact of Kurt Lewin's life on the place of social issues in his work. *Journal of Social Issues*, 48(2), 15–29.

Lewis, R (1994) From chaos to complexity: implications for organizations. *Executive Development*, 7(4), 16–17.

Lichtenstein, BM (1997) Grace, magic and miracles: a 'chaotic logic' of organizational transformation. *Journal of Organizational Change Management*, 10(5), 393–411.

Likert, R (1961) *New Patterns of Management*. McGraw-Hill: New York, USA.

Likert, R (1967) *The Human Organization: Its Management and Values*. McGraw-Hill: New York, USA.

Lincoln, JR and Kalleberg, AL (1985) Work organisation and workforce commitment: a study of plants and employees in the US and Japan. *American Sociological Review*, 50, 738–60.

Lindblom, CE (1959) The science of muddling through. *Public Administration Review*, 19, Spring, 79–88.

Lindblom, CE (1968) *The Policy-Making Process*. Prentice-Hall: Englewood Cliffs, NJ, USA.

Lines, WL (2002) *Open Air Essays*. New Holland Publishers: Sydney, Australia.

Linneman, RE and Klein, HE (1979) The use of multiple scenarios by US industrial companies. *Long Range Planning*, 12, February, 83–90.

Linstead, S (1993) From postmodern anthropology to deconstructive ethnography. *Human Relations*, 46(1), 97–120.

Lippitt, G (1982) Management development as the key to organisational renewal. *Journal of Management Development*, 1(2).

Lippitt, R and White, R (1960) *Autocracy and Democracy: An Experimental Inquiry*. Harper & Row: New York, USA.

Lippitt, R, Watson, J and Westley, B (1958) *The Dynamics of Planned Change*. Harcourt, Brace and World: New York.

Litschert, R and Nicholson, E (1974) Corporate long range planning groups – some different approaches. *Long Range Planning*, 7, August, 62–6.

Little, R (1984) Conglomerates are doing better than you think. *Fortune*, 28 May, 60.

Littler, CR (1978) Understanding Taylorism. *British Journal of Sociology*, 29(2), 185–202.

Lloyd, AR, Dale, BG and Burnes, B (1994) A study of Nissan Motor Manufacturing (UK) Supplier Development Team Activities. *Proceedings of the Institute of Mechanical Engineers, 208, Part D: Journal of Automobile Engineering*, 63–8.

Locke, EW (1982) The ideas of Frederick W Taylor. *Academy of Management Review*, 7(1), 14–24.

Loden, M (1986) *Feminine Leadership, or How to Succeed in Business without Being One of the Boys*. Time Books: New York, NY.

Long, P (1986) *Performance Appraisal Revisited*. IPM (Institute of Personnel Management): London.

Lorenz, E (1979) *Predictability: Does the Flap of a Butterfly's Wing in Brazil Set off a Tornado in Texas?* Address at the American Association for the Advancement of Science, Washington, DC, USA.

Lorenz, E (1993) *The Essence of Chaos*. UCL Press: London.

Lorsch, JW (1970) Introduction to the structural design of organizations. In GW Dalton, PR Lawrence and JW Lorsch (eds): *Organization Structure and Design*. Irwin-Dorsey: London.

Lorsch, JW (1986) Managing culture: the invisible barrier to strategic change. *California Management Review*, 28(2), 95–109.

Lovell, R (1980) *Adult Learning*. Croom Helm: London.

Lowe, S, Moore, F and Carr, AN (2007) Paradigmapping studies of culture and organization. *International Journal of Cross Cultural Management*, 7(2), 237–51.

Lu, DJ (1987) *Inside Corporate Japan*. Productivity Press: Cambridge, MA, USA.

Luthans, F (1989) Conversation with Edgar H Schein. *Organizational Dynamics*, 17, Spring, 70–5.

Luthans, F, McCaul, HS and Dodd, NG (1985) Organizational commitment: a comparison of American, Japanese and Korean employees. *Academy of Management Journal*, 28, 213–19.

Lynch, R (1997) *Corporate Strategy*. Pitman: London.

Lyon, D (2000) Post-modernity. In G Browning, A Halcli and F Webster (eds): *Understanding Contemporary Society*. Sage: London.

Lyotard, J-F (1984) *The Postmodern Condition*. Manchester University Press: Manchester.

Mabey, C and Mayon-White, B (1993) *Managing Change* (2nd edition). The Open University/Paul Chapman Publishing: London.

Macalister, T (1999) Fury over further 6000 job cuts in utilities. *Guardian*, 15 December, available at www.guardian.co.uk.

Macalister, T (2003) Swiss join oil bribery inquiry. *Guardian*, 7 May, available at www.guardian.co.uk.

Macbeth, DK (2002) Emergent strategy in managing cooperative supply chain change. *International Journal of Operations and Producton Management*, 22(7), 728–40.

Macdonald, M, Sprenger, E and Dubel, I (1999) *Gender and Organizational Change: Bridging the Gap between Policy and Practice*. Royal Tropical Institute: Amsterdam.

Machiavelli, N (1515) *The Prince*. Available at www.constitution.org/mac/prince06.htm.

MacIntosh, R and MacLean, D (1999) Conditioned emergence: a dissipative structures approach to transformation. *Strategic Management Journal*, 20(4), 297–316.

MacIntosh, R and MacLean, D (2001) Conditioned emergence: researching change and changing research. *International Journal of Operations and Production Management*, 21(10), 1343–57.

Maddock, S (1999) *Challenging Women*. Sage: London.

Magex (2000a) Liberating the digital economy – creating commercial success in the digital marketplace. Magex.com Whitepaper, 21 February, available at www.magex.com/downloads/W_Paper_1(1).pdf.

Magex (2000b) Online music piracy. Magex.com Whitepaper, 22 June, available at www.magex.com/news/library/list.

Maguire, K, Milner, M and Watt, N (2000) The secret deal that left Rover a museum piece. *The Guardian*, 18 March, 4–5.

Mahoney, MJ (1974) *Cognition and Behavior Modification*. Ballinger: Cambridge, MA, USA.

Maitland, A (2001) Managers resort to old tools in a crisis. *Financial Times*, 18 July, 10.

Malaska, P, Malmivirta, M, Meristo, T and Hansen, SO (1984) Scenarios in Europe – who uses them and why? *Long Range Planning*, 17, October, 45–9.

Mallory, G (1997) March, James Gardner (1928–) and Cyert, Richard Michael (1921–). In A Sorge and M Warner (eds): *The IEBM Handbook of Organizational Behaviour*. International Thompson Business Press: London.

Mangham Working Party (1987) *The Mangham Working Party Report: A Survey of the In-house Activities of Ten Major Companies*. British Institute of Management/ Confederation of British Industry: London.

Manicas, P (1980) The concept of social structure. *Journal of the Theory of Social Behaviour*, 10(2), 65–82.

Mansfield, R (1984) Formal and informal structures. In M Gruneberg and T Wall (eds): *Social Psychology and Organizational Behaviour*. Wiley: Chichester.

Mantoux, P (1964) *The Industrial Revolution in the Eighteenth Century*. Cape: London.

Marczewski, J (1963) The take-off hypothesis and French experience. In WW Rostow: *The Economics of Take-Off into Sustained Growth*. Macmillan: London.

Marglin, SA (1976) What do bosses do? In A Gorz (ed): *The Division of Labour: The Labour Process and Class Struggle in Modern Capitalism*. Harvester: Brighton.

Markus, LM, Manville, B and Agres, CE (2000) What makes virtual organisations work? Lessons from the open-source world. *Sloan Management Review*, Fall, 13–26.

Marrow, AJ (1957) *Making Management Human*. McGraw-Hill: New York, NY.

Marrow, AJ (1967) Events leading to the establishment of the National Training Laboratories. *The Journal of Applied Behavioral Science*, 3, 144–50.

Marrow, AJ (1969) *The Practical Theorist: The Life and Work of Kurt Lewin*. Teachers College Press: New York, USA.

Marrow, AJ (1972) The effects of participation on performance. In AJ Marrow (ed), *The Failure of Success*. Amacom: New York, NY.

Marsh, N (1986) Management development and strategic management change. *Journal of Management Development*, 5(1).

Marsh, RM and Mannari, H (1976) *Modernization and the Japanese Factory*. Princeton University Press: Princeton, NJ, USA.

Marshak, RJ (1993) Lewin meets Confucius: a re-view of the OD model of change. *The Journal of Applied Behavioral Science*, 29(4), 393–415.

Martin, J (1992) *Cultures in Organizations: Three Perspectives*. Oxford University Press: Oxford.

Martin, J, Feldman, MS, Hatch, MJ and Sitkin, SB (1983) The uniqueness paradox in organizational stories. *Administrative Science Quarterly*, 28, 438–53.

Martin, R (2000) Breaking the code of change: observations and critique. In M Beer and N Nohria (eds): *Breaking the Code of Change*. Harvard Business School Press: Boston, MA, USA.

Masayoshi, I (1998) Globalisation's impact on the subcontracting system. In H Harukiyo and GD Hook (eds): *Japanese Business Management: Restructuring for Low Growth and Globalization*. Routledge: London.

Masayuki, M (1998) The end of the 'mass production system' and changes in work practices. In H Harukiyo and GD Hook (eds): *Japanese Business Management: Restructuring for Low Growth and Globalization*. Routledge: London.

Maslow, AH (1943) A theory of human motivation. *Psychology Review*, 50, 370–96.

Massie, JL (1965) Management theory. In JG March (ed): *Handbook of Organizations*. Rand McNally: Chicago, IL, USA.

Mathias, P (1969) *The First Industrial Nation*. Methuen: London.

Mathias, P and Davis, JA (eds) (1989) *The First Industrial Revolutions*. Blackwell: Cambridge.

Matthews, R (2002) Competition, archetypes and creative imagination. *Journal of Organizational Change Management*, 15(5), 461–76.

May, B and Singer, M (2001) Unchained melody. *The McKinsey Quarterly*, 1, available at www.Mckinseyquarterly.com.

Mayes, BT and Allen, RW (1977) Towards a definition of organizational politics. *Academy of Management Review*, October, 672–8.

Mayo, E (1933) *The Human Problems of Industrial Civilization*. Macmillan: New York, USA.

Mayon-White, B (1993) Problem-solving in small groups: team members as agents of change. In C Mabey and B Mayon-White (eds): *Managing Change* (2nd edition). The Open University/Paul Chapman Publishing: London.

McCalman, J and Paton, RA (1992) *Change Management: A Guide to Effective Implementation*. Paul Chapman Publishing: London.

McCormick, K (2007) Sociologists and 'the Japanese model': a passing enthusiasm? *Work, Employment and Society*, 21(4), 751–71.

McDougall, D (2008). Working flat out – the child labour behind your Egyptian cotton sheets. The Observer, 8 June. www.guardian.co.uk

McGill, I and Beaty, L (1995) *Action Learning*. Kogan Page: London.

McGregor, D (1960) *The Human Side of Enterprise*. McGraw-Hill: New York, USA.

McGregor, D (1967) *The Professional Manager*. McGraw-Hill: New York, USA.

McIvor, G (1995) Retuned Volvo rises from the ashes. *Guardian*, 24 June, 37.

McKenna, S (1988) 'Japanisation' and recent developments in Britain. *Employee Relations*, 10(4).

McKiernan, P (1992) *Strategies for Growth: Maturity, Recovery and Internationalization*. Routledge: London.

McKinsey & Company (2008) Creating organizational transformations. *The McKinsey Quarterly*, July, 1–7, available at www.mckinseyquarterly.com

McKracken, JK (1986) Exploitation of FMS technology to achieve strategic objectives. Paper to the 5th International Conference on Flexible Manufacturing Systems, Stratford-upon-Avon.

McLaughlin, H and Thorpe, R (1993) Action Learning – a paradigm in emergence. *British Journal of Management*, 4(1), 19–27.

McLennan, R (1989) *Managing Organizational Change*. Prentice-Hall: Englewood Cliffs, NJ, USA.

McMillan, J (1985) *The Japanese Industrial System*. De Gruyter: Berlin.

McNamee, BP (1985) *Tools and Techniques of Strategic Management*. Pergamon: Oxford.

McNiff, J (ed) (2000) *Action Research in Organisations*. Routledge: London.

McNulty, CAR (1977) Scenario development for corporate planning. *Futures*, 9(2), 128–38.

McSweeney, B (2002) Hofstede's model of national cultural differences and their consequences: a triumph of faith – a failure of analysis. *Human Relations*, 55(1), 89–118.

Meek, VL (1988) Organizational culture: origins and weaknesses. *Organization Studies*, 9(4), 453–73.

Meyer, MW and Zucker, LG (1989) *Permanently Failing Organizations*. Sage: Beverly Hills, CA, USA.

Meyerson, D and Martin, J (1987) Cultural change: an integration of three different views. *Journal of Management Studies*, 24(6), 623–47.

Michaels, A (2004) Survey reveals changing culture at the Big Four. *FT.Com*, 8 February. www.ft.com

Michaelson, GA (2001) *Sun Tzu: The Art of War for Managers: 50 Strategic Rules*. Adams Media: Avon, MA, USA.

Miewald, RD (1970) The greatly exaggerated death of bureaucracy. *California Management Review*, Winter, 65–9.

Miles, RE and Snow, CC (1978) *Organizational Strategy, Structure and Process*. McGraw-Hill: New York, USA.

Milgrom, P and Roberts, J (1982) Predation, reputation and entry deterrence. *Journal of Economic Theory*, 27, 280–313.

Mill, J (1994) No pain, no gain. *Computing*, 3 February, 26–7.

Miller, D (1992) The generic strategy trap. *Journal of Business Strategy*, 13(1), 37–41.

Miller, D (1993) The architecture of simplicity. *Academy of Management Review*, 18(1), 116–38.

Miller, D (1994) What happens after success: the perils of excellence. *Journal of Management Studies*, 31(3), 325–58.

Miller, D and Friesen, PH (1984) *Organizations: A Quantum View*. Prentice-Hall: Englewood Cliffs, NJ, USA.

Miller, E (1967) *Systems of Organisation*. Tavistock: London.

Miller, E (1993) *From Dependency to Autonomy – Studies in Organization and Change*. Free Association Books: London.

Milner, M (1998) Productivity as seen by hamsters. *Guardian*, 22 October, 27.

Milward, A and Saul, SB (1973) *The Economic Development of Continental Europe 1780–1870*. George Allen & Unwin: London.

Minett, S (1992) *Power, Politics and Participation in the Firm*. Ashgate: Brookfield, VT, USA.

Mink, OG (1992) Creating new organizational paradigms for change. *International Journal of Quality and Reliability Management*, 9(3), 21–35.

Mintzberg, H (1973) *The Nature of Managerial Work*. Harper & Row: New York, USA.

Mintzberg, H (1975) The manager's job: folklore and fact. *Harvard Business Review*, 53(4), 49–61.

Mintzberg, H (1976) Planning on the left side and managing on the right. *Harvard Business Review*, July/August, 49–58.

Mintzberg, H (1978) Patterns in strategy formation. *Management Science*, 24(9), 934–48.

Mintzberg, H (1979) *The Structure of Organizations*. Prentice-Hall: Englewood Cliffs, NJ, USA.

Mintzberg, H (1983) *Power in and around Organizations*. Prentice-Hall: Englewood Cliffs, NJ, USA.

Mintzberg, H (1987) Crafting strategy. *Harvard Business Review*, 19(2), 66–75.

Mintzberg, H (1994) *The Rise and Fall of Strategic Planning*. Prentice Hall: London.

Mintzberg, H (1998) Covert leadership: notes on managing professionals. *Harvard Business Review*, 76(6), 140–7.

Mintzberg, H (2001) Decision-making: it's not what you think. *Sloan Management Review*, 42(3), 89–93.

Mintzberg, H (2007) *Tracking Strategies: Toward a General Theory*. Oxford University Press: Oxford.

Mintzberg, H and Lampel, J (1999) Reflecting on the strategy process. *Sloan Management Review*, 40(3), 21–30.

Mintzberg, H and Quinn, JB (1991) *The Strategy Process: Concepts, Contexts and Cases*. Prentice Hall: London.

Mintzberg, H and Westley, F (1992) Cycles of organizational change. *Strategic Management Journal*, 13, Winter, 39–59.

Mintzberg, H, Ahlstrand, B and Lampel, J (1998a). *Strategy Safari*. Prentice Hall: Hemel Hempstead.

Mintzberg, H, Quinn, JB and Ghoshal, S (1998b) *The Strategy Process*. Prentice Hall: London.

Mirvis, P (1988) Organizational development: an evolutionary perspective. In W Pasmore and R Woodman (eds): *Research in Organizational Change and Development*, Vol. 2. JAI Press: Greenwich, CT, USA.

Mirvis, PH (1990) Organization development: Part 2 – a revolutionary perspective. *Research in Organizational Change and Development*, 4, 1–66.

Mitroff, II and Mason, RO (1981) *Challenging Strategic Planning Assumptions*. Wiley: New York, USA.

Moore, JI (1992) *Writers on Strategy and Strategic Management*. Penguin: Harmondsworth.

Morgan, G (1986) *Images of Organizations*. Sage: Beverly Hills, CA, USA.

Morgan, G (1988) *Riding the Waves of Change*. Jossey-Bass: San Francisco, CA, USA.

Morgan, G (1990) *Organisations in Society*. Macmillan: London.

Morgan, G (1997) *Images of Organization* (2nd edition). Sage: London.

Morieux, YUH and Sutherland, E (1988) The interaction between the use of information technology and organization change. *Behaviour and Information Technology*, 7(2), 205–13.

Morris, J and Imrie, R (1992) *Transforming Buyer–Supplier Relationships*. Macmillan: Basingstoke.

Mougayar, W (1998) *Opening Digital Markets: Battle Plans and Business Strategies for Internet Commerce*. McGraw-Hill: Maidenhead.

Mullins, L (1989) *Management and Organisational Behaviour*. Pitman: London.

Mullins, LJ (1993) *Management and Organisational Behaviour* (3rd edition). Pitman: London.

Mullins, L (2002) *Management and Organisational Behaviour* (6th edition). Financial Times Pearson: Harlow.

Mumford, A (1987) Myths and reality in developing directors. *Personnel Management*, 19(2), February, 29–33.

Mumford, E (1979) The design of work: new approaches and new needs. In JE Rijnsdorp (ed): *Case Studies in Automation Related to Humanization of Work*. Pergamon: Oxford.

Mumford, MD, Marks, MA, Connelly, MS, Zaccaro, SJ and Reiter-Palmon, R (2000) Development of leadership skills: experience and timing. *Leadership Quarterly*, 11, 87–114.

Murray, F (1989) The organizational politics of information technology: studies from the UK financial services industry. *Technology Analysis and Strategic Management*, 1(30), 285–97.

Myers, CS (1934) *An Account of the Work Carried out at the National Institute of Industrial Psychology during the Years 1921–34*. NIIP: London.

Nadler, DA (1988) Concepts for the management of organizational change. In ML Tushman and WL Moore (eds): *Readings in the Management of Innovation*. Ballinger: New York, USA.

Nadler, DA (1993) Concepts for the management of strategic change. In C Mabey and B Mayon-White (eds): *Managing Change* (2nd edition). The Open University/Paul Chapman Publishing: London.

Nadworthy, M (1957) Frederick Taylor and Frank Gilbreth: competition in scientific management. *Business History Review*, 31(1), 23–34.

Nahavandi, A (2000) *The Art and Science of Leadership* (2nd edition). Prentice-Hall: Upper Saddle River, NJ, USA.

NAO (1995) *Interim Report: PSA Services, The Sale of PSA Projects. Report by the National Audit Office*. HMSO: London.

NAO (1996) *PSA Services: The Transfer of PSA Building Management to the Private Sector. Report by the National Audit Office*. HMSO: London.

NAO (1999) *The United Kingdom Passport Agency. The Passport Delays of Summer of 1999. Report by the National Audit Office*. HMSO: London.

Naoi, A and Schooler, C (1985) Occupational conditions and psychological functioning in Japan. *American Journal of Sociology*, 90, 729–52.

Naylor, TH (1979) *Simulation Models in Corporate Measuring*. Draeger: New York, USA.

Naylor, TH (1981) Strategic planning models. *Managerial Planning*, 30, July/August, 3–11.

NEDC (1991a) *The Experience of Nissan Suppliers: Lessons for the United Kingdom Engineering Industry*. NEDC: London.

NEDC (1991b) *Winning Together: Collaborative Sourcing in Practice*. NEDC: London.

Nelson, RR and Winter, SG (1982) *An Evolutionary Theory of Economic Change*. Harvard University Press: Cambridge, MA, USA.

New, C (1989) The challenge of transformation. In B Burnes and B Weekes (eds): *AMT: A Strategy for Success?* NEDO: London.

New, S and Burnes, B (1998) Developing effective customer–supplier relationships: more than one way to skin a cat. *Journal of Quality and Reliability Management*, 15(4), 377–88.

Newman, S (ed) (2008) *The Final Energy Crisis*. Pluto Press: London.

Newstrom, J (1985) Modern management: does it deliver? *Journal of Management Development*, 4(1).

Nonaka, I (1988) Creating organizational order out of chaos: self-renewal in Japanese firms. *California Management Review*, 30(3), 57–73.

Nonaka, I (1991) The knowledge-creating company. *Harvard Business Review*, 69 (6, November/December), 96–104.

Nord, W (1985) Can organizational culture be managed: a synthesis. In R Kilmann, M Saxton, R Serpa and Associates (eds): *Gaining Control of Corporate Culture*. Jossey-Bass: San Francisco, CA, USA.

Norrie, J (1993) *Winning by Continuous Improvement: Facilitators' Guide*. Norrie: Northampton.

Norse, D (1979) Scenario analysis in interfutures. *Futures*, 11(5), 412–22.

Nwabueze, U (2001) An industry betrayed: the case of total quality management in manufacturing. *The TQM Magazine*, 13(6), 400–9.

Nystrom, PC and Starbuck, WH (1984) To avoid crises, unlearn. *Organizational Dynamics*, 12(4), 53–65.

O'Brien, GE and Kabanoff, B (1981) The effects of leadership style and group structure upon small group productivity: a test of discrepancy theory of leader effectiveness. *Australian Journal of Psychology*, 33(2), 157–8.

Observer (2008). Tesco in numbers. *The Observer*, 29 June, 25.

Odaka, K (1975) *Towards Industrial Democracy: Management and Workers in Modern Japan*. Harvard University Press: Cambridge, MA, USA.

OECD (1996) *The OECD Economic Survey: the UK 1996*. OECD: Paris, France.

Ogbonna, E and Harris, LC (2002) Managing organisational culture: insights from the hospitality industry. *Human Resource Management Journal*, 12(1), 33–53.

O'Hara, M (2008) Prophet for a new age. *The Guardian*: Society Guardian, 12 November, 1.

Ohmae, K (1986) *The Mind of the Strategist*. Penguin: Harmondsworth.

Ohmae, K (1990) Untitled article in *Special Report 1202, The Management Briefing, Economist*, London.

Ohmi, N (1997) The public sector and privatisation. In M Sako and H Sato (eds): *Japanese Labour and Management in Transition*. Routledge: London.

Ojiako, U and Maguire, (2008) Success criteria for systems led transformation: managerial implications for global operations management. *Industrial Management and Data Systems*, 108(7), 887–908.

Olsen, BD (2002) Applied social and community interventions for crisis in times of national and international conflict. *Analyses of Social Issues and Public Policy* 2(1), 119–29.

Ordanini, A and Rubera, G (2008) Strategic capabilities and internet resources in procurement: a resource-based view of B-to-B buying process. *International Journal of Operations and Production Management*, 28(1), 27–52.

O'Reilly, C (1989) Corporations, culture and commitment. *California Management Review*, 31(4), 9–24.

Orlikowski, WJ (1996) Improvising organizational transformation over time: a situated change perspective. *Information Systems Research*, 7(1), 63–92.

Orlikowski, WJ and Yates, JA (2006) ICT and organizational change: a commentary. *Journal of Applied Behavioral Science*, 42(1), 127–34.

O'Shaughnessy, J. (1984) *Competitive Marketing*. Allen & Unwin: Boston, MA, USA.

Osborne, D and Gaebler, T (1992) *Reinventing Government: How the Entrepreneurial Spirit Is Transforming the Public Sector*. Addison-Wesley: Reading, MA, USA.

Oticon (1994) *Oticon's Fundamental Human Values – Vision and Reality*. Oticon: Copenhagen, Denmark.

Ouchi, W (1981) *Theory Z: How American Business Can Meet the Japanese Challenge*. Addison-Wesley: Reading, MA, USA.

Outhwaite, W (1987) *New Philosophies of Social Science: Realism, Hermeneutics and Critical Theory*. Macmillan: London.

Owen, G (2002) The man who built GEC into an industrial giant. *Financial Times*, 24 July, 23.

Pang, K and Oliver, N (1988) Personnel strategy in eleven Japanese manufacturing companies. *Personnel Review*, 17(3).

Parikh, M (1999) The music industry in the digital world: waves of changes. *Putting the 'e' in Entertainment: e-Music as a Case in Point, Industry Round Table*, June 17. The New York Information Technology Center, available at www.ite.poly.edu.

Parker, D (1998) Privatisation in the European Union: an overview. In D Parker (ed): *Privatisation in the European Union: Theory and Policy Perspectives*. Routledge: London.

Parker, D (2003) Performance, risk and strategy in privatised, regulated industries: the UK's experience. *International Journal of Public Sector Management*, 16(1), 75–100.

Parker, M (2000) *Thatcherism and the Fall of Coal: Politics and Economics of UK Coal*. Cambridge University Press: Cambridge.

Parsons, T (1947) Introduction. In M Weber (ed): *The Theory of Social and Economic Organization*. Free Press: Glencoe, IL, USA.

Partnership Sourcing Ltd (1991a) *Case Studies in Partnership Sourcing*. Partnership Sourcing Ltd: London.

Partnership Sourcing Ltd (1991b) *Partnership Sourcing*. Partnership Sourcing Ltd: London.

Partnoy, F (2003) When greed is fact and control is fiction. *Guardian*, 14 February, available at www.guardian.co.uk.

Pascale, RT (1993) The benefit of a clash of opinions. *Personnel Management*, October, 38–41.

Pascale, RT and Athos, AG (1982) *The Art of Japanese Management*. Penguin: Harmondsworth.

Pasmore, W and Fagans, M (1992) Participation, individual development, and organizational change: a review and synthesis. *Journal of Management*, 18(2), 375–97.

Patel, P and Younger, M (1978) A frame of reference for strategy development. *Long Range Planning*, 11, April, 6–12.

Paton, N (2003) Leadership skills hold Britain back. *Guardian: Jobs and Money*, 22 February, 23.

Paton, R, Clark, G, Jones, G, Lewis, J and Quintas, P (eds) (1996) *The New Management Reader*. Routledge/Open University: London.

Patwardhan, A and Patwardhan, D (2008) Business process re-engineering – saviour or just another fad?: One UK health care perspective. *International Journal of Health Care Quality Assurance*, 21(3), 289–96.

Pavlov, IP (1927) *Conditioned Reflexes* (trans). Oxford University Press: London.

Peacock, A (1984) Privatisation in perspective. *Three Banks Review*, December, 3–25.

Pearson, AE (1987) Muscle-build the organization. *Harvard Business Review*, 65(4), 49–55.

Pearson, B (1977) How to manage turnarounds. *Management Today*, April, 75.

Pedler, M (1996) *Action Learning for Managers*. Lemos & Crane: London.

Pedler, M, Boydell, T and Burgoyne, JG (1989) Towards the learning company. *Management Education and Development*, 20(1), 1–8.

Pelling, H (1960) *American Labor*. Chicago University Press: Chicago, IL, USA.

Penrose, E (1959) *The Theory of Growth of the Firm*. Blackwell: Oxford.

Perez, C (1983) Structural change and the assimilation of new technologies in the economic and social systems. *Futures*, 15, 357–75.

Perrow, C (1967) A framework for the comparative analysis of organizations. *American Sociological Review*, 32, 194–208.

Perrow, C (1970) *Organizational Analysis: A Sociological View*. Tavistock: London.

Perrow, C (1983) The organizational context of human factors engineering. *Administrative Science Quarterly*, 28, 521–41.

Peters, T (1989) *Thriving on Chaos*. Pan: London.

Peters, T (1993) *Liberation Management*. Pan: London.

Peters, T (1995) *The Pursuit of WOW!* Macmillan: London.

Peters, T (1997a) *The Circle of Innovation: You Can't Shrink Your Way to Greatness*. Alfred A Knopf: New York, USA.

Peters, T (1997b) Foreword. In RM Kanter, J Kao and F Wiersema (eds): *Innovation: Breakthrough Thinking at 3M, DuPont, GE, Pfizer, and Rubbermaid*. HarperBusiness: New York, USA.

Peters, T (2006) *Re-imagine! Business Excellence in a Disruptive Age*. Dorling Kindersley: London.

Peters, T and Waterman, RH (1982) *In Search of Excellence: Lessons from America's Best-Run Companies*. Harper & Row: London.

Pettigrew, AM (1973) *The Politics of Decision-Making*. Tavistock: London.

Pettigrew, AM (1979) On studying organizational culture. *Administrative Science Quarterly*, 24(4), 570–81.

Pettigrew, AM (1980) The politics of organisational change. In NB Anderson (ed): *The Human Side of Information Processing*. North-Holland: Amsterdam, The Netherlands.

Pettigrew, AM (1985) *The Awakening Giant: Continuity and Change at ICI*. Blackwell: Oxford.

Pettigrew, AM (1987) Context and action in the transformation of the firm. *Journal of Management Sciences*, 24(6), 649–70.

Pettigrew, AM (1990a) Longitudinal field research on change: theory and practice. *Organizational Science*, 3(1), 267–92.

Pettigrew, AM (1990b) Studying strategic choice and strategic change. *Organizational Studies*, 11(1), 6–11.

Pettigrew, AM (1997) What is a processual analysis? *Scandinavian Journal of Management*, 13(4), 337–48.

Pettigrew, AM (2000) Linking change processes and outcomes: a commentary on Ghosal, Bartlett and Weick. In M Beer and N Nohria (eds): *Breaking the Code of Change*. Harvard Business School Press: Boston, MA, USA.

Pettigrew, AM and Whipp, R (1991) *Managing Change for Competitive Success*. Blackwell: Oxford.

Pettigrew, AM and Whipp, R (1993) Understanding the environment. In C Mabey and B Mayon-White (eds): *Managing Change* (2nd edition). The Open University/Paul Chapman Publishing: London.

Pettigrew, AM, Ferlie, E and McKee, L (1992) *Shaping Strategic Change*. Sage: London.

Pettigrew, AM, Hendry, C and Sparrow, P (1989) *Training in Britain: Employers' Perspectives on Human Resources*. HMSO: London.

Pettigrew, AM, Woodman, RW and Cameron, KS (2001) Studying organizational change and development: challenges for future research. *Academy of Management Journal*, 44(4), 697–713.

Pfeffer, J (1978) *Organizational Design*. AHM Publishing: Arlington Heights, IL, USA.

Pfeffer, J (1981) *Power in Organizations*. Pitman: Cambridge, MA, USA.

Pfeffer, J (1992) *Managing with Power: Politics and Influence in Organizations*. Harvard Business School Press: Boston, MA, USA.

Pfeffer, J (1996) *Competitive Advantage through People: Unleashing the Power of the Work Force*. Harvard Business School Press: Boston, MA.

Pfeffer, J (1997) *New Directions for Organization Theory*. Oxford University Press: Oxford.

Phillips, A (2003) Childcare before money: as BA has discovered, working mothers will not give up their childcare arrangements without a fight. *Guardian*, 30 July, 17.

Pilling, D (2003) How could a corporate sector that dominated the world a decade ago have become so unproductive? *Financial Times*, 21 April, 15.

Piore, M and Sabel, C (1984) *The Second Industrial Divide*. Basic Books: New York, USA.

Plowden, The Lord (1961) *Control of Public Expenditure*, Cmnd 1432. HMSO: London.

Pollard, S (1965) *The Genesis of Modern Management*. Pelican: Harmondsworth.

Pollard, S (1981) *Peaceful Conquest: The Industrialization of Europe, 1760–1970*. Oxford University Press: Oxford.

Pontusson, J (1990) The politics of new technology and job redesign: a comparison of Volvo and British Leyland. *Economic and Industrial Democracy*, 11, 311–36.

Porter, LW (1976) Organizations as political animals. *Presidential Address, Division of Industrial Organizational Psychology, 84th Annual Meeting of the American Psychological Association,* Washington, DC, USA.

Porter, LW, Allen, RW and Angle, HL (1983) The politics of upward influence in organizations. In R W Allen and L W Porter (eds): *Organizational Influence Processes*. Scott, Foresman and Co: Glenview, IL, USA.

Porter, M (1980) *Competitive Strategy*. Free Press: New York, USA.

Porter, M (1985) *Competitive Advantage*. Free Press: New York, USA.

Porter, ME (2001) Strategy and the Internet. *Harvard Business Review*, March, 63–78.

Prahalad, CK and Hamel, G (1990) The core competence of the corporation. *Harvard Business Review*, May/June, 71–91.

Price, TL (2003) The ethics of authentic transformational leadership. *The Leadership Quarterly*, 14(1), 67–81.

Priem, RL and Butler, JE (2001) Is the resource-based view a useful perspective for strategic management research? *Academy of Management Review*, 26(1), 22–40.

Prigogine, I (1997) *The End of Certainty: Time, Chaos, and the New Laws of Nature*. Free Press: New York, NY.

Prigogine, I and Stengers, I (1984) *Order out of Chaos: Man's New Dialogue with Nature*. Bantam Books: New York, USA.

Probst, G and Buchel, B (1997) *Organizational Learning*. Prentice Hall: London.

Pruijt, HD (1997) *Job Design and Technology: Taylorism vs Anti-Taylorism*. Routledge: London.

PSA [Property Services Agency] (1988) *PSA Annual Report 1987–88*. HMSO: London.

PSA [Property Services Agency] (1989) *PSA to be Privatised*. PSA Press Release No. 96, 27 September. DoE: London.

Public Power Corporation (1999) *Human Resource Management*. The PPC Sector of Education: Athens, Greece.

Public Power Corporation (2001) *Offering Circular: 35,000,000 Shares in the Form of Shares and Global Depository Receipts*. Hellenic Republic: Athens, Greece.

Pugh, DS (ed) (1984) *Organization Theory*. Penguin: Harmondsworth.

Pugh, DS (1993) Understanding and managing organizational change. In C Mabey and B Mayon-White (eds): *Managing Change* (2nd edition). The Open University/Paul Chapman Publishing: London.

Pugh, DS and Hickson, DJ (1976) *Organizational Structure in its Context: The Aston Programme 1*. Saxon House: Farnborough.

Pugh, DS, Hickson, DJ, Hinings, CR and Turner, C (1969a) The context of organization structures. *Administrative Science Quarterly*, 14, 91–114.

Pugh, DS, Hickson, DJ and Hinings, CR (1969b) An empirical taxonomy of structures of work organisation. *Administrative Science Quarterly*, 14, 115–26.

Quinn, JB (1980a) Managing strategic change. *Sloan Management Review*, 21(4), 3–20.

Quinn, JB (1980b) *Strategies for Change: Logical Incrementalism*. Irwin: Homewood, IL, USA.

Quinn, JB (1982) Managing strategies incrementally. *Omega*, 10(6), 613–27.

Quinn, JB (1993) Managing strategic change. In C Mabey and B Mayon-White (eds): *Managing Change* (2nd edition). The Open University/Paul Chapman Publishing: London.

Quinn, RE (1996) *Deep Change: Discovering the Leader Within*. Jossey-Bass: San Francisco, CA, USA.

Quinn, RE and McGrath, MR (1985) The transformation of organizational cultures: a competing values perspective. In PJ Frost, LF Moore, MR Louis, CC Lundberg and J Martin (eds): *Organizational Culture*. Sage: Newbury Park, CA, USA.

Rafferty, K (1995) Tokyo and Mitsubishi banks to merge to create world's largest bank. *Guardian*, 25 March, 15.

Raven, BH (1965) Social influence and power. In ID Steiner and M Fishbein (eds): *Current Studies in Social Psychology*. Holt, Rinehart, Winston: New York, USA.

Raven, BH (1993) The bases of power – origins and recent developments. *Journal of Social Issues*, 49(4), 227–51.

Raven, BH (1999) Kurt Lewin address: influence, power, religion, and the mechanisms of social control. *Journal of Social Issues*, 55(1), 161–89.

Reed, M (1992) *The Sociology of Organizations*. Harvester Wheatsheaf: Hemel Hempstead.

Reed, M and Hughes, M (eds) (1992) *Rethinking Organization: New Directions in Organization Theory and Analysis*. Sage: London.

Reed, MI (2000) In praise of duality and dualism: rethinking agency and structure in organisational analysis. In S Ackroyd and S Fleetwood (eds): *Realist Perspectives on Management and Organisations*. Routledge: London.

Reich, R (1997) The menace of prosperity: widening inequality poses a threat to US and other societies. *Financial Times*, 3 March, 20.

Reich, S (1998) *What is Globalization? Four Possible Answers*. Working paper No 261. The Helen Kellogg Institute for International Studies, University of Notre Dame, IN, USA.

Rescher, N (1996) *Complexity: A Philosophical Overview*. Transaction Publishers: New York, USA.

Reynolds, CW (1987) Flocks, herds and schools: a distributed behaviour model. Proceedings of SIGGRAPH '87'. *Computer Graphics*, 21(4), 25–34.

Ricks, DA (1999) *Blunders in International Business*. Blackwell: Oxford.

Rigby, D (2001) *Management Tools 2001: An Executive's Guide*. Bain & Company: Boston, MA, USA.

Rigby, D and Bilodeau, B (2007) *Management Tools and Trends 2007*. Bain & Company: Boston, MA, USA.

Rigby, D and Gillies, C (2000) Making the most of management tools and techniques: a survey from Bain & Company. *Strategic Change*, 9, 269–74.

Ringland, G (1998) *Scenario Planning: Managing for the Future*. Wiley: Chichester.

Robbins, SP (1986) *Organizational Behavior: Concepts, Controversies, and Applications*. Prentice-Hall: Englewood Cliffs, NJ, USA.

Robbins, SP (1987) *Organization Theory: Structure, Design, and Applications*. Prentice-Hall: Englewood Cliffs, NJ, USA.

Robbins, SP (1997) *Managing Today!* Prentice-Hall: Upper Saddle River, NJ, USA.

Roberts, Y (2008) The NHS isn't Ikea. *The Guardian*, 7 July. www.guardian.co.uk

Roethlisberger, F and Dickson, WJ (1938) *Management and the Worker*. Wiley: New York, USA.

Rogers, P, Meehan, P and Tanner, S (2006). *Building a Winning Culture*. Bain & Company: Boston, MA, USA.

Rogers, R (1997) Handy man. *Training*, November, 19.

Roll, E (1930) An early experiment in industrial organisation: Boulton and Watt, 1775–1805. Reprinted in M Berg (ed) (1979): *Technology and Toil in Nineteenth Century Britain*. CSE Books: London.

Rollinson, D (2002) *Organisational Behaviour and Analysis* (2nd edition). Financial Times Prentice Hall: Harlow.

Romanelli, E and Tushman, ML (1994) Organizational transformation as punctuated equilibrium: an empirical test. *Academy of Management Journal*, 37(5), 1141–66.

Rose, M (1988) *Industrial Behaviour*. Penguin: Harmondsworth.

Rosenbrock, H (1982) *Unmanned Engineering*. Report 12 to the FMS Steering Committee. UMIST: Manchester.

Rosenzweig, PM (1994) When can management science research be generalized internationally? *Management Science*, 40(1), 28–39.

Rost, JC (1991) *Leadership for the Twenty-First Century*. Greenwood: Westport, CT, USA.

Rost, JC (1993) Leadership development in the new millennium. *The Journal of Leadership Studies*, 1(1), 92–110.

Rothwell, S (1994) Human resources management. *Manager Update*, 5(3), Spring, 22–35.

Rubin, I (1967) Increasing self-acceptance: a means of reducing prejudice. *Journal of Personality and Social Psychology*, 5, 233–8.

Rumelt, RP (1991) How much does industry matter? *Strategic Management Journal*, 12(3), 167–85.

Rumelt, RP (1997) The evaluation of business strategy. In H Mintzberg and JB Quinn, *The Strategy Process* (3rd edition). Prentice-Hall: Englewood Cliffs, NJ, USA.

Saigol, L (2003) Sex discrimination case could spell the end for City's secretive pay structure. *The Financial Times*, 4 April, 8.

Sakai, K (1992) The feudal world of Japanese manufacturing. In RM Kanter, BA Stein and TD Jick: *The Challenge of Organizational Change*. Free Press: New York.

Sako, M (1997) Introduction. In M Sako and H Sato (eds): *Japanese Labour and Management in Transition*. Routledge: London.

Sako, M and Sato, H (eds) (1997) *Japanese Labour and Management in Transition*. Routledge: London.

Salaman, G (1979) *Work Organisations*. Longman: London.

Salauroo, M and Burnes, B (1998) The impact of a market system on public sector organisations: a study of organisational change in the NHS. *The International Journal of Public Sector Management*, 11(6), 451–67.

Sashkin, M and Burke, W (1987) Organization development in the nineteen-eighties. *Journal of Management*, 13, 393–417.

Sathe, V (1983) Some action implications of corporate culture: a manager's guide to action. *Organizational Dynamics*, Autumn, 4–23.

Saul, JR (1997) *The Unconscious Civilization*. Penguin: London.

Saunders, M (1997) *Strategic Purchasing and Supply Chain Management* (2nd edition). Pitman: London.

Sayer, A (1989) Post-Fordism in question. *International Journal of Urban and Regional Research*, 13(4), 666–95.

Sayer, A (2000) *Realism and Social Science*. Sage: London.

Schein, EH (1969) *Process Consultation*. Addison-Wesley: Reading, MA, USA.

Schein, EH (1984) Coming to a new awareness of organizational culture. *Sloan Management Review*, 25(2), 3–16.

Schein, EH (1985) *Organizational Culture and Leadership: A Dynamic View*. Jossey-Bass: San Francisco, CA, USA.

Schein, EH (1988) *Organizational Psychology* (3rd edition). Prentice-Hall: Englewood Cliffs, NJ, USA.

Schein, EH (1989) Organizational culture: what it is and how to change it. In P Evans, T Doz and A Laurent (eds): *Human Resource Management in International Firms*. Macmillan: London.

Schein, EH (1996) Kurt Lewin's change theory in the field and in the classroom: notes towards a model of management learning. *Systems Practice*, 9(1), 27–47.

Schein, VE and Mueller, R (1992) Sex role stereotyping and requisite management characteristics: a cross cultural look. *Journal of Organizational Behaviour*, 13, 439–47.

Schilit, WK and Locke, EA (1982) A study of upward influence in organizations. *Administrative Science Quarterly*, June, 304–16.

Schmalensee, R (1983) Advertising and entry deterrence: an exploratory model. *Journal of Political Economy*, 91(4), 636–53.

Schmuck, R and Miles, M (1971) *Organizational Development in Schools*. National Press: Palo Alto, CA, USA.

Schoeffler, S (1980) *Nine Basic Findings on Business Strategy*. The Strategic Planning Institute: Cambridge, MA, USA.

Schonberger, RJ (1982) *Japanese Manufacturing Techniques*. Free Press: New York, USA.

Schriesheim, CA and Murphy, CJ (1976) Relationships between leader behavior and subordinate satisfaction and performance: a test of some situational moderators. *Journal of Applied Psychology*, 61, 634–41.

Schumacher, EF (1973) *Small Is Beautiful: A Study of Economics as if People Mattered*. Vintage Books: London.

Schuyt, TNM and Schuijt, JJM (1998) Rituals and rules: about magic in consultancy. *Journal of Organizational Change Management*, 11(5), 399–406.

Schwartz, H and Davis, S (1981) Matching corporate culture and business strategy. *Organizational Dynamics*, 10, 30–48.

Schwartz, P and Leyden, P (1997) The long boom: a history of the future, 1980–2020. *Wired*, July, 1–16, available at www.wired.com.

Scott, WR (1987) *Organizations: Rational, Natural and Open Systems*. Prentice-Hall: Englewood Cliffs, NJ, USA.

Seike, A (1997) Ageing workers. In M Sako and H Sato (eds): *Japanese Labour and Management in Transition*. Routledge: London.

Selznick, P (1948) Foundations of the theory of organization. *American Sociological Review*, 13, 25–35.

Senge, PM (1990) *The Fifth Discipline: The Art and Practice of the Learning Organization*. Century Business: London.

Senge, PM (2000) The puzzles and paradoxes of how living companies create wealth: why single-valued objective functions are not quite enough. In M Beer and N Nohria (eds): *Breaking the Code of Change*. Harvard Business School Press: Boston, MA, USA.

Senior, B (1997) *Organisational Change*. Pitman: London.

Senior, B (2002) *Organisational Change* (2nd edition). Financial Times Prentice Hall: Harlow.

Senturia, T, Flees, L and Maceda, M (2008) *Leading Change Management Requires Sticking to the PLOT*. Bain & Company: London.

Shapiro, C (1989) The theory of business strategy. *RAND Journal of Economics*, 20(1), 125–37.

Sheahan, J (1969) *An Introduction to the French Economy*. Merill: Columbus, OH, USA.

Sheldrake, J (1996) *Management Theory: From Taylorism to Japanization*. International Thompson Business Press: London.

Shelton, CK and Darling, JR (2001) The quantum skills model in management: a new paradigm to enhance effective leadership. *Leadership and Organization Development Journal*, 22(6), 264–73.

Sheridan, K (1993) *Governing the Japanese Economy*. Polity Press: Oxford.

Shiflett, SC (1973) The contingency model of leadership effectiveness: some implications of its statistical and methodological properties. *Behavioral Science*, 18(6), 429–40.

Shirai, T (1997) Foreword. In M Sako and H Sato (eds): *Japanese Labour and Management in Transition*. Routledge: London.

Short, JE and Venkatraman, N (1992) Beyond business process redesign: redefining Baxter's business network. *Sloan Management Review*, Fall, 7–21.

Shortell, S and Zajac, E (1990) Perceptual and archival measures of Miles and Snow's strategic types: a comprehensive assessment of reliability and validity. *Academy of Management Journal*, 33, 817–32.

Silverman, D (1970) *The Theory of Organizations*. Heinemann: London.

Silverman, D and Jones, J (1976) *Organizational Work*. Macmillan: London.

Silverman, S (2002) Weill wields his power at Citigroup: revamp represents ongoing structural changes. *Financial Times*, 13 June, 30.

Simon, HA (1947) *Administrative Behavior: A Study of Decision-making Processes in Administrative Organizations*. Macmillan: New York, USA.

Sirower, M (2003) When mergers can be a scandal. *Financial Times*, 14 August, 17.

Sissons, K (ed) (1989) *Personnel Management in Britain*. Blackwell: Oxford.

Sissons, K and Storey, J (1988) Developing effective managers: a review of the issues and an agenda for research. *Personnel Review*, 17(4), 3–8.

Sjöstrand, SV (1997) *The Two Faces of Management: The Janus Factor*. Thomson: London.

Skinner, BF (1974) *About Behaviourism*. Cape: London.

Sloan, AP (1986) *My Years with General Motors*. Penguin: Harmondsworth.

Smircich, L and Calás, M (1987) Organizational culture: a critical assessment. In F Jabin, L Putnam, K Roberts and L Porter (eds): *Handbook of Organizational Communication*. Sage: Newbury Park, CA, USA.

Smith, A (1776) *The Wealth of Nations*, Volume 1. Methuen (1950 edition): London.

Smith, A (2008) Working lives: cultural control, collectivism, *Karoshi*. *Sociology*, 42(1), 179–85.

Smith, JG (1985) *Business Strategy*. Blackwell: Oxford.

Smith, JH (1987) Elton Mayo and the hidden Hawthorne. *Work, Employment and Society*, 1(1), 107–20.

Smith, JH (1998) The enduring legacy of Elton Mayo. *Human Relations*, 51(3), 221–49.

Smith, M, Beck, J, Cooper, CL, Cox, C, Ottaway, D and Talbot, R (1982) *Introducing Organizational Behaviour*. Macmillan: London.

Smith, MK (2001) Kurt Lewin: groups, experiential learning and action research. *The Encyclopedia of Informal Education*, 1–15, available at www.infed.org/thinkers/et-lewin.htm.

Smith, PB and Misumi, J (1989) Japanese management – a sun rising in the West. In CL Cooper and I Robertson (eds): *The International Review of Industrial and Organizational Psychology*. Wiley: London.

Smith, S and Tranfield, D (1987) The implementation and exploitation of advanced manufacturing technology – an outline methodology. *Change Management Research Unit, Research Paper No 2*, Sheffield Business School.

Smith, T (1994) Flexible production and capital/wage labour relation in manufacturing. *Capital and Class*, 53, Summer, 39–63.

Smithers, R (1995) Power chiefs pay themselves £72m in share options. *Guardian*, 13 February, 20.

Snow, C, Miles, R and Coleman, H (1993) Managing 21st century network organizations. In C Mabey and B Mayon-White (eds): *Managing Change* (2nd edition). The Open University/Paul Chapman Publishing: London.

Sorge, A (1997) Organization behaviour. In A Sorge and M Warner (eds): *The IEBM Handbook of Organizational Behaviour*. International Thompson Business Press: London.

Sosik, JJ and Megerian, LE (1999) Understanding leader emotional intelligence and performance: the role of self–other agreement in transformational leadership perceptions. *Group and Organization Management*, 24(3), 367–90.

Speed, RJ (1996) Oh Mr Porter! A re-appraisal of competitive strategy. *Marketing Intelligence and Planning*, 7(5/6), 8–11.

Speller, S (2001) The Best Value initiative. In G Johnson and K Scholes (eds): *Exploring Public Sector Strategy*. Financial Times Prentice Hall: Harlow.

Spiller, K (2003) Realism replaces grand visions. *Financial Times*, 12 March, 2.

Stace, DA and Dunphy, DD (1994) *Beyond the Boundaries: Leading and Re-Creating the Successful Enterprise*. McGraw-Hill: Sydney, Australia.

Stace, D and Dunphy, D (2001) *Beyond the Boundaries: Leading and Re-Creating the Successful Enterprise* (2nd edition). McGraw-Hill: Sydney, Australia.

Stacey, R (1990) *Dynamic Strategic Management for the 1990s*. Kogan Page: London.

Stacey, R (1992) *Managing Chaos: Dynamic Business Strategies in an Unpredictable World*. Kogan Page: London.

Stacey, R (1993) *Strategic Management and Organisational Dynamics*. Pitman: London.

Stacey, RD (2003) *Strategic Management and Organisational Dynamics: The Challenge of Complexity*. Financial Times Prentice Hall: Harlow.

Stacey, RD, Griffin, D and Shaw, P (2002) *Complexity and Management: Fad or Radical Challenge to Systems Thinking*. Routledge: London.

Stalk, G, Evans, P and Shulman, LE (1992) Competing on capabilities – the new rules of corporate strategy. *Harvard Business Review*, March–April, 57–69.

Stata, R (1989) Organization learning – the key to management innovation. *Sloan Management Review*, Spring, 63–74.

Statistics Bureau (2003) *Labour Force Survey – Monthly Results, June 2003*. Ministry of Public Management, Home Affairs, Posts and Telecommunications, available at www.stat.go.jp.

Steiner, GA (1969) *Top Management Planning*. Macmillan: London.

Stewart, H (2003) The day investors said enough is enough. *Guardian*, 20 May, available at www.guardian.co.uk.

Stewart, R (1976) *Contrasts in Management*. McGraw-Hill: London.

Stewart, R (1982) *Choices for the Manager: A Guide to Understanding Managerial Work*. Prentice-Hall: Englewood Cliffs, NJ, USA.

Stickland, F (1998) *The Dynamics of Change: Insights into Organisational Transition from the Natural World*. Routledge: London.

Stiglitz, J (2007). *Making Globalization Work: The Next Steps to Global Justice*. Penguin: Harmondsworth.

Stogdill, RM (1948) Personal factors associated with leadership: a survey of the literature. *Journal of Psychology*, 25, 35–71.

Stogdill, RM (1974) *A Handbook of Leadership: A Survey of Theory and Research*. Free Press: New York, NY, USA.

Stohl, C and Cheney, G (2001) Participatory processes/paradoxical practices. *Management Communication Quarterly*, 14(3), 349–407.

Storey, J (1989) Management development: a literature review and implications for future research – Part 1: conceptualisations and practices. *Personnel Review*, 18(6), 3–19.

Storey, J (1990) Management development: a literature review and implications for future research – Part 2: profiles and context. *Personnel Review*, 19(1), 3–11.

Storey, J (1992) *Developments in the Management of Human Resources*. Blackwell: Oxford.

Storey, J (ed) (2004) *Leadership in Organizations: Current Issues and Key Trends*. Routledge: London.

Stournaras, Y (1999) *The Converging Greek Economy: Developments, Policies and Prospects*. Ministry of National Economy: Athens.

Strahan, D (2008) *The Last Oil Shock: A Survival Guide to the Imminent Extinction of Petroleum Man*. John Murray: London.

Streeck, W (1987) The uncertainties of management and the management of uncertainties: employers, labour relations and industrial adjustments in the 1980s. *Work, Employment and Society*, 1(3), 281–308.

Stuart, R (1986) Social learning. *Management Decision*, 24(6), 32–5.

Student, J (1968) Supervisory influence and work-group performance. *Journal of Applied Psychology*, June, 188–94.

Styhre, A (2002) Non-linear change in organizations: organization change management informed by complexity theory. *Leadership and Organization Development Journal*, 23(6), 343–51.

Sugeno, K and Suwa, Y (1997) Labour law issues in a changing labour market: in search of a new support system. In M Sako and H Sato (eds): *Japanese Labour and Management in Transition*. Routledge: London.

Sullivan, J (1983) A critique of Theory Z. *Academy of Management Review*, 8, 132–42.

Sullivan, J and Nonaka, I (1986) The application of organizational learning theory to Japanese and American management. *Journal of International Business Studies*, Fall, 127–47.

Sullivan, TJ (1999) Leading people in a chaotic world. *Journal of Educational Administration*, 37(5), 408–23.

Sviokla, JJ (1998) Virtual value and the birth of virtual markets. In SP Bradley and RL Nolan (eds): *Sense and Respond: Capturing Value in the Network Era*. Harvard Business School Press: Boston, MA, USA.

Taguchi, G (1986) *Introduction to Quality Engineering*. Asian Production Organization: Dearborn, MI, USA.

Talbot, C (2001) UK public services and management (1979–2000): evolution or revolution? *International Journal of Public Sector Management*, 14(4), 281–303.

Talbot, R (1993) Creativity in the organizational context: implications for training. In SG Isaksen, MC Murdock, RL Firestien and DJ Treffinger (eds): *Nurturing and Developing Creativity*. Ablex: Norwood, NJ, USA.

Talbot, R (1997) Taking style on board. *Creativity and Innovation Management*, 6(3), 177–84.

Tarokh, MJ, Sharifi, E and Nazem, E (2008) Survey of BPR experiences in Iran: reasons for success and failure. *Journal of Business and Industrial Marketing*, 23(5), 350–62.

Taylor, FW (1911a) *The Principles of Scientific Management*. Dover (1998 edition): New York, NY.

Taylor, FW (1911b) *Shop Management*. Harper (1947 edition): New York, USA.

Teather, D (2002) Trying to close a can of worms. *Guardian*, 11 October, available at www.guardian.co.uk.

Teather, D (2003) US labels to sue individuals for net music piracy. *Guardian*, 26 June, 13.

Teece, DJ, Pisano, G and Shuen, A (1997) Dynamic capabilities and strategic management. *Strategic Management Journal*, 18(7), 509–33.

Terry, PT (1976) The contingency theory and the development of organisations. *Paper presented to the British Sociological Association.*

Tetenbaum, TJ (1998) Shifting paradigms: from Newton to chaos. *Organizational Dynamics*, 26(4), 21–32.

Tett, G (1994) Partnerships in business grow. *Financial Times*, 28 June, 12.

Thickett, M (1970) Gilbreth and the measurement of work. In A Tillett, T Kempner and G Willis (eds): *Management Thinkers*. Pelican: Harmondsworth.

Thomas, AB (1993) *Controversies in Management*. Routledge: London.

Thomas, AB (2003) *Controversies in Management: Issues, Debates, Answers*. Routledge: London.

Thompkins, JM (1990) Politics – the illegitimate discipline. *Management Decision*, 28(4), 23–8.

Thompson, AA Jnr and Strickland, AJ (1983) *Strategy Formulation and Implementation*. Business Publications Inc: Illinois, USA.

Thompson, J (1967) *Organizations in Action*. McGraw-Hill: New York, USA.

Thompson, JW (1995) The renaissance of learning in business. In S Chawla and J Renesch (eds): *Learning Organizations: Developing Cultures for Tomorrow's Workplace*. Productivity Press: Portland, OR, USA.

Thompson, M (1996) Effective purchasing strategy: the untapped source of competitiveness. *Supply Chain Management*, 1(3), 6–8.

Thompson, M (2008) *Introduction to Strategic Management*. MDP (Management Development Partnership): Bangor, Wales.

Thornberry, NE (1987) Training the engineer as project manager. *Training and Development Journal*, 41(10).

Tibbs, H and Bailey, K (2008) Empty threat. *The Guardian*, 11 June. www.guardian.co.uk.

Tighe, C (2002) Less means more in engineering. *Financial Times*, 17 October, 15.

Tillett, A (1970) Industry and management. In A Tillett, T Kempner and G Willis (eds): *Management Thinkers*. Pelican: Harmondsworth.

Tobach, E (1994) Personal is political is personal is political. *Journal of Social Issues*, 50(1), 221–44.

Toffler, A (1970) *Future Shock*. Random House: New York, USA.

Tomaney, J (1990) The reality of workplace flexibility. *Capital and Class*, 40, Spring, 29–60.

Total Quality Engineering Inc (2003) Hoshin Kanri, available at www.tqe.com/hoshinTR.html.

Trade (2003) 15 facts to remember about trade, wealth and the unequal world we live in. *Trade*. The Guardian/Action Aid: London.

Tran, M (2003) $1.4 bn Wall Street settlement finalised. *Guardian*, 28 April, available at www.guardian.co.uk.

Treanor, J and Finch, J (2003) Directors gains stir revolt by investors. *Guardian*, 31 July, 4.

Treanor, J and Wray, R (2003) Marconi chiefs defy FSA censure: no apology for shareholders in wake of City watchdog's warning on rules breach. *Guardian*, 12 April, available at www.guardian.co.uk.

Trice, HM and Beyer, JM (1984) Studying organizational cultures through rites and ceremonials. *Academy of Management Review*, 9, 653–69.

Trice, HM and Beyer, JM (1990) Using six organizational rites to change culture. In RH Kilmann, MJ Saxton, R Serpa and Associates (eds): *Gaining Control of the Corporate Culture*. Jossey-Bass: San Francisco, CA, USA.

Trist, EL, Higgin, GW, Murray, H and Pollock, AB (1963) *Organisational Choice*. Tavistock: London.

Trompenaars, F (1993) *Riding the Waves of Culture*. Nicholas Brealey: London.

Tsang, EWK (1997) Organizational learning and the learning organization: a dichotomy between descriptive and prescriptive research. *Human Relations*, 50(1), 73–89.

Tschacher, W and Brunner, EJ (1995) Empirical-studies of group-dynamics from the point-of-view of self-organization theory. *Zeitschrift fur Sozialpsychologie*, 26(2), 78–91.

Tsoukas, H (1989) The validity of idiographic research explanations. *Academy of Management Review*, 14(4), 551–61.

Tsoukas, H (1992) Postmodernism, reflexive rationalism and organisation studies. *Organisation Studies*, 13(4), 643–9.

Tsoukas, H (2000) What is management? An outline of a metatheory. In S Ackroyd and S Fleetwood (eds): *Realist Perspectives on Management and Organisations*. Routledge: London.

Tuckman, BW (1965) Developmental sequence in small groups. *Psychological Bulletin*, 63, 384–99.

Tuckman, BW and Jensen, MAC (1977) Stages of small group development revisited. *Group and Organizational Studies*, 2, 419–27.

Turnbull, P (1986) The Japanisation of production and industrial relations at Lucas Electrical. *Industrial Relations Journal*, 17(3), 193–206.

Turner, B (1971) *Exploring the Industrial Subculture*. Macmillan: London.

Turner, B (1986) Sociological aspects of organizational symbolism. *Organization Studies*, 7(2), 101–17.

Turner, D (2003) Unemployment falls to two-year low. *Financial Times*, 17 July, 3.

Turner, I (1990) Strategy and organisation. *Manager Update*, 1(3), 1–10.

Tushman, M and Virany, B (1986) Changing characteristics of executive teams in an emerging industry. *Journal of Business Venturing*, 37–49.

Tushman, ML and Romanelli, E (1985) Organizational evolution: a metamorphosis model of convergence and reorientation. In LL Cummings and BM Staw (eds): *Research in Organizational Behavior*, 7, 171–222. JAI Press: Greenwich, CT, USA.

Udy, SH Jnr (1959) 'Bureaucracy' and 'rationality' in Weber's organization theory. *American Sociological Review*, 24, December, 791–5.

United Nations Development Programme (2007) *Human Development Report 2007/2008*. Palgrave Macmillan: Basingstoke.

Urabe, K (1986) Innovation and the Japanese management system. Keynote address, First International Symposium on Management, Japan Society for the Study of Business Administration, Kobe University, 11–49.

Ure, A (1835) *The Philosophy of Manufactures*. Frank Cass (1967 edition): London.

Ure, A (1836) *The Cotton Manufacture of Great Britain*, Vol. 1. Johnson (1970 edition): London.

Urwick, L (1949) Introduction. In H Fayol (ed): *General and Industrial Management* (trans). Pitman: London.

Uttal, B (1983) The corporate culture vultures. *Fortune*, 17 October, 66–72.

Van der Wiele, A (1998) *Beyond Fads*. Eburon: Delft, The Netherlands.

Van Maanen, J (1991) The smile factory: work at Disneyland. In PJ Frost, L Moore, M Louis, C Lundberg and J Martin (eds): *Reframing Organizational Culture*. Sage: Beverly Hills, CA, USA.

Van Maanen, J and Kunda, G (1989) Real feelings: emotional expression and organisational culture. In B Staw and L Cummings (eds): *Research in Organizational Behaviour*, 11, 43–103.

Vecchio, RP (1983) Assessing the validity of Fielder's contingency model of leadership effectiveness: a closer look at Strube and Garcia. *Psychological Bulletin*, 93, 404–8.

Vickers, J and Yarrow, G (1991) Economic perspectives on privatisation. *Journal of Economic Perspectives*, 5(2), 111–32.

Vidler, E and Clarke, J (2005) Creating citizen-consumers: New Labour and the remaking of public services. *Public Policy and Administration*, 20(2), 19–37.

Vinnecombe, S (1987) What exactly are the differences in male and female working styles? *Women in Management Review*, 3(1).

Virgin.com (2008) *About Virgin*. www.virgin.com.

von Clausewitz, C, von Ghyczy, T, von Oetinger, C and Bassford, C (2001) *Clausewitz on Strategy: Inspiration and Insight from a Master Strategist*. Wiley: Chichester.

Voss, CA (1985) *Success and Failure in Advanced Manufacturing Technology*. Warwick University Working Paper.

Vroom, VH and Jago, AG (1988) *The New Leadership: Managing Participation in Organizations*. Prentice-Hall: Englewood Cliffs, NJ, USA.

Vroom, VH and Yetton, PW (1973) *Leadership and Decision Making*. Pittsburgh Press: Pittsburgh, PA, USA.

Wack, P (1985) Scenarios: uncharted waters ahead. *Harvard Business Review*, September/October, 73–89.

Waclawski, J (2002) Large-scale organizational change and performance: an empirical examination. *Human Resource Development Quarterly*, 13(3), 289–305.

Wagner, JA (1994) Participation's effects on performance and satisfaction: a reconsideration of research evidence. *Academy of Management Review*, 19, 312–30.

Wahba, A and Bridgewell, L (1976) Maslow reconsidered: a review of research on the need hierarchy theory. *Organizational Behavior and Human Performance*, 15(2), 212–40.

Wakisata, A (1997) Women at work. In M Sako and H Sato (eds): *Japanese Labour and Management in Transition*. Routledge: London.

Waldersee, R and Sheather, S (1996) The effects of strategy type on strategy implementation actions. *Human Relations*, 49(1), 105–22.

Wall, TD, Burnes, B, Clegg, CW and Kemp, NJ (1984) New technology, old jobs. *Work and People*, 10(2), 15–21.

Wallace, J and Erickson, J (1992) *Hard Drive: Bill Gates and the Making of the Microsoft Empire*. Wiley: New York, USA.

Waller, DL (1999) *Operations Management: A Supply Chain Approach*. International Thompson: London.

Wang, CL and Ahmed, PK (2003) Organisational learning: a critical review. *The Learning Organization*, 10(1), 8–17.

Warner, M (1984) New technology, work organisation and industrial relations. *Omega*, 12(3), 203–10.

Warner, M (1997) The year of the very big deals. *Fortune*, 24, November, 3.

Warr, P (ed) (1987) *Psychology at Work*. Penguin: Harmondsworth.

Warwick, DP and Thompson, JT (1980) Still crazy after all these years. *Training and Development Journal*, 34(2), 16–22.

Wastell, DG, White, P and Kawalek, P (1994) A methodology for business process redesign: experience and issues. *Journal of Strategic Information Systems*, 3(1), 23–40.

Watson, G (1994) The flexible workforce and patterns of working hours in the UK. *Employment Gazette*, July, 239–47.

Watson, T (1982) Group ideologies and organisational change. *Journal of Management Studies*, 19(3), 259–77.

Watson, TJ (1986) *Management Organisation and Employment Strategy: New Directions in Theory and Practice*. Routledge and Kegan Paul: London.

Watson, TJ (1997) *Sociology, Work and Industry* (3rd edition). Routledge: London.

Watts, J (1998) Japanese 'bullied' out of work. *Guardian*, 29 August, 13.

Weber, M (1928) *General Economic History*. George Allen & Unwin: London.

Weber, M (1947) *The Theory of Social and Economic Organization* (trans). Free Press: Glencoe, IL, USA.

Weber, M (1948) *From Max Weber: Essays in Sociology* (translated, edited and with an introduction by HH Gerth and C Wright Mills). Routledge and Kegan Paul: London.

Weick, KE (1979) *The Social Psychology of Organizing*. Addison-Wesley: Reading, MA, USA.

Weick, KE (1987) Substitute for corporate strategy. In DJ Teece (ed) *The Competitive Challenge: Strategies for Industrial Innovation and Renewal*. Ballinger: Cambridge, MA, USA.

Weick, KE (1995) *Sensemaking in Organizations*. Sage: London.

Weick, KE (2000) Emergent change as a universal in organizations. In M Beer and N Nohria (eds): *Breaking the Code of Change*. Harvard Business School Press: Boston, MA, USA.

Weick, KE and Quinn, RE (1999) Organizational change and development. *Annual Review of Psychology*, 50, 361–86.

Wernerfelt, B (1984) A resource-based view of the firm. *Strategic Management Journal*, 15(2), 171–80.

Wernerfelt, B (1995) The resource-based view of the firm: ten years after. *Strategic Management Journal*, 16, 171–4.

West, P (1994) The concept of the learning organization. *Journal of European Industrial Training*, 18(1), 15–21.

Wetlaufer, S (1999) Organizing for empowerment: an interview with AES's Roger Sante and Dennis Bakke. *Harvard Business Review*, January–February, 120–1.

Wheatley, MJ (1992a) *The Future of Middle Management*. British Institute of Management: London.

Wheatley, MJ (1992b) *Leadership and the New Science: Learning about Organization from an Orderly Universe*. Berrett-Koehler: San Francisco, CA, USA.

Wheelan, SA, Pepitone, EA and Abt, V (eds) (1990) *Advances in Field Theory*. Sage: Newbury Park: CA, USA.

Wheelen, TL and Hunger, DJ (1989) *Strategic Management and Business Policy*. Addison-Wesley: Reading, MA, USA.

Whitaker, A (1992) The transformation in work: post-Fordism revisited. In M Reed and M Hughes (eds): *Rethinking Organization: New Directions in Organization Theory and Analysis*. Sage: London.

White, M (1999) PM's deadline to end child poverty. *Guardian*, 19 March, 10.

White, S and Mitchell, T (1976) Organization development: a review of research content and research design. *Academy of Management Review*, 1(2), 57–73.

Whitehill, AM (1991) *Japanese Management: Tradition and Transition*. Routledge: London.

Whitley, R (1998) *Divergent Capitalisms*. Oxford University Press: London.

Whittington, R (1989) *Corporate Strategies in Recovery and Recession: Social Structure and Strategic Choice*. Unwin Hyman: London.

Whittington, R (1993) *What Is Strategy and Does it Matter?* Routledge: London.

Whittington, R (1994) Sociological pluralism, institutions and managerial agency. In J Hassard and M Parker (eds): *Towards a New Theory of Organisation*. Routledge: London.

Whittington, R (2001) *What Is Strategy and Does it Matter?* (2nd edition). Thomson Learning: London.

Whyte, J and Witcher, B (1992) *The Adoption of Total Quality Management in Northern England*. Durham University Business School: Durham.

Whyte, WH (1960) *The Organization of Man*. Penguin: Harmondsworth.

Wickens, P (1987) *The Road to Nissan*. Macmillan: London.

Wickens, P (1995) *The Ascendent Organization: Combining Commitment and Control for Long Term Sustainable Business Success*. Macmillan: London.

Wilkinson, A (1991) *TQM and HRM*. Working Paper, Manchester School of Management, UMIST.

Wilkinson, HE and Orth, DC (1986) Soft skill training in management development. *Training and Development Journal*, 40(3).

Willbur, J (1987) Does mentoring breed success? *Training and Development Journal*, 41(11).

Willcocks, SG (1994) Organizational analysis: a health service commentary. *Leadership and Organization Development Journal*, 15(1), 29–32.

Williams, K, Cutler, T and Haslan, C (1987) The end of mass production? *Economy and Society*, 1(3), 404–39.

Williams, K, Haslam, C and Williams, J (1991) Management Accounting: the Western Problematic against the Japanese Application. *9th Annual Conference of the Labour Process*, UMIST, Manchester.

Williamson, O (1991) Strategizing, economizing and economic organization. *Strategic Management Journal*, 12, 75–94.

Willmott, H (1995) Strength is ignorance; slavery is freedom: managing culture in modern organizations. *Journal of Management Studies*, 30(40), 511–12.

Willmott, R (2000) Structure, culture and agency: rejecting the current orthodoxy of organisational theory. In S Ackroyd and S Fleetwood (eds): *Realist Perspectives on Management and Organisations*. Routledge: London.

Wilson, AM (2001) Understanding organisational culture and the implications for corporate marketing. *European Journal of Marketing*, 35(3/4), 353–67.

Wilson, DC (1992) *A Strategy of Change*. Routledge: London.

Wilson, JF (1995) *British Business History, 1720–1994*. Manchester University Press: Manchester.

Wisdom, J (ed) (2001) *Digital Futures: Living in a Dot-Com World*. Earthscan: London.

Witcher, B (1993) *The Adoption of Total Quality Management in Scotland*. Durham University Business School: Durham.

Witzel, M (2002) The sustainable business: continuous search for improvement. *Financial Times*, 19 August, 9.

Witzel, M (2003a) *Fifty Key Figures in Management*. Routledge: London.

Witzel, M (2003b) The master strategist: Michael Porter. *Financial Times*, 15 August, 11.

Witzel, M (2003c) The great iconoclast: Henry Mintzberg. *Financial Times*, 5 August, 11.

Womack, JP, Jones, DT and Roos, D (1990) *The Machine that Changed the World*. Rawson Associates: New York, USA.

Wood, S (1979) A reappraisal of the contingency approach to organization. *Journal of Management Studies*, 16, 334–54.

Wood, S (1991) Japanisation and/or Toyotaism? *Work, Employment and Society*, 5(4), 567–600.

Woodman, R (1989) Organization change and development: new arenas for inquiry and action. *Journal of Management*, 15, 205–28.

Woodward, J (1965) *Industrial Organization: Theory and Practice*. Oxford University Press: London.

Woodward, J (1970) *Industrial Organization: Behaviour and Control*. Oxford University Press: London.

Wooten, KC and White, LP (1999) Linking OD's philosophy with justice theory: postmodern implications. *Journal of Organizational Change Management*, 12(1), 7–20.

Worley, GC and Feyerhern, AE (2003) Reflections on the future of organization development. *The Journal of Applied Behavioral Science*, 39(1), 97–115.

Worrall, L and Cooper, CL (1997) *The Quality of Working Life: The 1997 Survey of Managers' Changing Experiences*. Institute of Management: London.

Worrall, L and Cooper, CL (1998) *The Quality of Working Life: The 1998 Survey of Managers' Changing Experiences*. Institute of Management: London.

Wren, D (1994) *The Evolution of Management Thought* (4th edition). Wiley: Chichester.

www.dei.gr. The official website of PPC SA.

www.rae.gr. The official website of the Greek Regulatory Authority for Energy.

Yammarino, FI and Dansereau, F (2002) *The Many Faces of Multi-Level Issues: Research in Multi-level Issues Vol 1*. JAI Press: London.

Yaniv, E and Farkas, F (2005) The impact of person–organization fit on the corporate brand perception of employees and of customers. *Journal of Change Management*, 5(4), 447–61.

Young, H (1990) *The Iron Lady: A Biography of Margaret Thatcher*. Farrar Straus and Giroux: London.

Yukl, G (1994) *Leadership in Organizations* (3rd edition). Prentice-Hall: Englewood Cliffs, NJ, USA.

Yukl, G (2002) *Leadership in Organizations* (5th edition). Prentice-Hall: Upper Saddle River, NJ, USA.

Yukl, G (2006) *Leadership in Organizations* (6th edition). Prentice Hall: London.

Yukl, G and Van Fleet, DD (1992) Theory and research on leadership in organizations. In MD Dunnette and LM Hough (eds): *Handbook of Industrial and Organizational Psychology*, Vol. 3 (2nd edition). Consulting Psychologists Press: Palo Alto, CA, USA.

Yutaka, N (1998) Japanese-style industrial relations in historical perspective. In H Harukiyo and GD Hook (eds): *Japanese Business Management: Restructuring for Low Growth and Globalization*. Routledge: London.

Zairi, M, Letza, S and Oakland, J (1994) Does TQM impact on bottom line results? *TQM Magazine*, 6(1), 38–43.

Zaleznik, A (1970) Power and politics in organizational life. *Harvard Business Review*, May–June, 47–60.

Zell, D (2003) Organizational change as a process of death, dying, and rebirth. *Journal of Applied Behavioral Science*, 39(1), 73–96.

Zentner, RD (1982) Scenarios, past, present and future. *Long Range Planning*, 15, June, 12–20.

Zimmerman, BJ (1992) *Chaos and Self-Renewing Organizations: Designing Transformation Processes for Co-evolution*. Faculty of Administrative Studies, York University: Ontario, Canada.

Zinn, H (1980) *A People's History of the United States*. Longman: London.

Zwerman, WL (1970) *New Perspectives in Organization Theory*. Greenwood: Westport, CT, USA.

Glossary

Action Learning   This approach to management development was devised in the 1940s in the UK by Reg Revans and involves small groups of managers tackling a set problem or case study. The aim is not only that managers learn how to approach problems together, but also that they learn about themselves and challenge the appropriateness of their own attitudes and behaviours.

Action Research   This is an approach to change which, first, emphasises that change requires action, and is directed at achieving this; and second, recognises that successful action is based on analysing the situation correctly, identifying all the possible alternative solutions and choosing the one most appropriate to the situation at hand. It is one of the four elements of Lewin's Planned approach to change (*see* **Planned change**).

Activity planning   This involves constructing a schedule or 'road map' for a change programme, citing the main activities and events that must occur if the change is to be successful.

Adaptation–Innovation theory   This maintains not only that people exhibit different degrees of creativity, but also that they express their **creativity** in different ways, along a spectrum which runs from adaptors to innovators. Those who tend towards the adaptor end of the spectrum prefer to work within the existing system to improve things. Innovators tend to ignore or challenge the system and to come up with radical proposals for change.

Analytical stream   This phrase is used to describe writers on strategy and change who are more interested in understanding how organisations actually formulate **strategy** and manage change than prescribing how they should conduct these activities (*see* **Prescriptive stream**).

Artefacts   At the highest level of cultural awareness are the artefacts and creations that are visible manifestations of the other levels of culture. These include observable behaviours of members, as well as the structures, systems, procedures, rules and physical aspects of the organisation (*see* **organisational culture**).

Aston Group   The work of this group constitutes one of the key building blocks of **Contingency Theory**. Working in the 1960s, they found that size was the most powerful predictor of specialisation, use of procedures and reliance on paperwork. In effect, what they found was that the larger the organisation, the more likely it was to adopt (and need) a **mechanistic** (bureaucratic) **structure**. The reverse was also found: the smaller the organisation, the more likely it was to adopt (and need) an **organic** (flexible) **structure**.

Audits and post-audits   During and after a change initiative, an audit or a post-audit should be carried out (a) to establish that the objectives have really been met, and (b) to ascertain what lessons can be learned for future projects.

Authority   In organisational terms, authority is the right to act, or command others to act, towards the attainment of organisational goals. The right to act is given legitimacy by the authority figure's position in the organisation. Therefore, the level of authority a person possesses is related to their job.

Autonomy   This is the ability or requirement of individuals, groups and organisations to act independently and proactively, and without seeking the permission of higher authority, when pursuing organisational goals. Peters and Waterman link it to entrepreneurship and it is seen as an essential attribute of excellent organisations (*see* **Culture–Excellence approach**).

Backstaging   This is concerned with the exercise of power skills during the change process. In particular, it involves influencing the recipients of change to accept it. Buchanan and Boddy (1992) see this as being an essential skill of a **change agent**.

Basic assumptions   These are seen as one of the core components of **organisational culture**. They operate at the deepest level of cultural awareness and are unconscious, taken-for-granted assumptions about how organisational problems should be solved, as well as about the nature of human beings, human activity and human relationships.

Behaviourist psychology   This maintains that all human behaviour is learned and that the individual is the passive recipient of external and objective data. One of the basic principles of the Behaviourists is that human actions are conditioned by their expected consequences. Behaviour that is rewarded tends to be repeated, and behaviour that is ignored tends not to be. Therefore, in order to change behaviour, it is necessary to change the conditions that cause it.

Benchmarking   This is the term given to the process of comparing an organisation's performance, or the performance of part of an organisation, e.g. a product or service, against a range of internal and external comparators.

Bias for action   This is one of Peters and Waterman's eight key attributes of excellent companies. Even though such companies may have an analytical approach to problems, they are predisposed towards taking rapid and appropriate action rather than getting bogged down in analysis (*see* **Culture–Excellence approach**).

Bold Strokes   These are major strategic or economic initiatives, e.g. restructuring an organisation. They can have a clear and rapid impact on an organisation's performance, but they rarely lead to any long-term change in habits or culture. Bold Strokes are initiatives taken by a few senior managers, sometimes only one; they do not rely on the support of the rest of the organisation for their success (*see* **Long Marches**; **Culture–Excellence approach**).

Boston Consulting Group   *See* **Growth-Share Matrix**.

Bottom-up change   This is the opposite of top-down change. Instead of change being driven by a few senior managers from the top, this approach sees change as coming from bottom-up initiatives which emerge from local responses to issues, threats or opportunities in the environment. The size of such responses will vary but, because they are local responses, they can never be large-scale (*see* **Emergent change**).

BPR   *See* **Business Process Re-engineering.**

Bureaucracy   This form of organisational structure is characterised by the **division of labour,** a clear hierarchical authority structure, formal and unbiased selection procedures, employment decisions based on merit, career tracks for employees, detailed rules and regulations, impersonal relationships, and a distinct separation of members' organisational and personal lives. It is one of the core elements of the **Classical approach to organisations** and corresponds with the **mechanistic structure** identified by **Contingency theorists** (*see* **Contingency Theory**).

Business ethics   These are moral principles or beliefs about what is right or wrong. These beliefs guide managers and others in organisations in their dealings with other individuals, groups and organisations, and provide a basis for deciding whether behaviour is socially responsible.

Business Process Re-engineering (BPR)   This is an approach that aims to achieve a radical rethinking and redesign of organisational processes in order to significantly improve key performance measures, such as quality, cost and delivery.

Cash-cows   These are companies whose rate of market growth is in decline but which still achieve significant cash surpluses. They became market leaders, during the early days when the market was rapidly growing, and have maintained that position as the growth tapered off. They are regarded as businesses with low growth but high market share (*see* **Growth-Share Matrix**).

Causal mechanisms   According to the realist perspective, these are the (usually hidden) processes or pathways through which an outcome is caused to be brought about. An example of a causal mechanism is the process by which a rise in interest rates leads to a fall in house prices. In this case, the causal mechanism linking cause to effect involves decisions by each individual house purchaser about the mortgage repayments they can and cannot afford. It is the aggregate behaviour of these individuals that leads to the overall fall in house prices (*see* **realism**).

Causal powers   These are the capabilities or potential for systems and mechanisms to act in a particular way, or to be capable of acting in a particular way (*see* **realism**).

Change agents   These are the people responsible for directing, organising and facilitating change in organisations (*see* **backstaging**).

Chaordic   This term was coined by Hock (1999) to describe organisations which are poised between **order** and **chaos** (*see* **edge of chaos; complexity theories**).

Chaos   For **complexity theorists,** chaos describes a complex, unpredictable and orderly disorder in which patterns of behaviour unfold in irregular but similar forms (*see* **edge of chaos; complexity theories**).

Chaos Theory   This is one of the main **complexity theories.** It seeks to construct mathematical models of systems at the macro level (i.e. whole systems and populations). It portrays natural systems as both **non-linear** and **self-organising.**

Classical approach to organisations   This approach to organisations is characterised by the horizontal and hierarchical **division of labour,** the minimisation of human skills and discretion, and the attempt to construe organisations as rational–scientific entities. It comprises the work of Frederick Taylor (*see* **Scientific Management**), Henri Fayol (*see* **principles of organisation**) and Max Weber (*see* **bureaucracy**).

Classical approach to strategy   This is the oldest and most influential approach to **strategy**. It portrays strategy as a rational process, based on analysis and quantification, and aimed at achieving the maximum level of profit for an organisation.

Closed systems   This is a view of organisations which sees them as being relatively unaffected by events outside their boundaries. It considers organisations to be closed, changeless entities. Once organisations have structured themselves in accordance with the correct precepts, then, regardless of external or even internal developments, no further changes are necessary or desirable (*see* **Open Systems school**).

Coercive power   The use of threats, sanctions or force to gain compliance.

Cognitive dissonance   This theory states that people try to be consistent in both their attitudes and behaviour. When they sense an inconsistency either between two or more attitudes or between their attitudes and behaviour, people experience dissonance; that is, they feel frustrated and uncomfortable with the situation, sometimes extremely so.

Competitive Forces model   This is an approach to **strategy** which stresses the need to align the organisation with its **environment**, the key aspect of which is the industry or industries in which it competes. Proponents of this view believe that industry structure strongly influences the competitive rules of the game as well as the range of strategies open to the organisation. This model is most closely associated with the work of Michael Porter (1980, 1985).

Complexity theories   These are concerned with how order is created in dynamic **non-linear systems**. In particular, those applying this approach to organisations maintain that successful organisations need to operate at the '**edge of chaos**' and can only maintain this position by the presence of appropriate **order-generating rules**.

Contextual approach to leadership   This is an approach which argues that effective leadership is situation-dependent, i.e. a manager's performance will depend on his or her personal characteristics and the overall context within which they operate (*see* **transactional management** and **convergent state**, and **transformational leadership** and **divergent state**).

Contingency Theory   This maintains that the structures and practices of an organisation, and therefore its performance, are dependent (i.e. contingent) on the circumstances it faces. The main contingencies – **situational variables** – identified by its proponents are environmental uncertainty and dependence, technology and organisation size (*see* **environment**).

Continuous change   This model of change, also referred to as the continuous transformation model, is based on the assertion that the **environment** in which organisations operate is changing, and will continue to change, rapidly, radically and unpredictably. Consequently, only by continuous transformation will organisations be able to keep aligned with their environment and thus survive.

Contracting out   *See* **outsourcing**.

Control   The ability to impose a desired pattern of activity or behaviour on processes and people (*see* **authority** and **power**).

Convergent state   This occurs when an organisation is operating under stable conditions, where there are established and accepted goals, and a predictable external and internal environment (*see* **transactional management**).

Creativity   The ability to produce new, novel or original ideas and solutions.

Cross Impact method   This is a **scenario-building** technique which asks a panel of experts to assign subjective probabilities and time priorities to a list of potential future events and developments supplied by an organisation.

Culture   *See* **organisational culture**.

Culture–Excellence approach   Based on the work of Peters and Waterman, Kanter and Handy, this maintains that an organisation's performance (excellence) is determined by the possession of an appropriate, strong and clearly articulated culture. It is culture which ensures that the members of the organisation focus on those activities which lead to effective performance.

Delphi method   This is a **scenario-building** technique which uses a panel of experts, who, independently of each other, are interrogated about a number of future issues within their area of expertise.

Design school   The proponents of this approach to **strategy** emphasise the need to achieve a fit between the internal capabilities of an organisation and the external possibilities it faces. Flowing from this, they place primary emphasis on the appraisal of an organisation's external and internal situations.

Dissipative structures   These are systems that exist in far-from-equilibrium conditions (i.e. are in a state of constant fluctuation) and which, therefore, use (dissipate) energy. The concept of dissipative structures is one of the core ideas in **complexity theories**. They are most closely associated with the work of the Nobel Prize-winning physicist, Ilya Prigogine (Prigogine and Stengers, 1984; Prigogine, 1997).

Divergent state   This situation occurs when environmental changes challenge the efficiency and appropriateness of an organisation's established goals, structures and ways of working (*see* **contextual approach to leadership** and **transformational leadership**).

Diversity   *See* **workforce diversity**.

Division of labour   The hierarchical and horizontal separation of tasks and responsibilities into their component parts so that individuals are only responsible for a limited set of activities instead of the whole task.

Dogs   These are businesses that have low market share and which operate in markets with low growth potential (*see* **Growth-Share Matrix**).

Double-loop learning   This process involves challenging the appropriateness of an organisation's basic **norms, values**, policies and operating procedures (*see* **single-loop learning; triple-loop learning**).

Edge of chaos   This is a state where systems are constantly poised between order and disorder (*see* **complexity theories**).

Emergent change This approach to change is based on the assumption that change is a continuous, open-ended and unpredictable process of aligning and realigning an organisation to its changing **environment**.

Empowerment   The delegation of power and responsibility to subordinates.

Entrepreneurship   The encouragement and pursuit of innovative ideas, products and services (*see* **Culture–Excellence approach**).

Environment   Those forces external to an organisation, such as markets, customers, the economy, etc., which influence its decisions and internal operations.

Equifinality   This concept, coined by Child (1972), states that different sorts of internal arrangements and structures can be perfectly compatible with identical contextual or environmental states. Put simply, this means that there is more than one way for organisations to structure themselves in order to achieve their goals.

Esteem needs   These reflect a person's desire to be respected – esteemed – for their achievements (*see* **hierarchy of needs**).

Excellence   *See* **Culture–Excellence approach.**

Extrinsic motivators   These are material rewards, such as money and promotion, provided by others (*see* **intrinsic motivators** and **physiological needs**).

Felt-need   This is an individual's inner realisation that change is necessary. If felt-need is low in a group or organisation, introducing change becomes problematic.

Field Theory   This is an approach to understanding group behaviour by trying to map out the totality and complexity of the field in which the behaviour takes place. It is one of the four elements of Lewin's Planned approach to change (*see* **Planned change**).

Firm-in-sector perspective   This view of **strategy**, developed by Child and Smith (1987), maintains that the conditions operating in a sector shape and constrain the strategies which organisations in that sector can pursue.

Fordism   This is named after Henry Ford's approach to car assembly. Fordism is seen as the application of **Scientific Management** to mass production industries through the utilisation of automation, e.g. the moving assembly line.

Game theory   This approach to **strategy** can be traced back to the study of war. Game theory has two core assumptions: first, that competitors are rational and will try to win; second, that each competitor is in an interdependent relationship with the other competitors. So all competitors are affected by and will react to what other competitors do.

Generative structures   *See* **causal mechanisms.**

Gestalt-Field psychology   This sees an individual's behaviour as the product of their environment and reason. Behaviour arises from the way in which an individual uses reason to interpret external stimuli. Consequently, to change behaviour, individuals must be helped to change their understanding of themselves and the situation in question.

Globalisation   There is a great deal of dispute as to what this term means. However, at its most basic, it refers to the worldwide integration of markets and cultures, the removal of legal and political barriers to trade, the 'death of distance' as a factor limiting material and cultural exchanges.

Group Dynamics   This concept refers to the forces operating in groups. It is concerned with what gives rise to these forces, their consequence and how to modify them. Group Dynamics stresses that group behaviour, rather than that of individuals, should be the main focus of change. It is one of the four elements of Lewin's Planned approach to change (*see* **Planned change**).

Group Dynamics school   As a component of change theory, this school originated with the work of Kurt Lewin and has the longest history. Its emphasis is on bringing about organisational change through teams or work groups, rather than individuals.

Growth-Share Matrix   This is a strategic planning tool developed by the Boston Consulting Group. Using pictorial analogies, it posits that businesses in an organisation's portfolio can be classified into **stars**, **cash-cows**, **dogs** and **problem children**.

Hawthorne Experiments   These were carried out at Western Electric's Hawthorne Works in Chicago in the 1920s and 1930s. As a result of this work, two major propositions were put forward: that work is a collective, cooperative activity which is influenced by formal and informal aspects of an organisation; and that humans have a deep need for recognition, security and belonging, rather than being purely economic beings (*see* **Human Relations approach**).

Hierarchy of needs   Developed by Maslow (1943), this sees human motivation as based on an ascending order of needs: **physiological needs**; **safety needs**; **social needs**; **esteem needs** and **self-actualisation needs**. Only when a lower-order need has been met, does the next level of need begin to motivate an individual.

Hoshin Kanri   Also known as policy deployment, this is a Japanese approach to communicating a company's policy, goals and objectives throughout its hierarchy in a structured and consistent fashion in order to ensure that its strategic priorities inform decision-making at all levels in the organisation.

Human Relations approach   This was a reaction against the mechanistic view of organisations and the pessimistic view of human nature put forward in the **Classical approach to organisations**. It reintroduces the human element into organisational life by contending that people have emotional as well as economic needs, and that organisations are cooperative systems which comprise informal structures and **norms** as well as formal ones (*see* **hierarchy of needs** and **Hawthorne Experiments**).

Humanisation of work   *See* **Job Design**.

Incremental model of change   Advocates of this view see change as being a process whereby individual parts of an organisation deal incrementally and separately with one problem and one goal at a time.

Individual Perspective school   This school of thought is concerned with understanding and promoting behaviour change in individuals. It is split into two camps: the **Behaviourists** and the **Gestalt-Field psychologists**.

Informal organisations   *See* **Human Relations approach.**

Intrinsic motivators   These are non-material rewards, such as praise, satisfaction and recognition which are internal to the individual (*see* **extrinsic motivators, esteem needs** and **social needs**).

Japanese approach   Pascale and Athos (1982) argue that the effectiveness and uniqueness of the Japanese approach to **management** comes from their ability to combine 'soft' (personnel/industrial relations) elements and 'hard' (business/manufacturing) practices (*see* **7 S framework**).

Job Design   Also called work humanisation, and arising from the work of the **Human Relations** approach, proponents of this view argue that the fragmentation of jobs promoted by the **Classical approach to organisations** creates boring, monotonous, meaningless and de-motivating jobs. To reverse this, and to make jobs interesting and intrinsically motivating, they should be designed to provide variety, task completeness and, above all, **autonomy.**

Kaizen   This is a Japanese process of incremental, systematic, gradual, orderly and continuous improvement which utilises a range of techniques, tools and concepts, such as quality circles.

Knowledge power   This is **power** based on the control of unique information that is necessary for decision-making.

Leadership   The process of establishing goals and motivating others to pursue and achieve these goals.

Long Marches   The Long March approach to change favours relatively small-scale and operationally focused initiatives, which are slow to implement and whose full benefits are achieved in the long term rather than the short term. The Long March approach can impact on culture over time but it does require the involvement and commitment of most of the organisation (*see* **Bold Strokes**).

Long-range planning   This is an approach to **strategy** based on plotting trends and planning the actions required to achieve the identified growth targets. It is heavily biased towards financial targets and budgetary controls.

Management   The process of planning, organising and controlling resources and people in order to produce goods or provide services.

Management development   This is concerned with the training and education of managers so as to equip them with the competences and skills necessary to carry out their duties effectively.

Mechanistic structure   This forms one end of the structure continuum identified by **Contingency theorists**, the other end being **organic structure**. A mechanistic structure equates to the bureaucratic-type structure advocated by the **Classical approach to organisations** (*see* **bureaucracy**).

Metaphor   This is a linguistic device for describing or seeing one type of experience by suggestion that it is similar to something else, e.g. using the metaphor of a machine to describe a bureaucratic type of organisational structure.

Mission statement   This states an organisation's major strategic purpose or reason for existing. It can indicate such factors as the organisation's products, markets and core competences. It is part of an organisation's **vision**.

Modernism   This is a term used to describe the values, rationale and institutions that have dominated Western societies since the Age of Enlightenment in the eighteenth century. The essence of modernism is a strong belief in progress, economic and **scientific rationality**, a search for the fundamental rules and laws which govern both the natural world and human nature, and a commitment to a secular, rationalist and progressive individualism (*see* **postmodernism**; **realism**).

Moving   This is the second step in Lewin's **Three-Step model** of change. It involves identifying and evaluating the various types of change on offer, and implementing the chosen one (*see* **unfreezing**; **refreezing**).

Non-linear systems   This is a term used by **complexity theorists** to describe constantly changing systems where the laws of cause and effect appear not to apply. **Order** in such systems is seen as manifesting itself in a largely unpredictable fashion, in which patterns of behaviour emerge in irregular but similar forms through a process of **self-organisation**, which is governed by a small number of simple **order-generating rules**.

Normative power   This describes the allocation and manipulation of symbolic rewards, such as status symbols, as inducements to obey.

Norms   These are one of the key components of culture. They represent unwritten rules of behaviour which guide how members of an organisation should behave in particular situations (*see* **organisational culture**).

OD (Organization Development)   This is an approach to change developed in the USA. It is based on the work of Kurt Lewin and, originally at least, was concerned with improving the effectiveness of the human side of the organisation through participative change programmes.

'One best way' approach   This is a term used to describe any theory or approach which claims to be universally superior to all others on offer, e.g. the **Classical approach to organisations**.

Open-ended change   This is a term used especially by proponents of **Emergent change** to indicate that change is a continuous and unpredictable process which does not have a beginning, middle and end.

Open Systems school   Proponents of this view see organisations as systems composed of a number of interconnected sub-systems, where any change to one part of the system will have an impact on other parts of the system, and, in turn, on its overall performance. Organisations are seen as open systems in that they are open to, and interact with, their external **environment** (*see* **closed systems**).

Order   From a **complexity** perspective, order refers to the patterns of behaviour which emerge in irregular but similar forms in **non-linear systems** through a process of **self-organisation**.

Order-generating rules   In complex systems, the emergence of **order** is seen as being based on the operation of simple **order-generating rules** which permit limited chaos whilst providing relative order (*see* **Complexity theories**).

Organic structure   This forms one end of the structure continuum identified by **Contingency theorists**, the other end being **mechanistic structure**. An organic structure is seen as being flat, informal, flexible and highly adaptable, i.e. the reverse of a bureaucratic structure.

Organisational culture   This is the name given to the collection of **basic assumptions, values, norms** and **artefacts** that are shared by and influence the behaviour of an organisation's members.

Organisational learning This term describes the process of collective, as opposed to individual, learning in an organisation. Its aim is to improve the performance of the organisation by involving everyone in collecting, studying, learning from and acting on information.

Organization Development   *See* **OD**.

Outsourcing   This is the practice of seeking outside organisations to take over activities and services previously carried out within an organisation, e.g. catering, security and IT.

Paradigm   This is a way of looking at and interpreting the world, a framework of basic assumptions, theories and models that are commonly and strongly accepted and shared within a particular field of activity at a particular point in time.

Participation   This is the process of involving people in decision-making and change activities within organisations.

Person culture   The individual and his or her wishes are the central focus of this form of culture. It is associated with a minimalistic structure, the purpose of which is to assist those individuals who choose to work together (*see* **organisational culture**).

Phases of change   This is an elaboration of **Planned change** based on a four-phase model which describes change in terms of two major dimensions: change phases, which are distinct states through which an organisation moves as it undertakes **Planned change**; and change processes, which are the methods used to move an organisation from one state to another.

Physiological needs   These relate to hunger, thirst, sleep, etc. (*see* **hierarchy of needs**).

PIMS (Profit Impact on Marketing Strategy)   This is a quantitative strategic planning tool based upon the belief that there are three major factors which determine a business unit's performance: its **strategy**, its competitive position, and the market/industry characteristics of the field in which it competes.

Planned change   This term was coined by Kurt Lewin in the 1940s to distinguish change that was consciously embarked upon and planned by an organisation, as opposed to types of change that might come about by accident or by impulse or that might be forced on an organisation. Lewin's Planned approach to change consists of four interrelated elements: **Field Theory, Group Dynamics, Action Research** and the **Three-Step model** of change.

Politics   This describes the efforts of people in organisations to gain support for or against policies, rules, goals, or other decisions where the outcome will have some effect on them. Politics is seen as the exercise of **power**.

Population ecology   This concept is borrowed from the life sciences. It is a Darwinist-type approach that focuses on how organisations adapt and evolve in order to survive within the general population of organisations to which they belong.

Positioning school   This approach to **strategy** is based on the argument that organisations which enjoy higher profits than their competitors do so because they have achieved advantageous and easily defended positions in their markets.

Postmodernism   This is a loosely defined philosophical movement which, though originally based in the arts, has become increasingly influential in the social sciences over the last 20 years. It is a way of looking at the world that rejects the rationality of **modernism** and concentrates on the ways in which human beings attempt to shape reality and invent their world (*see* **realism**).

Power   An individual's capacity to influence decisions, to exert their will and achieve outcomes consistent with their goals and priorities.

Power culture   This is frequently found in small entrepreneurial organisations such as some property, trading and finance companies. It is associated with a web structure with one or more powerful figures at the centre, wielding **control** (*see* **organisational culture**).

Prescriptive stream   This phrase is used to describe writers on **strategy** and change who are more interested in developing prescriptions for telling organisations what they should do rather than analysing what they actually do (*see* **Analytical stream**).

Principles of organisation   These are a set of rules governing the running of organisations developed by Fayol (1949). He claimed that they were universally applicable to all organisations. The principles of organisation form one of the core elements of the **Classical approach to organisations**.

Privatisation   The process of transferring state assets from the public to the private sector.

Problem children   Also known as **question marks**, these are units or businesses which have a high growth rate and low market share. They have high cash requirements to keep them on course, but their profitability is low because of their low market share. They are so named because, most of the time, the appropriate **strategy** to adopt is not clear (*see* **Growth-Share Matrix**).

Processual approach to change   This approach sees change as a complex and dynamic process which cannot be solidified or treated as a series of linear events. In particular, it focuses on the need to analyse the **politics** of managing change.

Processual approach to strategy   This perspective concentrates on the nature of organisational and market processes. It views organisations and their members as shifting coalitions of individuals and groups with different interests, imperfect knowledge and short attention spans.

Profit Impact on Marketing Strategy   *See* **PIMS**.

Psychological contract This concept is based on the assertion that there is an unwritten set of expectations operating at all times between every member of an organisation and the various managers and others in that organisation.

Punctuated equilibrium model This view of change sees organisations as evolving through relatively long periods of stability (equilibrium periods) in their basic patterns of activity that are punctuated by relatively short bursts of fundamental change (revolutionary periods).

Question marks *See* **problem children.**

Rationality The use of scientific reasoning and logical arguments to arrive at decisions.

Realism This philosophical perspective asserts that social entities, such as markets, class relations, gender relations, ethnic groupings, social rules, etc., exist, are real and can be discovered. However, whilst it rejects the notion of multiple realities, it still acknowledges that social entities arise though a process of **social construction**. This distinguishes it from both **modernism** and **postmodernism**.

Refreezing This is the third step in Lewin's **Three-Step model** of change. It seeks to stabilise new behaviours in order to ensure that they are relatively safe from regression (*see* **unfreezing; moving**).

Remunerative power This is the use or promise of material rewards as inducements in order to gain people's cooperation.

Resource-Based model This approach to **strategy** sees competitiveness as coming from the effective deployment of superior or unique resources, such as equipment, patents, brands and competences, which allow firms to have lower costs or better products than their competitors.

Ringi system This is a Japanese approach to decision-making which promotes extensive and open debate over decisions, in order to ensure that they fit in with the company's objectives rather than those of sectional interests.

Role A set of observable behaviours associated with, and expected of, an identifiable position or job in an organisation.

Role culture This type of **organisational culture** is appropriate to bureaucracies, and organisations with **mechanistic**, rigid structures and narrow jobs. Such cultures stress the importance of procedures and rules, hierarchical position and **authority**, security and predictability. In essence, role cultures create situations in which those in the organisation stick rigidly to their **role**.

Safety needs The desire for security and protection against danger (*see* **hierarchy of needs**).

Scenario-building This is an approach to strategy development that allows organisations to construct and test pictures of possible futures and to select the one which is most likely to meet their needs. It is based on the assumption that, if you cannot predict the future, then by considering a range of possible futures, an organisation's strategic horizons can be broadened, and managers can be receptive to new ideas (*see* **vision-building**).

Scientific Management   This is an approach to work organisation developed by Frederick Taylor in the early twentieth century. He claimed that this approach to designing jobs and supervising workers is based on the scientific study of work. It emphasises the **division of labour,** the removal of workers' discretion and the right of management to make what changes it thinks are necessary for efficient working. It is one of the core elements of the **Classical approach to organisations.**

Scientific–Rational approach   This is an alternative title used to describe the **Classical approach to organisations.**

Self-actualisation needs   These constitute the need to achieve one's full potential. According to Maslow (1943), this will vary from person to person, and may differ over time as a person reaches a level of potential previously considered unattainable and so goes on to strive for new heights (*see* **hierarchy of needs**).

Self-organisation   This is a term used by **complexity theorists** to describe how **order** emerges and is maintained in complex systems (*see* **order-generating rules**).

Semistructures   This is a term used by **complexity theorists** to describe structures which are sufficiently rigid that change can be organised, but not so rigid that it cannot occur.

7 S framework   This is a tool for analysing organisational performance and was developed by Tom Peters, Robert Waterman, Richard Pascale and Anthony Athos when they all worked at McKinsey in the late 1970s. The seven Ss comprise four 'soft' Ss (staff, style, shared values and skills) and three 'hard' Ss (**strategy**, structure and systems) (*see* **Japanese approach**).

Simple order-generating rules   *See* **order-generating rules.**

Single-loop learning   This is adaptive learning which involves detecting and rectifying errors or exceptions within the scope of the organisation's existing practices, policies and **norms** of behaviour (*see* **double-loop learning; triple-loop learning; organisational learning**).

Situational variables   *See* **Contingency Theory.**

Size   *See* **Contingency Theory.**

Social construction   This is an approach concerned with the processes by which people construct, maintain and change social and organisational reality. It is a term used in both **postmodernism** and **realism**. For postmodernists, social construction is seen as creating a number of competing 'realities', none of which possess ultimate truth or reality. Realists, on the other hand, believe in just one socially constructed reality which does exist.

Social needs   The need to belong, to gain love and affection; to be in the company of others, especially friends (*see* **hierarchy of needs**).

Socio-Technical Systems theory   This is a variant on **Job Design** which involves a shift of focus from the individual job to the organisation as a whole. It sees organisations as being composed of interdependent social and technical systems.

Stars   These are business units, industries or products with high growth and high market share. Because of this, stars are assumed to use and generate large amounts of cash. However, they are also likely to be very profitable (*see* **Growth-Share Matrix**).

Strategic Conflict model   This is an approach to strategy which harks back to the military metaphor, and portrays competition as war between rival firms. In particular, this model draws on the work of military strategists, and attempts to apply their military aphorisms to modern business organisations.

Strategic intent   This is a term which was originally coined to describe the commitment of Japanese managers to create and pursue a **vision** of their desired future.

Strategic management   Though often used as a generic term to describe the process by which managers identify and implement their organisation's **strategy**, it was originally applied only to quantitative, mathematical approaches to strategy.

Strategy   This is a plan of action stating how an organisation will achieve its long-term objectives.

Sustainability   This term was originally coined by environmental and ecological campaigners to describe the development of economic, social and industrial practices which would contribute to sustaining the natural environment. It has been extended to include the promotion of organisational practices that contribute to the health of the planet, the survival of humans and other species, the development of a just and humane society, and the creation of work that brings dignity and self-fulfilment (Dunphy *et al*, 2007).

SWOT analysis   This is a strategic planning tool which assesses the Strengths, Weaknesses, Opportunities and Threats possessed and faced by an organisation.

Systems Theory   *See* **closed systems** and **Open Systems school**.

Task culture   This type of **organisational culture** is job- or project-orientated; the onus is on getting the job in hand (the task) done rather than prescribing how it should be done. Such types of culture are appropriate to organisations with **organic structures** where flexibility and teamworking are encouraged.

Taylorism   *See* **Scientific Management**.

Technology   *See* **Contingency Theory**.

Theory X   This is a management theory expounded by Douglas McGregor (1960) which states that the average person dislikes work and will avoid it wherever possible, unless coerced to do so (*see* **Theory Y**).

Theory Y   This is a management theory expounded by Douglas McGregor (1960) which states that most people can view work as being as natural as rest or play, they are willing to take responsibility, and are capable of exercising self-direction and self-control (*see* **Theory X**).

Three-Step model   This model of change was developed by Kurt Lewin and sees change as going through three stages: **unfreezing, moving** and **refreezing**. It is one of the four elements of Lewin's Planned approach to change (*see* **Planned change**).

Total Quality Management (TQM)   This was developed in Japan and is the systematic application of quality management principles to all aspects of an organisation's activities, including customers and suppliers, and their integration with key business processes.

Transactional management This approach stems from the notion that the manager–subordinate relationship is based on a transaction between the two, whereby managers exchange rewards for subordinates' performance. Transactional managers focus on task completion, goal clarification and optimising the performance of the organisation through incremental changes within the confines of existing policy, structures and practices – basically, they seek to work within and maintain the status quo. This approach to management is seen as being appropriate in **convergent states** (*see* **contextual approach to leadership; transformational leadership**).

Transformational leadership This approach portrays leaders as charismatic or visionary individuals who seek to overturn the status quo and bring about radical change. Such leaders use the force of their personality to motivate followers to identify with the leader's **vision** and to sacrifice their self-interest in favour of that of the group or organisation. Transformational leadership is seen as being appropriate to **divergent states** (*see* **contextual approach to leadership** and **transactional management**).

Triple-loop learning This involves questioning the rationale for the organisation and, in the light of this, radically transforming it (*see* **single-loop learning; double-loop learning; organisational learning**).

Uncertainty This relates to the degree of doubt, unpredictability and ambiguity that exists in any situation.

Unfreezing This is the first step in Lewin's **Three-Step model** of change. It seeks to destabilise (unfreeze) the complex field of driving and restraining forces which prevent human behaviour from changing (*see* **moving** and **refreezing**).

Values These are one of the key components of culture. They relate to how things ought to be done in an organisation; they tell members what is important in the organisation (*see* **organisational culture**).

Vision This is a view of an organisation's desired future state. It generally has two components: a description of the organisation's core **values** and purpose; and a strong and bold picture of the organisation's future which identifies specific goals and actions (*see* **vision-building**).

Vision-building This is the process of creating a **vision**. It is an iterative process which involves the conception by a company's senior management team of an 'ideal' future state for their organisation; the identification of the organisation's **mission**, its rationale for existence; and a clear statement of desired outcomes and the desired conditions and competences needed to achieve these.

Workforce diversity This term refers to the dissimilarities – differences – among an organisation's workforce owing to age, gender, race, ethnicity, religion, sexual orientation, nationality, socio-economic background, capabilities/disabilities, etc. It draws attention to the need to take account of these differences when seeking to recruit, retain and motivate staff. In particularly, it identifies the need to treat different groups differently if an organisation is to treat all its employees in an ethical and fair manner.

Index